μC/USB Device™
Universal Serial Bus Device Stack

The Micrium USB Team

Micrium
Press

Weston, FL 33326

Micriµm Press
1290 Weston Road, Suite 306
Weston, FL 33326
USA
www.micrium.com

For bulk orders, please contact Micriµm Press at: +1 954 217 2036

Micriµm
Press

ISBN: 978-1-935772-01-9
100-uC-USB-Device-Renesas-RX63N-001

Table of Contents

Part I: µC/USB: The Universal Serial Bus Device Stack

Part II: µC/USB and the Renesas RX63N

1

Introduction to USB

This chapter presents a quick introduction to USB. The first section in this chapter introduces the basic concepts of the USB specification Revision 2.0. The second section explores the data flow model. The third section gives details about the device operation. Lastly, the fourth section describes USB device logical organization. The full protocol is described extensively in the USB Specification Revision 2.0 at `http://www.usb.org`.

1-1 A BRIEF HISTORY OF USB

The Universal Serial Bus (USB) is an industry standard maintained by the USB Implementers Forum (USB-IF) for serial bus communication. The USB specification contains all the information about the protocol such as the electrical signaling, the physical dimension of the connector, the protocol layer, and other important aspects. USB provides several benefits compared to other communication interfaces such as ease of use, low cost, low power consumption and, fast and reliable data transfer.

USB CONSORTIUM

In 1994, seven companies joined forces to define the USB standard: Compaq, Digital Equipment, IBM, Intel, NEC, Microsoft, Nortel. Each company had its own reasons to join the consortium, but they had thee common goals:

■ To be fundamentally easier for users to connect peripheral devices to a computer while using a common infrastructure

■ To simplify the software configuration of any peripheral connected to the computer

■ To increase the achievable transfer bandwidth between the computer and the peripheral and vice-versa

USB 1.0 was released in 1996. It proposed Low Speed (LS) at 1.5 Mbits/sec and Full Speed (FS) at 12 Mbits/sec. In 1998, USB 1.1 was released to correct and clarify a few elements of the initial USB specification.

LS was, and still is, used for human interface devices that do not require a lot of bandwidth, such as keyboard, mouse and joystick. FS was widely adopted for mass storage devices, printers, scanners and audio devices.

The market increasing need for bigger storage and faster communication links lead to the development of USB 2.0 in early 2000. This new USB standard kept the compatibility with LS and FS and added High Speed (HS) at 480 Mbits/sec.

TIMELINE

1969	Development of the serial port (RS-232C).
1994	The USB consortium is formed by Compaq, DEC, IBM, Intel, Microsoft, NEC and Nortel.
1996	USB 1.0 standard is released, with data rates of 1.5 Mbit/s (Low-Bandwidth) and 12 Mbit/s (Full-Bandwidth).
1999	USB 1.1 is released. Corrected bugs.
2000	USB 2.0 is released, specifying the implementation of a 480 Mbps bus.
2001	USB On-The-Go (OTG) supplement is added, which allows devices to communicate with each other.
2005	Wireless USB standard is released, which is a point to point wireless communications link.
2008	USB 3.0 is released, which delivers a transmission speed of up to 5 Gbit/s.

This book covers USB 1.1 and USB 2.0, as these are the standards commonly used in embedded systems. USB 3.0 requires resources not often available in typical embedded systems, and so will not be discussed in any detail.

1-2 MECHANICAL SPECIFICATIONS

This section covers cabling and connectors, electrical specifications, and bus-powered devices for USB 1.1 and USB 2.0.

1-2-1 CABLING AND CONNECTORS

USB cables are made of four 28-AWG conductors. A USB twisted pair, where the "D+" and "D−" conductors are twisted together in a double helix. The wires are enclosed in a further layer of shielding. Maximum cable length is five meters.

TYPE A AND B CONNECTORS

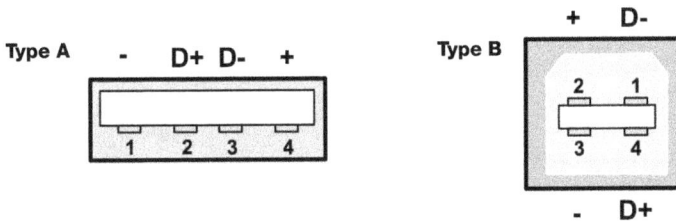

Figure 1-1 **Type A and Type B USB connectors**

Name	Usage	Color
VBus	Power	Red
Gnd	Power	Black
D+	Data	Green
D-	Data	White

Table 1-1 **USB Type A and B cable pinouts**

Connector Type A connects to the host (upstream ports), while connector Type B is often used to connect to devices (downstream ports).

The pins carrying electrical power (VBus and Gnd) are physically longer than the other two pins. So when connecting a device, the supply pins are connected first before the data pins. And when unplugging, the data pins disconnect before the power supply pins.

USB MINI CONNECTORS

Mini connectors were added in USB 2.0. They are an alternative to the standard B connector, and are used on handheld and portable devices; the Type B connector is too large to be easily integrated into these devices. The mini-B connecter has a fifth pin, named ID. but it is not connected.

Mini connectors have fallen out of use with the development of micro connectors for smaller handheld devices.

Figure 1-2 **Mini-B USB Connector**

Name	Usage	Color
VBus	Power	Red
Gnd	Power	Black
D+	Data	Green
D-	Data	White
Shell	Drain wire	
ID	No connection	

Table 1-2 **USB mini-B cable pinouts**

USB ON-THE-GO (MICRO) CONNECTORS

USB OTG devices use Micro-USB connectors. These connectors are smaller, which makes them more useful for handheld devices, and support the use of the ID pin to determine the device type. An OTG device is required to be able to detect whether a Micro-A or Micro-B plug is inserted by determining if the ID pin resistance to ground is less than 10Ω MAX or if the resistance to ground is greater than $100K\Omega$. If the electrical resistance on the ID pin is less than 10Ω MAX, the pin shall be treated as ID = FALSE, and a resistance greater than $100k\Omega$ MIN shall be treated as ID = TRUE.

"USB Stacks" on page 61 for more details about OTG usage in embedded systems.

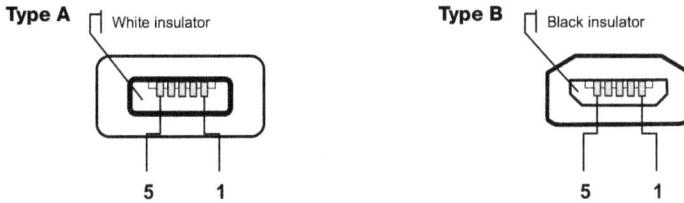

Figure 1-3 **Micro USB Connectors**

Contact Number	Signal Name	Typical Wiring Assignment
1	VBus	Red
2	D-	White
3	D+	Green
4	ID	<10Ω = Micro-A >100kΩ = Micro-B
5	GND	Black
Shell	Shield	Drain Wire

Table 1-3 **USB micro cable pinouts**

1-2-2 ELECTRICAL SPECIFICATIONS

In most embedded system designs, adherence to the USB electrical specifications is guaranteed by the USB controller used, whether that is an external controller, or one that is integrated into an MCU. Most USB controller vendors provide excellent reference materials that you can use as the basis of your product design.

So, the main issue you should consider is compliance testing, if you want to get the USB logo on your product. See "Compliance" on page 64 for more information.

Once a device has indicated its presence by setting the signal lines with the correct set of pull-ups resistors, the host controller is responsible for all further traffic on the bus.

A high-speed device begins by connecting to the host/hub as a full-speed device. Once attached, it will perform a high speed chirp during reset, and if the hub supports it, the device establishes a high speed connection. If the device operates in high speed mode, then the D+ line is pulled high to balance the line.

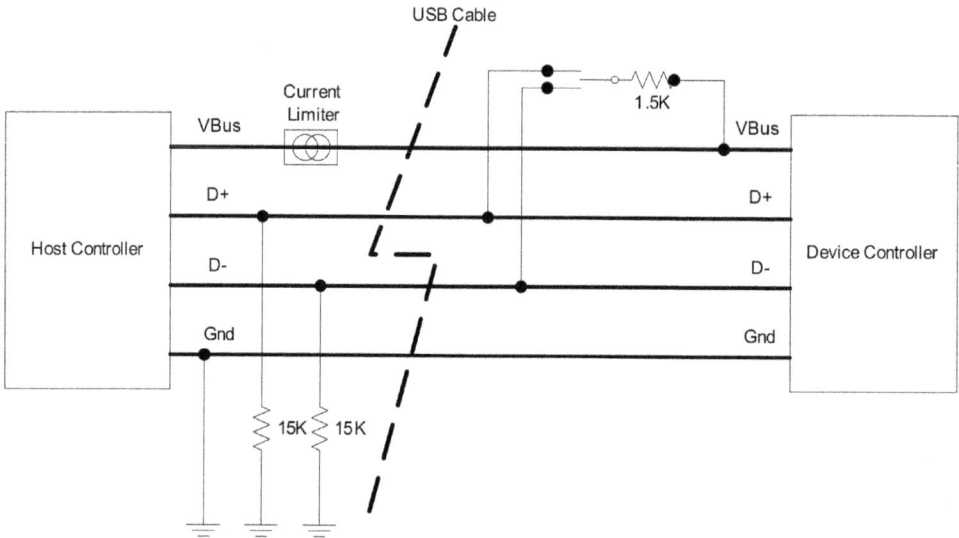

Figure 1-4 **USB cabling electrical specifications**

Note: A high speed device must not support low speed mode. A USB 2.0 compliant downstream-facing hub or host must support all three modes: high speed, full speed and low speed.

USB supports hot-plugging with dynamically loadable and unloadable drivers. The user simply plugs the device into the bus, and the host detects this addition, interrogates the newly inserted device, and loads the appropriate driver (provided a driver is installed for your device).

Quick facts about the electrical characteristics of USB cabling:

- In USB 2.0, a unit load is defined as 100 mA. A device may draw a maximum of five unit loads, for a total of 500 mA from a single port.

- Either the D+ or the D- line will be pulled high. If D+ is high, the device is Full or High Speed. If D- is high, the device is Low Speed.

- High Speed negotiation protocol occurs during the Bus Reset phase

- After detecting the reset signal, a high speed device will signal the host with a 480 Mbps chirp.

1-2-3 HIGH SPEED

High speed additions to the USB specification were introduced in USB 2.0 as a response to the higher speed of FireWire. It was added as an afterthought, and was designed to maintain compatibility without compromising performance. High Speed provides a maximum theoretical throughput of 480 Mb/s using the same cables as Low/Full Speed USB.

This is achieved by having each end of D+ and each end of D- terminated with a 45 Ohm resistance to ground when the link is conveying high speed data

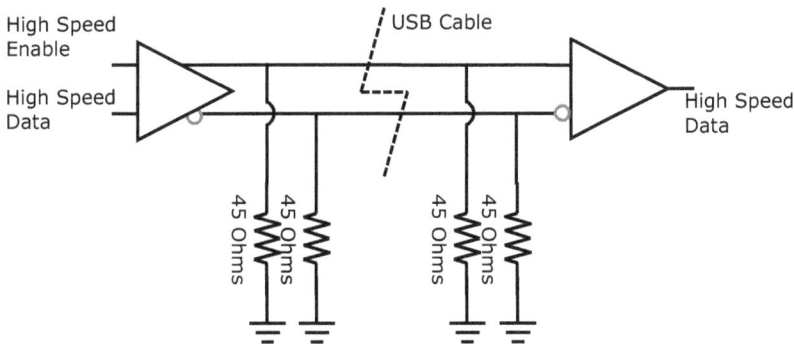

Figure 1-5 **High Speed USB**

A high speed transceiver current source injects a current of 17.78 mA (derived from the positive supply) into either the D+ or the D- line. A voltage of 400mV on the line is generated. A differential receiver detects the differential state of the line

In fact, the 45 ohm resistors are provided by the Full Speed / Low Speed circuitry, at each end of the link, applying a Single Ended Zero. The FS/LS controller is designed to provide as accurate a termination resistance as possible. Removing the high speed transceiver current source from the circuit re-establish the line conditions as defined for Low/Full Speed USB.

1-3 POWERING USB DEVICES

This section covers both *bus-powered* devices and *self-powered* devices.

■   A bus-powered device draws all of its power from the bus. It may draw up to 500 mA, if permitted to do so by the host.

■   A self-powered device does not draw the bulk of its power from the bus, but rather from an external power supply.

Any USB device (or hub) can consume current from the bus only from its upstream port.

Device	A device is a logical or physical entity that performs one of more functions.
Composite device	A composite device has one address but multiple interfaces or association of interfaces each providing a function
Compound device	A compound device contains a hub with one or more permanently attached devices. A host treats the hub and its functions as if they were separate physical devices.

Table 1-4 **Types of USB devices**

1-3-1 BUS-POWERED DEVICES

USB provides a power supply of between 4.75 and 5.25 volts and up to 500 milliAmperes to any device plugged into the port.

■   Supply voltage can fall to a minimum of 4.35V at the device.

■   When other devices are being plugged in, there can be transients lowering the supply voltage by 0.4V.

■   Devices can be classified as bus-powered, self-powered, or hybrid-powered.

A USB device specifies its power consumption in units of 2 mA in the configuration descriptor. A device cannot increase its power consumption to a value that is greater than what it specifies during enumeration.

There are two classes of bus-powered functions:

Function	Current demands
Low power	Draw maximum 100mA
High power	Self-powered hubs: Draw maximum 100mA initially. Must supply 500mA to each port

Table 1-5 **Bus-powered functions**

- **Low-power functions** draw power from the VBus, and cannot draw any more than one unit load. The USB specification defines a unit load as 100mA. Low-power functions must also be designed to work down to a VBus voltage of 4.40V and up to a maximum voltage of 5.25V as measured at the upsteam plug of the device. For many 3.3V devices, LDO regulators are mandatory.

- **High-power functions** draw power from the VBus, and cannot draw more than one unit load until it has been configured, after which it can then draw up to five unit loads (500mA Max), provided this is specified in the descriptor. High-power functions must be capable of being detected and enumerated at a minimum 4.40V. When operating at a full unit load, the VBus provides a minimum of 4.75V and a maximum of 5.25V. Once again, these measurements are taken at the upstream plug.

A device which has been *suspended*, as a result of no bus activity, must reduce its current consumption to 0.5 mA or less. If a device is configured for high power (up to 500 mA), and has its remote wakeup feature enabled, it is allowed to draw up to 2.5 mA during suspend.

1-3-2 SELF-POWERED DEVICES

Self-powered functions are devices that require more than 500 mA of current. These devices may draw up to one unit load (100 mA) from the bus, and must derive the rest of its power from an external source. Should this external source fail, the device must have provisions in place to draw no more than one unit load from the bus.

The one unit load from the bus allows devices to be detected and enumerated without requiring external power.

POWERED USB

Powered USB (also known as Retail USB, USB Plus Power, and USB + Power) is a proprietary variant of USB that adds new powering modes to the USB specification. Powered USB uses standard USB signaling, but with the addition of extra power lines. it is commonly used for point-of-sale terminals. IBM owns the intellectual rights to Powered USB and charges a licensing fee for its use.

Powered USB can provide:

- +5 volts DC at up to 6 amps per connector (up to 30 watts)

- +12 volts DC at up to 6 amps per connector (up to 72 watts)

- +24 volts DC at up to 6 amps per connector (up to 144 watts)

1-4 BUS STATES

As there are two data lines, there are a variety of different conditions that can be signaled.

Bus State	Levels
Differential '1'	D+ high, D- low
Differential '0'	D- high, D+ low
Single Ended Zero (SE0)	D+ and D- low
Single Ended One (SE1)	D+ and D- high
Data J State: Low-speed Full-speed	 Differential '0' Differential '1'
Data K State: Low-speed Full-speed	 Differential '1' Differential '0'
Idle State: Low-speed Full-speed	 D- high, D+ low D+ high, D- low
Resume State	Data K state
Start of Packet (SOP)	Data lines switch from idle to K state
End of Packet (EOP)	SE0 for 2 bit times followed by J state for 1 bit time
Disconnect	SE0 for >= 2 µs
Connect	Idle for 2.5 µs
Reset	SE0 for >= 2.5 µs

Table 1-6 **Bus states**

DETACHED STATE

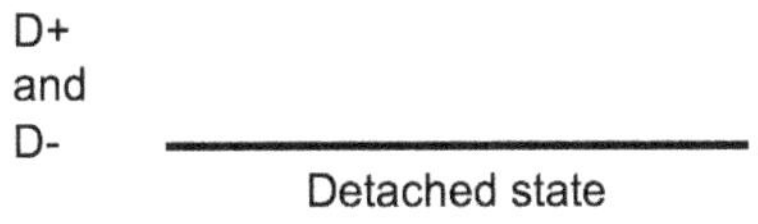

D+
and
D-   —————————————————
              Detached state

Figure 1-6 **Detached state**

When no device is plugged in, the host will see both data lines low, as its 15 kohm resistors are pulling each data line low.

ATTACHED STATE

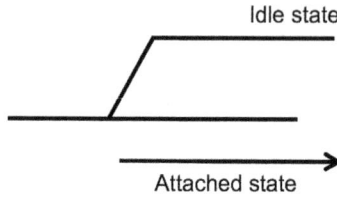

Figure 1-7 **Attached state**

When the device is plugged in to the host, the host will see either D+ or D- go to a '1' level, and will know that a device has been plugged in. The '1' level will be on D- for a low speed device, and D+ for a full (or high) speed device.

IDLE STATE

Figure 1-8 **Idle state**

The state of the data lines when the pulled up line is high, and the other line is low, is called the idle state. This is the state of the lines before and after a packet is sent.

J AND K STATES

The *J State* is the same polarity as the idle state (the line with the pull-up resistor is high, and the other line is low), but is being driven to that state by either host or device.

The *K state* is just the opposite polarity to the J state.

The J and K terms are used because for Full Speed and Low Speed links, they are of opposite polarity.

SE0 STATE

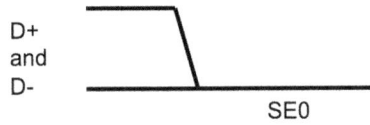

Figure 1-9 **SE0 state**

The Single Ended Zero (SE0) is when both lines are being pulled low.

EOP STATE

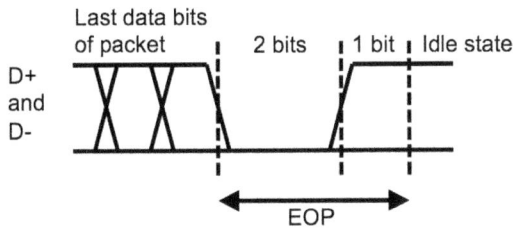

Figure 1-10 **EOP state**

The End of Packet (EOP) is an SE0 state for 2 bit times, followed by a J state for 1 bit time.

SINGLE ENDED ONE (SE1) STATE

Figure 1-11 **Single Ended One (SE1) state**

This is the illegal condition where both lines are high. It should never occur on a properly functioning link.

RESET STATE

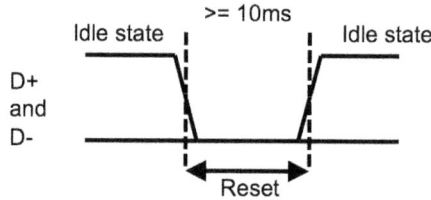

Figure 1-12 **Reset state**

When the host wants to start communicating with a device it will start by applying a 'Reset' condition which sets the device to its default unconfigured state.

The Reset condition involves the host pulling down both data lines to low levels (SE0) for at least 10 ms. The device may recognize the reset condition after 2.5 us.

This 'Reset' should not be confused with a micro-controller power-on type reset. It is a USB protocol reset to ensure that the device USB signaling starts from a known state.

SUSPENDED STATE

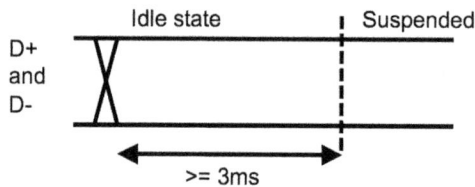

Figure 1-13 **Suspended state**

With today's emphasis on energy saving, the USB suspend mode is very useful. It allows to power down an unused device.

Suspending a device is achieved by not sending anything to the device for 3 ms.

A Start-Of-Frame packet (at full speed, see Packets section) or a Keep Alive signal (at low speed) is sent by the host every 1 ms to keep the device awake.

A suspended device must recognize the resume signal and the reset signal.

KEEP ALIVE STATE

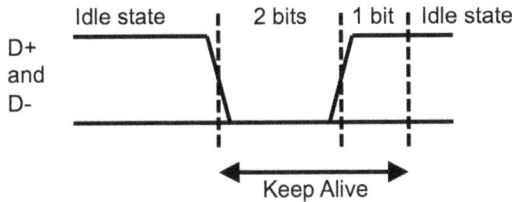

Figure 1-14 **Keep alive state**

This is represented by a Low speed EOP. It is sent at least once every millisecond on a Low speed link, in order to keep the device from suspending.

RESUME STATE

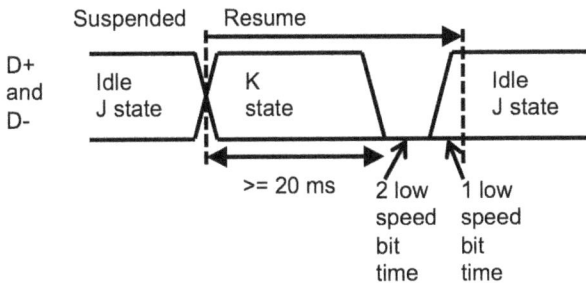

Figure 1-15 **Resume state**

When the host wants to wake the device up after a suspend, it does so by reversing the polarity of the signal on the data lines for at least 20ms. The signal is completed with a low speed end of packet signal.

It is also possible for a device with its remote wakeup feature set, to initiate a resume itself. It must have been in the idle state for at least 5ms, and must apply the wakeup K condition for between 1 and 15 ms. The host takes over the driving of the resume signal within 1 ms.

1-5 USB TOPOLOGY

USB can connect a series of devices using a tiered star topology. The key elements in USB topology are the *host*, *hubs*, and *devices*, as illustrated in Figure 1-16. Each node in the illustration represents a USB hub or a USB device. At the top level of the graph is the root hub, which is part of the host. There is only one host in the system. The specification allows up to seven tiers and a maximum of five non-root hubs in any path between the host and a device. Each tier must contain at least one hub except for the last tier where only devices are present. Each USB device in the system has a unique address assigned by the host through a process called *enumeration* (see section 1-12 on page 58 for more details on enumeration).

The host learns about the device capabilities during enumeration, which allows the host operating system to load a specific driver for a particular USB device. The maximum number of peripherals that can be attached to a host is 127, including the root hub.

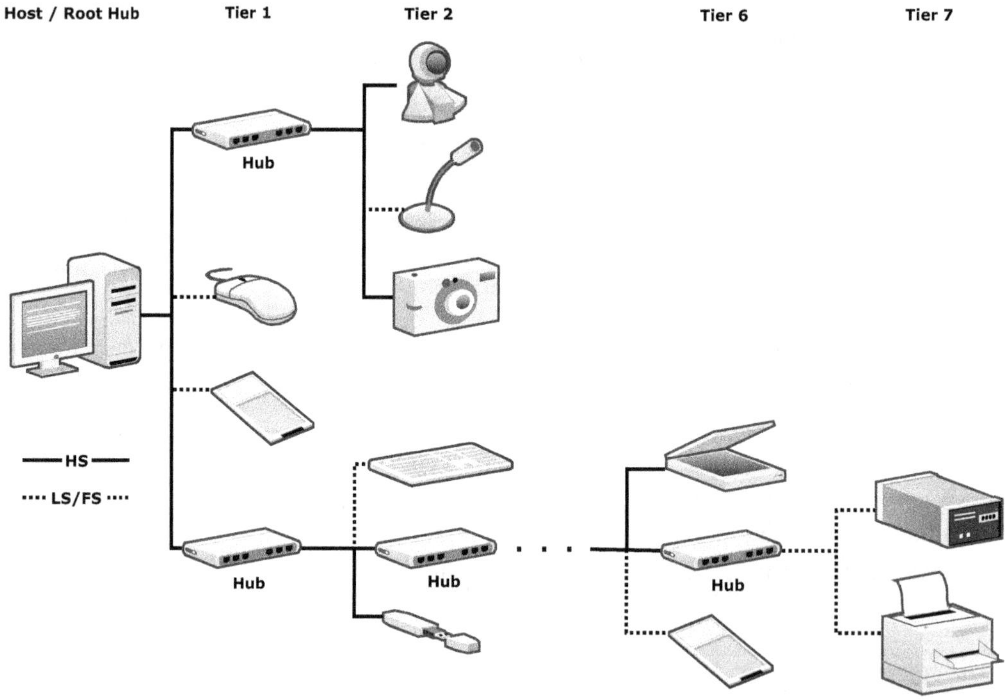

Figure 1-16 **USB topology**

- Star network configuration

- Only one host

- Maximum of seven levels of tiers, with each tier formed from a hub

- Host and hubs provide power to slaves

- Maximum of 5 metres per cable

- Maximum of 127 devices (hubs and root hub included)

- The host schedules and initiates data transfers.

1-5-1 USB HOST

The USB host communicates with the devices using a *USB host controller*. The host is responsible for detecting and enabling devices, managing bus access, performing error checking, providing and managing power, and exchanging data with the devices. Since USB devices are not responsible for these tasks, designing a USB device is a simpler job.

The host's communication with devices consist mainly of queries. For example, on power up, or when a device is connected to the host, the host queries the device capabilities during a process called *enumeration* (see section 1-12 "Enumeration" on page 58).

1-5-2 USB DEVICE

A USB device implements one or more USB *functions*, where a function provides one specific capability to the system. Examples of USB functions are keyboards, webcam, speakers, or a mouse. The requirements of each USB function are described in the USB class specification. For example, keyboards and mice are implemented using the Human Interface Device (HID) specification.

A device cannot initiate a transaction, nor can two devices communicate directly with each other; these activities are mediated by the host. There are a variety of transaction methods for data transmission (see transfer modes), and a token-based protocol is used (see packets). When the host identifies the presence of a device on the bus, the host start transmitting frames to the device (see Frames).

> It is worth emphasizing that the host is always responsible for scheduling and initiating data transfers; the device never initiates communication. The device must wait for a host query to send any data.

1-5-3 USB DEVICE STRUCTURE

From the host's point of view, USB devices are internally organized as a collection of configurations, interfaces and endpoints.

CONFIGURATION

A USB configuration specifies the capabilities of a device. A configuration consists of a collection of USB interfaces that implement one or more USB functions. Typically only one configuration is required for a given device. However, the USB specification allows up to 255 different configurations. During enumeration, the host selects a configuration. Only one configuration can be active at a time. The device uses a *configuration descriptor* to inform the host about a specific configuration's capabilities.

INTERFACE

A USB interface or a group of interfaces provides information about a function or class implemented by the device. An interface can contain multiple mutually exclusive settings called *alternate settings*. The device uses an *interface descriptor* to inform the host about a specific interface's capabilities. Each interface descriptor contains a class, subclass, and protocol codes defined by the USB-IF, and the number of endpoints required for a particular class implementation.

ALTERNATE SETTINGS

Alternate settings are used by the device to specify mutually exclusive settings for each interface. The default alternate settings contain the default settings of the device. The device also uses an interface descriptor to inform the host about an interface's alternate settings.

ENDPOINT

An interface requires a set of endpoints to communicate with the host. Each interface has different requirements in terms of the number of endpoints, transfer type, direction, maximum packet size, and maximum polling interval. The device sends an *endpoint descriptor* to notify the host about endpoint capabilities.

Figure 1-17 shows the hierarchical organization of a USB device. Configurations are grouped based on the device's speed. A high-speed device might have a particular configuration in both high-speed and low/full speed.

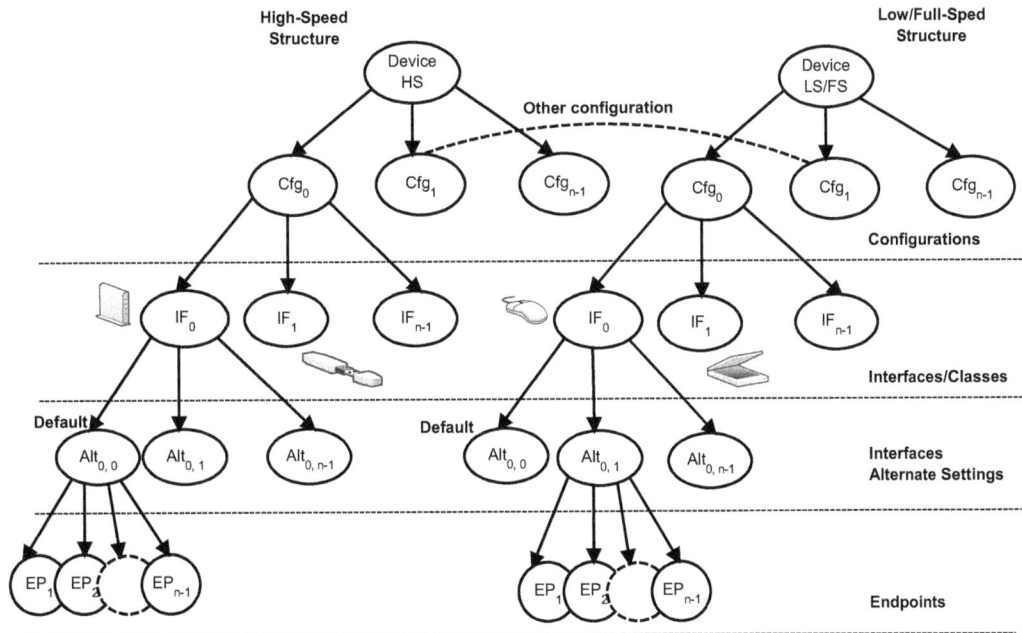

Figure 1-17 **USB device structure**

1-5-4 DEVICE STATES

The USB 2.0 specification defines six different states and are listed in Table 1-7.

Device States	Description
Attached	The device is in the Attached state when it is connected to the host or a hub port. The hub must be connected to the host or to another hub.
Powered	A device is considered in the Powered state when it starts consuming power from the bus. Only bus-powered devices use power from the host. Self-powered devices are in the Powered state after port attachment.
Default	After the device has been powered, it should not respond to any request or transactions until it receives a reset signal from the host. The device enters in the Default state when it receives a reset signal from the host. In the Default state, the device responds to standard requests at the default address 0.
Address	During enumeration, the host assigns a unique address to the device. When this occurs, the device moves from the Default state to the Address state.
Configured	After the host assigns an address to the device, the host must select a configuration. After the host selects a configuration, the device enters the Configured state. In this state, the device is ready to communicate with the host applications.
Suspended	The device enters into Suspended state when no traffic has been seen over the bus for a specific period of time. The device retains the address assigned by the host in the Suspended state. The device returns to the previous state after traffic is present in the bus.

Table 1-7 **USB Device States**

1-5-5 HOST CONTROLLERS

On typical desktop/laptop today, we can typically find multiple USB ports. These ports are driven by USB *host controllers*.

Speed	Controller Interface Type
LS and FS	OHCI (Open Host Controller Interface) or UHCI (Universal Host Controller Interface)
HS	EHCI (Enhanced Host Controller Interface)

Table 1-8 **Host controller speed**

Each host controller can drive one bus by itself (up to 127 devices on one host port). It can provide current up to 500 mA at 5 Volts. The host controller is responsible for complete bus management. When the host controller does not recognizes a device, it can reset the device. The controller can shut down USB ports to save power.

A host needs to check the following three items before authorizing a device on the bus:

- Can it supply the power required by the device?

- Does it have the driver matching the configuration requirements provided by the device during enumeration?

- Does the bus have sufficient bandwidth to satisfy the requirements of the device?

If these three elements are not met, the host will not enable the device on the bus.

When the host transmits a packet of data, the packet is sent to every device connected to a given port. Only one device, the addressed one, actually accepts the data. And only one device at a time is able to transmit data to the host, in response to a direct request from the host. Each hub in the chain repeats and resynchronizes the data as it relays it.

As stated above a maximum of 127 devices (including hubs) may be connected. This is because the address field in a packet is 7 bits long, and the address 0 cannot be used as it has special significance. (In most systems the bus would be running out of bandwidth, or other resources, long before the 127 devices was reached.)

Although host controllers that adhere to the OHCI, UHCI and EHCI standards are common on desktops and laptop computers, many of the MCUs that feature integrated USB host controllers do not follow these standards. Sometimes, the host controller does not include certain hardware-managed operations that are defined in the standard, or sometimes additional hardware is added to the MCU for customized automation. The result is that standard USB host drivers cannot be used with such MCUs, which complicates product development.

1-6 USB PACKETS

The fundamental element of communications is the packet.

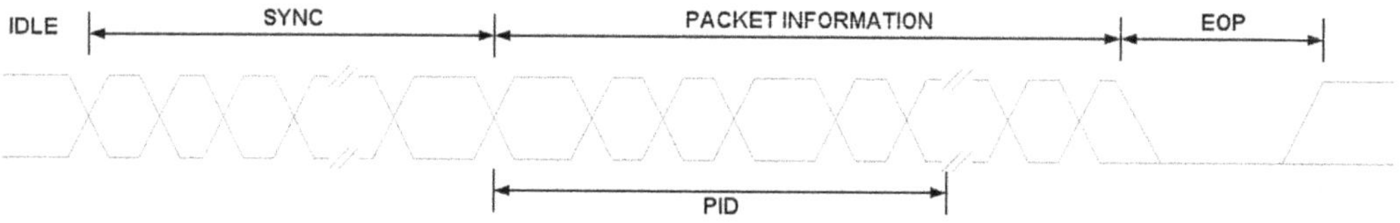

Figure 1-18 **USB Packet**

A packet is made of three parts: SYNC, INFORMATION, and END-OF-PACKET (EOP).

SYNC

The SYNC field is 8 bits long at low and full speed, or 32 bits long at high speed. It is used to synchronize the clock of the receiver with that of the transmitter. The SYNC pattern is a chirp of either 8 bits (full-/low-speed) or 32 bits (high-speed) where each bit is a J or K state:

KJKJKJKJKJKJKJKJKJKJKJKJKJKJKJKK

The last two bits indicate where the PID fields starts.

INFORMATION

The INFORMATION field varies from 1 byte up to 1024 bytes

- Packet Identifier (PID) – 4bits + complement

- Payload and CRC – Not present in handshake packets

EOP

End of packet. The EOP field is indicated by having both D+ and D- low for 3 bits (full-/low-speed) or 8 bits (high-speed).

1-7 USB PACKET TYPES

USB has four different packet types.

Packet Type	Packet ID Value	Packet Identifier
Token	0001 1001 0101 1101	OUT IN SOF SETUP
Data	0011 1011 0111 1111	DATA0 DATA1 DATA2 MDATA
Handshake	0010 1010 1110 0110	ACK NAK STALL NYET
Special (Split Transaction)	1100 1100 1000 0100	PRE ERR Split Ping

Table 1-9 **USB Packet types**

The first byte in every packet is the Packet Identifier (PID) byte. This byte needs to be recognized quickly by the USB controller. This is why it is not included in any CRC checks. It has its own validity check.

There are 4 bits to the PID. The check method uses the PID 4 bits by repeating and complementing them, making an 8 bit PID field in total.

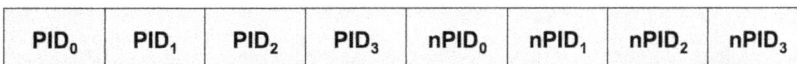

PID_0	PID_1	PID_2	PID_3	$nPID_0$	$nPID_1$	$nPID_2$	$nPID_3$

Figure 1-19 **PIDs shown in transmission order, LSB first**

1-7-1 TOKEN PACKETS

Token packets signal the type of transaction to follow. They are always the first packet in a transaction, identifying the targeted endpoint, and the purpose of the transaction.

There are four types of token packets:

Packet Type	Description
SOF	Start of Frame. Consists of an 11-bit frame number, is sent by the host every 1ms ± 500ns on a full-speed bus, or every 125 µs ± 0.0625 µs on a high speed bus. An SOF packet allows endpoints to identify the start of the frame and synchronize internal endpoint clocks to the host.
IN	Informs the USB device that the host wishes to read information.
OUT	Informs the USB device that the host wishes to send information.
SETUP	Used to begin control transfers.

Table 1-10 **Token packets**

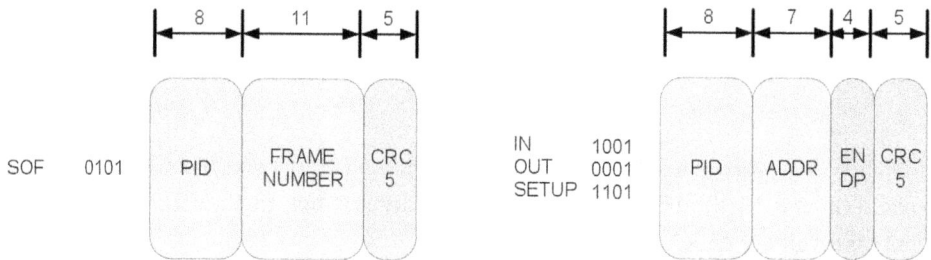

Figure 1-20 **SOF token packet (left) and IN / OUT / SETUP token packet (right)**

1-7-2 DATA PACKETS — LOW AND FULL SPEED

Data packets contain the payload. There are two types of data packets used in low speed and full speed connections: *DATA0* and *DATA1*. Each capable of transmitting up to 1024 bytes of data.

DATA0 and DATA1 PIDs are used together as part of an error-checking system. All data packets on a particular endpoint use an alternating pattern of DATA0 / DATA1 so that the endpoint knows if a received packet is the one it is expecting. If it is not the expected packet, it will still acknowledge (ACK) the packet as it is correctly received, but will then discard the data, assuming that it has been retransmitted because the host missed seeing the ACK after the previous data packet.

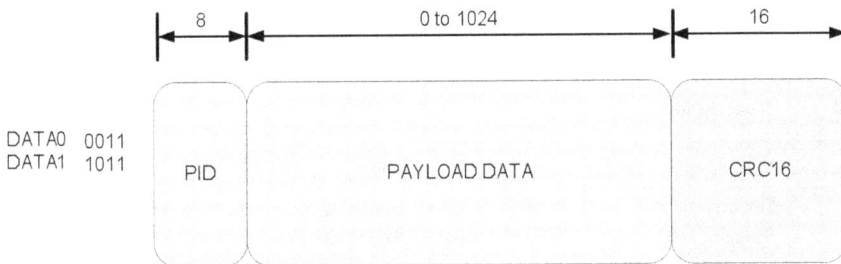

	8	0 to 1024	16
DATA0 0011 DATA1 1011	PID	PAYLOAD DATA	CRC16

Figure 1-21 **Low and full speed data packet**

1-7-3 DATA PACKETS — HIGH SPEED

High Speed mode defines two additional data PIDs: *DATA2* and *MDATA*.

Packet ID	Description
DATA2	This data packet token is part of a system for controlling multiple isochronous IN packets during one microframe. For each isochronous IN packet requested, the suffix of the DATAx PID represents the remaining number of packets to be transferred during the current micro-frame.
MDATA	This data packet token is part of a system for controlling multiple isochronous OUT packets during one microframe at high speed. All but the last packet sent during a microframe use the MDATA PID. The last packet sent uses DATA0, DATA1 or DATA2 depending on whether one, two or three packets were sent.

Table 1-11 **High speed data packets**

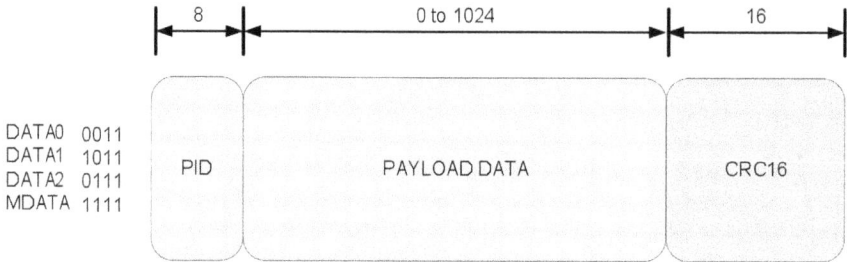

```
              8                    0 to 1024                    16

DATA0  0011
DATA1  1011      PID            PAYLOAD DATA              CRC16
DATA2  0111
MDATA  1111
```

Figure 1-22 **High speed data packet**

1-7-4 HANDSHAKE PACKETS

Handshake packets are used for acknowledging data or reporting errors. There are four type of handshake packets which consist simply of the PID.

Packet ID	Description
ACK	Acknowledgment that the packet has been successfully received.
NAK	Reports that the device temporary cannot send or receive data. Also used during interrupt transactions to inform the host there is no data to send.
STALL	The device finds itself in a state that requires intervention from the host (Endpoint is halted, or control pipe request is not supported)
NYET	No response yet. The device is not ready to answer (High Speed only).

Table 1-12 **Handshake packets**

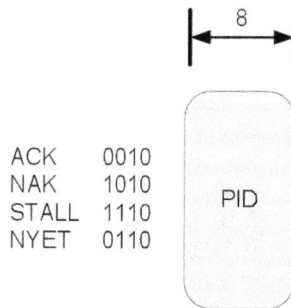

```
            8

ACK    0010
NAK    1010      PID
STALL  1110
NYET   0110
```

Figure 1-23 **Handshake packet**

1-7-5 SPLIT TRANSACTION SPECIAL TOKEN PACKETS

The split transaction token is used to support split transactions between the host controller communicating with a hub operating at high speed with full-/low-speed devices to some of its downstream facing ports. The SPLIT packet is the first packet in either a Start Split transaction or a Complete Split transaction, sent to a high speed hub when it is handling a low or full speed device.

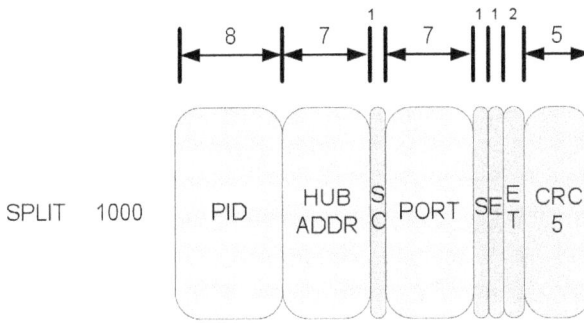

Figure 1-24 **Special packet**

SC	Start / Complete	0 = Start, 1 = Complete
S	Speed	0 = Full, 1 = Low
E	not used	0
ET	Endpoint Type	00 = Control 01 = Isochronous 10 = Bulk 11 = Interrupt

Table 1-13 **Control, Interrupt or Bulk Endpoints**

SC	Start / Complete	0 = Start, 1 = Complete
S and E	Start and End	00 = HS data is middle of FS data payload 01 = HS data is end of FS data payload 10 = HS data is start of FS data payload 11 = HS data is all of FS data payload
ET	Endpoint Type	00 = Control 01 = Isochronous 10 = Bulk 11 = Interrupt

Table 1-14 **Isochronous Endpoints**

47

1-8 DATA FLOW MODEL

This section defines the elements involved in the transmission of data across USB.

1-8-1 ENDPOINT

Endpoints function as the point of origin or the point of reception for data. An endpoint is a logical entity identified using an endpoint address. The endpoint address of a device is fixed, and is assigned when the device is designed, as opposed to the device address, which is assigned by the host dynamically during enumeration. An endpoint address consists of an endpoint number field (0 to 15), and a direction bit that indicates if the endpoint sends data to the host (IN) or receives data from the host (OUT). The maximum number of endpoints allowed on a single device is 32.

> Because RAM is allocated for buffers for each endpoint USB controllers fond on MCUs often don't implement 32 endpoints. You will find USB controllers with 4 endpoints only.

Endpoints contain configurable characteristics that define the behavior of a USB device:

- Bus access requirements

- Bandwidth requirement

- Error handling

- Maximum packet size that the endpoint is able to send or receive

- Transfer type

- Direction in which data is sent and receive from the host

ENDPOINT ZERO REQUIREMENT

Endpoint zero (also known as Default Endpoint) is a bi-directional endpoint used by the USB host system to get information, and configure the device via standard requests. All devices must implement an endpoint zero configured for control transfers (see section "Control Transfers" on page 49 for more information).

1-8-2 PIPES

A USB pipe is a logical association between an endpoint and a software structure in the USB host software system. USB pipes are used to send data from the host software to the device's endpoints. A USB pipe is associated to a unique endpoint address, type of transfer, maximum packet size, and interval for transfers.

The USB specification defines two types of pipes based on the communication mode:

▪ Stream Pipes: Data carried over the pipe is unstructured.

▪ Message Pipes: Data carried over the pipe has a defined structure.

The USB specification requires a default control pipe for each device. A default control pipe uses endpoint zero. The default control pipe is a bi-directional message pipe.

1-8-3 TRANSFERS

The USB specification defines four transfer types that match the bandwidth and services requirements of the host and the device application using a specific pipe. Each USB transfer encompasses one or more transactions that send data to and from the endpoint. The notion of transactions is related to the maximum payload size defined by each endpoint type, that is when a transfer is greater than this maximum, it will be split into one or more transactions to fulfill the action.

CONTROL TRANSFERS

Control transfers are used to configure and retrieve information about the device capabilities. They are used by the host to send standard requests during and after enumeration. Standard requests allow the host to learn about the device capabilities; for example, how many and which functions the device contains. Control transfers are also used for class-specific and vendor-specific requests.

A control transfer contains three stages: Setup, Data, and Status. These stages are listed in Table 1-15.

Stage	Description
Setup	The Setup stage includes information about the request. This SETUP stage represents one transaction.
Data	The Data stage contains data associated with request. Some standard and class-specific request may not require a Data stage. This stage is an IN or OUT directional transfer and the complete Data stage represents one ore more transactions.
Status	The Status stage, representing one transaction, is used to report the success or failure of the transfer. The direction of the Status stage is opposite to the direction of the Data stage. If the control transfer has no Data stage, the Status stage always is from the device (IN).

Table 1-15 **Control Transfer Stages**

BULK TRANSFERS

Bulk transfers are intended for devices that exchange large amounts of data where the transfer can take all of the available bus bandwidth. Bulk transfers are reliable, as error detection and retransmission mechanisms are implemented in hardware to guarantee data integrity. However, bulk transfers offer no guarantee on timing. Printers and mass storage devices are examples of devices that use bulk transfers.

INTERRUPT TRANSFERS

Interrupt transfers are designed to support devices with latency constrains. Devices using interrupt transfers can schedule data at any time. Devices using interrupt transfer provide a polling interval which determines when the scheduled data is transferred over the bus. Interrupt transfers are typically used for event notifications.

ISOCHRONOUS TRANSFERS

Isochronous transfers are used by devices that require data delivery at a constant rate with a certain degree of error-tolerance. Retransmission is not supported by isochronous transfers. Audio and video devices use isochronous transfers.

USB DATA FLOW MODEL

Figure 1-25 shows a graphical representation of the data flow model.

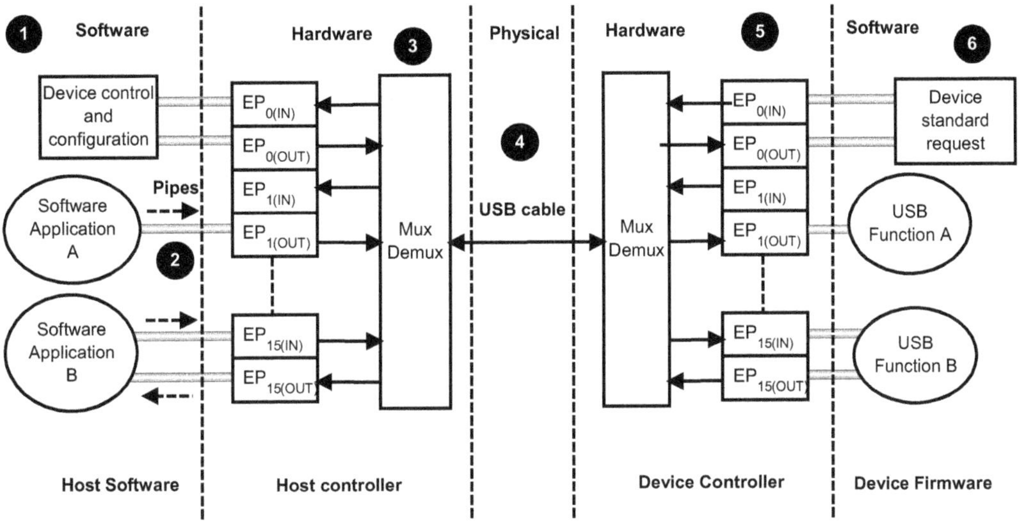

Figure 1-25 **USB data flow**

F1-25(1)   The host software uses standard requests to query and configure the device using the default pipe. The default pipe uses endpoint zero (EP0).

F1-25(2)   USB pipes allow associations between the host application and the device's endpoints. Host applications send and receive data through USB pipes.

F1-25(3)   The host controller is responsible for the transmission, reception, packing and unpacking of data over the bus.

F1-25(4)   Data is transmitted via the physical media.

F1-25(5)   The device controller is responsible for the transmission, reception, packing and unpacking of data over the bus. The USB controller informs the USB device software layer about several events such as bus events and transfer events.

F1-25(6)   The device software layer responds to the standard request, and implements one or more USB functions as specified in the USB class document.

TRANSFER COMPLETION

The notion of transfer completion is only relevant for control, bulk and interrupt transfers as isochronous transfers occur continuously and periodically by nature. In general, control, bulk and interrupt endpoints must transmit data payload sizes that are less than or equal to the endpoint's maximum data payload size. When a transfer's data payload is greater than the maximum data payload size, the transfer is split into several transactions whose payload is maximum-sized except the last transaction which contains the remaining data. A transfer is deemed complete when:

- The endpoint transfers exactly the amount of data expected.

- The endpoint transfers a short packet, that is a packet with a payload size less than the maximum.

- The endpoint transfers a zero-length packet.

DATA PACKET SIZE, TYPES, AND SPEED

Endpoints have several attributes in addition to their type, one of them being the maximum quantity of data that the endpoint can provide or consume in a single transaction.

A single transfer can involve less than the maximum quantity of data an endpoint can handle.

Transfer Type	Attributes	High Speed	Full Speed	Low Speed	Uses
Control	Quality + time	64 bytes	8,16,32 or 64 bytes	8 bytes	System control
Bulk	Quality	<512 bytes	8,16,32 or 64 bytes	NA	Printer, scanner
Interrupt	Quality + time	<1024 bytes	<64 bytes	8 bytes	Mouse, keyboard
Isochronous	Time	<3072 bytes	<1023 bytes	NA	Audio, video

Table 1-16 **Maximum DATA packet size**

1-9 TRANSACTIONS, TRANSFERS, AND FRAMES

A *transfer* is the largest unit of communication in USB, and consists of one or more *transactions* that can carry data to or from an endpoint. A transaction is made up of a sequence of three packets: token, data, and (in most cases) a handshake packet.

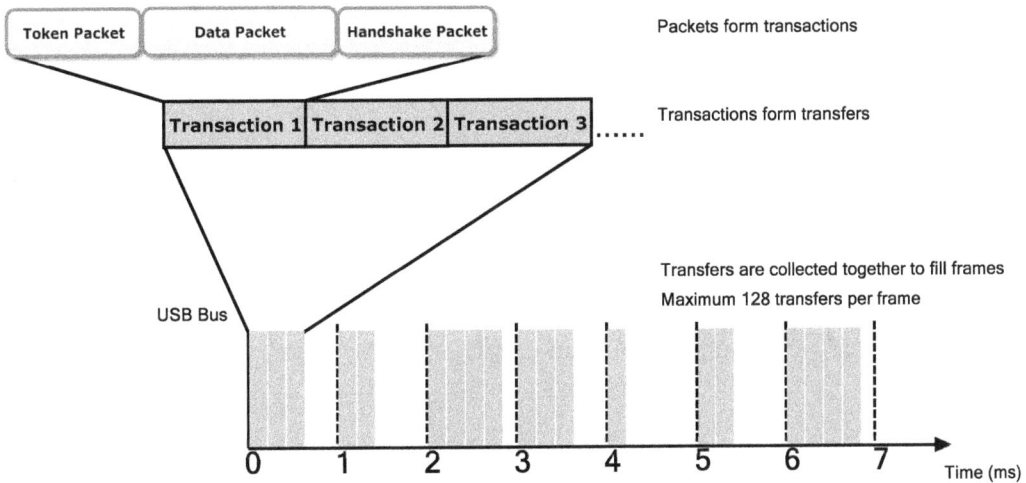

Figure 1-26 **Packets, transactions, and transfers**

For IN and OUT transactions used for isochronous transfers, there are only two packets. The handshake packet on the end is omitted. This is because error-checking is not required for IN and OUT transactions.

1-10 FRAMES AND MICROFRAMES

To ensure that the host and devices remain synchronized, bus timing is broken down into segments of a fixed duration. For low- or full-speed buses, the bus time is divided into 1 millisecond units, called *frames*. For a high-speed bus, the bus time is divided into 125 microsecond units, called microframes.

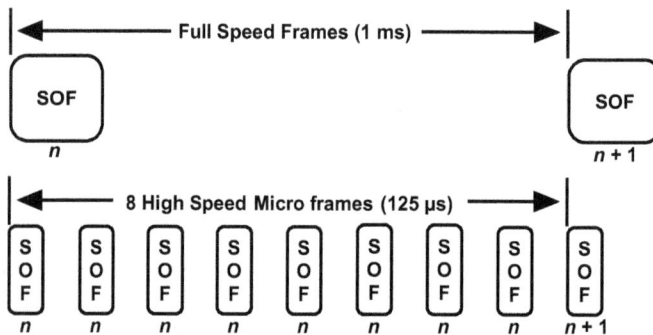

Figure 1-27 **Packets per microframe**

The first packet of each frame is the Start-Of-Frame packet (SOF). In low and full speed, a frame is transmitted every 1 ms.

At high speed the 1 ms frame is divided into eight microframes. A SOF packet is sent at the start of each of these eight microframes, each having the same frame number, which then increments every 1 ms.

On a low speed link, to preserve bandwidth, a Keep Alive signal is sent every millisecond, instead of a Start of Frame packet. In fact Keep Alives may be sent by a hub on a low speed link whenever the hub sees a full speed token packet.

1-10-1 PACKETS PER (MICRO)FRAME

At high speed it is possible to specify up to three isochronous or interrupt transfers per microframe, rather than the 1 transfer per frame of full speed; giving a maximum possible isochronous or interrupt transfer rate of 192 Mb/s.

No more than 90% of any frame to be allocated for periodic transfers (Interrupt and Isochronous) on a full speed bus. (80% in high speed)

In a highly saturated bus with periodic transfers, the remaining 10% is left for control transfers and once those have been allocated, bulk transfers will get its slice of what is left.

> *i*
>
> It is important when designing an embedded system to determine which transfer mode will be used as it can have a high impact on the product performance. For example, using the Interrupt transfer can guarantee a good bandwidth usage. And, it also allows the vendor to use HID drivers from the General Purpose Operating Systems (GPOS) for its product. Using a Bulk transfer requires a custom driver on the GPOS.

All USB transactions are performed in 1mSec frames (LS and FS) or 125 μsec frames (HS) initiated by the Host. Time Division Multiplexing is used to separate packets or transactions from different sources within each frame.

1-11 USB'S ACTUAL THROUGHPUT

The actual throughput on the bus is a function of:

■ The target device's ability to send or receive data (processor clock, DMA support)

■ The bandwidth consumption of other devices on the bus

■ The efficiency of the host's USB software stack

Assuming that only the device endpoint consumes bus bandwidth, and that both the device and the host are able to send or receive data as fast as USB can move it, then the maximum attainable bandwidth is a function of the transfer type and signaling rate.

Each transfer type determines various characteristics of the communication flow, including the following:

■ Data format imposed by the bus

■ Direction of communication flow

■ Packet size constraints

■ Bus access constraints

■ Latency constraints

■ Required data sequences

■ Error handling

The capabilities of a device's endpoints are determined by the device's designers.

The achievable bandwidth under various circumstances is defined and described in Chapter 5 of the USB Specification. Multiple tables provide the required calculation to determine the achievable bandwidth per bus speed and transfer type. Each table shows the protocol overhead required for the specific transfer type (and speed), and sample data payload sizes. The following is one example:

Protocol Overhead (55 bytes)		(3x4 SYNC bytes, 3 PID bytes, 2 EP/ADDR+CRC bytes, 2 CRC16, and a 3x(1+11) byte interpacket delay (EOP, etc.))			
Data Payload	Max Bandwidth (bytes/second)	Microframe Bandwidth per Transfer	Max Transfers	Bytes Remaining	Bytes/ Microframe Useful Data
1	1064000	1%	133	52	133
2	2096000	1%	131	33	262
4	4064000	1%	127	7	508
8	7616000	1%	119	3	952
16	13440000	1%	105	45	1680
32	22016000	1%	86	18	2752
64	32256000	2%	63	3	4032
128	40960000	2%	40	180	5120
256	49152000	4%	24	36	6144
512	53248000	8%	13	129	6656
Max	**60000000**				**7500**

Table 1-17 **High-speed Bulk Transaction Limits (source: USB Specification, chapter 5)**

A transaction of a particular transfer type typically requires multiple packets. The protocol overhead for each packet includes:

■ An 8-bits (FS/LS) or 32-bits (HS) SYNC field

■ A PID byte

■ A 3-bit (FS/LS) or 8-bit (HS) EOP

■ In a token packet: endpoint number + device address + CRC5 = 16 bits

■ In a data packet: 16-bits CRC16 + any data field (8 bits per byte)

■ For transaction with multiple packets, the inter packet gap or bus turnaround time required.

For these calculations, there is assumed to be no bit-stuffing required.

1-12 ENUMERATION

Enumeration is the process where the host configures the device and learns about the device's capabilities. The host starts enumeration after the device is attached to one of the root or external hub ports.

Device enumeration follows these steps:

1   Device Attachment

2   Reset Device

3   Get Device Descriptor

4   Reset Device (again)

5   Assign Address

6   Get Configuration and Other Descriptors

7   Select Device Driver

8   Set Configuration

DEVICE ATTACHMENT

The host or hub detects the connection of a new device when a cable is connected between the host/hub port and the device. On first detection of the signal, the host/hub waits for at least 100ms, making sure the connector is inserted completely and power is not fluctuating on the device.

RESET DEVICE

The host then sends a USB Reset packet to the device to make sure the device is in a known state. While In this state, the device responds to the default address 0. Because of the master/slave nature of the protocol, one device is reset at a time. Thus, one device can respond to address 0.

GET DEVICE DESCRIPTOR

The next step is for the host to send a request to endpoint 0 of device address 0 to determine the maximum packet size. The Get Descriptor (Device) command is used for that purpose. There are a few requests like this one where the device must answer when using address 0.

RESET DEVICE (AGAIN)

The host resets the device a second time.

ASSIGN ADDRESS

At this stage, this is when a unique address will be assigned to the device using the Set Address request.

GET CONFIGURATION AND OTHER DESCRIPTORS

The following step is for the host to collect the remaining device information that will be used for the device configuration. The standard requests used are:

- Get Device Descriptor

- Get Configuration Descriptor

- Get String Descriptor

SELECT DEVICE DRIVER

At this stage, we start talking about device driver, because now that the host knows everything he needs to know about the device, it will start interacting with the device using the specific device driver.

SET CONFIGURATION

The Set Configuration request is then send to the device by the device driver.

Even if from this point moving forward in time, the device is configured and can now perform the functions (classes) it is designed to do, it still is required to respond to standard requests.

When writing a USB device driver for connecting to a Windows host, you may notice that the first request sent by the host has an unexpectedly large wLength of 64 bytes. The Windows host will then request a single IN packet, but will reset the device immediately, regardless of the value of the max packet length. The purpose of this transaction is to provide the Windows host with the packet size for all upcoming control transfers. That value is contained only in the first eight bytes of the IN packet.

So, a reset after the first 8 bytes of the IN packet is not a problem on Windows. It is expected behavior.

Because the device stack may be confused after not being able to complete the transmission of all the 18 bytes of the device descriptor a second reset places the device in a known good state.

ENUMERATION FAILURE

According to the USB protocol specification, a host will attempt to read a descriptor three times when something is wrong with a descriptor. The three reads with be spaced with long pauses between requests. If it is not successful after the third attempt, the host reports an error with the device enumeration.

Other cases of when a Host can decide to not enumerate a device are:

- If the appropriate driver for the device is not present in the host,

- If the interface description does not match what the host can do,

In these cases, the host should reset the bus or even power down the port (connector).

1-13 USB STACKS

1-13-1 DEVICE STACK

The USB device stack is smaller than the host stack. A typical implementation with one device function has a footprint of 5 to 10K and a RAM usage of 1 to 2K.

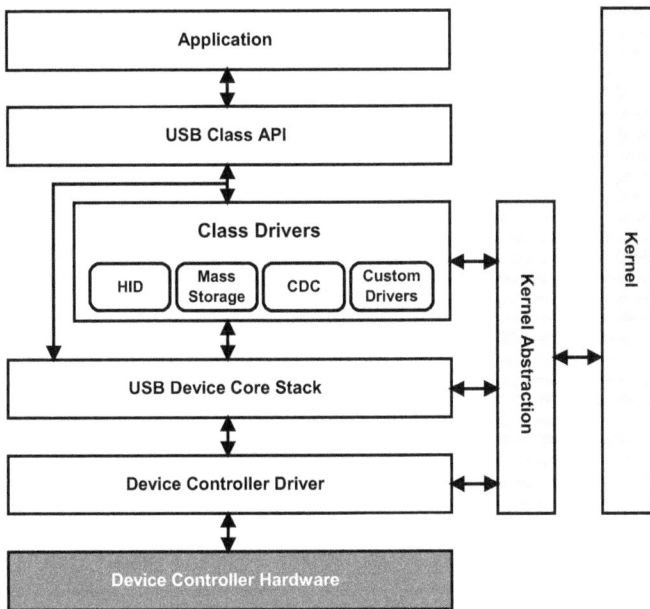

Figure 1-28 **USB device stack**

A device normally consists of three layers: A driver for hardware access, the core and at least a USB class driver or the bulk communication component.

61

1-13-2 HOST STACK

A USB host stack is more complex than a USB device stack, mainly because the host is required to manage the root hub and all bandwidth.

A typical footprint for a USB host stack is in the range of 35 to 45K of code space. For the RAM requirements is depends greatly of the USB class used. Some classes, such as HID or MSC, may require pools of memory to process large amount of data.

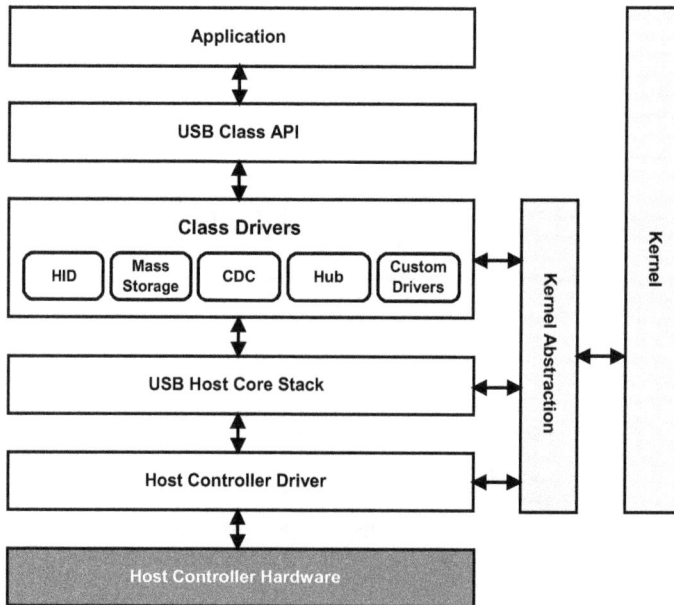

Figure 1-29 **USB host stack**

1-13-3 USB OTG STACK

The advent of the personal digital assistant (PDA) and the cellphone/smartphone introduced the need for equipment able to operate as either a host or a device. Within the general USB specification, it is not possible to configure the bus in a multimaster arrangement. A supplement to USB 2.0 defines a Host Negotiation Protocol (HNP) to allow two devices to negotiate for the role of host.

USB OTG allows for devices to function as both host and peripheral. The devices connect to either a PC or other portable devices through the same smaller connectors, but with an added pin (ID). The protocol provides enhancements for dynamic switching with the definition of the Session Request Protocols (SRP).

When two dual role (OTG) devices are connected together with the special OTG cable, the cable sets a default host and default peripheral depending on which end of the cable is used. If the software application requires the roles to be reversed, this is when HNP enters into action, and reverse the roles.

The complete information on USB OTG is found on the USB-IF website's OTG Developer's page at www.usb.org/developers/onthego/.

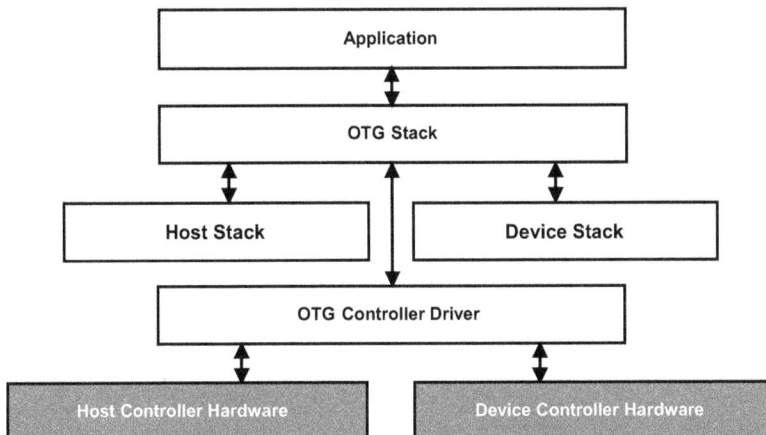

Figure 1-30 **USB OTG stack**

i

As seen on Figure 1-30, a USB OTG stack is the sum of a USB Device stack, a USB Host stack, a USB Device driver, a USB Host driver and some OTG software (HNP, SRP and driver switcher). This means that a USB OTG stack is more expensive then the combination of a USB Device and USB Host. When presented this way, and reviewing the product design objectives, many embedded developers will opt to implement the two stacks with two physical connectors (host and device) versus the single OTG connector. An exception would be a mobile device such as a PDA or smartphone, which have tight space requirements.

OTG was popular when introduced. Today, we see that its deployment has drastically slowed. The equipment for which OTG was designed (PDA and smartphones) are now using wireless protocols to achieve the same goals.

1-14 COMPLIANCE

When a manufacturer wants to have a USB logo on its product, the product needs to be certified by the USB organization. This is why the USB organization has created a compliance program. It contains two main criteria: checklists and compliance testing. The checklists contain questions relating to a product and its behavior. The USB-IF Compliance Program is accessible for a small membership fee.

Figure 1-31 **Official certified USB logos**

1-14-1 USB DEVICE TESTING

The USB Implementer's Forum offers free diagnostic tools including the compliance test tool USB Command Verifier (USBCV).

Module	USB-CV test suite
USB Device Core Stack	Chapter 9 tests
Human interface device class	HID class tests
Mass Storage Class	MSC tests
Personal Healthcare Device Class	PHDC tests

Figure 1-32 **Device testing suites**

All the drivers offered by Micriµm have been tested with all the above USB-CV test suites.

1-14-2 USB GOLD TREE

To verify interoperability and functionality of a USB device, the USB-IF uses a USB equipment setup of known, good, USB devices. When all interconnected together it is referred to as the Gold-tree (see Figure 1-33).

The gold-tree is supposed to consist of USB-IF certified consumer devices that are widely available in the market. Unfortunately, the shelf-life of consumer products is limited and some items become difficult to find as time goes by. As a result, the USB-IF will no longer identify specific makes and models of products for the gold-tree. The shelf life and availability of consumer products is just too short and is difficult to maintain. Because there is nothing special about the peripherals and hubs, except being USB Certified, product classes and types are specified.

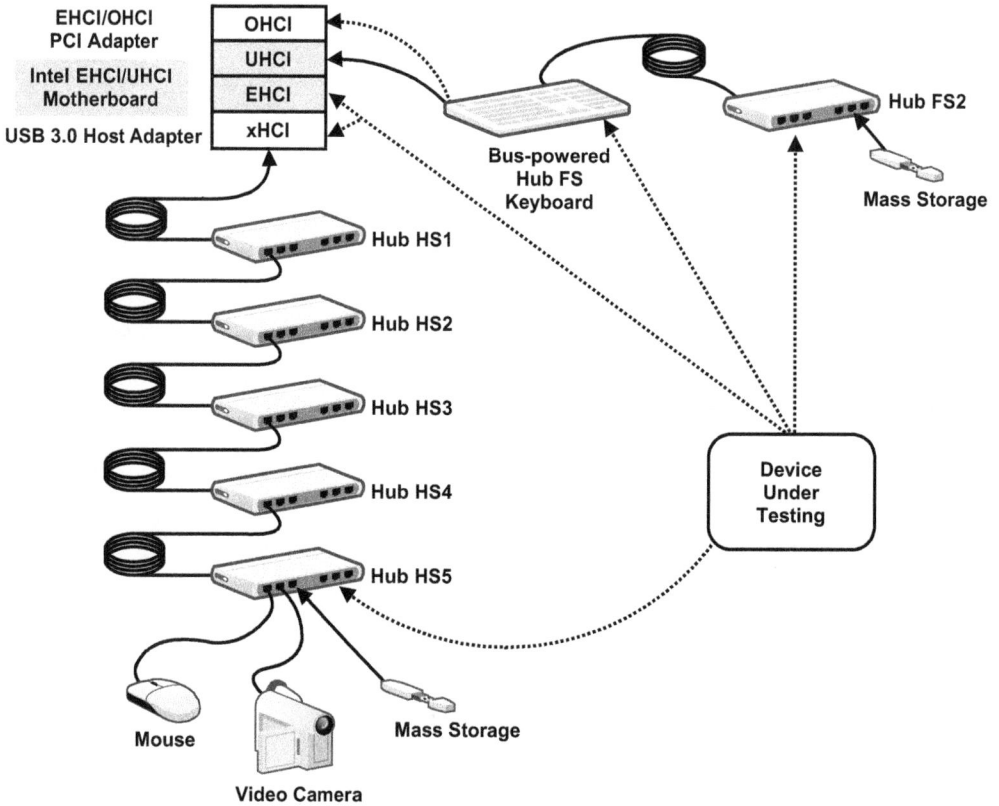

Figure 1-33 **Gold tree**

GOLD TREE COMPONENT LIST

▦ A Host PC with different USB controllers

    ▦ EHCI

    ▦ OHCI

    ▦ UHCI

    ▦ xHCI (USB 3.0)

    ▦ 5 HS self powered hubs

▦ One FS self-powered hub

▦ One FS keyboard/hub

- Five 5-meter USB cables

- One mouse

- Two mass storage devices

- One video camera

Additional information can be found at:
`http://compliance.usb.org/index.asp?UpdateFile=Interoperability`

1-14-3 USB HOST TESTING

Unfortunately, there are no standards to test a USB host. Because the USB bus is a master/slave bus, a device can be tested with a host. but a host cannot test a host. A manufacturer wanting to validate the operation and performance of a USB host based product will have to develop his own testing methods.

If you are using a commercial USB host stack, the vendor will be able to help you with the software validation. But for the hardware validation, you are on your own when validating a USB host based product.

Getting Started

This chapter gives you some insight into how to install and use the µC/USB-Device stack. The following topics are explained in this chapter:

■ Prerequisites

■ Downloading the source code files

■ Installing the files

■ Building the sample application

■ Running the sample application

After the completion of this chapter, you should be able to build and run your first USB application using the µC/USB-Device stack.

2-1 PREREQUISITES

Before running your first application, you must ensure that you have the minimal set of required tools and components:

▓ Toolchain for your specific microcontroller.

▓ Development board.

▓ µC/USB-Device stack with the source code of at least one of the Micrium USB classes.

▓ USB device controller driver compatible with your hardware for the µC/USB-Device stack.

▓ Board support package (BSP) for your development board.

▓ Example project for your selected RTOS (that is µC/OS-II or µC/OS-III).

If Micrium does not support your USB device controller or BSP, you will have to write your own device driver. Refer to Chapter 6, "Device Driver Guide" on page 125 for more information on writing your own USB device driver.

2-2 DOWNLOADING THE SOURCE CODE FILES

µC/USB-Device can be downloaded from the Micrium customer portal. The distribution package includes the full source code and documentation. You can log into the Micrium customer portal at the address below to begin your download (you must have a valid license to gain access to the file):

http://micrium.com/login

µC/USB-Device depends on other modules, and you need to install all the required modules before building your application. Depending on the availability of support for your hardware platform, ports and drivers may or may not be available for download from the customer portal. Table 2-1 shows the module dependency for µC/USB-Device.

Module Name	Required	Note(s)
µC/USB-Device Core	YES	Hardware independent USB stack.
µC/USB-Device Driver	YES	USB device controller driver. Available only if Micrium supports your controller, otherwise you have to develop it yourself.
µC/USB-Device Vendor Class	Optional	Available only if you purchased the Vendor class.
µC/USB-Device MSC	Optional	Available only if you purchased the Mass Storage Class (MSC).
µC/USB-Device HID Class	Optional	Available only if you purchased the Human Interface Device (HID) class.
µC/USB-Device CDC ACM	Optional	Available only if you purchased the Communication Device Class (CDC) with the Abstract Control Model (ACM) subclass.
µC/USB-Device PHDC	Optional	Available only if you purchased the Personal Healthcare Device Class (PHDC).
µC/CPU Core	YES	
µC/CPU Port	YES	Available only if Micrium has support for your processor architecture.
µC/LIB Core	YES	Micrium run-time library.
µC/LIB Port	Optional	Available only if Micrium has support for your processor architecture.
µC/OS-II Core	Optional	Available only if your application is using µC/OS-II
µC/OS-II Port	Optional	Available only if Micrium has support for your processor architecture.
µC/OS-III Core	Optional	Available only if your application is using µC/OS-III
µC/OS-III Port	Optional	Available only if Micrium has support for your processor architecture.

Table 2-1 **µC/USB-Device Module Dependency**

Table 2-1 indicates that all the µC/USB-Device classes are optional because there is no mandatory class to purchase with the µC/USB-Device Core and Driver. The class to purchase will depend on your needs. But don't forget that you need a class to build a complete USB project. Table 2-1 also indicates that µC/OS-II and -III Core and Port are optional. Indeed, µC/USB-Device stack does not assume a specific real-time operating system to work with, but it still requires one.

2-3 INSTALLING THE FILES

Once all the distribution packages have been downloaded to your host machine, extract all the files at the root of your C:\ drive for instance. The package may be extracted to any location. After extracting all the files, the directory structure should look as illustrated in Figure 2-1. In the example, all Micrium products sub-folders shown in Figure 2-1 will be located in C:\Micrium\Software\.

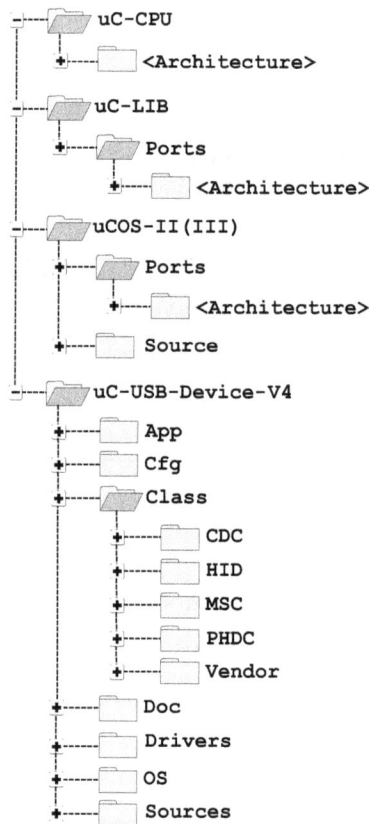

Figure 2-1 **Directory Tree for µC/USB-Device**

2-4 BUILDING THE SAMPLE APPLICATION

This section describes all the steps required to build a USB-based application. The instructions provided in this section are not intended for any particular toolchain, but instead are described in a generic way that can be adapted to any toolchain.

The best way to start building a USB-based project is to start from an existing project. If you are using µC/OS-II or µC/OS-III, Micrium provides example projects for multiple development boards and compilers. If your target board is not listed on Micrium's web site, you can download an example project for a similar board or microcontroller.

The purpose of the sample project is to allow a host to enumerate your device. You will add a USB class instance to both, full-speed and high-speed configurations (if both are supported by your controller). Refer to section 7-1 "Class Instance Concept" on page 147 for more details about the class instance concept. After you have successfully completed and run the sample project, you can use it as a starting point to run other USB class demos you may have purchased.

µC/USB-Device requires a Real-Time Operating System (RTOS). The following assumes that you have a working example project running on µC/OS-II or µC/OS-III.

2-4-1 UNDERSTANDING MICRIUM EXAMPLES

A Micrium example project is usually placed in the following directory structure.

```
\Micrium
    \Software
        \EvalBoards
            \<manufacturer>
                \<board_name>
                    \<compiler>
                        \<project name>
                            \*.*
```

Note that Micrium does *not* provide by default an example project with the µC/USB-Device distribution package. Micrium examples are provided to customers in specific situations. If it happens that you receive a Micrium example, the directory structure shown above is generally used by Micrium. You may use a different directory structure to store the application and toolchain projects files.

\Micrium

This is where Micrium places all software components and projects. This directory is generally located at the root directory.

\Software

This sub-directory contains all software components and projects.

\EvalBoards

This sub-directory contains all projects related to evaluation boards supported by Micrium.

\<manufacturer>

This is the name of the manufacturer of the evaluation board. In some cases this can also be the name of the microcontroller manufacturer.

\<board name>

This is the name of the evaluation board.

\<compiler>

This is the name of the compiler or compiler manufacturer used to build the code for the evaluation board.

\<project name>

The name of the project that will be demonstrated. For example a simple µC/USB-Device with µC/OS-III project might have the project name 'uCOS-III-USBD'.

.

These are the source files for the project. This directory contains configuration files **app_cfg.h**, **os_cfg.h**, **os_cfg_app.h**, **cpu_cfg.h** and other project-required sources files.

> **os_cfg.h** is a configuration file used to configure µC/OS-III (or µC/OS-II) parameters such as the maximum number of tasks, events, objects, which µC/OS-III services are enabled (semaphores, mailboxes, queues), and so on. **os_cfg.h** is a required file for any µC/OS-III application. See the µC/OS-III documentation and books for further information.

> **app.c** contains the application code for the example project. As with most C programs, code execution starts at **main()**. At a minimum, **app.c** initializes µC/OS-III and creates a startup task that initializes other Micrium modules.

> **app_cfg.h** is a configuration file for your application. This file contains **#defines** to configure the priorities and stack sizes of your application and the Micrium modules' tasks.

> **app_<module>.c** and **app_<module>.h** These optional files contain the Micrium modules' (µC/TCP-IP, µC/FS, µC/USB-Host, etc) initialization code. They may or may not be present in the example projects.

2-4-2 COPYING AND MODIFYING TEMPLATE FILES

Copy the files from the application template and configuration folders into your application as illustrated in Figure 2-2.

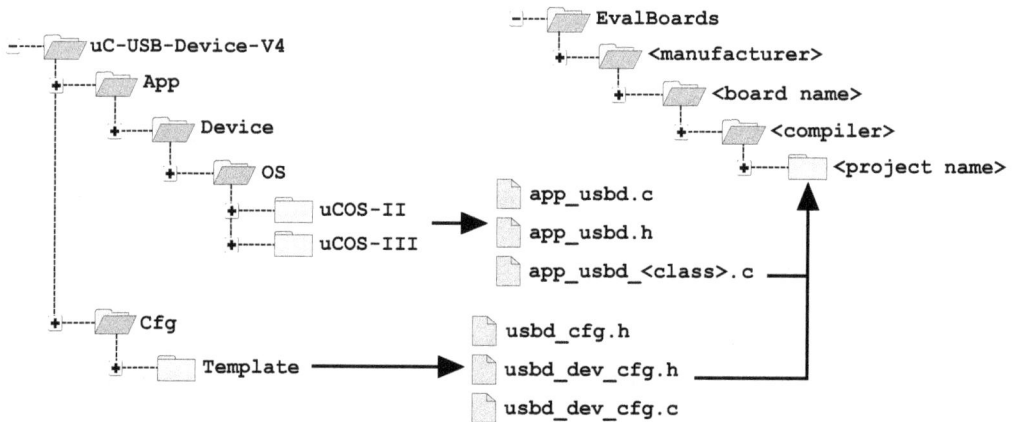

Figure 2-2 **Copying Template Files.**

app_usbd.* is the master template for USB application-specific initialization code. This file contains the function **App_USBD_Init()**, which initializes the USB stack and class-specific demos.

app_usbd_<class>.c contains a template to initialize and use a certain class. This file contains the class demo application. In general, the class application initializes the class, creates a class instance, and adds the instance to the full-speed and high-speed configurations. Refer to the chapter(s) of the USB class(es) you purchased for more details about the USB class demos.

usbd_cfg.h is a configuration file used to setup µC/USB-Device stack parameters such as the maximum number of configurations, interfaces, or class-related parameters.

usbd_dev_cfg.c and **usbd_dev_cfg.h** are configuration files used to set device parameters such as vendor ID, product ID, and device release number. They are also necessary to configure the USB device controller driver parameters, such as base address, dedicated memory base address and size, controller's speed, and endpoint capabilities.

MODIFY DEVICE CONFIGURATION

Modify the device configuration file (**usbd_cfg.c**) as needed for your application. See the coding listing below for details.

```
USBD_DEV_CFG  USBD_DevCfg_Template = {            (1)
    0xFFFE,                                        (2)
    0x1234,
    0x0100,
    "OEM MANUFACTURER",                            (3)
    "OEM PRODUCT",
    "1234567890ABCDEF",
    USBD_LANG_ID_ENGLISH_US                        (4)
};
```

Listing 2-1 **Device Configuration Template**

L2-1(1)   Give your device configuration a meaningful name by replacing the word "**Template**".

L2-1(2)   Assign the Vendor ID, Product ID and Device Release Number. For development purposes you can use the default values, but once you decide to release your product, you must contact the USB Implementers Forum (USB-IF) at *www.usb.org* in order to get valid IDs. USB-IF is a non-profit organization that among other activities, maintains all USB Vendor ID and Product ID numbers.

L2-1(3)   Specify human readable Vendor ID, Product ID, and Device Release Number strings.

L2-1(4)   A USB device can store strings in multiple languages. Specify the language used in your strings. The #defines for the other languages are defined in the file **usbd_core.h** in the section "Language Identifiers".

MODIFY DRIVER CONFIGURATION

Modify the driver configuration (**usbd_dev_cfg.c**) as needed for your controller. See Listing 2-2 below for details.

```
USBD_DRV_CFG  USBD_DrvCfg_Template = {          (1)
    0x00000000,                                  (2)
    0x00000000,                                  (3)
            0u,
    USBD_DEV_SPD_FULL,                           (4)
    USBD_DrvEP_InfoTbl_Template                  (5)
};
```

Listing 2-2 **Driver Configuration Template**

L2-2(1)   Give your driver configuration a meaningful name by replacing the word "**Template**".

L2-2(2)   Specify the base address of your USB device controller.

L2-2(3)   If your target has dedicated memory for the USB controller, you can specify its base address and size here. Depending on the USB controller, dedicated memory can be used to allocate driver buffers or DMA descriptors.

L2-2(4)   Specify the USB device controller speed: **USBD_DEV_SPD_HIGH** if your controller supports high-speed or **USBD_DEV_SPD_FULL** if your controller supports only full-speed.

L2-2(5)   Specify the endpoint information table. The endpoint information table should be defined in your USB device controller BSP files. Refer to section 6-5-1 "Endpoint Information Table" on page 135 for more details on the endpoint information table.

MODIFY USB APPLICATION INITIALIZATION CODE

Listing 2-3 shows the code that you should modify based on your specific configuration done previously. You should modify the parts that are highlighted by the text in bold. The code snippet is extracted from the function **App_USBD_Init()** defined in **app_usbd.c**. The complete initialization sequence performed by **App_USBD_Init()** is presented in Listing 2-5.

```
#include  <usbd_bsp_template.h>                         (1)

CPU_BOOLEAN  App_USBD_Init (void)
{
    CPU_INT08U   dev_nbr;
    CPU_INT08U   cfg_fs_nbr;
    USBD_ERR     err;


    USBD_Init(&err);                                     (2)

    dev_nbr = USBD_DevAdd(&USBD_DevCfg_Template,         (3)
                          &App_USBD_BusFncts,
                          &USBD_DrvAPI_Template,          (4)
                          &USBD_DrvCfg_Template,          (5)
                          &USBD_DrvBSP_Template,          (6)
                          &err);

    if (USBD_DrvCfg_Template.Spd == USBD_DEV_SPD_HIGH) {  (7)

        cfg_hs_nbr = USBD_CfgAdd( dev_nbr,
                          USBD_DEV_ATTRIB_SELF_POWERED,
                          100u,
                          USBD_DEV_SPD_HIGH,
                          "HS configuration",
                          &err);
    }
    ....
}
```

Listing 2-3 **App_USBD_Init() in app_usbd.c**

L2-3(1)   Include the USB driver BSP header file that is specific to your board. This file can be found in the following folder:

\Micrium\Software\uC-USB-Device\Drivers\<controller>\BSP\<board name>

L2-3(2)   Initialize the USB device stack's internal variables, structures and core RTOS port.

L2-3(3)   Specify the address of the device configuration structure that you modified in section "Modify Device Configuration" on page 77.

L2-3(4)   Specify the address of the driver's API structure. The driver's API structure is defined in the driver's header file named **usbd_drv_<controller>.h**.

L2-3(5)   Specify the address of the driver configuration structure that you modified in the section "Modify Driver Configuration" on page 78.

L2-3(6)   Specify the endpoint information table. The endpoint information table should be defined in your USB device controller BSP files.

L2-3(7)   If the device controller supports high-speed, create a high-speed configuration for the specified device.

2-4-3 INCLUDING USB DEVICE STACK SOURCE CODE

First, include the following files in your project from the µC/USB-Device source code distribution, as indicated in Figure 2-3.

```
---- uC-USB-Device-V4
  +---- Class
  |   +---- <class>
  |           usbd_<class>.c
  +---- Driver
  |   +---- <controller>
  |           usbd_drv_<controller>.c
  |       +---- BSP
  |           +---- <board name>
  |                   usbd_bsp_<controller>.c
  +---- OS
  |   +---- <RTOS>
  |           usbd_os.c
  +---- Source
          usbd_os.c
          usbd_ep.c
          usbd_core.c
```

Figure 2-3 µC/USB-Device Source Code

Second, add the following include paths to your project's C compiler settings:

```
\Micrium\Software\uC-USB-Device\Source\
\Micrium\Software\uC-USB-Device\Class\<class>\
\Micrium\Software\uC-USB-Device\Drivers\<controller>
\Micrium\Software\uC-USB-Device\Drivers\<controller>\BSP\<board name>
```

2-4-4 MODIFYING THE APPLICATION CONFIGURATION FILE

The USB application initialization code templates assume the presence of **app_cfg.h**. The following **#defines** must be present in **app_cfg.h** in order to build the sample application.

```
#define  APP_CFG_USBD_EN                        DEF_ENABLED        (1)

#define  USBD_OS_CFG_CORE_TASK_PRIO                   6u           (2)
#define  USBD_OS_CFG_TRACE_TASK_PRIO                  7u
#define  USBD_OS_CFG_CORE_TASK_STK_SIZE            256u
#define  USBD_OS_CFG_TRACE_TASK_STK_SIZE           256u

#define  APP_CFG_USBD_CDC_EN                    DEF_ENABLED        (3)
#define  APP_CFG_USBD_HID_EN                    DEF_DISABLED
#define  APP_CFG_USBD_MSC_EN                    DEF_DISABLED
#define  APP_CFG_USBD_PHDC_EN                   DEF_DISABLED
#define  APP_CFG_USBD_VENDOR_EN                 DEF_DISABLED

#define  LIB_MEM_CFG_OPTIMIZE_ASM_EN            DEF_DISABLED       (4)
#define  LIB_MEM_CFG_ARG_CHK_EXT_EN             DEF_ENABLED
#define  LIB_MEM_CFG_ALLOC_EN                   DEF_ENABLED
#define  LIB_MEM_CFG_HEAP_SIZE                      1024u

#define  TRACE_LEVEL_OFF                             0u            (5)
#define  TRACE_LEVEL_INFO                            1u
#define  TRACE_LEVEL_DBG                             2u

#define  APP_CFG_TRACE_LEVEL                    TRACE_LEVEL_DBG    (6)
#define  APP_CFG_TRACE                          printf             (7)

#define  APP_TRACE_INFO(x)    \
 ((APP_CFG_TRACE_LEVEL >= TRACE_LEVEL_INFO)  ? (void)(APP_CFG_TRACE x) : (void)0)
#define  APP_TRACE_DBG(x)     \
 ((APP_CFG_TRACE_LEVEL >= TRACE_LEVEL_DBG)   ? (void)(APP_CFG_TRACE x) : (void)0)
```

Listing 2-4 **Application Configuration #defines**

L2-4(1)   **APP_CFG_USBD_EN** enables or disables the USB application initialization code.

L2-4(2)   These #defines relate to the µC/USB-Device OS port. The µC/USB-Device core requires only one task to manage control requests and asynchronous transfers, and a second, optional task to output trace events (if trace capability is enabled). To properly set the priority of the core and debug tasks, refer to section 5-2-1 "Task Priorities" on page 117.

L2-4(3)   This **#define** enables the USB class-specific demo. You can enable one or more USB class-specific demos. If you enable several USB class-specific demos, your device will be a composite device.

L2-4(4)   Configure the desired size of the heap memory. Heap memory is only used for µC/USB-Device drivers that use internal buffers and DMA descriptors which are allocated at run-time. Refer to the µC/LIB documentation for more details on the other µC/LIB constants.

L2-4(5)   Most Micrium examples contain application trace macros to output human-readable debugging information. Two levels of tracing are enabled: INFO and DBG. INFO traces high-level operations, and DBG traces high-level operations and return errors. Application-level tracing is different from µC/USB-Device tracing (refer to Chapter 13, "Debug and Trace" on page 289 for more details).

L2-4(6)   Define the application trace level.

L2-4(7)   Specify which function should be used to redirect the output of human-readable application tracing. You can select the standard output via **printf()**, or another output such as a text terminal using a serial interface.

Every USB class also needs to have certain constants defined to work correctly. Table 2-2 presents the section to refer to based on the USB class.

Communications Device Class (CDC)	section 8-3-1 "General Configuration" on page 169
Human Interface Device Class (HID)	section 9-3-1 "General Configuration" on page 193
Mass Storage Class (MSC)	section 10-4-1 "General Configuration" on page 226
Personal Healthcare Device Class (PHDC)	section 11-2-1 "General configuration" on page 244
Vendor Class	section 12-2-1 "General Configuration" on page 265

Table 2-2 **USB Class Configuration References**

2-5 RUNNING THE SAMPLE APPLICATION

The first step to integrate the demo application into your application code is to call `App_USBD_Init()`. This function is responsible for the following steps:

- Initializing the USB device stack.

- Creating and adding a device instance.

- Creating and adding configurations.

- Calling USB class-specific application code.

- Starting the USB device stack.

The `App_USBD_Init()` function is described in Listing 2-5.

```
CPU_BOOLEAN  App_USBD_Init (void)
{
    CPU_INT08U   dev_nbr;
    CPU_INT08U   cfg_hs_nbr;
    CPU_INT08U   cfg_fs_nbr;
    CPU_BOOLEAN  ok;
    USBD_ERR     err;


    USBD_Init(&err);                          (1)
    if (err != USBD_ERR_NONE) {
        /* $$$$ Handle error. */
        return (DEF_FAIL);
    }
```

```
dev_nbr = USBD_DevAdd(&USBD_DevCfg_<controller>,              (2)
                      &App_USBD_BusFncts,
                      &USBD_DrvAPI_<controller>,
                      &USBD_DrvCfg_<controller>,
                      &USBD_DrvBSP_<board name>,
                      &err);
if (err != USBD_ERR_NONE) {
    /* $$$$ Handle error. */
    return (DEF_FAIL);
}


cfg_hs_nbr = USBD_CFG_NBR_NONE;
cfg_fs_nbr = USBD_CFG_NBR_NONE;

if (USBD_DrvCfg_<controller>.Spd == USBD_DEV_SPD_HIGH) {

    cfg_hs_nbr = USBD_CfgAdd( dev_nbr,                         (3)
                             USBD_DEV_ATTRIB_SELF_POWERED,
                             100u,
                             USBD_DEV_SPD_HIGH,
                             "HS configuration",
                             &err);
    if (err != USBD_ERR_NONE) {
        /* $$$$ Handle error. */
        return (DEF_FAIL);
    }
}


cfg_fs_nbr = USBD_CfgAdd( dev_nbr,                             (4)
                         USBD_DEV_ATTRIB_SELF_POWERED,
                         100u,
                         USBD_DEV_SPD_FULL,
                         "FS configuration",
                         &err);
if (err != USBD_ERR_NONE) {
    /* $$$$ Handle error. */
    return (DEF_FAIL);
}
```

```
        if ((cfg_fs_nbr != USBD_CFG_NBR_NONE) &&
            (cfg_hs_nbr != USBD_CFG_NBR_NONE)) {
            USBD_CfgOtherSpeed(dev_nbr,                                  (5)
                               cfg_hs_nbr,
                               cfg_fs_nbr,
                               &err);
            if (err != USBD_ERR_NONE) {
                /* $$$$ Handle error. */
                return (DEF_FAIL);
            }
        }

#if (APP_CFG_USBD_XXXX_EN == DEF_ENABLED)                               (6)
    ok = App_USBD_XXXX_Init(dev_nbr,
                            cfg_hs_nbr,
                            cfg_fs_nbr);
    if (ok != DEF_OK) {
        /* $$$$ Handle error. */
        return (DEF_FAIL);
    }
#endif

    if (APP_CFG_USBD_XXXX_EN == DEF_ENABLED)                            (6)
        .
        .
        .
#endif

    USBD_DevStart(dev_nbr, &err);                                       (7)

    (void)ok;
    return (DEF_OK);
}
```

Listing 2-5 **App_USBD_Init() Function**

L2-5(1)   **USBD_Init()** initializes the USB device stack. This must be the first USB
           function called by your application's initialization code. If µC/USB-Device is
           used with µC/OS-II or -III, **OSInit()** must be called prior to **USBD_Init()** in
           order to initialize the kernel services.

L2-5(2)   **USBD_DevAdd()** creates and adds a USB device instance. A given USB device
           instance is associated with a single USB device controller. µC/USB-Device can
           support multiple USB device controllers concurrently. If your target supports

multiple controllers, you can create multiple USB device instances for them. The function `USBD_DevAdd()` returns a device instance number; this number is used as a parameter for all subsequent operations.

L2-5(3)   Create and add a high-speed configuration to your device. `USBD_CfgAdd()` creates and adds a configuration to the USB device stack. At a minimum, your USB device application only needs one full-speed and one high-speed configuration if your device is a high-speed capable device. For a full-speed device, only a full-speed configuration will be required. You can create as many configurations as needed by your application, and you can associate multiple instances of USB classes to these configurations. For example, you can create a configuration to contain a mass storage device, and another configuration for a human interface device such as a keyboard, and a vendor specific device.

L2-5(4)   Create and add a full-speed configuration to your device.

L2-5(5)   Associate the high-speed configuration to it's full-speed counterpart. This inform the stack that both configurations offer comparable functionality regardless of speed. This is useful to generate the "Other Speed Configuration" descriptor.

L2-5(6)   Initialize the class-specific application demos by calling the function `App_USBD_XXXX_Init()` where `XXXX` can be `CDC`, `HID`, `MSC`, `PHDC` or `VENDOR`. Class-specific demos are enabled and disabled using the `APP_CFG_USB_XXXX_EN` #define.

L2-5(7)   After all the class instances are created and added to the device configurations, the application should call `USBD_DevStart()`. This function connects the device with the host by enabling the pull-up resistor on the D+ line.

Table 2-3 lists the sections you should refer to for more details about each `App_USBD_XXXX_Init()` function.

Class	Function	Refer to...
CDC ACM	App_USBD_CDC_Init()	section 8-3-1 "General Configuration" on page 169
HID	App_USBD_HID_Init()	section 9-3-2 "Class Instance Configuration" on page 194
MSC	App_USBD_MSC_Init()	section 10-4-2 "Class Instance Configuration" on page 227
PHDC	App_USBD_PHDC_Init()	section 11-2-2 "Class instance configuration" on page 245
Vendor	App_USBD_Vendor_Init()	section 12-2-2 "Class Instance Configuration" on page 266

Table 2-3 **USB Class Demos References**

After building and downloading the application into your target, you should be able to successfully connect your target to a host PC through USB. Once the USB sample application is running, the host detects the connection of a new device and starts the enumeration process. If you are using a Windows PC, it will load a driver which will manage your device. If no driver is found for your device, Windows will display the "found new hardware" wizard so that you can specify which driver to load. Once the driver is loaded, your device is ready for communication. Table 2-4 lists the different section(s) you should refer to for more details on each USB class demo.

Class	Refer to...
CDC ACM	section 8-4-6 "Using the Demo Application" on page 178
HID	section 9-4 "Using the Demo Application" on page 204
MSC	section 10-5 "Using the Demo Application" on page 231
PHDC	section 11-5 "Using the Demo Application" on page 257
Vendor	section 12-4 "Using the Demo Application" on page 279

Table 2-4 **USB Class Demos References**

3

Host Operating Systems

The major host operating systems (OS), such as Microsoft Windows, Apple Mac OS and Linux, recognize a wide range of USB devices that belong to standard classes defined by the USB Implementers Forum. Upon connection of the USB device, any host operating system performs the following general steps:

1   Enumerating the USB device to learn about its characteristics.

2   Loading a proper driver according to its characteristics' analysis in order to manage the device.

3   Communicating with the device.

Step 2, where a driver is loaded to handle the device is performed differently by each major host operating system. Usually, a native driver provided by the operating system manages a device complying to a standard class (for instance, Audio, HID, MSC, Video, etc.) In this case, the native driver loading process is transparent to you. In general, the OS won't ask you for specific actions during the driver loading process. On the other hand, a vendor-specific device requires a vendor-specific driver provided by the device manufacturer. Vendor-specific devices don't fit into any standard class or don't use the standard protocols for an existing standard class. In this situation, the OS may explicitly ask for your intervention during the driver loading process.

During step 3, your application may have to find the USB device attached to the OS before communication with it. Each major OS uses a different method to allow you to find a specific device.

This chapter gives you the necessary information in case your intervention is required during the USB device driver loading process and in case your application needs to find a device attached to the computer. For the moment, this chapter describes this process only for the Windows operating system.

3-1 MICROSOFT WINDOWS

Microsoft offers class drivers for some standard USB classes. These drivers can also be called native drivers. A complete list of the native drivers can be found in the MSDN online documentation on the page titled "Drivers for the Supported USB Device Classes" (`http://msdn.microsoft.com/en-us/library/ff538820(VS.85).aspx`). If a connected device belongs to a class for which a native driver exists, Windows automatically loads the driver without any additional actions from you. If a vendor-specific driver is required for the device, a manufacturer's INF file giving instructions to Windows for loading the vendor-specific driver is required. In some cases, a manufacturer's INF file may also be required to load a native driver.

When the device has been recognized by Windows and is ready for communication, your application may need to use a Globally Unique IDentifier (GUID) to retrieve a device handle that allows your application to communicate with the device.

The following sections explain the use of INF files and GUIDs. Table 3-1 shows the USB classes to which the information in the following sub-sections applies.

Section	Micrium USB classes
section 3-1-1 "About INF Files" on page 90	CDC, PHDC and Vendor
section 3-1-2 "Using GUIDs" on page 95	HID, PHDC and Vendor.

Table 3-1 **Micrium USB Classes Concerned by Windows USB Device Management**

3-1-1 ABOUT INF FILES

An INF file is a setup information file that contains information used by Windows to install software and drivers for one or more devices. The INF file also contains information to store in the Windows registry. Each of the drivers provided natively with the operating system has an associated INF file stored in `C:\WINDOWS\inf`. For instance, when an HID or MSC device is connected to the PC, Windows enumerates the device and implicitly finds an INF file associated to an HID or MSC class that permits loading the proper driver. INF files for native drivers are called system INF files. Any new INF files provided by manufacturers for vendor-specific devices are copied into the folder `C:\WINDOWS\inf`. These INF files can be called vendor-specific INF files. An INF file allows Windows to load one or more drivers for a device. A driver can be native or provided by the device manufacturer.

Table 3-2 shows the Windows driver(s) loaded for each Micrium USB class:

Micrium class	Windows driver	Driver type	INF file type
CDC ACM	usbser.sys	Native	Vendor-specific INF file
HID	Hidclass.sys Hidusb.sys	Native	System INF file
MSC	Usbstor.sys	Native	System INF file
PHDC	winusb.sys (for getting started purpose only).	Native	Vendor-specific INF file
Vendor	winusb.sys	Native	Vendor-specific INF file

Table 3-2 **Windows Drivers Loaded for each Micrium USB Class**

When a device is first connected, Windows searches for a match between the information contained in system INF files and the information retrieved from device descriptors. If there is no match, Windows asks you to provide an INF file for the connected device.

An INF file is arranged in sections whose names are surrounded by square brackets []. Each section contains one or several entries. If the entry has a predefined keyword such as "Class", "Signature", etc, the entry is called a directive. Listing 3-1 presents an example of an INF file structure:

```
; ================== Version section ==================
[Version]                                              (1)
Signature = "$Windows NT$"
Class     = Ports
ClassGuid = {4D36E978-E325-11CE-BFC1-08002BE10318}

Provider=%ProviderName%
DriverVer=01/01/2012,1.0.0.0

; ========== Manufacturer/Models sections ==========

[Manufacturer]                                         (2)
%ProviderName% = DeviceList, NTx86, NTamd64

[DeviceList.NTx86]                                     (3)
%PROVIDER_CDC% = DriverInstall, USB\VID_fffe&PID_1234&MI_00
```

```
[DeviceList.NTamd64]                                                    (3)
%PROVIDER_CDC% = DriverInstall, USB\VID_fffe&PID_1234&MI_00


; =============== Installation sections ===================     (4)

[DriverInstall]
include   = mdmcpq.inf
CopyFiles = FakeModemCopyFileSection
AddReg    = LowerFilterAddReg,SerialPropPageAddReg

[DriverInstall.Services]
include    = mdmcpq.inf
AddService = usbser, 0x00000002, LowerFilter_Service_Inst

[SerialPropPageAddReg]
HKR,,EnumPropPages32,,"MsPorts.dll,SerialPortPropPageProvider"

; ================= Strings section ======================

[Strings]                                                               (5)
ProviderName = "Micrium"
PROVIDER_CDC = "Micrium CDC Device"
```

Listing 3-1 **Example of INF File Structure**

L3-1(1)   The section [**Version**] is mandatory and informs Windows about the provider, the version and other descriptive information about the driver package.

L3-1(2)   The section [**Manufacturer**] is mandatory. It identifies the device's manufacturer.

L3-1(3)   The following two sections are called Models sections and are defined on a per-manufacturer basis. They give more detailed instructions on the driver(s) to install for the device(s). A section name can use extensions to specify OSes and/or CPUs the entries apply to. In this example, **.NTx86** and **.NTamd64** indicate that the driver can be installed on an NT-based Windows (that is Windows 2000 and later), on x86- and x64-based PC respectively.

L3-1(4)   The installation sections actually install the driver(s) for each device described in the Model section(s). The driver installation may involve reading existing information from the Windows registry, modifying existing entries of the registry or creating new entries into the registry.

L3-1(5)   The section [Strings] is mandatory and it is used to define each string key token indicated by %string name% in the INF file.

Refer to the MSDN online documentation on this web page for more details about INF sections and directives: http://msdn.microsoft.com/en-us/library/ff549520.aspx.

You will be able to modify some sections in order to match the INF file to your device characteristics, such as Vendor ID, Product ID and human-readable strings describing the device. The sections are:

▪ Models section

▪ [Strings] section

To identify possible drivers for a device, Windows looks in the Models section for a *device identification string* that matches a string created from information in the device's descriptors. Every USB device has a device ID, that is a *hardware ID* created by the Windows USB host stack from information contained in the Device descriptor. A device ID has the following form:

USB\Vid_xxxx&Pid_yyyy

xxxx, **yyyy**, represent the value of the Device descriptor fields "idVendor" and "idProduct" respectively (refer to the Universal Serial Bus Specification, revision 2.0, section 9.6.1 for more details about the Device descriptor fields). This string allows Windows to load a driver for the device. You can modify **xxxx** and **yyyy** to match your device's Vendor and Product IDs. In Listing 2-1, the hardware ID defines the Vendor ID **0xFFFE** and the Product ID **0x1234**.

Composite devices, formed of several functions, can specify a driver for each function. In this case, the device has a device ID for each interface that represents a function. A device ID for an interface has the following form:

USB\Vid_xxxx&Pid_yyyy&MI_ww

ww is equal to the "bInterfaceNumber" field in the Interface descriptor (refer to the Universal Serial Bus Specification, revision 2.0, section 9.6.5 for more details on the Interface descriptor fields). You can modify ww to match the position of the interface in the Configuration descriptor. If the interface has the position #2 in the Configuration descriptor, ww is equals to 02.

The [Strings] section contains a description of your device. In Listing 3-1, the strings define the name of the device driver package provider and the device name. You can see these device description strings in the Device Manager. For instance, Figure 3-1 shows a virtual COM port created with the INF file from Listing 3-1. The string "Micrium" appears under the "Driver Provider" name in the device properties. The string "Micrium CDC Device" appears under the "Ports" group and in the device properties dialog box.

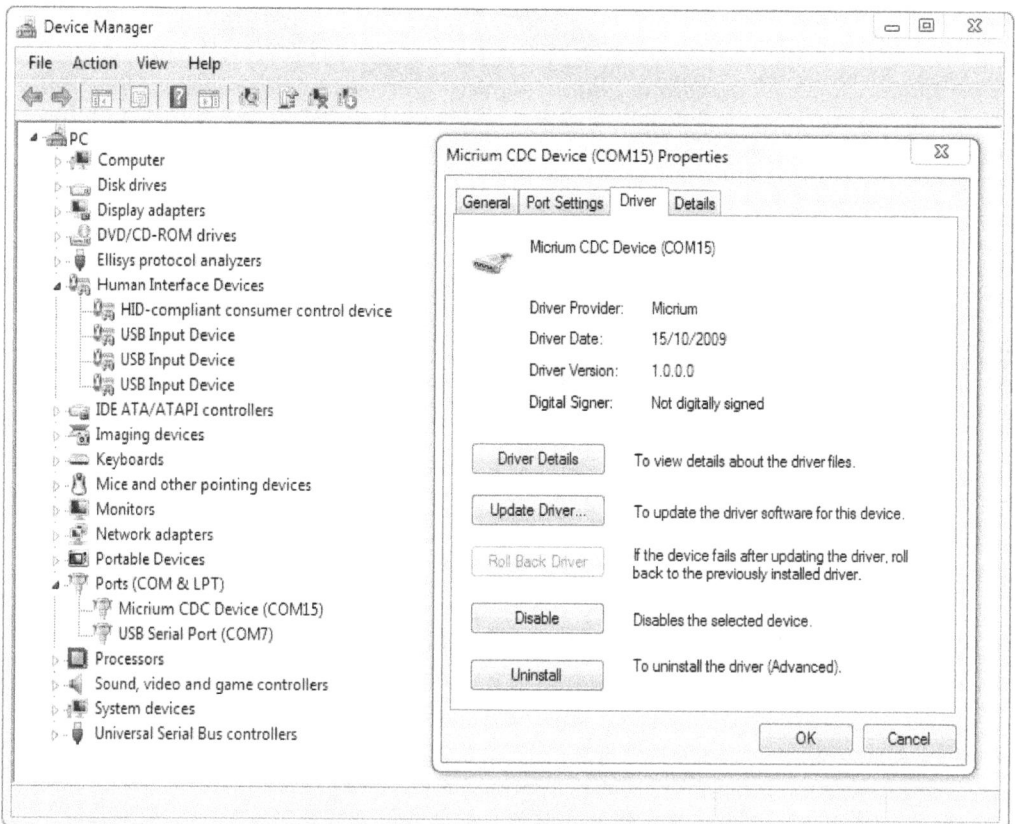

Figure 3-1 **Windows Device Manager Example for a CDC Device**

3-1-2 USING GUIDS

A Globally Unique IDentifier (GUID) is a 128-bit value that uniquely identifies a class or other entity. Windows uses GUIDs for identifying two types of device classes:

▪ Device setup class

▪ Device interface class

A device setup GUID encompasses devices that Windows installs in the same way and using the same class installer and co-installers. Class installers and co-installers are DLLs that provide functions related to device installation. There is a GUID associated with each device setup class. System-defined setup class GUIDs are defined in devguid.h. The device setup class GUID defines the `..\CurrentControlSet\Control\Class\ClassGuid` registry key under which to create a new subkey for any particular device of a standard setup class. A complete list of system-defined device setup classes offered by Microsoft Windows® is available on MSDN online documentation:

`http://msdn.microsoft.com/en-us/library/windows/hardware/ff553426(v=vs.85).aspx`

A device interface class GUID provides a mechanism for applications to communicate with a driver assigned to devices in a class. A class or device driver can register one or more device interface classes to enable applications to learn about and communicate with devices that use the driver. Each device interface class has a device interface GUID. Upon a device's first attachment to the PC, the Windows I/O manager associates the device and the device interface class GUID with a symbolic link name, also called a device path. The device path is stored in the Windows registry and persists across system reboot. An application can retrieve all the connected devices within a device interface class. If the application has gotten a device path for a connected device, this device path can be passed to a function that will return a handle. This handle is passed to other functions in order to communicate with the corresponding device.

Three of Micrium's USB classes are provided with Visual Studio 2010 projects. These Visual Studio projects build applications that interact with a USB device. They use a device interface class GUID to detect any attached device belonging to the class. Table 3-3 shows the Micrium class and the corresponding device interface class GUID used in the class Visual Studio project.

Micrium USB class	Device interface class GUID	Defined in
HID	{4d1e55b2–f16f–11cf–88cb–001111000030}	app_hid_common.h
PHDC	{143f20bd–7bd2–4ca6–9465–8882f2156bd6}	usbdev_guid.h
Vendor	{143f20bd–7bd2–4ca6–9465–8882f2156bd6}	usbdev_guid.h

Table 3-3 **Micrium Class and Device Interface Class GUID**

The interface class GUID for the HID class is provided by Microsoft as part of system-defined device interface classes, whereas the interface class GUID for PHDC and Vendor classes have been generated with Visual Studio 2010 using the utility tool, **guidgen.exe**. This tool is accessible from the menu Tools and the option Create GUID or, through the command-line by selecting the menu Tools, option Visual Studio Command Prompt and by typing **guidgen** at the prompt.

4

Architecture

µC/USB-Device was designed to be modular and easy to adapt to a variety of Central Processing Units (CPUs), Real-Time Operating Systems (RTOS), USB device controllers, and compilers.

Figure 4-1 shows a simplified block diagram of all the µC/USB-Device modules and their relationships.

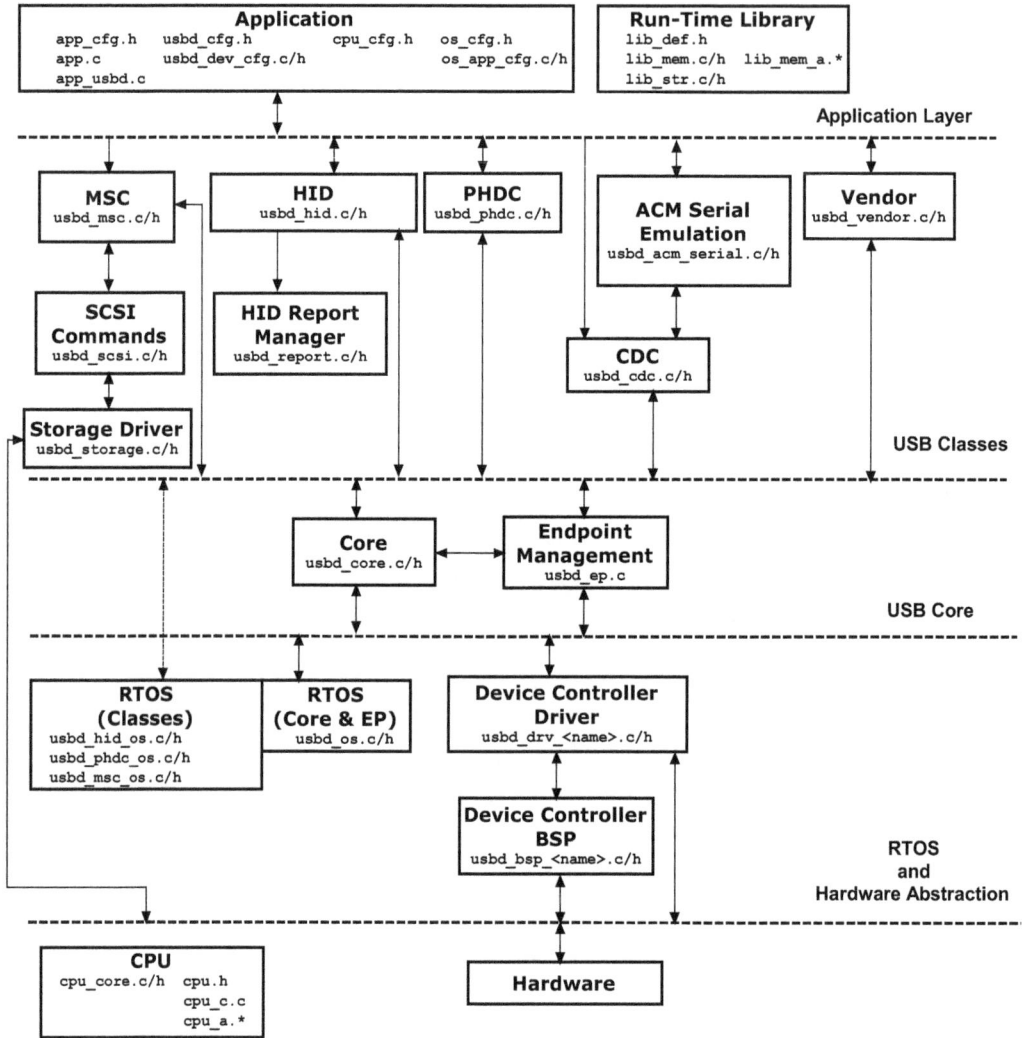

Figure 4-1 **µC/USB-Device Architecture Block Diagram**

4-1 MODULES RELATIONSHIP

4-1-1 APPLICATION

Your application layer needs to provide configuration information to µC/USB-Device in the form of four C files: **app_cfg.h**, **usbd_cfg.h**, **usbd_dev_cfg.c** and **usbd_dev_cfg.h**:

■ **app_cfg.h** is an application-specific configuration file. It contains #defines to specify task priorities and the stack size of each of the task within the application and the task required by µC/USB-Device. Some small Micrium modules like µC/LIB (run-time library) use **app_cfg.h** to configure parameters such as the heap size.

■ Configuration data in **usbd_cfg.h** consists of specifying the number of devices supported in the stack, the maximum number of configurations, the maximum number of interfaces and alternate interfaces, maximum number of opened endpoints per device, class-specific configuration parameters and more. In all, there are approximately 20 #defines to set.

■ Finally, **usbd_dev_cfg.c/.h** consists of device-specific configuration requirements such as vendor ID, product ID, device release number and its respective strings. It also contains device controller specific configurations such as base address, dedicated memory base address and size, and endpoint management table.

Refer to Chapter 5, "Configuration" on page 109 for more information on how to configure µC/USB-Device.

4-1-2 LIBRARIES

Given that µC/USB-Device is designed to be used in safety critical applications, some of the "standard" library functions such as **strcpy()**, **memset()**, etc. have been rewritten to conform to the same quality standards as the rest of the USB device stack. All these standard functions are part of a separate Micrium product called µC/LIB. µC/USB-Device depends on this product. In addition, some data objects in USB controller drivers are created at run-time which implies the use of memory allocation from the heap function **Mem_HeapAlloc()**.

4

4-1-3 USB CLASS LAYER

Your application will interface with μC/USB-Device using the class layer API. In this layer, four classes defined by the USB-IF are implemented. In case you need to implement a vendor-specific class, a fifth class, the "vendor" class, is available. This class provides functions for simple communication via endpoints. The classes that μC/USB-Device currently supports are the following:

- Communication Device Class (CDC)

    - CDC Abstract Control Model (ACM) subclass

- Human Interface Device Class (HID)

- Mass Storage Class (MSC)

- Personal Healthcare Device Class (PHDC)

- Vendor Class

You can also create other classes defined by the USB-IF. Refer to Chapter 7, "USB Classes" on page 147 for more information on how a USB class interacts with the core layer.

4-1-4 USB CORE LAYER

USB core layer is responsible for creating and maintaining the logical structure of a USB device. The core layer manages the USB configurations, interfaces, alternate interfaces and allocation of endpoints based on the application or USB classes requirements and the USB controller endpoints available. Standard requests, bus events (reset, suspend, connect and disconnect) and enumeration process are also handled by the Core layer.

4-1-5 ENDPOINT MANAGEMENT LAYER

The endpoint management layer is responsible for sending and receiving data using endpoints. Control, interrupt and bulk transfers are implemented in this layer. This layer provides synchronous API for control, bulk and interrupt I/O operations and asynchronous API for bulk and interrupt I/O operations.

4-1-6 REAL-TIME OPERATING SYSTEM (RTOS) ABSTRACTION LAYER

μC/USB-Device assumes the presence of an RTOS, and an RTOS abstraction layer allows μC/USB-Device to be independent of a specific RTOS. The RTOS abstraction layer is composed of several RTOS ports, a core layer port and some class layer ports.

CORE LAYER PORT

At the very least, the RTOS for the core layer:

- Creates at least one task for the core operation and one optional task for the debug trace feature.

- Provides semaphore management (or the equivalent). Semaphores are used to signal completion or error in synchronous I/O operations and trace events.

- Provides queue management for I/O and bus events.

μC/USB-Device is provided with ports for μC/OS-II and μC/OS-III. If a different RTOS is used, you can use the files for μC/OS-II or μC/OS-III as a template to interface to the RTOS of your choice. For more information on how to port μC/USB-Device to an RTOS, see Chapter 14, "Porting μC/USB-Device to your RTOS" on page 295.

CLASS LAYER PORTS

Some USB classes require an RTOS port (i.e., MSC, PHDC and HID). Refer to Table 14-2 on page 297 for a list of sections containing more information on the RTOS port of each of these classes.

4-1-7 HARDWARE ABSTRACTION LAYER

μC/USB-Device works with nearly any USB device controller. This layer handles the specifics of the hardware, e.g., how to initialize the device, how to open and configure endpoints, how to start reception and transmission of USB packets, how to read and write USB packets and how to report USB events to the core, among others. The USB device driver controller functions are encapsulated and implemented in the `usbd_drv_<controller>.c` file.

4

In order to have independent configuration for clock gating, interrupt controller and general purpose I/O, a USB device controller driver needs an additional file. This file is called a Board Support Package (BSP). The name of this file is **usbd_bsp_<controller>.c**. This file contains all the details that are closely related to the hardware on which the product is used. This file also defines the *endpoints information table*. This table is used by the core layer to allocate endpoints according to the hardware capabilities.

4-1-8 CPU LAYER

μC/USB-Device can work with either an 8, 16, 32 or even 64-bit CPU, but it must have information about the CPU used. The CPU layer defines such information as the C data type corresponding to 16-bit and 32-bit variables, whether the CPU has little or big endian memory organization, and how interrupts are disabled and enabled on the CPU.

CPU-specific files are found in the **\uC-CPU** directory and are used to adapt μC/USB-Device to a different CPU.

4-2 TASK MODEL

μC/USB-Device requires two tasks: One core task and one optional task for tracing debug events. The core task has three main responsibilities:

- Process USB bus events: Bus events such as reset, suspend, connect and disconnect are processed by the core task. Based on the type of bus event, the core task sets the state of the device.

- Process USB requests: USB requests are sent by the host using the default control endpoint. The core task processes all USB requests. Some requests are handled by the USB class driver, for those requests the core calls the class-specific request handler.

- Process I/O asynchronous transfers: Asynchronous I/O transfers are handled by the core. Under completion, the core task invokes the respective callback for the transfer.

Figure 4-2 shows a simplified task model of μC/USB-Device along with application tasks.

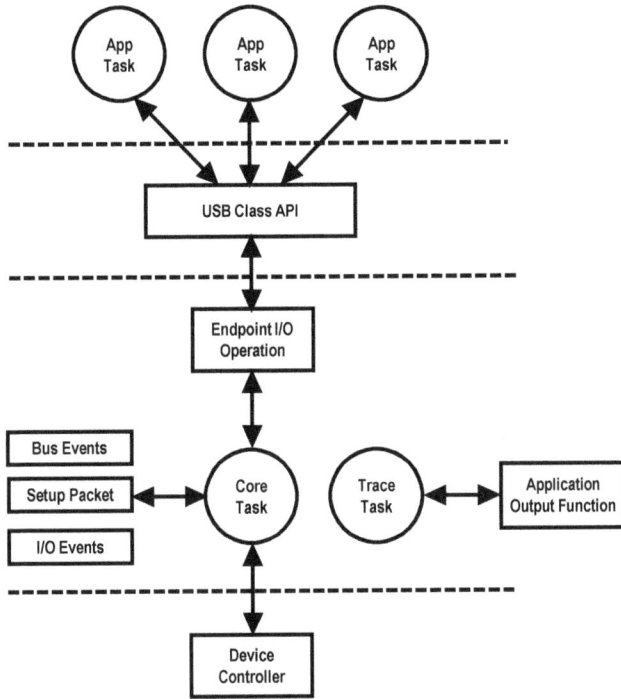

Figure 4-2 **μC/USB-Device Task Model**

4-2-1 **SENDING AND RECEIVING DATA**

Figure 4-3 shows a simplified task model of μC/USB-Device when data is transmitted and received through the USB device controller. With μC/USB-Device, data can be sent asynchronously or synchronously. In a synchronous operation, the application blocks execution until the transfer operation completes, or an error or a time-out has occurred. In an asynchronous operation, the application does not block. The core task notifies the application when the transfer operation has completed through a callback function.

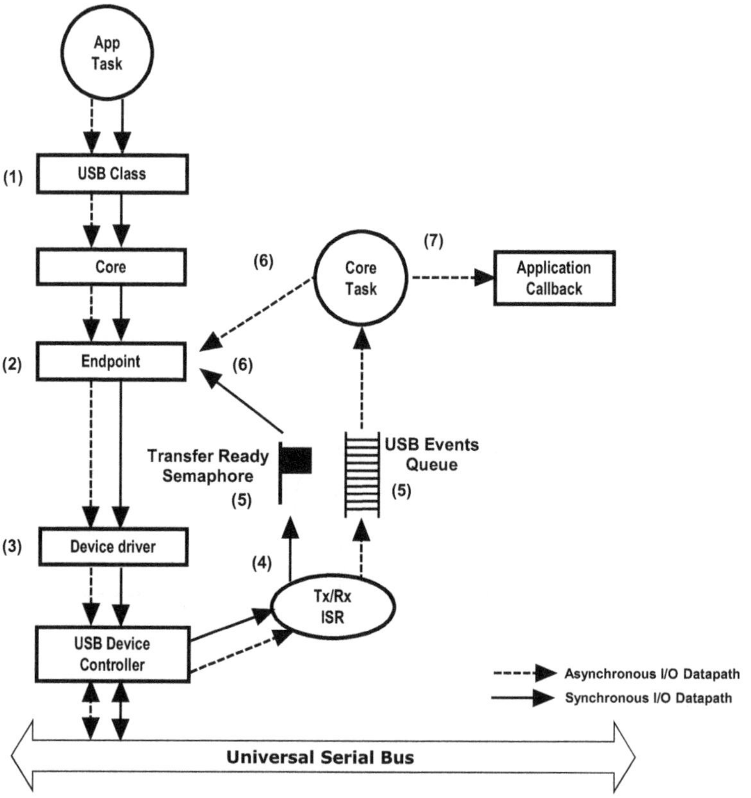

Figure 4-3 **Sending and Receiving a Packet**

F4-3(1)   An application task that wants to receive or send data, interfaces with µC/USB-Device through the USB classes API. The USB classes API interfaces with the core API, which in turn, interfaces with the endpoint layer API.

F4-3(2)   The endpoint layer API prepares the data depending on the endpoint characteristics.

F4-3(3)   When the USB device controller is ready, the driver prepares the transmission or the reception.

F4-3(4)   Once the transfer has completed, the USB device controller generates an interrupt. Depending on the operation (transmission or reception) the USB device controller's driver ISR invokes the transmit complete or receive complete function from the core.

F4-3(5)   If the operation is synchronous, the transmit or receive complete function will signal the transfer ready counting semaphore. If the operation is asynchronous, the transmit or receive complete function will put a message in the USB core event queue for deferred processing by the USB core task.

F4-3(6)   If the operation is synchronous, the endpoint layer will wait on the counting semaphore. The operation repeats steps 2 to 5 until the whole transfer has completed.

F4-3(7)   The core task waits on events to be put in the core event queue. In asynchronous transfers, the core task will call the endpoint layer until the operation is completed.

F4-3(8)   In asynchronous mode, after the transfer has completed, the core task will call the application completion callback to notify the end of the I/O operation.

4-2-2 PROCESSING USB REQUESTS AND BUS EVENTS

USB requests are processed by the core task. Figure 4-4 shows a simplified task diagram of a USB request processing. USB bus events such as reset, resume, connect, disconnect, and suspend are processed in the same way as the USB requests. The core processes the USB bus events to modify and update the current state of the device.

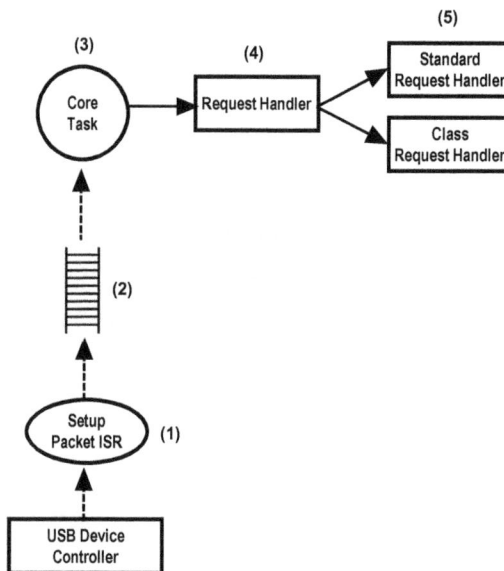

Figure 4-4 **Processing USB Requests**

F4-4(1)   USB requests are sent using control transfers. During the setup stage of the control transfer, the USB device controller generates an interrupt to notify the driver that a new setup packet has arrived.

F4-4(2)   The USB device controller driver ISR notifies the core by pushing the event in the core event queue.

F4-4(3)   The core task receives the message from the queue, and starts parsing the USB request by calling the request handler.

F4-4(4)   The request handler analyzes the request type and determines if the request is a standard, vendor or class specific request.

F4-4(5)   Standard requests are processed by the core layer. Vendor and class specific requests are processed by the class driver, in the class layer.

4-2-3 PROCESSING DEBUG EVENTS

μC/USB-Device contains an optional debug and trace feature. Debug events are managed in the core layer using a dedicated task. Figure 4-5 shows how the core manages debug events.

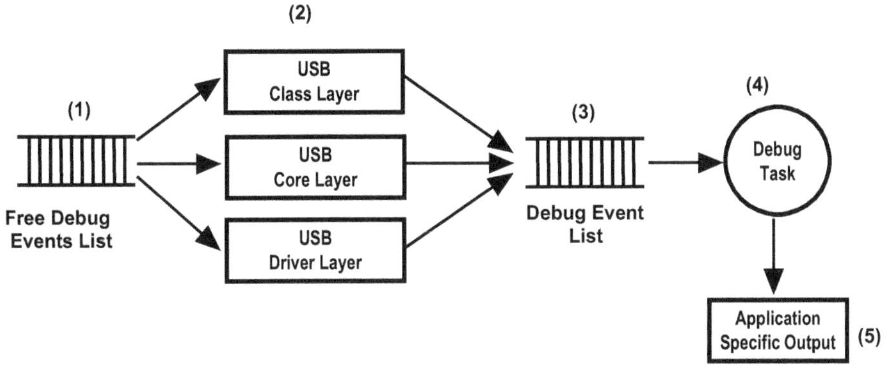

Figure 4-5 **Processing USB Debug Events**

F4-5(1)   The debug and trace module in the core contains a free list of USB debug events. The debug events objects contain useful information such as the endpoint number, interface number or the layer that generates the events.

F4-5(2)   Multiple μC/USB-Device layers take available debug event objects to trace useful information about different USB related events.

F4-5(3)   Trace and debug information events are pushed in the debug event `list.ggg`

F4-5(4)   The debug task is dormant until a new debug event is available in the debug event list. The debug task will parse the information contained in the debug event object and it will output it in a human readable format using the application specific output trace function `USBD_Trace()`.

F4-5(5)   The application specific output function outputs the debug trace information.

For more information on the debug and trace module, see Chapter 13, "Debug and Trace" on page 289.

Configuration

Prior to usage, µC/USB-Device must be properly configured. There are three groups of configuration parameters:

■ Static stack configuration

■ Application specific configuration

■ Device and device controller driver configuration

This chapter explains how to setup all these groups of configuration. The last section of this chapter also provides examples of configuration following examples of typical usage.

5-1 STATIC STACK CONFIGURATION

µC/USB-Device is configurable at compile time via approximately 20 **#defines** in the application's copy of **usbd_cfg.h**. µC/USB-Device uses **#defines** when possible, because they allow code and data sizes to be scaled at compile time based on enabled features and the configured number of USB objects. This allows the Read-Only Memory (ROM) and Random-Access Memory (RAM) footprints of µC/USB-Device to be adjusted based on application requirements.

It is recommended that the configuration process begins with the default configuration values which in the next sections will be shown in **bold**.

The sections in this chapter are organized following the order in µC/USB-Device's template configuration file, **usbd_cfg.h**.

5

5-1-1 GENERIC CONFIGURATION

USBD_CFG_OPTIMIZE_SPD

Selected portions of µC/USB-Device code may be optimized for either better performance or for smallest code size by configuring USBD_CFG_OPTIMIZE_SPD:

DEF_ENABLED   Optimizes µC/USB-Device for best speed performance

DEF_DISABLED   Optimizes µC/USB-Device for best binary image size

USBD_CFG_MAX_NBR_DEV

USBD_CFG_MAX_NBR_DEV configures the maximum number of devices. This value should be set to the number of device controllers used on your platform. Default value is **1**.

USBD_CFG_BUF_ALIGN_OCTETS

USBD_CFG_BUF_ALIGN_OCTETS configures the alignment in octets that internal stack's buffer needs. This value should be set in function of your platform/hardware requirements. If your platform does not require buffer alignment, this should be set to the size of a CPU word (sizeof(CPU_DATA)). Default value is **sizeof(CPU_DATA)**.

USBD_ERR_CFG_ARG_CHK_EXT_EN

USBD_ERR_CFG_ARG_CHK_EXT_EN allows code to be generated to check arguments for functions that can be called by the user and, for functions which are internal but receive arguments from an API that the user can call. USBD_ERR_CFG_ARG_CHK_EXT_EN can be set to either DEF_DISABLED or **DEF_ENABLED**.

5-1-2 USB DEVICE CONFIGURATION

USBD_CFG_MAX_NBR_CFG

USBD_CFG_MAX_NBR_CFG sets the maximum number of USB configurations used by your device. Keep in mind that if you use a high-speed USB device controller, you will need at least two USB configurations, one for low and full-speed and another for high-speed. Refer to the *Universal Serial Bus specification, Revision 2.0, section 9.2.3* for more details on USB configuration. Default value is **2**.

USBD_CFG_HS_EN

Selected portions of µC/USB-Device code required only for high-speed operation may be disabled to reduce the code size by configuring USBD_CFG_HS_EN:

DEF_ENABLED   High-speed operation is supported, code size is larger

DEF_DISABLED   High-speed operation is not supported, code size is smaller

5-1-3 INTERFACE CONFIGURATION

USBD_CFG_MAX_NBR_IF

USBD_CFG_MAX_NBR_IF configures the maximum number of interfaces available. This value should at least be equal to USBD_CFG_MAX_NBR_CFG and greatly depends on the USB class(es) used. Each class instance requires at least one interface, while CDC-ACM requires two. Refer to the *Universal Serial Bus specification, Revision 2.0, section 9.2.3* for more details on USB interfaces. Default value is **2**.

USBD_CFG_MAX_NBR_IF_ALT

USBD_CFG_MAX_NBR_IF_ALT defines the maximum number of alternate interfaces (alternate settings) available. This value should at least be equal to USBD_CFG_MAX_NBR_IF. Refer to the *Universal Serial Bus specification, Revision 2.0, section 9.2.3* for more details on alternate settings. Default value is **2**.

USBD_CFG_MAX_NBR_IF_GRP

USBD_CFG_MAX_NBR_IF_GRP sets the maximum number of interface groups or associations available. For the moment, Micrium offers only one USB class (CDC-ACM) that requires interface groups. Refer to the Interface Association Descriptors USB Engineering Change Notice for more details about interface associations. Default value is **0** (should be equal to the number of instances of CDC-ACM).

USBD_CFG_MAX_NBR_EP_DESC

USBD_CFG_MAX_NBR_EP_DESC sets the maximum number of endpoint descriptors available. This value greatly depends on the USB class(es) used. For information on how many endpoints are needed for each class, refer to the class specific chapter. Keep in mind that control endpoints do not need any endpoint descriptors. Default value is **2**.

USBD_CFG_MAX_NBR_EP_OPEN

USBD_CFG_MAX_NBR_EP_OPEN configures the maximum number of opened endpoints per device. If you use more than one device, set this value to the worst case. This value greatly depends on the USB class(es) used. For information on how many endpoints are needed for each class, refer to the class specific chapter. Default value is **4** (2 control plus 2 other endpoints).

5-1-4 STRING CONFIGURATION

USBD_CFG_MAX_NBR_STR

USBD_CFG_MAX_NBR_STR configures the maximum number of string descriptors supported. Default value is **3** (1 Manufacturer string, 1 product string and 1 serial number string). This value can be increased if, for example, you plan to add interface specific strings.

5-1-5 DEBUG CONFIGURATION

Configurations in this section only need to be set if you use the core debugging service. For more information on that service, see Chapter 13, "Debug and Trace" on page 289.

USBD_CFG_DBG_TRACE_EN

USBD_CFG_DBG_TRACE_EN enables or disables the core debug trace engine.

DEF_ENABLED   Core debug trace engine is enabled.

DEF_DISABLED   Core debug trace engine is disabled.

USBD_CFG_DBG_TRACE_NBR_EVENTS

USBD_CFG_DBG_TRACE_NBR_EVENTS indicates the maximum number of debug trace events that can be queued by the core debug trace engine. Default value is **10**.

This configuration constant has no effect and will not allocate any memory if USBD_CFG_DBG_TRACE_EN is set to DEF_DISABLED.

5-1-6 COMMUNICATION DEVICE CLASS (CDC) CONFIGURATION

USBD_CDC_CFG_MAX_NBR_DEV

Configures the maximum number of class instances. Each associated subclass also defines a maximum number of subclass instances. The sum of all the maximum numbers of subclass instances must not be greater than USBD_CDC_CFG_MAX_NBR_DEV. Default value is **1**.

USBD_CDC_CFG_MAX_NBR_CFG

Configures the maximum number of configurations in which CDC class is used. Keep in mind that if you use a high-speed device, two configurations will be built, one for full-speed and another for high-speed. Default value is **2**.

USBD_CDC_CFG_MAX_NBR_DATA_IF

Configures the maximum number of Data interfaces. The minimum value is **1**.

5

5-1-7 CDC ABSTRACT CONTROL MODEL (ACM) SERIAL CLASS CONFIGURATION

USBD_ACM_SERIAL_CFG_MAX_NBR_DEV

Configures the maximum number of ACM subclass instances. The constant value cannot be greater than USBD_CDC_CFG_MAX_NBR_DEV. Unless you plan on having multiple configurations or interfaces using different class instances, this can be set to the default value (**1**).

5-1-8 HUMAN INTERFACE DEVICE (HID) CLASS CONFIGURATION

USBD_HID_CFG_MAX_NBR_DEV

Configures the maximum number of class instances. Unless you plan on having multiple configurations or interfaces using different class instances, this can be set to the default value (**1**).

USBD_HID_CFG_MAX_NBR_CFG

Configures the maximum number of configurations in which HID class is used. Keep in mind that if you use a high-speed device, two configurations will be built, one for full-speed and another for high-speed. Default value is **2.**

USBD_HID_CFG_MAX_NBR_REPORT_ID

Configures the maximum number of report IDs allowed in a report. The value should be set properly to accommodate the number of report ID to be used in the report. The minimum value is **1**.

USBD_HID_CFG_MAX_NBR_REPORT_PUSHPOP

Configures the maximum number of Push and Pop items used in a report. If the constant is set to **0**, no Push and Pop items are present in the report.

The HID class uses an internal task to manage periodic input reports. The following constants are defined in the application configuration file, **app_cfg.h**.

USBD_HID_OS_CFG_TMR_TASK_PRIO

Configures the priority of the HID periodic input reports task

USBD_HID_OS_CFG_TMR_TASK_STK_SIZE

Configures the stack size of the HID periodic input reports task.

5-1-9 MASS STORAGE CLASS (MSC) CONFIGURATION

USBD_MSC_CFG_MAX_NBR_DEV

Configures the maximum number of class instances. Unless you plan having multiple configuration or interfaces using different class instances, this should be set to **1**.

USBD_MSC_CFG_MAX_NBR_CFG

Configures the maximum number of configuration in which MSC is used. Keep in mind that if you use a high-speed device, two configurations will be built, one for full-speed and another for high-speed. DEfault value is **2**.

USBD_MSC_CFG_MAX_LUN

Configures the maximum number of logical units. This value must be at least **1**.

USBD_MSC_CFG_DATA_LEN

Configures the read/write data length in octets. The default value set is **2048**.

Since MSC device relies on a task handler to implement the MSC protocol, this OS-task's priority and stack size constants need to be configured in the application configuration file, **app_cfg.h**.

USBD_MSC_OS_CFG_TASK_PRIO

MSC task handler's priority level. The priority level must be lower (higher valued) than the start task and core task priorities.

USBD_MSC_OS_CFG_TASK_STK_SIZE

MSC task handler's stack size. Default value is set to **256**.

5

5-1-10 PERSONAL HEALTHCARE DEVICE CLASS (PHDC) CONFIGURATION

USBD_PHDC_CFG_MAX_NBR_DEV

Configures the maximum number of class instances. Unless you plan having multiple configuration or interfaces using different class instances, this can be set to **1**.

USBD_PHDC_CFG_MAX_NBR_CFG

Configures the maximum number of configuration in which PHDC is used. Keep in mind that if you use a high-speed device, two configurations will be built, one for full-speed and another for high-speed. Default value is **2**.

USBD_PHDC_CFG_DATA_OPAQUE_MAX_LEN

Maximum length in octets that opaque data can be. Must always be equal or less to MaxPacketSize - 21. Default value is **43**.

USBD_PHDC_OS_CFG_SCHED_EN

If using μC/OS-II or μC/OS-III RTOS port, enable or disable the scheduler feature. You should set it to `DEF_DISABLED` if device only use one QoS level to send data, for instance. (See section 11-4 "RTOS QoS-based scheduler" on page 253) Default value is **DEF_ENABLED**.

WARNING: If you set this constant to `DEF_ENABLED`, you MUST ensure that the scheduler's task has a lower priority (i.e. higher priority value) than any task that can write PHDC data.

If you set `USBD_PHDC_OS_CFG_SCHED_EN` to `DEF_ENABLED` and you use a μC/OS-II or μC/OS-III RTOS port, PHDC will need an internal task for the scheduling operations. There are two application specific configurations that must be set in this case. They should be defined in the **app_cfg.h** file.

USBD_PHDC_OS_CFG_SCHED_TASK_PRIO

QoS based scheduler's task priority.

You must ensure that the scheduler's task has a lower priority (i.e. higher priority value) than any task writing PHDC data.

USBD_PHDC_OS_CFG_SCHED_TASK_STK_SIZE

QoS based scheduler's task stack size. Default value is **512**.

5-1-11 VENDOR CLASS CONFIGURATION

USBD_VENDOR_CFG_MAX_NBR_DEV

Configures the maximum number of class instances. Unless you plan on having multiple configurations or interfaces using different class instances, this can be set to **1**.

USBD_VENDOR_CFG_MAX_NBR_CFG

Configures the maximum number of configuration in which Vendor class is used. Keep in mind that if you use a high-speed device, two configurations will be built, one for full-speed and another for high-speed. Default value is **2**.

5-2 APPLICATION SPECIFIC CONFIGURATION

This section defines the configuration constants related to µC/USB-Device but that are application-specific. All these configuration constants relate to the RTOS. For many OSs, the µC/USB-Device task priorities and stack sizes will need to be explicitly configured for the particular OS (consult the specific OS's documentation for more information).

These configuration constants should be defined in an application's **app_cfg.h** file.

5-2-1 TASK PRIORITIES

As mentioned in section 4-2 "Task Model" on page 102, µC/USB-Device needs one core task and one optional debug task for its proper operation. The priority of µC/USB-Device's core task greatly depends on the USB requirements of your application. For some applications, it might be better to set it at a high priority, especially if your application requires a lot of tasks and is CPU intensive. In that case, if the core task has a low priority, it might not be able to process the bus and control requests on time. On the other hand, for some applications, you might want to give the core task a low priority, especially if you plan on using asynchronous communication and if you know you will have quite a lot of code in your callback functions. For more information on the core task, see section 4-2 "Task Model" on page 102.

5

The priority of the debug task should generally be low since it is not critical and the task performed can be executed in the background.

For the µC/OS-II and µC/OS-III RTOS ports, the following macros must be configured within **app_cfg.h**:

- USBD_OS_CFG_CORE_TASK_PRIO

- USBD_OS_CFG_TRACE_TASK_PRIO

Note: if USBD_CFG_DBG_TRACE_EN is set to DEF_DISABLED, USBD_OS_CFG_TRACE_TASK_PRIO should not be defined.

5-2-2 TASK STACK SIZES

For the µC/OS-II and µC/OS-III RTOS ports, the following macros must be configured within **app_cfg.h** to set the internal task stack sizes:

- USBD_OS_CFG_CORE_TASK_STK_SIZE   **1000**

- USBD_OS_CFG_TRACE_TASK_STK_SIZE   **1000**

Note: if USBD_CFG_DBG_TRACE_EN is set to DEF_DISABLED, USBD_OS_CFG_TRACE_TASK_STK_SIZE should not be defined.

The arbitrary stack size of **1000** is a good starting point for most applications.

The only guaranteed method of determining the required task stack sizes is to calculate the maximum stack usage for each task. Obviously, the maximum stack usage for a task is the total stack usage along the task's most-stack-greedy function path plus the (maximum) stack usage for interrupts. Note that the most-stack-greedy function path is not necessarily the longest or deepest function path.

The easiest and best method for calculating the maximum stack usage for any task/function should be performed statically by the compiler or by a static analysis tool since these can calculate function/task maximum stack usage based on the compiler's actual code generation and optimization settings. So for optimal task stack configuration, we recommend to invest in a task stack calculator tool compatible with your build toolchain.

5-3 DEVICE AND DEVICE CONTROLLER DRIVER CONFIGURATION

In order to finalize the configuration of your device, you need to declare two structures: one will contain information about your device (Vendor ID, Product ID, etc.) and another will contain information useful to the device controller driver. A reference to both of these structures needs to be passed to the **USBD_DevAdd()** function, which allocates a device controller.

For more information on how to modify device and device controller driver configuration, see section 2-4-2 "Copying and Modifying Template Files" on page 76.

5-4 CONFIGURATION EXAMPLES

This section provides examples of configuration for µC/USB-Device stack based on some typical usages. This section will only give examples of static stack configuration, as the application-specific configuration greatly depends on your application. Also, the device configuration is related to your product's context, and the device controller driver configuration depends on the hardware you use.

The examples of typical usage that will be treated are the following:

- A simple full-speed USB device. This device uses Micrium's vendor class.

- A composite high-speed USB device. This device uses Micrium's PHDC and MSC classes.

- A complex composite high-speed USB device. This device uses an instance of Micrium's HID class in two different configurations plus a different instance of Micrium's CDC-ACM class in each configuration. This device also uses an instance of Micrium's vendor class in the second configuration.

5-4-1 SIMPLE FULL-SPEED USB DEVICE

Table 5-1 shows the values that should be set for the different configuration constants described earlier if you build a simple full-speed USB device using Micrium's vendor class.

Configuration	Value	Explanation
USBD_CFG_MAX_NBR_CFG	1	Since the device is full speed, only one configuration is needed.
USBD_CFG_MAX_NBR_IF	1	Since the device only uses the vendor class, only one interface is needed.
USBD_CFG_MAX_NBR_IF_ALT	1	No alternate interfaces are needed, but this value must at least be equal to USBD_CFG_MAX_NBR_IF.
USBD_CFG_MAX_NBR_IF_GRP	0	No interface association needed.
USBD_CFG_MAX_NBR_EP_DESC	2 or 4	Two bulk endpoints and two optional interrupt endpoints.
USBD_CFG_MAX_NBR_EP_OPEN	4 or 6	Two control endpoints for the device's standard requests. Two bulk endpoints and two optional interrupt endpoints.
USBD_VENDOR_CFG_MAX_NBR_DEV	1	Only one instance of vendor class is needed.
USBD_VENDOR_CFG_MAX_NBR_CFG	1	Vendor class instance will only be used in one configuration.

Table 5-1 **Configuration Example of a Simple Full-Speed USB Device**

5-4-2 COMPOSITE HIGH-SPEED USB DEVICE

Table 5-2 shows the values that should be set for the different configuration constants described earlier if you build a composite high-speed USB device using Micrium's PHDC and MSC classes. The structure of this device is described in Figure 5-1.

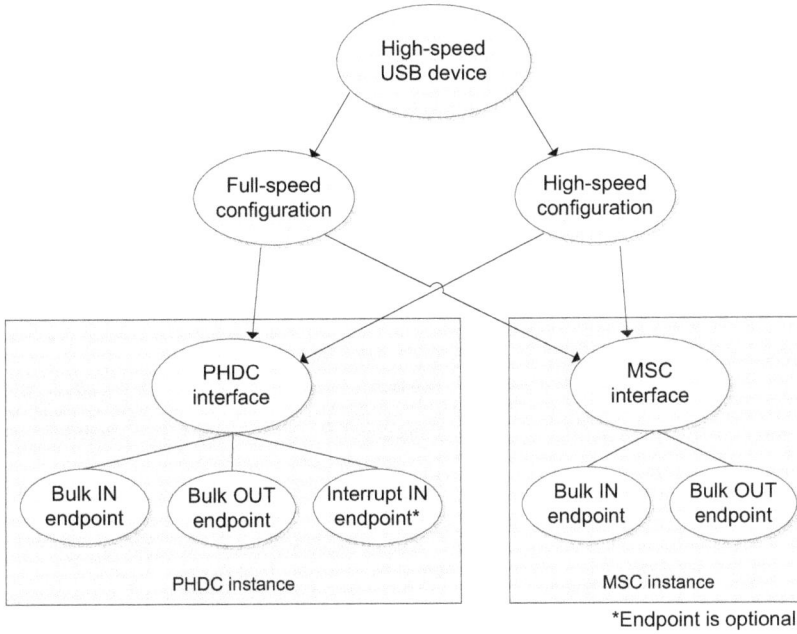

Figure 5-1 **Composite High-Speed USB Device Structure**

Configuration	Value	Explanation
USBD_CFG_MAX_NBR_CFG	2	One configuration for full/low-speed and another for high-speed.
USBD_CFG_MAX_NBR_IF	4	One interface for PHDC and another for MSC. A different interface for each configuration is also needed.
USBD_CFG_MAX_NBR_IF_ALT	4	No alternate interface needed, but this value must at least be equal to USBD_CFG_MAX_NBR_IF.
USBD_CFG_MAX_NBR_IF_GRP	0	No interface association needed.
USBD_CFG_MAX_NBR_EP_DESC	4 or 5	Two bulk endpoints for MSC. Two bulk plus one optional interrupt endpoint for PHDC.
USBD_CFG_MAX_NBR_EP_OPEN	6 or 7	Two control endpoints for device's standard requests. Two bulk endpoints for MSC. Two bulk plus 1 optional interrupt endpoint for PHDC.
USBD_PHDC_CFG_MAX_NBR_DEV	1	Only one instance of PHDC is needed. It will be shared between all the configurations.
USBD_PHDC_CFG_MAX_NBR_CFG	2	PHDC instance can be used in both of device's configurations.
USBD_MSC_CFG_MAX_NBR_DEV	1	Only one instance of MSC is needed. It will be shared between all the configurations.
USBD_MSC_CFG_MAX_NBR_CFG	2	MSC instance can be used in both of device's configurations.

Table 5-2 **Configuration Example of a Composite High-Speed USB Device**

5-4-3 COMPLEX COMPOSITE HIGH-SPEED USB DEVICE

Table 5-3 shows the values that should be set for the different configuration constants described earlier if you build a composite high-speed USB device using a single instance of Micrium's HID class in two different configurations plus a different instance of Micrium's CDC-ACM class in each configuration. The device also uses an instance of Micrium's vendor class in its second configuration. See Figure 5-2 for a graphical description of this USB device.

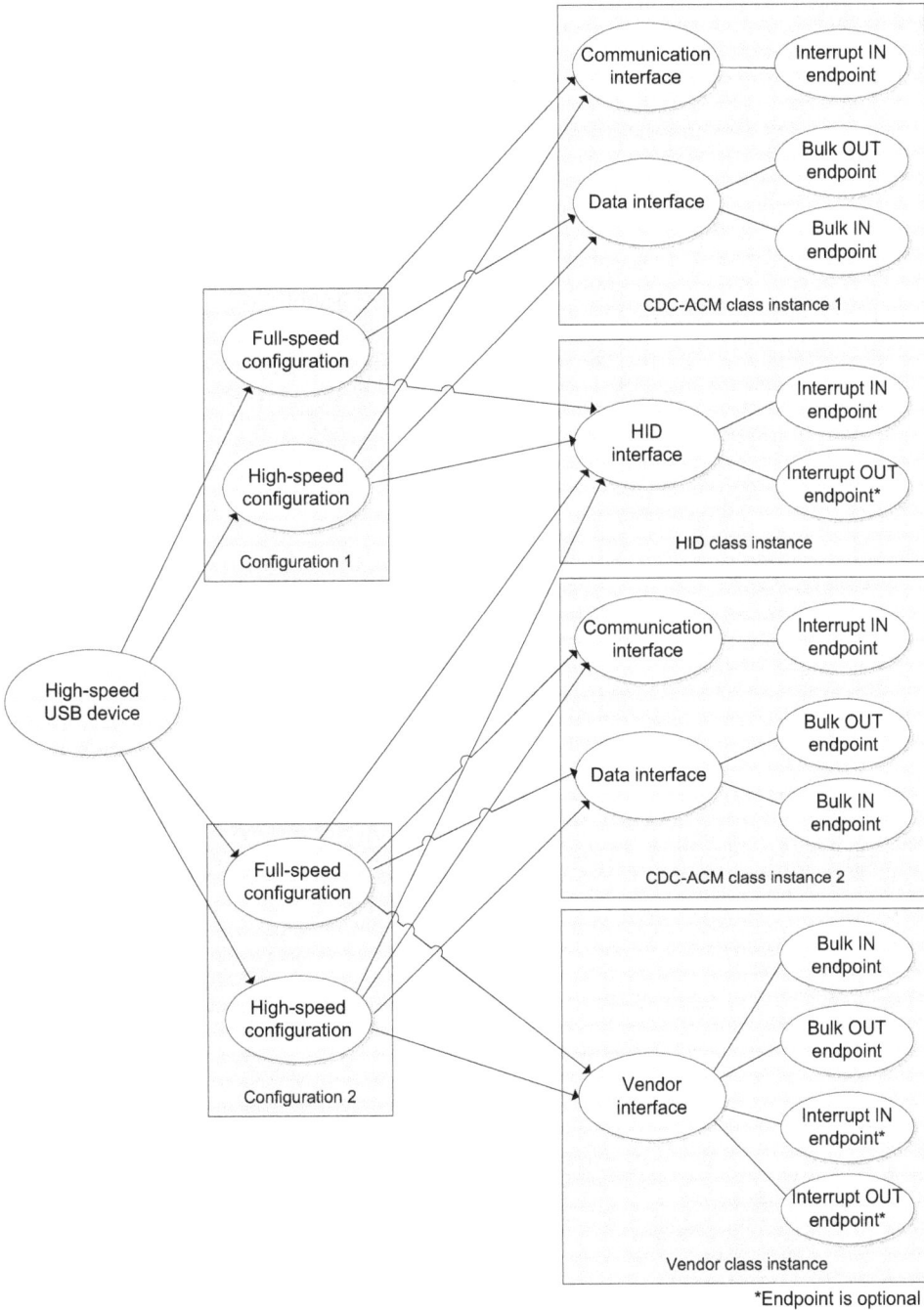

Figure 5-2 **Complex Composite High-Speed USB Device Structure**

Configuration	Value	Explanation
USBD_CFG_MAX_NBR_CFG	4	Two configurations for full/low-speed and two others for high-speed.

USBD_CFG_MAX_NBR_IF	7	First configuration:
		   One interface for HID.
		   Two interfaces for CDC-ACM.
		Second configuration:
		   One interface for HID.
		   Two interfaces for CDC-ACM.
		   One interface for vendor.

USBD_CFG_MAX_NBR_IF_ALT	7	No alternate interface needed, but this value must at least be equal to USBD_CFG_MAX_NBR_IF.
USBD_CFG_MAX_NBR_IF_GRP	2	CDC-ACM needs to group its communication and data interfaces into a single USB function. Since there are two CDC-ACM class instances, there will be two interface groups.
USBD_CFG_MAX_NBR_EP_DESC	9, 10, 11 or 12	One IN and (optional) OUT interrupt endpoint for HID. Three endpoints for first CDC-ACM class instance. Three endpoints for second CDC-ACM class instance. Two bulk plus two optional interrupt endpoints for vendor.
USBD_CFG_MAX_NBR_EP_OPEN	8, 9, 10 or 11	In the worst case (host enables second configuration): Two control endpoints for device's standard requests. One IN and (optional) OUT interrupt endpoint for HID. Three endpoints for second CDC-ACM class instance. Two bulk plus two optional interrupt endpoints for vendor.
USBD_HID_CFG_MAX_NBR_DEV	1	Only one instance of HID class is needed. It will be shared between all the configurations.
USBD_HID_CFG_MAX_NBR_CFG	4	HID class instance can be used in all of device's configurations.
USBD_CDC_CFG_MAX_NBR_DEV	2	Two CDC base class instances are used.
USBD_CDC_CFG_MAX_NBR_CFG	2	Each CDC base class instance can be used in one full-speed and one high-speed configuration.
USBD_ACM_SERIAL_CFG_MAX_NBR_DEV	2	Two ACM subclass instances are used.
USBD_VENDOR_CFG_MAX_NBR_DEV	1	Only one vendor class instance is used.
USBD_VENDOR_CFG_MAX_NBR_CFG	2	The vendor class instance can be used in one full-speed and one high-speed configuration.

Table 5-3 **Configuration Example of a Complex Composite High-Speed USB Device**

Device Driver Guide

There are many USB device controllers available on the market and each requires a driver to work with µC/USB-Device. The amount of code necessary to port a specific device to µC/USB-Device greatly depends on the device's complexity.

If not already available, a driver can be developed, as described in this chapter. However, it is recommended to modify an already existing device driver with the new device's specific code following the Micrium coding convention for consistency. It is also possible to adapt drivers written for other USB device stacks, especially if the driver is short and it is a matter of simply copying data to and from the device.

6-1 DEVICE DRIVER ARCHITECTURE

This section describes the hardware (device) driver architecture for µC/USB-Device, including:

■ Device Driver API Definition(s)

■ Device Configuration

■ Memory Allocation

■ CPU and Board Support

Micrium provides sample configuration code free of charge; however, the sample code will likely require modification depending on the combination of processor, evaluation board, and USB device controller(s).

6-2 DEVICE DRIVER MODEL

No particular memory interface is required by µC/USB-Device's driver model. Therefore, the USB device controller may use the assistance of a Direct Memory Access (DMA) controller to transfer data or handle the data transfers directly.

6-3 DEVICE DRIVER API

All device drivers must declare an instance of the appropriate device driver API structure as a global variable within the source code. The API structure is an ordered list of function pointers utilized by µC/USB-Device when device hardware services are required.

A sample device driver API structure is shown below.

```
const  USBD_DRV_API  USBD_DrvAPI_<controller> = { USBD_DrvInit,              (1)
                                                   USBD_DrvStart,             (2)
                                                   USBD_DrvStop,              (3)
                                                   USBD_DrvAddrSet,           (4)
                                                   USBD_DrvAddrEn,            (5)
                                                   USBD_DrvCfgSet,            (6)
                                                   USBD_DrvCfgClr,            (7)
                                                   USBD_DrvGetFrameNbr,       (8)
                                                   USBD_DrvEP_Open,           (9)
                                                   USBD_DrvEP_Close,          (10)
                                                   USBD_DrvEP_RxStart,        (11)
                                                   USBD_DrvEP_Rx,             (12)
                                                   USBD_DrvEP_RxZLP,          (13)
                                                   USBD_DrvEP_Tx,             (14)
                                                   USBD_DrvEP_TxStart,        (15)
                                                   USBD_DrvEP_TxZLP,          (16)
                                                   USBD_DrvEP_Abort,          (17)
                                                   USBD_DrvEP_Stall,          (18)
                                                   USBD_DrvISR_Handler        (19)
};
```

Listing 6-1 **Device Driver Interface API**

Note: It is the device driver developers' responsibility to ensure that all of the functions listed within the API are properly implemented and that the order of the functions within the API structure is correct. The different function pointers are:

6

L6-1(1)   Device initialization/add

L6-1(2)   Device start

L6-1(3)   Device stop

L6-1(4)   Assign device address

L6-1(5)   Enable device address

L6-1(6)   Set device configuration

L6-1(7)   Clear device configuration

L6-1(8)   Retrieve frame number

L6-1(9)   Open device endpoint

L6-1(10) Close device endpoint

L6-1(11) Configure device endpoint to receive data

L6-1(12) Receive from device endpoint

L6-1(13) Receive zero-length packet from device endpoint

L6-1(14) Configure device endpoint to transmit data

L6-1(15) Transmit to device endpoint

L6-1(16) Transmit zero-length packet to device endpoint

L6-1(17) Abort device endpoint transfer

L6-1(18) Stall device endpoint

L6-1(19) Device interrupt service routine (ISR) handler

6

The details of each device driver API function are described in Appendix B, "Device Controller Driver API Reference" on page 391.

Note: µC/USB-Device device driver API function names may not be unique. Name clashes between device drivers are avoided by never globally prototyping device driver functions and ensuring that all references to functions within the driver are obtained by pointers within the API structure. The developer may arbitrarily name the functions within the source file so long as the API structure is properly declared. The user application should never need to call API functions. Unless special care is taken, calling device driver functions may lead to unpredictable results due to reentrancy.

When writing your own device driver, you can assume that each driver API function accepts a pointer to a structure of the type **USBD_DRV** as one of its parameters. Through this structure, you will be able to access the following fields:

```
typedef  struct  usbd_drv  USBD_DRV;

typedef  usb_drv {
    CPU_INT08U        DevNbr;                       (1)
    USBD_DRV_API      *API_Ptr;                     (2)
    USBD_DRV_CFG      *CfgPtr;                       (3)
    void              *DataPtr;                      (4)
    USBD_DRV_BSP_API  *BSP_API_Ptr;                 (5)
};
```

Listing 6-2 **USB Device Driver Data Type**

L6-2(1)   Unique index to identify device.

L6-2(2)   Pointer to USB device controller driver API.

L6-2(3)   Pointer to USB device controller driver configuration.

L6-2(4)   Pointer to USB device controller driver specific data.

L6-2(5)   Pointer to USB device controller BSP.

6-4 INTERRUPT HANDLING

Interrupt handling is accomplished using the following multi-level scheme.

1   Processor level kernel-aware interrupt handler

2   Device driver interrupt handler

During initialization, the device driver registers all necessary interrupt sources with the BSP interrupt management code. You can also accomplish this by plugging an interrupt vector table during compile time. Once the global interrupt vector sources are configured and an interrupt occurs, the system will call the first-level interrupt handler. The first-level interrupt handler is responsible for performing all kernel required steps prior to calling the USB device driver interrupt handler: `USBD_DrvISR_Handler()`. Depending on the platform architecture (that is the way the kernel handles interrupts) and the USB device controller interrupt vectors, the device driver interrupt handler implementation may follow the models below.

6-4-1 SINGLE USB ISR VECTOR WITH ISR HANDLER ARGUMENT

If the platform architecture allows parameters to be passed to ISR handlers and the USB device controller has a single interrupt vector for the USB device, the first-level interrupt handler may be defined as:

PROTOTYPE

```
void  USBD_BSP_<controller>_IntHandler (void  *p_arg);
```

ARGUMENTS

p_arg   Pointer to USB device driver structure that must be typecast to a pointer to USBD_DRV.

129

6-4-2 SINGLE USB ISR VECTOR

If the platform architecture does not allow parameters to be passed to ISR handlers and the USB device controller has a single interrupt vector for the USB device, the first-level interrupt handler may be defined as:

PROTOTYPE

```
void  USBD_BSP_<controller>_IntHandler (void);
```

ARGUMENTS

None.

NOTES / WARNINGS

In this configuration, the pointer to the USB device driver structure must be stored globally in the driver. Since the pointer to the USB device structure is never modified, the BSP initialization function, USBD_BSP_Init(), can save its address for later use.

6-4-3 MULTIPLE USB ISR VECTORS WITH ISR HANDLER ARGUMENTS

If the platform architecture allows parameters to be passed to ISR handlers and the USB device controller has multiple interrupt vectors for the USB device (e.g., USB events, DMA transfers), the first-level interrupt handler may need to be split into multiple sub-handlers. Each sub-handler would be responsible for managing the status reported to the different vectors. For example, the first-level interrupt handlers for a USB device controller that redirects USB events to one interrupt vector and the status of DMA transfers to a second interrupt vector may be defined as:

PROTOTYPE

```
void  USBD_BSP_<controller>_EventIntHandler (void  *p_arg);
void  USBD_BSP_<controller>_DMAIntHandler   (void  *p_arg);
```

ARGUMENTS

p_arg   Pointer to USB device driver structure that must be typecast to a pointer to USBD_DRV.

6-4-4 MULTIPLE USB ISR VECTORS

6

If the platform architecture does not allow parameters to be passed to ISR handlers and the USB device controller has multiple interrupt vectors for the USB device (e.g., USB events, DMA transfers), the first-level interrupt handler may need to be split into multiple sub-handlers. Each sub-handler would be responsible for managing the status reported to the different vectors. For example, the first-level interrupt handlers for a USB device controller that redirects USB events to one interrupt vector and the status of DMA transfers to a second interrupt vector may be defined as:

PROTOTYPE

```
void  USBD_BSP_<controller>_EventIntHandler (void);
void  USBD_BSP_<controller>_DMAIntHandler   (void);
```

ARGUMENTS

None.

NOTES / WARNINGS

In this configuration, the pointer to the USB device driver structure must be stored globally in the driver. Since the pointer to the USB device structure is never modified, the BSP initialization function, `USBD_BSP_Init()`, can save its address for later use.

6-4-5 USBD_DrvISR_HANDLER()

The device driver interrupt handler must notify the USB device stack of various status changes. Table 6-1 shows each type of status change and the corresponding notification function.

Connect Event	`USBD_EventConn()`
Disconnect Event	`USBD_EventDisconn()`
Reset Event	`USBD_EventReset()`
Suspend Event	`USBD_EventSuspend()`
Resume Event	`USBD_EventResume()`
High-Speed Handshake Event	`USBD_EventHS()`
Setup Packet	`USBD_EventSetup()`
Receive Packet Completed	`USBD_EP_RxCmpl()`
Transmit Packet Completed	`USBD_EP_TxCmpl()`

Table 6-1 **Status Notification API**

Each status notification API queues the event type to be processed by the USB stack's event processing task. Upon reception of a USB event, the interrupt service routine may perform some operations associated to the event before notifying the stack. For example, the USB device controller driver must perform the proper actions for the bus reset when an interrupt request for that event is triggered. Additionally, it must also notify the USB device stack about the bus reset event by invoking the proper status notification API. In general, the device driver interrupt handler must perform the following functions:

1   Determine which type of interrupt event occurred by reading an interrupt status register.

2   If a receive event has occurred, the driver must post the successful completion or the error status to the USB device stack by calling **USBD_EP_RxCmpl()** for each transfer received.

3   If a transmit complete event has occurred, the driver must post the successful completion or the error status to the USB device stack by calling **USBD_EP_TxCmpl()** for each transfer transmitted.

4   If a setup packet event has occurred, the driver must post the setup packet data in little-endian format to the USB device stack by calling **USBD_EventSetup()**.

5   All other events must be posted to the USB device stack by a call to their corresponding status notification API from Table 1. This allows the USB device stack to broadcast these event notifications to the classes.

6   Clear local interrupt flags.

6-5 DEVICE CONFIGURATION

The USB device characteristics must be shared with the USB device stack through configuration parameters. All of these parameters are provided through two global structures of type **USBD_DRV_CFG** and **USBD_DEV_CFG**. These structures are declared in the file **usbd_dev_cfg.h**, and defined in the file **usbd_dev_cfg.c** (refer to section 2-4-2 "Copying and Modifying Template Files" on page 76 for an example of initializing these structures). These files are distributed as templates, and you should modify them to have the proper configuration for your USB device controller. The fields of the following structure are the parameters needed to configure the USB device controller driver:

```
typedef const struct usb_drv_cfg {
    CPU_ADDR          BaseAddr;                          (1)
    CPU_ADDR,         MemAddr;                            (2)
    CPU_ADDR,         MemSize;                            (3)
    USBD_DEV_SPD,     Spd;                                (4)
    USBD_DRV_EP_INFO  *EP_InfoTbl;                        (5)
} USBD_DRV_CFG;
```

Listing 6-3 **USB Device Controller Driver Configuration Structure**

L6-3(1)   Base address of the USB device controller hardware registers.

L6-3(2)   Base address of the USB device controller dedicated memory.

L6-3(3)   Size of the USB device controller dedicated memory.

L6-3(4)   Speed of the USB device controller. Can be set to either **USBD_DEV_SPD_LOW**, **USBD_DEV_SPD_FULL** or **USBD_DEV_SPD_HIGH**.

L6-3(5)   USB device controller endpoint information table (see section 6-5-1 "Endpoint Information Table" on page 135).

The fields of the following structure are the parameters needed to configure the USB device:

```
typedef  const  struct  usb_dev_cfg {
              CPU_INT16U   VendorID;                          (1)
              CPU_INT16U   ProductID;                         (2)
              CPU_INT16U   DeviceBCD;                         (3)
      const   CPU_CHAR    *ManufacturerStrPtr;               (4)
      const   CPU_CHAR    *ProductStrPtr;                    (5)
      const   CPU_CHAR    *SerialNbrStrPtr;                  (6)
              CPU_INT16U   LangID;                            (7)
} USBD_DEV_CFG;
```

Listing 6-4 **USB Device Configuration Structure**

L6-4(1)   Vendor ID.

L6-4(2)   Product ID.

L6-4(3)   Device release number.

L6-4(4)   Pointer to manufacturer string.

L6-4(5)   Pointer to product string.

L6-4(6)   Pointer to serial number ID.

L6-4(7)   Language ID.

6-5-1 ENDPOINT INFORMATION TABLE

The endpoint information table provides the hardware endpoint characteristics to the USB device stack. When an endpoint is opened, the USB device stack's core iterates through the endpoint information table entries until the endpoint type and direction match the requested endpoint characteristics. The matching entry provides the physical endpoint number and maximum packet size information to the USB device stack. The entries on the endpoint information table are organized as follows:

```
typedef  const  struct  usbd_drv_ep_info {
    CPU_INT08U  Attrib;                            (1)
    CPU_INT08U  Nbr;                               (2)
    CPU_INT16U  MaxPktSize;                         (3)
} USBD_DRV_EP_INFO;
```

Listing 6-5 **Endpoint Information Table Entry**

L6-5(1)   The endpoint Attrib is a combination of the endpoint type USBD_EP_INFO_TYPE and endpoint direction USBD_EP_INFO_DIR attributes. The endpoint type can be defined as: USBD_EP_INFO_TYPE_CTRL, USBD_EP_INFO_TYPE_INTR, USBD_EP_INFO_TYPE_BULK, or USBD_EP_INFO_TYPE_ISOC. The endpoint direction can be defined as either USBD_EP_INFO_DIR_IN or USBD_EP_INFO_DIR_OUT.

L6-5(2)   The endpoint **Nbr** is the logical endpoint number used by the USB device controller.

L6-5(3)   The endpoint **MaxPktSize** defines the maximum packet size supported by the hardware. The maximum packet size used by the USB device stack is validated to comply with the USB standard guidelines.

An example of an endpoint information table for a high-speed capable device is provided below.

```
const  USBD_DRV_EP_INFO  USBD_DrvEP_InfoTbl_<controller>[] = {
   {USBD_EP_INFO_TYPE_CTRL                                  | USBD_EP_INFO_DIR_OUT, 0u,   64u},   (1)
   {USBD_EP_INFO_TYPE_CTRL                                  | USBD_EP_INFO_DIR_IN,  0u,   64u},
   {USBD_EP_INFO_TYPE_BULK | USBD_EP_INFO_TYPE_INTR | USBD_EP_INFO_DIR_OUT, 1u, 1024u},   (2)
   {USBD_EP_INFO_TYPE_BULK | USBD_EP_INFO_TYPE_INTR | USBD_EP_INFO_DIR_IN,  1u, 1024u},
   {DEF_BIT_NONE                                                         ,  0u,    0u}    (3)
};
```

Listing 6-6 **Example of Endpoint Information Table Configuration**

L6-6(1)   An endpoint described only by one type and one direction is a *dedicated* endpoint. Most of the device controllers will have a dedicated endpoint for control OUT and IN endpoints. That's why the table **USBD_DrvEP_InfoTbl_<controller>** is first initialized with two dedicated control endpoints.

L6-6(2)   An endpoint indicating several types and two possible directions is a *configurable* endpoint. In this example, the endpoint can be configured as a bulk or interrupt OUT endpoint. An endpoint fully configurable in terms of type and direction would be OR'ed with this format:
USBD_EP_INFO_TYPE_CTRL | USBD_EP_INFO_TYPE_INTR | USBD_EP_INFO_TYPE_BULK | USBD_EP_INFO_TYPE_ISOC | USBD_EP_INFO_DIR_IN | USBD_EP_INFO_DIR_OUT.

L6-6(3)   The last entry on the endpoint information table must be an empty entry to allow the USB device stack to determine the end of the table.

6-6 MEMORY ALLOCATION

Memory allocation in the driver can be simplified by the use of memory allocation functions available from Micrium's μC/LIB module. μC/LIB's memory allocation functions provide allocation of memory from dedicated memory space (e.g., USB RAM) or general purpose heap. The driver may use the pool functionality offered by μC/LIB. Memory pools use fixed-sized blocks that can be dynamically allocated and freed during application execution. Memory pools may be convenient to manage objects needed by the driver. The objects could be for instance data structures mandatory for DMA operations. For more information on using μC/LIB memory allocation functions, consult the μC/LIB documentation.

6-7 CPU AND BOARD SUPPORT

The USB device stack supports big-endian and little-endian CPU architectures. The setup packet received as part of a control transfer must provide the content of the setup packet in little-endian format to the stack. Therefore, if the USB device controller provides the content in big-endian format, device drivers must swap the endianness of the setup packet's content.

In order for device drivers to be platform-independent, it is necessary to provide a layer of code that abstracts details such as clocks, interrupt controllers, general-purpose input/output (GPIO) pins, and other hardware modules configuration. With this board support package (BSP) code layer, it is possible for the majority of the USB device stack to be independent of any specific hardware, and for device drivers to be reused on different architectures and bus configurations without the need to modify stack or driver source code. These procedures are also referred as the USB BSP for a particular development board.

A sample device BSP interface API structure is shown below.

```
const  USBD_DRV_BSP_API  USBD_DrvBSP_<controller> = { USBD_BSP_Init,        (1)
                                                      USBD_BSP_Conn,        (2)
                                                      USBD_BSP_Disconn      (3)
};
```

Listing 6-7 **Device BSP Interface API**

L6-7(1)   Device BSP initialization function pointer

L6-7(2)   Device BSP connect function pointer

L6-7(3)   Device BSP disconnect function pointer

The details of each device BSP API function are described in section B-2 "Device Driver BSP Functions" on page 418.

6-8 USB DEVICE DRIVER FUNCTIONAL MODEL

The USB device controller can operate in distinct modes while transferring data. This section describes the common sequence of operations for the receive and transmit API functions in the device driver, highlighting potential differences when the controller is operating on FIFO or DMA mode. While there are some controllers that are strictly FIFO based or DMA based, there are controllers that can operate in both modes depending on hardware characteristics. For this type of controller, the device driver will employ the appropriate sequence of operations depending, for example, on the endpoint type.

6-8-1 DEVICE SYNCHRONOUS RECEIVE

The device synchronous receive operation is initiated by the calls: USBD_BulkRx(), USBD_CtrlRx(), and USBD_IntrRx(). Figure 6-1 shows an overview of the device synchronous receive operation.

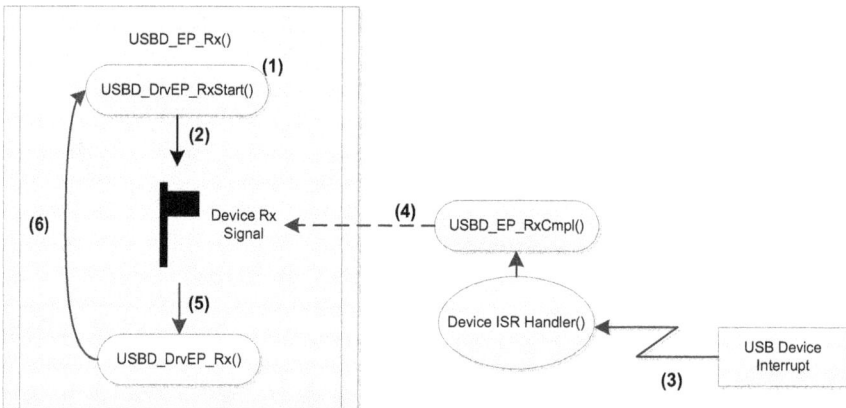

Figure 6-1 **Device Synchronous Receive Diagram**

F6-1(1)   The upper layer API's, USBD_BulkRx(), USBD_CtrlRx(), and USBD_IntrRx(), call USBD_EP_Rx(), in which USBD_DrvEP_RxStart() is invoked.

On DMA-based controllers, this device driver API is responsible for queuing a receive transfer. The queued receive transfer does not need to satisfy the whole requested transfer length at once. If multiple transfers are queued only the last queued transfer must be signaled to the USB device stack. This is required since the USB device stack iterates through the receive process until all requested data or a short packet has been received.

On FIFO-based controllers, this device driver API is responsible for enabling data to be received into the endpoint FIFO, including any related ISR's.

F6-1(2) While data is being received, the device synchronous receive operation waits on the device receive signal.

F6-1(3) The USB device controller triggers an interrupt request when it is finished receiving the data. This invokes the USB device driver interrupt service routine (ISR) handler, directly or indirectly, depending on the architecture.

F6-1(4) Inside the USB device driver ISR handler, the type of interrupt request is determined to be a receive interrupt. **USBD_EP_RxCmpl()** is called to unblock the device receive signal.

F6-1(5) The device receive operation reaches the **USBD_EP_Rx()**, which internally calls **USBD_DrvEP_Rx()**.

On DMA-based controllers, this device driver API is responsible for de-queuing the completed receive transfer and returning the amount of data received. In case the DMA-based controller requires the buffered data to be placed in a dedicated USB memory region, the buffered data must be transferred into the application buffer area.

On FIFO-based controllers, this device driver API is responsible for reading the amount of data received by copying it into the application buffer area and returning the data back to its caller.

F6-1(6) The device receive operation iterates through the process until the amount of data received matches the amount requested, or a short packet is received.

6

6-8-2 DEVICE ASYNCHRONOUS RECEIVE

The device asynchronous receive operation is initiated by the calls: **USBD_BulkRxAsync()** and **USBD_IntrRxAsync()**. Figure 6-2 shows an overview of the device asynchronous receive operation.

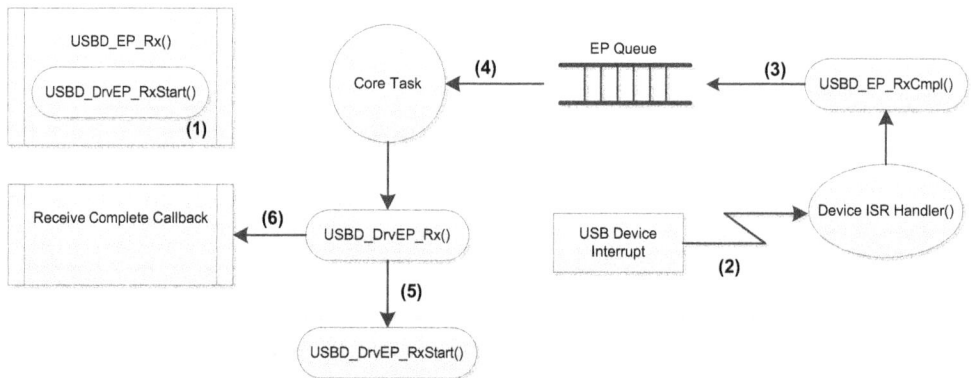

Figure 6-2 **Device Asynchronous Receive Diagram**

F6-2(1)   The upper layer API's, **USBD_BulkRxAsync()** and **USBD_IntrRxAsync()**, call **USBD_EP_Rx()** passing a receive complete callback function as an argument. In **USBD_EP_Rx()**, the **USBD_DrvEP_RxStart()** function is invoked in the same way as for the synchronous operation.

On DMA-based controllers, this device driver API is responsible for queuing a receive transfer. The queued receive transfer does not need to satisfy the whole requested transfer length at once. If multiple transfers are queued only the last queued transfer must be signaled to the USB device stack. This is required since the USB device stack iterates through the receive process until all requested data or a short packet has been received.

On FIFO-based controllers, this device driver API is responsible for enabling data to be received into the endpoint FIFO, including any related ISRs.

The call to **USBD_EP_Rx()** returns immediately to the application (without blocking) while data is being received.

6

F6-2(2)   The USB device controller triggers an interrupt request when it is finished receiving the data. This invokes the USB device driver interrupt service routine (ISR) handler, directly or indirectly, depending on the architecture.

F6-2(3)   Inside the USB device driver ISR handler, the type of interrupt request is determined to be a receive interrupt. `USBD_EP_RxCmpl()` is called to queue the endpoint that had its transfer completed.

F6-2(4)   The core task de-queues the endpoint that completed a transfer and invokes `USBD_EP_Process()`, which internally calls `USBD_DrvEP_Rx()`.

On DMA-based controllers, this device driver API is responsible for de-queuing the completed receive transfer and returning the amount of data received. In case the DMA-based controller requires the buffered data to be placed in a dedicated USB memory region, the buffered data must be transferred into the application buffer area.

On FIFO-based controllers, this device driver API is responsible for reading the amount of data received by copying it into the application buffer area and returning the data back to its caller.

F6-2(5)   If the overall amount of data received is less than the amount requested and the current transfer is not a short packet, `USBD_DrvEP_RxStart()` is called to request the remaining data.

On DMA-based controllers, this device driver API is responsible for queuing a receive transfer. The queued receive transfer does not need to satisfy the whole requested transfer length at once. If multiple transfers are queued only the last queued transfer must be signaled to the USB device stack. This is required since the USB device stack iterates through the receive process until all requested data or a short packet has been received.

On FIFO-based controllers, this device driver API is responsible for enabling data to be received into the endpoint FIFO, including any related ISRs.

F6-2(6)   The receive operation finishes when the amount of data received matches the amount requested, or a short packet is received. The receive complete callback is invoked to notify the application about the completion of the process.

6-8-3 DEVICE SYNCHRONOUS TRANSMIT

The device synchronous transmit operation is initiated by the calls: **USBD_BulkTx()**, **USBD_CtrlTx()**, and **USBD_IntrTx()**. Figure 6-3 shows an overview of the device synchronous transmit operation.

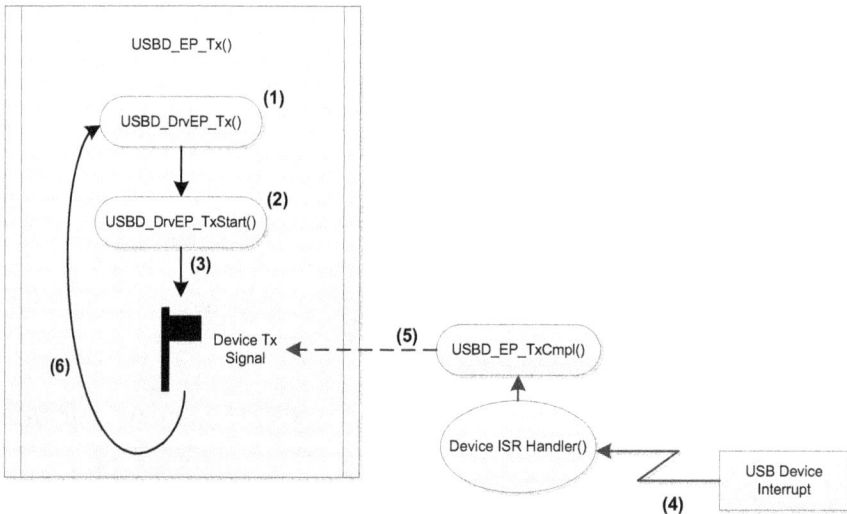

Figure 6-3 **Device Synchronous Transmit Diagram**

F6-3(1)   The upper layer API's, **USBD_BulkTx()**, **USBD_CtrlTx()**, and **USBD_IntrTx()**, call **USBD_EP_Tx()**, where **USBD_DrvEP_Tx()** is invoked.

On DMA-based controllers, this device driver API is responsible for preparing the transmit transfer/descriptor and returning the amount of data to transmit. In case the DMA-based controller requires the buffered data to be placed in a dedicated USB memory region, the contents of the application buffer area must be transferred into the dedicated memory region.

On FIFO-based controllers, this device driver API is responsible for writing the amount of data to transfer into the FIFO and returning the amount of data to transmit.

F6-3(2)   The **USBD_DrvEP_TxStart()** API starts the transmit process.

On DMA-based controllers, this device driver API is responsible for queuing the DMA transmit descriptor and enabling DMA transmit complete ISR's.

On FIFO-based controllers, this device driver API is responsible for enabling transmit complete ISR's.

F6-3(3)   While data is being transmitted, the device synchronous transmit operation waits on the device transmit signal.

F6-3(4)   The USB device controller triggers an interrupt request when it is finished transmitting the data. This invokes the USB device driver interrupt service routine (ISR) handler, directly or indirectly, depending on the architecture.

F6-3(5)   Inside the USB device driver ISR handler, the type of interrupt request is determined as a transmit interrupt. **USBD_EP_TxCmpl()** is called to unblock the device transmit signal.

On DMA-based controllers, the transmit transfer is de-queued from a list of completed transfers.

F6-3(6)   The device transmit operation iterates through the process until the amount of data transmitted matches the requested amount.

6

6-8-4 DEVICE ASYNCHRONOUS TRANSMIT

The device asynchronous transmit operation is initiated by the calls: `USBD_BulkTxAsync()` and `USBD_IntrTxAsync()`. Figure 6-4 shows an overview of the device asynchronous transmit operation

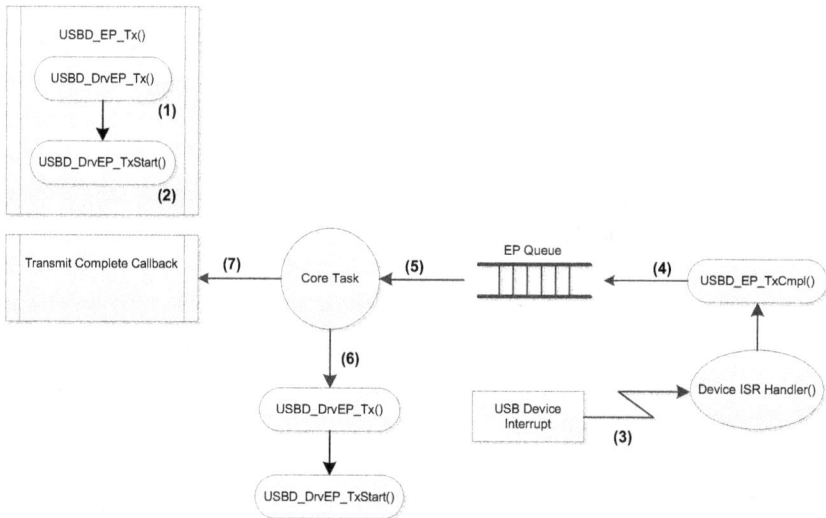

Figure 6-4 **Device Asynchronous Transmit Diagram**

F6-4(1)   The upper layer API's, `USBD_BulkTxAsync()` and `USBD_IntrTxAsync()`, call `USBD_EP_Tx()` passing a transmit complete callback function as an argument. In `USBD_EP_Tx()`, the `USBD_DrvEP_Tx()` function is invoked in the same way as for the synchronous operation.

On DMA-based controllers, this device driver API is responsible for preparing the transmit transfer/descriptor and returning the amount of data to transmit. In case the DMA-based controller requires the buffered data to be placed in a dedicated USB memory region, the contents of the application buffer area must be transferred into the dedicated memory region.

On FIFO-based controllers, this device driver API is responsible for writing the amount of data to transfer into the FIFO and returning the amount of data to transmit.

F6-4(2)   The **USBD_DrvEP_TxStart()** API starts the transmit process.

On DMA-based controllers, this device driver API is responsible for queuing the DMA transmit descriptor and enabling DMA transmit complete ISR's.

On FIFO-based controllers, this device driver API is responsible for enabling transmit complete ISR's.

The call to **USBD_EP_Tx()** returns immediately to the application (without blocking) while data is being transmitted.

F6-4(3)   The USB device controller triggers an interrupt request when it is finished transmitting the data. This invokes the USB device driver interrupt service routine (ISR) handler, directly or indirectly, depending on the architecture.

F6-4(4)   Inside the USB device driver ISR handler, the type of interrupt request is determined as a transmit interrupt. **USBD_EP_TxCmpl()** is called to queue the endpoint that had its transfer completed.

On DMA-based controllers, the transmit transfer is de-queued from the list of completed transfers.

F6-4(5)   The core task de-queues the endpoint that completed a transfer.

F6-4(6)   If the overall amount of data transmitted is less than the amount requested, **USBD_DrvEP_Tx()** and **USBD_DrvEP_TxStart()** are called to transmit the remaining amount of data.

F6-4(7)   The device transmit operation finishes when the amount of data transmitted matches the amount requested. The transmit complete callback is invoked to notify the application about the completion of the process.

6-8-5 DEVICE SET ADDRESS

The device set address operation is performed by the setup transfer handler when a **SET_ADDRESS** request is received. Figure 6-5 shows an overview of the device set address operation.

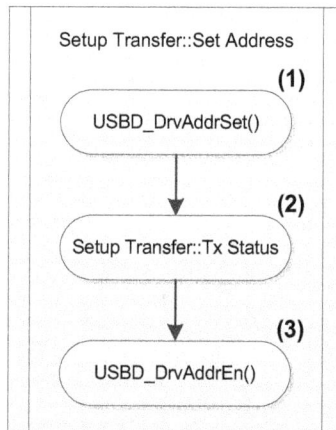

Figure 6-5 **Device Set Address Diagram**

F6-5(1)   Once the arguments of the setup request are validated, **USBD_DrvAddrSet()** is called to inform the device driver layer of the new address. For controllers that have hardware assistance in setting the device address after the status stage, this device driver API is used to configure the device address and enable the transition after the status stage. For controllers that activate the device address as soon as configured, this device driver API should not perform any action.

F6-5(2)   The setup request status stage is transmitted to acknowledge the address change.

F6-5(3)   After the status stage, the **USBD_DrvAddrEn()** is called to inform the device driver layer to enable the new device address. For controllers that activate the device address as soon as configured, this device driver API is responsible for setting and enabling the new device address. For controllers that have hardware assistance in setting the device address after the status stage, this device driver API should not perform any action, since **USBD_DrvAddrSet()** has already taken care of setting the new device.

USB Classes

The USB classes available for the µC/USB-Device stack have some common characteristics. This chapter explains these characteristics and the interactions with the core layer allowing you to better understand the operation of classes.

7-1 CLASS INSTANCE CONCEPT

The USB classes available with the µC/USB-Device stack implement the concept of class instances. A class instance represents one function within a device. The function can be described by one interface or by a group of interfaces and belongs to a certain class.

Each USB class implementation has some configuration and functions in common based on the concept of class instance. The common configuration and functions are presented in Table 7-1. In the column title 'Constants or Function', the placeholder **XXXX** can be replaced by the name of the class: CDC, HID, MSC, PHDC or VENDOR (Vendor for function names).

Constant or function	Description
USBD_XXXX_CFG_MAX_NBR_DEV	Configures the maximum number of class instances.
USBD_XXXX_CFG_MAX_NBR_CFG	Configures the maximum number of configurations per device. During the class initialization, a created class instance will be added to one or more configurations.
USBD_XXXX_Add()	Creates a new class instance.
USBD_XXXX_CfgAdd()	Adds an existing class instance to the specified device configuration.

Table 7-1 **Constants and Functions Related to the Concept of Multiple Class Instances**

7

In terms of code implementation, the class will declare a local global table that contains a class control structure. The size of the table is determined by the constant **USBD_XXXX_CFG_MAX_NBR_DEV**. This class control structure is associated with one class instance and will contain certain information to manage the class instance. See section 7-2 "Class Instance Structures" on page 156 for more details about this class control structure.

The following illustrations present several case scenarios. Each illustration is followed by a code listing showing the code corresponding to the case scenario. Figure 7-1 represents a typical USB device. The device is Full-Speed (FS) and contains one single configuration. The function of the device is described by one interface composed of a pair of endpoints for the data communication. One class instance is created and it will allow you to manage the entire interface with its associated endpoint.

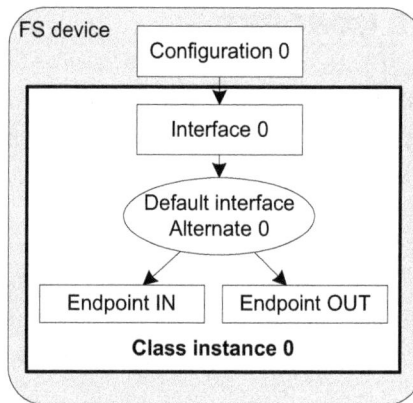

Figure 7-1 **Multiple Class Instances - FS Device (1 Configuration with 1 Interface)**

The code corresponding to Figure 7-1 is shown in Listing 7-1.

```
USBD_ERR     err;
CPU_INT08U   class_0;


USBD_XXXX_Init(&err);                                (1)
if (err != USBD_ERR_NONE) {
    /* $$$$ Handle the error. */
}


class_0 = USBD_XXXX_Add(&err);                       (2)
if (err != USBD_ERR_NONE) {
    /* $$$$ Handle the error. */
}


USBD_XXXX_CfgAdd(class_0, dev_nbr, cfg_0, &err);     (3)
if (err != USBD_ERR_NONE) {
    /* $$$$ Handle the error. */
}
```

Listing 7-1 **Multiple Class Instances - FS Device (1 Configuration with 1 Interface) - Code**

L7-1(1)   Initialize the class. Any internal variables, structures, and class Real-Time Operating System (RTOS) port will be initialized.

L7-1(2)   Create the class instance, **class_0**. The function **USBD_XXXX_Add( )** allocates a class control structure associated to **class_0**. Depending on the class, besides the parameter for an error code, **USBD_XXXX_Add( )** may have additional parameters representing class-specific information stored in the class control structure.

L7-1(3)   Add the class instance, **class_0**, to the specified configuration number, **cfg_0**. **USBD_XXXX_CfgAdd( )** will create the interface 0 and its associated endpoints IN and OUT. As a result, the class instance encompasses the interface 0 and its endpoints. Any communication done on the interface 0 will use the class instance number, **class_0**.

Figure 7-2 represents an example of a high-speed capable device. The device can support High-Speed (HS) and Full-Speed (FS). The device will contain two configurations: one valid if the device operates at full-speed and another if it operates at high-speed. In each configuration, interface 0 is the same but its associated endpoints are different. The difference will be the endpoint maximum packet size which varies according to the speed.

If a high-speed host enumerates this device, by default, the device will work in high-speed mode and thus the high-speed configuration will be active. The host can learn about the full-speed capabilities by getting a *Device_Qualifier* descriptor followed by an *Other_Speed_Configuration* descriptor. These two descriptors describe a configuration of a high-speed capable device if it were operating at its other possible speed (refer to Universal Serial Bus 2.0 Specification revision 2.0, section 9.6, for more details about these descriptors). In our example, the host may want to reset and enumerate the device again in full-speed mode. In this case, the full-speed configuration is active. Whatever the active configuration, the same class instance is used. Indeed, the same class instance can be added to different configurations. A class instance cannot be added several times to the same configuration.

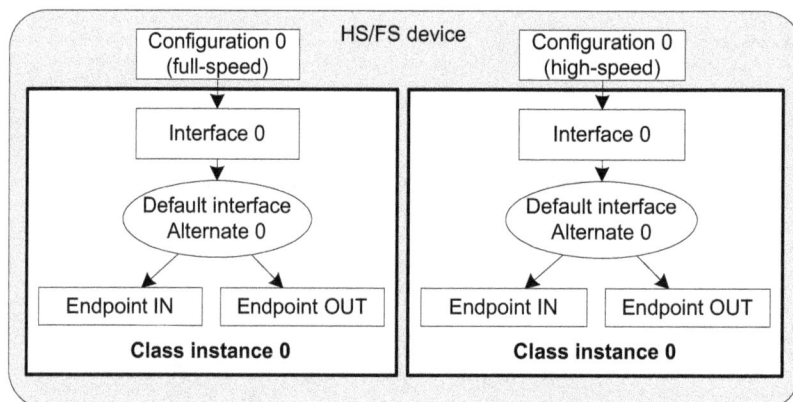

Figure 7-2 **Multiple Class Instances - HS/FS Device (2 Configurations and 1 Single Interface)**

The code corresponding to Figure 7-2 is shown in Listing 7-2.

```
USBD_ERR    err;
CPU_INT08U  class_0;


USBD_XXXX_Init(&err);                                        (1)
if (err != USBD_ERR_NONE) {
    /* $$$$ Handle the error. */
}

class_0 = USBD_XXXX_Add(&err);                               (2)
if (err != USBD_ERR_NONE) {
    /* $$$$ Handle the error. */
}

USBD_XXXX_CfgAdd(class_0, dev_nbr, cfg_0_fs, &err);          (3)
if (err != USBD_ERR_NONE) {
    /* $$$$ Handle the error. */
}

USBD_XXXX_CfgAdd(class_0, dev_nbr, cfg_0_hs, &err);          (4)
if (err != USBD_ERR_NONE) {
    /* $$$$ Handle the error. */
}
```

Listing 7-2 **Multiple Class Instances - HS/FS Device (2 Configurations and 1 Single Interface) - Code**

L7-2(1)   Initialize the class. Any internal variables, structures, and class RTOS port will be initialized.

L7-2(2)   Create the class instance, **class_0**. The function **USBD_XXXX_Add()** allocates a class control structure associated to **class_0**. Depending on the class, besides the parameter for an error code, **USBD_XXXX_Add()** may have additional parameters representing class-specific information stored in the class control structure.

L7-2(3)   Add the class instance, **class_0**, to the full-speed configuration, **cfg_0_fs**. **USBD_XXXX_CfgAdd()** will create the interface 0 and its associated endpoints IN and OUT. If the full-speed configuration is active, any communication done on the interface 0 will use the class instance number, **class_0**.

L7-2(4)   Add the class instance, **class_0**, to the high-speed configuration, **cfg_0_hs**.

7

In the case of the high-speed capable device presented in Figure 7-2, in order to enable the use of *Device_Qualifier* and *Other_Speed_Configuration* descriptors, the function USBD_CfgOtherSpeed() should be called during the µC/USB-Device initialization. Listing 2-5 presents the function **App_USBD_Init()** defined in **app_usbd.c**. This function shows an example of the µC/USB-Device initialization sequence. USBD_CfgOtherSpeed() should be called after the creation of a high-speed and a full-speed configurations with USBD_CfgAdd(). Listing 7-3 below shows the use of USBD_CfgOtherSpeed() based on Listing 2-5. Error handling is omitted for clarity.

```
CCPU_BOOLEAN  App_USBD_Init (void)
{
    CPU_INT08U   dev_nbr;
    CPU_INT08U   cfg_0_fs;
    CPU_INT08U   cfg_0_hs;
    USBD_ERR     err;


    ...                                                      (1)


    if (USBD_DrvCfg_<controller>.Spd == USBD_DEV_SPD_HIGH) {

        cfg_0_hs = USBD_CfgAdd( dev_nbr,                      (2)
                        USBD_DEV_ATTRIB_SELF_POWERED,
                        100u,
                        USBD_DEV_SPD_HIGH,
                        "HS configuration",
                        &err);
    }
    cfg_0_fs = USBD_CfgAdd( dev_nbr,                          (3)
                        USBD_DEV_ATTRIB_SELF_POWERED,
                        100u,
                        USBD_DEV_SPD_FULL,
                        "FS configuration",
                        &err);

    USBD_CfgOtherSpeed(dev_nbr,                               (4)
                        cfg_0_hs,
                        cfg_0_fs,
                        &err);

    return (DEF_OK);
}
```

Listing 7-3 **Use of USBD_CfgOtherSpeed()**

L7-3(1)   Refer to Listing 2-5 for the beginning of the initialization.

L7-3(2)   Add the high-speed configuration, **cfg_0_hs**, to your high-speed capable device.

L7-3(3)   Add the full-speed configuration, **cfg_0_fs**, to your high-speed capable device.

L7-3(4)   Associate the high-speed configuration **cfg_0_hs** with its other-speed counterpart, **cfg_0_fs**.

Figure 7-3 represents a more complex example. A full-speed device is composed of two configurations. The device has two functions which belong to the same class. Each function is described by two interfaces. Each interface has a pair of bidirectional endpoints. In this example, two class instances are created. Each class instance is associated with a group of interfaces as opposed to Figure 7-1 and Figure 7-2 where the class instance was associated to a single interface.

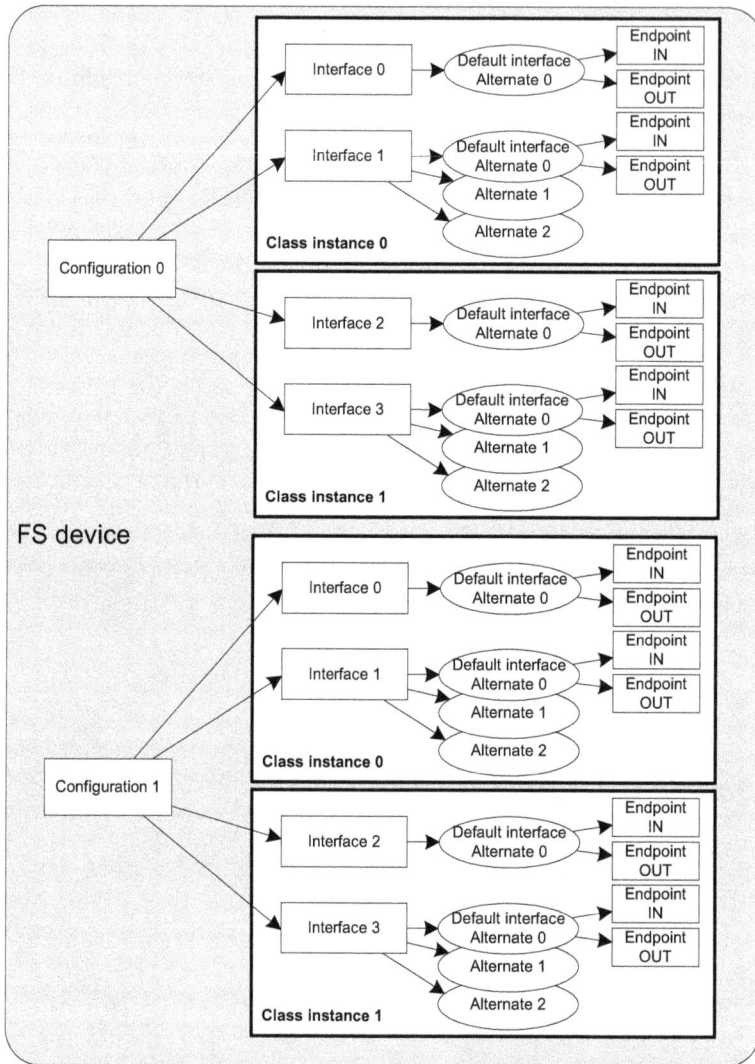

Figure 7-3 **Multiple Class Instances - FS Device (2 Configurations and Multiple Interfaces)**

The code corresponding to Figure 7-3 is shown in Listing 7-4. The error handling is omitted for clarity.

```
USBD_ERR    err;
CPU_INT08U  class_0;
CPU_INT08U  class_1;


USBD_XXXX_Init(&err);                                   (1)

class_0 = USBD_XXXX_Add(&err);                          (2)
class_1 = USBD_XXXX_Add(&err);                          (3)

USBD_XXXX_CfgAdd(class_0, dev_nbr, cfg_0, &err);        (4)
USBD_XXXX_CfgAdd(class_1, dev_nbr, cfg_0, &err);        (5)

USBD_XXXX_CfgAdd(class_0, dev_nbr, cfg_1, &err);        (6)
USBD_XXXX_CfgAdd(class_1, dev_nbr, cfg_1, &err);        (6)
```

Listing 7-4 **Multiple Class Instances - FS Device (2 Configurations and Multiple Interfaces) - Code**

L7-4(1)   Initialize the class. Any internal variables, structures, and class RTOS port will be initialized.

L7-4(2)   Create the class instance, **class_0**. The function **USBD_XXXX_Add( )** allocates a class control structure associated to **class_0**.

L7-4(3)   Create the class instance, **class_1**. The function **USBD_XXXX_Add( )** allocates another class control structure associated to **class_1**.

L7-4(4)   Add the class instance, **class_0**, to the configuration, **cfg_0**. **USBD_XXXX_CfgAdd( )** will create the interface 0, interface 1, alternate interfaces, and the associated endpoints IN and OUT. The class instance number, **class_0**, will be used for any data communication on interface 0 or interface 1.

L7-4(5)   Add the class instance, **class_1**, to the configuration, **cfg_0**. **USBD_XXXX_CfgAdd( )** will create the interface 2, interface 3 and their associated endpoints IN and OUT. The class instance number, **class_1**, will be used for any data communication on interface 2 or interface 3.

L7-4(6)   Add the same class instances, **class_0** and **class_1**, to the other configuration, **cfg_1**.

You can refer to section 5-4 "Configuration Examples" on page 119 for some configuration examples showing multiple class instances applied to composite devices. Composite devices use at least two different classes provided by the µC/USB-Device stack. The section 5-4-2 "Composite High-Speed USB device" on page 120 gives a concrete example based on Figure 7-2. See section 5-4-3 "Complex Composite High-Speed USB device" on page 122 for a hybrid example that corresponds to Figure 7-2 and Figure 7-3.

7-2 CLASS INSTANCE STRUCTURES

When a class instance is created, a control structure is allocated and associated to a specific class instance. The class uses this control structure for its internal operations. All the Micrium USB classes define a class control structure data type. Listing 7-5 shows the declaration of such data structure.

```
struct usbd_xxxx_ctrl {
    CPU_INT08U      DevNbr;                              (1)
    CPU_INT08U      ClassNbr;                            (2)
    USBD_XXXX_STATE State;                               (3)
    USBD_XXXX_COMM  *CommPtr;                            (4)
    ...                                                  (5)
};
```

Listing 7-5 **Class Instance Control Structure**

L7-5(1)   The device number to which the class instance is associated with.

L7-5(2)   The class instance number.

L7-5(3)   The class instance state.

L7-5(4)   A pointer to a class instance communication structure. This structure holds information regarding the interface's endpoints used for data communication. Listing 7-6 presents the communication structure.

L7-5(5)   Class-specific fields.

During the communication phase, the class communication structure is used by the class for data transfers on the endpoints. It allows you to route the transfer to the proper endpoint within the interface. There will be one class communication structure per configuration to which the class instance has been added. Listing 7-6 presents this structure.

```
struct usbd_xxxx_comm {
    USBD_XXXX_CTRL   *CtrlPtr;                        (1)
    CPU_INT08U       ClassEpInAddr;                   (2)
    CPU_INT08U       ClassEpOutAdd2;                  (2)
    ...                                               (2)
};
```

Listing 7-6 **Class Instance Communication Structure**

L7-6(1)   A pointer to the class instance control structure to which the communication relates to.

L7-6(2)   Class-specific fields. In general, this structure stores mainly endpoint addresses related to the class. Depending on the class, the structure may store other types of information. For instance, the Mass Storage Class stores information about the Command Block and Status Wrappers.

Micrium's USB classes define a class state for each class instance created. The class state values are implemented in the form of an enumeration:

```
typedef  enum  usbd_xxxx_state {
    USBD_XXXX_STATE_NONE = 0,
    USBD_XXXX_STATE_INIT,
    USBD_XXXX_STATE_CFG
} USBD_XXXX_STATE;
```

Figure 7-4 defines a class state machine which applies to all the Micrium classes. Three class states are used.

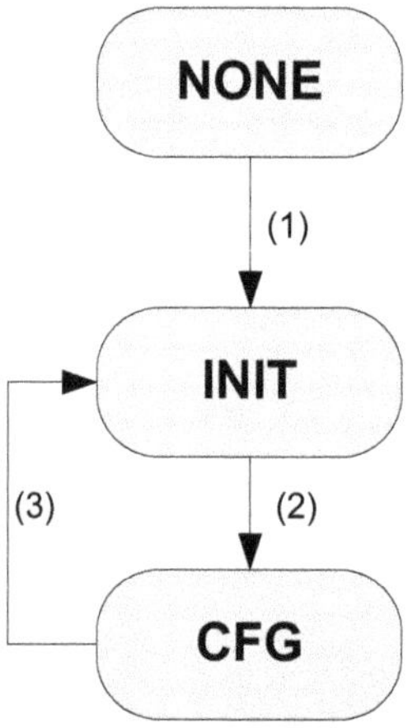

Figure 7-4 **Class State Machine**

F7-4(1)   A class instance has been added to a configuration, the class instance state transitions to the 'Init' state. No data communication on the class endpoint(s) can occur yet.

F7-4(2)   The host has sent the **SET_CONFIGURATION** request to activate a certain configuration. The Core layer calls a class callback informing about the completion of the standard enumeration. The class instance state transitions to the 'Cfg' state. This state indicates that the device has transitioned to the 'Configured' state defined by the Universal Serial Bus Specification revision 2.0. The data communication may begin. Some classes such as the MSC class may require that the host sends some class-specific requests before the communication on the endpoints really starts.

F7-4(3)   The Core layer calls another class callback informing that the host has sent a **SET_CONFIGURATION** request with a new configuration number or with the value 0 indicating a configuration reset, or that the device has been physically disconnected from the host. In all these cases, the current active configuration becomes inactive. The class instance state transitions to the 'Init' state. Any ongoing transfers on the endpoints managed by the class instance have been aborted by the Core layer. No more communication is possible until the host sends a new **SET_CONFIGURATION** request with a non-null value or until the device is plugged again to the host.

7-3 CLASS AND CORE LAYERS INTERACTION THROUGH CALLBACKS

Upon reception of standard, class-specific and/or vendor requests, the Core layer can notify the Class layer about the event associated with the request via the use of class callbacks. Each Micrium class must define a class callbacks structure of type USBD_CLASS_DRV that contains function pointers. Each callback allows the class to perform a specific action if it is required. Listing 7-7 shows a generic example of class callback structure. In the listing, XXXX could be replaced with CDC, HID, MSC, PHDC or Vendor.

```
static  USBD_CLASS_DRV  USBD_XXXX_Drv = {
        USBD_XXXX_Conn,                         (1)
        USBD_XXXX_Disconn,                      (2)
        USBD_XXXX_UpdateAltSetting,             (3)
        USBD_XXXX_UpdateEPState,                (4)
        USBD_XXXX_IFDesc,                       (5)
        USBD_XXXX_IFDescGetSize,                (6)
        USBD_XXXX_EPDesc,                       (7)
        USBD_XXXX_EPDescGetSize,                (8)
        USBD_XXXX_IFReq,                        (9)
        USBD_XXXX_ClassReq,                     (10)
        USBD_XXXX_VendorReq                     (11)
};
```

Listing 7-7 **Class Callback Structure**

L7-7(1)   Notify the class that a configuration has been activated.

L7-7(2)   Notify the class that a configuration has been deactivated.

L7-7(3)   Notify the class that an alternate interface setting has been updated.

L7-7(4)   Notify the class that an endpoint state has been updated by the host. The state is generally stalled or not stalled.

L7-7(5)   Ask the class to build the interface class-specific descriptors.

L7-7(6)   Ask the class for the total size of interface class-specific descriptors.

L7-7(7)   Ask the class to build endpoint class-specific descriptors.

L7-7(8)   Ask the class for the total size of endpoint class-specific descriptors.

L7-7(9)   Ask the class to process a standard request whose recipient is an interface.

L7-7(10)   Ask the class to process a class-specific request.

L7-7(11)   Ask the class to process a vendor-specific request.

A class is not required to provide all the callbacks. If a class for instance does not define alternate interface settings and does not process any vendor requests, the corresponding function pointer will be a null-pointer. Listing 7-8 presents the callback structure for that case.

```
static  USBD_CLASS_DRV  USBD_XXXX_Drv = {
    USBD_XXXX_Conn,
    USBD_XXXX_Disconn,
    0,
    USBD_XXXX_UpdateEPState,
    USBD_XXXX_IFDesc,
    USBD_XXXX_IFDescGetSize,
    USBD_XXXX_EPDesc,
    USBD_XXXX_EPDescGetSize,
    USBD_XXXX_IFReq,
    USBD_XXXX_ClassReq,
    0
};
```

Listing 7-8 **Class Callback Structure with Null Function Pointers**

If a class is composed of one interface then one class callback structure is required. If a class is composed of several interfaces then the class may define several class callback structures. In that case, a callback structure may be linked to one or several interfaces. For instance, the Communication Device Class (CDC) is composed of one Communication Interface and one or more Data Interfaces. The Communication interface will be linked to a callback structure. The Data interfaces may be linked to another callback structure common to all Data interfaces.

The class callbacks are called by the core task when receiving a request from the host sent over control endpoints (refer to section 4-2 "Task Model" on page 102 for more details on the core task). Table 7-2 indicates which callbacks are mandatory and optional and upon reception of which request the core task calls a specific callback.

Request type	Callback	Request	Mandatory? / Note
Standard	`Conn()`	`SET_CONFIGURATION`	Yes / Host selects a non-null configuration number.
Standard	`Disconn()`	`SET_CONFIGURATION`	Yes / Host resets the current configuration or device physically detached from host.
Standard	`UpdateAltSetting()`	`SET_INTERFACE`	No / Callback skipped if no alternate settings are defined for one or more interfaces.
Standard	`UpdateEPState()`	`SET_FEATURE` `CLEAR_FEATURE`	No / Callback skipped if the state of the endpoint is not used.
Standard	`IFDesc()`	`GET_DESCRIPTOR`	No / Callback skipped if no class-specific descriptors for one or more interfaces.
Standard	`IFDescGetSize()`	`GET_DESCRIPTOR`	No / Callback skipped if no class-specific descriptors for one or more interfaces.
Standard	`EPDesc()`	`GET_DESCRIPTOR`	No / Callback skipped if no class-specific descriptors for one or more endpoints.
Standard	`EPDescGetSize()`	`GET_DESCRIPTOR`	No / Callback skipped if no class-specific descriptors for one or more endpoints.
Standard	`IFReq()`	`GET_DESCRIPTOR`	No / Callback skipped if no standard descriptors provided by a class.
Class	`ClassReq()`	–	No / Callback skipped if no class-specific requests defined by the class specification.
Vendor	`VendorReq()`	–	No / Callback skipped if no vendor requests.

Table 7-2 **Class Callbacks and Requests Mapping**

Communications Device Class

This chapter describes the Communications Device Class (CDC) class and the associated CDC subclass supported by μC/USB-Device. μC/USB-Device currently supports the Abstract Control Model (ACM) subclass, which is especially used for serial emulation.

The CDC and the associated subclass implementation complies with the following specifications:

▪ *Universal Serial Bus, Class Definitions for Communications Devices, Revision 1.2,* November 3 2010.

▪ *Universal Serial Bus, Communications, Subclass for PSTN Devices, revision 1.2,* February 9, 2007.

CDC includes various telecommunication and networking devices. Telecommunication devices encompass analog modems, analog and digital telephones, ISDN terminal adapters, etc. Networking devices contain, for example, ADSL and cable modems, Ethernet adapters and hubs. CDC defines a framework to encapsulate existing communication services standards, such as V.250 (for modems over telephone network) and Ethernet (for local area network devices), using a USB link. A communication device is in charge of device management, call management when needed and data transmission. CDC defines seven major groups of devices. Each group belongs to a model of communication which may include several subclasses. Each group of devices has its own specification besides the CDC base class. The seven groups are:

▪ Public Switched Telephone Network (PSTN), devices including voiceband modems, telephones and serial emulation devices.

▪ Integrated Services Digital Network (ISDN) devices, including terminal adaptors and telephones.

8

■ Ethernet Control Model (ECM) devices, including devices supporting the IEEE 802 family (for instance cable and ADSL modems, WiFi adaptors).

■ Asynchronous Transfer Mode (ATM) devices, including ADLS modems and other devices connected to ATM networks (workstations, routers, LAN switches).

■ Wireless Mobile Communications (WMC) devices, including multi-function communications handset devices used to manage voice and data communications.

■ Ethernet Emulation Model (EEM) devices which exchange Ethernet-framed data.

■ Network Control Model (NCM) devices, including high-speed network devices (High Speed Packet Access modems, Line Terminal Equipment)

8-1 OVERVIEW

A CDC device is composed of several interfaces to implement a certain function, that is communication capability. It is formed by the following interfaces:

■ Communications Class Interface (CCI)

■ Data Class Interface (DCI)

A CCI is responsible for the device management and optionally the call management. The device management enables the general configuration and control of the device and the notification of events to the host. The call management enables calls establishment and termination. Call management might be multiplexed through a DCI. A CCI is mandatory for all CDC devices. It identifies the CDC function by specifying the communication model supported by the CDC device. The interface(s) following the CCI can be any defined USB class interface, such as Audio or a vendor-specific interface. The vendor-specific interface is represented specifically by a DCI.

A DCI is responsible for data transmission. The data transmitted and/or received do not follow a specific format. Data could be raw data from a communication line, data following a proprietary format, etc. All the DCIs following the CCI can be seen as subordinate interfaces.

A CDC device must have at least one CCI and zero or more DCIs. One CCI and any subordinate DCI together provide a feature to the host. This capability is also referred to as a function. In a CDC composite device, you could have several functions. And thus, the device would be composed of several sets of CCI and DCI(s) as shown in Figure 8-1.

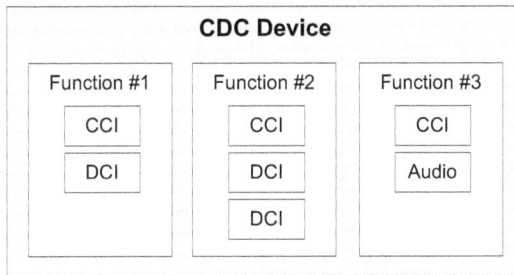

```
┌─────────────────────────────────────────────────────┐
│                    CDC Device                         │
│  ┌──────────────┐ ┌──────────────┐ ┌──────────────┐  │
│  │  Function #1 │ │  Function #2 │ │  Function #3 │  │
│  │  ┌────────┐  │ │  ┌────────┐  │ │  ┌────────┐  │  │
│  │  │  CCI   │  │ │  │  CCI   │  │ │  │  CCI   │  │  │
│  │  └────────┘  │ │  └────────┘  │ │  └────────┘  │  │
│  │  ┌────────┐  │ │  ┌────────┐  │ │  ┌────────┐  │  │
│  │  │  DCI   │  │ │  │  DCI   │  │ │  │ Audio  │  │  │
│  │  └────────┘  │ │  └────────┘  │ │  └────────┘  │  │
│  │              │ │  ┌────────┐  │ │              │  │
│  │              │ │  │  DCI   │  │ │              │  │
│  │              │ │  └────────┘  │ │              │  │
│  └──────────────┘ └──────────────┘ └──────────────┘  │
└─────────────────────────────────────────────────────┘
```

Figure 8-1 **CDC Composite Device**

A CDC device is likely to use the following combination of endpoints:

- A pair of control IN and OUT endpoints called the default endpoint.

- An optional bulk or interrupt IN endpoint.

- A pair of bulk or isochronous IN and OUT endpoints.

Table 8-1 indicates the usage of the different endpoints and by which interface of the CDC they are used:

Endpoint	Direction	Interface	Usage
Control IN	Device-to-host	CCI	Standard requests for enumeration, class-specific requests, device management and optionally call management.
Control OUT	Host-to-device	CCI	Standard requests for enumeration, class-specific requests, device management and optionally call management.
Interrupt or bulk IN	Device-to-host	CCI	Events notification, such as ring detect, serial line status, network status.
Bulk or isochronous IN	Device-to-host	DCI	Raw or formatted data communication.
Bulk or isochronous OUT	Host-to-device	DCI	Raw or formatted data communication.

Table 8-1 **CDC Endpoint Usage**

Most communication devices use an interrupt endpoint to notify the host of events. Isochronous endpoints should not be used for data transmission when a proprietary protocol relies on data retransmission in case of USB protocol errors. Isochronous communication can inherently loose data since it has no retry mechanisms.

The seven major models of communication encompass several subclasses. A subclass describes the way the device should use the CCI to handle the device management and call management. Table 8-2 shows all the possible subclasses and the communication model they belong to.

Subclass	Communication model	Example of devices using this subclass
Direct Line Control Model	PSTN	Modem devices directly controlled by the USB host
Abstract Control Model	PSTN	Serial emulation devices, modem devices controlled through a serial command set
Telephone Control Model	PSTN	Voice telephony devices
Multi-Channel Control Model	ISDN	Basic rate terminal adaptors, primary rate terminal adaptors, telephones
CAPI Control Model	ISDN	Basic rate terminal adaptors, primary rate terminal adaptors, telephones
Ethernet Networking Control Model	ECM	DOC-SIS cable modems, ADSL modems that support PPPoE emulation, Wi-Fi adaptors (IEEE 802.11-family), IEEE 802.3 adaptors
ATM Networking Control Model	ATM	ADSL modems
Wireless Handset Control Model	WMC	Mobile terminal equipment connecting to wireless devices
Device Management	WMC	Mobile terminal equipment connecting to wireless devices
Mobile Direct Line Model	WMC	Mobile terminal equipment connecting to wireless devices
OBEX	WMC	Mobile terminal equipment connecting to wireless devices
Ethernet Emulation Model	EEM	Devices using Ethernet frames as the next layer of transport. Not intended for routing and Internet connectivity devices
Network Control Model	NCM	IEEE 802.3 adaptors carrying high-speed data bandwidth on network

Table 8-2 **CDC Subclasses**

8
8-2 ARCHITECTURE

Figure 8-2 shows the general architecture between the host and the device using CDC available from Micrium.

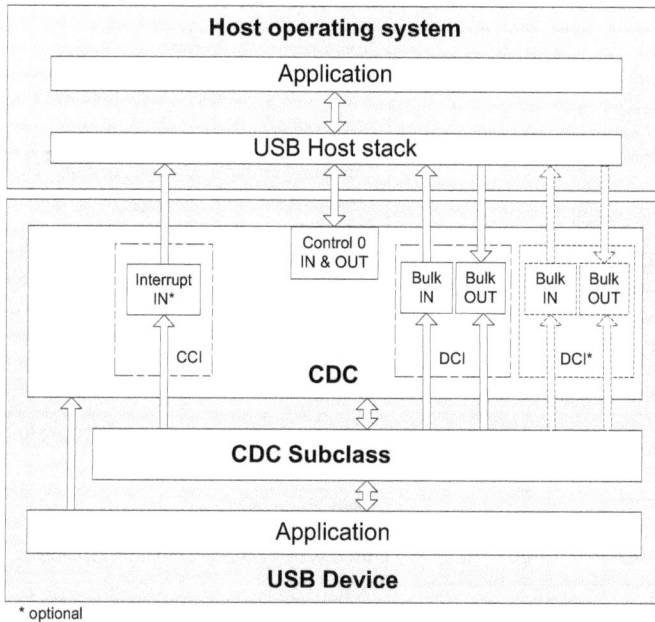

Figure 8-2 **General Architecture between a Host and Micrium's CDC**

The host operating system (OS) enumerates the device using the control endpoints. Once the enumeration phase is done, the host can configure the device by sending class-specific requests to the Communications Class Interface (CCI) via the control endpoints. The class-specific requests vary according to the CDC subclasses. Micrium's CDC base class offers the possibility to allocate an interrupt endpoint for event notification, depending on the subclass needs.

Following enumeration and configuration of the device, the host can start the transmission/reception of data to/from the device using the bulk endpoints belonging to the Data Class Interface (DCI). Isochronous endpoints are not supported in the current implementation. The CDC base class enables you to have several DCIs along with the CCI. The application can communicate with the host using the communication API offered by the CDC subclass.

8-3 CONFIGURATION

8-3-1 GENERAL CONFIGURATION

Some constants are available to customize the CDC base class. These constants are located in the USB device configuration file, **usbd_cfg.h**. Table 8-3 shows their description.

Constant	Description
USBD_CDC_CFG_MAX_NBR_DEV	Configures the maximum number of class instances. Each associated subclass also defines a maximum number of subclass instances. The sum of all the maximum numbers of subclass instances must *not* be greater than USBD_CDC_CFG_MAX_NBR_DEV.
USBD_CDC_CFG_MAX_NBR_CFG	Configures the maximum number of configurations in which CDC class is used. Keep in mind that if you use a high-speed device, two configurations will be built, one for full-speed and another for high-speed.
USBD_CDC_CFG_MAX_NBR_DATA_IF	Configures the maximum number of Data interfaces. The minimum value is 1.

Table 8-3 **CDC Class Configuration Constants**

Listing 8-1 shows the **App_USBD_CDC_Init()** function defined in the application template file **app_usbd_cdc.c**. This function performs CDC and associated subclass initialization.

```
CPU_BOOLEAN  App_USBD_CDC_Init (CPU_INT08U  dev_nbr,
                                CPU_INT08U  cfg_hs,
                                CPU_INT08U  cfg_fs)
{
    USBD_ERR    err;


    USBD_CDC_Init(&err);                                    (1)


    ...                                                     (2)
}
```

Listing 8-1 **CDC Initialization Example**

8

L8-1(1)   Initialize CDC internal structures and variables. This is the first function you should call and you should do it only once.

L8-1(2)   Call all the required functions to initialize the subclass(es). Refer to section 8-4-2 "General Configuration" on page 172 for ACM subclass initialization.

8-4 ACM SUBCLASS

The ACM subclass is used by two types of communication devices:

▨ Devices supporting AT commands (for instance, voiceband modems).

▨ Serial emulation devices which are also called Virtual COM port devices.

Micrium's ACM subclass implementation complies with the following specification:

▨ *Universal Serial Bus, Communications, Subclass for PSTN Devices, revision 1.2, February 9, 2007.*

8-4-1 OVERVIEW

The general characteristics of the CDC base class in terms of Communications Class Interface (CCI) and Data Class Interface (DCI) were presented in section 8-1 "Overview" on page 164. In this section, a CCI of type ACM is considered. It will consist of a default endpoint for the management element and an interrupt endpoint for the notification element. A pair of bulk endpoints is used to carry unspecified data over the DCI.

Several subclass-specific requests exists for the ACM subclass. They allow you to control and configure the device. The complete list and description of all ACM requests can be found in the specification "*Universal Serial Bus, Communications, Subclass for PSTN Devices, revision 1.2, February 9, 2007*", section 6.2.2. From this list, Micrium's ACM subclass supports:

8

Subclass request	Description
SetCommFeature	The host sends this request to control the settings for a particular communications feature. Not used for serial emulation.
GetCommFeature	The host sends this request to get the current settings for a particular communications feature. Not used for serial emulation.
ClearCommFeature	The host sends this request to clear the settings for a particular communications feature. Not used for serial emulation.
SetLineCoding	The host sends this request to configure the ACM device settings in terms of baud rate, number of stop bits, parity type and number of data bits. For a serial emulation, this request is sent automatically by a serial terminal each time you configure the serial settings for an open virtual COM port.
GetLineCoding	The host sends this request to get the current ACM settings (baud rate, stop bits, parity, data bits). For a serial emulation, serial terminals send this request automatically during virtual COM port opening.
SetControlLineState	The host sends this request to control the carrier for half duplex modems and indicate that Data Terminal Equipment (DTE) is ready or not. In the serial emulation case, the DTE is a serial terminal. For a serial emulation, certain serial terminals allow you to send this request with the controls set.
SetBreak	The host sends this request to generate an RS-232 style break. For a serial emulation, certain serial terminals allow you to send this request.

Table 8-4 **ACM Requests Supported by Micrium**

Micrium's ACM subclass uses the interrupt IN endpoint to notify the host about the current *serial line state*. The serial line state is a bitmap informing the host about:

- Data discarded because of overrun

- Parity error

- Framing error

- State of the ring signal detection

- State of break detection mechanism

- State of transmission carrier

- State of receiver carrier detection

8

8-4-2 GENERAL CONFIGURATION

Table 8-5 shows the constant available to customize the ACM serial emulation subclass. This constant is located in the USB device configuration file, **usbd_cfg.h**.

Constant	Description
USBD_ACM_SERIAL_CFG_MAX_NBR_DEV	Configures the maximum number of subclass instances. The constant value cannot be greater than USBD_CDC_CFG_MAX_NBR_DEV. Unless you plan on having multiple configurations or interfaces using different class instances, this can be set to 1.

Table 8-5 **ACM Serial Emulation Subclass Configuration Constants**

8-4-3 SUBCLASS INSTANCE CONFIGURATION

Before starting the communication phase, your application needs to initialize and configure the class to suit its needs. Table 8-6 summarizes the initialization functions provided by the ACM subclass. For more details about the functions' parameters, refer to section C-2 "CDC ACM Subclass Functions" on page 437.

Function name	Operation
USBD_ACM_SerialInit()	Initializes ACM subclass internal structures and variables.
USBD_ACM_SerialAdd()	Creates a new instance of ACM subclass.
USBD_ACM_SerialCfgAdd()	Adds an existing ACM instance to the specified device configuration.
USBD_ACM_SerialLineCodingReg()	Registers line coding notification callback.
USBD_ACM_SerialLineCtrlReg()	Registers line control notification callback.

Table 8-6 **ACM Subclass Initialization API Summary**

You need to call these functions in the order shown below to successfully initialize the ACM subclass:

1 Call **USBD_ACM_SerialInit()**

This function initializes all internal structures and variables that the ACM subclass needs. You should call this function only once even if you use multiple class instances.

8

2   Call `USBD_ACM_SerialAdd()`

This function allocates an ACM subclass instance. Internally, this function allocates a CDC class instance. It also allows you to specify the line state notification interval expressed in milliseconds.

3   Call `USBD_ACM_SerialLineCodingReg()`

This function allows you to register a callback used by the ACM subclass to notify the application about a change in the serial line coding settings (that is baud rate, number of stop bits, parity and number of data bits).

4   Call `USBD_ACM_SerialLineCtrlReg()`

This function allows you to register a callback used by the ACM subclass to notify the application about a change in the serial line state (that is carrier control and a flag indicating that data equipment terminal is present or not).

5   Call `USBD_ACM_SerialCfgAdd()`

Finally, once the ACM subclass instance has been created, you must add it to a specific configuration.

Listing 8-2 illustrates the use of the previous functions for initializing the ACM subclass. Note that the error handling has been omitted for clarity.

8

```
                                                        (4)
static  void         App_USBD_CDC_SerialLineCtrl (CPU_INT08U                      subclass_nbr,
                                                  CPU_INT08U                      events,
                                                  CPU_INT08U                      events_chngd,
                                                  void                            *p_arg);
                                                        (5)
static  CPU_BOOLEAN  App_USBD_CDC_SerialLineCoding(CPU_INT08U                     subclass_nbr,
                                                   USBD_ACM_SERIAL_LINE_CODING    *p_line_coding,
                                                   void                           *p_arg);


CPU_BOOLEAN  App_USBD_CDC_Init (CPU_INT08U  dev_nbr,
                                CPU_INT08U  cfg_hs,
                                CPU_INT08U  cfg_fs)
{
    USBD_ERR    err;
    CPU_INT08U  subclass_nbr;

    USBD_CDC_Init(&err);                                    (1)

    USBD_ACM_SerialInit(&err);                              (2)

    subclass_nbr = USBD_ACM_SerialAdd(100u, &err);          (3)
                                                            (4)
    USBD_ACM_SerialLineCodingReg(      subclass_nbr,
                                       App_USBD_CDC_SerialLineCoding,
                               (void *)0,
                                       &err);
                                                            (5)
    USBD_ACM_SerialLineCtrlReg(        subclass_nbr,
                                       App_USBD_CDC_SerialLineCtrl,
                               (void *)0,
                                       &err);


    if (cfg_hs != USBD_CFG_NBR_NONE) {
        USBD_ACM_SerialCfgAdd(subclass_nbr, dev_nbr, cfg_hs, &err); (6)
    }

    if (cfg_fs != USBD_CFG_NBR_NONE) {
        USBD_ACM_SerialCfgAdd(subclass_nbr, dev_nbr, cfg_fs, &err); (7)
    }
}
```

Listing 8-2 **CDC ACM Subclass Initialization Example**

L8-2(1)   Initialize CDC internal structures and variables.

L8-2(2)   Initialize CDC ACM internal structures and variables.

L8-2(3)   Create a new CDC ACM subclass instance. In this example, the line state notification interval is 100 ms. In the CCI, an interrupt IN endpoint is used to asynchronously notify the host of the status of the different signals forming the serial line. The line state notification interval corresponds to the interrupt endpoint's polling interval.

L8-2(4)   Register the application callback, **App_USBD_CDC_SerialLineCoding()**. It is called by the ACM subclass when the class-specific request **SET_LINE_CODING** has been received by the device. This request allows the host to specify the serial line settings (baud rate, stop bits, parity and data bits). Refer to "*CDC PSTN Subclass, revision 1.2*", section 6.3.10 for more details about this class-specific request.

L8-2(5)   Register the application callback, **App_USBD_CDC_SerialLineCtrl()**. It is called by the ACM subclass when the class-specific request **SET_CONTROL_LINE_STATE** has been received by the device. This request generates RS-232/V.24 style control signals. Refer to "*CDC PSTN Subclass, revision 1.2*", section 6.3.12 for more details about this class-specific request.

L8-2(6)   Check if the high-speed configuration is active and proceed to add the ACM subclass instance to this configuration.

L8-2(7)   Check if the full-speed configuration is active and proceed to add the ACM subclass instance to this configuration.

Listing 8-2 also illustrates an example of multiple configurations. The functions **USBD_ACM_SerialAdd()** and **USBD_ACM_SerialCfgAdd()** allow you to create multiple configurations and multiple instances architecture. Refer to section 7-1 "Class Instance Concept" on page 147 for more details about multiple class instances.

8

8-4-4 SUBCLASS NOTIFICATION AND MANAGEMENT

You have access to some functions provides in the ACM subclass which relate to the ACM requests and the serial line state previously presented in section 8-4-1 "Overview" on page 170. Table 8-7 shows these functions. Refer to section C-2 "CDC ACM Subclass Functions" on page 437 for more details about the functions' parameters.

Function	Relates to...	Description
USBD_ACM_SerialLineCodingGet()	SetLineCoding	Application can get the current line coding settings set either by the host with SetLineCoding requests or by USBD_ACM_SerialLineCodingSet()
USBD_ACM_SerialLineCodingSet()	GetLineCoding	Application can set the line coding. The host can retrieve the settings with the GetLineCoding request.
USBD_ACM_SerialLineCodingReg()	SetLineCoding	Application registers a callback called by the ACM subclass upon reception of the SetLineCoding request. Application can perform any specific operations.
USBD_ACM_SerialLineCtrlGet()	SetControlLineState	Application can get the current control line state set by the host with the SetControlLineState request.
USBD_ACM_SerialLineCtrlReg()	SetControlLineState	Application registers a callback called by the ACM subclass upon reception of the SetControlLineState request. Application can perform any specific operations.
USBD_ACM_SerialLineStateSet()	Serial line state	Application can set any line state event(s). While setting the line state, an interrupt IN transfer is sent to the host to inform about it a change in the serial line state.
USBD_ACM_SerialLineStateClr()	Serial line state	Application can clear two events of the line state: transmission carrier and receiver carrier detection. All the other events are self-cleared by the ACM serial emulation subclass.

Table 8-7 **ACM Subclass Functions Related to the Subclass Requests and Notifications**

Micrium's ACM subclass always uses the interrupt endpoint to notify the host of the serial line state. You cannot disable the interrupt endpoint.

8-4-5 SUBCLASS INSTANCE COMMUNICATION

Micrium's ACM subclass offers the following functions to communicate with the host. For more details about the functions' parameters, refer to section C-2 "CDC ACM Subclass Functions" on page 437.

Function name	Operation
USBD_ACM_SerialRx()	Receives data from host through a bulk OUT endpoint. This function is blocking.
USBD_ACM_SerialTx()	Sends data to host through a bulk IN endpoint. This function is blocking.

Table 8-8 **CDC ACM Communication API Summary**

USBD_ACM_SerialRx() and USBD_ACM_SerialTx() provide synchronous communication which means that the transfer is blocking. Upon calling the function, the application blocks until transfer completion with or without an error. A timeout can be specified to avoid waiting forever. Listing 8-3 presents a read and write example to receive data from the host using the bulk OUT endpoint and to send data to the host using the bulk IN endpoint.

```
CPU_INT08U  rx_buf[2];
CPU_INT08U  tx_buf[2];
USBD_ERR    err;

(void)USBD_ACM_SerialRx(subclass_nbr,                    (1)
                        &rx_buf[0],                      (2)
                        2u,
                        0u,                              (3)
                        &err);
if (err != USBD_ERR_NONE) {
    /* Handle the error. */
}


(void)USBD_ACM_SerialTx(subclass_nbr,                    (1)
                        &tx_buf[0],                      (4)
                        2u,
                        0u,                              (3)
                        &err);
if (err != USBD_ERR_NONE) {
    /* Handle the error. */
}
```

Listing 8-3 **Serial Read and Write Example**

8

L8-3(1)   The class instance number created with **USBD_ACM_SerialAdd()** will serve internally to the ACM subclass to route the transfer to the proper bulk OUT or IN endpoint.

L8-3(2)   The application must ensure that the buffer provided to the function is large enough to accommodate all the data. Otherwise, synchronization issues might happen.

L8-3(3)   In order to avoid an infinite blocking situation, a timeout expressed in milliseconds can be specified. A value of '0' makes the application task wait forever.

L8-3(4)   The application provides the initialized transmit buffer.

8-4-6 USING THE DEMO APPLICATION

Micrium provides a demo application that lets you test and evaluate the class implementation. Source template files are provided for the device.

CONFIGURING DEVICE APPLICATION

The *serial* demo allows you to send and/or receive serial data to and/or from the device through a virtual COM port. The demo is implemented in the application file, **app_usbd_cdc.c**, provided for µC/OS-II and µC/OS-III. **app_usbd_cdc.c** is located in these two folders:

▨ \Micrium\Software\uC-USB-Device-V4\App\Device\OS\uCOS-II

▨ \Micrium\Software\uC-USB-Device-V4\App\Device\OS\uCOS-III

Table 8-9 describes the constants usually defined in **app_cfg.h** which allows you to use the serial demo.

Constant	Description
APP_CFG_USBD_CDC_EN	General constant to enable the CDC ACM demo application. Must be set to DEF_ENABLED.
APP_CFG_USBD_CDC_SERIAL_TEST_EN	Constant to enable the serial demo. Must be set to DEF_ENABLED.

Constant	Description
APP_CFG_USBD_CDC_SERIAL_TASK_PRIO	Priority of the task used by the serial demo.
APP_CFG_USBD_CDC_SERIAL_TASK_STK_SIZE	Stack size of the task used by the serial demo. A default value can be 256.

Table 8-9 **Device Application Configuration Constants**

RUNNING THE DEMO APPLICATION

In this section, we will assume Windows as the host operating system. Upon connection of your CDC ACM device, Windows will enumerate your device and load the native driver **usbser.sys** to handle the device communication. The first time you connect your device to the host, you will have to indicate to Windows which driver to load using an INF file (refer to section 3-1-1 "About INF Files" on page 90 for more details about INF). The INF file tells Windows to load the **usbser.sys** driver. Indicating the INF file to Windows has to be done only once. Windows will then automatically recognize the CDC ACM device and load the proper driver for any new connection. The process of indicating the INF file may vary according to the Windows operating system version:

- Windows XP directly opens the Found New Hardware Wizard. Follow the different steps of the wizard until you reach the page where you can indicate the path of the INF file.

- Windows Vista and later won't open a "Found New Hardware Wizard". It will just indicate that no driver was found for the vendor device. You have to manually open the wizard. When you open the Device Manager, your CDC ACM device should appear with a yellow icon. Right-click on your device and choose 'Update Driver Software...' to open the wizard. Follow the different steps of the wizard until the page where you can indicate the path of the INF file.

The INF file is located in:

`\Micrium\Software\uC-USB-Device-V4\App\Host\OS\Windows\CDC\INF`

Refer to section 3-1-1 "About INF Files" on page 90 for more details about how to edit the INF file to match your Vendor ID (VID) and Product ID (PID). The provided INF files define, by default, `0xFFFE` for VID and `0x1234` for PID. Once the driver is loaded, Windows creates a virtual COM port as shown in Figure 8-3.

179

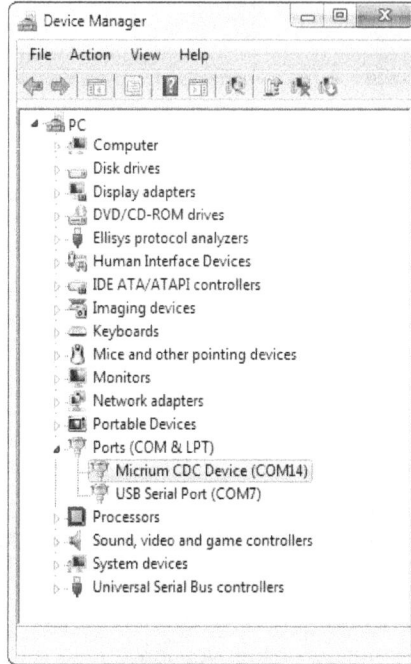

Figure 8-3 **Windows Device Manager and Created Virtual COM Port**

Figure 8-4 presents the steps to follow to use the serial demo.

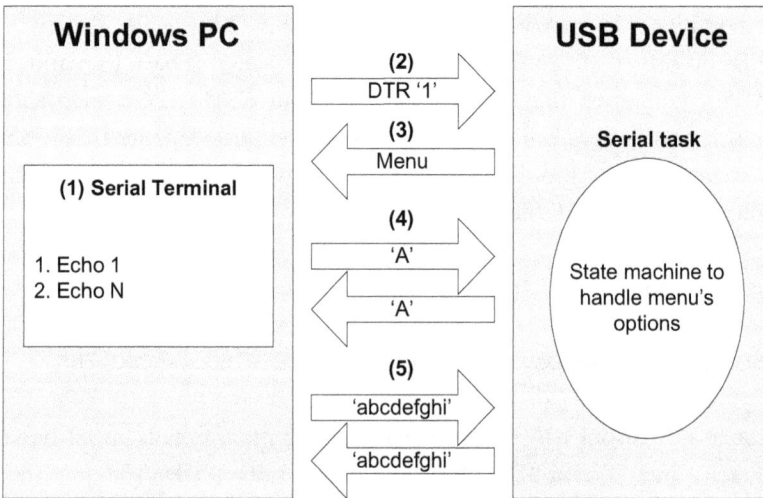

Figure 8-4 **Serial Demo**

F8-4(1)   Open a serial terminal (for instance, HyperTerminal). Open the COM port matching to your CDC ACM device with the serial settings (baud rate, stop bits, parity and data bits) you want. This operation will send a series of CDC ACM class-specific requests (`GET_LINE_CODING`, `SET_LINE_CODING`, `SET_CONTROL_LINE_STATE`) to your device. Note that Windows Vista and later don't provide HyperTerminal anymore. You may use other free serial terminals such *TeraTerm* (`http://ttssh2.sourceforge.jp/`), *Hercules* (`http://www.hw-group.com/products/hercules/index_en.html`), *RealTerm* (`http://realterm.sourceforge.net/`), etc.

F8-4(2)   In order to start the communication with the serial task on the device side, the Data Terminal Ready (DTR) signal must be set and sent to the device. The DTR signal prevents the serial task from sending characters if the terminal is not ready to receive data. Sending the DTR signal may vary depending on your serial terminal. For example, *HyperTerminal* sends a properly set DTR signal automatically upon opening of the COM port. *Hercules* terminal allows you to set and clear the DTR signal from the graphical user interface (GUI) with a checkbox. Other terminals do not permit to set/clear DTR or the DTR set/clear's functionality is difficult to find and to use.

F8-4(3)   Once the serial task receives the DTR signal, the task sends a menu to the serial terminal with two options as presented in Figure 8-5.

F8-4(4)   The menu option #1 is the *Echo 1 demo*. It allows you to send one unique character to the device. This character is received by the serial task and sent back to the host.

F8-4(5)   The menu options #2 is the *Echo N demo*. It allows you to send several characters to the device. All the characters are received by the serial task and sent back to the host. The serial task can receive a maximum of 512 characters.

8

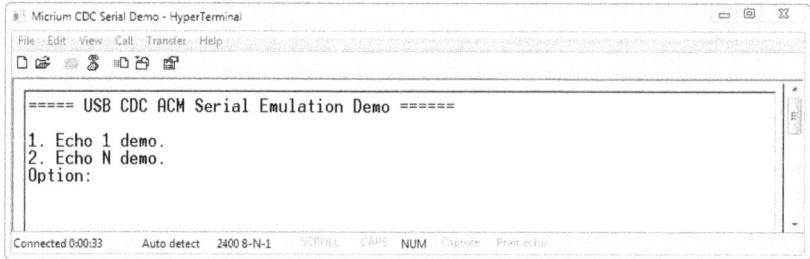

Figure 8-5 **CDC Serial Demo Menu in HyperTerminal**

To support the two demos, the serial task implements a state machine as shown in Figure 8-6. Basically, the state machine has two paths corresponding to the user choice in the serial terminal menu.

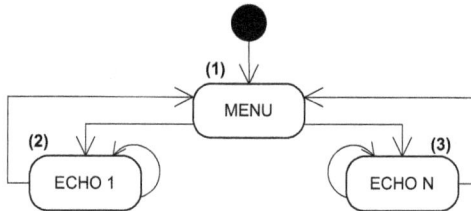

Figure 8-6 **Serial Demo State Machine**

F8-6(1)   Once the DTR signal has been received, the serial task is in the MENU state.

F8-6(2)   If you choose the menu option #1, the serial task will echo back any single character sent by the serial terminal as long as "Ctrl+C" is not pressed.

F8-6(3)   If you choose the menu option #2, the serial task will echo all the received characters sent by the serial terminal as long as "Ctrl+C" is not pressed.

Table 8-10 shows four possible serial terminals which you may use to test the CDC ACM class.

Terminal	DTR set/clear	Menu option(s) usable
HyperTerminal	Yes (properly set DTR signal automatically sent upon COM port opening)	1 and 2
Hercules	Yes (a checkbox in the GUI allows you to set/clear DTR)	1 and 2
RealTerm	Yes (Set/Clear DTR buttons in the GUI)	1 and 2
TeraTerm	Yes (DTR can be set using a macro. GUI does NOT allows you to set/clear DTR easily)	1 and 2

Table 8-10 **Serial Terminals and CDC Serial Demo**

8

Human Interface Device Class

This chapter describes the Human Interface Device (HID) class supported by μC/USB-Device. The HID implementation complies with the following specifications:

- *Device Class Definition for Human Interface Devices (HID), 6/27/01, Version 1.11.*

- *Universal Serial Bus HID Usage Tables, 10/28/2004, Version 1.12.*

The HID class encompasses devices used by humans to control computer operations. Keyboards, mice, pointing devices, game devices are some examples of typical HID devices. The HID class can also be used in a composite device that contains some controls such as knobs, switches, buttons and sliders. For instance, mute and volume controls in an audio headset are controlled by the HID function of the headset. The headset also has an audio function. HID data can exchange data for any purpose using only control and interrupt transfers. The HID class is one of the oldest and most popular USB classes. All the major host operating systems provide a native driver to manage HID devices. That's why a variety of vendor-specific devices work with the HID class. This class also includes various types of output directed to the user information (e.g. LEDs on a keyboard).

9-1 OVERVIEW

A HID device is composed of the following endpoints:

■ A pair of control IN and OUT endpoints called the default endpoint.

■ An interrupt IN endpoint.

■ An optional interrupt OUT endpoint.

Table 9-1 describes the usage of the different endpoints:

Endpoint	Direction	Usage
Control IN	Device-to-host	Standard requests for enumeration, class-specific requests, and data communication (Input, Feature reports sent to the host with GET_REPORT request).
Control OUT	Host-to-device	Standard requests for enumeration, class-specific requests and data communication (Output, Feature reports received from the host with SET_REPORT request).
Interrupt IN	Device-to-host	Data communication (Input and Feature reports).
Interrupt OUT	Host-to-device	Data communication (Output and Feature reports).

Table 9-1 **HID Class Endpoints Usage**

9-1-1 REPORT

A host and a HID device exchange data using reports. A report contains formatted data giving information about controls and other physical entities of the HID device. A control is manipulable by the user and operates an aspect of the device. For instance, a control can be a button on a mouse or a keyboard, a switch, etc. Other entities inform the user about the state of certain device's features. For instance, LEDs on a keyboard notify the user about the caps lock on, about the numeric keypad active, etc.

The format and the use of a report data is understood by the host by analyzing the content of a *Report descriptor.* Analyzing the content is done by a parser. The Report descriptor describes the data provided by each control in a device. It is composed of *items.* An item is a piece of information about the device and consists of a 1-byte prefix and variable-length data. Refer to *"Device Class Definition for Human Interface Devices (HID) Version 1.11"*, section 5.6 and 6.2.2 for more details about the item format.

There are three principal types of items:

- *Main item* defines or groups certain types of data fields.

- *Global item* describes data characteristics of a control.

- *Local item* describes data characteristics of a control.

Each item type is defined by different functions. An item function can also be called an item. An item function can be seen as a sub-item that belongs to one of the 3 principal item types. Table 9-2 gives a brief overview of the item's functions in each item type. For a complete description of the items in each category, refer to "Device Class Definition for Human Interface Devices (HID) Version 1.11", section 6.2.2.

Item type	Item function	Description
Main	Input	Describes information about the data provided by one ore more physical controls.
	Output	Describes data sent to the device.
	Feature	Describes device configuration information sent to or received from the device which influences the overall behavior of the device or one of its components.
	Collection	Group related items (Input, Output or Feature).
	End of Collection	Closes a collection.

Item type	Item function	Description
Global	Usage Page	Identifies a function available within the device.
	Logical Minimum	Defines the lower limit of the reported values in logical units.
	Logical Maximum	Defines the upper limit of the reported values in logical units.
	Physical Minimum	Defines the lower limit of the reported values in physical units, that is the Logical Minimum expressed in physical units.
	Physical Maximum	Defines the upper limit of the reported values in physical units, that is the Logical Maximum expressed in physical units.
	Unit Exponent	Indicates the unit exponent in base 10. The exponent ranges from -8 to +7.
	Unit	Indicates the unit of the reported values. For instance, length, mass, temperature units, etc.
	Report Size	Indicates the size of the report fields in bits.
	Report ID	Indicates the prefix added to a particular report.
	Report Count	Indicates the number of data fields for an item.
	Push	Places a copy of the global item state table on the CPU stack.
	Pop	Replaces the item state table with the last structure from the stack.

Item type	Item function	Description
Local	Usage	Represents an index to designate a specific Usage within a Usage Page. It indicates the vendor's suggested use for a specific control or group of controls. A usage supplies information to an application developer about what a control is actually measuring.
	Usage Minimum	Defines the starting usage associated with an array or bitmap.
	Usage Maximum	Defines the ending usage associated with an array or bitmap.
	Designator Index	Determines the body part used for a control. Index points to a designator in the Physical descriptor.
	Designator Minimum	Defines the index of the starting designator associated with an array or bitmap.
	Designator Maximum	Defines the index of the ending designator associated with an array or bitmap.
	String Index	String index for a String descriptor. It allows a string to be associated with a particular item or control.
	String Minimum	Specifies the first string index when assigning a group of sequential strings to controls in an array or bitmap.
	String Maximum	Specifies the last string index when assigning a group of sequential strings to controls in an array or bitmap.
	Delimiter	Defines the beginning or end of a set of local items.

Table 9-2 **Item's Function Description for each Item Type**

A control's data must define at least the following items:

▦ Input, Output or Feature Main items.

▦ Usage Local item.

▦ Usage Page Global item.

▦ Logical Minimum Global item.

▦ Logical Maximum Global item.

▦ Report Size Global item.

▦ Report Count Global item.

9

Table 9-1 shows the representation of a Mouse Report descriptor content from a host HID parser perspective. The mouse has three buttons (left, right and wheel). The code presented in Listing 9-2 is an example of code implementation corresponding to this mouse Report descriptor representation.

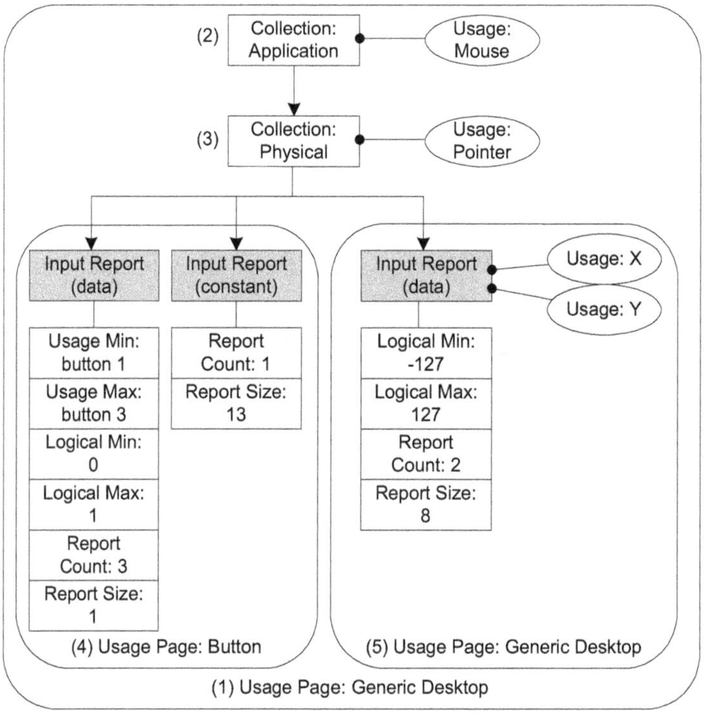

Figure 9-1 **Report Descriptor Content from a Host HID Parser View**

F9-1(1)   The *Usage Page* item function specifies the general function of the device. In this example, the HID device belongs to a generic desktop control.

F9-1(2)   The *Collection Application* groups Main items that have a common purpose and may be familiar to applications. In the diagram, the group is composed of three Input Main items. For this collection, the suggested use for the controls is a mouse as indicated by the *Usage* item.

F9-1(3)   Nested collections may be used to give more details about the use of a single control or group of controls to applications. In this example, the Collection Physical, nested into the Collection Application, is composed of the same 3

Input items forming the Collection Application. The *Collection Physical* is used for a set of data items that represent data points collected at one geometric point. In the example, the suggested use is a pointer as indicated by the Usage item. Here the pointer usage refers to the mouse position coordinates and the system software will translate the mouse coordinates in movement of the screen cursor.

F9-1(4) Nested usage pages are also possible and give more details about a certain aspect within the general function of the device. In this case, two Inputs items are grouped and correspond to the buttons of the mouse. One Input item defines the three buttons of the mouse (right, left and wheel) in terms of number of data fields for the item (*Report Count* item), size of a data field (*Report Size* item) and possible values for each data field (*Usage Minimum* and *Maximum*, *Logical Minimum* and *Maximum* items). The other Input item is a 13-bit constant allowing the Input report data to be aligned on a byte boundary. This Input item is used only for padding purpose.

F9-1(5) Another nested usage page referring to a generic desktop control is defined for the mouse position coordinates. For this usage page, the Input item describes the data fields corresponding to the x- and y-axis as specified by the two Usage items.

After analyzing the previous mouse Report descriptor content, the host's HID parser is able to interpret the Input report data sent by the device with an interrupt IN transfer or in response to a **GET_REPORT** request. The Input report data corresponding to the mouse Report descriptor shown in Figure 9-1 is presented in Table 9-3. The total size of the report data is 4 bytes. Different types of reports may be sent over the same endpoint. For the purpose of distinguishing the different types of reports, a 1-byte report ID prefix is added to the data report. If a report ID was used in the example of the mouse report, the total size of the report data would be 5 bytes.

Bit offset	Bit count	Description
0	1	Button 1 (left button).
1	1	Button 2 (right button).
2	1	Button 3 (wheel button).
3	13	Not used.
16	8	Position on axis X.
24	8	Position on axis Y.

Table 9-3 **Input Report Sent to Host and Corresponding to the State of a 3-Buttons Mouse.**

A Physical descriptor indicates the part or parts of the body intended to activate a control or controls. An application may use this information to assign a functionality to the control of a device. A Physical descriptor is an optional class-specific descriptor and most devices have little gain for using it. Refer to "Device Class Definition for Human Interface Devices (HID) Version 1.11" section 6.2.3 for more details about this descriptor.

9-2 ARCHITECTURE

Figure 9-2 shows the general architecture between the host and the device using the HID class offered by Micrium.

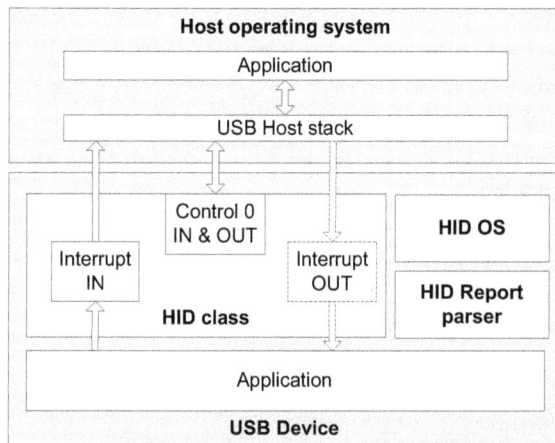

Figure 9-2 **General Architecture Between a Host and HID Class**

The host operating system (OS) enumerates the device using the control endpoints. Once the enumeration phase is done, the host starts the transmission/reception of reports to/from the device using the interrupt endpoints.

On the device side, the HID class interacts with an OS layer specific to this class. The HID OS layer provides specific OS services needed for the internal functioning of the HID class. This layer does not assume a particular OS. By default, Micrium provides the HID OS layer for µC/OS-II and µC/OS-III. If you need to port the HID class to your own OS, refer to section 9-5 "Porting the HID Class to an RTOS" on page 210 for more details about the HID OS layer.

During the HID class initialization phase, a report parser module is used to validate the report provided by the application. If any error is detected during the report validation, the initialization will fail.

9-3 CONFIGURATION

9-3-1 GENERAL CONFIGURATION

Some constants are available to customize the class. These constants are located in the USB device configuration file, **usbd_cfg.h** . Table 9-4 shows their description.

Constant	Description
USBD_HID_CFG_MAX_NBR_DEV	Configures the maximum number of class instances. Unless you plan on having multiple configurations or interfaces using different class instances, this can be set to 1.
USBD_HID_CFG_MAX_NBR_CFG	Configures the maximum number of configurations in which HID class is used. Keep in mind that if you use a high-speed device, two configurations will be built, one for full-speed and another for high-speed.
USBD_HID_CFG_MAX_NBR_REPORT_ID	Configures the maximum number of report IDs allowed in a report. The value should be set properly to accommodate the number of report ID to be used in the report. The minimum value is 1.
USBD_HID_CFG_MAX_NBR_REPORT_PUSHPOP	Configures the maximum number of Push and Pop items used in a report. If the constant is set to 0, no Push and Pop items are present in the report.

Table 9-4 **HID Class Configuration Constants**

The HID class uses an internal task to manage periodic input reports. The task priority and stack size shown in Table 9-5 are defined in the application configuration file, `app_cfg.h`. Refer to section 9-6 "Periodic Input Reports Task" on page 211 for more details about the HID internal task.

Constant	Description
USBD_HID_OS_CFG_TMR_TASK_PRIO	Configures the priority of the HID periodic input reports task.
USBD_HID_OS_CFG_TMR_TASK_STK_SIZE	Configures the stack size of the HID periodic input reports task.

Table 9-5 **HID Internal Task's Configuration Constants**

9-3-2 CLASS INSTANCE CONFIGURATION

Before starting the communication phase, your application needs to initialize and configure the class to suit its needs. Table 9-6 summarizes the initialization functions provided by the HID class. For more details about the functions parameters, refer to Appendix D, "HID API Reference" on page 455.

Function name	Operation
USBD_HID_Init()	Initializes HID class internal structures, variables and the OS layer.
USBD_HID_Add()	Creates a new instance of HID class.
USBD_HID_CfgAdd()	Adds an existing HID instance to the specified device configuration.

Table 9-6 **HID Class Initialization API Summary**

You need to call these functions in the order shown below to successfully initialize the HID class:

1   Call `USBD_HID_Init()`

This is the first function you should call and you should do it only once even if you use multiple class instances. This function initializes all internal structures and variables that the class needs and also the HID OS layer.

2   Call **USBD_HID_Add( )**

This function allocates an HID class instance. It also allows you to specify the following instance characteristics:

▤   The country code of the localized HID hardware.

▤   The Report descriptor content and size.

▤   The Physical descriptor content and size.

▤   The polling internal for the interrupt IN endpoint.

▤   The polling internal for the interrupt OUT endpoint.

▤   A flag enabling or disabling the Output reports reception with the control endpoint. When the control endpoint is not used, the interrupt OUT endpoint is used instead to receive Output reports.

▤   A structure that contains 4 application callbacks used for class-specific requests processing.

3   Call **USBD_HID_CfgAdd( )**

Finally, once the HID class instance has been created, you must add it to a specific configuration.

Listing 9-1 illustrates the use of the previous functions for initializing the HID class.

```
static  USBD_HID_CALLBACK  App_USBD_HID_Callback = {          (3)
    App_USBD_HID_GetFeatureReport,
    App_USBD_HID_SetFeatureReport,
    App_USBD_HID_GetProtocol,
    App_USBD_HID_SetProtocol,
};
```

```
CPU_BOOLEAN  App_USBD_HID_Init (CPU_INT08U  dev_nbr,
                                CPU_INT08U  cfg_hs,
                                CPU_INT08U  cfg_fs)
{
    USBD_ERR    err;
    CPU_INT08U  class_nbr;

    USBD_HID_Init(&err);                                        (1)
    if (err != USBD_ERR_NONE) {
        /* Handle the error. */
    }
                                                                (2)

    class_nbr = USBD_HID_Add(           USBD_HID_SUBCLASS_BOOT,
                                        USBD_HID_PROTOCOL_MOUSE,
                                        USBD_HID_COUNTRY_CODE_NOT_SUPPORTED,
                                        &App_USBD_HID_ReportDesc[0],
                                        sizeof(App_USBD_HID_ReportDesc),
                            (CPU_INT08U *)0,
                                        0u,
                                        2u,
                                        2u,
                                        DEF_YES,
                                        &App_USBD_HID_Callback,  (3)
                                        &err);
    if (err != USBD_ERR_NONE) {
        /* Handle the error. */
    }

    if (cfg_hs != USBD_CFG_NBR_NONE) {
        USBD_HID_CfgAdd(class_nbr, dev_nbr, cfg_hs, &err);      (4)
        if (err != USBD_ERR_NONE) {
            /* Handle the error. */
        }
    }
    if (cfg_fs != USBD_CFG_NBR_NONE) {
        USBD_HID_CfgAdd(class_nbr, dev_nbr, cfg_fs, &err);      (5)
        if (err != USBD_ERR_NONE) {
            /* Handle the error. */
        }
    }
}
```

Listing 9-1 **HID Class Initialization Example**

L9-1(1)   Initialize HID internal structures, variables and OS layer.

L9-1(2)   Create a new HID class instance. In this example, the subclass is "Boot", the protocol is "Mouse" and the country code is unknown. A table, **App_USBD_HID_ReportDesc**[], representing the Report descriptor is passed to the function (refer to Listing 9-2 for an example of Report descriptor content and section 9-1-1 "Report" on page 186 for more details about the Report descriptor format). No Physical descriptor is provided by the application. The interrupt IN endpoint is used and has a 2 frames or microframes polling interval. The use of the control endpoint to receive Output reports is enabled. The interrupt OUT endpoint will not be used. And therefore, the interrupt OUT polling interval of 2 is ignored by the class. The structure **App_USBD_HID_Callback** is also passed and references 4 application callbacks which will be called by the HID class upon processing of the class-specific requests.

L9-1(3)   There are 4 application callbacks for class-specific requests processing. There is one callback for each of the following requests: **GET_REPORT, SET_REPORT, GET_PROTOCOL** and **SET_PROTOCOL**. Refer to "Device Class Definition for Human Interface Devices (HID) Version 1.11", section 7.2 for more details about these class-specific requests.

L9-1(4)   Check if the high-speed configuration is active and proceed to add the HID instance previously created to this configuration.

L9-1(5)   Check if the full-speed configuration is active and proceed to add the HID instance to this configuration.

Listing 9-1 also illustrates an example of multiple configurations. The functions **USBD_HID_Add()** and **USBD_HID_CfgAdd()** allow you to create multiple configurations and multiple instances architecture. Refer to section Table 7-1 "Constants and Functions Related to the Concept of Multiple Class Instances" on page 147 for more details about multiple class instances.

Listing 9-2 presents an example of table declaration defining a Report descriptor corresponding to a mouse. The example matches the mouse report descriptor viewed by the host HID parser in Figure 9-1. The mouse report represents an Input report. Refer to section 9-1-1 "Report" on page 186 for more details about the Report descriptor format. The items inside a collection are intentionally indented for code clarity.

9

```
static  CPU_INT08U  App_USBD_HID_ReportDesc[] = {                                    (1)
    USBD_HID_GLOBAL_USAGE_PAGE               + 1, USBD_HID_USAGE_PAGE_GENERIC_DESKTOP_CONTROLS, (2)
    USBD_HID_LOCAL_USAGE                     + 1, USBD_HID_CA_MOUSE,                   (3)
    USBD_HID_MAIN_COLLECTION                 + 1, USBD_HID_COLLECTION_APPLICATION,     (4)
        USBD_HID_LOCAL_USAGE                 + 1, USBD_HID_CP_POINTER,                 (5)
        USBD_HID_MAIN_COLLECTION             + 1, USBD_HID_COLLECTION_PHYSICAL,        (6)
                                                                                       (7)
            USBD_HID_GLOBAL_USAGE_PAGE       + 1, USBD_HID_USAGE_PAGE_BUTTON,
            USBD_HID_LOCAL_USAGE_MIN         + 1, 0x01,
            USBD_HID_LOCAL_USAGE_MAX         + 1, 0x03,
            USBD_HID_GLOBAL_LOG_MIN          + 1, 0x00,
            USBD_HID_GLOBAL_LOG_MAX          + 1, 0x01,
            USBD_HID_GLOBAL_REPORT_COUNT     + 1, 0x03,
            USBD_HID_GLOBAL_REPORT_SIZE      + 1, 0x01,
            USBD_HID_MAIN_INPUT              + 1, USBD_HID_MAIN_DATA       |
                                                  USBD_HID_MAIN_VARIABLE  |
                                                  USBD_HID_MAIN_ABSOLUTE,
                                                                                       (8)
            USBD_HID_GLOBAL_REPORT_COUNT     + 1, 0x01,
            USBD_HID_GLOBAL_REPORT_SIZE      + 1, 0x0D,
            USBD_HID_MAIN_INPUT              + 1, USBD_HID_MAIN_CONSTANT,
                                                                                       (9)
            USBD_HID_GLOBAL_USAGE_PAGE       + 1, USBD_HID_USAGE_PAGE_GENERIC_DESKTOP_CONTROLS,
            USBD_HID_LOCAL_USAGE             + 1, USBD_HID_DV_X,
            USBD_HID_LOCAL_USAGE             + 1, USBD_HID_DV_Y,
            USBD_HID_GLOBAL_LOG_MIN          + 1, 0x81,
            USBD_HID_GLOBAL_LOG_MAX          + 1, 0x7F,
            USBD_HID_GLOBAL_REPORT_SIZE      + 1, 0x08,
            USBD_HID_GLOBAL_REPORT_COUNT     + 1, 0x02,
            USBD_HID_MAIN_INPUT              + 1, USBD_HID_MAIN_DATA       |
                                                  USBD_HID_MAIN_VARIABLE  |
                                                  USBD_HID_MAIN_RELATIVE,
        USBD_HID_MAIN_ENDCOLLECTION,                                                   (10)
    USBD_HID_MAIN_ENDCOLLECTION                                                        (11)
};
```

Listing 9-2 **Mouse Report Descriptor Example**

L9-2(1)   The table representing a mouse Report descriptor is initialized in such way that each line corresponds to a short item. The latter is formed from a 1-byte prefix and a 1-byte data. Refer to "Device Class Definition for Human Interface Devices (HID) Version 1.11", sections 5.3 and 6.2.2.2 for more details about short items format. This table content corresponds to the mouse Report descriptor content viewed by a host HID parser in Figure 9-1.

L9-2(2)   The Generic Desktop Usage Page is used.

L9-2(3)   Within the Generic Desktop Usage Page, the usage tag suggests that the group of controls is for controlling a mouse. A mouse collection typically consists of two axes (X and Y) and one, two, or three buttons.

L9-2(4)   The mouse collection is started.

L9-2(5)   Within the mouse collection, a usage tag suggests more specifically that the mouse controls belong to the pointer collection. A pointer collection is a collection of axes that generates a value to direct, indicate, or point user intentions to an application.

L9-2(6)   The pointer collection is started.

L9-2(7)   The Buttons Usage Page defines an Input item composed of three 1-bit fields. Each 1-bit field represents the mouse's button 1, 2 and 3 respectively and can return a value of 0 or 1.

L9-2(8)   The Input Item for the Buttons Usage Page is padded with 13 other bits.

L9-2(9)   Another Generic Desktop Usage Page is indicated for describing the mouse position with the axes X and Y. The Input item is composed of two 8-bit fields whose value can be between -127 and 127.

L9-2(10)   The pointer collection is closed.

L9-2(11)   The mouse collection is closed.

9

9-3-3 CLASS INSTANCE COMMUNICATION

The HID class offers the following functions to communicate with the host. For more details about the functions parameters, refer to Appendix D, "HID API Reference" on page 455.

Function name	Operation
USBD_HID_Rd()	Receives data from host through interrupt OUT endpoint. This function is blocking.
USBD_HID_Wr()	Sends data to host through interrupt IN endpoint. This function is blocking.
USBD_HID_RdAsync()	Receives data from host through interrupt OUT endpoint. This function is non-blocking.
USBD_HID_WrAsync()	Sends data to host through interrupt IN endpoint. This function is non-blocking.

Table 9-7 **HID Communication API Summary**

9-3-4 SYNCHRONOUS COMMUNICATION

Synchronous communication means that the transfer is blocking. Upon function call, the applications blocks until the transfer completion with or without an error. A timeout can be specified to avoid waiting forever.

Listing 9-3 presents a read and write example to receive data from the host using the interrupt OUT endpoint and to send data to the host using the interrupt IN endpoint.

```
CPU_INT08U  rx_buf[2];
CPU_INT08U  tx_buf[2];
USBD_ERR    err;

(void)USBD_HID_Rd(          class_nbr,                          (1)
                  (void *)&rx_buf[0],                           (2)
                  2u,
                  0u,                                           (3)
                  &err);
if (err != USBD_ERR_NONE) {
   /* $$$$ Handle the error. */
}


(void)USBD_HID_Wr(          class_nbr,                          (1)
                  (void *)&tx_buf[0],                           (4)
                  2u,
                  0u,                                           (3)
                  &err);
if (err != USBD_ERR_NONE) {
   /* $$$$ Handle the error. */
}
```

Listing 9-3 **Synchronous Bulk Read and Write Example**

L9-3(1)   The class instance number created from **USBD_HID_Add()** will serve internally for the HID class to route the transfer to the proper interrupt OUT or IN endpoint.

L9-3(2)   The application must ensure that the buffer provided to the function is large enough to accommodate all the data. Otherwise, synchronization issues might happen. Internally, the read operation is done either with the control endpoint or with the interrupt endpoint depending on the control read flag set when calling **USBD_HID_Add()**.

L9-3(3)   In order to avoid an infinite blocking situation, a timeout expressed in milliseconds can be specified. A value of '0' makes the application task wait forever.

L9-3(4)   The application provides the initialized transmit buffer.

9-3-5 ASYNCHRONOUS COMMUNICATION

Asynchronous communication means that the transfer is non-blocking. Upon function call, the application passes the transfer information to the device stack and does not block. Other application processing can be done while the transfer is in progress over the USB bus. Once the transfer is completed, a callback is called by the device stack to inform the application about the transfer completion.

Listing 9-4 shows an example of an asynchronous read and write.

```
void App_USBD_HID_Comm (CPU_INT08U  class_nbr)
{
    CPU_INT08U  rx_buf[2];
    CPU_INT08U  tx_buf[2];
    USBD_ERR    err;

    USBD_HID_RdAsync(          class_nbr,                    (1)
                     (void *)&rx_buf[0],                     (2)
                               2u,
                               App_USBD_HID_RxCmpl,          (3)
                     (void *) 0u,                            (4)
                               &err);
    if (err != USBD_ERR_NONE) {
        /* Handle the error. */
    }

    USBD_HID_WrAsync(          class_nbr,                    (1)
                     (void *)&tx_buf[0],                     (5)
                               2u,
                               App_USBD_HID_TxCmpl,          (3)
                     (void *) 0u,                            (4)
                               &err);
    if (err != USBD_ERR_NONE) {
        /* $$$$ Handle the error. */
    }
}
                                                            (3)
static  void  App_USBD_HID_RxCmpl (CPU_INT08U  class_nbr,
                                   void        *p_buf,
                                   CPU_INT32U  buf_len,
                                   CPU_INT32U  xfer_len,
                                   void        *p_callback_arg,
                                   USBD_ERR    err)
```

```
{
    (void)class_nbr;
    (void)p_buf;
    (void)buf_len;
    (void)xfer_len;
    (void)p_callback_arg;                                        (4)

    if (err == USBD_ERR_NONE) {
        /* $$$$ Do some processing. */
    } else {
        /* $$$$ Handle the error. */
    }
}

                                                                 (3)
static  void  App_USBD_HID_TxCmpl (CPU_INT08U   class_nbr,
                                   void        *p_buf,
                                   CPU_INT32U   buf_len,
                                   CPU_INT32U   xfer_len,
                                   void        *p_callback_arg,
                                   USBD_ERR     err)
{
    (void)class_nbr;
    (void)p_buf;
    (void)buf_len;
    (void)xfer_len;
    (void)p_callback_arg;                                        (4)

    if (err == USBD_ERR_NONE) {
        /* $$$$ Do some processing. */
    } else {
        /* $$$$ Handle the error. */
    }
}
```

Listing 9-4 **Asynchronous Bulk Read and Write Example**

L9-4(1)   The class instance number serves internally for the HID class to route the transfer to the proper interrupt OUT or IN endpoint.

L9-4(2)   The application must ensure that the buffer provided to the function is large enough to accommodate all the data. Otherwise, synchronization issues might happen. Internally, the read operation is done either with the control endpoint or with the interrupt endpoint depending on the control read flag set when calling **USBD_HID_Add( )**.

9

L9-4(3)   The application provides a callback passed as a parameter. Upon completion of the transfer, the device stack calls this callback so that the application can finalize the transfer by analyzing the transfer result. For instance, upon read operation completion, the application may do a certain processing with the received data. Upon write completion, the application may indicate if the write was successful and how many bytes were sent.

L9-4(4)   An argument associated to the callback can be also passed. Then in the callback context, some private information can be retrieved.

L9-4(5)   The application provides the initialized transmit buffer.

9-4 USING THE DEMO APPLICATION

Micrium provides a demo application that lets you test and evaluate the class implementation. Source template files are provided for the device. Executable and source files are provided for Windows host PC.

9-4-1 CONFIGURING PC AND DEVICE APPLICATIONS

The HID class provides two demos:

- *Mouse* demo exercises Input reports sent to the host. Each report gives periodically the current state of a simulated mouse.

- *Vendor-specific* demo exercises Input and Output reports. The host sends an Output report or receives an Input report according to your choice.

On the device side, the demo application file, **app_usbd_hid.c**, offering the two HID demos is provided for μC/OS-II and μC/OS-III. It is located in these two folders:

- \Micrium\Software\uC-USB-Device-V4\App\Device\OS\uCOS-II

- \Micrium\Software\uC-USB-Device-V4\App\Device\OS\uCOS-III

The use of these constants usually defined in **app_cfg.h** allows you to use one of the HID demos.

Constant	Description
APP_CFG_USBD_HID_EN	General constant to enable the Vendor class demo application. Must be set to DEF_ENABLED.
APP_CFG_USBD_HID_TEST_MOUSE_EN	Enables or disables the mouse demo. The possible values are DEF_ENABLED or DEF_DISABLED. If the constant is set to DEF_DISABLED, the vendor-specific demo is enabled.
APP_CFG_USBD_HID_MOUSE_TASK_PRIO	Priority of the task used by the mouse demo.
APP_CFG_USBD_HID_READ_TASK_PRIO	Priority of the read task used by the vendor-specific demo.
APP_CFG_USBD_HID_WRITE_TASK_PRIO	Priority of the write task used by the vendor-specific demo.
APP_CFG_USBD_HID_TASK_STK_SIZE	Stack size of the tasks used by mouse or vendor-specific demo. A default value can be 256.

Table 9-8 **Device Application Constants Configuration**

On the Windows side, the mouse demo influences directly the cursor on your monitor while the vendor-specific demo requires a custom application. The latter is provided by a Visual Studio solution located in this folder:

▣ \Micrium\Software\uC-USB-Device-V4\App\Host\OS\Windows\HID\Visual
   Studio 2010

The solution **HID.sln** contains two projects:

▣ "HID - Control" tests the Input and Output reports transferred through the control endpoints. The class-specific requests **GET_REPORT** and **SET_REPORT** allows the host to receive Input reports and send Output reports respectively.

▣ "HID - Interrupt" tests the Input and Output reports transferred through the interrupt IN and OUT endpoints.

An HID device is defined by a Vendor ID (VID) and Product ID (PID). The VID and PID will be retrieved by the host during the enumeration to build a string identifying the HID device. The "HID - Control" and "HID - Interrupt" projects contain both a file named **app_hid_common.c**. This file declares the following local constant:

```
static  const  TCHAR  App_DevPathStr[] = _TEXT("hid#vid_fffe&pid_1234");          (1)
```

Listing 9-5 **Windows Application and String to Detect a Specific HID Device**

L9-5(1)   This constant allows the application to detect a specified HID device connected to the host. The VID and PID given in **App_DevPathStr** variable must match with device side values. The device side VID and PID are defined in the **USBD_DEV_CFG** structure in the file **usbd_dev_cfg.c**. Refer to the section "Modify Device Configuration" on page 77 for more details about the **USBD_DEV_CFG** structure. In this example, **VID** = **fffe** and **PID** = **1234** in hexadecimal format.

9-4-2 RUNNING THE DEMO APPLICATION

The *mouse demo* does not require anything on the Windows side. You just need to plug the HID device running the mouse demo to the PC and see the screen cursor moving.

Figure 9-3 presents the mouse demo with the host and device interactions:

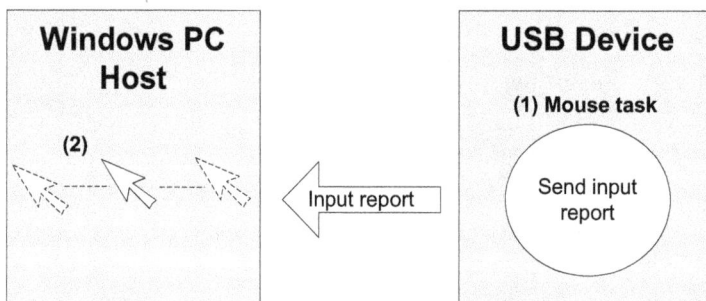

Figure 9-3 **HID Mouse Demo**

F9-3(1)   On the device side, the task **App_USBD_HID_MouseTask()** simulates a mouse movement by setting the coordinates X and Y to a certain value and by sending the Input report that contains these coordinates. The Input report is sent by calling the **USBD_HID_Wr()** function through the interrupt IN endpoint. The mouse demo does not simulate any button clicks; only mouse movement.

F9-3(2) The host Windows PC polls the HID device periodically following the polling interval of the interrupt IN endpoint. The polling interval is specified in the Endpoint descriptor matching to the interrupt IN endpoint. The host receives and interprets the Input report content. The simulated mouse movement is translated into a movement of the screen cursor. While the device side application is running, the screen cursor moves endlessly.

9

The *vendor-specific demo* requires you to launch a Windows executable. Two executables are already provided in the following folder:

- `\Micrium\Software\uC-USB-Device-V4\App\Host\OS\Windows\HID\Visual    Studio 2010\exe\`

The two executables have been generated with a Visual Studio 2010 project available in `\Micrium\Software\uC-USB-Device-V4\App\Host\OS\Windows\HID\Visual Studio 2010\`.

- *HID - Control.exe* for the vendor-specific demo utilizing the control endpoints to send Output reports or receive Input reports.

- *HID - Interrupt.exe* for the vendor-specific demo utilizing the interrupt endpoints to send Output reports or receive Input reports.

Figure 9-4 presents the vendor-specific demo with the host and device interactions:

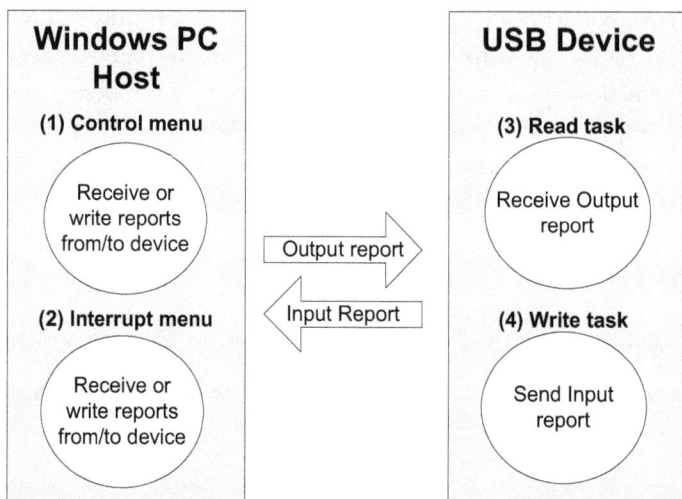

Figure 9-4 **HID Vendor-Specific Demo**

F9-4(1)   A menu will appear after launching *HID - Control.exe*. You will have three choices: "1. Sent get report", "2. Send set report" and "3. Exit". Choice 1 will send a **GET_REPORT** request to obtain an Input report from the device. The content of the Input report will be displayed in the console. Choice 2 will send a **SET_REPORT** request to send an Output report to the device.

F9-4(2)   A menu will appear after launching *HID - Interrupt.exe*. You will have three choices: "1. Read from device", "2. Write from device" and "3. Exit". The choice 1 will initiate an interrupt IN transfer to obtain an Input report from the device. The content of the Input report will be displayed in the console. Choice 2 will initiate an interrupt OUT transfer to send an Output report to the device.

F9-4(3)   On the device side, the task **App_USBD_HID_ReadTask()** is used to receive Output reports from the host. The synchronous HID read function, **USBD_HID_Rd()**, will receive the Output report data. Nothing is done with the received data. The Output report has a size of 4 bytes.

F9-4(4)   Another task, **App_USBD_HID_WriteTask()**, will send Input reports to the host using the synchronous HID write function, **USBD_HID_Wr()**. The Input report has a size of 4 bytes.

Figure 9-5 and Figure 9-6 show screenshot examples corresponding to HID - Control.exe and HID - Interrupt.exe respectively.

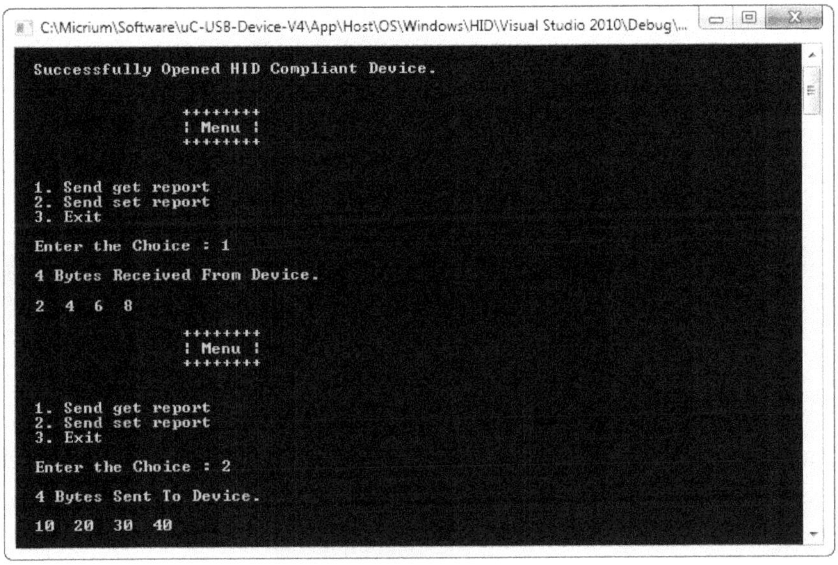

Figure 9-5 **HID - Control.exe (Vendor-Specific Demo)**

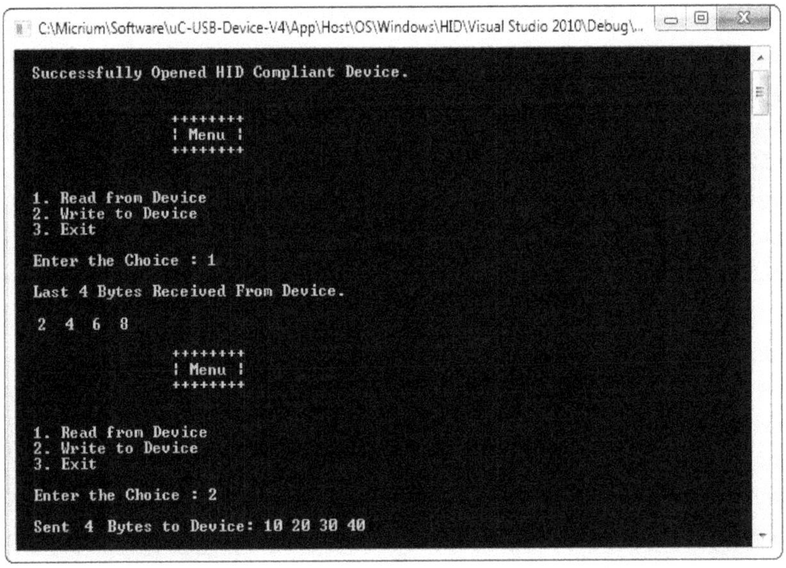

Figure 9-6 **HID - Interrupt.exe (Vendor-Specific Demo)**

9

9-5 PORTING THE HID CLASS TO AN RTOS

The HID class uses its own RTOS layer for different purposes:

- A locking system is used to protect a given Input report. A host can get an Input report by sending a **GET_REPORT** request to the device using the control endpoint or with an interrupt IN transfer. **GET_REPORT** request processing is done by the device stack while the interrupt IN transfer is done by the application. When the application executes the interrupt IN transfer, the Input report data is stored internally. This report data stored will be sent via a control transfer when **GET_REPORT** is received. The locking system ensures the data integrity between the Input report data storage operation done within an application task context and the **GET_REPORT** request processing done within the device stack's internal task context.

- A locking system is used to protect the Output report processing between an application task and the device stack's internal task when the control endpoint is used. The application provides to the HID class a receive buffer for the Output report in the application task context. This receive buffer will be used by the device stack's internal task upon reception of a **SET_REPORT** request. The locking system ensures the receive buffer and related variables integrity.

- A locking system is used to protect the interrupt IN endpoint access from multiple application tasks.

- A synchronization mechanism is used to implement the blocking behavior of **USBD_HID_Rd()** when the control endpoint is used.

- A synchronization mechanism is used to implement the blocking behavior of **USBD_HID_Wr()** because the HID class internally uses the asynchronous interrupt API for HID write.

- A task is used to process periodic Input reports. Refer to section 9-6 "Periodic Input Reports Task" on page 211 for more details about this task.

By default, Micrium will provide an RTOS layer for both µC/OS-II and µC/OS-III. However, it is possible to create your own RTOS layer. Your layer will need to implement the functions listed in Table 9-9. For a complete API description, refer to Appendix D, "HID API Reference" on page 455.

Function name	Operation
USBD_HID_OS_Init()	Creates and initializes the task and semaphores.
USBD_HID_OS_InputLock()	Locks Input report.
USBD_HID_OS_InputUnlock()	Unlocks Input report.
USBD_HID_OS_InputDataPend()	Waits for Input report data write completion.
USBD_HID_OS_InputDataPendAbort()	Aborts the wait for Input report data write completion.
USBD_HID_OS_InputDataPost()	Signals that Input report data has been sent to the host.
USBD_HID_OS_OutputLock()	Locks Output report.
USBD_HID_OS_OutputUnlock()	Unlocks Output report.
USBD_HID_OS_OutputDataPend()	Waits for Output report data read completion.
USBD_HID_OS_OutputDataPendAbort()	Aborts the wait for Output report data read completion.
USBD_HID_OS_OutputDataPost()	Signals that Output report data has been received from the host.
USBD_HID_OS_TxLock()	Locks class transmit.
USBD_HID_OS_TxUnlock()	Unlocks class transmit.
USBD_HID_OS_TmrTask()	Task processing periodic input reports. Refer to section 9-6 "Periodic Input Reports Task" on page 211 for more details about this task.

Table 9-9 **HID OS Layer API Summary**

9-6 PERIODIC INPUT REPORTS TASK

In order to save bandwidth, the host has the ability to silence a particular report in an interrupt IN endpoint by limiting the reporting frequency. The host sends the SET_IDLE request to realize this operation. The HID class implemented by Micrium contains an internal task responsible for respecting the reporting frequency limitation applying to one or several input reports. Figure 9-7 shows the periodic input reports tasks functioning.

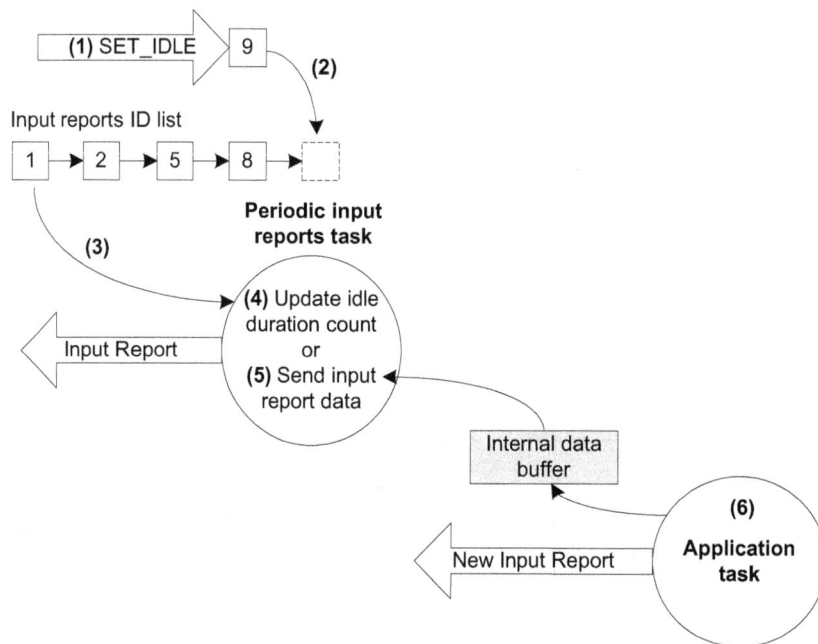

Figure 9-7 **Periodic Input Reports Task**

F9-7(1)   The device receives a **SET_IDLE** request. This request specifies an idle duration for a given report ID. Refer to "Device Class Definition for Human Interface Devices (HID) Version 1.11", section 7.2.4 for more details about the **SET_IDLE** request. A report ID allows you to distinguish among the different types of reports sent over the same endpoint.

F9-7(2)   A report ID structure allocated during the HID class initialization phase is updated with the idle duration. An idle duration counter is initialized with the idle duration value. Then the report ID structure is inserted at the end of a linked list containing input reports ID structures. The idle duration value is expressed in 4-ms unit which gives a range of 4 to 1020 ms. If the idle duration is less than the interrupt IN endpoint polling interval, the reports are generated at the polling interval.

F9-7(3)   Every 4 ms, the periodic input report task browses the input reports ID list. For each input report ID, the task performs one of two possible operations. The task period matches the 4-ms unit used for the idle duration. If no **SET_IDLE** requests have been sent by the host, the input reports ID list is empty and the task has nothing to process. The task processes only report IDs different from 0 and with an idle duration greater than 0.

F9-7(4)   For a given input report ID, the task verifies if the idle duration has elapsed. If the idle duration has not elapsed, the counter is decremented and no input report is sent to the host.

F9-7(5)   If the idle duration has elapsed, that is the idle duration counter has reached zero, an input report is sent to the host by calling the USBD_HID_Wr() function via the interrupt IN endpoint.

F9-7(6)   The input report data sent by the task comes from an internal data buffer allocated for each input report described in the Report descriptor. An application task can call the USBD_HID_Wr() function to send an input report. After sending the input report data, USBD_HID_Wr() updates the internal buffer associated to an input report ID with the data just sent. Then, the periodic input reports task always sends the same input report data after each idle duration elapsed and until the application task updates the data in the internal buffer. There is some locking mechanism to avoid corruption of the input report ID data in the event of a modification happening at the exact time of transmission done by the periodic input report task.

The periodic input reports task is implemented in the HID OS layer in the function USBD_HID_OS_TmrTask(). Refer to section D-2 "HID OS Functions" on page 470 for more details about this function.

9

Mass Storage Class

This section describes the mass storage device class (MSC) supported by μC/USB-Device. The MSC implementation offered by μC/USB-Device is in compliance with the following specifications:

- *Universal Serial Bus Mass Storage Class Specification Overview*, Revision 1.3 Sept. 5, 2008.

- *Universal Serial Bus Mass Storage Class Bulk-Only Transport*, Revision 1.0 Sept. 31, 1999.

MSC is a protocol that enables the transfer of information between a USB device and a host. The information is anything that can be stored electronically: executable programs, source code, documents, images, configuration data, or other text or numeric data. The USB device appears as an external storage medium to the host, enabling the transfer of files via drag and drop.

A file system defines how the files are organized in the storage media. The USB mass storage class specification does not require any particular file system to be used on conforming devices. Instead, it provides a simple interface to read and write sectors of data using the Small Computer System Interface (SCSI) transparent command set. As such, operating systems may treat the USB drive like a hard drive and can format it with any file system they like.

The USB mass storage device class supports two transport protocols:

- Bulk-Only Transport (BOT)

- Control/Bulk/Interrupt (CBI) Transport.

10

The mass storage device class supported by µC/USB-Device implements the SCSI transparent command set using the BOT protocol only, which signifies that only bulk endpoints will be used to transmit data and status information. The MSC implementation supports multiple logical units and provides a high-level lock mechanism for storage media shared with an embedded file system.

10-1 OVERVIEW

10-1-1 MASS STORAGE CLASS PROTOCOL

The MSC protocol is composed of three phases:

- The Command Transport

- The Data Transport

- The Status Transport

Mass storage commands are sent by the host through a structure called the Command Block Wrapper (CBW). For commands requiring a data transport stage, the host will attempt to send or receive the exact number of bytes from the device as specified by the length and flag fields of the CBW. After the data transport stage, the host attempts to receive a Command Status Wrapper (CSW) from the device detailing the status of the command as well as any data residue (if any). For commands that do not include a data transport stage, the host attempts to receive the CSW directly after CBW is sent. The protocol is detailed in Figure 10-1.

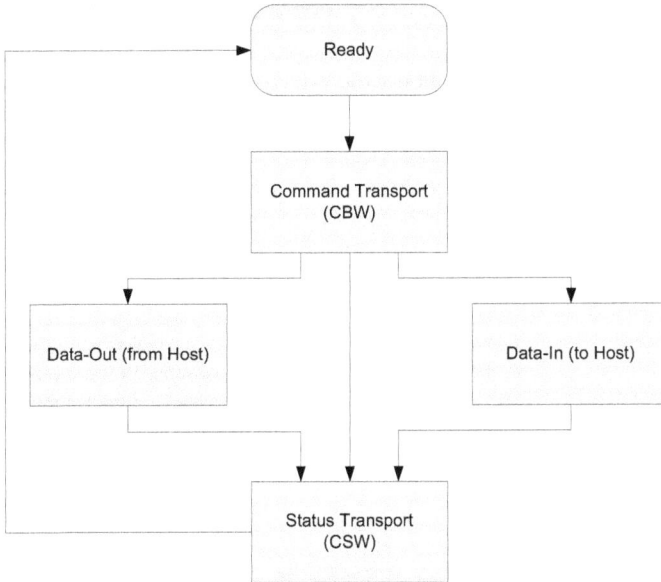

Figure 10-1 **MSC Protocol**

10-1-2 ENDPOINTS

On the device side, in compliance with the BOT specification, the MSC is composed of the following endpoints:

▪ A pair of control IN and OUT endpoints called default endpoint.

▪ A pair of bulk IN and OUT endpoints.

Table 10-1indicates the different usages of the endpoints.

Endpoint	Direction	Usage
Control IN Control OUT	Device to Host Host to Device	Enumeration and MSC class-specific requests
Bulk IN Bulk OUT	Device to Host Host to Device	Send CSW and data Receive CBW and data

Table 10-1 **MSC Endpoint Usage**

217

10-1-3 MASS STORAGE CLASS REQUESTS

There are two defined control requests for the MSC BOT protocol. These requests and their descriptions are detailed in Table 10-2.

Class Requests	Description
Bulk-Only Mass Storage Reset	This request is used to reset the mass storage device and its associated interface. This request readies the device to receive the next command block.
Get Max LUN	This request is used to return the highest logical unit number (LUN) supported by the device. For example, a device with LUN 0 and LUN 1 will return a value of 1. A device with a single logical unit will return 0 or stall the request. The maximum value that can be returned is 15.

Table 10-2 **Mass Storage Class Requests**

10-1-4 SMALL COMPUTER SYSTEM INTERFACE (SCSI)

SCSI is a set of standards for handling communication between computers and peripheral devices. These standards include commands, protocols, electrical interfaces and optical interfaces. Storage devices that use other hardware interfaces such as USB, use SCSI commands for obtaining device/host information and controlling the device's operation and transferring blocks of data in the storage media.

SCSI commands cover a vast range of device types and functions and as such, devices need a subset of these commands. In general, the following commands are necessary for basic communication:

- INQUIRY

- READ CAPACITY (10)

- READ(10)

- REQUEST SENSE

- TEST UNIT READY

- WRITE(10)

Refer to Table 10-3 to see the full list of implemented SCSI commands by μC/USB-Device.

10-2 ARCHITECTURE

10-2-1 MSC ARCHITECTURE

Figure 10-2 shows the general architecture of a USB Host and a USB MSC Device.

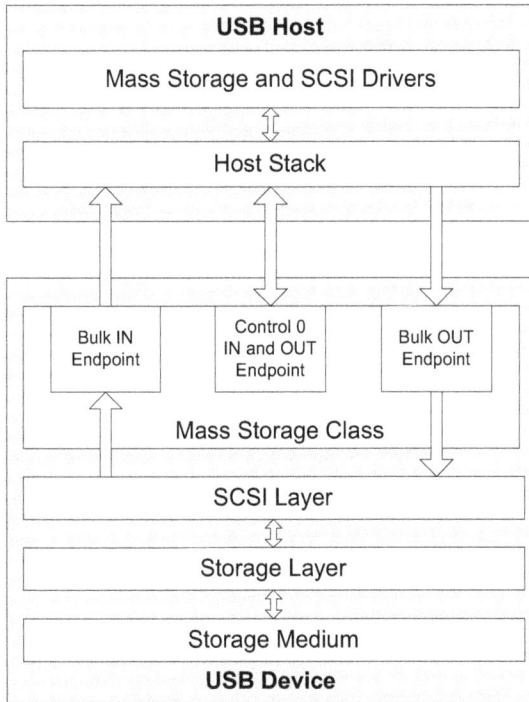

Figure 10-2 **MSC Architecture**

On the host side, the application communicates with the MSC device by interacting with the native mass storage drivers and SCSI drivers. In compliance with the BOT specification, the host utilizes the default control endpoint to enumerate the device and the Bulk IN/OUT endpoints to communicate with the device.

10

10-2-2 SCSI COMMANDS

The host sends SCSI commands to the device via the Command Descriptor Block (CDB). These commands set specific requests for transfer of blocks of data and status, and control information such as a device's capacity and readiness to exchange data. The μC/USB MSC Device supports the following subset of SCSI Primary and Block Commands listed in Table 10-3.

SCSI Command	Function
INQUIRY	Requests the device to return a structure that contains information about itself. A structure shall be returned by the device despite of the media's readiness to respond to other commands. Refer to SCSI Primary Commands documentation for the full command description.
TEST UNIT READY	Requests the device to return a status to know if the device is ready to use. Refer to SCSI Primary Commands documentation for the full command description.
READ CAPACITY (10) READ CAPACITY (16)	Requests the device to return how many bytes a device can store. Refer to SCSI Block Commands documentation for the full command description.
READ (10) READ (12) READ (16)	Requests to read a block of data from the device's storage media. Please refer to SCSI Block Commands documentation for the full command description.
WRITE (10) WRITE (12) WRITE (16)	Requests to write a block of data to the device's storage media. Refer to SCSI Block Commands documentation for the full command description.
VERIFY (10) VERIFY (12) VERIFY (16)	Requests the device to test one or more sectors. Refer to SCSI Block Commands documentation for the full command description.
MODE SENSE (6) MODE SENSE (10)	Requests parameters relating to the storage media, logical unit or the device itself. Refer to SCSI Primary Commands documentation for the full command description.
REQUEST SENSE	Requests a structure containing sense data. Refer to SCSI Primary Commands documentation for the full command description.

SCSI Command	Function
PREVENT ALLOW MEDIA REMOVAL	Requests the device to prevent or allow users to remove the storage media from the device. Refer to SCSI Primary Commands documentation for the full command description.
START STOP UNIT	Requests the device to load or eject the medium. Refer to SCSI Block Commands documentation for the full command description.

10

Table 10-3 **SCSI Commands**

10-2-3 STORAGE LAYER AND STORAGE MEDIUM

The storage layer shown in Figure 10-2 is the interface between the MSC and the storage medium. The storage layer is responsible for initializing the storage medium, performing read / write operations on it, as well as obtaining information regarding its capacity and status. The storage medium could be:

- RAM

- SD/CF card

- NAND flash

- NOR flash

- IDE hard disk drive

The MSC can interface with three types of storage layer:

- RAM disk

- µC/FS

- Vendor-specific file system

By default, Micrium will provide a storage layer implementation (named RAMDisk) by utilizing the hardware's platform memory as storage medium. Aside from this implementation, you have the option to use Micrium's µC/FS or even utilize your own file system referred as vendor-specific file system storage layer. In the event you use your own file system, you will need to create a storage layer port to communicate with the storage medium. Please refer to section 10-6 "Porting MSC to a Storage Layer" on page 236 to learn how to implement this storage layer.

Figure 10-3 shows how the µC/FS storage layer interfaces with µC/FS.

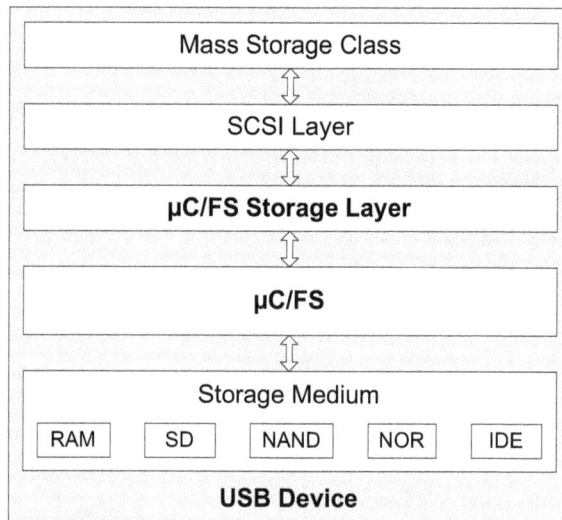

```
┌──────────────────────────────────────────────────┐
│  ┌────────────────────────────────────────────┐  │
│  │            Mass Storage Class                │  │
│  └────────────────────────────────────────────┘  │
│                        ⇕                           │
│  ┌────────────────────────────────────────────┐  │
│  │              SCSI Layer                      │  │
│  └────────────────────────────────────────────┘  │
│                        ⇕                           │
│  ┌────────────────────────────────────────────┐  │
│  │          µC/FS Storage Layer                 │  │
│  └────────────────────────────────────────────┘  │
│                        ⇕                           │
│  ┌────────────────────────────────────────────┐  │
│  │                 µC/FS                        │  │
│  └────────────────────────────────────────────┘  │
│                        ⇕                           │
│  ┌────────────────────────────────────────────┐  │
│  │            Storage Medium                    │  │
│  │ ┌─────┐ ┌────┐ ┌──────┐ ┌─────┐ ┌─────┐    │  │
│  │ │ RAM │ │ SD │ │ NAND │ │ NOR │ │ IDE │    │  │
│  │ └─────┘ └────┘ └──────┘ └─────┘ └─────┘    │  │
│  └────────────────────────────────────────────┘  │
│                  USB Device                        │
└──────────────────────────────────────────────────┘
```

Figure 10-3 **µC/FS Storage layer**

µC/FS storage layer implementation has two main characteristics:

- High-level lock mechanism.

- Insertion/removal detection of removable media.

The high-level lock mechanism protects the storage medium from concurrent accesses that could occur between a host computer and an embedded µC/FS application. On one hand, if a mass storage device is connected to a host computer and the storage medium is available, the host computer has the exclusive control of the storage medium. No embedded µC/FS application can access the storage medium. The µC/FS application will wait until the lock has been released. The lock is released upon device disconnection from the host or by a software eject done on the medium from the host side. On the other hand, if a µC/FS application has already the lock on the storage medium, upon device connection, the host won't have access. Each time the host requests the storage medium presence status, the mass storage device will indicate that the medium is not present. This status is returned as long as µC/FS application holds the lock. As soon as the lock is released, the host takes it and no more µC/FS operations on the storage medium are possible.

µC/FS storage layer is able to detect the insertion or removal of a removable media such as SD card. A task is used to detect the insertion or removal. The task checks periodically the presence or absence of a removable media. When the mass storage device is connected and the removable media is not present, the mass storage device indicates to the host that the storage medium is not present. As soon as the removable media is inserted in its slot, the task in µC/FS storage layer updates the removable media presence status. Next time the host requests the presence status, the mass storage device returns a good status and the host can access the content of the removable media. The opposite reasoning applies to media removal. If your product uses only fixed media, the task in µC/FS storage layer can be disabled. You can also configure the task's period. Refer to section 10-4-1 "General Configuration" on page 226 for more details about µC/FS storage layer configuration.

10-2-4 MULTIPLE LOGICAL UNITS

The MSC class supports multiple logical units. A logical unit designates usually an entire media type or a partition within the same media type. Figure 10-4 illustrates the different multiple logical units configurations supported.

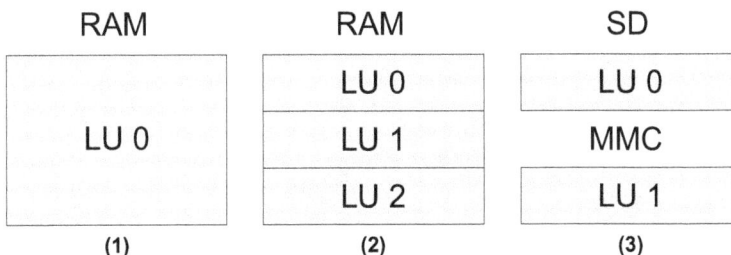

RAM	RAM	SD
	LU 0	LU 0
LU 0	LU 1	MMC
	LU 2	LU 1
(1)	(2)	(3)

Figure 10-4 **Example of Logical Units Configurations**

10

F10-4(1)   Configuration #1 is an example of single logical unit. The whole RAM region represents one unique logical unit. This configuration is a typical example of USB memory sticks. When the device is connected to a host, this one will display a media icon.

F10-4(2)   Configuration #2 is an example of multiple logical units within the same media. Each logical unit could be seen as a partition. This configuration is a typical example of USB external hard drive. When the device is connected to the host, this one will display three media icons.

F10-4(3)   Configuration #3 is an example of multiple logical units of different type. This configuration a a typical example of multi-card reader.

Configurations #1 and #2 are supported by the RAMDisk storage layer. Configurations #1 and #3 are supported by the µC/FS storage layer. The configuration #2 is currently not supported by the µC/FS storage layer.

Each logical unit is added to the MSC at initialization. Refer to section 10-4-2 "Class Instance Configuration" on page 227 for more details about the multiple logical units initialization and to section 10-5-2 "USB Host Application" on page 233 for a Windows example of multiple logical units.

10-3 RTOS LAYER

MSC device communication relies on a task handler that implements the MSC protocol. This task handler needs to be notified when the device is properly enumerated before communication begins. Once communication begins, the task must also keep track of endpoint update statuses to correctly implement the MSC protocol. These types of notification are handled by RTOS signals. For the MSC RTOS layer, there are two semaphores created. One for enumeration process and one for communication process. By default, Micrium will provide RTOS layers for both µC/OS-II and µC/OS-III. However, it is also possible to create your own RTOS layer. Please refer to section 10-7 "Porting MSC to an RTOS" on page 237 to learn how to port to a different RTOS.

10-3-1 MASS STORAGE TASK HANDLER

The MSC task handler implements the MSC protocol, responsible for the communication between the device and the host. The task handler is initialized when `USBD_MSC_Init()` is called. The MSC protocol is handled by a state machine comprised of 9 states. The transition between these states are detailed in Figure 10-5.

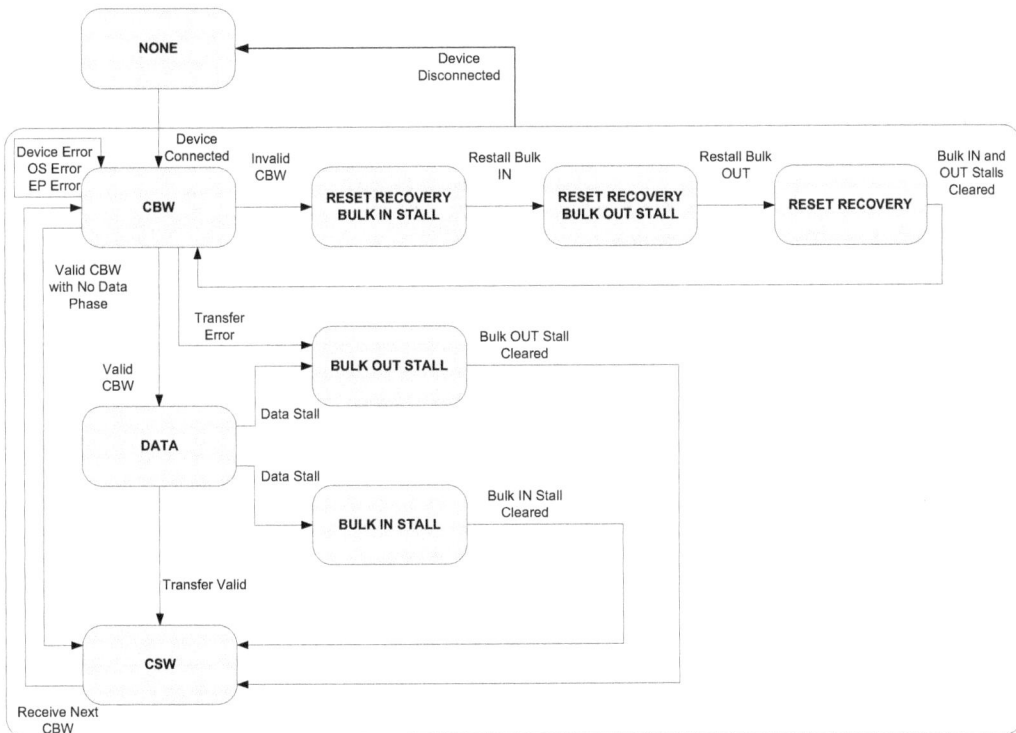

Figure 10-5 **MSC State Machine**

Upon detecting that the MSC device is connected, the device enters an infinite loop, waiting to receive the first CBW from the host. Depending on the command received, the device will either enter the data phase or transmit CSW phase. In the event of any stall conditions in the data phase, the host must clear the respective endpoint before transitioning to the CSW phase. If an invalid CBW is received from the host, the device enters the reset recovery state, where both endpoints are stalled, to complete the full reset with the host issuing the Bulk-Only Mass Storage Reset Class Request. After a successful CSW phase or a reset recovery, the task will return to receive the next CBW command. If at any stage the device is disconnected from the host, the state machine will transition to the None state.

225

10-4 CONFIGURATION

10-4-1 GENERAL CONFIGURATION

There are various configuration constants necessary to customize the MSC device. These constants are located in the `usbd_cfg.h` file. Table 10-4 shows a description of each constant.

Constant	Description
USBD_MSC_CFG_MAX_NBR_DEV	Configures the maximum number of class instances. Unless you plan having multiple configuration or interfaces using different class instances, this should be set to 1.
USBD_MSC_CFG_MAX_NBR_CFG	Configures the maximum number of configuration in which MSC is used. Keep in mind that if you use a high-speed device, two configurations will be built, one for full-speed and another for high-speed.
USBD_MSC_CFG_MAX_LUN	Configures the maximum number of logical units. This value must be at least 1.
USBD_MSC_CFG_DATA_LEN	Configures the read/write data length in octets. The default value set is 2048
USBD_MSC_CFG_FS_REFRESH_TASK_EN	Enables or disables the use of a task in µC/FS storage layer for removable media insertion/removal detection. The default value is DEF_DISABLED. If only fixed media such as RAM, NAND are used, this constant should be set to DEF_DISABLED. Otherwise, DEF_ENABLED should be set.
USBD_MSC_CFG_DEV_POLL_DLY_mS	Configures the period of the µC/FS storage layer's task. It is expressed in milliseconds. The default value is 100 ms. If USBD_MSC_CFG_FS_REFRESH_TASK_EN is set to DEF_DISABLED, this constant has no effect. A faster period may improve the delay to detect the removable media insertion/removal resulting in a host computer displaying the removable media icon promptly. But the CPU will be interrupted often to check the removable media status. A slower period may result in a certain delay for the host computer to display the removable media icon. But the CPU will spend less time verifying the removable media status.

Table 10-4 **MSC Configuration Constants**

Since MSC device relies on a task handler to implement the MSC protocol, this OS-task's priority and stack size constants need to be configured if µC/OS-II or µC/OS-III RTOS is used. Moreover if **USBD_MSC_CFG_FS_REFRESH_TASK_EN** is set to **DEF_ENABLED**, the µC/FS storage layer task's priority and stack size need also to be configured. These constants are summarized in Table 10-5.

Constant	Description
USBD_MSC_OS_CFG_TASK_PRIO	MSC task handler's priority level. The priority level must be lower (higher valued) than the start task and core task priorities.
USBD_MSC_OS_CFG_TASK_STK_SIZE	MSC task handler's stack size. Default value is set to 256.
USBD_MSC_OS_CFG_REFRESH_TASK_PRIO	µC/FS storage layer task's priority level. The priority level must be lower (higher valued) than the MSC task.
USBD_MSC_OS_CFG_REFRESH_TASK_STK_SIZE	µC/FS storage layer task's stack size. Default value is set to 256.

Table 10-5 **MSC OS-Task Handler Configuration Constants**

10-4-2 CLASS INSTANCE CONFIGURATION

Before starting the communication phase, your application needs to initialize and configure the class to suit its needs. Table 10-6 summarizes the initialization functions provided by the MSC implementation. Please refer to section E-1 "Mass Storage Class Functions" on page 488 for a full listing of the MSC API.

Function name	Operation
USBD_MSC_Init()	Initializes MSC internal structures and variables.
USBD_MSC_Add()	Adds a new instance of the MSC.
USBD_MSC_CfgAdd()	Adds existing MSC instance into USB device configuration.
USBD_MSC_LunAdd()	Adds a LUN to the MSC interface.

Table 10-6 **Class Instance API Functions**

To successfully initialize the MSC, you need to follow these steps:

1   Call **USBD_MSC_Init( )**

This is the first function you should call, and it should be called only once regardless of the number of class instances you intend to have. This function will initialize all internal structures and variables that the class will need. It will also initialize the real-time operating system (RTOS) layer.

2   Call **USBD_MSC_Add( )**

This function will add a new instance of the MSC.

3   Call **USBD_MSC_CfgAdd( )**

Once the class instance is correctly configured and initialized, you will need to add it to a USB configuration. High speed devices will build two separate configurations, one for full speed and one for high speed by calling **USBD_MSC_CfgAdd( )** for each speed configuration.

4   Call **USBD_MSC_LunAdd( )**

Lastly, you add a logical unit to the MSC interface by calling this function. You will specify the type and volume of the logical unit you want to add as well as device details such as vendor ID string, product ID string, product revision level and read only flag. Logical units are identified by a string name composed of the storage device driver name and the logical unit number as follows: *<device_driver_name>:<logical_unit_number>:*. The logical unit number starts counting from number 0. For example, if a device has only one logical unit, the *<logical_unit_number>* specified in this field should be 0. Examples of logical units string name are **ram:0:**, **sdcard:0:**, etc. This function is called several times when a multiple logical unit configuration is created.

Listing 10-1 shows how the latter functions are called during MSC initialization. Listing 10-1 also shows an example of multiple logical units initialization.

```
USBD_ERR    err;
CPU_INT08U  msc_nbr;
CPU_BOOLEAN valid;

USBD_MSC_Init(&err);                                        (1)
if (err != USBD_ERR_NONE){
    return (DEF_FAIL);
}

msc_nbr = USBD_MSC_Add(&err);                               (2)
if (cfg_hs != USBD_CFG_NBR_NONE){
    valid = USBD_MSC_CfgAdd (msc_nbr,                       (3)
                             dev_nbr,
                             cfg_hs,
                             &err);
    if (valid != DEF_YES) {
        return (DEF_FAIL);
    }
}

if (cfg_fs != USBD_CFG_NBR_NONE){
    valid = USBD_MSC_CfgAdd (msc_nbr,                       (4)
                             dev_nbr,
                             cfg_fs,
                             &err);
    if (valid != DEF_YES) {
        return (DEF_FAIL);
    }
}

USBD_MSC_LunAdd((void *)"ram:0:",                           (5)
                         msc_nbr,
                        "Micrium",
                        "MSC LUN 0 RAM",
                        0x0000,
                        DEF_TRUE,
                        &err);
if (err != USBD_ERR_NONE){
    return (DEF_FAIL);
}
```

```
USBD_MSC_LunAdd((void *)"sdcard:0:",                          (6)
                        msc_nbr,
                        "Micrium",
                        "MSC LUN 1 SD",
                        0x0000,
                        DEF_FALSE,
                        &err);
if (err != USBD_ERR_NONE){
    return (DEF_FAIL);
}

return(DEF_OK);
```

Listing 10-1 **MSC Initialization**

L10-1(1)   Initialize internal structures and variables used by MSC BOT.

L10-1(2)   Add a new instance of the MSC.

L10-1(3)   Check if high speed configuration is active and proceed to add an existing MSC instance to the USB configuration.

L10-1(4)   Check if full speed configuration is active and proceed to add an existing MSC instance to the USB configuration.

L10-1(5)   Add a logical unit number to the MSC instance by specifying the type and volume. Note that in this example the *<device_driver_name>* string is "ram" and *<logical_unit_number>* string is "0" and the logical unit is read-only (**DEF_TRUE** specified).

L10-1(6)   Add another logical unit number to the MSC instance by specifying the type and volume. Note that in this example the *<device_driver_name>* string is "sdcard" and *<logical_unit_number>* string is "0" and the logical unit is read-write (**DEF_FALSE** specified). When the host will enumerate the mass storage device, this one will report two logical units of different type, one RAM and one SD.

10-5 USING THE DEMO APPLICATION

The MSC demo consists of two parts:

- Any file explorer application (Windows, Linux, Mac) from a USB host. For instance, in Windows, mass-storage devices appear as drives in *My Computer*. From Windows Explorer, users can copy, move, and delete files in the devices.

- The USB Device application on the target board which responds to the request of the host.

µC/USB Device allows the explorer application to access a MSC device such as a NAND/NOR Flash memory, RAM disk, Compact Flash, Secure Digital etc. Once the device is configured for MSC and is connected to the PC host, the operating system will try to load the necessary drivers to manage the communication with the MSC device. For example, Windows loads the built-in drivers *disk.sys* and *PartMgr.sys*. You will be able to interact with the device through the explorer application to validate the device stack with MSC.

10-5-1 USB DEVICE APPLICATION

On the target side, the user configures the application through the `app_cfg.h` file. Table 10-7 lists a few preprocessor constants that must be defined.

Preprocessor Constants	Description	Default Value
APP_CFG_USBD_EN	Enables µC/USB Device in the application.	DEF_ENABLED
APP_CFG_USBD_MSC_EN	Enables MSC in the application.	DEF_ENABLED

Table 10-7 **Application Preprocessor Constants**

If RAMDisk storage is used, ensure that the associated storage layer files are included in the project and configure the following constants listed in Table 10-8.

Preprocessor Constants	Description	Default Value
USBD_RAMDISK_CFG_NBR_UNITS	Number of RAMDISK units.	1
USBD_RAMDISK_CFG_BLK_SIZE	RAMDISK block size.	512
USBD_RAMDISK_CFG_NBR_BLKS	RAMDISK number of blocks.	(4*1024*1)
USBD_RAMDISK_CFG_BASE_ADDR	RAMDISK base address in memory. This constant is optional and is used to define the data area of the RAMDISK. If it is defined, RAMDISK's data area will be set from this base address directly. If it is not defined, RAMDISK's data area will be represented as a table from the program's data area.	0XA000000

Table 10-8 **RAM Disk Preprocessor Constants**

If µC/FS storage is used, ensure that the associated µC/FS storage layer files are included in the project and configure the following constants listed in Table 10-8:

Preprocessor Constant	Description	Default Value
APP_CFG_FS_EN	Enables µC/FS in the application	DEF_ENABLED
APP_CFG_FS_DEV_CNT	File system device count.	1
APP_CFG_FS_VOL_CNT	File system volume count.	1
APP_CFG_FS_FILE_CNT	File system file count.	2
APP_CFG_FS_DIR_CNT	File system directory count.	1
APP_CFG_FS_BUF_CNT	File system buffer count.	(2 * APP_CFG_FS_VOL_CNT)
APP_CFG_FS_DEV_DRV_CNT	File system device driver count.	1
APP_CFG_FS_WORKING_DIR_CNT	File system working directory count.	0
APP_CFG_FS_MAX_SEC_SIZE	File system max sector size.	512
APP_CFG_FS_RAM_NBR_SEC	File system number of RAM sectors.	8192
APP_CFG_FS_RAM_SEC_SIZE	File system RAM sector size.	512
APP_CFG_FS_NBR_TEST	File system number of tests.	10
APP_CFG_FS_IDE_EN	Enables IDE device in file system.	DEF_DISABLED
APP_CFG_FS_MSC_EN	Enables MSC device in file system.	DEF_DISABLED
APP_CFG_FS_NOR_EN	Enables NOR device in file system.	DEF_DISABLED
APP_CFG_FS_RAM_EN	Enables RAM device in file system.	DEF_ENABLED

Preprocessor Constant	Description	Default Value
APP_CFG_FS_SD_EN	Enables SD device in file system.	DEF_DISABLED
APP_CFG_FS_SD_CARD_EN	Enables SD card device in file system.	DEF_ENABLED

Table 10-9 **uC/FS Preprocessor Constants**

10-5-2 USB HOST APPLICATION

To test the µC/USB-Device stack with MSC, the user can use for instance the Windows Explorer as a USB Host application on a Windows PC.

When the device configured for the MSC demo is connected to the PC, Windows loads the appropriate drivers as shown in Figure 10-6.

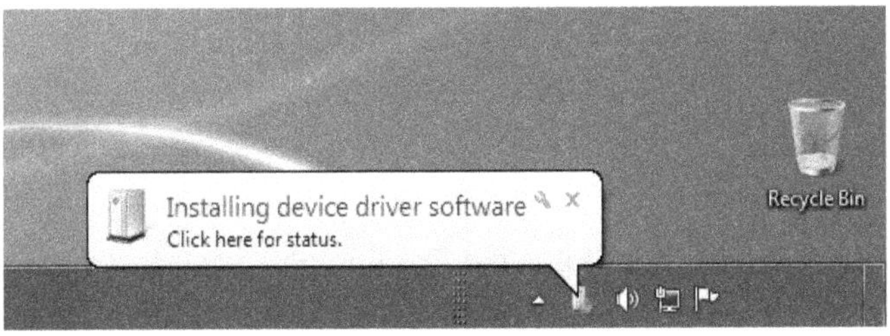

Figure 10-6 **MSC Device Driver Detection on Windows Host**

Open a Windows Explorer and a removable disk appears as shown in Figure 10-7. If the MSC demo is modified to configure a mass storage device composed of multiple logical units as shown in Listing 10-1, Windows Explorer will show a removable disk icon per logical unit.

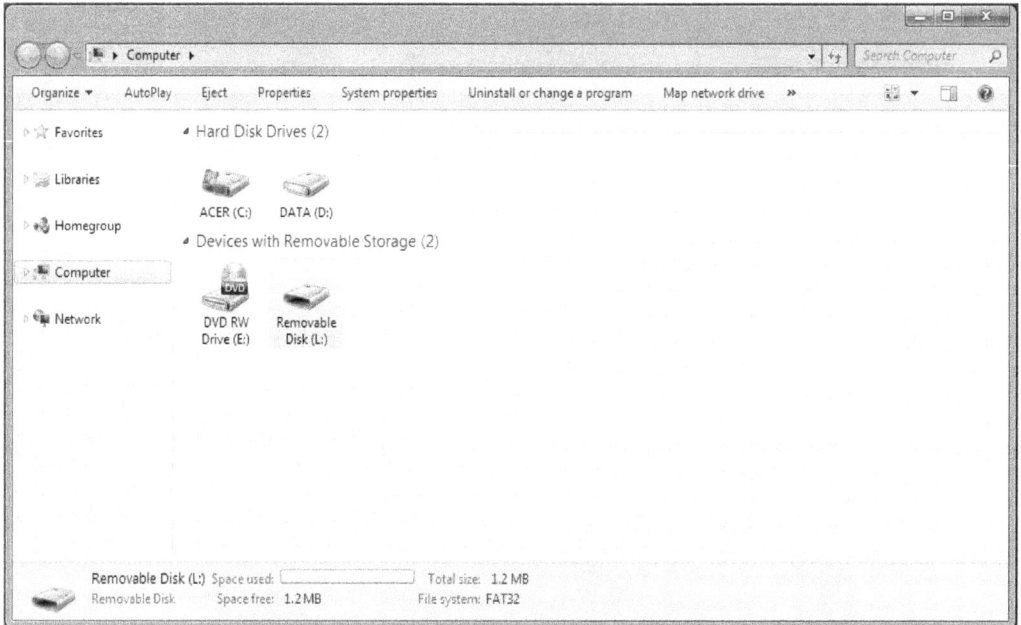

Figure 10-7 **MSC Device on Windows 7 Explorer**

When you open the removable disk, if it is the first time the MSC device is connected to the PC and is not formatted, Windows will ask to format it to handle files on the mass storage. When formatting, choose the File System you want. In embedded systems, the most widespread file system is the FAT.

If the mass storage device is a *volatile memory* such as a SDRAM, every time the target board is switched off, the data of the memory is lost, and so is the file system data information. As a result, the next time the target is switched on, the SDRAM is blank and reconnecting the mass storage to the PC, you will have to format again the mass storage device.

Once the device is correctly formatted, you are ready to test the MSC demo. Below are a few examples of what you can do:

▨ You can create one or more text files.

▨ You can write data in these files.

- You can open them to read the content of the files.

- You can copy/paste data.

- You can delete one or more files.

All of these actions will generate SCSI commands to write and read the mass storage device.

The MSC class supports the removable storage eject option offered by any major operating systems. Figure 10-8 shows an example of Eject option available in Windows Explorer. When you right-click on the removable disk, you can choose the *Eject* option. Eject option will send to the mass storage device some special SCSI commands. The mass storage device will stop the access to the storage. Hence, Windows will modify the removable disk icon by removing the size information. If you double-click on the icon after the eject operation, Windows will display a message saying that no disk is inserted. After an eject operation, you cannot reactivate the removable media. The only way is to disconnect the device and reconnect it so that Windows will re-enumerate it and refresh the Windows explorer's content.

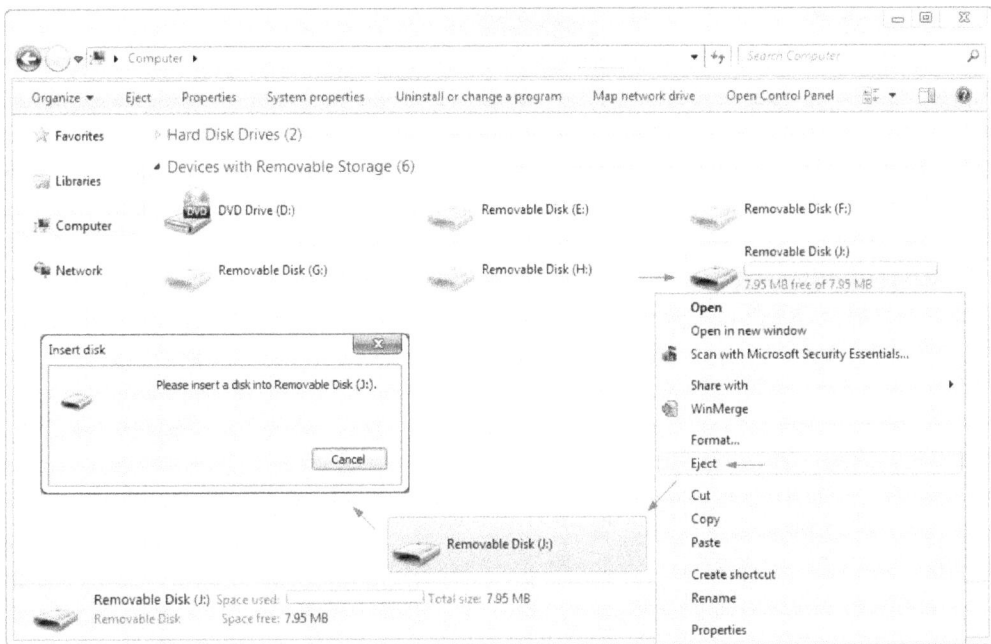

Figure 10-8 **Windows Removable Storage Eject Option Example**

10-6 PORTING MSC TO A STORAGE LAYER

The storage layer port must implement the API functions summarized in Table 10-10. You can start by referencing to the storage port template located under:

```
Micrium\Software\uC-USB-Device-V4\Class\MSC\Storage\Template
```

You can also refer to the RAMDisk storage and μC/FS storage located in `Micrium\Software\uC-USB-Device-V4\Class\MSC\Storage\` for a more detailed example of storage layer implementation.

Please refer to section E-3 "MSC Storage Layer Functions" on page 504 for a full description of the storage layer API.

Function Name	Operation
`USBD_StorageInit()`	Initializes internal tables used by the storage layer.
USBD_StorageAdd()	Initializes storage medium.
`USBD_StorageCapacityGet()`	Gets the storage medium's capacity.
`USBD_StorageRd()`	Reads data from the storage medium.
`USBD_StorageWr()`	Writes data to the storage medium.
`USBD_StorageStatusGet()`	Gets storage medium's status. If the storage medium is a removable device such as an SD/MMC card, this function will return if the storage is inserted or removed.
USBD_StorageLock()	Locks access to the storage medium.
USBD_StorageUnlock()	Unlocks access to the storage medium.
USBD_StorageRefreshTaskHandler()	Checks the removable media presence status, that is insertion/removal detection. Defined only for the μC/FS storage layer.

Table 10-10 **Storage API Functions**

10-7 PORTING MSC TO AN RTOS

The RTOS layer must implement the API functions listed in Table 10-11. You can start by referencing the RTOS port template located under:

`Micrium\Software\uC-USB-Device-V4\Class\MSC\OS\Template`

Please refer to section E-2 "MSC OS Functions" on page 496 for a full API description.

Function	Operation
`USBD_MSC_OS_Init()`	Initializes MSC OS interface. This function will create both signals (semaphores) for communication and enumeration processes. Furthermore, this function will create the MSC task used for the MSC protocol. If µC/FS storage layer is used with removable media, the Refresh task will be created.
`USBD_MSC_OS_CommSignalPost()`	Posts a semaphore used for MSC communication,
`USBD_MSC_OS_CommSignalPend()`	Waits on a semaphore to become available for MSC communication.
`USBD_MSC_OS_CommSignalDel()`	Deletes a semaphore if no tasks are waiting for it for MSC communication.
`USBD_MSC_OS_EnumSignalPost()`	Posts a semaphore used for MSC enumeration process.
`USBD_MSC_OS_EnumSignalPend()`	Waits for a semaphore to become available for MSC enumeration process.
USBD_MSC_OS_Task()	Task processing the MSC protocol. Refer to section 10-3 "RTOS Layer" on page 224 for more details about this task.
USBD_MSC_OS_RefreshTask()	Task responsible for removable media insertion/removal detection. This task is only present when µC/FS storage layer is used with removable media.

Table 10-11 **RTOS API Functions**

10

237

Chapter 10

Personal Healthcare Device Class

This section describes the Personal Healthcare Device Class (PHDC) supported by µC/USB-Device. The implementation offered refers to the following USB-IF specification:

■ *USB Device Class Definition for Personal Healthcare Devices, release 1.0, Nov. 8 2007.*

PHDC allows you to build USB devices that are meant to be used to monitor and improve personal healthcare. Lots of modern personal healthcare devices have arrived on the market in recent years. Glucose meter, pulse oximeter and blood-pressure monitor are some examples. A characteristic of these devices is that they can be connected to a computer for playback, live monitoring or configuration. One of the typical ways to connect these devices to a computer is by using a USB connection, and that's why PHDC has been developed.

Although PHDC is a standard, most modern Operating Systems (OS) do not provide any specific driver for this class. When working with Microsoft Windows®, developers can use the WinUsb driver provided by Microsoft to create their own driver. The Continua Health Alliance also provides an example of a PHDC driver based on libusb (an open source USB library, for more information, see `http://www.libusb.org/`). This example driver is part of the Vendor Assisted Source-Code (VASC).

11-1 OVERVIEW

11-1-1 DATA CHARACTERISTICS

Personal healthcare devices, due to their nature, may need to send data in 3 different ways:

▦ Episodic: data is sent sporadically each time the user accomplishes a specific action.

▦ Store and forward: data is collected and stored on the device while it is not connected. The data is then forwarded to the host once it is connected.

▦ Continuous: data is sent continuously to the host for continuous monitoring.

Considering these needs, data transfers will be defined in terms of latency and reliability. PHDC defines three levels of reliability and four levels of latency:

▦ Reliability: Good, better and best.

▦ Latency: Very-high, high, medium and low.

For example, a device that sends continuous data for monitoring will send them as low latency and good reliability.

PHDC does not support all latency/reliability combinations. Here is a list of supported combinations:

▦ Low latency, good reliability.

▦ Medium latency, good reliability.

▦ Medium latency, better reliability.

▦ Medium latency, best reliability.

▦ High latency, best reliability.

▦ Very high latency, best reliability.

These combinations are called quality of service (QoS).

QoS (Latency / reliability)	Latency	Raw info rate	Transfer direction(s)	Typical use
Low / good	< 20ms	50 bits/sec to 1.2M bits/sec	IN	Real-time monitoring, with fast analog sampling rate.
Medium / good	< 200ms	50 bits/sec to 1.2M bits/s	IN	
Medium / better	< 200ms	10s of byte range	IN	Data from measured parameter collected off-line and replayed or sent real-time.
Medium / best	< 200ms	10s of byte range	IN, OUT	Events, notifications, request, control and status of physiological and equipment functionality.
High / best	< 2s	10s of byte range	IN, OUT	Physiological and equipment alarms.
Very high / best	< 20s	10s of byte range to gigabytes of data	IN, OUT	Transfer reports, histories or off-line collection of data.

Table 11-1 **QoS Levels Description**

Transfers from a PHDC device will also contain a preamble, in which there is the possibility to include opaque data. Opaque data is data that should not be treated as actual data, but instead acts as a header, allowing the receiving host application to know what type of data it receives, for example. See Table 11-3 on page 243 for more details about the content of a preamble.

11-1-2 OPERATIONAL MODEL

The requirements for data transfer QoS in personal healthcare devices can be accomplished by PHDC using bulk endpoints and, optionally, an interrupt endpoint. Table 11-2 and Figure 11-1 show the mapping between QoS and endpoint types.

Endpoint	Usage
Bulk OUT	All QoS host to device data transfers.
Bulk IN	Very high, high and medium latency device to host data transfers.
Interrupt IN	Low latency device to host data transfers.

Table 11-2 **Endpoint - QoS Mapping**

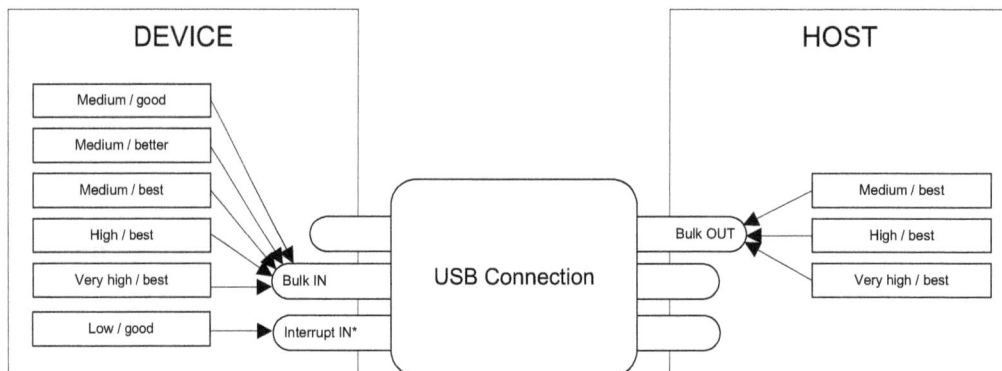

Figure 11-1 **QoS - Endpoint Mapping**

PHDC does not define a protocol for data and messaging. It is only intended to be used as a communication layer. Developers can use either data and messaging protocol defined in ISO/IEEE 11073-20601 base protocol or a vendor-defined protocol. Figure 11-2 shows the different software layers needed in a personal healthcare device.

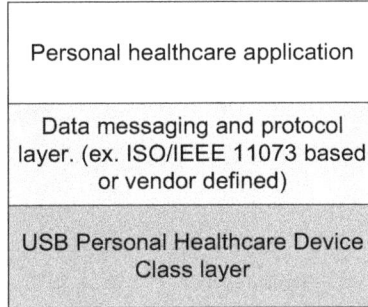

Figure 11-2 **Personal Healthcare Device Software Layers**

Since transfers having different QoS will have to share a single bulk endpoint, host and device need a way to inform each other what is the QoS of the current transfer. A metadata message preamble will then be sent before a single or a group of regular data transfers. This preamble will contain the information listed in Table 11-3.

Offset	Field	Size (bytes)	Description
0	aSignature	16	Constant used to verify preamble validity. Always set to "PhdcQoSSignature" string.
16	bNumTransfers	1	Count of following transfers to which QoS setting applies.
17	bQoSEncodingVersion	1	QoS information encoding version. Should be 0x01.
18	bmLatencyReliability	1	Bitmap that refers to latency / reliability bin for data.
19	bOpaqueDataSize	1	Length, in bytes, of opaque data.
20	bOpaqueData	[0 .. MaxPacketSize - 21]	Optional data usually application specific that is opaque to the class.

Table 11-3 **Metadata Preamble**

11

11-2 CONFIGURATION

11-2-1 GENERAL CONFIGURATION

Some constants are available to customize the class. These constants are located in the usbd_cfg.h file. Table 11-4 shows a description of each of them.

Constant	Description
USBD_PHDC_CFG_MAX_NBR_DEV	Configures the maximum number of class instances. Unless you plan on having multiple configuration or interfaces using different class instances, this can be set to 1.
USBD_PHDC_CFG_MAX_NBR_CFG	Configures the maximum number of configuration in which PHDC is used. Keep in mind that if you use a high-speed device, two configurations will be built, one for full-speed and another for high-speed.
USBD_PHDC_CFG_DATA_OPAQUE_MAX_LEN	Maximum length in octets that opaque data can be. Must always be equal or less than MaxPacketSize - 21.
USBD_PHDC_OS_CFG_SCHED_EN	If using µC/OS-II or µC/OS-III RTOS port, enable or disable the scheduler feature. You should set it to DEF_DISABLED if the device only uses one QoS level to send data, for instance. (See section 11-4 "RTOS QoS-based scheduler" on page 253) WARNING: If you set this constant to DEF_ENABLED, you MUST ensure that the scheduler's task has a lower priority (i.e. higher priority value) than any task that can write PHDC data.

Table 11-4 **Configuration Constants Summary**

If you set USBD_PHDC_OS_CFG_SCHED_EN to DEF_ENABLED and you use a µC/OS-II or µC/OS-III RTOS port, PHDC will need an internal task for the scheduling operations. There are two application specific configurations that must be set in this case. They should be defined in the app_cfg.h file. Table 11-5 describes these configurations.

Constant	Description
USBD_PHDC_OS_CFG_SCHED_TASK_PRIO	QoS based scheduler's task priority. WARNING: You *must* ensure that the scheduler's task has a lower priority (i.e. higher priority value) than any task writing PHDC data.
USBD_PHDC_OS_CFG_SCHED_TASK_STK_SIZE	QoS based scheduler's task stack size. Default value is 512.

Table 11-5 **Application-Specific Configuration Constants**

11-2-2 CLASS INSTANCE CONFIGURATION

Before starting the communication phase, your application needs to initialize and configure the class to suit its needs. Table 11-6 summarizes the initialization functions provided by the PHDC implementation. For a complete API reference, see section F-1 "PHDC Functions" on page 516.

Function name	Operation
USBD_PHDC_Init()	Initializes PHDC internal structures and variables.
USBD_PHDC_Add()	Adds a new instance of PHDC.
USBD_PHDC_RdCfg()	Configures read communication pipe parameters.
USBD_PHDC_WrCfg()	Configures write communication pipe parameters.
USBD_PHDC_11073_ExtCfg()	Configures IEEE 11073 function extension(s).
USBD_PHDC_CfgAdd()	Adds PHDC instance into USB device configuration.

Table 11-6 **PHDC Initialization API Summary**

You need to follow these steps to successfully initialize PHDC:

1   Call **USBD_PHDC_Init()**

This is the first function you should call, and you should do it only once, even if you use multiple class instances. This function will initialize all internal structures and variables that the class will need. It will also initialize the real-time operating system (RTOS) layer.

11

2   Call `USBD_PHDC_Add( )`

This function will allocate a PHDC instance. This call will also let you determine if the PHDC instance is capable of sending / receiving the metadata message preamble and if it uses a vendor-defined or ISO/IEEE-11073 based data and messaging protocol.

Another parameter of this function lets you specify a callback function that the class will call when the host enables / disables metadata message preambles. This is useful for the application as the behavior in communication will differ depending on the metadata message preamble state.

If your application needs to send low latency / good reliability data, the class will need to allocate an interrupt endpoint. The endpoint's interval will be specified in this call as well.

3   Call `USBD_PHDC_RdCfg( )` and `USBD_PHDC_WrCfg( )`

The next step is to call `USBD_PHDC_RdCfg( )` and `USBD_PHDC_WrCfg( )`. These functions will let you set the latency / reliability bins that the communication pipe will carry. Bins are listed in Table 11-7. It will also be used to specify opaque data to send within extra endpoint metadata descriptors (see "USB Device Class Definition for Personal Healthcare Devices", Release 1.0, Section 5 for more details on PHDC extra descriptors)..

Name	Description
`USBD_PHDC_LATENCY_VERYHIGH_RELY_BEST`	Very-high latency, best reliability.
`USBD_PHDC_LATENCY_HIGH_RELY_BEST`	High latency, best reliability.
`USBD_PHDC_LATENCY_MEDIUM_RELY_BEST`	Medium latency, best reliability.
`USBD_PHDC_LATENCY_MEDIUM_RELY_BETTER`	Medium latency, better reliability.
`USBD_PHDC_LATENCY_MEDIUM_RELY_GOOD`	Medium latency, good reliability.
`USBD_PHDC_LATENCY_LOW_RELY_GOOD`	Low latency, good reliability.

Table 11-7 **Listing of QoS Bins**

4   Call **USBD_PHDC_11073_ExtCfg()** (optional)

If the PHDC instance uses ISO/IEEE 11073-based data and messaging protocol, a call to this function will let you configure the device specialization code(s).

5   Call **USBD_PHDC_CfgAdd()**

Finally, once the class instance is correctly configured and initialized, you will need to add it to a USB configuration. This is done by calling **USBD_PHDC_CfgAdd()**.

Listing shows an example of initialization and configuration of a PHDC instance. If you need more than one class instance of PHDC for your application, refer to section 7-1 "Class Instance Concept" on page 147 for generic examples of how to build your device.

```
CPU_BOOLEAN  App_USBD_PHDC_Init(CPU_INT08U  dev_nbr,
                                CPU_INT08U  cfg_hs,
                                CPU_INT08U  cfg_fs)
{
    USBD_ERR    err;
    CPU_INT08U  class_nbr;


    USBD_PHDC_Init(&err);                                               (1)
    class_nbr = USBD_PHDC_Add(DEF_YES,                                  (2)
                        DEF_YES,
                        App_USBD_PHDC_SetPreambleEn,
                        10,
                        &err);


    latency_rely_flags = USBD_PHDC_LATENCY_VERYHIGH_RELY_BEST |
                         USBD_PHDC_LATENCY_HIGH_RELY_BEST     |
                         USBD_PHDC_LATENCY_MEDIUM_RELY_BEST;
    USBD_PHDC_RdCfg(class_nbr,                                          (3)
                    latency_rely_flags,
                    opaque_data_rx,
                    sizeof(opaque_data_rx),
                    &err);
```

```
USBD_PHDC_WrCfg(class_nbr,                                          (3)
                USBD_PHDC_LATENCY_VERYHIGH_RELY_BEST,
                opaque_data_tx,
                sizeof(opaque_data_tx),
                &err);

    USBD_PHDC_11073_ExtCfg(class_nbr, dev_specialization, 1, &err);     (4)
    valid_cfg_hs = USBD_PHDC_CfgAdd(class_nbr, dev_nbr, cfg_hs, &err);  (5)
    valid_cfg_fs = USBD_PHDC_CfgAdd(class_nbr, dev_nbr, cfg_fs, &err);  (6)
}
```

Listing 11-1 **PHDC Instance Initialization and Configuration Example**

L11-1(1)   Initialize PHDC internal members and variables.

L11-1(2)   Create a PHDC instance, this instance support preambles and ISO/IEEE 11073 based data and messaging protocol.

L11-1(3)   Configure read and write pipes with correct QoS and opaque data.

L11-1(4)   Add ISO/IEEE 11073 device specialization to PHDC instance.

L11-1(5)   Add class instance to high-speed configuration.

L11-1(6)   Add class instance to full-speed configuration.

11-3 CLASS INSTANCE COMMUNICATION

Now that the class instance has been correctly initialized, it's time to exchange data. PHDC offers 4 functions to do so. Table 11-8 summarizes the communication functions provided by the PHDC implementation. See Appendix F, "PHDC API Reference" on page 515 for a complete API reference.

Function name	Operation
USBD_PHDC_RdPreamble()	Reads metadata preamble.
USBD_PHDC_Rd()	Reads PHDC data.
USBD_PHDC_WrPreamble()	Writes metadata preamble.
USBD_PHDC_Wr()	Writes PHDC data.

Table 11-8 **PHDC Communication API Summary**

11-3-1 COMMUNICATION WITH METADATA PREAMBLE

Via the preamble enabled callback, the application will be notified once the host enables the metadata preamble. If metadata preambles are enabled, you should use the following procedure to perform a read:

▪ Call **USBD_PHDC_RdPreamble()**. Device expects metadata preamble from the host. This function will return opaque data and the number of incoming transfers that the host specified. Note that if the host disables preamble while the application is pending on that function, it will immediately return with error "**USBD_ERR_OS_ABORT**".

▪ Call **USBD_PHDC_Rd()** a number of times corresponding to the number of incoming transfers returned by **USBD_PHDC_RdPreamble()**. The application must ensure that the buffer provided to the function is large enough to accommodate all the data. Otherwise, synchronization issues might happen. Note that if the host enables preamble while the application is pending on that function, it will immediately return with error "**USBD_ERR_OS_ABORT**".

11

```
CPU_INT16U  App_USBD_PHDC_Rd(CPU_INT08U   class_nbr,
                             CPU_INT08U  *p_data_opaque_buf
                             CPU_INT08U  *p_data_opaque_len,
                             CPU_INT08U  *p_buf,
                             USBD_ERR    *p_err)
{
    CPU_INT08U  nbr_xfer;
    CPU_INT16U  xfer_len;


    *p_data_opaque_len = USBD_PHDC_RdPreamble(           class_nbr,                (1)
                                         (void *)p_data_opaque_buf,                (2)
                                              USBD_PHDC_CFG_DATA_OPAQUE_MAX_LEN,
                                              &nbr_xfer,                           (3)
                                              0,                                   (4)
                                              p_err);

    for (i = 0; i < nbr_xfers; i++) {                                             (5)
        xfer_len = USBD_PHDC_Rd(          class_nbr,
                           (void *)p_buf,                                          (6)
                           APP_USBD_PHDC_ITEM_DATA_LEN_MAX,
                           0,                                                      (4)
                           p_err);

        /* Handle received data. */
    }

    return (xfer_len);
}
```

Listing 11-2 **PHDC Read Procedure**

L11-2(1)   The class instance number obtained with **USBD_PHDC_Add( )** will serve internally to the PHDC class to route the data to the proper endpoints.

L11-2(2)   Buffer that will contain opaque data. The application must ensure that the buffer provided is large enough to accommodate all the data. Otherwise, synchronization issues might happen.

L11-2(3)   Variable that will contain the number of following transfers to which this preamble applies.

L11-2(4)   In order to avoid an infinite blocking situation, a timeout expressed in milliseconds can be specified. A value of '0' makes the application task wait forever.

L11-2(5)   Read all the USB transfers to which the preamble applies.

L11-2(6)   Buffer that will contain the data. The application must ensure that the buffer provided is large enough to accommodate all the data. Otherwise, synchronization issues might happen.

You should use the following procedure to perform a write:

▪ Call **USBD_PHDC_WrPreamble()**. The host expects metadata preamble from the device. The application will have to specify opaque data, transfer's QoS (see Table 11-7), and a number of following transfers to which the selected QoS applies.

▪ Call **USBD_PHDC_Wr()** a number of times corresponding to the number of transfers following the preamble.

```
CPU_INT16U  App_USBD_PHDC_Wr(CPU_INT08U          class_nbr,
                             LATENCY_RELY_FLAGS  latency_rely,
                             CPU_INT08U          nbr_xfer,
                             CPU_INT08U          *p_data_opaque_buf
                             CPU_INT08U          data_opaque_buf_len,
                             CPU_INT08U          *p_buf,
                             CPU_INT08U          buf_len,
                             USBD_ERR            *p_err)


{
    (void)USBD_PHDC_WrPreamble(         class_nbr,                 (1)
                               (void *)p_data_opaque_buf,          (2)
                                       data_opaque_buf_len,
                                       latency_rely,               (3)
                                       nbr_xfer,                   (4)
                                       0,                          (5)
                                       p_err);
```

```
      for (i = 0; i < nbr_xfer; i++) {                              (6)
          /* Prepare data to send. */

          xfer_len = USBD_PHDC_Wr(          class_nbr,              (1)
                                 (void *)p_buf,                     (7)
                                  buf_len,
                                  latency_rely,                     (3)
                                  0,
                                  p_err);
      }
}
```

Listing 11-3 **PHDC Write Procedure**

L11-3(1)   The class instance number obtained with **USBD_PHDC_Add()** will serve internally to the PHDC class to route the data to the proper endpoints.

L11-3(2)   Buffer that contains opaque data.

L11-3(3)   Latency / reliability (QoS) of the following transfer(s).

L11-3(4)   Variable that contains the number of following transfers to which this preamble will apply.

L11-3(5)   In order to avoid an infinite blocking situation, a timeout expressed in milliseconds can be specified. A value of '0' makes the application task wait forever.

L11-3(6)   Write all the USB transfers to which the preamble will apply.

L11-3(7)   Buffer that contains the data.

11-3-2 COMMUNICATION WITHOUT METADATA PREAMBLE

If the device does not support metadata preamble or if it supports them but it has not been enabled by the host, you should not call `USBD_PHDC_RdPreamble()` and `USBD_PHDC_WrPreamble()`.

11-4 RTOS QOS-BASED SCHEDULER

Since it is possible to send data with different QoS using a single bulk endpoint, you might want to prioritize the transfers by their QoS latency (medium latency transfers processed before high latency transfers, for instance). This kind of prioritization is implemented inside PHDC µC/OS-II and µC/OS-III RTOS layer. Table 11-9 shows the priority value associated with each QoS latency (the lowest priority value will be treated first).

QoS latency	QoS based scheduler associated priority
Very high latency	3
High latency	2
Medium latency	1

Table 11-9 **QoS Based Scheduler Priority Values**

For instance, let's say that your application has 3 tasks. Task A has an OS priority of 1, task B has an OS priority of 2 and task C has an OS priority of 3. Note that a low priority number indicates a high priority task. Now say that all 3 tasks want to write PHDC data of different QoS latency. Task A wants to write data that can have very high latency, task B wants to write data that can have medium latency, and finally, task C wants to write data that can have high latency. Table 11-10 shows a summary of the tasks involved in this example.

Task	QoS latency of data to write	OS priority	QoS priority of data to write
A	Very high	1	3
B	Medium	2	1
C	High	3	2

Table 11-10 **QoS-Based Scheduling Example**

253

If no QoS based priority management is implemented, the OS will then resume the tasks in the order of their OS priority. In this example, the task that has the higher OS priority, A, will be resumed first. However, that task wants to write data that can have very high latency (QoS priority of 3). A better choice would be to resume task B first, which wants to send data that can have medium latency (QoS priority of 1). Figure 11-3 and Figure 11-4 represent this example without and with a QoS-based scheduler, respectively.

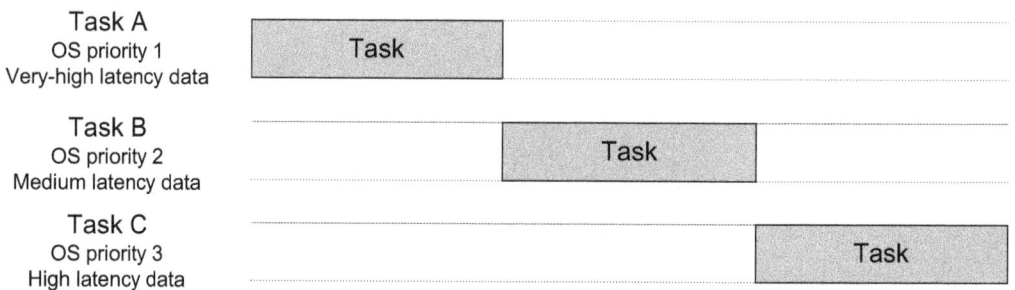

Figure 11-3 **Task Execution Order, Without QoS Based Scheduling**

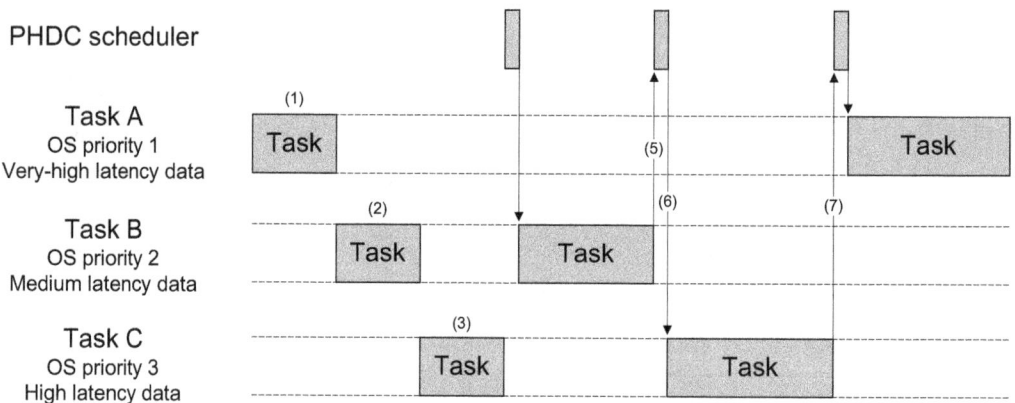

Figure 11-4 **Task Execution Order, with QoS Based Scheduling**

F11-4(1)

F11-4(2)

F11-4(3)   A task currently holds the lock on the write bulk endpoint, task A, B and C are added to the wait list until the lock is released.

F11-4(4)   The lock has been released. The QoS based scheduler's task is resumed, and finds the task that should be resumed first (according to the QoS of the data it wants to send). Task B is resumed.

F11-4(5)   Task B completes its execution and releases the lock on the pipe. This resumes the scheduler's task.

F11-4(6)   Again, the QoS based scheduler finds the next task that should be resumed. Task C is resumed.

F11-4(7)   Task C has completed its execution and releases the lock. Scheduler task is resumed and determines that task A is the next one to be resumed.

The QoS-based scheduler is implemented in the RTOS layer. Three functions are involved in the execution of the scheduler.

Function name	Called by	Operation
USBD_PHDC_OS_WrBulkLock()	USBD_PHDC_Wr() or USBD_PHDC_WrPreamble(), depending if preambles are enabled or not.	Locks write bulk pipe.
USBD_PHDC_OS_WrBulkUnlock()	USBD_PHDC_Wr().	Unlocks write bulk pipe.
USBD_PHDC_OS_WrBulkSchedTask()	N/A.	Determines next task to resume.

Table 11-11 **QoS-Based Scheduler API Summary**

The pseudocode for these three functions is shown in Listing 11-4, Listing 11-5 and Listing 11-6.

```
void  USBD_PHDC_OS_WrBulkLock (CPU_INT08U   class_nbr,
                               CPU_INT08U   prio,
                               CPU_INT16U   timeout_ms,
                               USBD_ERR     *p_err)
{
    Increment transfer count of given priority (QoS);
    Post scheduler lock semaphore;
    Pend on priority specific semaphore;
    Decrement transfer count of given priority (QoS);
}
```

Listing 11-4 **Pseudocode for USBD_PHDC_OS_WrBulkLock()**

```
void  USBD_PHDC_OS_WrBulkUnlock (CPU_INT08U  class_nbr)
{
    Post scheduler release semaphore;
}
```

Listing 11-5 **Pseudocode for USBD_PHDC_OS_WrBulkUnlock()**

```
static  void  USBD_PHDC_OS_WrBulkSchedTask (void *p_arg)
{
    Pend on scheduler lock semaphore;

    Get next highest QoS ready;
    PostSem(SemList[QoS]);

    Pend on scheduler release semaphore;
}
```

Listing 11-6 **Pseudocode for QoS-Based Scheduler's Task**

11-5 USING THE DEMO APPLICATION

Micrium provides a demo application that lets you test and evaluate the class implementation. Source files are provided for the device (for µC/OS-II and µC/OS-III only). Executable and source files are provided for the host (Windows only).

11-5-1 SETUP THE APPLICATION

On the target side, two applications are available: **app_usbd_phdc_single.c** and **app_usbd_phdc_multiple.c**. You should compile only one of these files with your project. Table 11-12 provides a description of each one. Both files are located in the following folders:

\Micrium\Software\uC-USB-Device-V4\App\Device\OS\uCOS-II
\Micrium\Software\uC-USB-Device-V4\App\Device\OS\uCOS-III

File	Description
app_usbd_phdc_single.c	Only one task is used to send all data of different QoS. Usually used with USBD_PHDC_OS_CFG_SCHED_EN set to DEF_DISABLED.
app_usbd_phdc_multiple.c	One task per QoS level is used to send data. Usually used with USBD_PHDC_OS_CFG_SCHED_EN set to DEF_ENABLED.

Table 11-12 **Device Demo Application Files**

Several constants are available to customize the demo application on both device and host (Windows) side. Table 11-13 describe device side constants that are located in the **app_cfg.h** file. Table 11-14 describe host side constants that are located in the **app_phdc.c** file.

Constant	Description
APP_CFG_USBD_PHDC_EN	Set to DEF_ENABLED to enable the demo application.
APP_CFG_USBD_PHDC_TX_COMM_TASK_PRIO	Priority of the write task.
APP_CFG_USBD_PHDC_RX_COMM_TASK_PRIO	Priority of the read task.
APP_CFG_USBD_PHDC_TASK_STK_SIZE	Stack size of both read and write tasks. Default value is 512.
APP_CFG_USBD_PHDC_ITEM_DATA_LEN_MAX	Set this constant to the maximum number of bytes that can be transferred as data. Must be >= 5.
APP_CFG_USBD_PHDC_ITEM_NBR_MAX	Set this constant to the maximum number of items that the application should support. Must be >= 1.

Table 11-13 **Device Side Demo Application's Configuration Constants**

Constant	Description
APP_ITEM_DATA_LEN_MAX	Set this constant to the maximum number of bytes that can be transferred as data. Must be >= 5.
APP_ITEM_DATA_OPAQUE_LEN_MAX	Set this constant to the maximum number of bytes that can be transferred as opaque data. Must be <= (*MaxPacketSize* - 21).
APP_ITEM_NBR_MAX	Set this constant to the maximum number of items that the application should support. Must be >= 1.
APP_STAT_COMP_PERIOD	Set this constant to the period (in ms) on which the statistic of each transfer (mean and standard deviation) should be computed.
APP_ITEM_PERIOD_MIN	Set this constant to the minimum period (in ms) that a user can specify for an item.
APP_ITEM_PERIOD_MAX	Set this constant to the maximum period (in ms) that a user can specify for an item.
APP_ITEM_PERIOD_MULTIPLE	Set this constant to a multiple (in ms) that periodicity of items specified by the user must comply.

Table 11-14 **Host Side (Windows) Demo Application's Configuration Constants**

Since Microsoft does not provide any specific driver for PHDC, you will have to indicate to windows which driver to load using an "inf" file. The "inf" file will ask Windows to load the WinUSB generic driver (provided by Microsoft). The application uses the USBDev_API, which is a wrapper of the WinUSB driver (refer to section 12-3 "USBDev_API" on page 273).

Windows will ask for the INF file (refer to section 3-1-1 "About INF Files" on page 90) the first time the device will be plugged-in. It is located in the following folder:

`\Micrium\Software\uC-USB-Device-V4\App\Host\OS\Windows\PHDC\INF`

Once the driver is successfully loaded, the Windows host application is ready to be launched. The executable is located in the following folder:

`\Micrium\Software\uC-USB-Device-V4\App\Host\OS\Windows\PHDC\Visual    Studio`
`2010\exe`

11-5-2 RUNNING THE DEMO APPLICATION

In this demo application, you can ask the device to continuously send data of different QoS level and using a given periodicity. Each requested transfer is called an "item". Using the monitor, you can see each transfer's average periodicity and standard deviation. The monitor will also show the data and opaque data that you specified. At startup, the application will always send a default item with a periodicity of 100 ms. This item will send the device CPU usage and the value of a counter that is incremented each time the item is sent. The default item uses low latency / good reliability as QoS. Figure 11-5 shows the demo application at startup.

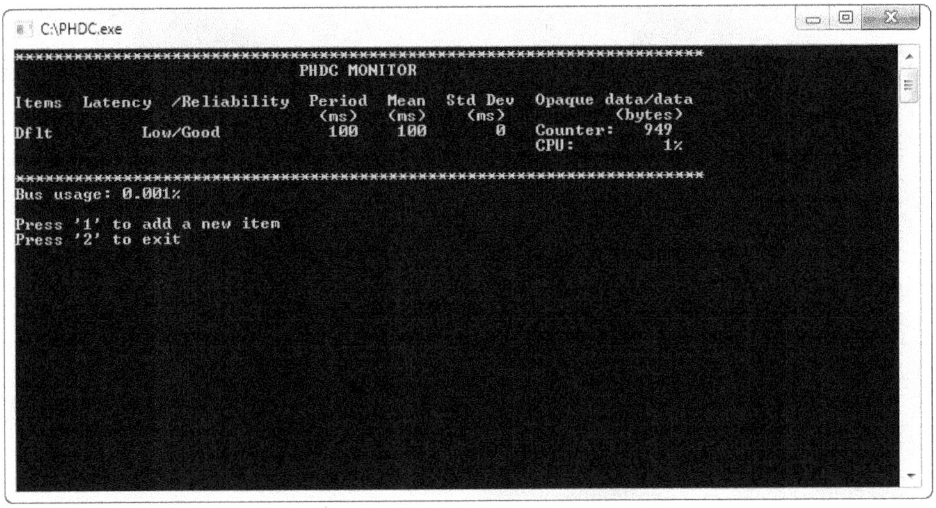

Figure 11-5 **Demo Application at Startup**

11

At this point, you have the possibility to add a new item by pressing 1. You will be prompted to specify the following values:

■ Periodicity of the transfer: the period at which the transfer will attempt to occur.

■ QoS (Latency / reliability) of the transfer: the type of QoS desired for this transfer.

■ Opaque data (if QoS is not low latency / good reliability): the opaque data that will be included in this transfer.

■ Data: the actual data that will be transferred.

Figure 11-6 shows the demo application with a few items added.

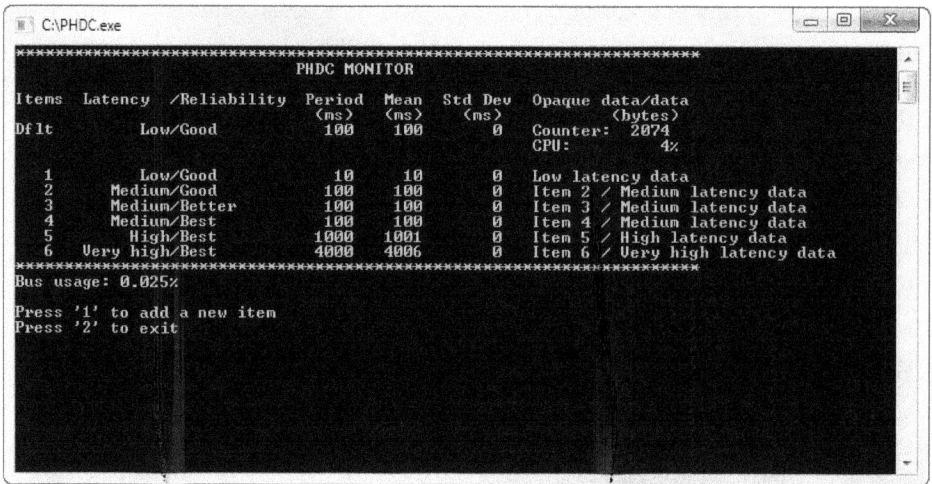

Figure 11-6 **Demo Application with Five Items Added**

Once an item has been added, the application provides statistics about every transfer. From left to right, there is the item's number, the type of QoS, the ideal period, the mean period value, the standard deviation value and the opaque data/data. The mean and standard deviation values are calculated by the host application, based on a sampling of the actual period value obtained for every single transfer.

11-6 PORTING PHDC TO AN RTOS

Since PHDC communication functions can be called from different tasks at application level, there is a need to protect the resources they use (in this case, the endpoint). Furthermore, since it is possible to send data with different QoS using a single bulk endpoint, an application might want to prioritize the transfers by their QoS (i.e. medium latency transfers processed before high latency transfers). This kind of prioritization can be implemented/customized inside the RTOS layer (see Section 11-4, "RTOS QoS-based scheduler" on page 253, for more information). By default, Micrium will provide an RTOS layer for both μC/OS-II and μC/OS-III. However, it is possible to create your own RTOS layer. Your layer will need to implement the functions listed in Table 11-15. For a complete API description, see Appendix F, "PHDC API Reference" on page 515.

Function name	Operation
USBD_PHDC_OS_Init()	Initializes all internal members / tasks.
USBD_PHDC_OS_RdLock()	Locks read pipe.
USBD_PHDC_OS_RdUnlock()	Unlocks read pipe.
USBD_PHDC_OS_WrBulkLock()	Locks write bulk pipe.
USBD_PHDC_OS_WrBulkUnlock()	Unlocks write bulk pipe.
USBD_PHDC_OS_WrIntrLock()	Locks write interrupt pipe.
USBD_PHDC_OS_WrIntrUnlock()	Unlocks write interrupt pipe.
USBD_PHDC_OS_Reset()	Resets OS layer members.

Table 11-15 **OS Layer API Summary**

11

Vendor Class

The Vendor class allows you to build vendor-specific devices implementing for instance a proprietary protocol. It relies on a pair of bulk endpoints to transfer data between the host and the device. Bulk transfers are typically convenient for transferring large amounts of unstructured data and provides reliable exchange of data by using an error detection and retry mechanism. Besides bulk endpoints, an optional pair of interrupt endpoints can also be used. Any operating system (OS) can work with the Vendor class provided that the OS has a driver to handle the Vendor class. Depending on the OS, the driver can be native or vendor-specific. For instance, under Microsoft Windows®, your application interacts with the WinUSB driver provided by Microsoft to communicate with the vendor device.

12-1 OVERVIEW

Figure 12-1 shows the general architecture between the host and the device using the Vendor class. In this example, the host operating system is Windows.

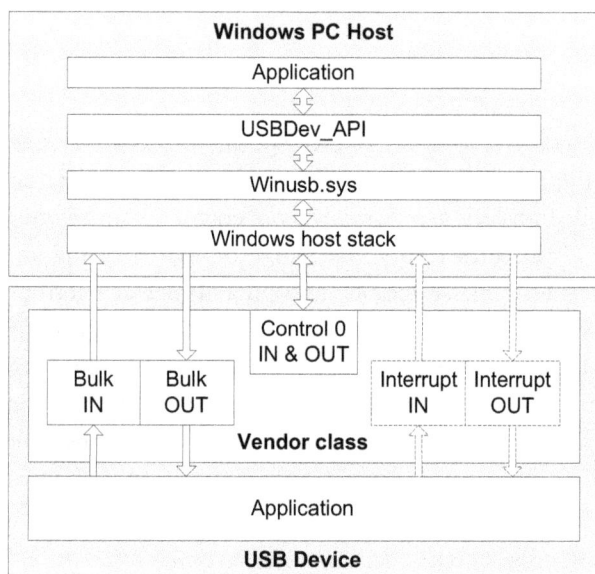

Figure 12-1 **General Architecture Between Windows Host and Vendor Class**

On the Windows side, the application communicates with the vendor device by interacting with the USBDev_API library. This library provided by Micrium offers an API to manage a device and its associated pipes, and to communicate with the device through control, bulk and interrupt endpoints. USBDev_API is a wrapper that allows the use of the WinUSB functions exposed by Winusb.dll.

On the device side, the Vendor class is composed of the following endpoints:

■ A pair of control IN and OUT endpoints called the default endpoint.

■ A pair of bulk IN and OUT endpoints.

■ A pair of interrupt IN and OUT endpoints. This pair is optional.

Table 12-1 indicates the usage of the different endpoints:

Endpoint	Direction	Usage
Control IN Control OUT	Device-to-host Host-to-device	Standard requests for enumeration and vendor-specific requests.
Bulk IN Bulk OUT	Device-to-host Host-to-device	Raw data communication. Data can be structured according to a proprietary protocol.
Interrupt IN Interrupt OUT	Device-to-host Host-to-device	Raw data communication or notification. Data can be structured according to a proprietary protocol.

Table 12-1 **Vendor Class Endpoints Usage**

The device application can use bulk and interrupt endpoints to send or receive data to or from the host. It can only use the default endpoint to decode vendor-specific requests sent by the host. The standard requests are managed internally by the Core layer of µC/USB-Device.

12-2 CONFIGURATION

12-2-1 GENERAL CONFIGURATION

Some constants are available to customize the class. These constants are located in the USB device configuration file, **usbd_cfg.h**. Table 12-2 shows their description.

Constant	Description
USBD_VENDOR_CFG_MAX_NBR_DEV	Configures the maximum number of class instances. Unless you plan on having multiple configurations or interfaces using different class instances, this can be set to 1.
USBD_VENDOR_CFG_MAX_NBR_CFG	Configures the maximum number of configuration in which Vendor class is used. Keep in mind that if you use a high-speed device, two configurations will be built, one for full-speed and another for high-speed.

Table 12-2 **General Configuration Constants Summary**

12

12-2-2 CLASS INSTANCE CONFIGURATION

Before starting the communication phase, your application needs to initialize and configure the class to suit its needs. Table 12-3 summarizes the initialization functions provided by the Vendor class. For more details about the functions parameters, refer to section G-1 "Vendor Class Functions" on page 548.

Function name	Operation
USBD_Vendor_Init()	Initializes Vendor class internal structures and variables.
USBD_Vendor_Add()	Creates a new instance of Vendor class.
USBD_Vendor_CfgAdd()	Adds Vendor instance to the specified device configuration.

Table 12-3 **Vendor Class Initialization API Summary**

You need to call these functions in the order shown below to successfully initialize the Vendor class:

1   Call **USBD_Vendor_Init( )**

This is the first function you should call and you should do it only once even if you use multiple class instances. This function initializes all internal structures and variables that the class needs.

2   Call **USBD_Vendor_Add( )**

This function allocates a Vendor class instance. This function allows you to include a pair of interrupt endpoints for the considered class instance. If the interrupt endpoints are included, the polling interval can also be indicated. The polling interval will be the same for interrupt IN and OUT endpoints. Moreover, another parameter lets you specify a callback function used when receiving vendor requests. This callback allows the decoding of vendor-specific requests utilized by a proprietary protocol.

3   Call **USBD_Vendor_CfgAdd( )**

Finally, once the Vendor class instance has been created, you must add it to a specific configuration.

Listing 12-1 illustrates the use of the previous functions for initializing the Vendor class.

```
                                                    (1)
static  CPU_BOOLEAN  App_USBD_Vendor_VendorReq (        CPU_INT08U      class_nbr,
                                                const  USBD_SETUP_REQ  *p_setup_req);


CPU_BOOLEAN  App_USBD_Vendor_Init (CPU_INT08U  dev_nbr,
                                   CPU_INT08U  cfg_hs,
                                   CPU_INT08U  cfg_fs)
{
    USBD_ERR     err;
    CPU_INT08U  class_nbr;

    USBD_Vemdor_Init(&err);                             (2)
    if (err != USBD_ERR_NONE) {
        /* $$$$ Handle the error. */
    }
                                                        (3)
    class_nbr = USBD_Vendor_Add(DEF_FALSE,
                                0u,
                                App_USBD_Vendor_VendorReq,  (1)
                                &err);
    if (err != USBD_ERR_NONE) {
        /* $$$$ Handle the error. */
    }

    if (cfg_hs != USBD_CFG_NBR_NONE) {
        USBD_Vendor_CfgAdd(class_nbr, dev_nbr, cfg_hs, &err);   (4)
        if (err != USBD_ERR_NONE) {
            /* $$$$ Handle the error. */
        }
    }

    if (cfg_fs != USBD_CFG_NBR_NONE) {
        USBD_Vendor_CfgAdd(class_nbr, dev_nbr, cfg_fs, &err);   (5)
        if (err != USBD_ERR_NONE) {
            /* $$$$ Handle the error. */
        }
    }
}
```

Listing 12-1 **Vendor Class Initialization Example**

L12-1(1)   Provide an application callback for vendor requests decoding.

L12-1(2)   Initialize Vendor internal structures, variables.

L12-1(3)   Create a new Vendor class instance. In this example, **DEF_FALSE** indicates that no interrupt endpoints are used. Thus, the polling interval is set to 0. The callback **App_USBD_Vendor_VendorReq( )** is passed to the function.

L12-1(4)   Check if the high-speed configuration is active and proceed to add the Vendor instance previously created to this configuration.

L12-1(5)   Check if the full-speed configuration is active and proceed to add the Vendor instance to this configuration.

Code Listing 12-1 also illustrates an example of multiple configurations. The functions **USBD_Vendor_Add( )** and **USBD_Vendor_CfgAdd( )** allow you to create multiple configurations and multiples instances architecture. Refer to section 7-1 "Class Instance Concept" on page 147 for more details about multiple class instances.

12-2-3 CLASS INSTANCE COMMUNICATION

The Vendor class offers the following functions to communicate with the host. For more details about the functions parameters, refer to section G-1 "Vendor Class Functions" on page 548.

Function name	Operation
USBD_Vendor_Rd( )	Receives data from host through bulk OUT endpoint. This function is blocking.
USBD_Vendor_Wr( )	Sends data to host through bulk IN endpoint. This function is blocking.
USBD_Vendor_RdAsync( )	Receives data from host through bulk OUT endpoint. This function is non-blocking.
USBD_Vendor_WrAsync( )	Sends data to host through bulk IN endpoint. This function is non-blocking.
USBD_Vendor_IntrRd( )	Receives data from host through interrupt OUT endpoint. This function is blocking.
USBD_Vendor_IntrWr( )	Sends data to host through interrupt IN endpoint. This function is blocking.
USBD_Vendor_IntrRdAsync( )	Receives data from host through interrupt OUT endpoint. This function is non-blocking.
USBD_Vendor_IntrWrAsync( )	Sends data to host through interrupt IN endpoint. This function is non-blocking.

Table 12-4 **Vendor Communication API Summary**

12-2-4 SYNCHRONOUS COMMUNICATION

Synchronous communication means that the transfer is blocking. Upon function call, the application blocks until the transfer completes with or without an error. A timeout can be specified to avoid waiting forever.

Listing 12-2 presents a read and write example to receive data from the host using the bulk OUT endpoint and to send data to the host using the bulk IN endpoint.

```
CPU_INT08U  rx_buf[2];
CPU_INT08U  tx_buf[2];
USBD_ERR    err;

(void)USBD_Vendor_Rd(          class_nbr,                    (1)
                     (void *)&rx_buf[0],                     (2)
                     2u,
                     0u,                                     (3)
                     &err);
if (err != USBD_ERR_NONE) {
    /* $$$$ Handle the error. */
}


(void)USBD_Vendor_Wr(          class_nbr,                    (1)
                     (void *)&tx_buf[0],                     (4)
                     2u,
                     0u,                                     (3)
                     DEF_FALSE,                              (5)
                     &err);
if (err != USBD_ERR_NONE) {
    /* $$$$ Handle the error. */
}
```

Listing 12-2 **Synchronous Bulk Read and Write Example**

L12-2(1)   The class instance number created with **USBD_Vendor_Add()** will serve internally to the Vendor class to route the transfer to the proper bulk OUT or IN endpoint.

L12-2(2)   The application must ensure that the buffer provided to the function is large enough to accommodate all the data. Otherwise, synchronization issues might happen.

L12-2(3)   In order to avoid an infinite blocking situation, a timeout expressed in milliseconds can be specified. A value of '0' makes the application task wait forever.

L12-2(4)   The application provides the initialized transmit buffer.

L12-2(5)   If this flag is set to **DEF_TRUE** and the transfer length is multiple of the endpoint maximum packet size, the device stack will send a zero-length packet to the host to signal the end of the transfer.

The use of interrupt endpoint communication functions, **USBD_Vendor_IntrRd()** and **USBD_Vendor_IntrWr()**, is similar to bulk endpoint communication functions presented in Listing 12-2.

12-2-5 ASYNCHRONOUS COMMUNICATION

Asynchronous communication means that the transfer is non-blocking. Upon function call, the application passes the transfer information to the device stack and does not block. Other application processing can be done while the transfer is in progress over the USB bus. Once the transfer has completed, a callback function is called by the device stack to inform the application about the transfer completion. Listing 12-3 shows an example of asynchronous read and write.

```
void App_USBD_Vendor_Comm (CPU_INT08U  class_nbr)
{
    CPU_INT08U  rx_buf[2];
    CPU_INT08U  tx_buf[2];
    USBD_ERR    err;

    USBD_Vendor_RdAsync(          class_nbr,                (1)
                        (void *)&rx_buf[0],                 (2)
                              2u,
                              App_USBD_Vendor_RxCmpl,       (3)
                        (void *) 0u,                        (4)
                              &err);
    if (err != USBD_ERR_NONE) {
        /* $$$$ Handle the error. */
    }
```

```
    USBD_Vendor_WrAsync(         class_nbr,                  (1)
                        (void *)&tx_buf[0],                  (5)
                                 2u,
                                 App_USBD_Vendor_TxCmpl,     (3)
                        (void *) 0u,                         (4)
                                 DEF_FALSE,                  (6)
                                &err);

    if (err != USBD_ERR_NONE) {
        /* $$$$ Handle the error. */
    }
}


                                                             (3)
static  void  App_USBD_Vendor_RxCmpl (CPU_INT08U  class_nbr,
                                       void        *p_buf,
                                       CPU_INT32U  buf_len,
                                       CPU_INT32U  xfer_len,
                                       void        *p_callback_arg,
                                       USBD_ERR    err)
{
    (void)class_nbr;
    (void)p_buf;
    (void)buf_len;
    (void)xfer_len;
    (void)p_callback_arg;                                    (4)

    if (err == USBD_ERR_NONE) {
        /* $$$$ Do some processing. */
    } else {
        /* $$$$ Handle the error. */
    }
}


                                                             (3)
static  void  App_USBD_Vendor_TxCmpl (CPU_INT08U  class_nbr,
                                       void        *p_buf,
                                       CPU_INT32U  buf_len,
                                       CPU_INT32U  xfer_len,
                                       void        *p_callback_arg,
                                       USBD_ERR    err)
```

```
{
    (void)class_nbr;
    (void)p_buf;
    (void)buf_len;
    (void)xfer_len;
    (void)p_callback_arg;                                     (4)
    if (err == USBD_ERR_NONE) {
        /* $$$$ Do some processing. */
    } else {
        /* $$$$ Handle the error. */
    }
}
```

Listing 12-3 Asynchronous Bulk Read and Write Example

L12-3(1)   The class instance number serves internally to the Vendor class to route the transfer to the proper bulk OUT or IN endpoint.

L12-3(2)   The application must ensure that the buffer provided is large enough to accommodate all the data. Otherwise, there may be synchronization issues.

L12-3(3)   The application provides a callback function pointer passed as a parameter. Upon completion of the transfer, the device stack calls this callback function so that the application can finalize the transfer by analyzing the transfer result. For instance, upon read operation completion, the application may do a certain processing with the received data. Upon write completion, the application may indicate if the write was successful and how many bytes were sent.

L12-3(4)   An argument associated to the callback can be also passed. Then in the callback context, some private information can be retrieved.

L12-3(5)   The application provides the initialized transmit buffer.

L12-3(6)   If this flag is set to **DEF_TRUE** and the transfer length is a multiple of the endpoint maximum packet size, the device stack will send a zero-length packet to the host to signal the end of transfer.

The use of interrupt endpoint communication functions, **USBD_Vendor_IntrRdAsync()** and **USBD_Vendor_IntrWrAsync()**, is similar to bulk endpoint communication functions presented in Listing 12-3.

12-3 USBDEV_API

The Windows host application communicates with a vendor device through *USBDev_API*. The latter is a wrapper developed by Micrium allowing the application to access the WinUSB functionalities to manage a USB device. Windows USB (WinUSB) is a generic driver for USB devices. The WinUSB architecture consists of a kernel-mode driver (`winusb.sys`) and a user-mode dynamic link library (`winusb.dll`) that exposes WinUSB functions. USBDev_API eases the use of WinUSB by providing a comprehensive API (refer to section G-2 on page 572 for the complete list). Figure 12-2 shows the USBDev_API library and WinUSB.

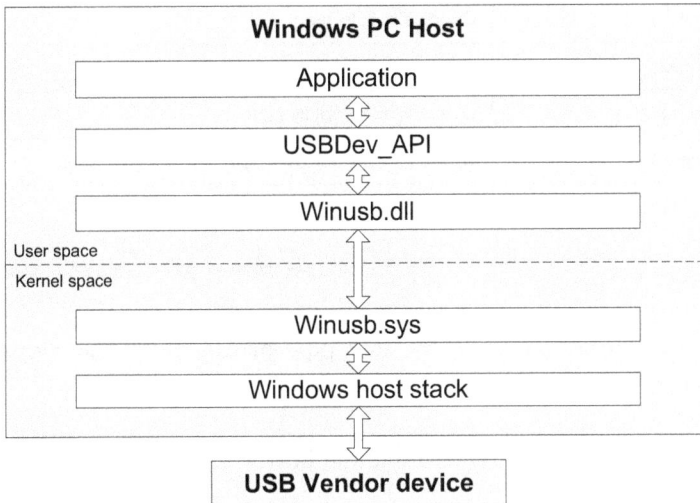

12

Figure 12-2 **USBDev_API and WinUSB**

For more about WinUSB architecture, refer to Microsoft's MSDN online documentation at:
`http://msdn.microsoft.com/en-us/library/ff540207(v=VS.85).aspx`

12-3-1 DEVICE AND PIPE MANAGEMENT

USBDev_API offers the following functions to manage a device and its function's pipes.

Function name	Operation
USBDev_GetNbrDev()	Gets number of devices belonging to a specified Globally Unique IDentifier (GUID) and connected to the host. Refer to section 12-4-4 "GUID" on page 287 for more details about the GUID.
USBDev_Open()	Opens a device.
USBDev_Close()	Closes a device.
USBDev_BulkIn_Open()	Opens a bulk IN pipe.
USBDev_BulkOut_Open()	Opens a bulk OUT pipe.
USBDev_IntIn_Open()	Opens an interrupt IN pipe.
USBDev_IntOut_Open()	Opens an interrupt OUT pipe.
USBDev_PipeClose()	Closes a pipe.

Table 12-5 **USBDev_API Device and Pipe Management API**

Listing 12-4 shows an example of device and pipe management. The steps to manage a device typically consist in:

- Opening the vendor device connected to the host.

- Opening required pipes for this device.

- Communicating with the device via the open pipes.

- Closing pipes.

- Closing the device.

```
HANDLE   dev_handle;
HANDLE   bulk_in_handle;
HANDLE   bulk_out_handle;
DWORD    err;
DWORD    nbr_dev;

nbr_dev = USBDev_GetNbrDev(USBDev_GUID, &err);              (1)
if (err != ERROR_SUCCESS) {
    /* $$$$ Handle the error. */
}

dev_handle = USBDev_Open(USBDev_GUID, 1, &err);            (2)
if (dev_handle == INVALID_HANDLE_VALUE) {
    /* $$$$ Handle the error. */
}

bulk_in_handle = USBDev_BulkIn_Open(dev_handle, 0, 0, &err);    (3)
if (bulk_in_handle == INVALID_HANDLE_VALUE) {
    /* $$$$ Handle the error. */
}

bulk_out_handle = USBDev_BulkOut_Open(dev_handle, 0, 0, &err);  (3)
if (bulk_out_handle == INVALID_HANDLE_VALUE) {
    /* $$$$ Handle the error. */
}

/* Communicate with the device. */                         (4)

                                                           (5)
USBDev_PipeClose(bulk_in_handle, &err);
if (err != ERROR_SUCCESS) {
    /* $$$$ Handle the error. */
}

USBDev_PipeClose(bulk_out_handle, &err);
if (err != ERROR_SUCCESS) {
    /* $$$$ Handle the error. */
}

USBDev_Close(dev_handle, &err);                            (6)
if (err != ERROR_SUCCESS) {
    /* $$$$ Handle the error. */
}
```

Listing 12-4 **USBDev_API Device and Pipe Management Example**

L12-4(1)   Get the number of devices connected to the host under the specified GUID. A GUID provides a mechanism for applications to communicate with a driver assigned to devices in a class. The number of devices could be used in a loop to open at once all the devices. In this example, one device is assumed.

L12-4(2)   Open the device by retrieving a general device handle. This handle will be used for pipe management and communication.

L12-4(3)   Open a bulk pipe by retrieving a pipe handle. In the example, a bulk IN and a bulk OUT pipes are open. If the pipe does not exist for this device, an error is returned. When opening a pipe, the interface number and alternate setting number are specified. In the example, bulk IN and OUT pipes are part of the default interface. Opening an interrupt IN and OUT pipes with `USBDev_IntIn_Open()` or `USBDev_IntOut_Open()` is similar to bulk IN and OUT pipes.

L12-4(4)   Transferring data on the open pipes can take place now. The pipe communication is described in section 12-3-2 "Device Communication" on page 277.

L12-4(5)   Close a pipe by passing the associated handle. The closing operation aborts any transfer in progress for the pipe and frees any allocated resources.

L12-4(6)   Close the device by passing the associated handle. The operation frees any allocated resources for this device. If a pipe has not been closed by the application, this function will close any forgotten open pipes.

12-3-2 DEVICE COMMUNICATION

SYNCHRONOUS COMMUNICATION

Synchronous communication means that the transfer is blocking. Upon function call, the application blocks until the end of transfer is completed with or without an error. A timeout can be specified to avoid waiting forever. Listing 12-5 presents a read and write example using a bulk IN pipe and a bulk OUT pipe.

```
UCHAR  rx_buf[2];
UCHAR  tx_buf[2];
DWORD  err;

(void)USBDev_PipeRd(bulk_in_handle,                      (1)
                    &rx_buf[0],                          (2)
                    2u,
                    5000u,                               (3)
                    &err);
if (err != ERROR_SUCCESS) {
    /* $$$$ Handle the error. */
}

(void)USBDev_PipeWr(bulk_out_handle,                     (1)
                    &tx_buf[0],                          (4)
                    2u,
                    5000u,                               (3)
                    &err);
if (err != ERROR_SUCCESS) {
    /* $$$$ Handle the error. */
}
```

Listing 12-5 **USBDev_API Synchronous Read and Write Example**

L12-5(1)   The pipe handle gotten with `USBDev_BulkIn_Open()` or `USBDev_BulkOut_Open()` is passed to the function to schedule the transfer for the desired pipe.

L12-5(2)   The application provides a receive buffer to store the data sent by the device.

L12-5(3)   In order to avoid an infinite blocking situation, a timeout expressed in milliseconds can be specified. A value of '0' makes the application thread wait forever. In the example, a timeout of 5 seconds is set.

L12-5(4)   The application provides the transmit buffer that contains the data for the device.

12

ASYNCHRONOUS COMMUNICATION

Asynchronous communication means that the transfer is non-blocking. Upon function call, the application passes the transfer information to the device stack and does not block. Other application processing can be done while the transfer is in progress over the USB bus. Once the transfer has completed, a callback is called by USBDev_API to inform the application about the transfer completion.

Code Listing 12-6 presents a read example. The asynchronous write is not offered by USBDev_API.

```
UCHAR   rx_buf[2];
DWORD   err;

USBDev_PipeRdAsync(          bulk_in_handle,                      (1)
                             &rx_buf[0],                          (2)
                             2u,
                             App_PipeRdAsyncComplete,             (3)
                  (void *)0u,                                     (4)
                             &err);
if (err != ERROR_SUCCESS) {
    /* $$$$ Handle the error. */
}
                                                                  (3)

static void App_PipeRdAsyncComplete(void   *p_buf,
                                    DWORD   buf_len,
                                    DWORD   xfer_len,
                                    void   *p_callback_arg,
                                    DWORD   err)
{
    (void)p_buf;
    (void)buf_len;
    (void)xfer_len;
    (void)p_callback_arg;                                         (4)

    if (err == ERROR_SUCCESS) {
        /* $$$$ Process the received data. */
    } else {
        /* $$$$ Handle the error. */
    }
}
```

Listing 12-6 **USBDev_API Asynchronous Read Example**

L12-6(1)   The pipe handle gotten with `USBDev_BulkIn_Open()` is passed to the function to schedule the transfer for the desired pipe.

L12-6(2)   The application provides a receive buffer to store the data sent by the device.

L12-6(3)   The application provides a callback passed as a parameter. Upon completion of the transfer, USBDev_API calls this callback so that the application can finalize the transfer by analyzing the transfer result. For instance, upon read operation completion, the application may do a certain processing with the received data.

L12-6(4)   An argument associated to the callback can also be passed. Then, in the callback context, some private information can be retrieved.

12-4 USING THE DEMO APPLICATION

Micrium provides a demo application that lets you test and evaluate the class implementation. Source template files are provided for the device. Executable and source files are provided for Windows host PC.

12-4-1 CONFIGURING PC AND DEVICE APPLICATIONS

The demo used between the host and the device is the *Echo* demo. This demo implements a simple protocol allowing the device to echo the data sent by the host.

On the device side, the demo application file, **app_usbd_vendor.c**, provided for µC/OS-II and µC/OS-III is located in these two folders:

- \Micrium\Software\uC-USB-Device-V4\App\Device\OS\uCOS-II

- \Micrium\Software\uC-USB-Device-V4\App\Device\OS\uCOS-III

app_usbd_vendor.c contains the Echo demo available in two versions:

- The *Echo Sync* demo exercises the synchronous communication API described in section 12-2-4 "Synchronous Communication" on page 269.

- The *Echo Async* demo exercises the asynchronous communication API described in section 12-2-5 "Asynchronous Communication" on page 270.

The use of these constants defined usually in **app_cfg.h** allows you to use the vendor demo application.

Constant	Description
APP_CFG_USBD_VENDOR_EN	General constant to enable the Vendor class demo application. Must be set to DEF_ENABLED.
APP_CFG_USBD_VENDOR_ECHO_SYNC_EN	Enables or disables the Echo Sync demo. The possible values are DEF_ENABLED or DEF_DISABLED.
APP_CFG_USBD_VENDOR_ECHO_ASYNC_EN	Enables or disables the Echo Async demo. The possible values are DEF_ENABLED or DEF_DISABLED.
APP_CFG_USBD_VENDOR_ECHO_SYNC_TASK_PRIO	Priority of the task used by the Echo Sync demo.
APP_CFG_USBD_VENDOR_ECHO_ASYNC_TASK_PRIO	Priority of the task used by the Echo Async demo.
APP_CFG_USBD_VENDOR_TASK_STK_SIZE	Stack size of the tasks used by Echo Sync and Async demos. A default value can be 256.

Table 12-6 **Device Application Constants Configuration**

APP_CFG_USBD_VENDOR_ECHO_SYNC_EN and APP_CFG_USBD_VENDOR_ECHO_ASYNC_EN can be set to **DEF_ENABLED** at the same time. The vendor device created will be a composite device formed with two vendor interfaces. One will represent the Echo Sync demo and the other the Echo Async demo.

On the Windows side, the demo application file, **app_vendor_echo.c**, is part of a Visual Studio solution located in this folder:

\Micrium\Software\uC-USB-Device-V4\App\Host\OS\Windows\Vendor\Visual
Studio 2010

app_vendor_echo.c allows you to test:

- One single device. That is Echo Sync or Async demo is enabled on the device side.

- One composite device. That is Echo Sync and Async demos are both enabled on the device side.

- Multiple devices (single or composite devices).

`app_vendor_echo.c` contains some constants to customize the demo.

Constant	Description
APP_CFG_RX_ASYNC_EN	Enables or disables the use of the asynchronous API for IN pipe. The possible values are TRUE or FALSE.
APP_MAX_NBR_VENDOR_DEV	Defines the maximum number of connected vendor devices supported by the demo.

Table 12-7 **Windows Application Constants Configuration**

The constants configuration for the Windows application are independent from the device application constants configuration presented in Table 12-6.

12-4-2 EDITING AN INF FILE

An INF file contains directives telling to Windows how to install one or several drivers for one or more devices. Refer to section 3-1-1 "About INF Files" on page 90 for more details about INF file use and format. The Vendor class includes two INF files located in \Micrium\Software\uC-USB-Device-V4\App\Host\OS\Windows\Vendor\INF:

- **WinUSB_single.inf**, used if the device presents only one Vendor class interface.

- **WinUSB_composite.inf**, used if the device presents at least one Vendor class interface along with another interface.

The two INF files allows you to load the **WinUSB.sys** driver provided by Windows. **WinUSB_single.inf** defines this default hardware ID string:

USB\VID_FFFE&PID_1003

While **WinUSB_composite.inf** defines this one:

USB\VID_FFFE&PID_1001&MI_00

The hardware ID string contains the Vendor ID (VID) and Product ID (PID). In the default strings, the VID is FFFE and the PID is either 1003 or 1001. The VID/PID values should match the ones from the USB device configuration structure defined in **usb_dev_cfg.c**. Refer to section "Modify Device Configuration" on page 77 for more details about the USB device configuration structure.

If you want to define your own VID/PID, you must modify the previous default hardware ID strings with your VID/PID.

In the case of a composite device formed of several vendor interfaces, in order to load WinUSB.sys for each vendor interface, the manufacturer section in **WinUSB_composite.inf** can be modified as shown in Listing 12-7. Let's assume a device with two vendor interfaces.

```
[MyDevice_WinUSB.NTx86]
%USB\MyDevice.DeviceDesc% =USB_Install, USB\VID_FFFE&PID_1001&MI_00
%USB\MyDevice.DeviceDesc% =USB_Install, USB\VID_FFFE&PID_1001&MI_01

[MyDevice_WinUSB.NTamd64]
%USB\MyDevice.DeviceDesc% =USB_Install, USB\VID_FFFE&PID_1001&MI_00
%USB\MyDevice.DeviceDesc% =USB_Install, USB\VID_FFFE&PID_1001&MI_01

[MyDevice_WinUSB.NTia64]
%USB\MyDevice.DeviceDesc% =USB_Install, USB\VID_FFFE&PID_1001&MI_00
%USB\MyDevice.DeviceDesc% =USB_Install, USB\VID_FFFE&PID_1001&MI_01
```

Listing 12-7 **INF File Example for Composite Device Formed of Several Vendor Interfaces.**

You can also modify the [Strings] section of the INF file in order to add the strings that best describe your device. Listing 12-8 shows the editable **[Strings]** section common to **WinUSB_single.inf** and **WinUSB_composite.inf**.

```
[Strings]
ProviderName           ="Micrium"                        (1)
USB\MyDevice.DeviceDesc ="Micrium Vendor Specific Device" (2)
ClassName              ="USB Sample Class"               (3)
```

Listing 12-8 **Editable Strings in the INF File to Describe the Vendor Device.**

L12-8(1)   Specify the name of your company as the driver provider.

L12-8(2)   Write the name of your device.

L12-8(3)   You can modify this string to give a new name to the device group in which your device will appear under Device Manager. In this example, "Micrium Vendor Specific Device" will appear under the "USB Sample Class" group. Refer to Figure 3-1 "Windows Device Manager Example for a CDC Device" on page 94 for an illustration of the strings used by Windows.

12-4-3 RUNNING THE DEMO APPLICATION

Figure 12-3 illustrates the Echo demo with host and device interactions:

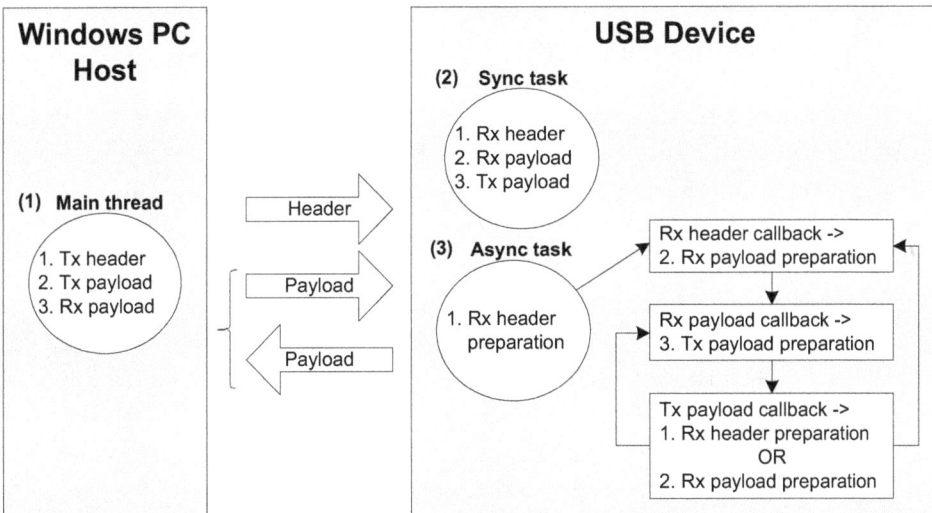

Figure 12-3 **Echo Demo**

F12-3(1)   The Windows application executes a simple protocol consisting of sending a header indicating the total payload size, sending the data payload to the device and receiving the same data payload from the device. The entire transfer for data payload is split into small chunks of write and read operations of 512 bytes. The write operation is done using a bulk OUT endpoint and the read uses a bulk IN endpoint.

F12-3(2)   On the device side, the Echo Sync uses a task that complements the Windows application execution. Each step is done synchronously. The read and write operation is the opposite of the host side in terms of USB transfer direction. Read operation implies a bulk OUT endpoint while a write implies a bulk IN endpoint.

F12-3(3)   If the Echo Async is enabled, the same steps done by the Sync task are replicated but using the asynchronous API. A task is responsible to start the first asynchronous OUT transfer to receive the header. The task is also used in case of error during the protocol communication. The callback associated to the header reception is called by the device stack. It prepares the next asynchronous OUT transfer to receive the payload. The read payload callback sends back the payload to the host via an asynchronous IN transfer. The write payload callback is called and either prepares the next header reception if the entire payload has been sent to the host, or prepares a next OUT transfer to receive a new chunk of data payload.

Upon the first connection of the vendor device, Windows enumerates the device by retrieving the standard descriptors. Since Microsoft does not provide any specific driver for the Vendor class, you have to indicate to Windows which driver to load using an INF file (refer to section 3-1-1 "About INF Files" on page 90 to for more details about INF). The INF file tells Windows to load the WinUSB generic driver (provided by Microsoft). Indicating the INF file to Windows has to be done only once. Windows will then automatically recognize the vendor device and load the proper driver for any new connection. The process of indicating the INF file may vary according to the Windows operating system version:

- Windows XP directly opens the "Found New Hardware Wizard". Follow the different steps of the wizard until the page where you can indicate the path of the INF file.

- Windows Vista and later won't open a "Found New Hardware Wizard". It will just indicate that no driver was found for the vendor device. You have to manually open the wizard. Open the Device Manager, the vendor device connected appears under the category 'Other Devices' with a yellow icon. Right-click on your device and choose 'Update Driver Software...' to open the wizard. Follow the different steps of the wizard until the page where you can indicate the path of the INF file.

The INF file is located in:

`\Micrium\Software\uC-USB-Device-V4\App\Host\OS\Windows\Vendor\INF`

Refer to section 3-1-1 "About INF Files" on page 90 for more details about how to edit the INF file to match your Vendor and Product IDs.

Once the driver is successfully loaded, the Windows host application is ready to be launched. The executable is located in the following folder:

`\Micrium\Software\uC-USB-Device-V4\App\Host\OS\Windows\Vendor\Visual Studio 2010\exe\`

There are two executables:

■ *EchoSync.exe* for the Windows application with the synchronous communication API of USBDev_API.

■ *EchoAsync.exe* for the Windows application with the asynchronous IN API of USBDev_API.

The Windows application interacts with WinUSB driver via USBDev_API which is a wrapper of WinUSB driver. USBDev_API is provided by Micrium. Refer to section 12-3 "USBDev_API" on page 273 for more details about USBDev_API and WinUSB driver.

The Echo Sync or Async demo will first determine the number of vendor devices connected to the PC. For each detected device, the demo will open a bulk IN and a bulk OUT pipe. Then the demo is ready to send/receive data to/from the device. You will have to enter the maximum number of transfers you want as shown by Figure 12-4.

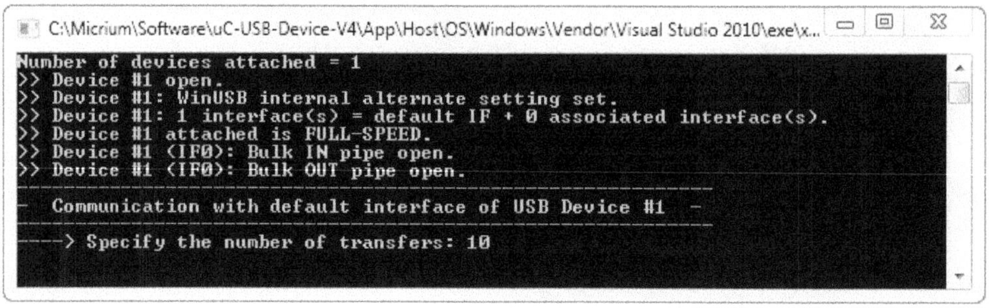

Figure 12-4 **Demo Application at Startup**

In the example of Figure 12-4, the demo will handle 10 transfers. Each transfer is sent after the header following the simple protocol described in Figure 12-3. The first transfer will have a data payload of 1 byte. Then, subsequent transfers will have their size incremented by 1 byte until the last transfer. In our example, the last transfer will have 10 bytes. Figure 12-5 presents the execution.

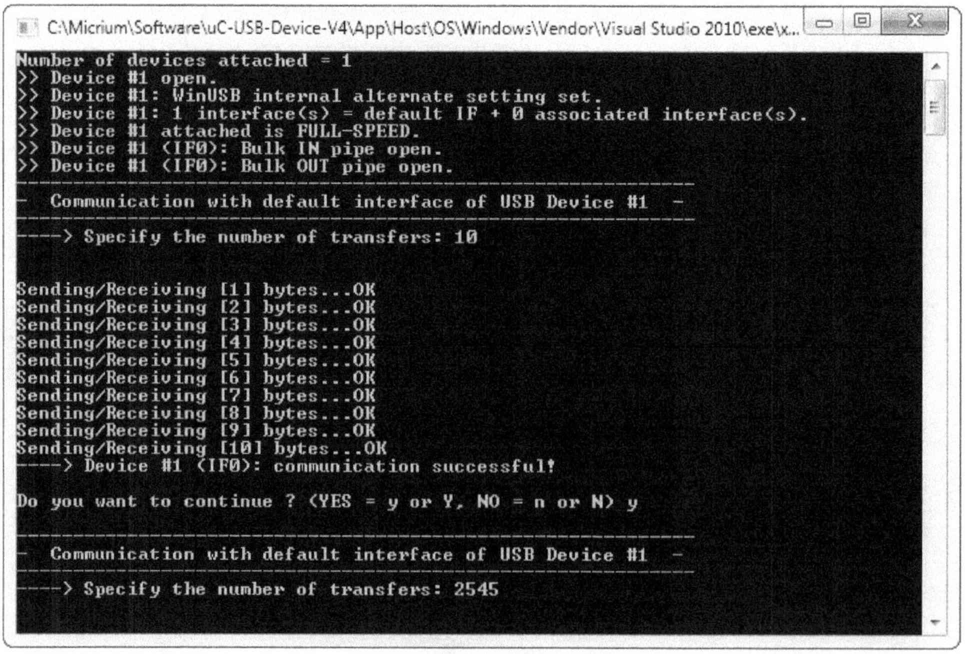

Figure 12-5 **Demo Application Execution (Single Device)**

The demo will propose to do a new execution. Figure 12-5 shows the example of a single device with 1 vendor interface. The demo is able to communicate with each vendor interface in the case of a composite device. In that case, the demo will open bulk IN and OUT pipes for each interface. You will be asked the maximum number of transfers for each interface composing the device. Figure 12-6 shows an example of a composite device.

```
C:\Micrium\Software\uC-USB-Device-V4\App\Host\OS\Windows\Vendor\Visual Studio 2010\exe\x...
Number of devices attached = 1
>> Device #1 open.
>> Device #1: WinUSB internal alternate setting set.
>> Device #1: 2 interface(s) = default IF + 1 associated interface(s).
>> Device #1 attached is FULL-SPEED.
>> Device #1 (IF0): Bulk IN pipe open.
>> Device #1 (IF0): Bulk OUT pipe open.
>> Device #1 (IF1): Bulk OUT pipe open.
>> Device #1 (IF1): Bulk OUT pipe open.
-------------------------------------------------------------------
- Communication with default interface of USB Device #1 -
-------------------------------------------------------------------
----> Specify the number of transfers: 5

Sending/Receiving [1] bytes...OK
Sending/Receiving [2] bytes...OK
Sending/Receiving [3] bytes...OK
Sending/Receiving [4] bytes...OK
Sending/Receiving [5] bytes...OK
----> Device #1 (IF0): communication successful!
-------------------------------------------------------------------
- Communication with associated interface #1 of USB Device #1 -
-------------------------------------------------------------------
----> Specify the number of transfers: 5

Sending/Receiving [1] bytes...OK
Sending/Receiving [2] bytes...OK
Sending/Receiving [3] bytes...OK
Sending/Receiving [4] bytes...OK
Sending/Receiving [5] bytes...OK
----> Device #1 (IF1): communication successful!

Do you want to continue ? (YES = y or Y, NO = n or N) _
```

Figure 12-6 **Demo Application Execution (Composite Device)**

12-4-4 GUID

A Globally Unique IDentifier (GUID) is a 128-bit value that uniquely identifies a class or other entity. Windows uses GUIDs for identifying two types of devices classes:

- Device setup class

- Device interface class

12

A device setup GUID encompasses devices that Windows installs in the same way and using the same class installer and co-installers. Class installers and co-installers are DLLs that provide functions related to the device installation. A device interface class GUID provides a mechanism for applications to communicate with a driver assigned to devices in a class. Refer to section 3-1-2 "Using GUIDs" on page 95 for more details about the GUID.

Device setup class GUID is used in **WinUSB_single.inf** and **WinUSB_composite.inf** located in **\Micrium\Software\uC-USB-Device-V4\App\Host\OS\Windows\Vendor\INF.** These INF files define a new device setup class that will be added in the Windows registry under **HKEY_LOCAL_MACHINE\System\CurrentControlSet\Control\Class** upon first connection of a vendor device. The following entries in the INF file define the new device setup class.

```
Class    = MyDeviceClass                              ; Name of the device setup class.
ClassGuid = {11111111-2222-3333-4444-555555555555}    ; Device setup class GUID
```

The INF file allows Windows to register in the registry base all the information necessary to associate the driver Winusb.sys with the connected vendor device.

The Windows Echo application is able to retrieve the attached vendor device thanks to the device interface class GUID. **WinUSB_single.inf** and **WinUSB_composite.inf** define the following device interface class GUID: {143f20bd-7bd2-4ca6-9465-8882f2156bd6}. The Echo application includes a header file called **usbdev_guid.h**. This header file defines the following variable:

```
GUID USBDev_GUID = {0x143f20bd,0x7bd2,0x4ca6,{0x94,0x65,0x88,0x82,0xf2,0x15,0x6b,0xd6}};
```

USBDev_GUID is a structure whose fields represent the device interface class GUID defined in **WinUSB_single.inf** and **WinUSB_composite.inf**. The **USBDev_GUID** variable will be passed as a parameter to the function **USBDev_Open()**. A handle will be returned by **USBDev_Open()**. And the application uses this handle to access the device.

Chapter

13

Debug and Trace

µC/USB-Device provides an option to enable debug traces to output transactional activity via an output port of your choice such as the console or serial port. Debugging traces allows you to see how the USB device stack behaves and is a useful troubleshooting tool when trying to debug a problem. This chapter will show you the debug and trace tools available in the USB device core as well as how to go about using them.

13-1 USING DEBUG TRACES

13-1-1 DEBUG CONFIGURATION

There are several configuration constants necessary to customize the core level debugging traces. These constants are found in **usbd_cfg.h** and are summarized in Table 13-1.

Constant	Description
USBD_CFG_DBG_TRACE_EN	This constant enables core level debugging traces in the program so that transactional activity can be outputted.
USBD_CFG_DBG_TRACE_NBR_EVENTS	This constant configures the size of the debug event pool to store debug events.

Table 13-1 **General Configuration Constants**

13-1-2 DEBUG TRACE OUTPUT

Core level debug traces are outputted from the debug task handler via an application defined trace function USBD_Trace(). This function is located in **app_usbd.c** and it is up to you to define how messages are outputted whether through console terminal printf() statements or serial printf() statements for example. Listing 13-1 shows an example of an implementation for USBD_Trace() with a serial printf() function.

```
void USBD_Trace (const CPU_CHAR *p_str)
{
    App_SerPrintf("%s", (CPU_CHAR *)p_str);
}
```

Listing 13-1 **USBD_Trace() Example**

13-1-3 DEBUG FORMAT

The debug task handler follows a simple format when outputting debug events. The format is as follows:

USB <timestamp> <endpoint address> <interface number> <error/info message>

In the event that timestamp, endpoint address, interface number or error messages are not provided, they are left void in the output. An example output is shown in Listing 13-2. This example corresponds to traces placed in the USB device core and device driver functions. This trace shows the enumeration process where bus events are received and related endpoints are opened in the device driver. Next, a setup event is sent to the core task followed by receiving the first Get Device Descriptor standard request.

```
USB          0                Bus Reset
USB          0   80             Drv EP DMA Open
USB          0    0             Drv EP DMA Open
USB          0                Bus Suspend
USB          0                Bus Reset
USB          0   80             Drv EP DMA Close
USB          0    0             Drv EP DMA Close
USB          0   80             Drv EP DMA Open
USB          0    0             Drv EP DMA Open
USB          0                  Drv ISR Rx (Fast)
USB          0    0            Setup pkt
USB          0    0              Drv ISR Rx Cmpl (Fast)
USB          0                  Drv ISR Rx (Fast)
USB          0    0            Get descriptor(Device)
USB          0   80             Drv EP FIFO Tx Len: 18
USB          0   80             Drv EP FIFO Tx Start Len: 18
USB          0                  Drv ISR Rx (Fast)
USB          0   80             Drv ISR Tx Cmpl (Fast)
USB          0    0             Drv ISR Rx Cmpl (Fast)
USB          0                  Drv ISR Rx (Fast)
USB          0    0             Drv EP FIFO RxZLP
USB          0                  Drv ISR Rx (Fast)
...
```

Listing 13-2 **Sample Debug Output**

13-2 HANDLING DEBUG EVENTS

13-2-1 DEBUG EVENT POOL

A pool is used to keep track of debugging events. This pool is made up of debug event structures where the size of the pool is specified by **USBD_CFG_DBG_TRACE_NBR_EVENTS** in the application configuration. Within the core, each time a new debug standard request is received, the message's details will be set into a debug event structure and queued into the pool. Once the debug event is properly queued, a ready signal is invoked to notify the debug task handler that an event is ready to be processed.

13-2-2 DEBUG TASK

An OS-dependent task is used to process debug events. The debug task handler simply pends until an event ready signal is received and obtains a pointer to the first debug event structure from the pool. The details of the debug event structure is then formatted and outputted via the application trace function. At the end of the output, the debug event structure is then subsequently freed and the debug task will pend and process the next debug event structure ready. Refer to section 4-2-3 "Processing Debug Events" on page 107 for details on processing debug events.

13-2-3 DEBUG MACROS

Within the core, several macros are created to set debug messages. These macros are defined in **usbd_core.h** and make use of the core functions **USBD_Dbg()** and **USBD_DbgArg()** that will set up a debug event structure and put the event into the debug event pool. These macros are defined in Listing 13-3.

```
#define USBD_DBG_GENERIC(msg, ep_addr, if_nbr)                   USBD_Dbg((msg),            \
                                                                         (ep_addr),        \
                                                                         (if_nbr),         \
                                                                          USBD_ERR_NONE)

#define USBD_DBG_GENERIC_ERR(msg, ep_addr, if_nbr, err)         USBD_Dbg((msg),            \
                                                                         (ep_addr),        \
                                                                         (if_nbr),         \
                                                                         (err))

#define USBD_DBG_GENERIC_ARG(msg, ep_addr, if_nbr, arg)         USBD_DbgArg((msg),         \
                                                                            (ep_addr),     \
                                                                            (if_nbr),      \
                                                                            (CPU_INT32U)(arg),\
                                                                            (USBD_ERR_NONE))

#define USBD_DBG_GENERIC_ARG_ERR(msg, ep_addr, if_nbr, arg, err) USBD_DbgArg((msg),        \
                                                                             (ep_addr),    \
                                                                             (if_nbr),     \
                                                                             (CPU_INT32U)(arg),\
                                                                             (err))
```

Listing 13-3 **Core Level Debug Macros**

There are subtle yet important differences between each debug macro. The first debug macro is the most simple, specifying just the debug message, endpoint address and interface number as parameters. The second and third macros differ in the last parameter where one specifies the error and the other specifies an argument of choice. The last macro lets the caller specify all details including both error and argument.

Furthermore, core level debug macros can be further mapped to other macros to simplify the repetition of endpoint address and interface number parameters. Listing 13-4 shows an example of a bus specific debug macro and a standard debug macro found in `usbd_core.c`.

13

```
# define  USBD_DBG_CORE_BUS(msg)        USBD_DBG_GENERIC((msg),          \
                                            USBD_EP_ADDR_NONE,  \
                                            USBD_IF_NBR_NONE)

# define  USBD_DBG_CORE_STD(msg)        USBD_DBG_GENERIC((msg),          \
                                            0u,                 \
                                            USBD_IF_NBR_NONE)
```

Listing 13-4 **Mapped Core Tracing Macros**

13

14

Porting µC/USB-Device to your RTOS

µC/USB-Device requires a Real-Time Operating System (RTOS). In order to make it usable with nearly any RTOS available on the market, it has been designed to be easily portable. Micrium provides ports for both µC/OS-II and µC/OS-III and recommends using one of these RTOS. In case you need to use another RTOS, this chapter will explain you how to port µC/USB-Device to your RTOS.

14-1 OVERVIEW

µC/USB-Device uses some RTOS abstraction ports to interact with the RTOS. Instead of being a simple wrapper for common RTOS service functions (**TaskCreate()**, **SemaphorePost()**, etc...), those ports are in charge of allocating and managing all the OS resources needed. All the APIs are related to the µC/USB-Device module feature that uses it. This offers you a better flexibility of implementation as you can decide which OS services can be used for each specific action. Table 14-1 gives an example of comparison between a simple RTOS functions wrapper port and a features-oriented RTOS port.

Operation	Example of feature-oriented function (current implementation)	Equivalent function in a simple wrapper (not used)
Create a task	The stack is not in charge of creating tasks. This should be done in the RTOS abstraction layer within a USBD_OS_Init( ) function, for example.	USBD_OS_TaskCreate( ). The stack would need to explicitly create the needed tasks and to manage them.
Create a signal for an endpoint	USBD_OS_EP_SignalCreate( ). You are free to use another OS service than a typical Semaphore.	USBD_OS_SemCreate( ). The stack would need to explicitly choose the OS service to use.
Put a core event in a queue	USBD_OS_CoreEventPut( ). If you prefer not using typical OS queues, you could still implement it using a chained list and a semaphore, for instance.	USBD_OS_Q_Post( ). Again, the stack would need to explicitly choose the OS service to use.

Table 14-1 **Comparison between a wrapper and a features-oriented RTOS port**

Because of the features oriented RTOS port design, some µC/USB-Device modules will need their own OS port. These modules are listed here:

- µC/USB-Device core layer

- Personal Healthcare Device Class (PHDC)

- Human Interface Device Class (HID)

- Mass Storage Class (MSC)

Moreover, all the demo applications for each USB class that Micrium provides interact with the RTOS. The demo applications do not benefit from an RTOS port. Therefore, if you plan to use them with an RTOS other than µC/OS-II or µC/OS-III, you will have to modify them.

Figure 14-1 summarizes the interactions between the different µC/USB-Device modules and the RTOS.

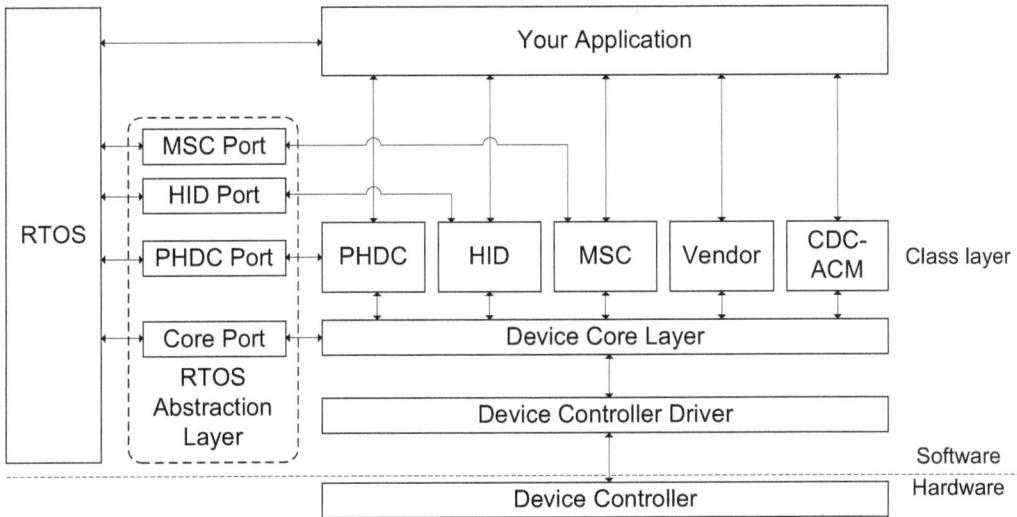

Figure 14-1 **µC/USB-Device architecture with RTOS interactions**

14-2 PORTING MODULES TO AN RTOS

Table 14-2 lists the section of this manual to which you should refer to for an explanation on how to port µC/USB-Device modules to an RTOS.

Module	Refer to...
Core layer	Section 14-4 "Porting The Core Layer to an RTOS" on page 300
PHDC	Section 11-6 "Porting PHDC to an RTOS" on page 261
HID	Section 9-5 "Porting the HID Class to an RTOS" on page 210
MSC	Section 10-7 "Porting MSC to an RTOS" on page 237

Table 14-2 **References to Port a Module to an RTOS**

14-3 CORE LAYER RTOS MODEL

The core layer of µC/USB-Device needs an RTOS for three purposes:

▤ Signal the completion of synchronous transfers.

▤ Manage core events.

▤ Manage debug events (optional).

14-3-1 SYNCHRONOUS TRANSFER COMPLETION SIGNALS

The core layer needs a way to signal the application about the synchronous transfer completion. The core will need one signal per endpoint. The RTOS resources usually used for this signal is a semaphore. Figure 14-2 describes a synchronous transfer completion notification.

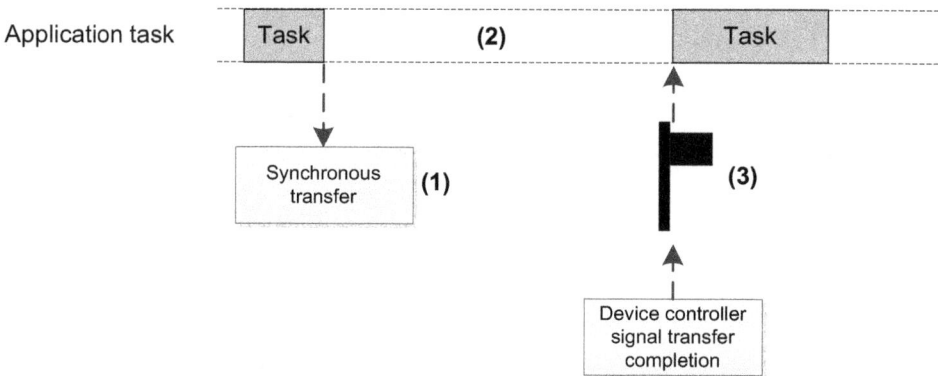

Figure 14-2 **Synchronous transfer completion notification**

F14-2(1)   Application task calls a synchronous transfer function.

F14-2(2)   While the transfer is in progress, the application task pends on the transfer completion signal.

F14-2(3)   Once the transfer is completed, the core will post the transfer completion signal which will resume the application task.

14-3-2 CORE EVENTS MANAGEMENT

For proper operation, the core layer needs an OS task that will manage the core events. For more information on the purpose of this task or on what a core event is, refer to section 4-2 "Task Model" on page 102. The core events must be queued in a data structure and be processed by the core. This allows the core to process the events in a task context instead of in an ISR context, as most of the events will be raised by the device driver's ISR. The core task also needs to be informed when a new event is queued. Figure 14-3 describes the core events management within the RTOS port.

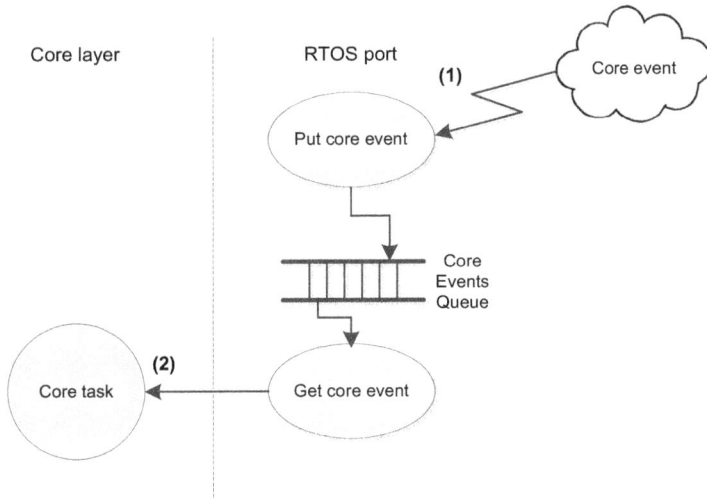

Figure 14-3 **Core events management within RTOS port**

F14-3(1)   A core event is added to the queue.

F14-3(2)   The core task of the core layer pends on the queue. Whenever an event is added, the core task is resumed to process it.

14-3-3 DEBUG EVENTS MANAGEMENT

The core layer of μC/USB-Device offers an optional feature to do tracing and debugging. For more information on this feature, see Chapter 13, "Debug and Trace" on page 289. This feature requires an OS task. For more information on the purpose of this task or on debug events, refer to section 4-2 "Task Model" on page 102. The behavior of this task is similar to the core task described in Section 14-3-2. The difference is that the RTOS port does not need to manage the queue, as it is handled within the core layer. The RTOS port only needs to provide a signal that will inform of a debug event insertion.

14-4 PORTING THE CORE LAYER TO AN RTOS

The core RTOS port is located in a separate file named **usbd_os.c**. A template file can be found in the following folder:

`\Micrium\Software\uC-USB-Device-V4\OS\Template`

Table 14-3 summarizes all the functions that need to be implemented in the RTOS port file. For more information on how these functions should be implemented, refer to section 14-3 on page 298 and to section A-5 "Core OS Functions" on page 365.

Function name	Operation
USBD_OS_Init()	Initializes all internal members / tasks.
USBD_OS_EP_SignalCreate()	Creates OS signal used to synchronize synchronous transfers.
USBD_OS_EP_SignalDel()	Deletes OS signal used to synchronize synchronous transfers.
USBD_OS_EP_SignalPend()	Pends on OS signal used to synchronize synchronous transfers.
USBD_OS_EP_SignalAbort()	Aborts OS signal used to synchronize synchronous transfers.
USBD_OS_EP_SignalPost()	Posts OS signal used to synchronize synchronous transfers.
USBD_OS_DbgEventRdy()	Posts signal used to resume debug task.
USBD_OS_DbgEventWait()	Pends on signal used to resume debug task.
USBD_OS_CoreEventGet()	Retrieves the next core event to process.
USBD_OS_CoreEventPut()	Adds a core event to be processed by the core.

Table 14-3 **Core OS port API summary**

Note that you must declare at least one task for the core events management within your RTOS port. This task should simply call the core function **USBD_CoreTaskHandler()** in an infinite loop. Furthermore, if you plan using the debugging feature, you must also create a task for this purpose. This task should simply call the core function **USBD_DbgTaskHandler()** in an infinite loop. Listing 14-1 shows how these two task functions body should be implemented.

```
static  void  USBD_OS_CoreTask (void *p_arg)
{
    p_arg = p_arg;

    while (DEF_ON) {
        USBD_CoreTaskHandler();
    }
}

static  void  USBD_OS_TraceTask (void *p_arg)
{
    p_arg = p_arg;

    while (DEF_ON) {
        USBD_DbgTaskHandler();
    }
}
```

Listing 14-1 **Core task and debug task typical implementation**

14

14

Core API Reference

This appendix provides a reference to the µC/USB-Device core layer API. The following information is provided for each of the services:

■ A brief description

■ The function prototype

■ The filename of the source code

■ A description of the arguments passed to the function

■ A description of returned value(s)

■ Specific notes and warnings regarding use of the service

A-1 DEVICE FUNCTIONS

A-1-1 USBD_Init()

Initialize USB device stack. This function is called by the application exactly once. This function initializes all the internal variables and modules used by the USB device stack.

FILES

usbd_core.h/usbd_core.c

PROTOTYPE

```
static void USBD_Init (USBD_ERR *p_err);
```

ARGUMENTS

p_err   Pointer to variable that will receive the return error code from this function.

            USBD_ERR_NONE
            USBD_ERR_OS_INIT_FAIL

RETURNED VALUE

None.

CALLERS

Application.

NOTES / WARNINGS

USBD_Init( ) must be called:

■   Only once from a product's application.

■   After product's OS has been initialized

■   Before product's application calls any USB device stack function(s).

A-1-2 USBD_DevStart()

Starts device stack. This function connects the device to the USB host.

usbd_core.h/usbd_core.c

```
void  USBD_DevStart (CPU_INT08U   dev_nbr,
                     USBD_ERR    *p_err);
```

dev_nbr   Device number.

p_err   Pointer to variable that will receive the return error code from this function.

        USBD_ERR_NONE
        USBD_ERR_DEV_INVALID_NBR
        USBD_ERR_DEV_INVALID_STATE

None.

Application.

Device stack can be only started if the device is in either the USBD_DEV_STATE_NONE or USB_DEV_STATE_INIT states.

A-1-3 USBD_DevStop()

Stops device stack. This function disconnects the device from the USB host.

FILES

usbd_core.h/usbd_core.c

PROTOTYPE

```
void  USBD_DevStop (CPU_INT08U   dev_nbr,
                    USBD_ERR    *p_err);
```

ARGUMENTS

dev_nbr   Device number.

p_err   Pointer to variable that will receive the return error code from this function.

USBD_ERR_NONE
USBD_ERR_DEV_INVALID_NBR
USBD_ERR_DEV_INVALID_STATE

RETURNED VALUE

None.

CALLERS

Application.

NOTES / WARNINGS

None.

A-1-4 USBD_DevGetState()

Gets current device state.

FILES

usbd_core.h/usbd_core.c

PROTOTYPE

```
USBD_DEV_STATE  USBD_DevGetState (CPU_INT08U  dev_nbr,
                                  USBD_ERR   *p_err);
```

ARGUMENTS

dev_nbr   Device number.

p_err   Pointer to variable that will receive the return error code from this function.

            USBD_ERR_NONE
            USBD_ERR_DEV_INVALID_NBR

RETURNED VALUE

Current device state, if no error(s).

USBD_DEV_STATE_NONE, otherwise.

CALLERS

USBD_EP_BulkRx()
USBD_EP_BulkRxAsync()
USBD_EP_BulkTx()
USBD_EP_BulkTxAsync()
USBD_EP_CtrlRx()
USBD_EP_CtrlRxStatus()
USBD_EP_CtrlTx()
USBD_EP_IntrRx()

USBD_EP_IntrRxAsync()
USBD_EP_IntrTx()
USBD_EP_IntrTxAsync()

NOTES / WARNINGS

None.

A-1-5 USBD_DevSetSelfPwr()

Sets the powered state (self- or bus-powered) when the device is in the addressed state, before a configuration is set.

FILES

usbd_core.h/usbd_core.c

PROTOTYPE

```
void  USBD_DevSetSelfPwr (CPU_INT08U   dev_nbr,
                          CPU_BOOLEAN  self_pwr,
                          USBD_ERR     *p_err);
```

ARGUMENTS

dev_nbr   Device number.

self_pwr   The power source of the device:

            DEF_TRUE if device is self-powered.
            DEF_FALSE if device is bus-powered.

p_err   Pointer to variable that will receive the return error code from this function:

            USBD_ERR_NONE
            USBD_ERR_DEV_INVALID_NBR

RETURNED VALUE

None.

CALLERS

Application.

NOTES / WARNINGS

None.

A-1-6 USBD_DevAdd()

Adds device to the stack.

FILES

usbd_cdc.h/usbd_cdc.c

PROTOTYPE

```
CPU_INT08U  USBD_DevAdd (USBD_DEV_CFG      *p_dev_cfg,
                         USBD_BUS_FNCTS     *p_bus_fnct,
                         USBD_DRV_API       *p_drv_api,
                         USBD_DRV_CFG       *p_drv_cfg,
                         USBD_DRV_BSP_API   *p_bsp_api,
                         USBD_ERR           *p_err);
```

ARGUMENTS

p_dev_cfg   Pointer to specific USB device configuration

p_bus_fnct   Pointer to specific USB device configuration

p_drv_api   Pointer to specific USB device driver API.

p_drv_cfg   Pointer to specific USB device driver configuration.

p_bsp_api   Pointer to specific USB device board-specific API.

p_err   Pointer to variable that will receive the return error code from this function.

        USBD_ERR_NONE
        USBD_ERR_INVALID_ARG
        USBD_ERR_NULL_PTR
        USBD_ERR_DEV_ALLOC
        USBD_ERR_EP_NONE_AVAIL

RETURNED VALUE

Device number, If no error(s).

USBD_DEV_NBR_NONE, otherwise.

CALLERS

Application.

NOTES / WARNINGS

None.

A-1-7 USBD_DescDevGet()

Get the device descriptor.

FILES

usbd_core.h/usbd_core.c

PROTOTYPE

```
CPU_INT08U  USBD_DescDevGet (USBD_DRV    *p_drv,
                             CPU_INT08U  *p_buf,
                             CPU_INT08U   max_len,
                             USBD_ERR    *p_err);
```

ARGUMENTS

p_drv   Pointer to device driver structure.

p_buf   Pointer to the destination buffer.

max_len   Maximum number of bytes to write in destination buffer.

p_err   Pointer to variable that will receive the return error code from this function.

            USBD_ERR_NONE
            USBD_ERR_ALLOC
            USBD_ERR_INVALID_ARG
            USBD_ERR_DEV_INVALID_NBR
            USBD_ERR_DEV_INVALID_STATE

RETURNED VALUE

Number of bytes actually in the descriptor, if no error(s).

0, otherwise.

CALLERS

USB device driver's init function

NOTES / WARNINGS

This function should only be used by drivers supporting standard requests auto-reply, during the initialization process.

A-1-8 USBD_DescCfgGet()

Get a configuration descriptor.

FILES

usbd_core.h/usbd_core.c

PROTOTYPE

```
CPU_INT16U  USBD_DescCfgGet (USBD_DRV    *p_drv,
                             CPU_INT08U  *p_buf,
                             CPU_INT08U   max_len,
                             CPU_INT08U   cfg_ix,
                             USBD_ERR    *p_err);
```

ARGUMENTS

p_drv   Pointer to device driver structure.

p_buf   Pointer to the destination buffer.

max_len   Maximum number of bytes to write in destination buffer.

cfg_ix   Index of the desired configuration descriptor.

p_err   Pointer to variable that will receive the return error code from this function.

            USBD_ERR_NONE
            USBD_ERR_ALLOC
            USBD_ERR_INVALID_ARG
            USBD_ERR_DEV_INVALID_NBR
            USBD_ERR_DEV_INVALID_STATE

RETURNED VALUE

Number of bytes actually in the descriptor, if no error(s).

0, otherwise.

CALLERS

USB device driver's init function.

NOTES / WARNINGS

This function should only be used by drivers supporting standard requests auto-reply, during the initialization process.

A-1-9 USBD_DescStrGet()

Get a string descriptor.

FILES

usbd_core.h/usbd_core.c

PROTOTYPE

```
CPU_INT08U  USBD_DescStrGet (USBD_DRV    *p_drv,
                             CPU_INT08U  *p_buf,
                             CPU_INT08U   max_len,
                             CPU_INT08U   str_ix,
                             USBD_ERR    *p_err);
```

ARGUMENTS

p_drv   Pointer to device driver structure.

p_buf   Pointer to the destination buffer.

max_len   Maximum number of bytes to write in destination buffer.

str_ix   Index of the desired string descriptor.

p_err   Pointer to variable that will receive the return error code from this function.

USBD_ERR_NONE
USBD_ERR_ALLOC
USBD_ERR_INVALID_ARG
USBD_ERR_DEV_INVALID_NBR
USBD_ERR_DEV_INVALID_STATE

RETURNED VALUE

Number of bytes actually in the descriptor, if no error(s).

0, otherwise.

CALLERS

USB device driver's init function.

NOTES / WARNINGS

This function should only be used by drivers supporting standard requests auto-reply, during the initialization process.

A-2 CONFIGURATION FUNCTIONS

A-2-1 USBD_CfgAdd()

Adds a configuration to the device.

FILES

usbd_core.h/usbd_core.c

PROTOTYPE

```
CPU_INT08U  USBD_CfgAdd (        CPU_INT08U     dev_nbr,
                                 CPU_INT08U     attrib,
                                 CPU_INT16U     max_pwr,
                                 USBD_DEV_SPD   spd,
                           const CPU_CHAR       *p_name,
                                 USBD_ERR       *p_err);
```

ARGUMENTS

dev_nbr   Device number.

attrib   Configuration attributes.

USBD_DEV_ATTRIB_SELF_POWERED
USBD_DEV_ATTRIB_REMOTE_WAKEUP

max_pwr   Bus power required for this device (see Note #1).

spd   Configuration speed.

USBD_DEV_SPD_FULL
USBD_DEV_SPD_HIGH

p_name   Pointer to string describing the configuration (See Note #2).

p_err Pointer to variable that will receive the return error code from this function.

        USBD_ERR_NONE
        USBD_ERR_DEV_INVALID_NBR
        USBD_ERR_DEV_INVALID_STATE
        USBD_ERR_CFG_ALLOC
        USBD_ERR_CFG_INVALID_MAX_PWR

RETURNED VALUE

Configuration number, If no error(s).

USBD_CFG_NBR_NONE, otherwise.

CALLERS

Application.

NOTES / WARNINGS

- USB spec 2.0, section 7.2.1.3/4 defines power constrains for bus-powered devices:

  - "A low-power function is one that draws up to one unit load from the USB cable when operational"

  - "A function is defined as being high-power if, when fully powered, it draws over one but no more than five unit loads from the USB cable."

  - A unit load is defined as 100mA, thus **max_pwr** argument should be between 0 mA and 500mA.

- String support is optional, in this case 'p_name' can be a **NULL** string pointer.

- Configuration can only be added when the device is in either the USBD_DEV_STATE_NONE or USB_DEV_STATE_INIT states.

A-3 INTERFACE FUNCTIONS

A-3-1 USBD_IF_Add()

Send data on CDC data class interface.

FILES

usbd_cdc.h/usbd_cdc.c

PROTOTYPE

```
CPU_INT08U  USBD_IF_Add (      CPU_INT08U      dev_nbr,
                               CPU_INT08U      cfg_nbr,
                               USBD_CLASS_DRV  *p_class_drv,
                               void            *p_class_arg,
                               CPU_INT08U      class_code,
                               CPU_INT08U      class_sub_code,
                               CPU_INT08U      class_protocol_code,
                         const CPU_CHAR        *p_name,
                               USBD_ERR        *p_err);
```

ARGUMENTS

dev_nbr   Device number.

cfg_nbr   Configuration index to add the interface.

p_class_drv   Pointer to interface driver.

p_class_arg   Pointer to interface driver argument.

class_code   Class code assigned by the USB-IF.

class_sub_code   Subclass code assigned by the USB-IF.

class_protocol_code   Protocol code assigned by the USB-IF.

p_name   Pointer to string describing the Interface.

p_err   Pointer to variable that will receive the return error code from this function.

> USBD_ERR_NONE
> USBD_ERR_INVALID_ARG
> USBD_ERR_NULL_PTR
> USBD_ERR_DEV_INVALID_NBR
> USBD_ERR_DEV_INVALID_STATE
> USBD_ERR_CFG_INVALID_NBR
> USBD_ERR_IF_ALLOC
> USBD_ERR_IF_ALT_ALLOC

RETURNED VALUE

None.

CALLERS

USB Class drivers.

NOTES / WARNINGS

Interface number, If no error(s).

USBD_IF_NBR_NONE, otherwise.

A-3-2 USBD_IF_AltAdd()

Adds an alternate setting to a specific interface.

FILES

usbd_core.h/usbd_core.c

PROTOTYPE

```
CPU_INT08U  USBD_IF_AltAdd (       CPU_INT08U   dev_nbr,
                                   CPU_INT08U   cfg_nbr,
                                   CPU_INT08U   if_nbr,
                            const  CPU_CHAR     *p_name,
                                   USBD_ERR     *p_err);
```

ARGUMENTS

dev_nbr   Device number.

cfg_nbr   Configuration number.

if_nbr   Interface number.

p_name   Pointer to alternate setting name.

p_err   Pointer to variable that will receive the return error code from this function.

        USBD_ERR_NONE
        USBD_ERR_DEV_INVALID_NBR
        USBD_ERR_CFG_INVALID_NBR
        USBD_ERR_IF_INVALID_NBR
        USBD_ERR_IF_ALT_ALLOC

RETURNED VALUE

Interface alternate setting number, if no errors.

USBD_IF_ALT_NBR_NONE, otherwise.

CALLERS

USB class drivers.

NOTES / WARNINGS

None.

A-3-3 USBD_IF_Grp()

Creates an interface group.

FILES

usbd_core.h/usbd_core.c

PROTOTYPE

```
CPU_INT08U  USBD_IF_Grp (        CPU_INT08U   dev_nbr,
                                 CPU_INT08U   cfg_nbr,
                                 CPU_INT08U   class_code,
                                 CPU_INT08U   class_sub_code,
                                 CPU_INT08U   class_protocol_code,
                                 CPU_INT08U   if_start,
                                 CPU_INT08U   if_cnt,
                          const  CPU_CHAR     *p_name,
                                 USBD_ERR     *p_err);
```

ARGUMENTS

dev_nbr   Device number.

cfg_nbr   Configuration index to add the interface.

p_class_drv   Pointer to interface driver.

p_class_arg   Pointer to interface driver argument.

class_code   Class code assigned by the USB-IF.

class_sub_code   Subclass code assigned by the USB-IF.

class_protocol_code   Protocol code assigned by the USB-IF.

if_start   Interface number of the first interface that is associated with this group

if_cnt   Number of consecutive interfaces that are associated with this group.

p_err   Pointer to variable that will receive the return error code from this function.

           USBD_ERR_NONE
           USBD_ERR_DEV_INVALID_NBR
           USBD_ERR_CFG_INVALID_NBR
           USBD_ERR_IF_INVALID_NBR
           USBD_ERR_IF_GRP_NBR_IN_USE
           USBD_ERR_IF_GRP_ALLOC

RETURNED VALUE

Interface group number, if no errors.

USBD_IF_GRP_NBR_NONE, otherwise.

CALLERS

USB class drivers.

NOTES / WARNINGS

None.

A-4 ENDPOINTS FUNCTIONS

A-4-1 USBD_CtrlTx()

Sends data on control IN endpoint.

FILES

usbd_core.h/usbd_ep.c

PROTOTYPE

```
CPU_INT32U  USBD_CtrlTx (CPU_INT08U    dev_nbr,
                         void          *p_buf,
                         CPU_INT32U    buf_len,
                         CPU_INT16U    timeout_ms,
                         CPU_BOOLEAN   end,
                         USBD_ERR      *p_err);
```

ARGUMENTS

dev_nbr   Device number.

p_buf   Pointer to buffer of data that will be sent

buf_len   Number of octets to transmit.

timeout_ms   Timeout in milliseconds.

end   End-of-transfer flag (see Note #1).

p_err   Pointer to variable that will receive the return error code from this function.

        USBD_ERR_NONE
        USBD_ERR_INVALID_ARG
        USBD_ERR_DEV_INVALID_NBR
        USBD_ERR_DEV_INVALID_STATE
        USBD_ERR_EP_INVALID_ADDR
        USBD_ERR_EP_INVALID_STATE

```
USBD_ERR_EP_INVALID_TYPE
USBD_ERR_OS_TIMEOUT
USBD_ERR_OS_ABORT
USBD_ERR_OS_FAIL
```

RETURNED VALUE

Number of octets transmitted, if no errors.

0, otherwise.

CALLERS

USBD_DescWrReq()
USBD_DescWrStop()
USBD_StdReqDev()
USBD_StdReqEP()
USBD_StdReqIF()
USB device class drivers

NOTES / WARNINGS

■ If end-of-transfer is set and transfer length is multiple of maximum packet size, a zero-length packet is transferred to indicate a short transfer to the host.

■ This function can be only called from USB device class drivers during class specific setup request callbacks.

A-4-2 USBD_CtrlRx()

Receive data on control OUT endpoint.

FILES

usbd_core.h/usbd_ep.c

PROTOTYPE

```
CPU_INT32U  USBD_CtrlRx (CPU_INT08U    dev_nbr,
                         void          *p_buf,
                         CPU_INT32U    buf_len,
                         CPU_INT16U    timeout_ms,
                         USBD_ERR      *p_err);
```

ARGUMENTS

dev_nbr   Device number.

p_buf   Pointer to buffer of data that will be sent

buf_len   Number of octets to transmit.

timeout_ms   Timeout in milliseconds.

p_err   Pointer to variable that will receive the return error code from this function.

             USBD_ERR_NONE
             USBD_ERR_DEV_INVALID_NBR
             USBD_ERR_DEV_INVALID_STATE
             USBD_ERR_EP_INVALID_ADDR
             USBD_ERR_EP_INVALID_STATE
             USBD_ERR_EP_INVALID_TYPE
             USBD_ERR_OS_TIMEOUT
             USBD_ERR_OS_ABORT
             USBD_ERR_OS_FAIL

RETURNED VALUE

Number of octets received If no error(s).

0, otherwise.

CALLERS

USB device class drivers.

NOTES / WARNINGS

This function can be only called from USB device class drivers during class specific setup request callbacks.

A-4-3 USBD_BulkAdd()

Adds a bulk endpoint to alternate setting interface.

FILES

usbd_core.h/usbd_core.c

PROTOTYPE

```
CPU_INT08U  USBD_BulkAdd (CPU_INT08U   dev_nbr,
                          CPU_INT08U   cfg_nbr,
                          CPU_INT08U   if_nbr,
                          CPU_INT08U   if_alt_nbr,
                          CPU_BOOLEAN  dir_in,
                          CPU_INT16U   max_pkt_len,
                          USBD_ERR     *p_err);
```

ARGUMENTS

dev_nbr   Device number.

cfg_nbr   Configuration number.

if_nbr   Interface number.

if_alt_nbr   Interface alternate setting number.

dir_in   Endpoint direction.

      DEF_YES   IN direction.

      DEF_NO   OUT direction.

max_pkt_len Endpoint maximum packet length (see Note #1).

p_err   Pointer to variable that will receive the return error code from this function.

          USBD_ERR_NONE
          USBD_ERR_INVALID_ARG
          USBD_ERR_DEV_INVALID_NBR
          USBD_ERR_CFG_INVALID_NBR
          USBD_ERR_IF_INVALID_NBR
          USBD_ERR_EP_NONE_AVAIL
          USBD_ERR_EP_ALLOC

RETURNED VALUE

Endpoint address,   if no error(s).

USBD_EP_ADDR_NONE,   otherwise.

CALLERS

USB device class drivers.

NOTES / WARNINGS

If the max_pkt_len argument is '0', the stack will allocate the first available bulk endpoint regardless its maximum packet size.

A-4-4 USBD_BulkRx()

Receives data on bulk OUT endpoint.

FILES

usbd_core.h/usbd_ep.c

PROTOTYPE

```
CPU_INT32U  USBD_BulkRx (CPU_INT08U   dev_nbr,
                         CPU_INT08U   ep_addr,
                         void        *p_buf,
                         CPU_INT32U   buf_len,
                         CPU_INT16U   timeout_ms,
                         USBD_ERR    *p_err);
```

ARGUMENTS

dev_nbr   Device number.

ep_addr   Endpoint address.

p_buf   Pointer to destination buffer to receive data

buf_len   Number of octets to receive.

timeout_ms   Timeout in milliseconds.

p_err   Pointer to variable that will receive the return error code from this function.

        USBD_ERR_NONE
        USBD_ERR_DEV_INVALID_NBR
        USBD_ERR_DEVINVALID_STATE
        USBD_ERR_EP_INVALID_ADDR
        USBD_ERR_EP_INVALID_STATE
        USBD_ERR_EP_INVALID_TYPE
        USBD_ERR_OS_TIMEOUT
        USBD_ERR_OS_ABORT
        USBD_ERR_OS_FAIL

RETURNED VALUE

Number of octets received, If no error(s).

0, otherwise.

CALLERS

USB device class drivers.

NOTES / WARNINGS

This function blocks until:

- All data is received, or

- An error occurred.

- Transfer does not complete in the period specified by `timeout_ms`.

A-4-5 USBD_BulkRxAsync()

Receives data on bulk OUT endpoint asynchronously.

FILES

usbd_core.h/usbd_core.c

PROTOTYPE

```
void  USBD_BulkRxAsync (CPU_INT08U        dev_nbr,
                        CPU_INT08U        ep_addr,
                        void              *p_buf,
                        CPU_INT32U        buf_len,
                        USBD_ASYNC_FNCT   async_fnct,
                        void              *p_async_arg,
                        USBD_ERR          *p_err);
```

ARGUMENTS

dev_nbr   Device number.

ep_addr   Endpoint address.

p_buf   Pointer to destination buffer to receive data

buf_len   Number of octets to receive.

async_fnct   Function that will be invoked upon completion of receive operation

p_async_arg Pointer to argument that will be passed as parameter of **async_fnct**.

p_err   Pointer to variable that will receive the return error code from this function.

    USBD_ERR_NONE
    USBD_ERR_DEV_INVALID_NBR
    USBD_ERR_DEV_INVALID_STATE
    USBD_ERR_EP_INVALID_ADDR
    USBD_ERR_EP_INVALID_STATE

```
        USBD_ERR_EP_INVALID_TYPE
        USBD_ERR_OS_TIMEOUT
        USBD_ERR_OS_ABORT
        USBD_ERR_OS_FAIL
```

RETURNED VALUE

None.

CALLERS

USB device class drivers.

NOTES / WARNINGS

The callback specified by **async_fnct** has the following prototype.

```
void  USB_AsyncFnct (CPU_INT08U   dev_nbr,
                     CPU_INT08U   ep_addr,
                     void         *p_buf,
                     CPU_INT32U   buf_len,
                     CPU_INT32U   xfer_len,
                     void         *p_arg,
                     USBD_ERR     err);
```

Argument(s):

dev_nbr   Device number.

ep_addr   Endpoint address.

p_buf   Pointer to destination buffer to receive data.

buf_len   Buffer length.

xfer_len   Number of byte received.

p_arg   Pointer to function argument.

err   Error status.

USBD_ERR_NONE
USBD_ERR_EP_ABORT

A-4-6 USBD_BulkTx()

Sends data on bulk IN endpoint.

FILES

usbd_core.h/usbd_ep.c

PROTOTYPE

```
CPU_INT32U  USBD_BulkTx (CPU_INT08U    dev_nbr,
                         CPU_INT08U    ep_addr,
                         void          *p_buf,
                         CPU_INT32U    buf_len,
                         CPU_INT16U    timeout_ms,
                         CPU_BOOLEAN   end,
                         USBD_ERR      *p_err);
```

ARGUMENTS

dev_nbr   Device number.

ep_addr   Endpoint address.

p_buf   Pointer to buffer of data that will be transmitted.

buf_len   Number of octets to transmit.

timeout_ms   Timeout in milliseconds.

end   End-of-transfer flag (see Note #2).

p_err   Pointer to variable that will receive the return error code from this function.

             USBD_ERR_NONE
             USBD_ERR_DEV_INVALID_NBR
             USBD_ERR_DEV_INVALID_STATE
             USBD_ERR_EP_INVALID_ADDR
             USBD_ERR_EP_INVALID_STATE
             USBD_ERR_EP_INVALID_TYPE

```
USBD_ERR_OS_TIMEOUT
USBD_ERR_OS_ABORT
USBD_ERR_OS_FAIL
```

RETURNED VALUE

Number of octets transmitted, If no error(s).

0, otherwise.

CALLERS

USB device class drivers.

NOTES / WARNINGS

- This function blocks until:

    - All data is transmitted, or

    - An error occurred.

    - Transfer does not complete in the period specified by `timeout_ms`.

- If end-of-transfer is set and transfer length is multiple of maximum packet size, a zero-length packet is transferred to indicate a short transfer to the host.

A-4-7 USBD_BulkTxAsync()

Receives data on bulk OUT endpoint asynchronously.

FILES

usbd_core.h/usbd_core.c

PROTOTYPE

```
void  USBD_BulkTxAsync (CPU_INT08U       dev_nbr,
                        CPU_INT08U       ep_addr,
                        void             *p_buf,
                        CPU_INT32U       buf_len,
                        USBD_ASYNC_FNCT  async_fnct,
                        void             *p_async_arg,
                        CPU_BOOLEAN      end,
                        USBD_ERR         *p_err);
```

ARGUMENTS

dev_nbr   Device number.

ep_addr   Endpoint address.

p_buf   Pointer to buffer of data that will be transmitted

buf_len   Number of octets to transmit.

async_fnct   Function that will be invoked upon completion of transmit operation.

p_async_arg   Pointer to argument that will be passed as parameter of async_fnct.

end   End-of-transfer flag (see Note #2).

p_err   Pointer to variable that will receive the return error code from this function.

          USBD_ERR_NONE
          USBD_ERR_DEV_INVALID_NBR
          USBD_ERR_DEV_INVALID_STATE
          USBD_ERR_EP_INVALID_ADDR
          USBD_ERR_EP_INVALID_STATE
          USBD_ERR_EP_INVALID_TYPE
          USBD_ERR_OS_TIMEOUT
          USBD_ERR_OS_ABORT
          USBD_ERR_OS_FAIL

RETURNED VALUE

None.

CALLERS

USB device class drivers.

NOTES / WARNINGS

The callback specified by **async_fnct** has the following prototype.

```
void  USB_AsyncFnct (CPU_INT08U   dev_nbr,
                     CPU_INT08U   ep_addr,
                     void         *p_buf,
                     CPU_INT32U   buf_len,
                     CPU_INT32U   xfer_len,
                     void         *p_arg,
                     USBD_ERR     err);
```

Argument(s):

dev_nbr   Device number.

ep_addr   Endpoint address.

p_buf   Pointer to buffer of data that will be transmitted.

buf_len   Buffer length.

xfer_len   Number of byte transmitted.

p_arg   Pointer to function argument.

err   Error status.

          USBD_ERR_NONE
          USBD_ERR_EP_ABORT

If end-of-transfer is set and transfer length is multiple of maximum packet size, a zero-length packet is transferred to indicate a short transfer to the host.

A-4-8 USBD_IntrAdd()

Adds an interrupt endpoint to alternate setting interface.

FILES

usbd_core.h/usbd_core.c

PROTOTYPE

```
CPU_INT08U  USBD_IntrAdd (CPU_INT08U   dev_nbr,
                          CPU_INT08U   cfg_nbr,
                          CPU_INT08U   if_nbr,
                          CPU_INT08U   if_alt_nbr,
                          CPU_BOOLEAN  dir_in,
                          CPU_INT16U   max_pkt_len,
                          CPU_INT16U   interval,
                          USBD_ERR     *p_err);
```

ARGUMENTS

dev_nbr   Device number.

cfg_nbr   Configuration number.

if_nbr   Interface number.

if_alt_nbr   Interface alternate setting number.

dir_in   Endpoint direction.

     DEF_YES   IN direction.

     DEF_NO   OUT direction.

max_pkt_len Endpoint maximum packet length (see Note #1).

interval   Endpoint interval in frames/microframes.

p_err   Pointer to variable that will receive the return error code from this function.

> USBD_ERR_NONE
> USBD_ERR_INVALID_ARG
> USBD_ERR_DEV_INVALID_NBR
> USBD_ERR_CFG_INVALID_NBR
> USBD_ERR_IF_INVALID_NBR
> USBD_ERR_EP_NONE_AVAIL
> USBD_ERR_EP_ALLOC

RETURNED VALUE

Endpoint address, if no error(s).

USBD_EP_ADDR_NONE, otherwise.

CALLERS

USB device class drivers.

NOTES / WARNINGS

If the **max_pkt_len** argument is '0', the stack will allocate the first available interrupt endpoint regardless its maximum packet size.

A-4-9 USBD_IntrRx()

Receives data on interrupt OUT endpoint.

FILES

usbd_core.h/usbd_ep.c

PROTOTYPE

```
CPU_INT32U  USBD_IntrRx (CPU_INT08U   dev_nbr,
                         CPU_INT08U   ep_addr,
                         void        *p_buf,
                         CPU_INT32U   buf_len,
                         CPU_INT16U   timeout_ms,
                         USBD_ERR    *p_err);
```

ARGUMENTS

dev_nbr   Device number.

ep_addr   Endpoint address.

p_buf   Pointer to destination buffer to receive data

buf_len   Number of octets to receive.

timeout_ms   Timeout in milliseconds.

p_err   Pointer to variable that will receive the return error code from this function.

             USBD_ERR_NONE
             USBD_ERR_DEV_INVALID_NBR
             USBD_ERR_DEVINVALID_STATE
             USBD_ERR_EP_INVALID_ADDR
             USBD_ERR_EP_INVALID_STATE
             USBD_ERR_EP_INVALID_TYPE
             USBD_ERR_OS_TIMEOUT
             USBD_ERR_OS_ABORT
             USBD_ERR_OS_FAIL

RETURNED VALUE

Number of octets received, If no error(s).

0, otherwise.

CALLERS

USB device class drivers.

NOTES / WARNINGS

This function blocks until:

- All data is received, or

- An error occurred.

- Transfer does not complete in the period specified by `timeout_ms`.

A-4-10 USBD_IntrRxAsync()

Receives data on interrupt OUT endpoint asynchronously.

FILES

usbd_core.h/usbd_core.c

PROTOTYPE

```
void   USBD_IntrRxAsync (CPU_INT08U      dev_nbr,
                         CPU_INT08U      ep_addr,
                         void            *p_buf,
                         CPU_INT32U      buf_len,
                         USBD_ASYNC_FNCT async_fnct,
                         void            *p_async_arg,
                         USBD_ERR        *p_err);
```

ARGUMENTS

dev_nbr   Device number.

ep_addr   Endpoint address.

p_buf   Pointer to destination buffer to receive data

buf_len   Number of octets to receive.

async_fnct   Function that will be invoked upon completion of receive operation

p_async_arg Pointer to argument that will be passed as parameter of **async_fnct**.

p_err   Pointer to variable that will receive the return error code from this function.

        USBD_ERR_NONE
        USBD_ERR_DEV_INVALID_NBR
        USBD_ERR_DEV_INVALID_STATE
        USBD_ERR_EP_INVALID_ADDR

USBD_ERR_EP_INVALID_STATE
USBD_ERR_EP_INVALID_TYPE
USBD_ERR_OS_TIMEOUT
USBD_ERR_OS_ABORT
USBD_ERR_OS_FAIL

RETURNED VALUE

None.

CALLERS

USB device class drivers.

NOTES / WARNINGS

The callback specified by **async_fnct** has the following prototype.

```
void  USB_AsyncFnct (CPU_INT08U   dev_nbr,
                     CPU_INT08U   ep_addr,
                     void        *p_buf,
                     CPU_INT32U   buf_len,
                     CPU_INT32U   xfer_len,
                     void        *p_arg,
                     USBD_ERR     err);
```

Argument(s):

dev_nbr   Device number.

ep_addr   Endpoint address.

p_buf   Pointer to destination buffer to receive data.

buf_len   Buffer length.

xfer_len   Number of byte received.

p_arg   Pointer to function argument.

---

err   Error status.

              USBD_ERR_NONE
              USBD_ERR_EP_ABORT

A-4-11 USBD_IntrTx()

Sends data on interrupt IN endpoint.

FILES

usbd_core.h/usbd_ep.c

PROTOTYPE

```
CPU_INT32U  USBD_IntrTx (CPU_INT08U    dev_nbr,
                         CPU_INT08U    ep_addr,
                         void          *p_buf,
                         CPU_INT32U    buf_len,
                         CPU_INT16U    timeout_ms,
                         CPU_BOOLEAN   end,
                         USBD_ERR      *p_err);
```

ARGUMENTS

dev_nbr   Device number.

ep_addr   Endpoint address.

p_buf   Pointer to buffer of data that will be transmitted.

buf_len   Number of octets to transmit.

timeout_ms   Timeout in milliseconds.

end   End-of-transfer flag (see Note #2).

p_err   Pointer to variable that will receive the return error code from this function.

              USBD_ERR_NONE
              USBD_ERR_DEV_INVALID_NBR
              USBD_ERR_DEV_INVALID_STATE
              USBD_ERR_EP_INVALID_ADDR
              USBD_ERR_EP_INVALID_STATE
              USBD_ERR_EP_INVALID_TYPE

```
USBD_ERR_OS_TIMEOUT
USBD_ERR_OS_ABORT
USBD_ERR_OS_FAIL
```

RETURNED VALUE

Number of octets transmitted, If no error(s).

0, otherwise.

CALLERS

USB device class drivers.

NOTES / WARNINGS

- This function blocks until:

    - All data is transmitted, or

    - An error occurred.

    - Transfer does not complete in the period specified by **timeout_ms**.

- If end-of-transfer is set and transfer length is multiple of maximum packet size, a zero-length packet is transferred to indicate a short transfer to the host.

A-4-12 USBD_IntrTxAsync()

Receives data on interrupt OUT endpoint asynchronously.

usbd_core.h/usbd_core.c

```
void  USBD_IntrTxAsync (CPU_INT08U       dev_nbr,
                        CPU_INT08U       ep_addr,
                        void             *p_buf,
                        CPU_INT32U       buf_len,
                        USBD_ASYNC_FNCT  async_fnct,
                        void             *p_async_arg,
                        CPU_BOOLEAN      end,
                        USBD_ERR         *p_err);
```

dev_nbr   Device number.

ep_addr   Endpoint address.

p_buf   Pointer to buffer of data that will be transmitted

buf_len   Number of octets to transmit.

async_fnct   Function that will be invoked upon completion of transmit operation.

p_async_arg   Pointer to argument that will be passed as parameter of async_fnct.

end   End-of-transfer flag (see Note #2).

p_err   Pointer to variable that will receive the return error code from this function.

               USBD_ERR_NONE
               USBD_ERR_DEV_INVALID_NBR
               USBD_ERR_DEV_INVALID_STATE

USBD_ERR_EP_INVALID_ADDR

USBD_ERR_EP_INVALID_STATE

USBD_ERR_EP_INVALID_TYPE

USBD_ERR_OS_TIMEOUT

USBD_ERR_OS_ABORT

USBD_ERR_OS_FAIL

RETURNED VALUE

None.

CALLERS

USB device class drivers.

NOTES / WARNINGS

The callback specified by **async_fnct** has the following prototype.

```
void  USB_AsyncFnct (CPU_INT08U   dev_nbr,
                     CPU_INT08U   ep_addr,
                     void        *p_buf,
                     CPU_INT32U   buf_len,
                     CPU_INT32U   xfer_len,
                     void        *p_arg,
                     USBD_ERR     err);
```

Argument(s):

dev_nbr   Device number.

ep_addr   Endpoint address.

p_buf   Pointer to buffer of data that will be transmitted.

buf_len   Buffer length.

xfer_len   Number of byte transmitted.

p_arg   Pointer to function argument.

err   Error status.

      USBD_ERR_NONE
      USBD_ERR_EP_ABORT

If end-of-transfer is set and transfer length is multiple of maximum packet size, a zero-length packet is transferred to indicate a short transfer to the host.

A-4-13 USBD_EP_RxZLP()

Receives zero-length packet from the host.

FILES

usbd_core.h/usbd_ep.c

PROTOTYPE

```
void  USBD_EP_RxZLP (CPU_INT08U   dev_nbr,
                     CPU_INT08U   ep_addr,
                     CPU_INT16U   timeout_ms,
                     USBD_ERR     *p_err);
```

ARGUMENTS

dev_nbr   Pointer to USB device driver structure.

ep_addr   Pointer to buffer of data that will be transmitted.

timeout_ms   Timeout in milliseconds.

p_err   Pointer to variable that will receive the return error code from this function.

             USBD_ERR_OS_NONE
             USBD_ERR_DEV_INVALID_NBR
             USBD_ERR_EP_INVALID_ADDR
             USBD_ERR_EP_INVALID_STATE
             USBD_ERR_OS_TIMEOUT
             USBD_ERR_OS_ABORT
             USBD_ERR_OS_FAIL

RETURNED VALUE

None.

CALLERS

USBD_CtrlRx()
USBD_CtrlRxStatus()
USB device class drivers.

NOTES / WARNINGS

None.

A-4-14 USBD_EP_TxZLP()

Sends zero-length packet from the host.

FILES

usbd_core.h/usbd_ep.c

PROTOTYPE

```
void  USBD_EP_RxZLP (CPU_INT08U   dev_nbr,
                     CPU_INT08U   ep_addr,
                     CPU_INT16U   timeout_ms,
                     USBD_ERR    *p_err);
```

ARGUMENTS

dev_nbr   Pointer to USB device driver structure.

ep_addr   Pointer to buffer of data that will be transmitted.

timeout_ms   Timeout in milliseconds.

p_err   Pointer to variable that will receive the return error code from this function.

        USBD_ERR_OS_NONE
        USBD_ERR_DEV_INVALID_NBR
        USBD_ERR_EP_INVALID_ADDR
        USBD_ERR_EP_INVALID_STATE
        USBD_ERR_OS_TIMEOUT
        USBD_ERR_OS_ABORT
        USBD_ERR_OS_FAIL

RETURNED VALUE

None.

CALLERS

USBD_CtrlTxStatus()
USB device class drivers.

NOTES / WARNINGS

None.

A-4-15 USBD_EP_Abort()

Abort I/O transfer on endpoint.

FILES

usbd_core.h/usbd_ep.c

PROTOTYPE

```
void  USBD_EP_Abort (CPU_INT08U   dev_nbr,
                     CPU_INT08U   ep_addr,
                     USBD_ERR    *p_err);
```

ARGUMENTS

dev_nbr   Device number.

ep_addr   Endpoint address.

p_err   Pointer to variable that will receive the return error code from this function.

          USBD_ERR_NONE
          USBD_ERR_DEV_INVALID_NBR
          USBD_ERR_EP_INVALID_ADDR
          USBD_ERR_EP_INVALID_STATE
          USBD_ERR_EP_ABORT
          USBD_ERR_EP_OS_FAIL

RETURNED VALUE

None.

CALLERS

USBD_EP_Stall( )
USB device class drivers.

NOTES / WARNINGS

None.

A-4-16 USBD_EP_Stall()

Modify stall state condition on non-control endpoints.

FILES

usbd_core.h/usbd_ep.c

PROTOTYPE

```
void  USBD_EP_Stall (CPU_INT08U    dev_nbr,
                     CPU_INT08U    ep_addr,
                     CPU_BOOLEAN   state,
                     USBD_ERR      *p_err)
```

ARGUMENTS

dev_nbr   Device number.

ep_addr   Line control change notification callback (see note #1).

state   Endpoint stall state.

DEF_SET	Set stall condition.
DEF_NO	Clear stall condition.

p_err   Pointer to variable that will receive the return error code from this function.

USBD_ERR_NONE
USBD_ERR_DEV_INVALID_ARG
USBD_ERR_EP_INVALID_ADDR
USBD_ERR_EP_INVALID_STATE
USBD_ERR_EP_STALL
USBD_ERR_EP_ABORT
USBD_ERR_OS_FAIL

RETURNED VALUE

None.

CALLERS

USBD_EP_Close( )
USBD_StdReqEP( )
USB device class drivers.

NOTES / WARNINGS

None.

A-4-17 USBD_EP_IsStalled()

Gets stall status of non-control endpoint

usbd_core.h/usbd_ep.c

```
CPU_BOOLEAN  USBD_EP_IsStalled (CPU_INT08U   dev_nbr,
                                CPU_INT08U   ep_addr,
                                USBD_ERR     *p_err);
```

dev_nbr   Device number.

ep_addr   Pointer to the structure where the current line coding will be stored.

p_err   Pointer to variable that will receive the return error code from this function.

            USBD_ERR_NONE
            USBD_ERR_DEV_INVALID_ARG
            USBD_ERR_EP_INVALID_ADDR

DEF_TRUE,   if endpoint is stalled.

DEF_FALSE,   otherwise.

USBD_StdReqEP()
USB device class drivers.
Application.

None.

A-4-18 USBD_EP_GetMaxPktSize()

Retrieves endpoint's maximum packet size

FILES

usbd_core.h/usbd_ep.c

PROTOTYPE

```
CPU_INT16U  USBD_EP_GetMaxPktSize (CPU_INT08U   dev_nbr,
                                   CPU_INT08U   ep_addr,
                                   USBD_ERR    *p_err);
```

ARGUMENTS

dev_nbr   Device number.

ep_addr   Endpoint address.

p_err   Pointer to variable that will receive the return error code from this function.

        USBD_ERR_NONE
        USBD_ERR_DEV_INVALID_NBR
        USBD_ERR_EP_INVALID_ADDR
        USBD_ERR_EP_INVALID_STATE

RETURNED VALUE

Maximum packet size,   If no error(s).

0,   otherwise.

CALLERS

Application.

NOTES / WARNINGS

None.

A-4-19 USBD_EP_GetMaxPhyNbr()

Get the maximum physical endpoint number.

FILES

usbd_core.h/usbd_ep.c

PROTOTYPE

```
CPU_INT08U  USBD_EP_GetMaxPhyNbr (CPU_INT08U  dev_nbr)
```

ARGUMENTS

dev_nbr   Device number.

RETURNED VALUE

Maximum physical endpoint number, If no error(s).

USBD_EP_PHY_NONE, otherwise.

CALLERS

USB device controllers drivers.

Application.

NOTES / WARNINGS

None.

A-4-20 USBD_EP_GetMaxNbrOpen()

Retrieve maximum number of opened endpoints

FILES

usbd_core.h/usbd_ep.c

PROTOTYPE

```
CPU_INT08U  USBD_EP_GetMaxNbrOpen (CPU_INT08U dev_nbr);
```

ARGUMENTS

dev_nbr   Device number.

RETURNED VALUE

Maximum number of opened endpoints, If no errors.

0, otherwise.

CALLERS

USB device controllers drivers.

Application.

NOTES / WARNINGS

None.

A-5 CORE OS FUNCTIONS

A-5-1 USBD_OS_Init()

Initialize USB RTOS layer internal objects.

FILES

usbd_internal.h/usbd_os.c

PROTOTYPE

```
void  USBD_OS_Init (USBD_ERR  *p_err);
```

ARGUMENTS

p_err   Pointer to variable that will receive the return error code from this function.

RETURNED VALUE

None.

CALLERS

USBD_Init()

IMPLEMENTATION GUIDELINES

- The followings RTOS resources are required by the stack and should be allocated in when this function is called.

  - One task for core and asynchronous events.

  - One queue that can hold up to **USBD_CORE_EVENT_NBR_TOTAL** events.

  - **USBD_CFG_MAX_NBR_DEV** x **USBD_CFG_MAX_NBR_EP_OPEN** semaphores for endpoints operations.

- If tracing is enabled, a semaphore and a task to manage debug events allocation and debug events processing respectively.

If any error happen, **USBD_ERR_OS_INIT_FAIL** should be assigned to **p_err** and the function should return immediately. Otherwise, **USBD_ERR_NONE** should be assigned to **p_err**.

A-5-2 USBD_CoreTaskHandler()

Process all core events and operations.

FILES

usbd_internal.h/usbd_core.c

PROTOTYPE

```
void  USBD_CoreTaskHandler (void);
```

ARGUMENTS

None.

RETURNED VALUE

None.

CALLERS

USB RTOS layer.

IMPLEMENTATION GUIDELINES

Typically, the RTOS layer should create a shell task for core events. The primary purpose of the shell task is to run USBD_CoreTaskHandler().

A-5-3 USBD_DbgTaskHandler()

Process all pending debug events generated by the core.

FILES

usbd_internal.h/usbd_core.c

PROTOTYPE

```
void  USBD_DbgTaskHandler (void);
```

ARGUMENTS

None.

RETURNED VALUE

None.

CALLERS

USB RTOS layer.

IMPLEMENTATION GUIDELINES

- Typically, the RTOS layer code should create a shell task to process debug events generated by the core. The primary purpose of the shell task is to run USBD_DbgTaskHandler().

- This function is only present in the code if trace option is enabled in the stack.

A-5-4 USBD_OS_EP_SignalCreate()

Creates a signal/semaphore for endpoints operations.

FILES

usbd_internal.h/usbd_os.c

PROTOTYPE

```
void USBD_OS_EP_SignalCreate (CPU_INT08U   dev_nbr,
                              CPU_INT08U   ep_ix,
                              USBD_ERR    *p_err);
```

ARGUMENTS

dev_nbr   Device number.

ep_ix   Endpoint index.

p_err   Pointer to variable that will receive the return error code from this function.

RETURNED VALUE

None.

CALLERS

Endpoints open functions.

IMPLEMENTATION GUIDELINES

■   The purpose of this function is to allocate a signal or a semaphore for the specified endpoint.

- Typically, the RTOS layer code should create a two-dimensional array to store the signals/semaphores handlers. The **dev_nbr** and **ep_ix** are used to index this array.

  - **dev_nbr** ranges between 0 and **USBD_CFG_MAX_NBR_DEV**.

  - **ep_ix** ranges between 0 and **USBD_CFG_MAX_NBR_EP_OPEN**.

- In case the creation fails, **USBD_ERR_OS_SIGNAL_CREATE** should be assigned to **p_err.** Otherwise, **USBD_ERR_NONE** should be assigned to **p_err**.

A-5-5 USBD_OS_EP_SignalDel()

Deletes a signal/semaphore.

usbd_internal.h/usbd_os.c

```
void  USBD_OS_EP_SignalDel (CPU_INT08U  dev_nbr,
                            CPU_INT08U  ep_ix);
```

dev_nbr   Device number.

ep_ix   Endpoint index.

None.

Endpoints close functions.

A call to this function should delete the signal / semaphore associated to the specified endpoint.

A-5-6 USBD_OS_EP_SignalPend()

Waits for a signal/semaphore to become available.

FILES

usbd_internal.h/usbd_os.c

PROTOTYPE

```
void  USBD_OS_EP_SignalPend (CPU_INT08U   dev_nbr,
                             CPU_INT08U   ep_ix,
                             CPU_INT16U   timeout_ms,
                             USBD_ERR     *p_err);
```

ARGUMENTS

dev_nbr   Device number.

ep_ix   Endpoint index.

timeout_ms   Timeout in milliseconds.

p_err   Pointer to variable that will receive the return error code from this function.

RETURNED VALUE

None.

CALLERS

Endpoints Rx/Tx functions.

IMPLEMENTATION GUIDELINES

A call to this function should pend on the signal / semaphore associated to the specified endpoint.

Table A-1 describes the error codes that should be assigned to **p_err** depending on the operation result.

Operation result	Error code
No error.	USBD_ERR_NONE
Pend timeout	USBD_ERR_OS_TIMEOUT
Pend aborted	USBD_ERR_OS_ABORT
Pend failed for any other reason	USBD_ERR_OS_FAIL

Table A-1 **p_err assignment in function of operation result.**

A-5-7 USBD_OS_EP_SignalAbort()

Aborts any wait operation on signal/semaphore.

FILES

usbd_internal.h/usbd_os.c

PROTOTYPE

```
void  USBD_OS_EP_SignalAbort (CPU_INT08U   dev_nbr,
                              CPU_INT08U   ep_ix,
                              USBD_ERR    *p_err);
```

ARGUMENTS

dev_nbr   Device number.

ep_ix   Endpoint index.

p_err   Pointer to variable that will receive the return error code from this function.

RETURNED VALUE

None.

CALLERS

Endpoints abort functions.

IMPLEMENTATION GUIDELINES

This function should abort all pend operations performed on the signal / semaphore associated to the specified endpoint.

If any error happen, USBD_ERR_OS_FAIL should be assigned to p_err. Otherwise, USBD_ERR_NONE should be assigned to p_err.

A-5-8 USBD_OS_EP_SignalPost()

Makes a signal/semaphore available.

usbd_internal.h/usbd_os.c

```
void    USBD_OS_EP_SignalPost (CPU_INT08U   dev_nbr,
                               CPU_INT08U   ep_ix,
                               USBD_ERR     *p_err);
```

dev_nbr   Device number.

ep_ix   Endpoint index.

p_err   Pointer to variable that will receive the return error code from this function.

None.

Endpoints transfer complete functions.

A call to this function should post the signal / semaphore associated to the specified endpoint.

In case the post fail, USBD_ERR_OS_FAIL should be assigned to p_err. Otherwise, USBD_ERR_NONE should be assigned to p_err.

A-5-9 USBD_OS_CoreEventPut()

Queues a core event.

FILES

usbd_internal.h/usbd_os.c

PROTOTYPE

```
void  USBD_OS_CoreEventPut (void  *p_event);
```

ARGUMENTS

p_event   Pointer to core event.

RETURNED VALUE

None.

CALLERS

Endpoints and bus event handlers.

IMPLEMENTATION GUIDELINES

A call to this function should add the passed event to the core events queue.

A-5-10 USBD_OS_CoreEventGet()

Wait until a core event is ready.

FILES

usbd_internal.h/usbd_os.c

PROTOTYPE

```
void  *USBD_OS_CoreEventGet (CPU_INT32U   timeout_ms,
                             USBD_ERR     *p_err);
```

ARGUMENTS

timeout_ms   Timeout in milliseconds.

p_err   Pointer to variable that will receive the return error code from this function.

RETURNED VALUE

Pointer to core event,   if no errors.

Null pointer,   otherwise.

CALLERS

USBD_CoreTaskHandler()

IMPLEMENTATION GUIDELINES

A call to this function should block until an event is added to queue and return it.

Table A-1 describes the error codes that should be assigned to **p_err** depending on the operation result.

A-5-11 USBD_OS_DbgEventRdy()

Signals debug event handler task.

FILES

usbd_internal.h/usbd_os.c

PROTOTYPE

```
void  USBD_OS_DbgEventRdy (void);
```

ARGUMENTS

None.

RETURNED VALUE

None.

CALLERS

Debug functions.

IMPLEMENTATION GUIDELINES

A call to this function should post the signal / semaphore that resume the debug task.

A-5-12 USBD_OS_DbgEventWait ()

Waits until a trace event is available.

FILES

usbd_internal.h/usbd_os.c

PROTOTYPE

```
void  USBD_OS_DbgEventWait (void);
```

ARGUMENTS

None.

RETURNED VALUE

None.

CALLERS

USBD_DbgTaskHandler()

IMPLEMENTATION GUIDELINES

A call to this function should pend on the signal / semaphore that resume the debug task.

A-6 DEVICE DRIVERS CALLBACKS FUNCTIONS

A-6-1 USBD_EP_RxCmpl()

Notifies the stack that an OUT transfer is completed.

FILES

usbd_core.h/usbd_ep.c

PROTOTYPE

```
void  USBD_EP_RxCmpl (USBD_DRV    *p_drv,
                      CPU_INT08U   ep_log_nbr);
```

ARGUMENTS

p_drv   Pointer to device driver structure.

ep_log_nbr Endpoint logical number.

RETURNED VALUE

None.

CALLERS

USB device controller driver ISR

NOTES / WARNINGS

None.

A-6-2 USBD_EP_TxCmpl()

Notifies the stack that an IN transfer is completed.

FILES

usbd_core.h/usbd_ep.c

PROTOTYPE

```
void  USBD_EP_RxCmpl (USBD_DRV    *p_drv,
                      CPU_INT08U   ep_log_nbr);
```

ARGUMENTS

p_drv   Pointer to device driver structure.

ep_log_nbr   Endpoint logical number.

RETURNED VALUE

None.

CALLERS

USB device controller driver ISR

NOTES / WARNINGS

None.

A-6-3 USBD_EventConn()

Notifies the stack the device is connected to the host.

FILES

usbd_core.h/usbd_core.c

PROTOTYPE

```
void  USBD_EventConn (USBD_DRV  *p_drv);
```

ARGUMENTS

p_drv   Pointer to device driver structure.

RETURNED VALUE

None.

CALLERS

USB device controller driver ISR

NOTES / WARNINGS

None.

A-6-4 USBD_EventDisconn()

Notifies the stack the device is disconnected from the host.

FILES

usbd_core.h/usbd_core.c

PROTOTYPE

```
void  USBD_EventDisconn (USBD_DRV  *p_drv);
```

ARGUMENTS

p_drv   Pointer to device driver structure.

RETURNED VALUE

None.

CALLERS

USB device controller driver ISR

NOTES / WARNINGS

None.

A-6-5 USBD_EventReset()

Notifies the stack a reset event in the bus.

FILES

usbd_core.h/usbd_core.c

PROTOTYPE

```
void  USBD_EventReset(USBD_DRV  *p_drv);
```

ARGUMENTS

p_drv   Pointer to device driver structure.

RETURNED VALUE

None.

CALLERS

USB device controller driver ISR

NOTES / WARNINGS

None.

A-6-6 USBD_EventHS()

This function notifies the stack that a host is high speed capable.

FILES

usbd_core.h/usbd_core.c

PROTOTYPE

```
void  USBD_EventHS(USBD_DRV  *p_drv);
```

ARGUMENTS

p_drv   Pointer to device driver structure.

RETURNED VALUE

None.

CALLERS

USB device controller driver ISR

NOTES / WARNINGS

None.

A-6-7 USBD_EventSuspend()

Notifies the stack a suspend event in the bus.

FILES

usbd_core.h/usbd_core.c

PROTOTYPE

```
void  USBD_EventSuspend (USBD_DRV  *p_drv);
```

ARGUMENTS

p_drv   Pointer to device driver structure.

RETURNED VALUE

None.

CALLERS

USB device controller driver ISR

NOTES / WARNINGS

None.

A-6-8 USBD_EventResume()

Notifies the stack a resume event in the bus.

FILES

usbd_core.h/usbd_core.c

PROTOTYPE

```
void  USBD_EventResume (USBD_DRV  *p_drv);
```

ARGUMENTS

p_drv   Pointer to device driver structure.

RETURNED VALUE

None.

CALLERS

USB device controller driver ISR

NOTES / WARNINGS

None.

A-6-9 USBD_EventSetup()

Notifies the stack that a setup transfer has been received.

FILES

usbd_core.h/usbd_core.c

PROTOTYPE

```
void  USBD_EventSetup (USBD_DRV  *p_drv,
                       void      *p_buf);
```

ARGUMENTS

p_drv   Pointer to device driver structure.

p_buf   Pointer to the setup packet.

RETURNED VALUE

None.

CALLERS

USB device controller driver ISR

NOTES / WARNINGS

None.

A-7 TRACE FUNCTIONS

A-7-1 USBD_Trace()

Outputs debug information from the core. Users must implement this function if trace functionality is enabled (USBD_CFG_DBG_TRACE is defined to DEF_ENABLED).

FILES

usbd_core.h

PROTOTYPE

```
void  USBD_Trace (const CPU_CHAR  *p_str);
```

ARGUMENTS

p_drv   Pointer to the string containing debug information.

RETURNED VALUE

None.

CALLERS

USB core debug task handler.

NOTES / WARNINGS

None.

Appendix A

B

Device Controller Driver API Reference

This appendix provides a reference to the Device Controller Driver API. Each user-accessible service is presented in alphabetical order. The following information is provided for each of the services:

- A brief description

- The function prototype

- The filename of the source code

- A description of the arguments passed to the function

- A description of returned value(s)

- Specific notes and warnings regarding use of the service

B-1 DEVICE DRIVER FUNCTIONS

B-1-1 USBD_DrvInit()

The first function within the Device Driver API is the device driver initialization/**Init()** function. This function is called by **USBD_DevStart()** exactly once for each specific device added by the application. If multiple instances of the same device are present on the development board, then this function is called for each instance of the device. However, applications should not try to add the same specific device more than once. If a device fails to initialize, it is recommend debugging to find and correct the cause of failure.

Note: This function relies heavily on the implementation of several device board support package (BSP) functions. See section B-2 "Device Driver BSP Functions" on page 418 for more information on device BSP functions.

FILES

Every device driver's **usbd_drv.c**

PROTOTYPE

```
static void USBD_DrvInit (USBD_DRV   *p_drv
                          USBD_ERR   *p_err);
```

Note that since every device driver function is accessed only by function pointer via the device driver's API structure, they do not need to be globally available and should therefore be declared as '**static**'.

ARGUMENTS

p_drv   Pointer to USB device driver structure.

p_err   Pointer to variable that will receive the return error code from this function.

RETURNED VALUE

None.

USBD_DevInit() via 'p_drv_api->Init()'.

NOTES / WARNINGS

The **Init()** function generally performs the following operations, however, depending on the device being initialized, functionality may need to be added or removed:

■ Configure clock gating to the USB device, configure all necessary I/O pins, and configure the host interrupt controller. This is generally performed via the device's BSP function pointer, **Init()**, implemented in **usbd_bsp.c** (see section B-2-1 "USBD_BSP_Init()" on page 418).

■ Reset USB controller or USB controller registers.

■ Disable and clear pending interrupts (should already be cleared).

■ Set the device address to zero.

■ For DMA devices: Allocate memory for all necessary descriptors. This is performed via calls to µC/LIB's memory module. If memory allocation fails, set **p_err** to **USBD_ERR_ALLOC** and return.

■ Set **p_err** to **USBD_ERR_NONE** if initialization proceeded as expected. Otherwise, set **p_err** to an appropriate device error code.

B-1-2 USBD_DrvStart()

The second function is the device driver **Start()** function. This function is called once each time a device is started.

FILES

Every device driver's **usbd_drv.c**

PROTOTYPE

```
static void USBD_DrvStart (USBD_DRV  *p_drv
                           USBD_ERR  *p_err);
```

ARGUMENTS

p_drv   Pointer to USB device driver structure.

p_err   Pointer to variable that will receive the return error code from this function.

RETURNED VALUE

None.

CALLERS

USBD_DevStart() via 'p_drv_api->Start()'.

NOTES / WARNINGS

The **Start()** function performs the following items:

- Typically, activates the pull-up on the D+ pin to simulate attachment to host. Some MCUs/MPUs have an internal pull-up that is activated by a device controller register; for others, this may be a general purpose I/O pin. This is generally performed via the device's BSP function pointer, **Conn()**, implemented in **usbd_bsp.c** (see section B-2-2 on page 419). The device's BSP ConnO is also responsible for enabling the host interrupt controller.

- Clear all interrupt flags.

- Locally enable interrupts on the hardware device. The host interrupt controller should have already been configured within the device driver **Init()** function.

- Enable the controller.

- Set **p_err** equal to **USBD_ERR_NONE** if no errors have occurred. Otherwise, set **p_err** to an appropriate device error code.

B-1-3 USBD_DrvStop()

The next function within the device API structure is the device **Stop()** function. This function is called once each time a device is stopped.

FILES

Every device driver's **usbd_drv.c**

PROTOTYPE

```
static void USBD_DrvStop (USBD_DRV  *p_drv);
```

ARGUMENTS

p_drv   Pointer to USB device driver structure.

RETURNED VALUE

None.

CALLERS

USBD_DevStop() via 'p_drv_api->Stop()'.

NOTES / WARNINGS

Typically, the **Stop()** function performs the following operations:

■ Disable the controller.

■ Clear and locally disable interrupts on the hardware device.

■ Disconnect from the USB host (e.g, reset the pull-up on the D+ pin). This is generally performed via the device's BSP function pointer, **Disconn()**, implemented in **usbd_bsp.c** (see section B-2-3 on page 420).

B-1-4 USBD_DrvAddrSet()

The next API function to implement is the device address set/**AddrSet()** function. The device address set function is called while processing a **SET_ADDRESS** setup request.

FILES

Every device driver's **usbd_drv.c**

PROTOTYPE

```
static CPU_BOOLEAN USBD_DrvAddrSet (USBD_DRV    *p_drv,
                                    CPU_INT08U   dev_addr);
```

ARGUMENTS

p_drv   Pointer to USB device driver structure.

dev_addr   Device address assigned by the host.

RETURNED VALUE

DEF_OK,   if NO error(s).

DEF_FAIL, otherwise.

CALLERS

USBD_StdReqDev() via 'p_drv_api->AddrSet()'.

NOTES / WARNINGS

■ For device controllers that have hardware assistance to enable the device address after the status stage has completed, the assignment of the device address can also be combined with enabling the device address mode.

■ For device controllers that change the device address immediately, without waiting the status phase to complete, see USBD_DrvAddrEn().

B-1-5 USBD_DrvAddrEn()

The next function in the device API structure is the device address enable/**AddrEn( )** function.

FILES

Every device driver's **usbd_drv.c**

PROTOTYPE

```
static CPU_BOOLEAN USBD_DrvAddrEn (USBD_DRV    *p_drv
                                   CPU_INT08U   dev_addr);
```

ARGUMENTS

p_drv   Pointer to USB device driver structure.

dev_addr   Device address assigned by the host.

RETURNED VALUE

None.

CALLERS

USBD_StdReqHandler( ) via 'p_drv_api->AddrEn( )'.

NOTES / WARNINGS

■   For device controllers that have hardware assistance to enable the device address after the status stage has completed, no operation needs to be performed.

■   For device controllers that change the device address immediately, without waiting the status phase to complete, the device address must be set and enabled.

B-1-6 USBD_DrvCfgSet()

Bring device into configured state.

Every device driver's **usbd_drv.c**

```
static CPU_BOOLEAN USBD_DrvCfgSet (USBD_DRV    *p_drv,
                                   CPU_INT08U   cfg_val);
```

p_drv   Pointer to USB device driver structure.

cfg_val   Configuration value.

DEF_OK,   if NO error(s).

DEF_FAIL,   otherwise.

USBD_CfgOpen() via 'p_drv_api->CfgSet()'.

Typically, the set configuration function sets the device as configured. For some controllers, this may not be necessary.

B-1-7 USBD_DrvCfgClr()

Bring device into de-configured state.

FILES

Every device driver's **usbd_drv.c**

PROTOTYPE

```
static void USBD_DrvCfgClr (USBD_DRV   *p_drv,
                           CPU_INT08U  cfg_val);
```

ARGUMENTS

p_drv   Pointer to USB device driver structure.

cfg_val   Configuration value.

RETURNED VALUE

None.

CALLERS

USBD_CfgClose() via '**p_drv_api->CfgClr()**'.

NOTES / WARNINGS

- Typically, the clear configuration function sets the device as not being configured. For some controllers, this may not be necessary.

- This functions in invoked after a bus reset or before the status stage of some **SET_CONFIGURATION** requests.

B-1-8 USBD_DrvGetFrameNbr()

Retrieve current frame number.

FILES

Every device driver's **usbd_drv.c**

PROTOTYPE

```
static CPU_INT16U USBD_DrvGetFrameNbr (USBD_DRV  *p_drv);
```

ARGUMENTS

p_drv   Pointer to USB device driver structure.

RETURNED VALUE

Frame number.

CALLERS

None.

NOTES / WARNINGS

None.

B-1-9 USBD_DrvEP_Open()

Open and configure a device endpoint, given its characteristics (e.g., endpoint type, endpoint address, maximum packet size, etc).

FILES

Every device driver's **usbd_drv.c**

PROTOTYPE

```
static void USBD_DrvEP_Open (USBD_DEV    *p_drv,
                             CPU_INT08U   ep_addr,
                             CPU_INT08U   ep_type,
                             CPU_INT16U   max_pkt_size,
                             CPU_INT08U   transaction_frame,
                             USBD_ERR    *p_err);
```

ARGUMENTS

p_drv   Pointer to USB device driver structure.

ep_addr   Endpoint address.

ep_type   Endpoint type:

  USB_EP_TYPE_CTRL,
  USB_EP_TYPE_ISOC,
  USB_EP_TYPE_BULK,
  USB_EP_TYPE_INTR.

max_pkt_size   Maximum packet size.

transaction_frame   Endpoint transactions per frame.

p_err   Pointer to variable that will receive the return error code from this function.

RETURNED VALUE

None.

- USBD_EP_Open( ) via 'p_drv_api->EP_Open( )'

- USBD_CtrlOpen( )

NOTES / WARNINGS

- Typically, the endpoint open function performs the following operations:

  - Validate endpoint address, type and maximum packet size.

  - Configure endpoint information in the device controller. This may include not only assigning the type and maximum packet size, but also making certain that the endpoint is successfully configured (or *realized* or *mapped*). For some device controllers, this may not be necessary.

- If the endpoint address is valid, then the endpoint open function should validate the attributes allowed by the hardware endpoint.

  - **max_pkt_size** is the maximum packet size the endpoint can send or receive. The endpoint open function should validate the maximum packet size to match hardware capabilities.

B-1-10 USBD_DrvEP_Close()

Close a device endpoint, and un-initialize/clear endpoint configuration in hardware.

FILES

Every device driver's **usbd_drv.c**

PROTOTYPE

```
static void USBD_DrvEP_Close (USBD_DRV    *p_drv,
                              CPU_INT08U   ep_addr);
```

ARGUMENTS

p_drv   Pointer to USB device driver structure.

ep_addr   Endpoint address.

RETURNED VALUE

None.

CALLERS

▧ USBD_EP_Close() via 'p_drv_api->EP_Close()'

▧ USBD_CtrlOpen()

NOTES / WARNINGS

Typically, the endpoint close function clears the endpoint information in the device controller. For some controllers, this may not be necessary.

B-1-11 USBD_DrvEP_RxStart()

Configure endpoint with buffer to receive data.

FILES

Every device driver's **usbd_drv.c**

PROTOTYPE

```
static void USBD_DrvEP_RxStart (USBD_DRV    *p_drv,
                                CPU_INT08U   ep_addr,
                                CPU_INT08U  *p_buf,
                                CPU_INT32U   buf_len,
                                USBD_ERR    *p_err);
```

ARGUMENTS

p_drv   Pointer to USB device driver structure.

ep_addr   Endpoint address.

p_buf   Pointer to data buffer.

buf_len   Length of the buffer.

p_err   Pointer to variable that will receive the return error code from this function.

RETURNED VALUE

None.

CALLERS

■ USBD_EP_Rx() via 'p_drv_api->EP_Rx()'

■ USBD_EP_Process()

NOTES / WARNINGS

Typically, the function to configure the endpoint receive transaction performs the following operations:

- Determine maximum transaction length, given the specified length of the buffer (`buf_len`).

- Setup receive transaction.

B-1-12 USBD_DrvEP_Rx()

Receive the specified amount of data from device endpoint.

FILES

Every device driver's **usbd_drv.c**

PROTOTYPE

```
static CPU_INT32U USBD_DrvEP_Rx (USBD_DRV    *p_drv,
                                 CPU_INT08U   ep_addr,
                                 CPU_INT08U  *p_buf,
                                 CPU_INT32U   buf_len,
                                 USBD_ERR    *p_err);
```

ARGUMENTS

p_drv   Pointer to USB device driver structure.

ep_addr   Endpoint address.

p_buf   Pointer to data buffer.

buf_len   Length of the buffer.

p_err   Pointer to variable that will receive the return error code from this function.

RETURNED VALUE

Number of octets received,   if NO error(s)

0,   otherwise

CALLERS

▪ USBD_EP_Rx() via 'p_drv_api->EP_Rx()'

▪ USBD_EP_Process()

NOTES / WARNINGS

Typically, the receive from endpoint function performs the following operations:

▣ Check if packet has been received and is ready to be read.

▣ Determine packet length.

▣ Copy the data received into the buffer referenced by **p_buf**. If the USB device controller is working in DMA mode, no CPU copy will be required as it was already done by the DMA engine of the USB device controller.

▣ If an error occurred during the transfer (i.e. overflow or buffer error), the function must set the value of **p_err** to **USBD_ERR_RX** and treat the transfer data as invalid.

▣ Clear endpoint buffer to allow next packet to be received. For some controllers, this may not be necessary.

B-1-13 USBD_DrvEP_RxZLP()

Receive zero-length packet from endpoint.

FILES

Every device driver's **usbd_drv.c**

PROTOTYPE

```
static void USBD_DrvEP_RxZLP (USBD_DRV    *p_drv,
                             CPU_INT08U   ep_addr,
                             USBD_ERR    *p_err);
```

ARGUMENTS

p_drv   Pointer to USB device driver structure.

ep_addr   Endpoint address.

p_err   Pointer to variable that will receive the return error code from this function.

RETURNED VALUE

None.

CALLERS

USBD_EP_RxZLP() via 'p_drv_api->EP_RxZLP()'

NOTES / WARNINGS

None.

B-1-14 USBD_DrvEP_Tx()

Configure endpoint with buffer to transmit data.

FILES

Every device driver's **usbd_drv.c**

PROTOTYPE

```
static CPU_INT32U USBD_DrvEP_Tx (USBD_DRV    *p_drv,
                                 CPU_INT08U   ep_addr,
                                 CPU_INT08U  *p_buf,
                                 CPU_INT32U   buf_len,
                                 USBD_ERR    *p_err);
```

ARGUMENTS

p_drv   Pointer to USB device driver structure.

ep_addr   Endpoint address.

p_buf   Pointer to data buffer.

buf_len   Length of the buffer.

p_err   Pointer to variable that will receive the return error code from this function.

RETURNED VALUE

Number of octets transmitted,   if NO error(s).

0,   otherwise.

CALLERS

▪   USBD_EP_Tx( ) via 'p_drv_api->EP_Tx( )'

▪   USBD_EP_Process( )

NOTES / WARNINGS

Typically, the function to configure the endpoint receive transaction performs the following operations:

▪ Check if data can be transmitted.

▪ Write data to device endpoint.

▪ Configure the packet length in USB device controller. This is often necessary when the packet is shorter than the maximum packet size. Depending on the USB controller, this operation may need to be performed prior to writing the data to the device endpoint.

B-1-15 USBD_DrvEP_TxStart()

Transmit the specified amount of data to device endpoint.

FILES

Every device driver's **usbd_drv.c**

PROTOTYPE

```
static void USBD_DrvEP_TxStart (USBD_DRV    *p_drv,
                                CPU_INT08U   ep_addr,
                                CPU_INT08U  *p_buf,
                                CPU_INT32U   buf_len,
                                USBD_ERR    *p_err);
```

ARGUMENTS

p_drv   Pointer to USB device driver structure.

ep_addr   Endpoint address.

p_buf   Pointer to data buffer.

buf_len   Length of the buffer.

p_err   Pointer to variable that will receive the return error code from this function.

RETURNED VALUE

Number of octets transmitted,   if NO error(s).

0,   otherwise.

CALLERS

■ USBD_EP_Tx() via 'p_drv_api->EP_TxStart()'

■ USBD_EP_Process()

NOTES / WARNINGS

Typically, the function to configure the endpoint receive transaction performs the following operations:

▪ Trigger packet transmission.

B-1-16 USBD_DrvEP_TxZLP()

Transmit zero-length packet to endpoint.

FILES

Every device driver's **usbd_drv.c**

PROTOTYPE

```
static void USBD_DrvEP_TxZLP (USBD_DRV    *p_drv,
                             CPU_INT08U   ep_addr,
                             USBD_ERR    *p_err);
```

ARGUMENTS

p_drv   Pointer to USB device driver structure.

ep_addr   Endpoint address.

p_err   Pointer to variable that will receive the return error code from this function.

RETURNED VALUE

None.

CALLERS

- USBD_EP_Tx() via 'p_drv_api->EP_TxZLP()'

- USBD_EP_TxZLP()

- USBD_EP_Process()

NOTES / WARNINGS

None.

B-1-17 USBD_DrvEP_Abort()

Abort any pending transfer on endpoint.

FILES

Every device driver's **usbd_drv.c**

PROTOTYPE

```
static CPU_BOOLEAN USBD_DrvEP_Abort (USBD_DRV    *p_drv,
                                     CPU_INT08U   ep_addr);
```

ARGUMENTS

p_drv   Pointer to USB device driver structure.

ep_addr   Endpoint Address.

RETURNED VALUE

DEF_OK,   if NO error(s).

DEF_FAIL,   otherwise.

CALLERS

USBD_URB_Abort() via 'p_drv_api->EP_Abort()'

NOTES / WARNINGS

None.

B-1-18 USBD_DrvEP_Stall()

Set or clear stall condition on endpoint.

FILES

Every device driver's **usbd_drv.c**

PROTOTYPE

```
static CPU_BOOLEAN USBD_DrvEP_Stall (USBD_DRV    *p_drv,
                                     CPU_INT08U   ep_addr,
                                     CPU_BOOLEAN  state);
```

ARGUMENTS

p_drv   Pointer to USB device driver structure.

ep_addr   Endpoint address.

state   Endpoint stall state.

RETURNED VALUE

DEF_OK,   if NO error(s).

DEF_FAIL,   otherwise.

CALLERS

▨ USBD_EP_Stall() via 'p_drv_api->EP_Stall()'

▨ USBD_CtrlStall()

NOTES / WARNINGS

None.

B-1-19 USBD_DrvISR_Handler()

USB device Interrupt Service Routine (ISR) handler.

FILES

Every device driver's **usbd_drv.c**

PROTOTYPE

```
static void USBD_DrvISR_Handler (USBD_DRV  *p_drv);
```

ARGUMENTS

p_drv   Pointer to USB device driver structure.

RETURNED VALUE

None.

CALLERS

Processor level kernel-aware interrupt handler.

NOTES / WARNINGS

None.

B-2 DEVICE DRIVER BSP FUNCTIONS

B-2-1 USBD_BSP_Init()

Initialize board-specific USB controller dependencies.

FILES

Every device driver's **usbd_bsp.c**

PROTOTYPE

```
static void USBD_BSP_Init (USBD_DRV  *p_drv);
```

ARGUMENTS

p_drv   Pointer to USB device driver structure.

RETURNED VALUE

None.

CALLERS

USBD_DrvInit( )

NOTES / WARNINGS

None.

B-2-2 USBD_BSP_Conn()

Enable USB controller connection dependencies.

Every device driver's **usbd_bsp.c**

```
static void USBD_BSP_Conn (void);
```

None.

None.

USBD_DrvStart()

None.

B-2-3 USBD_BSP_Disconn()

Disable USB controller connection dependencies.

FILES

Every device driver's **usbd_bsp.c**

PROTOTYPE

```
static void USBD_BSP_Disconn (void);
```

ARGUMENTS

None.

RETURNED VALUE

None.

CALLERS

USBD_DrvStop( )

NOTES / WARNINGS

None.

C

CDC API Reference

This appendix provides a reference to the µC/USB-Device Communications Device Class (CDC) API and Abstract Control Model (ACM) subclass API. The following information is provided for each of the services:

■ A brief description

■ The function prototype

■ The filename of the source code

■ A description of the arguments passed to the function

■ A description of returned value(s)

■ Specific notes and warnings regarding use of the service

C-1 CDC FUNCTIONS

C-1-1 USBD_CDC_Init()

This function initializes all the internal variables and modules used by the CDC. The initialization function is called by the application exactly once.

FILES

usbd_cdc.h/usbd_cdc.c

PROTOTYPE

```
static void USBD_CDC_Init (USBD_ERR  *p_err);
```

ARGUMENTS

p_err   Pointer to variable that will receive the return error code from this function:

USBD_ERR_NONE

RETURNED VALUE

None.

CALLERS

Application.

NOTES / WARNINGS

None.

C-1-2 USBD_CDC_Add()

This function creates a CDC instance.

usbd_cdc.h/usbd_cdc.c

```
CPU_INT08U  USBD_CDC_Add(CPU_INT08U              subclass,
                         USBD_CDC_SUBCLASS_DRV  *p_subclass_drv,
                         void                   *p_subclass_arg,
                         CPU_INT08U              protocol,
                         CPU_BOOLEAN             notify_en,
                         CPU_INT16U              notify_interval,
                         USBD_ERR               *p_err);
```

subclass   CDC subclass code.

USBD_CDC_SUBCLASS_RSVD	Reserved value
USBD_CDC_SUBCLASS_DLCM	Direct Line Control Model
USBD_CDC_SUBCLASS_ACM	Abstract Control Model
USBD_CDC_SUBCLASS_TCM	Telephone Control Model
USBD_CDC_SUBCLASS_MCC	Multi-Channel Control Model
USBD_CDC_SUBCLASS_CAPICM	CAPI Control Model
USBD_CDC_SUBCLASS_WHCM	Wireless Handset Control Model
USBD_CDC_SUBCLASS_DEV_MGMT	Device Management
USBD_CDC_SUBCLASS_MDLM	Device Management
USBD_CDC_SUBCLASS_OBEX	Obex
USBD_CDC_SUBCLASS_EEM	Ethernet Emulation Model
USBD_CDC_SUBCLASS_NCM	Network Control Model
USBD_CDC_SUBCLASS_VENDOR	Vendor specific

CDC subclass codes are defined in the Universal Serial Bus Class Definitions for Communication Devices Revision 2.1 Table 4.

p_subclass_drv   Pointer to CDC subclass driver.

p_subclass_arg   Pointer to CDC subclass driver argument.

protocol   CDC protocol code.

> USBD_CDC_COMM_PROTOCOL_NONE
> USBD_CDC_COMM_PROTOCOL_AT_V250
> USBD_CDC_COMM_PROTOCOL_AT_PCCA_101
> USBD_CDC_COMM_PROTOCOL_AT_PCCA_101_ANNEX
> USBD_CDC_COMM_PROTOCOL_AT_GSM_7_07
> USBD_CDC_COMM_PROTOCOL_AT_3GPP_27_07
> USBD_CDC_COMM_PROTOCOL_AT_TIA_CDMA
> USBD_CDC_COMM_PROTOCOL_EEM
> USBD_CDC_COMM_PROTOCOL_EXT
> USBD_CDC_COMM_PROTOCOL_VENDOR

> CDC protocol codes are defined in the Universal Serial Bus Class Definitions for Communication Devices Revision 2.1 Table 5.

notify_en   Notification enabled.

> DEF_ENABLED   CDC notifications are enabled.
> DEF_DISABLED   CDC notifications are disabled.

notify_interval   Notification interval in milliseconds.

p_err   Pointer to variable that will receive the return error code from this function.

> USBD_ERR_NONE
> USBD_ERR_ALLOC

RETURNED VALUE

CDC class interface number, if CDC class successfully created.

USBD_CDC_NBR_NONE, otherwise.

CALLERS

CDC Subclass drivers.

NOTES / WARNINGS

The CDC defines a communication class interface consisting of a management element and optionally a notification element. The notification element transports event to the host. The **enable_en** enable notifications in the CDC. The notification are sent to the host using an interrupt endpoint, the interval of the interrupt endpoint is specified by the **notify_interval** parameter.

C-1-3 USBD_CDC_CfgAdd()

Add a CDC instance to specific USB configuration.

usbd_cdc.h/usbd_cdc.c

```
CPU_BOOLEAN  USBD_CDC_CfgAdd (CPU_INT08U   class_nbr,
                              CPU_INT08U   dev_nbr,
                              CPU_INT08U   cfg_nbr,
                              USBD_ERR     *p_err);
```

class_nbr   CDC instance number.

dev_nbr   Device number.

cfg_nbr   Configuration number.

p_err   Pointer to variable that will receive the return error code from this function.

              USBD_ERR_NONE
              USBD_ERR_ALLOC
              USBD_ERR_INVALID_ARG
              USBD_ERR_DEV_INVALID_NBR
              USBD_ERR_DEV_INVALID_STATE
              USBD_ERR_CFG_INVALID_NBR
              USBD_ERR_IF_ALLOC
              USBD_ERR_IF_ALT_ALLOC
              USBD_ERR_IF_INVALID_NBR
              USBD_ERR_IF_GRP_NBR_IN_USE
              USBD_ERR_IF_GRP_ALLOC
              USBD_ERR_EP_NONE_AVAIL
              USBD_ERR_EP_ALLOC

RETURNED VALUE

DEF_OK,   if CDC class instance was added to device configuration successfully.

DEF_FAIL,   otherwise.

CALLERS

CDC Subclass drivers.

NOTES / WARNINGS

None.

C-1-4 USBD_CDC_IsConn()

Determine if CDC instance is connected.

FILES

usbd_cdc.h/usbd_cdc.c

PROTOTYPE

```
CPU_BOOLEAN  USBD_CDC_IsConn (CPU_INT08U  class_nbr)
```

ARGUMENTS

class_nbr   CDC instance number.

RETURNED VALUE

DEF_OK,   if CDC instance is connected and device is not in suspended state.

DEF_FAIL,   otherwise.

CALLERS

- CDC Subclass drivers

- Application

NOTES / WARNINGS

If the USBD_CDC_IsConn() returns DEF_OK, than the CDC instance is ready for management, notification, read and write operations.

C-1-5 USBD_CDC_DataIF_Add()

Add a data interface class to CDC.

FILES

usbd_cdc.h/usbd_cdc.c

PROTOTYPE

```
CPU_INT08U  USBD_CDC_DataIF_Add (CPU_INT08U   class_nbr,
                                 CPU_BOOLEAN  isoc_en,
                                 CPU_INT08U   protocol,
                                 USBD_ERR     *p_err);
```

ARGUMENTS

class_nbr   CDC instance number.

isoc_en   Data interface isochronous enable.

DEF_ENABLED	Data interface uses isochronous endpoints.
DEF_DISABLED	Data interface uses bulk endpoints.

protocol   Data interface protocol code:

USBD_CDC_DATA_PROTOCOL_NONE	No class specific protocol required.
USBD_CDC_DATA_PROTOCOL_NTB	Network Transfer Block.
USBD_CDC_DATA_PROTOCOL_PHY	Physical interface protocol for ISDN BRI.
USBD_CDC_DATA_PROTOCOL_HDLC	HDLC.
USBD_CDC_DATA_PROTOCOL_TRANS	Transparent.
USBD_CDC_DATA_PROTOCOL_Q921M	Management protocol for Q.921 data link protocol.
USBD_CDC_DATA_PROTOCOL_Q921	Data link protocol for Q.921.
USBD_CDC_DATA_PROTOCOL_Q921TM	TEI-multiplexor for Q.921 data link protocol
USBD_CDC_DATA_PROTOCOL_COMPRESS	Data compression procedures.
USBD_CDC_DATA_PROTOCOL_Q9131	Euro-ISDN protocol control.

`USBD_CDC_DATA_PROTOCOL_V24`	V.24 rate adaptation to ISDN.
`USBD_CDC_DATA_PROTOCOL_CAPI`	CAPI Commands.
`USBD_CDC_DATA_PROTOCOL_HOST`	Host based driver.
`USBD_CDC_DATA_PROTOCOL_CDC`	The protocol(s) are described using a Protocol Unit Function Communication Class Interface.
`USBD_CDC_DATA_PROTOCOL_VENDOR`	Vendor-specific.

CDC data interface class protocol codes are defined in the Universal Serial Bus Class Definitions for Communication Devices Revision 2.1 Table 7.

`p_err`   Pointer to variable that will receive the return error code from this function.

   `USBD_ERR_NONE`
   `USBD_ERR_ALLOC`
   `USBD_ERR_INVALID_ARG`

RETURNED VALUE

Data interface number, if no errors.

`USBD_CDC_DATA_IF_NBR_NONE`, otherwise.

CALLERS

CDC Subclass drivers.

NOTES / WARNINGS

None.

C-1-6 USBD_CDC_DataRx()

Receive data on CDC data interface.

FILES

usbd_cdc.h/usbd_cdc.c

PROTOTYPE

```
CPU_INT32U  USBD_CDC_DataRx (CPU_INT08U   class_nbr,
                             CPU_INT08U   data_if_nbr,
                             CPU_INT08U  *p_buf,
                             CPU_INT32U   buf_len,
                             CPU_INT16U   timeout,
                             USBD_ERR    *p_err);
```

ARGUMENTS

class_nbr   CDC instance number.

data_if_nbr CDC data interface number.

p_buf   Pointer to destination buffer to receive data.

buf_len   Number of octets to receive.

timeout_ms Timeout in milliseconds.

p_err   Pointer to variable that will receive the return error code from this function.

        USBD_ERR_NONE
        USBD_ERR_INVALID_ARG
        USBD_ERR_INVALID_CLASS_STATE
        USBD_ERR_DEV_INVALID_NBR
        USBD_ERR_DEV_INVALID_STATE
        USBD_ERR_EP_INVALID_ADDR
        USBD_ERR_EP_INVALID_STATE
        USBD_ERR_EP_INVALID_TYPE

```
USBD_ERR_OS_TIMEOUT
USBD_ERR_OS_ABORT
USBD_ERR_OS_FAIL
```

RETURNED VALUE

Numbers of octets received, if no errors.

0, otherwise.

CALLERS

CDC Subclass drivers.

NOTES / WARNINGS

None.

C-1-7 USBD_CDC_DataTx()

Send data on CDC data class interface.

FILES

usbd_cdc.h/usbd_cdc.c

PROTOTYPE

```
CPU_INT32U  USBD_CDC_DataTx (CPU_INT08U   class_nbr,
                             CPU_INT08U   data_if_nbr,
                             CPU_INT08U  *p_buf,
                             CPU_INT32U   buf_len,
                             CPU_INT16U   timeout,
                             USBD_ERR    *p_err);
```

ARGUMENTS

class_nbr   CDC instance number.

data_if_nbr   CDC data interface number.

p_buf   Pointer to buffer of data that will be transmitted.

buf_len   Number of octets to transmit.

timeout_ms   Timeout in milliseconds.

p_err   Pointer to variable that will receive the return error code from this function.

       USBD_ERR_NONE
       USBD_ERR_INVALID_ARG
       USBD_ERR_INVALID_CLASS_STATE
       USBD_ERR_DEV_INVALID_NBR
       USBD_ERR_DEV_INVALID_STATE
       USBD_ERR_EP_INVALID_ADDR
       USBD_ERR_EP_INVALID_STATE
       USBD_ERR_EP_INVALID_TYPE

USBD_ERR_OS_TIMEOUT
USBD_ERR_OS_ABORT
USBD_ERR_OS_FAIL

RETURNED VALUE

Numbers of octets transmitted, if no errors.

0, otherwise.

CALLERS

CDC Subclass drivers.

NOTES / WARNINGS

None.

C-1-8 USBD_CDC_Notify()

Send communication interface class notification to the host.

FILES

usbd_cdc.h/usbd_cdc.c

PROTOTYPE

```
CPU_BOOLEAN  USBD_CDC_Notify (CPU_INT08U   class_nbr,
                              CPU_INT08U   notification,
                              CPU_INT16U   value,
                              CPU_INT08U  *p_buf,
                              CPU_INT16U   data_len,
                              USBD_ERR    *p_err);
```

ARGUMENTS

class_nbr   CDC instance number.

notification   Notification code (see Note #1).

value   Notification value (see Note #1).

p_buf   Pointer to notification buffer (see Note #2).

data_len   Notification's data section length.

p_err   Pointer to variable that will receive the return error code from this function.

USBD_ERR_NONE
USBD_ERR_INVALID_ARG
USBD_ERR_INVALID_CLASS_STATE
USBD_ERR_DEV_INVALID_NBR
USBD_ERR_DEV_INVALID_STATE
USBD_ERR_EP_INVALID_ADDR
USBD_ERR_EP_INVALID_STATE
USBD_ERR_EP_INVALID_TYPE

```
USBD_ERR_OS_TIMEOUT
USBD_ERR_OS_ABORT
USBD_ERR_OS_FAIL
```

RETURNED VALUE

None.

CALLERS

CDC Subclass drivers.

NOTES / WARNINGS

1   The following table show the relationship between CDC request and the parameters passed in the **USBD_CDC_Notify()** function. The *bmRequestType* and *wIndex* fields are calculated internally in the CDC module.

bmRequestType	bNotificationCode	wValue	wIndex	wLength	Data
1010001b	notification	value	Interface	data_len	p_buf[7] to p_buf[data_len -1]

2   The notification buffer size *must* contain space for the notification header (8 bytes and the variable-length data portion.

C-2 CDC ACM SUBCLASS FUNCTIONS

C-2-1 USBD_ACM_SerialInit()

Initialize CDC ACM serial emulation subclass.

FILES

usbd_acm_serial.h/usbd_acm_serial.c

PROTOTYPE

```
void  USBD_ACM_SerialInit (USBD_ERR  *p_err);
```

ARGUMENTS

p_err   Pointer to variable that will receive the return error code from this function: USBD_ERR_NONE.

RETURNED VALUE

None.

CALLERS

Application.

NOTES / WARNINGS

None.

C-2-2 USBD_ACM_SerialAdd()

Add a new CDC ACM serial emulation instance.

FILES

usbd_acm_serial.h/usbd_acm_serial.c

PROTOTYPE

```
CPU_INT08U  USBD_ACM_SerialAdd (CPU_INT16U   line_state_interval,
                                USBD_ERR    *p_err);
```

ARGUMENTS

line_state_interval   Polling interval in frames or microframes for line state notification.

p_err   Pointer to variable that will receive the return error code from this function.

USBD_ERR_NONE
USBD_ERR_ALLOC
USBD_ERR_INVALID_ARG

RETURNED VALUE

CDC ACM serial emulation subclass instance number, if no errors.

USBD_ACM_SERIAL_NBR_NONE, otherwise.

CALLERS

Application.

NOTES / WARNINGS

None.

C-2-3 USBD_ACM_SerialCfgAdd()

Add CDC ACM subclass instance to USB device configuration.

FILES

usbd_acm_serial.h/usbd_acm_serial.c

PROTOTYPE

```
CPU_BOOLEAN  USBD_ACM_SerialCfgAdd (CPU_INT08U   subclass_nbr,
                                    CPU_INT08U   dev_nbr,
                                    CPU_INT08U   cfg_nbr,
                                    USBD_ERR    *p_err);
```

ARGUMENTS

subclass_nbr   CDC ACM serial emulation subclass instance number.

dev_nbr   Device number.

cfg_nbr   Configuration number.

p_err   Pointer to variable that will receive the return error code from this function.

   USBD_ERR_NONE
   USBD_ERR_INVALID_ARG
   USBD_ERR_ALLOC
   USBD_ERR_INVALID_CLASS_STATE
   USBD_ERR_DEV_INVALID_NBR
   USBD_ERR_CFG_INVALID_NBR
   USBD_ERR_IF_ALLOC
   USBD_ERR_IF_ALT_ALLOC
   USBD_ERR_EP_NONE_AVAIL
   USBD_ERR_EP_ALLOC

RETURNED VALUE

DEF_OK,   If CDC ACM serial emulation subclass instance was added to device configuration successfully.

DEF_FAIL,   Otherwise.

CALLERS

Application.

NOTES / WARNINGS

None.

C-2-4 USBD_ACM_SerialIsConn()

Determine if CDC ACM serial emulation class instance is connected.

FILES

usbd_acm_serial.h/usbd_acm_serial.c

PROTOTYPE

```
CPU_BOOLEAN  USBD_ACM_SerialIsConn (CPU_INT08U  subclass_nbr);
```

ARGUMENTS

subclass_nbr   CDC ACM serial emulation subclass instance number.

RETURNED VALUE

DEF_OK, if CDC ACM serial emulation subclass instance is connected and device is not in suspended state.

DEF_FAIL, otherwise.

CALLERS

Application.

NOTES / WARNINGS

None.

C-2-5 USBD_ACM_SerialRx()

Receive data on CDC ACM serial emulation subclass.

FILES

usbd_acm_serial.h/usbd_acm_serial.c

PROTOTYPE

```
CPU_INT32U  USBD_ACM_SerialRx (CPU_INT08U   subclass_nbr,
                               CPU_INT08U   *p_buf,
                               CPU_INT32U   buf_len,
                               CPU_INT16U   timeout,
                               USBD_ERR     *p_err);
```

ARGUMENTS

subclass_nbr   Pointer to USB device driver structure.

p_buf   Pointer to destination buffer to receive data.

buf_len   Number of octets to receive.

timeout_ms   Timeout in milliseconds.

p_err   Pointer to variable that will receive the return error code from this function.

> USBD_ERR_NONE
> USBD_ERR_INVALID_ARG
> USBD_ERR_INVALID_CLASS_STATE
> USBD_ERR_EP_INVALID_ADDR
> USBD_ERR_EP_INVALID_STATE
> USBD_ERR_EP_INVALID_TYPE
> USBD_ERR_OS_TIMEOUT
> USBD_ERR_OS_ABORT
> USBD_ERR_OS_FAIL

C

RETURNED VALUE

None.

CALLERS

Numbers of octets received, if NO error(s).

0, otherwise.

NOTES / WARNINGS

None.

C-2-6 USBD_ACM_SerialTx()

Send data on CDC ACM serial emulation subclass.

FILES

usbd_acm_serial.h/usbd_acm_serial.c

PROTOTYPE

```
CPU_INT32U  USBD_ACM_SerialTx (CPU_INT08U   subclass_nbr,
                               CPU_INT08U  *p_buf,
                               CPU_INT32U   buf_len,
                               CPU_INT16U   timeout,
                               USBD_ERR    *p_err);
```

ARGUMENTS

subclass_nbr   Pointer to USB device driver structure.

p_buf   Pointer to buffer of data that will be transmitted.

buf_len   Number of octets to receive.

timeout_ms   Timeout in milliseconds.

p_err   Pointer to variable that will receive the return error code from this function.

> USBD_ERR_NONE
> USBD_ERR_INVALID_ARG
> USBD_ERR_INVALID_CLASS_STATE
> USBD_ERR_EP_INVALID_ADDR
> USBD_ERR_EP_INVALID_STATE
> USBD_ERR_EP_INVALID_TYPE
> USBD_ERR_OS_TIMEOUT
> USBD_ERR_OS_ABORT
> USBD_ERR_OS_FAIL

RETURNED VALUE

Number of octets transmitted, if NO error(s).

0, otherwise.

CALLERS

Application.

NOTES / WARNINGS

None.

C-2-7 USBD_ACM_SerialLineCtrlGet()

Return current control line state.

FILES

usbd_acm_serial.h/usbd_acm_serial.c

PROTOTYPE

```
CPU_INT08U  USBD_ACM_SerialLineCtrlGet (CPU_INT08U   subclass_nbr,
                                        USBD_ERR     *p_err);
```

ARGUMENTS

subclass_nbr   CDC ACM serial emulation subclass instance number.

p_err   Pointer to variable that will receive the return error code from this function.

             USBD_ERR_NONE
             USBD_ERR_INVALID_ARG

RETURNED VALUE

Bit-field with the state of the control line.

USBD_ACM_SERIAL_CTRL_BREAK   Break signal is set.

USBD_ACM_SERIAL_CTRL_RTS   RTS signal is set.

USBD_ACM_SERIAL_CTRL_DTR   DTR signal is set.

CALLERS

Application.

NOTES / WARNINGS

None.

C-2-8 USBD_ACM_SerialLineCtrlReg()

Register line control change notification callback.

usbd_acm_serial.h/usbd_acm_serial.c

```
void  USBD_ACM_SerialLineCtrlReg (CPU_INT08U                      subclass_nbr,
                                  USBD_ACM_SERIAL_LINE_CTRL_CHNGD  line_ctrl_chngd,
                                  void                            *p_arg,
                                  USBD_ERR                        *p_err);
```

subclass_nbr   CDC ACM serial emulation subclass instance number.

line_ctrl_chngd   Line control change notification callback (see note #1).

p_arg   Pointer to callback argument.

p_err   Pointer to variable that will receive the return error code from this function.

        USBD_ERR_NONE
        USBD_ERR_INVALID_ARG

None.

Application.

The callback specified by line_ctrl_chngd argument is used to notify changes in the control signals to the application.

The line control notification function has the following prototype:

```
void AppLineCtrlChngd (CPU_INT08U  subclass_nbr,
                       CPU_INT08U  events,
                       CPU_INT08U  events_chngd,
                       void        *p_arg);
```

Argument(s):

subclass_nbr   CDC ACM serial emulation subclass instance number.

events   Current line state.

events_chngd   Line state flags that have changed.

events_chngd   Pointer to callback argument.

C-2-9 USBD_ACM_SerialLineCodingGet()

Get the current state of the line coding.

FILES

usbd_acm_serial.h/usbd_acm_serial.c

PROTOTYPE

```
void  USBD_ACM_SerialLineCodingGet (CPU_INT08U                subclass_nbr,
                                    USBD_ACM_SERIAL_LINE_CODING  *p_line_coding,
                                    USBD_ERR                   *p_err);
```

ARGUMENTS

subclass_nbr   CDC ACM serial emulation subclass instance number.

p_line_coding   Pointer to the structure where the current line coding will be
                      stored.

p_err   Pointer to variable that will receive the return error code from this function.

              USBD_ERR_NONE
              USBD_ERR_INVALID_ARG
              USBD_ERR_NULL_PTR

RETURNED VALUE

None.

CALLERS

Application.

NOTES / WARNINGS

None.

C-2-10 USBD_ACM_SerialLineCodingSet()

Set a new line coding.

usbd_acm_serial.h/usbd_acm_serial.c

```
void  USBD_ACM_SerialLineCodingSet (CPU_INT08U                  subclass_nbr,
                                    USBD_ACM_SERIAL_LINE_CODING  *p_line_coding,
                                    USBD_ERR                     *p_err);
```

subclass_nbr   CDC ACM serial emulation subclass instance number.

p_line_coding   Pointer to the structure where that contains the new line coding.

p_err   Pointer to variable that will receive the return error code from this function.

> USBD_ERR_NONE
> USBD_ERR_INVALID_ARG
> USBD_ERR_NULL_PTR

None.

Application.

None.

C-2-11 USBD_ACM_SerialLineCodingReg()

Register line coding change notification callback.

FILES

usbd_acm_serial.h/usbd_acm_serial.c

PROTOTYPE

```
void  USBD_ACM_SerialLineCodingReg(CPU_INT08U                        subclass_nbr,
                                   USBD_ACM_SERIAL_LINE_CODING_CHNGD  line_coding_chngd,
                                   void                              *p_arg,
                                   USBD_ERR                          *p_err);
```

ARGUMENTS

subclass_nbr   CDC ACM serial emulation subclass instance number.

line_coding_chngd   Line coding change notification callback (see Note #1).

p_arg   Pointer to callback argument.

p_err   Pointer to variable that will receive the return error code from this function.

       USBD_ERR_NONE
       USBD_ERR_INVALID_ARG

RETURNED VALUE

None.

CALLERS

Application.

NOTES / WARNINGS

■ The callback specified by line_coding_chngd argument is used to notify changes in the control signals to the application.

The line control notification function has the following prototype:

```
CPU_BOOLEAN AppLineCodingChngd (CPU_INT08U  subclass_nbr,
                                ...         *p_line_coding,
                                void        *p_arg);
```

Arguments:

subclass_nbr   CDC ACM serial emulation subclass instance number.

p_line_coding   Pointer to line coding structure.

p_arg   Pointer to callback argument.

Returned value:

DEF_OK,   If line coding is supported by the application.

DEF_FAIL,   Otherwise.

C-2-12 USBD_ACM_SerialLineStateSet()

Set one or several line state events.

FILES

usbd_acm_serial.h/usbd_acm_serial.c

PROTOTYPE

```
CPU_BOOLEAN  USBD_ACM_SerialLineStateSet (CPU_INT08U  subclass_nbr,
                                          CPU_INT08U  events);
```

ARGUMENTS

subclass_nbr   CDC ACM serial emulation subclass instance number.

events   Line state event(s) to set.

USBD_ACM_SERIAL_STATE_DCD	DCD (Rx carrier)
USBD_ACM_SERIAL_STATE_DSR	DSR (Tx carrier)
USBD_ACM_SERIAL_STATE_BREAK	Break
USBD_ACM_SERIAL_STATE_RING	Ring
USBD_ACM_SERIAL_STATE_FRAMING	Framing error
USBD_ACM_SERIAL_STATE_PARITY	Parity error
USBD_ACM_SERIAL_STATE_OVERUN	Overrun

RETURNED VALUE

DEF_OK,   if new line state event set successfully.

DEF_FAIL, otherwise.

CALLERS

Application.

NOTES / WARNINGS

None.

C-2-13 USBD_ACM_SerialLineStateClr()

Clear one or several line state event(s).

FILES

usbd_acm_serial.h/usbd_acm_serial.c

PROTOTYPE

```
CPU_BOOLEAN  USBD_ACM_SerialLineStateSet (CPU_INT08U  subclass_nbr,
                                          CPU_INT08U  events);
```

ARGUMENTS

subclass_nbr   CDC ACM serial emulation subclass instance number.

events   Line state event(s) to clear (see Note #1).

> USBD_ACM_SERIAL_STATE_DCD   DCD (Rx carrier)
> USBD_ACM_SERIAL_STATE_DSR   DSR (Tx carrier)

RETURNED VALUE

DEF_OK,   if new line state event clear successfully.

DEF_FAIL, otherwise.

CALLERS

Application.

NOTES / WARNINGS

- Universal Serial Bus Communications Class Subclass Specification for PSTN Devices version 1.2 states: "For the irregular signals like break, the incoming ring signal, or the overrun error state, this will reset their values to zero and again will not send another notification until their state changes". The irregular events are self-clear and cannot be clear using this function.

D

HID API Reference

This appendix provides a reference to the Human Interface Device (HID) class API. The following information is provided for each of the services:

■ A brief description

■ The function prototype

■ The filename of the source code

■ A description of the arguments passed to the function

■ A description of returned value(s)

■ Specific notes and warnings regarding use of the service

D-1 HID CLASS FUNCTIONS

D-1-1 USBD_HID_Init()

This function initializes all the internal variables and modules used by the HID class.

FILES

usbd_hid.c

PROTOTYPE

```
void USBD_HID_Init (USBD_ERR  *p_err);
```

ARGUMENTS

p_err   Pointer to variable that will receive the return error code from this function.

USBD_ERR_NONE

RETURNED VALUE

None.

CALLERS

Application.

NOTES / WARNINGS

The initialization function *must* be called only once by the application, and before calling any other HID API.

D-1-2 USBD_HID_Add()

This function adds a new instance of the HID class.

usbd_hid.c

```
void USBD_HID_Add (CPU_INT08U              subclass,
                   CPU_INT08U              protocol,
                   USBD_HID_COUNTRY_CODE   country_code,
                   CPU_INT08U              *p_report_desc,
                   CPU_INT16U              report_desc_len,
                   CPU_INT08U              *p_phy_desc,
                   CPU_INT16U              phy_desc_len,
                   CPU_INT16U              interval_in,
                   CPU_INT16U              interval_out,
                   CPU_BOOLEAN             ctrl_rd_en,
                   USBD_HID_CALLBACK       *p_hid_callback,
                   USBD_ERR                *p_err);
```

subclass   Subclass code.

protocol   Protocol code.

country_code   Country code ID.

p_report_desc   Pointer to report descriptor structure.

report_desc_len   Report descriptor length.

p_phy_desc   Pointer to physical descriptor structure.

phy_desc_len   Physical descriptor length.

interval_in   Polling interval for input transfers, in milliseconds.

interval_out   Polling interval for output transfers, in milliseconds. Used only when read operations are not through control transfers.

ctrl_rd_en   Enable read operations through control transfers.

p_hid_callback   Pointer to HID descriptor and request callback structure.

p_err   Pointer to variable that will receive the return error code from this function.

      USBD_ERR_NONE
      USBD_ERR_ALLOC
      USBD_ERR_NULL_PTR
      USBD_ERR_INVALID_ARG
      USBD_ERR_FAIL

RETURNED VALUE

Class interface number, if NO error(s).

USBD_CLASS_NBR_NONE, otherwise.

CALLERS

Application.

NOTES / WARNINGS

None.

D-1-3 USBD_HID_CfgAdd()

This function adds HID class instance into USB device configuration.

FILES

usbd_hid.c

PROTOTYPE

```
CPU_BOOLEAN USBD_HID_CfgAdd (CPU_INT08U  class_nbr,
                             CPU_INT08U  dev_nbr,
                             CPU_INT08U  cfg_nbr,
                             USBD_ERR    *p_err);
```

ARGUMENTS

class_nbr   Class instance number.

dev_nbr   Device number.

cfg_nbr   Configuration index to add class instance to.

p_err   Pointer to variable that will receive the return error code from this function.

USBD_ERR_NONE
USBD_ERR_ALLOC
USBD_ERR_INVALID_ARG
USBD_ERR_NULL_PTR
USBD_ERR_DEV_INVALID_NBR
USBD_ERR_DEV_INVALID_STATE
USBD_ERR_CFG_INVALID_NBR
USBD_ERR_IF_ALLOC
USBD_ERR_IF_ALT_ALLOC
USBD_ERR_EP_NONE_AVAIL
USBD_ERR_IF_INVALID_NBR
USBD_ERR_EP_ALLOC

RETURNED VALUE

DEF_YES, if NO error(s).

DEF_NO, otherwise.

CALLERS

Application.

NOTES / WARNINGS

This API may be called several times. This allows to create multiple instances of the HID class into different USB device configurations.

D-1-4 USBD_HID_IsConn()

This function returns the HID class connection state.

FILES

usbd_hid.c

PROTOTYPE

```
CPU_BOOLEAN USBD_HID_IsConn (CPU_INT08U   class_nbr);
```

ARGUMENTS

class_nbr   Class instance number.

RETURNED VALUE

DEF_YES, if class is connected.

DEF_NO, otherwise.

CALLERS

Application.

NOTES / WARNINGS

The class connected state also implies the USB device is in configured state.

D-1-5 USBD_HID_Rd()

This function receives data from the host through an interrupt OUT endpoint.

FILES

usbd_hid.c

PROTOTYPE

```
CPU_INT32U USBD_HID_Rd (CPU_INT08U   class_nbr,
                        void        *p_buf,
                        CPU_INT32U   buf_len,
                        CPU_INT16U   timeout,
                        USBD_ERR    *p_err);
```

ARGUMENTS

class_nbr   Class instance number.

p_buf   Pointer to receive buffer.

buf_len   Receive buffer length, in octets.

timeout   Timeout, in milliseconds.

p_err   Pointer to variable that will receive the return error code from this function.

        USBD_ERR_NONE
        USBD_ERR_NULL_PTR
        USBD_ERR_INVALID_ARG
        USBD_ERR_INVALID_CLASS_STATE
        USBD_ERR_DEV_INVALID_NBR
        USBD_ERR_EP_INVALID_NBR
        USBD_ERR_DEV_INVALID_STATE
        USBD_ERR_EP_INVALID_TYPE

RETURNED VALUE

Number of octets received, if NO error(s).

0, otherwise.

CALLERS

Application.

NOTES / WARNINGS

None.

D-1-6 USBD_HID_RdAsync()

This function receives data from the host asynchronously through an interrupt OUT endpoint.

FILES

usbd_hid.c

PROTOTYPE

```
void USBD_HID_RdAsync (CPU_INT08U          class_nbr,
                       void               *p_buf,
                       CPU_INT32U          buf_len,
                       USBD_HID_ASYNC_FNCT async_fnct,
                       void               *p_async_arg,
                       USBD_ERR           *p_err);
```

ARGUMENTS

class_nbr   Class instance number.

p_buf   Pointer to receive buffer.

buf_len   Receive buffer length, in octets.

async_fnct Receive callback.

p_async_arg Additional argument provided by application for receive callback.

p_err   Pointer to variable that will receive the return error code from this function.

USBD_ERR_NONE
USBD_ERR_NULL_PTR
USBD_ERR_INVALID_ARG
USBD_ERR_INVALID_CLASS_STATE
USBD_ERR_FAIL
USBD_ERR_DEV_INVALID_NBR
USBD_ERR_EP_INVALID_NBR

```
USBD_ERR_DEV_INVALID_STATE
USBD_ERR_EP_INVALID_TYPE
USBD_ERR_EP_INVALID_STATE
```

RETURNED VALUE

None.

CALLERS

Application.

NOTES / WARNINGS

This function is non-blocking and returns immediately after transfer preparation. Upon transfer completion, the callback provided is called to notify the application.

D-1-7 USBD_HID_Wr()

This function transmits data to the host through an interrupt IN endpoint.

FILES

usbd_hid.c

PROTOTYPE

```
CPU_INT32U USBD_HID_Wr (CPU_INT08U   class_nbr,
                        void        *p_buf,
                        CPU_INT32U   buf_len,
                        CPU_INT16U   timeout,
                        USBD_ERR    *p_err);
```

ARGUMENTS

class_nbr   Class instance number.

p_buf   Pointer to transmit buffer.

buf_len   Transmit buffer length, in octets.

timeout   Timeout, in milliseconds.

p_err   Pointer to variable that will receive the return error code from this function.

            USBD_ERR_NONE
            USBD_ERR_NULL_PTR
            USBD_ERR_INVALID_ARG
            USBD_ERR_INVALID_CLASS_STATE
            USBD_ERR_DEV_INVALID_NBR
            USBD_ERR_EP_INVALID_NBR
            USBD_ERR_DEV_INVALID_STATE
            USBD_ERR_EP_INVALID_TYPE

RETURNED VALUE

Number of octets transmitted, if NO error(s).

0, otherwise.

CALLERS

Application.

NOTES / WARNINGS

None.

D-1-8 USBD_HID_WrAsync()

This function transmits data to the host asynchronously through an interrupt IN endpoint.

FILES

usbd_hid.c

PROTOTYPE

```
void USBD_HID_WrAsync (CPU_INT08U         class_nbr,
                       void               *p_buf,
                       CPU_INT32U         buf_len,
                       USBD_HID_ASYNC_FNCT async_fnct,
                       void               *p_async_arg,
                       USBD_ERR           *p_err);
```

ARGUMENTS

class_nbr   Class instance number.

p_buf   Pointer to transmit buffer.

buf_len   Transmit buffer length, in octets.

async_fnct   Transmit callback.

p_async_arg   Additional argument provided by application for transmit callback.

p_err   Pointer to variable that will receive the return error code from this function.

              USBD_ERR_NONE
              USBD_ERR_NULL_PTR
              USBD_ERR_INVALID_ARG
              USBD_ERR_INVALID_CLASS_STATE
              USBD_ERR_FAIL
              USBD_ERR_DEV_INVALID_NBR
              USBD_ERR_EP_INVALID_NBR
              USBD_ERR_DEV_INVALID_STATE
              USBD_ERR_EP_INVALID_TYPE
              USBD_ERR_EP_INVALID_STATE

RETURNED VALUE

None.

CALLERS

Application.

NOTES / WARNINGS

This function is non-blocking and returns immediately after transfer preparation. Upon transfer completion, the callback provided is called to notify the application.

D

___

D-2 HID OS FUNCTIONS

D-2-1 USBD_HID_OS_Init()

Initialize HID OS interface.

FILES

usbd_hid_os.c

PROTOTYPE

```
void  USBD_HID_OS_Init (USBD_ERR  *p_err);
```

ARGUMENTS

p_err   Pointer to variable that will receive the return error code from this function.

             USBD_ERR_NONE
             OS error code(s) relevant to failure(s).

CALLERS

USBD_HID_Init()

IMPLEMENTATION GUIDELINES

The USBD_HID_Init() function is called only once by the HID class. It usually performs the following operations:

▪ For each class instance up to the maximum number of HID class instances defined by the constant USBD_HID_CFG_MAX_NBR_DEV, create all the required semaphores. If the any semaphore creation fails, set p_err to USBD_ERR_OS_SIGNAL_CREATE and return.

▪ Create a task used to manage periodic Input reports. If the task creation fails, set p_err to USBD_ERR_OS_INIT_FAIL and return.

▪ Set p_err to USBD_ERR_NONE if the initialization proceeded as expected.

D-2-2 USBD_HID_OS_InputLock()

Lock class input report.

FILES

usbd_hid_os.c

PROTOTYPE

```
void  USBD_HID_OS_InputLock (CPU_INT08U   class_nbr,
                             USBD_ERR    *p_err);
```

ARGUMENTS

class_nbr   Class instance number.

p_err   Pointer to variable that will receive the return error code from this function.

             USBD_ERR_NONE: OS error code(s) relevant to failure(s).

CALLERS

USBD_HID_Wr()
USBD_HID_WrAsync()
USBD_HID_ClassReq()

IMPLEMENTATION GUIDELINES

The lock operation typically consists in pending on a semaphore. If the semaphore is free, the task continues normally its execution, otherwise it waits until another task releases the semaphore. p_err argument should be assigned as described in Table D-1.

Operation result	Error code to assign
No error	USBD_ERR_NONE
Pend aborted	USBD_ERR_OS_ABORT
Pend failed for any other reason	USBD_ERR_OS_FAIL

Table D-1 **p_err assignment according to the pend operation result**

471

D

D-2-3 USBD_HID_OS_InputUnlock()

Unlock class input report.

FILES

usbd_hid_os.c

PROTOTYPE

```
void  USBD_HID_OS_InputUnlock (CPU_INT08U   class_nbr);
```

ARGUMENTS

class_nbr   Class instance number.

CALLERS

USBD_HID_Wr( )
USBD_HID_WrAsync( )
USBD_HID_ClassReq( )

IMPLEMENTATION GUIDELINES

The unlock operation simply consists in posting a semaphore.

D-2-4 USBD_HID_OS_InputDataPend()

Wait for input report data to complete.

FILES

usbd_hid_os.c

PROTOTYPE

```
void  USBD_HID_OS_InputDataPend (CPU_INT08U    class_nbr
                                 CPU_INT16U    timeout_ms,
                                 USBD_ERR      *p_err);
```

ARGUMENTS

class_nbr   Class instance number.

timeout_ms   Signal wait timeout in milliseconds

p_err   Pointer to variable that will receive the return error code from this function.

             USBD_ERR_NONE
             OS error code(s) relevant to failure(s)

CALLERS

USBD_HID_Wr()

IMPLEMENTATION GUIDELINES

The wait operation typically consists in pending on a semaphore. When the input report transfer has completed, the task is waken up by the Core layer internal task responsible for asynchronous communication. **p_err** argument should be assigned as described in Table D-2.

Operation result	Error code to assign
No error	`USBD_ERR_NONE`
Pend timeout	`USBD_ERR_OS_TIMEOUT`
Pend aborted	`USBD_ERR_OS_ABORT`
Pend failed for any other reason	`USBD_ERR_OS_FAIL`

Table D-2 **p_err assignment according to the pend operation result**

D-2-5 USBD_HID_OS_InputDataPendAbort()

Abort any operation on input report.

usbd_hid_os.c

```
void  USBD_HID_OS_InputDataPendAbort (CPU_INT08U  class_nbr);
```

class_nbr   Class instance number.

USBD_HID_WrSyncCmpl()

If the input report transfer completes with an error, the task waiting is waken up by aborting the active wait done with USBD_HID_OS_InputDataPend(). The active wait abortion is executed by the Core layer internal task responsible for asynchronous communication.

D-2-6 USBD_HID_OS_InputDataPost()

Signal that Input report data has been sent to the host.

FILES

usbd_hid_os.c

PROTOTYPE

```
void  USBD_HID_OS_InputDataPost (CPU_INT08U  class_nbr);
```

ARGUMENTS

class_nbr   Class instance number.

CALLERS

USBD_HID_WrSyncCmpl( )

IMPLEMENTATION GUIDELINES

If the input report transfer completes without an error, the task waiting is waken up by posting a semaphore. The semaphore post is executed by the Core layer internal task responsible for asynchronous communication.

D-2-7 USBD_HID_OS_OutputLock()

Lock class output report.

FILES

usbd_hid_os.c

PROTOTYPE

```
void  USBD_HID_OS_OutputLock (CPU_INT08U   class_nbr,
                              USBD_ERR    *p_err);
```

ARGUMENTS

class_nbr   Class instance number.

p_err   Pointer to variable that will receive the return error code from this function.

             USBD_ERR_NONE: OS error code(s) relevant to failure(s)

CALLERS

USBD_HID_Rd()
USBD_HID_RdAsync()
USBD_HID_ClassReq()

IMPLEMENTATION GUIDELINES

The lock operation typically consists in pending on a semaphore. If the semaphore is free, the task continues normally its execution, otherwise it waits until another task releases the semaphore. p_err argument should be assigned as described in Table D-3.

Operation result	Error code to assign
No error	USBD_ERR_NONE
Pend aborted	USBD_ERR_OS_ABORT
Pend failed for any other reason	USBD_ERR_OS_FAIL

Table D-3 **p_err assignment according to the pend operation result**

477

D-2-8 USBD_HID_OS_OutputUnlock()

Unlock class output report.

FILES

usbd_hid_os.c

PROTOTYPE

```
void  USBD_HID_OS_OutputUnlock (CPU_INT08U  class_nbr);
```

ARGUMENTS

class_nbr   Class instance number.

CALLERS

USBD_HID_Rd( )
USBD_HID_RdAsync( )
USBD_HID_ClassReq( )

IMPLEMENTATION GUIDELINES

The unlock operation simply consists in posting a semaphore.

D-2-9 USBD_HID_OS_OutputDataPend()

Wait for Output report data read completion.

FILES

usbd_hid_os.c

PROTOTYPE

```
void  USBD_HID_OS_OutputDataPend (CPU_INT08U   class_nbr
                                  CPU_INT16U   timeout_ms,
                                  USBD_ERR     *p_err);
```

ARGUMENTS

class_nbr   Class instance number.

timeout_ms   Signal wait timeout in milliseconds

p_err   Pointer to variable that will receive the return error code from this function.

             USBD_ERR_NONE
             OS error code(s) relevant to failure(s)

CALLERS

USBD_HID_Rd( )

IMPLEMENTATION GUIDELINES

The wait operation typically consists of pending on a semaphore. When the output report transfer is complete, the task is woken up by the Core layer internal task responsible for asynchronous communication. The **p_err** argument should be assigned as described in Table D-2.

Operation result	Error code to assign
No error	USBD_ERR_NONE
Pend aborted	USBD_ERR_OS_ABORT
Pend failed for any other reason	USBD_ERR_OS_FAIL

Table D-4 **p_err assignment according to the pend operation result**

D-2-10 USBD_HID_OS_OutputDataPendAbort()

Abort the wait for Output report data read completion.

FILES

usbd_hid_os.c

PROTOTYPE

```
void  USBD_HID_OS_OutputDataPendAbort (CPU_INT08U  class_nbr);
```

ARGUMENTS

class_nbr   Class instance number.

CALLERS

USBD_HID_OutputDataCmpl()

IMPLEMENTATION GUIDELINES

If the output report transfer completes with an error, the task waiting is waken up by aborting the active wait done with USBD_HID_OS_OutputDataPend(). The active wait abortion is executed by the Core layer internal task responsible for asynchronous communication.

D-2-11 USBD_HID_OS_OutputDataPost()

Signal that Output report data has been received from the host

FILES

usbd_hid_os.c

PROTOTYPE

```
void  USBD_HID_OS_OutputDataPost (CPU_INT08U  class_nbr);
```

ARGUMENTS

class_nbr   Class instance number.

CALLERS

USBD_HID_OutputDataCmpl()

IMPLEMENTATION GUIDELINES

If the output report transfer completes without an error, the task waiting is waken up by posting a semaphore. The semaphore post is executed by the Core layer internal task responsible for asynchronous communication.

D-2-12 USBD_HID_OS_TxLock()

Lock class transmit.

FILES

usbd_hid_os.c

PROTOTYPE

```
void  USBD_HID_OS_TxLock (CPU_INT08U  class_nbr,
                          USBD_ERR    *p_err);
```

ARGUMENTS

class_nbr   Class instance number.

p_err   Pointer to variable that will receive the return error code from this function.

      USBD_ERR_NONE: OS error code(s) relevant to failure(s).

CALLERS

USBD_HID_Wr()
USBD_HID_WrAsync()

IMPLEMENTATION GUIDELINES

The lock operation typically consists in pending on a semaphore. If the semaphore is free, the task continues normally its execution, otherwise it waits until another task releases the semaphore. p_err argument should be assigned as described in Table D-5.

Operation result	Error code to assign
No error	USBD_ERR_NONE
Pend aborted	USBD_ERR_OS_ABORT
Pend failed for any other reason	USBD_ERR_OS_FAIL

Table D-5 **p_err assignment according to the pend operation result**

D

D-2-13 USBD_HID_OS_TxUnlock()

Unlock class transmit.

FILES

usbd_hid_os.c

PROTOTYPE

```
void  USBD_HID_OS_TxUnlock (CPU_INT08U  class_nbr);
```

ARGUMENTS

class_nbr   Class instance number.

CALLERS

USBD_HID_Wr( )
USBD_HID_WrAsync( )

IMPLEMENTATION GUIDELINES

The unlock operation simply consists in posting a semaphore.

D-2-14 USBD_HID_OS_TmrTask()

Process periodic input reports according to idle duration set by the host with the SET_IDLE request.

FILES

usbd_hid_os.c

PROTOTYPE

```
static  void  USBD_HID_OS_TmrTask (void  *p_arg);
```

ARGUMENTS

p_arg   Pointer to task initialization argument.

CALLERS

This is a task.

IMPLEMENTATION GUIDELINES

The task body is usually implemented as an infinite loop. The task should perform the following steps:

- Delay for 4 ms. This delay corresponds to the 4 ms unit used to express the idle duration transported by the **SET_IDLE** request.

- Call **USBD_HID_Report_TmrTaskHandler()** function defined in the HID parser module. This function implements the periodic input reports processing.

MSC API Reference

This appendix provides a reference to the mass storage class API. Each user-accessible service is presented following a category order (i.e. initialization and communication categories). The following information is provided for each of the services:

■ A brief description

■ The function prototype

■ The filename of the source code

■ A description of the arguments passed to the function

■ A description of returned value(s)

■ Specific notes and warnings regarding use of the service.

E

E-1 MASS STORAGE CLASS FUNCTIONS

E-1-1 USBD_MSC_Init()

Initialize internal structures and local global variables used by the MSC bulk only transport.

FILES

usbd_msc.h / usbd_msc.c

PROTOTYPE

```
void  USBD_MSC_Init (USBD_ERR  *p_err);
```

ARGUMENTS

p_err   Pointer to variable that will receive the return error code from this function:
            USBD_ERR_NONE

RETURNED VALUE

None.

CALLERS

Application.

NOTES / WARNINGS

None.

E-1-2 USBD_MSC_Add()

Create a new instance of the MSC.

FILES

usbd_msc.h / usbd_msc.c

PROTOTYPE

```
CPU_INT08U  USBD_MSC_Add ( USBD_ERR    *p_err)
```

ARGUMENTS

p_err   Pointer to variable that will receive the return error code from this function.

            USBD_ERR_NONE
            USBD_ERR_ALLOC

RETURNED VALUE

Class instance number,   if NO error(s).

USBD_CLASS_NBR_NONE, otherwise.

CALLERS

Application.

NOTES / WARNINGS

None.

E

E-1-3 USBD_MSC_CfgAdd()

Add an existing MSC instance to the specified configuration and device. The MSC instance was previously created by the function **USBD_MSC_Add( )**.

FILES

usbd_msc.h / usbd_msc.c

PROTOTYPE

```
CPU_BOOLEAN  USBD_MSC_CfgAdd (CPU_INT08U   class_nbr,
                              CPU_INT08U   dev_nbr,
                              CPU_INT08U   cfg_nbr,
                              USBD_ERR     *p_err);
```

ARGUMENTS

class_nbr   MSC instance number.

dev_nbr   Device number.

cfg_nbr   Configuration index to add MSC instance to.

p_err   Pointer to variable that will receive the return error code from this function.

        USBD_ERR_NONE
        USBD_ERR_INVALID_ARG
        USBD_ERR_ALLOC
        USBD_ERR_NULL_PTR
        USBD_ERR_DEV_INVALID_NBR
        USBD_ERR_DEV_INVALID_STATE
        USBD_ERR_CFG_INVALID_NBR
        USBD_ERR_IF_ALLOC
        USBD_ERR_IF_ALT_ALLOC
        USBD_ERR_IF_INVALID_NBR
        USBD_ERR_EP_NONE_AVAIL
        USBD_ERR_EP_ALLOC

RETURNED VALUE

DEF_YES, if MSC instance is added to USB device configuration successfully.

DEF_NO, otherwise.

CALLERS

Application.

NOTES / WARNINGS

USBD_MSC_CfgAdd() basically adds an Interface descriptor and its associated Endpoint descriptor(s) to the Configuration descriptor. One call to USBD_MSC_CfgAdd() builds the Configuration descriptor corresponding to a MSC device with the following format:

```
Configuration Descriptor
|-- Interface Descriptor (MSC)
    |-- Endpoint Descriptor (Bulk OUT)
    |-- Endpoint Descriptor (Bulk IN)
```

If USBD_MSC_CfgAdd() is called several times from the application, it allows to create multiple instances and multiple configurations. For instance, the following architecture could be created for an high-speed device:

```
High-speed
|-- Configuration 0
    |-- Interface 0 (MSC 0)
|-- Configuration 1
    |-- Interface 0 (MSC 0)
    |-- Interface 1 (MSC 1)
```

In that example, there are two instances of MSC: 'MSC 0' and 'MSC 1', and two possible configurations for the device: 'Configuration 0' and 'Configuration 1'. 'Configuration 1' is composed of two interfaces. Each class instance has an association with one of the interfaces. If 'Configuration 1' is activated by the host, it allows the host to access two different functionalities offered by the device.

E

E-1-4 USBD_MSC_LunAdd()

Add a logical unit number to the MSC interface.

FILES

usbd_msc.h / usbd_msc.c

PROTOTYPE

```
void  USBD_MSC_LunAdd (CPU_CHAR    *p_store_name,
                       CPU_INT08U   class_nbr,
                       CPU_CHAR    *p_vend_id,
                       CPU_CHAR    *p_prod_id,
                       CPU_INT32U   prod_rev_level,
                       CPU_BOOLEAN  rd_only,
                       USBD_ERR    *p_err);
```

ARGUMENTS

p_store_name   Pointer to logical unit driver.

class_nbr   MSC instance number.

p_vend_id   Pointer to string containing vendor id.

p_prod_id   Pointer to string containing product id.

prod_rev_level   Product revision level.

rd_only   Boolean specifying if logical unit is read only or not.

p_err   Pointer to variable that will receive the return error code from this function.

> USBD_ERR_NONE
> USBD_ERR_INVALID_ARG
> USBD_ERR_MSC_MAX_LUN_EXCEED
> USBD_ERR_SCSI_LOG_UNIT_NOTRDY

RETURNED VALUE

None.

CALLERS

Application.

NOTES / WARNINGS

The pointer to logical unit driver specifies the type and volume of the logical unit to add. Valid logical unit driver names follow the pattern:

```
<device_driver_name>:<logical_unit_number>:
```

where `<device_driver_name>` is the name of the device driver and `<logical_unit_number>` is the device's logical unit number. Take special note that the logical unit number starts counting from number 0.

E

E-1-5   USBD_MSC_IsConn()

Get MSC connection state of the device.

FILES

usbd_msc.h / usbd_msc.c

PROTOTYPE

```
CPU_BOOLEAN  USBD_MSC_IsConn (CPU_INT08U  class_nbr);
```

ARGUMENTS

class_nbr   MSC instance number.

RETURNED VALUE

DEF_YES, if MSC is connected.
DEF_NO, otherwise.

CALLERS

Application.

NOTES / WARNINGS

USBD_MSC_IsConn() is typically used to verify that the device is in 'configured' state and that the MSC instance is ready for communication. The following code illustrates a typical example:

```
CPU_BOOLEAN  conn;

conn = USBD_MSC_IsConn(class_nbr);
if (conn != DEF_YES) {
    USBD_MSC_OS_EnumSignalPend((CPU_INT16U)0,
                                        &os_err);
}
```

Once the connected status is DEF_YES, the communication can start.

E-1-6 USBD_MSC_TaskHandler()

Task to handle transfers for the MSC bulk-only transport protocol.

usbd_msc.h / usbd_msc.c

```
void  USBD_MSC_TaskHandler (CPU_INT08U   class_nbr);
```

class_nbr   MSC instance number.

None.

OS layer.

None.

E-2 MSC OS FUNCTIONS

E-2-1 USBD_MSC_OS_Init()

Initialize MSC OS interface.

FILES

usbd_msc_os.h / usbd_msc_os.c

PROTOTYPE

```
void  USBD_MSC_OS_Init (USBD_ERR        *p_err)
```

ARGUMENTS

p_err   Pointer to variable that will receive the return error code from this function.

            USBD_ERR_NONE
            USBD_ERR_OS_FAIL

RETURNED VALUE

None.

CALLERS

USBD_OS_Init()

IMPLEMENTATION GUIDELINES

Initialization of the MSC OS interface must include creating:

1. Two semaphores, one for MSC communication and one for enumeration.

2. A MSC task to handle the MSC protocol.

3. A Refresh task if µC/FS storage layer is used with removable media.

E-2-2 USBD_MSC_OS_CommSignalPost()

Post a semaphore used for MSC communication.

FILES

usbd_msc_os.h / usbd_msc_os.c

PROTOTYPE

```
void  USBD_MSC_OS_CommSignalPost (CPU_INT08U   class_nbr,
                                  USBD_ERR     *p_err)
```

ARGUMENTS

class_nbr   MSC instance class number.

p_err   Pointer to variable that will receive the return error code from this function.

             USBD_ERR_NONE
             USBD_ERR_OS_FAIL

RETURNED VALUE

None.

CALLERS

Various.

NOTES / WARNINGS

None.

E-2-3 USBD_MSC_OS_CommSignalPend()

Wait on a semaphore to become available for MSC communication.

FILES

usbd_msc_os.h / usbd_msc_os.c

PROTOTYPE

```
void  USBD_MSC_OS_CommSignalPend (CPU_INT08U  class_nbr,
                                  CPU_INT32U  timeout,
                                  USBD_ERR    *p_err);
```

ARGUMENTS

class_nbr   MSC instance class number.

timeout   Timeout in milliseconds.

p_err   Pointer to variable that will receive the return error code from this function.

            USBD_ERR_NONE
            USBD_ERR_OS_TIMEOUT
            USBD_ERR_OS_FAIL

RETURNED VALUE

None.

CALLERS

Various.

NOTES / WARNINGS

None.

E-2-4 USBD_MSC_OS_CommSignalDel()

Delete a semaphore if no tasks are waiting on it for MSC communication.

FILES

usbd_msc_os.h / usbd_msc_os.c

PROTOTYPE

```
void  USBD_MSC_OS_CommSignalDel (CPU_INT08U  class_nbr,
                                 USBD_ERR    *p_err);
```

ARGUMENTS

class_nbr   MSC instance class number.

p_err   Pointer to variable that will receive the return error code from this function.

        USBD_ERR_NONE
        USBD_ERR_OS_FAIL

RETURNED VALUE

None.

CALLERS

Various.

NOTES / WARNINGS

None.

E

E-2-5 USBD_MSC_OS_EnumSignalPost()

Post a semaphore for MSC enumeration process.

FILES

usbd_msc_os.h / usbd_msc_os.c

PROTOTYPE

```
void  USBD_MSC_OS_EnumSignalPost (USBD_ERR  *p_err);
```

ARGUMENTS

p_err   Pointer to variable that will receive the return error code from this function.

             USBD_ERR_NONE
             USBD_ERR_OS_FAIL

RETURNED VALUE

None.

CALLERS

Various.

NOTES / WARNINGS

None.

E-2-6 USBD_MSC_OS_EnumSignalPend()

Wait on a semaphore to become available for MSC enumeration process.

FILES

usbd_msc_os.h / usbd_msc_os.c

PROTOTYPE

```
void  USBD_MSC_OS_EnumSignalPend (CPU_INT32U  timeout,
                                  USBD_ERR    *p_err);
```

ARGUMENTS

timeout   Timeout in milliseconds.

p_err   Pointer to variable that will receive the return error code from this function.

             USBD_ERR_NONE
             USBD_ERR_OS_TIMEOUT
             USBD_ERR_OS_FAIL

RETURNED VALUE

None.

CALLERS

Various.

NOTES / WARNINGS

None.

E

E-2-7 USBD_MSC_OS_Task()

Process the MSC protocol.

FILES

usbd_msc_os.c

PROTOTYPE

```
static void USBD_MSC_OS_Task (void *p_arg);
```

ARGUMENTS

p_arg   Pointer to task initialization argument.

CALLERS

This is a task.

IMPLEMENTATION GUIDELINES

The task should call **USBD_MSC_TaskHandler()** function defined in the MSC layer. This function implements the task body, usually an infinite loop, responsible for the MSC protocol management.

E-2-8 USBD_MSC_OS_RefreshTask()

Detect the insertion or removal of removable media. Defined only if the µC/FS storage layer is used.

usbd_msc_os.c

```
static  void  USBD_MSC_OS_RefreshTask (void  *p_arg);
```

p_arg   Pointer to task initialization argument.

This is a task.

The task body is usually implemented as an infinite loop. The task should perform the following steps:

■ Call **USBD_StorageRefreshTaskHandler()** function defined in the µC/FS storage layer. This function implements the removable media insertion/removable detection..

■ Delay for a certain period of time. This delay is configurable by you through the configuration constant, **USBD_MSC_CFG_DEV_POLL_DLY_mS**. Refer to section 10-4-1 "General Configuration" on page 226 fore more details about this constant.

E-3 MSC STORAGE LAYER FUNCTIONS

E-3-1 USBD_StorageInit()

Initialize internal structures and local global variables used by the storage medium.

FILES

usbd_storage.h / usbd_storage.c

PROTOTYPE

```
void  USBD_StorageInit (USBD_ERR        *p_err)
```

ARGUMENTS

p_err   Pointer to variable that will receive the return error code from this function.

        USBD_ERR_NONE

RETURNED VALUE

None.

CALLERS

USBD_SCSI_Init( )

NOTES / WARNINGS

None.

E-3-2 USBD_StorageAdd()

Initialize the storage medium.

FILES

usbd_storage.h / usbd_storage.c

PROTOTYPE

```
void  USBD_StorageAdd (USBD_STORAGE_LUN  *p_storage_lun);
                       USBD_ERR          *p_err)
```

ARGUMENTS

p_storage_lunPointer to logical unit storage structure.

p_err   Pointer to variable that will receive the return error code from this function.

            USBD_ERR_NONE
            USBD_ERR_SCSI_LU_NOTRDY

RETURNED VALUE

None.

CALLERS

USBD_SCSI_LunAdd()

NOTES / WARNINGS

None.

E

E-3-3 USBD_StorageCapacityGet()

Get the capacity of the storage medium.

FILES

usbd_storage.h / usbd_storage.c

PROTOTYPE

```
void  USBD_StorageCapacityGet (USBD_STORAGE_LUN  *p_storage_lun),
                               CPU_INT64U        *p_nbr_blks,
                               CPU_INT32U        *p_blk_size,
                               USBD_ERR          *p_err)
```

ARGUMENTS

p_storage_lun   Pointer to logical unit storage structure.

p_nbr_blks   Pointer to variable that will receive the number of logical blocks.

p_blk_size   Pointer to variable that will receive the size of each block, in bytes.

p_err   Pointer to variable that will receive the return error code from this function.

>   USBD_ERR_NONE
>   USBD_ERR_SCSI_MEDIUM_NOTPRESENT

RETURNED VALUE

None.

CALLERS

USBD_SCSI_ProcessCmd( )

NOTES / WARNINGS

None.

E-3-4 USBD_StorageRd()

Read data from the storage medium.

FILES

usbd_storage.h / usbd_storage.c

PROTOTYPE

```
void  USBD_StorageRd (USBD_STORAGE_LUN  *p_storage_lun,
                      CPU_INT32U         blk_addr,
                      CPU_INT32U         nbr_blks,
                      CPU_INT08U        *p_data_buf,
                      USBD_ERR          *p_err);
```

ARGUMENTS

p_storage_lun   Pointer to the logical unit storage structure.

blk_addr   Logical Block Address (LBA) of read block start.

nbr_blks   Number of logical blocks to read.

p_data_buf   Pointer to buffer in which data will be stored.

p_err   Pointer to variable that will receive the return error code from this function.

             USBD_ERR_NONE
             USBD_ERR_SCSI_MEDIUM_NOT_PRESENT

RETURNED VALUE

None.

E

CALLERS

USBD_SCSI_RdData()

NOTES / WARNINGS

None.

E-3-5 USBD_StorageWr()

Write data to the storage medium.

FILES

usbd_storage.h / usbd_storage.c

PROTOTYPE

```
void  USBD_StorageWr (USBD_STORAGE_LUN  *p_storage_lun,
                      CPU_INT32U         blk_addr,
                      CPU_INT32U         nbr_blks,
                      CPU_INT08U        *p_data_buf,
                      USBD_ERR          *p_err);
```

ARGUMENTS

p_storage_lun   Pointer to logical unit storage structure

blk_addr   Logical Block Address (LBA) of write block start.

nbr_blks   Number of logical blocks to write.

p_data_buf   Pointer to buffer in which data is stored.

p_err   Pointer to variable that receives the return error code from this function.

               USBD_ERR_NONE
               USBD_ERR_SCSI_MEDIUM_NOTPRESENT

RETURNED VALUE

None.

E

CALLERS

USBD_SCSI_WrData( )

NOTES / WARNINGS

None.

E-3-6 USBD_StorageStatusGet()

Get the presence of the storage medium.

FILES

usbd_storage.h / usbd_storage.c

PROTOTYPE

```
void  USBD_StorageStatusGet (USBD_STORAGE_LUN  *p_storage_lun,
                             USBD_ERR          *p_err);
```

ARGUMENTS

p_storage_lun   Pointer to logical unit storage structure

p_err   Pointer to variable that will receive the return error code from this function.

            USBD_ERR_NONE
            USBD_ERR_SCSI_MEDIUM_NOTPRESENT
            USBD_ERR_SCSI_MEDIUM_NOT_RDY_TO_RDY
            USBD_ERR_SCSI_MEDIUM_RDY_TO_NOT_RDY

RETURNED VALUE

None.

CALLERS

USBD_SCSI_ProcessCmd()

NOTES / WARNINGS

None.

E-3-7   USBD_StorageLock()

Lock the storage medium.

FILES

usbd_storage.h / usbd_storage.c

PROTOTYPE

```
void  USBD_StorageLock (USBD_STORAGE_LUN  *p_storage_lun,
                        CPU_INT32U         timeout_ms,
                        USBD_ERR          *p_err)
```

ARGUMENTS

p_storage_lun   Pointer to logical unit storage structure

timeout_ms   Timeout in milliseconds.

p_err   Pointer to variable that will receive the return error code from this function.

              USBD_ERR_NONE
              USBD_ERR_SCSI_LOCK_TIMEOUT
              USBD_ERR_SCSI_LOCK

RETURNED VALUE

None.

CALLERS

USBD_SCSI_ProcessCmd()

NOTES / WARNINGS

None.

E-3-8 USBD_StorageUnlock()

Unlock the storage medium.

FILES

usbd_storage.h / usbd_storage.c

PROTOTYPE

```
void  USBD_StorageLock (USBD_STORAGE_LUN  *p_storage_lun,
                        USBD_ERR          *p_err)
```

ARGUMENTS

p_storage_lun   Pointer to logical unit storage structure

p_err   Pointer to variable that will receive the return error code from this function.

         USBD_ERR_NONE
         USBD_ERR_SCSI_UNLOCK

RETURNED VALUE

None.

CALLERS

USBD_SCSI_ProcessCmd( )

USBD_SCSI_Unlock()

NOTES / WARNINGS

None.

E

E-3-9 USBD_StorageRefreshTaskHandler()

Check the removable media presence status, that is insertion/removal detection. Defined only for the µC/FS storage layer.

FILES

usbd_storage.h / usbd_storage.c

PROTOTYPE

```
void  USBD_StorageRefreshTaskHandler (void *p_arg)
```

ARGUMENTS

p_arg   Pointer to task initialization argument.

RETURNED VALUE

None.

CALLERS

USBD_MSC_OS_Refresh_Task()

NOTES / WARNINGS

None.

PHDC API Reference

This appendix provides a reference to the Personal Healthcare Device Class (PHDC) API. Each user-accessible service is presented following a category order (i.e. initialization, communication and RTOS layer categories). The following information is provided for each of the services:

■ A brief description

■ The function prototype

■ The filename of the source code

■ A description of the arguments passed to the function

■ A description of returned value(s)

Specific notes and warnings regarding use of the service.

F

F-1 PHDC FUNCTIONS

F-1-1 USBD_PHDC_Init()

Initialize internal structures and local global variables used by the PHDC.

FILES

usbd_phdc.h / usbd_phdc.c

PROTOTYPE

```
void  USBD_PHDC_Init (USBD_ERR  *p_err);
```

ARGUMENTS

p_err   Pointer to variable that will receive the return error code from this function.

              USBD_ERR_NONE

RETURNED VALUE

None.

CALLERS

Application.

NOTES / WARNINGS

None.

F-1-2 USBD_PHDC_Add()

Create a new instance of the PHDC.

FILES

usbd_phdc.h / usbd_phdc.c

PROTOTYPE

```
CPU_INT08U  USBD_PHDC_Add (CPU_BOOLEAN                data_fmt_11073,
                           CPU_BOOLEAN                preamble_capable,
                           USBD_PHDC_PREAMBLE_EN_NOTIFY  preamble_en_notify,
                           CPU_INT16U                 low_latency_interval,
                           USBD_ERR                   *p_err)
```

ARGUMENTS

data_fmt_11073   Variable that indicates whether the class instance uses IEEE 11073 or a vendor-defined data format.

                      DEF_YES   Class instance uses IEEE 11073 data format.

                      DEF_NO   Class instance uses vendor-defined data format.

preamble_capable   Variable that indicates whether the class instance support metadata message preamble or not.

                      DEF_YES   Class instance support metadata message preamble.

                      DEF_NO   Class instance doesn't support metadata message preamble.

preamble_en_notify   Pointer to a callback function that will notify the application if the host enable / disable metadata message preamble.

low_latency_interval   Interrupt endpoint interval in frames or microframes. Can be 0 if PHDC device will not send low latency data.

517

p_err   Pointer to variable that will receive the return error code from this function.

   USBD_ERR_NONE
   USBD_ERR_ALLOC

RETURNED VALUE

Class instance number,   if NO error(s).

USBD_CLASS_NBR_NONE, otherwise.

CALLERS

Application.

NOTES / WARNINGS

None.

F-1-3 USBD_PHDC_CfgAdd()

Add a PHDC instance into the specified configuration. The PHDC instance was previously created by the function USBD_PHDC_Add( ).

FILES

usbd_phdc.h / usbd_phdc.c

PROTOTYPE

```
void  USBD_PHDC_CfgAdd (CPU_INT08U   class_nbr,
                        CPU_INT08U   dev_nbr,
                        CPU_INT08U   cfg_nbr,
                        USBD_ERR     *p_err);
```

ARGUMENTS

class_nbr   PHDC instance number.

dev_nbr   Device number.

cfg_nbr   Configuration index to add PHDC instance to.

p_err   Pointer to variable that will receive the return error code from this function.

             USBD_ERR_NONE
             USBD_ERR_INVALID_ARG
             USBD_ERR_ALLOC
             USBD_ERR_NULL_PTR
             USBD_ERR_DEV_INVALID_NBR
             USBD_ERR_DEV_INVALID_STATE
             USBD_ERR_CFG_INVALID_NBR
             USBD_ERR_IF_ALLOC
             USBD_ERR_IF_ALT_ALLOC
             USBD_ERR_IF_INVALID_NBR
             USBD_ERR_EP_NONE_AVAIL
             USBD_ERR_EP_ALLOC

RETURNED VALUE

None.

CALLERS

Application.

NOTES / WARNINGS

USBD_PHDC_CfgAdd() basically adds an Interface descriptor and its associated Endpoint descriptor(s) to the Configuration descriptor. One call to USBD_PHDC_CfgAdd() builds the Configuration descriptor corresponding to a PHDC device with the following format:

```
Configuration Descriptor
|-- Interface Descriptor (PHDC)
    |-- Endpoint Descriptor (Bulk OUT)
    |-- Endpoint Descriptor (Bulk IN)
    |-- Endpoint Descriptor (Interrupt IN)  - optional
```

The Interrupt IN endpoint is optional. It will be added to the Interface descriptor if application specified that it will send low latency data when calling USBD_PHDC_WrCfg().

If USBD_PHDC_CfgAdd() is called several times from the application, it allows to create multiple instances and multiple configurations. For instance, the following architecture could be created for an high-speed device:

```
High-speed
|-- Configuration 0
    |-- Interface 0 (PHDC 0)
|-- Configuration 1
    |-- Interface 0 (PHDC 0)
    |-- Interface 1 (PHDC 1)
```

In that example, there are two instances of PHDC: 'PHDC 0' and 'PHDC 1', and two possible configurations for the device: 'Configuration 0' and 'Configuration 1'. 'Configuration 1' is composed of two interfaces. Each class instance has an association with one of the interfaces. If 'Configuration 1' is activated by the host, it allows the host to access two different functionalities offered by the device.

F-1-4 USBD_PHDC_IsConn()

Get PHDC connection state.

FILES

usbd_phdc.h / usbd_phdc.c

PROTOTYPE

```
CPU_BOOLEAN  USBD_PHDC_IsConn (CPU_INT08U  class_nbr);
```

ARGUMENTS

class_nbr   PHDC instance number.

RETURNED VALUE

DEF_YES, if PHDC is connected.

DEF_NO, otherwise.

CALLERS

Application.

F

NOTES / WARNINGS

USBD_PHDC_IsConn( ) is typically used to verify that the device is in 'configured' state and that the PHDC instance is ready for communication. The following code illustrates a typical example:

```
CPU_BOOLEAN  conn;

conn = USBD_PHDC_IsConn(class_nbr);
while (conn != DEF_YES) {
    OSTimeDlyHMSM(0, 0, 0, 250);

    conn = USBD_PHDC_IsConn(class_nbr);
}
```

Once the connected status is DEF_YES, the communication can start.

F-1-5 USBD_PHDC_RdCfg()

Initialize read communication pipe parameters.

FILES

usbd_phdc.h / usbd_phdc.c

PROTOTYPE

```
void  USBD_PHDC_RdCfg (CPU_INT08U          class_nbr,
                       LATENCY_RELY_FLAGS  latency_rely,
                       CPU_INT08U          *p_data_opaque,
                       CPU_INT08U          data_opaque_len,
                       USBD_ERR            *p_err);
```

ARGUMENTS

class_nbr   PHDC instance number.

latency_rely   Bitmap of transfer latency / reliability that this communication
                     pipe will carry. Can be one or more of these values:

                     USBD_PHDC_LATENCY_VERYHIGH_RELY_BEST
                     USBD_PHDC_LATENCY_HIGH_RELY_BEST
                     USBD_PHDC_LATENCY_MEDIUM_RELY_BEST

p_data_opaque   Pointer to a buffer that contains opaque data related to this
                     communication pipe.

data_opaque_len   Length of opaque data (in octets). If 0, no metadata descriptor
                     will be written for the endpoint.

p_err   Pointer to variable that will receive the return error code from this function.

                     USBD_ERR_NONE
                     USBD_ERR_NULL_PTR
                     USBD_ERR_INVALID_ARG

F

RETURNED VALUE

None.

CALLERS

Application.

NOTES / WARNINGS

USBD_PHDC_RdCfg() should be called after USBD_PHDC_Init() and USBD_PHDC_Add() but before USBD_PHDC_CfgAdd().

F-1-6 USBD_PHDC_WrCfg()

Initialize write communication pipe parameters.

FILES

usbd_phdc.h / usbd_phdc.c

PROTOTYPE

```
void  USBD_PHDC_WrCfg (CPU_INT08U          class_nbr,
                       LATENCY_RELY_FLAGS   latency_rely,
                       CPU_INT08U          *p_data_opaque,
                       CPU_INT08U           data_opaque_len,
                       USBD_ERR            *p_err);
```

ARGUMENTS

class_nbr   PHDC instance number.

latency_rely   Bitmap of transfer Latency / reliability that this communication
                        pipe will carry. Can be one or more of these values:

                        USBD_PHDC_LATENCY_VERYHIGH_RELY_BEST
                        USBD_PHDC_LATENCY_HIGH_RELY_BEST
                        USBD_PHDC_LATENCY_MEDIUM_RELY_BEST
                        USBD_PHDC_LATENCY_MEDIUM_RELY_BETTER
                        USBD_PHDC_LATENCY_MEDIUM_RELY_GOOD
                        USBD_PHDC_LATENCY_LOW_RELY_GOOD

p_data_opaque   Pointer to a buffer that contains opaque data related to this
                        communication pipe.

data_opaque_len   Length of opaque data (in octets). If 0, no metadata descriptor
                        will be written for the endpoint.

p_err   Pointer to variable that will receive the return error code from this function.

USBD_ERR_NONE
USBD_ERR_NULL_PTR
USBD_ERR_INVALID_ARG

RETURNED VALUE

None.

CALLERS

Application.

NOTES / WARNINGS

USBD_PHDC_WrCfg() should be called after USBD_PHDC_Init() and USBD_PHDC_Add() but before USBD_PHDC_CfgAdd().

Since low latency transfers will use a different endpoint, it is possible to set different opaque data for that endpoint. In case the application need different opaque data for low latency pipe, USBD_PHDC_WrCfg() should be called twice. Once with all the desired latency/reliability flags set except for low latency, opaque data passed at this call will be used for the Bulk endpoint metadata descriptor. USBD_PHDC_WrCfg() should then be called once again with only the low latency flag set, opaque data passed at this call will be used for interrupt endpoint metadata descriptor.

F-1-7 USBD_PHDC_11073_ExtCfg()

Configure function extension for given class instance.

FILES

usbd_phdc.h / usbd_phdc.c

PROTOTYPE

```
void  USBD_PHDC_11073_ExtCfg (CPU_INT08U   class_nbr,
                              CPU_INT16U  *p_dev_specialization,
                              CPU_INT08U   nbr_dev_specialization,
                              USBD_ERR    *p_err);
```

ARGUMENTS

class_nbr   PHDC instance number.

p_dev_specialization   Pointer to an array that contains a list of device
                                   specializations.

nbr_dev_specialization   Number of device specializations specified in
                                   p_dev_specialization.

p_err   Pointer to variable that will receive the return error code from this function.

             USBD_ERR_NONE
             USBD_ERR_INVALID_ARG

RETURNED VALUE

None.

CALLERS

Application.

F

NOTES / WARNINGS

`USBD_PHDC_11073_ExtCfg()` should be called only if PHDC instance uses 11073 data format.

`USBD_PHDC_11073_ExtCfg()` should be called after `USBD_PHDC_Init()` and `USBD_PHDC_Add()` but before `USBD_PHDC_CfgAdd()`.

For more information on 11073 device specialization, See 'Personal Healthcare Device Class specifications Revision 1.0', Appendix A. For a list of known device specialization, see 'Nomenclature code annex of ISO/IEEE 11073-20601'. Specific code are listed in the 'From Communication infrastructure (MDC_PART_INFRA)' section.

F-1-8 USBD_PHDC_RdPreamble()

Read metadata preamble. This function is blocking.

FILES

usbd_phdc.h / usbd_phdc.c

PROTOTYPE

```
CPU_INT08U  USBD_PHDC_RdPreamble (CPU_INT08U   class_nbr,
                                  void        *p_buf,
                                  CPU_INT08U   buf_len,
                                  CPU_INT08U  *p_nbr_xfer,
                                  CPU_INT16U   timeout,
                                  USBD_ERR    *p_err);
```

ARGUMENTS

class_nbr   PHDC instance number.

p_buf   Pointer to buffer that will contain data from metadata message preamble.

buf_len   Opaque data buffer length in octets.

p_nbr_xfer   Pointer to a variable that will contain the number of transfer the preamble
             will apply to. After this call, **USBD_PHDC_Rd** shall be called **nbr_xfer** times by
             the application.

timeout   Timeout in milliseconds.

p_err   Pointer to variable that will receive the return error code from this function.

             USBD_ERR_NONE
             USBD_ERR_INVALID_CLASS_STATE
             USBD_ERR_INVALID_ARG
             USBD_ERR_NULL_PTR
             USBD_ERR_ALLOC
             USBD_ERR_RX
             USBD_ERR_DEV_INVALID_NBR

F

USBD_ERR_EP_INVALID_NBR
USBD_ERR_DEV_INVALID_STATE
USBD_ERR_EP_INVALID_TYPE
USBD_OS_ERR_TIMEOUT
USBD_OS_ERR_ABORT
USBD_OS_ERR_FAIL

RETURNED VALUE

Length of opaque data read from metadata preamble, if no error.

0, otherwise

CALLERS

Application.

NOTES / WARNINGS

USBD_PHDC_RdPreamble() should always be called before **USBD_PHDC_Rd()** if metadata message preambles are enabled by the host. Application should then call **USBD_PHDC_Rd()** **p_nbr_xfer** times.

If host disable preamble while application is pending on this function, the call will immediately return with error '**USBD_OS_ERR_ABORT**'.

F-1-9 USBD_PHDC_Rd()

Read PHDC data. This function is blocking.

usbd_phdc.h / usbd_phdc.c

```
CPU_INT08U  USBD_PHDC_Rd (CPU_INT08U   class_nbr,
                          void        *p_buf,
                          CPU_INT16U   buf_len,
                          CPU_INT16U   timeout,
                          USBD_ERR    *p_err);
```

class_nbr   PHDC instance number.

p_buf   Pointer to buffer that will contain opaque data from metadata message preamble.

buf_len   Opaque data buffer length in octets.

timeout   Timeout in milliseconds.

p_err   Pointer to variable that will receive the return error code from this function.

            USBD_ERR_NONE
            USBD_ERR_INVALID_CLASS_STATE
            USBD_ERR_INVALID_ARG
            USBD_ERR_NULL_PTR
            USBD_ERR_RX
            USBD_ERR_DEV_INVALID_NBR
            USBD_ERR_EP_INVALID_NBR
            USBD_ERR_DEV_INVALID_STATE
            USBD_ERR_EP_INVALID_TYPE
            USBD_OS_ERR_TIMEOUT
            USBD_OS_ERR_ABORT
            USBD_OS_ERR_FAIL

RETURNED VALUE

Number of octets received, if no error(s).

0, otherwise.

CALLERS

Application.

NOTES / WARNINGS

`USBD_PHDC_Rd()` should always be called after `USBD_PHDC_RdPreamble()` if metadata message preambles are enabled by the host.

Application should ensure that the length of the buffer provided is large enough to accommodate the incoming transfer. Otherwise, synchronization with metadata preambles might be lost.

If host enable preamble while application is pending on this function, the call will immediately return with error '`USBD_OS_ERR_ABORT`'.

F-1-10 USBD_PHDC_Wrpreamble()

Write metadata preamble. This function is blocking.

usbd_phdc.h / usbd_phdc.c

```
void  USBD_PHDC_WrPreamble (CPU_INT08U           class_nbr,
                            void                 *p_data_opaque,
                            CPU_INT16U           data_opaque_len,
                            LATENCY_RELY_FLAGS   latency_rely
                            CPU_INT08U           nbr_xfers,
                            CPU_INT16U           timeout,
                            USBD_ERR             *p_err);
```

class_nbr   PHDC instance number.

p_data_opaque   Pointer to buffer that will supply opaque data.

data_opaque_len   Length of opaque data buffer in octets.

latency_rely   Latency reliability of related transfers.

nbr_xfers   Number of transfers this preamble will apply to.

timeout   Timeout in milliseconds.

p_err   Pointer to variable that will receive the return error code from this function.

             USBD_ERR_NONE
             USBD_ERR_INVALID_ARG
             USBD_ERR_NULL_PTR
             USBD_ERR_TX
             USBD_ERR_DEV_INVALID_NBR
             USBD_ERR_DEV_INVALID_STATE

F

```
USBD_ERR_EP_INVALID_ADDR
USBD_ERR_EP_INVALID_STATE
USBD_ERR_EP_INVALID_TYPE
USBD_OS_ERR_TIMEOUT
USBD_OS_ERR_ABORT
USBD_OS_ERR_FAIL
```

RETURNED VALUE

None.

CALLERS

Application.

NOTES / WARNINGS

USBD_PHDC_WrPreamble() should always be called before USBD_PHDC_Wr() if metadata message preambles are enabled by the host and if the latency of the transfer is not 'low'.

Application will have to call USBD_PHDC_Wr() 'nbr_xfers' of times with the same latency / reliability parameter after a call to USBD_PHDC_WrPreamble().

F-1-11 USBD_PHDC_Wr()

Write PHDC data. This function is blocking.

FILES

usbd_phdc.h / usbd_phdc.c

PROTOTYPE

```
void  USBD_PHDC_Wr (CPU_INT08U           class_nbr,
                    void                 *p_buf,
                    CPU_INT16U           buf_len,
                    LATENCY_RELY_FLAGS   latency_rely
                    CPU_INT16U           timeout,
                    USBD_ERR             *p_err);
```

ARGUMENTS

class_nbr   PHDC instance number.

p_buf   Pointer to buffer that will supply data.

buf_len   Buffer length in octets.

latency_rely   Latency / reliability of this transfer.

timeout   Timeout in milliseconds.

p_err   Pointer to variable that will receive the return error code from this function.

             USBD_ERR_NONE
             USBD_ERR_INVALID_ARG
             USBD_ERR_NULL_PTR
             USBD_ERR_TX
             USBD_ERR_INVALID_CLASS_STATE
             USBD_ERR_DEV_INVALID_NBR
             USBD_ERR_DEV_INVALID_STATE
             USBD_ERR_EP_INVALID_ADDR
             USBD_ERR_EP_INVALID_STATE

USBD_ERR_EP_INVALID_TYPE
USBD_OS_ERR_TIMEOUT
USBD_OS_ERR_ABORT
USBD_OS_ERR_FAIL

RETURNED VALUE

None.

CALLERS

Application.

NOTES / WARNINGS

USBD_PHDC_Wr() should always be called after USBD_PHDC_WrPreamble() if metadata message preambles are enabled by the host and if the latency of the transfer is not 'low'.

Application will have to call USBD_PHDC_Wr() 'nbr_xfers' of times with the same latency / reliability parameter after a call to USBD_PHDC_WrPreamble().

F-1-12 USBD_PHDC_Reset()

Reset PHDC instance.

FILES

usbd_phdc.h / usbd_phdc.c

PROTOTYPE

```
void  USBD_PHDC_Reset (CPU_INT08U  class_nbr);
```

ARGUMENTS

class_nbr   PHDC instance number.

RETURNED VALUE

None.

CALLERS

USBD_PHDC_Disconn() and Application.

NOTES / WARNINGS

USBD_PHDC_Reset() should be used to reset internal variables like the transmit priority queue of the PHDC instance.

This function should be called when the data layer above PHDC request to terminate communication. For instance, USBD_PHDC_Reset() should be called when the host send an '11073 Association abort' request.

F-2 PHDC OS LAYER FUNCTIONS

F-2-1 USBD_PHDC_OS_Init()

Initialize PHDC OS layer.

FILES

usbd_phdc_os.h / usbd_phdc_os.c

PROTOTYPE

```
void  USBD_PHDC_OS_Init (USBD_ERR  *p_err);
```

ARGUMENTS

p_err   Pointer to variable that will receive the return error code from this function.

RETURNED VALUE

None.

CALLERS

USBD_PHDC_Init()

IMPLEMENTATION GUIDELINES

This function should be used to initialize all RTOS layer's internal variables / tasks of every class instances. It will be called only once.

In case creation of semaphore, mutex, or other signal fails, the function should assign USBD_ERR_OS_SIGNAL_CREATE to p_err and return immediately. If any other error occurs, USBD_ERR_OS_INIT_FAIL should be assigned to p_err. Otherwise, USBD_ERR_NONE should be used.

F-2-2 USBD_PHDC_OS_RdLock()

Lock the read pipe.

FILES

usbd_phdc_os.h / usbd_phdc_os.c

PROTOTYPE

```
void  USBD_PHDC_OS_RdLock (CPU_INT08U  class_nbr,
                           CPU_INT16U  timeout,
                           USBD_ERR    *p_err);
```

ARGUMENTS

class_nbr   PHDC instance number.

timeout   Timeout.

p_err   Pointer to variable that will receive the return error code from this function.

RETURNED VALUE

None.

CALLERS

USBD_PHDC_Rd( ), USBD_PHDC_RdPreamble( )

IMPLEMENTATION GUIDELINES

Typical implementation will consist in pending on a semaphore that locks the read pipe.

p_err argument should be assigned as described in Table F-1.

F

Operation result	Error code to assign
No error	USBD_ERR_NONE
Pend timeout	USBD_ERR_OS_TIMEOUT
Pend aborted	USBD_ERR_OS_ABORT
Pend failed for any other reason	USBD_ERR_OS_FAIL

Table F-1 **p_err assignment in function of operation result**

F-2-3 USBD_PHDC_OS_RdUnLock()

Unlock the read pipe.

FILES

usbd_phdc_os.h / usbd_phdc_os.c

PROTOTYPE

```
void  USBD_PHDC_OS_RdUnlock (CPU_INT08U  class_nbr);
```

ARGUMENTS

class_nbr   PHDC instance number.

RETURNED VALUE

None.

CALLERS

USBD_PHDC_Rd( ), USBD_PHDC_RdPreamble( )

IMPLEMENTATION GUIDELINES

Typical implementation will consist in posting a semaphore that locks the read pipe.

F

F-2-4 USBD_PHDC_OS_WrIntrLock()

Lock the write interrupt pipe.

FILES

usbd_phdc_os.h / usbd_phdc_os.c

PROTOTYPE

```
void  USBD_PHDC_OS_WrIntrLock (CPU_INT08U  class_nbr,
                              CPU_INT16U  timeout,
                              USBD_ERR    *p_err);
```

ARGUMENTS

class_nbr   PHDC instance number.

timeout   Timeout.

p_err   Pointer to variable that will receive the return error code from this function.

RETURNED VALUE

None.

CALLERS

USBD_PHDC_Wr()

IMPLEMENTATION GUIDELINES

Typical implementation will consist in pending on a semaphore that locks the write interrupt pipe.

p_err argument should be assigned as described in Table F-1.

F-2-5 USBD_PHDC_OS_WrIntrUnLock()

Unlock the write interrupt pipe.

FILES

usbd_phdc_os.h / usbd_phdc_os.c

PROTOTYPE

```
void  USBD_PHDC_OS_WrIntrUnlock (CPU_INT08U  class_nbr);
```

ARGUMENTS

class_nbr   PHDC instance number.

RETURNED VALUE

None.

CALLERS

USBD_PHDC_Wr()

IMPLEMENTATION GUIDELINES

Typical implementation will consist in posting a semaphore that locks the write interrupt pipe.

F

F-2-6 USBD_PHDC_OS_WrBulkLock()

Lock the write bulk pipe.

FILES

usbd_phdc_os.h / usbd_phdc_os.c

PROTOTYPE

```
void  USBD_PHDC_OS_WrBulkLock (CPU_INT08U  class_nbr,
                               CPU_INT08U  prio,
                               CPU_INT16U  timeout,
                               USBD_ERR    *p_err);
```

ARGUMENTS

class_nbr   PHDC instance number.

prio   Priority of the transfer. This value is between 0 and 4 and is computed in function of the transfer's QoS by the caller.

timeout   Timeout.

p_err   Pointer to variable that will receive the return error code from this function.

RETURNED VALUE

None.

CALLERS

USBD_PHDC_Wr(), USBD_PHDC_WrPreamble().

IMPLEMENTATION GUIDELINES

Two typical implementations will be possible here. The first one consists in pending on a semaphore that locks the write bulk pipe, just as we saw previously.

But since different QoS data can travel using a single bulk IN endpoint, you might want to prioritize them in function of the QoS. See section 11-4 "RTOS QoS-based scheduler" on page 253 for more details on how a priority manager can be implemented.

p_err argument should be assigned as described in Table F-1.

F

F-2-7 USBD_PHDC_OS_WrBulkUnLock()

Unlock the write bulk pipe.

FILES

usbd_phdc_os.h / usbd_phdc_os.c

PROTOTYPE

```
void  USBD_PHDC_OS_WrBulkUnlock (CPU_INT08U  class_nbr);
```

ARGUMENTS

class_nbr   PHDC instance number.

RETURNED VALUE

None.

CALLERS

USBD_PHDC_Wr()

IMPLEMENTATION GUIDELINES

Two typical implementations will be possible here. The first one consists in posting the semaphore that locks the write bulk pipe, if no priority management is implemented. However, if priority management has been integrated, this call should release the scheduler (See Section 11-4, "RTOS QoS-based scheduler" on page 253).

Vendor Class API Reference

This appendix provides a reference to the Vendor class API. Each user-accessible service is presented following a category order (i.e., initialization and communication categories). The following information is provided for each of the services:

- A brief description

- The function prototype

- The filename of the source code

- A description of the arguments passed to the function

- A description of returned value(s)

- Specific notes and warnings regarding use of the service.

G

G-1 VENDOR CLASS FUNCTIONS

G-1-1 USBD_Vendor_Init()

Initialize internal structures and local global variables used by the Vendor class.

FILES

usbd_vendor.c

PROTOTYPE

```
void  USBD_Vendor_Init (USBD_ERR  *p_err);
```

ARGUMENTS

p_err   Pointer to variable that will receive the return error code from this function.

          USBD_ERR_NONE

RETURNED VALUE

None.

CALLERS

Application.

NOTES / WARNINGS

The initialization function *must* be called only once by the application, and before calling any other Vendor API.

G-1-2 USBD_Vendor_Add()

Create a new instance of the Vendor class.

FILES

usbd_vendor.c

PROTOTYPE

```
CPU_INT08U  USBD_Vendor_Add (CPU_BOOLEAN          intr_en,
                             CPU_INT16U           interval,
                             USBD_VENDOR_REQ_FNCT req_callback,
                             USBD_ERR             *p_err);
```

ARGUMENTS

intr_en   Interrupt endpoints IN and OUT flag:

DEF_TRUE   Pair of interrupt endpoints added to
                                    interface.

DEF_FALSE   Pair of interrupt endpoints not added to
                                    interface.

interval   Endpoint interval in frames or microframes.

req_callback   Vendor-specific request callback.

p_err   Pointer to variable that will receive the return error code from this function.

USBD_ERR_NONE
USBD_ERR_INVALID_ARG
USBD_ERR_ALLOC

RETURNED VALUE

Class instance number,   if NO error(s).

USBD_CLASS_NBR_NONE, otherwise.

G

CALLERS

Application.

NOTES / WARNINGS

None.

G-1-3 USBD_Vendor_CfgAdd()

Add a Vendor class instance into the specified configuration. The Vendor class instance was previously created by the function **USBD_Vendor_Add( )**.

FILES

usbd_vendor.c

PROTOTYPE

```
void  USBD_Vendor_CfgAdd (CPU_INT08U       class_nbr,
                          CPU_INT08U       dev_nbr,
                          CPU_INT08U       cfg_nbr,
                          USBD_ERR        *p_err);
```

ARGUMENTS

class_nbr   Class instance number.

dev_nbr   Device number.

cfg_nbr   Configuration index to add Vendor class instance to.

p_err   Pointer to variable that will receive the return error code from this function.

        USBD_ERR_NONE
        USBD_ERR_INVALID_ARG
        USBD_ERR_ALLOC
        USBD_ERR_NULL_PTR
        USBD_ERR_DEV_INVALID_NBR
        USBD_ERR_DEV_INVALID_STATE
        USBD_ERR_CFG_INVALID_NBR
        USBD_ERR_IF_ALLOC
        USBD_ERR_IF_ALT_ALLOC
        USBD_ERR_IF_INVALID_NBR
        USBD_ERR_EP_NONE_AVAIL
        USBD_ERR_EP_ALLOC

G

G

RETURNED VALUE

None.

CALLERS

Application.

NOTES / WARNINGS

USBD_Vendor_CfgAdd() basically adds an Interface descriptor and its associated Endpoint descriptor(s) to the Configuration descriptor. One call to USBD_Vendor_CfgAdd() builds the Configuration descriptor corresponding to a Vendor-specific device with the following format:

```
Configuration Descriptor
|-- Interface Descriptor (Vendor class)
    |-- Endpoint Descriptor (Bulk OUT)
    |-- Endpoint Descriptor (Bulk IN)
    |-- Endpoint Descriptor (Interrupt OUT) - optional
    |-- Endpoint Descriptor (Interrupt IN)  - optional
```

The pair of Interrupt endpoints are optional. They can be added to the Interface descriptor by setting the parameter intr_en to DEF_TRUE.

If USBD_Vendor_CfgAdd() is called several times from the application, it allows to create multiple instances and multiple configurations. For instance, the following architecture could be created for an high-speed device:

```
High-speed
|-- Configuration 0
    |-- Interface 0 (Vendor 0)
|-- Configuration 1
    |-- Interface 0 (Vendor 0)
    |-- Interface 1 (Vendor 1)
```

In that example, there are two instances of Vendor class: 'Vendor 0' and 'Vendor 1', and two possible configurations for the device: 'Configuration 0' and 'Configuration 1'. 'Configuration 1' is composed of two interfaces. Each class instance has an association with one of the interfaces. If 'Configuration 1' is activated by the host, it allows the host to access two different functionalities offered by the device.

G

G-1-4 USBD_Vendor_IsConn()

Get the vendor class connection state.

FILES

usbd_vendor.c

PROTOTYPE

```
CPU_BOOLEAN  USBD_Vendor_IsConn (CPU_INT08U  class_nbr);
```

ARGUMENTS

class_nbr   Class instance number.

RETURNED VALUE

DEF_YES, if Vendor class is connected.

DEF_NO, otherwise.

CALLERS

Application.

NOTES / WARNINGS

USBD_Vendor_IsConn() is typically used to verify that the device is in 'configured' state and that the vendor class instance is ready for communication. The following code illustrates a typical example:

```
CPU_BOOLEAN  conn;

conn = USBD_Vendor_IsConn(class_nbr);
while (conn != DEF_YES) {
    OSTimeDlyHMSM(0, 0, 0, 250);

    conn = USBD_Vendor_IsConn(class_nbr);
}
```

Once the connected status is **DEF_YES**, the communication using the Bulk endpoints can start.

G

G-1-5 USBD_Vendor_Rd()

Receive data from host through Bulk OUT endpoint. This function is blocking.

FILES

usbd_vendor.c

PROTOTYPE

```
CPU_INT32U  USBD_Vendor_Rd (CPU_INT08U   class_nbr,
                            void        *p_buf,
                            CPU_INT32U   buf_len,
                            CPU_INT16U   timeout,
                            USBD_ERR    *p_err);
```

ARGUMENTS

class_nbr   Class instance number.

p_buf   Pointer to receive buffer.

buf_len   Receive buffer length in octets.

timeout   Timeout in milliseconds.

p_err   Pointer to variable that will receive the return error code from this function.

USBD_ERR_NONE
USBD_ERR_NULL_PTR
USBD_ERR_INVALID_ARG
USBD_ERR_INVALID_CLASS_STATE
USBD_ERR_DEV_INVALID_NBR
USBD_ERR_EP_INVALID_NBR
USBD_ERR_DEV_INVALID_STATE
USBD_ERR_EP_INVALID_TYPE

RETURNED VALUE

Number of octets received, if NO error(s).

0, otherwise.

CALLERS

Application.

NOTES / WARNINGS

None.

G

G-1-6 USBD_Vendor_Wr()

Send data to host through Bulk IN endpoint. This function is blocking.

FILES

usbd_vendor.c

PROTOTYPE

```
CPU_INT32U  USBD_Vendor_Wr (CPU_INT08U    class_nbr,
                            void          *p_buf,
                            CPU_INT32U    buf_len,
                            CPU_INT16U    timeout,
                            CPU_BOOLEAN   end,
                            USBD_ERR      *p_err);
```

ARGUMENTS

class_nbr   Class instance number.

p_buf   Pointer to transmit buffer.

buf_len   Transmit buffer length in octets.

timeout   Timeout in milliseconds.

end   End-of-transfer flag.

p_err   Pointer to variable that will receive the return error code from this function.

USBD_ERR_NONE
USBD_ERR_NULL_PTR
USBD_ERR_INVALID_ARG
USBD_ERR_INVALID_CLASS_STATE
USBD_ERR_DEV_INVALID_NBR
USBD_ERR_EP_INVALID_NBR
USBD_ERR_DEV_INVALID_STATE
USBD_ERR_EP_INVALID_TYPE

RETURNED VALUE

Number of octets sent, if NO error(s).

0, otherwise.

CALLERS

Application.

NOTES / WARNINGS

If end-of-transfer flag is set and transfer length is multiple of maximum packet size, a zero-length packet is transferred to indicate the end of transfer to the host.

G

G-1-7 USBD_Vendor_RdAsync()

Receive data from host through Bulk OUT endpoint. This function is non-blocking. It returns immediately after transfer preparation. Upon transfer completion, a callback provided by the application will be called to finalize the transfer.

FILES

usbd_vendor.c

PROTOTYPE

```
void  USBD_Vendor_RdAsync (CPU_INT08U              class_nbr,
                           void                    *p_buf,
                           CPU_INT32U              buf_len,
                           USBD_VENDOR_ASYNC_FNCT  async_fnct,
                           void                    *p_async_arg,
                           USBD_ERR                *p_err);
```

ARGUMENTS

class_nbr   Class instance number.

p_buf   Pointer to receive buffer.

buf_len   Receive buffer length in octets.

async_fnct Receive callback.

p_async_arg Additional argument provided by application for receive callback.

p_err   Pointer to variable that will receive the return error code from this function.

  USBD_ERR_NONE
  USBD_ERR_NULL_PTR
  USBD_ERR_INVALID_ARG
  USBD_ERR_INVALID_CLASS_STATE
  USBD_ERR_DEV_INVALID_NBR
  USBD_ERR_EP_INVALID_NBR

```
USBD_ERR_DEV_INVALID_STATE
USBD_ERR_EP_INVALID_TYPE
USBD_ERR_EP_INVALID_STATE
```

G

RETURNED VALUE

None.

CALLERS

Application.

NOTES / WARNINGS

None.

G-1-8 USBD_Vendor_WrAsync()

Send data to host through Bulk IN endpoint. This function is non-blocking. It returns immediately after transfer preparation. Upon transfer completion, a callback provided by the application will be called to finalize the transfer.

FILES

usbd_vendor.c

PROTOTYPE

```
void   USBD_Vendor_WrAsync (CPU_INT08U                class_nbr,
                            void                      *p_buf,
                            CPU_INT32U                buf_len,
                            USBD_VENDOR_ASYNC_FNCT    async_fnct,
                            void                      *p_async_arg,
                            CPU_BOOLEAN               end,
                            USBD_ERR                  *p_err);
```

ARGUMENTS

class_nbr   Class instance number.

p_buf   Pointer to transmit buffer.

buf_len   Transmit buffer length in octets.

async_fnct Transmit callback.

p_async_arg Additional argument provided by application for transmit callback.

end   End-of-transfer flag.

p_err   Pointer to variable that will receive the return error code from this function.

        USBD_ERR_NONE
        USBD_ERR_NULL_PTR
        USBD_ERR_INVALID_ARG
        USBD_ERR_INVALID_CLASS_STATE

```
USBD_ERR_DEV_INVALID_NBR
USBD_ERR_EP_INVALID_NBR
USBD_ERR_DEV_INVALID_STATE
USBD_ERR_EP_INVALID_TYPE
USBD_ERR_EP_INVALID_STATE
```

RETURNED VALUE

Number of octets sent, if NO error(s).

0, otherwise.

CALLERS

Application.

NOTES / WARNINGS

If end-of-transfer flag is set and transfer length is multiple of maximum packet size, a zero-length packet is transferred to indicate the end of transfer to the host.

G

G-1-9 USBD_Vendor_IntrRd()

Receive data from host through Interrupt OUT endpoint. This function is blocking.

FILES

usbd_vendor.c

PROTOTYPE

```
CPU_INT32U  USBD_Vendor_IntrRd (CPU_INT08U   class_nbr,
                                void        *p_buf,
                                CPU_INT32U   buf_len,
                                CPU_INT16U   timeout,
                                USBD_ERR    *p_err);
```

ARGUMENTS

class_nbr   Class instance number.

p_buf   Pointer to receive buffer.

buf_len   Receive buffer length in octets.

timeout   Timeout in milliseconds.

p_err   Pointer to variable that will receive the return error code from this function.

             USBD_ERR_NONE
             USBD_ERR_NULL_PTR
             USBD_ERR_INVALID_ARG
             USBD_ERR_INVALID_CLASS_STATE
             USBD_ERR_DEV_INVALID_NBR
             USBD_ERR_EP_INVALID_NBR
             USBD_ERR_DEV_INVALID_STATE
             USBD_ERR_EP_INVALID_TYPE

RETURNED VALUE

Number of octets received, if NO error(s).

0, otherwise.

CALLERS

Application.

NOTES / WARNINGS

None.

G

G

G-1-10 USBD_Vendor_IntrWr()

Send data to host through Interrupt IN endpoint. This function is blocking.

FILES

usbd_vendor.c

PROTOTYPE

```
CPU_INT32U  USBD_Vendor_IntrWr (CPU_INT08U    class_nbr,
                                void          *p_buf,
                                CPU_INT32U    buf_len,
                                CPU_INT16U    timeout,
                                CPU_BOOLEAN   end,
                                USBD_ERR      *p_err);
```

ARGUMENTS

class_nbr   Class instance number.

p_buf   Pointer to transmit buffer.

buf_len   Transmit buffer length in octets.

timeout   Timeout in milliseconds.

end   End-of-transfer flag.

p_err   Pointer to variable that will receive the return error code from this function.

             USBD_ERR_NONE
             USBD_ERR_NULL_PTR
             USBD_ERR_INVALID_ARG
             USBD_ERR_INVALID_CLASS_STATE
             USBD_ERR_DEV_INVALID_NBR
             USBD_ERR_EP_INVALID_NBR
             USBD_ERR_DEV_INVALID_STATE
             USBD_ERR_EP_INVALID_TYPE

RETURNED VALUE

Number of octets sent, if NO error(s).

0, otherwise.

CALLERS

Application.

NOTES / WARNINGS

If end-of-transfer flag is set and transfer length is multiple of maximum packet size, a zero-length packet is transferred to indicate the end of transfer to the host.

G

G

G-1-11 USBD_Vendor_IntrRdAsync()

Receive data from host through Interrupt OUT endpoint. This function is non-blocking. It returns immediately after transfer preparation. Upon transfer completion, a callback provided by the application will be called to finalize the transfer.

FILES

usbd_vendor.c

PROTOTYPE

```
void  USBD_Vendor_IntrRdAsync (CPU_INT08U            class_nbr,
                               void                 *p_buf,
                               CPU_INT32U            buf_len,
                               USBD_VENDOR_ASYNC_FNCT  async_fnct,
                               void                 *p_async_arg,
                               USBD_ERR             *p_err);
```

ARGUMENTS

class_nbr   Class instance number.

p_buf   Pointer to receive buffer.

buf_len   Receive buffer length in octets.

async_fnct   Receive callback.

p_async_arg Additional argument provided by application for receive callback.

p_err   Pointer to variable that will receive the return error code from this function.

             USBD_ERR_NONE
             USBD_ERR_NULL_PTR
             USBD_ERR_INVALID_ARG
             USBD_ERR_INVALID_CLASS_STATE
             USBD_ERR_DEV_INVALID_NBR
             USBD_ERR_EP_INVALID_NBR

USBD_ERR_DEV_INVALID_STATE
USBD_ERR_EP_INVALID_TYPE
USBD_ERR_EP_INVALID_STATE

RETURNED VALUE

None.

CALLERS

Application.

NOTES / WARNINGS

None.

G-1-12 USBD_Vendor_IntrWrAsync()

Send data to host through Interrupt IN endpoint. This function is non-blocking. It returns immediately after transfer preparation. Upon transfer completion, a callback provided by the application will be called to finalize the transfer.

FILES

usbd_vendor.c

PROTOTYPE

```
void  USBD_Vendor_IntrWrAsync (CPU_INT08U            class_nbr,
                               void                  *p_buf,
                               CPU_INT32U            buf_len,
                               USBD_VENDOR_ASYNC_FNCT  async_fnct,
                               void                  *p_async_arg,
                               CPU_BOOLEAN           end,
                               USBD_ERR              *p_err);
```

ARGUMENTS

class_nbr   Class instance number.

p_buf   Pointer to transmit buffer.

buf_len   Transmit buffer length in octets.

async_fnct Transmit callback.

p_async_arg Additional argument provided by application for transmit callback.

end   End-of-transfer flag.

p_err   Pointer to variable that will receive the return error code from this function.

        USBD_ERR_NONE
        USBD_ERR_NULL_PTR
        USBD_ERR_INVALID_ARG
        USBD_ERR_INVALID_CLASS_STATE

```
USBD_ERR_DEV_INVALID_NBR
USBD_ERR_EP_INVALID_NBR
USBD_ERR_DEV_INVALID_STATE
USBD_ERR_EP_INVALID_TYPE
USBD_ERR_EP_INVALID_STATE
```

RETURNED VALUE

Number of octets sent, if NO error(s).

0, otherwise.

CALLERS

Application.

NOTES / WARNINGS

If end-of-transfer flag is set and transfer length is multiple of maximum packet size, a zero-length packet is transferred to indicate the end of transfer to the host.

G

G-2 USBDEV_API FUNCTIONS

USBDev_API is a library implemented under Windows operating system. Functions return values and parameters use Windows data types such as **DWORD**, **HANDLE**, **ULONG**. Refer to MSDN online documentation for more details about Windows data types (`http://msdn.microsoft.com/en-us/library/aa383751(v=VS.85).aspx`).

G-2-1 USBDev_GetNbrDev()

Get number of devices belonging to the specified GUID.

FILES

usbdev_api.c

PROTOTYPE

```
DWORD  USBDev_GetNbrDev (const  GUID    guid_dev_if,
                                DWORD  *p_err);
```

ARGUMENTS

guid_dev_if Device interface class GUID.

p_err   Pointer to variable that will receive the return error code from this function.

            ERROR_SUCCESS

RETURNED VALUE

Number of devices for the provided GUID, if NO error(s).

0, otherwise.

CALLERS

Application.

NOTES / WARNINGS

The function `USBDev_GetNbrDev()` uses the concept of device information set. A device information set consists of device information elements for all the devices that belong to some device setup class or device interface class. The GUID passed to `USBDev_GetNbrDev()` function is a device interface class. Internally by using some control options the function retrieves the device information set which represents a list of all devices present in the system and registered under the specified GUID. More details about the device information set can be found at `http://msdn.microsoft.com/en-us/library/ff541247(VS.85).aspx`.

G

G-2-2 USBDev_Open()

Open a device by retrieving a general device handle.

FILES

usbdev_api.c

PROTOTYPE

```
HANDLE  USBDev_Open (const  GUID    guid_dev_if,
                            DWORD   dev_nbr,
                            DWORD  *p_err);
```

ARGUMENTS

guid_dev_if Device interface class GUID.

dev_nbr   Device number.

p_err   Pointer to variable that will receive the return error code from this function:

　　　　　　ERROR_SUCCESS
　　　　　　ERROR_INVALID_PARAMETER
　　　　　　ERROR_NOT_ENOUGH_MEMORY
　　　　　　ERROR_BAD_DEVICE

RETURNED VALUE

Handle to device,   if NO error(s).

INVALID_HANDLE_VALUE, otherwise.

CALLERS

Application.

NOTES / WARNINGS

None.

G-2-3 USBDev_Close()

Close a device by freeing any allocated resources and by releasing any created handles.

FILES

usbdev_api.c

PROTOTYPE

```
void  USBDev_Close (HANDLE   dev,
                    DWORD    *p_err);
```

ARGUMENTS

dev   General handle to device.

p_err   Pointer to variable that will receive the return error code from this function:

             ERROR_SUCCESS
             ERROR_INVALID_HANDLE

RETURNED VALUE

None.

CALLERS

Application.

NOTES / WARNINGS

USBDev_Close() closes any remaining open pipes. The open pipes are usually closed from the application by calling the function USBDev_PipeClose().

G

G-2-4 USBDev_GetNbrAltSetting()

Get number of alternate settings for the specified interface.

FILES

usbdev_api.c

PROTOTYPE

```
UCHAR  USBDev_GetNbrAltSetting (HANDLE  dev,
                               UCHAR   if_nbr,
                               DWORD  *p_err);
```

ARGUMENTS

dev   General handle to device.

if_nbr   Interface number.

p_err   Pointer to variable that will receive the return error code from this function:

ERROR_SUCCESS
ERROR_INVALID_HANDLE
ERROR_INVALID_PARAMETER

RETURNED VALUE

Number of alternate setting, if NO error(s).

0, otherwise.

CALLERS

Application.

An interface may include alternate settings that allow the endpoints and/or their characteristics to be varied after the device has been configured. The default setting for an interface is always alternate setting zero. Alternate settings allow a portion of the device configuration to be varied while other interfaces remain in operation.

The number of alternate settings gotten can be used to open a pipe associated with a certain alternate interface.

G

G

G-2-5 USBDev_GetNbrAssociatedIF()

Get number of associated interfaces with the default interface. That is all the interfaces besides the default interface managed by **WinUSB.sys** and registered under the same GUID.

FILES

usbdev_api.c

PROTOTYPE

```
UCHAR  USBDev_GetNbrAssociatedIF (HANDLE   dev,
                                 DWORD   *p_err);
```

ARGUMENTS

dev   General handle to device.

p_err   Pointer to variable that will receive the return error code from this function:

                 ERROR_SUCCESS
                 ERROR_INVALID_HANDLE

RETURNED VALUE

Number of associated interfaces, if NO error(s).

0, otherwise.

CALLERS

Application.

NOTES / WARNINGS

Let's assume that a device has three interfaces managed by WinUSB.sys driver and belonging to the same GUID: Interface #0, #1 and #2. Interface #0 is the default interface. Interfaces #1 and #2 are the associated interfaces. In that example calling **USBDev_GetNbrAssociatedIF()** will return 2 associated interfaces.

G-2-6 USBDev_SetAltSetting()

Set the alternate setting of an interface.

usbdev_api.c

```
void  USBDev_SetAltSetting (HANDLE   dev,
                            UCHAR    if_nbr,
                            UCHAR    alt_set,
                            DWORD    *p_err);
```

dev   General handle to device.

if_nbr   Interface number.

alt_set   Alternate setting number.

p_err   Pointer to variable that will receive the return error code from this function:

             ERROR_SUCCESS
             ERROR_INVALID_HANDLE
             ERROR_INVALID_PARAMETER

None.

Application.

G

NOTES / WARNINGS

This function sets alternate setting number for WinUSB internal use. It does *not* send a SET_INTERFACE request to the device. To send SET_INTERFACE request to the device, the function USBDev_CtrlReq() must be used.

G-2-7 USBDev_GetCurAltSetting()

Get the current alternate setting for the specified interface.

FILES

usbdev_api.c

PROTOTYPE

```
UCHAR  USBDev_GetCurAltSetting (HANDLE   dev,
                                UCHAR    if_nbr,
                                DWORD    *p_err);
```

ARGUMENTS

dev   General handle to device.

if_nbr   Interface number.

p_err   Pointer to variable that will receive the return error code from this function:

             ERROR_SUCCESS
             ERROR_INVALID_HANDLE
             ERROR_INVALID_PARAMETER

RETURNED VALUE

Current alternate setting number, if NO error(s).

0, otherwise.

CALLERS

Application.

NOTES / WARNINGS

This function gets the current alternate setting number used internally by WinUSB and set by the function **USBDev_SetAltSetting( )**. It does NOT send a **GET_INTERFACE** request to the device. To send **GET_INTERFACE** request to the device, the function **USBDev_CtrlReq( )** must be used.

G-2-8 USBDev_IsHighSpeed()

Specify if the device attached to PC is high speed or not.

usbdev_api.c

```
BOOL  USBDev_IsHighSpeed (HANDLE   dev,
                          DWORD   *p_err);
```

dev   General handle to device.

p_err   Pointer to variable that will receive the return error code from this function:

            ERROR_SUCCESS
            ERROR_INVALID_HANDLE
            ERROR_INVALID_PARAMETER

TRUE, if device is high-speed.

FALSE, otherwise.

Application.

None.

G

G-2-9 USBDev_BulkIn_Open()

Open a Bulk IN pipe.

FILES

usbdev_api.c

PROTOTYPE

```
HANDLE  USBDev_BulkIn_Open (HANDLE  dev,
                           UCHAR   if_nbr,
                           UCHAR   alt_set,
                           DWORD   *p_err);
```

ARGUMENTS

dev   General handle to device.

if_nbr   Interface number.

alt_set   Alternate setting number for specified interface.

p_err   Pointer to variable that will receive the return error code from this function:

        ERROR_SUCCESS
        ERROR_INVALID_HANDLE
        ERROR_NO_MORE_ITEMS

RETURNED VALUE

Handle to Bulk IN pipe,   if NO error(s).

INVALID_HANDLE_VALUE, otherwise.

CALLERS

Application.

NOTES / WARNINGS

None.

G

G-2-10 USBDev_BulkOut_Open()

Open a Bulk OUT pipe.

FILES

usbdev_api.c

PROTOTYPE

```
HANDLE  USBDev_BulkOut_Open (HANDLE   dev,
                            UCHAR    if_nbr,
                            UCHAR    alt_set,
                            DWORD    *p_err);
```

ARGUMENTS

dev   General handle to device.

if_nbr   Interface number.

alt_set   Alternate setting number for specified interface.

p_err   Pointer to variable that will receive the return error code from this function:

           ERROR_SUCCESS
           ERROR_INVALID_HANDLE
           ERROR_NO_MORE_ITEMS

RETURNED VALUE

Handle to Bulk OUT pipe, if NO error(s).

INVALID_HANDLE_VALUE,   otherwise.

CALLERS

Application.

NOTES / WARNINGS

None.

G

G-2-11 USBDev_IntrIn_Open()

Open a Interrupt IN pipe.

FILES

usbdev_api.c

PROTOTYPE

```
HANDLE  USBDev_IntrIn_Open (HANDLE   dev,
                           UCHAR    if_nbr,
                           UCHAR    alt_set,
                           DWORD    *p_err);
```

ARGUMENTS

dev   General handle to device.

if_nbr   Interface number.

alt_set   Alternate setting number for specified interface.

p_err   Pointer to variable that will receive the return error code from this function:

            ERROR_SUCCESS
            ERROR_INVALID_HANDLE
            ERROR_NO_MORE_ITEMS

RETURNED VALUE

Handle to Interrupt IN pipe, if NO error(s).

INVALID_HANDLE_VALUE, otherwise.

CALLERS

Application.

NOTES / WARNINGS

None.

G

G

G-2-12 USBDev_IntrOut_Open()

Open a Interrupt OUT pipe.

FILES

usbdev_api.c

PROTOTYPE

```
HANDLE  USBDev_IntrOut_Open (HANDLE   dev,
                            UCHAR    if_nbr,
                            UCHAR    alt_set,
                            DWORD    *p_err);
```

ARGUMENTS

dev   General handle to device.

if_nbr   Interface number.

alt_set   Alternate setting number for specified interface.

p_err   Pointer to variable that will receive the return error code from this function:

           ERROR_SUCCESS
           ERROR_INVALID_HANDLE
           ERROR_NO_MORE_ITEMS

RETURNED VALUE

Handle to Interrupt OUT pipe, if NO error(s).

INVALID_HANDLE_VALUE, otherwise.

CALLERS

Application.

NOTES / WARNINGS

None.

G

G-2-13 USBDev_PipeGetAddr()

Get pipe address.

FILES

usbdev_api.c

PROTOTYPE

```
UCHAR USBDev_PipeGetAddr (HANDLE   pipe,
                          DWORD   *p_err);
```

ARGUMENTS

pipe   Pipe handle.

p_err   Pointer to variable that will receive the return error code from this function:

        ERROR_SUCCESS
        ERROR_INVALID_HANDLE

RETURNED VALUE

Pipe address, if NO error(s).

0, otherwise.

CALLERS

Application.

NOTES / WARNINGS

None.

G-2-14 USBDev_PipeClose()

Close a pipe.

FILES

usbdev_api.c

PROTOTYPE

```
void  USBDev_PipeClose (HANDLE   pipe,
                        DWORD   *p_err);
```

ARGUMENTS

pipe   Pipe handle.

p_err   Pointer to variable that will receive the return error code from this function:

        ERROR_SUCCESS
        ERROR_INVALID_HANDLE

RETURNED VALUE

None

CALLERS

Application.

NOTES / WARNINGS

None.

G

G-2-15 USBDev_PipeStall()

Stall a pipe or clear the stall condition of a pipe.

FILES

usbdev_api.c

PROTOTYPE

```
void  USBDev_PipeStall (HANDLE  pipe,
                        BOOL    stall,
                        DWORD  *p_err);
```

ARGUMENTS

pipe   Pipe handle.

stall   Indicate which action to do:

TRUE	Stall pipe.
FALSE	Clear stall condition of the pipe.

p_err   Pointer to variable that will receive the return error code from this function:

ERROR_SUCCESS
ERROR_INVALID_HANDLE
ERROR_NOT_ENOUGH_MEMORY

RETURNED VALUE

None.

CALLERS

Application.

NOTES / WARNINGS

The **SET_FEATURE** standard request is sent to the device to stall the pipe. The **CLEAR_FEATURE** standard request is sent to the device to clear the stall condition of the pipe.

G-2-16 USBDev_PipeAbort()

Aborts all of the pending transfers for a pipe.

FILES

usbdev_api.c

PROTOTYPE

```
void  USBDev_PipeAbort (HANDLE  pipe,
                        DWORD  *p_err);
```

ARGUMENTS

pipe   Pipe handle.

p_err   Pointer to variable that will receive the return error code from this function:

            ERROR_SUCCESS
            ERROR_INVALID_HANDLE

RETURNED VALUE

None.

CALLERS

Application.

NOTES / WARNINGS

None.

G-2-17 USBDev_CtrlReq()

Send control data over the default control endpoint.

FILES

usbdev_api.c

PROTOTYPE

```
ULONG  USBDev_CtrlReq (HANDLE   dev,
                       UCHAR    bm_req_type,
                       UCHAR    b_request,
                       USHORT   w_value,
                       USHORT   w_index,
                       UCHAR    *p_buf,
                       USHORT   buf_len,
                       DWORD    *p_err);
```

ARGUMENTS

dev   General handle to device

bm_req_type   Variable representing **bmRequestType** of setup packet. **bmRequestType** is a
               bitmap with the following characteristics:

               D7   Data transfer direction:

               '0': USB_DIR_HOST_TO_DEVICE
               '1': USB_DIR_DEVICE_TO_HOST

               D6...5   Request type:

               '00': USB_REQUEST_TYPE_STD (standard)
               '01': USB_REQUEST_TYPE_CLASS
               '10': USB_REQUEST_TYPE_VENDOR

               D4...0   Recipient:

'0000': USB_RECIPIENT_DEV (device)
'0001': USB_RECIPIENT_IF (interface)
'0010': USB_RECIPIENT_ENDPOINT

bm_req_type	Argument is a OR'ed of D7, D6...5 and D4...0 values.

b_request   Variable representing **bRequest** of setup packet. Possible values are:

GET_STATUS	Returns status for the specified recipient.
CLEAR_FEATURE	Clear or disable a specific feature.
SET_FEATURE	Set or enable a specific feature.
SET_ADDRESS	Set the device address for all future device accesses.
GET_DESCRIPTOR	Return the specified descriptor if the descriptor exists.
SET_DESCRIPTOR	Update existing descriptors or new descriptors may be added.
GET_CONFIGURATION	Return the current device configuration value.
SET_CONFIGURATION	Set the device configuration.
GET_INTERFACE	Return the selected alternate setting for the specified interface.
SET_INTERFACE	Select an alternate setting for the specified interface.
SYNCH_FRAME	Set and then report an endpoint's synchronization frame.

w_value   Variable representing wValue of setup packet.

w_index   Variable representing wIndex of setup packet.

p_buf   Pointer to transmit or receive buffer for data phase of control transfer.

buf_len   Length of transmit or receive buffer.

G

p_err   Pointer to variable that will receive the return error code from this function:

           ERROR_SUCCESS
           ERROR_INVALID_HANDLE
           ERROR_NOT_ENOUGH_MEMORY
           ERROR_GEN_FAILURE

RETURNED VALUE

None

CALLERS

Application.

NOTES / WARNINGS

The value of **w_value** and **w_index** arguments vary according to the specific request defined by **b_request** argument.

The following code shows an example using **USBDev_CtrlReq()** to send the **SET_INTERFACE** request:

```
DWORD   err;
                                /* Select alternate setting #1 for default interface.  */
USBDev_CtrlReq ( dev_handle,
               (USB_DIR_HOST_TO_DEVICE | USB_REQUEST_TYPE_STD | USB_RECIPIENT_IF),
               SET_INTERFACE,
               1,               /* Alternate setting #1.                                */
               0,               /* Interface #0 inside active configuration.            */
               0,               /* No data phase.                                       */
               0,
               &err);
if (err != ERROR_SUCCESS) {
    printf("[ERROR #%d] SET_INTERFACE(1) request failed.\n", err);
}
```

More details about USB device requests can be found in "Universal Serial Bus Specification, Revision 2.0, April 27, 2000", section 9.3.

G-2-18 USBDev_PipeWr()

Write data to device over the specified pipe.

FILES

usbdev_api.c

PROTOTYPE

```
DWORD   USBDev_PipeWr (HANDLE   pipe,
                       UCHAR    *p_buf,
                       DWORD    buf_len,
                       DWORD    timeout,
                       DWORD    *p_err);
```

ARGUMENTS

pipe   Pipe handle.

p_buf   Pointer to transmit buffer.

buf_len   Transmit buffer length.

timeout   Timeout in milliseconds. A value of 0 indicates a wait forever.

p_err   Pointer to variable that will receive the return error code from this function:

        ERROR_SUCCESS
        ERROR_INVALID_HANDLE
        ERROR_INVALID_USER_BUFFER
        ERROR_BAD_PIPE
        ERROR_INVALID_PARAMETER
        ERROR_NOT_ENOUGH_MEMORY
        ERROR_SEM_TIMEOUT

G

RETURNED VALUE

Number of bytes written, if NO error(s).

0, otherwise.

CALLERS

Application.

NOTES / WARNINGS

None.

G-2-19 USBDev_PipeRd()

Read data from device over the specified pipe.

FILES

usbdev_api.c

PROTOTYPE

```
DWORD  USBDev_PipeRd (HANDLE    pipe,
                      UCHAR    *p_buf,
                      DWORD     buf_len,
                      DWORD     timeout,
                      DWORD    *p_err);
```

ARGUMENTS

pipe   Pipe handle.

p_buf   Pointer to receive buffer.

buf_len   Receive buffer length.

timeout   Timeout in milliseconds. A value of 0 indicates a wait forever.

p_err   Pointer to variable that will receive the return error code from this function:

            ERROR_SUCCESS
            ERROR_INVALID_HANDLE
            ERROR_INVALID_USER_BUFFER
            ERROR_BAD_PIPE
            ERROR_INVALID_PARAMETER
            ERROR_NOT_ENOUGH_MEMORY
            ERROR_SEM_TIMEOUT7

RETURNED VALUE

Number of bytes received, if NO error(s).

0, otherwise.

CALLERS

Application.

NOTES / WARNINGS

None.

G-2-20 USBDev_PipeRdAsync()

Read data from device over the specified pipe. This function returns immediately if data is not present. The data will be retrieved later.

usbdev_api.c

```
void  USBDev_PipeRdAsync (HANDLE                   pipe,
                          UCHAR                    *p_buf,
                          DWORD                    buf_len,
                          USBDEV_PIPE_RD_CALLBACK  callback,
                          void                     *p_callback_arg,
                          DWORD                    *p_err);
```

pipe   Pipe handle.

p_buf   Pointer to receive buffer.

buf_len   Receive buffer length.

callback   Pointer to application callback called by Asynchronous thread upon completion.

p_callback_arg   Pointer to argument which can carry private information passed by application. This argument is used when the callback is called.

G

p_err   Pointer to variable that will receive the return error code from this function:

            ERROR_SUCCESS
            ERROR_INVALID_HANDLE
            ERROR_INVALID_USER_BUFFER
            ERROR_BAD_PIPE
            ERROR_NOT_ENOUGH_MEMORY
            ERROR_SEM_TIMEOUT

RETURNED VALUE

None.

CALLERS

Application.

NOTES / WARNINGS

When a IN pipe is open with one of the open functions **USBDev_xxxxIn_Open( )**, a thread is automatically created. This thread is in charge of informing the application about a completed asynchronous IN transfer. Upon completion of an asynchronous transfer, the thread is waken up and calls the application callback provided to **USBDev_API** library using the **callback** argument.

USBDev_API library allows to queue several asynchronous IN transfers for the same pipe.

Error Codes

This appendix provides a brief explanation of µC/USB-Device error codes defined in **usbd_core.h**. Any error codes not listed here may be searched in **usbd_core.h** for both their numerical value and usage. This appendix also contains class-specific error codes. Only MSC class defines class-specific error codes. There are defined in **usbd_msc.h**.

Each error has a numerical value. The error codes are grouped. The definition of the groups are:

Error code group	Numbering series
GENERIC	0
DEVICE	100
CONFIGURATION	200
INTERFACE	300
ENDPOINT	400
OS LAYER	500
MSC	800

H-1 GENERIC ERROR CODES

0	USBD_ERR_NONE	No error.
1	USBD_ERR_SHORT_XFER	Short transfer detected.
2	USBD_ERR_FAIL	Hardware error occurred.
3	USBD_ERR_RX	Generic receive error. A problem has occurred during read transfer preparation or after data has been received.
4	USBD_ERR_TX	Generic transmit error. A problem has occurred during write transfer preparation. No data transmitted or data transmitted with a certain problem.
5	USBD_ERR_ALLOC	Object/memory allocation failed.
6	USBD_ERR_NULL_PTR	Pointer argument(s) passed NULL pointer(s).
7	USBD_ERR_INVALID_ARG	Invalid argument(s).
8	USBD_ERR_INVALID_CLASS_STATE	Invalid class state.

H-2 DEVICE ERROR CODES

100	USBD_ERR_DEV_ALLOC	Device allocation failed.
101	USBD_ERR_DEV_INVALID_NBR	Invalid device number.
102	USBD_ERR_DEV_INVALID_STATE	Invalid device state.
103	USBD_ERR_DEV_INVALID_SPD	Invalid device speed.

H-3 CONFIGURATION ERROR CODES

200	USBD_ERR_CFG_ALLOC	Configuration allocation failed.
201	USBD_ERR_CFG_INVALID_NBR	Invalid configuration number.
202	USBD_ERR_CFG_INVALID_MAX_PWR	Invalid maximum power.
203	USBD_ERR_CFG_SET_FAIL	Device driver set configuration failed.

H-4 INTERFACE ERROR CODES

300	USBD_ERR_IF_ALLOC	Interface allocation failed.
301	USBD_ERR_IF_INVALID_NBR	Invalid interface number.
302	USBD_ERR_IF_ALT_ALLOC	Alternate interface setting allocation failed.
303	USBD_ERR_IF_ALT_INVALID_NBR	Invalid interface alternate setting number.
304	USBD_ERR_IF_GRP_ALLOC	Interface group allocation failed.
305	USBD_ERR_IF_GRP_NBR_IN_USE	Interface group number already in use.

H-5 ENDPOINT ERROR CODES

400	USBD_ERR_EP_ALLOC	Endpoint allocation failed.
401	USBD_ERR_EP_INVALID_ADDR	Invalid endpoint address.
402	USBD_ERR_EP_INVALID_STATE	Invalid endpoint state.
403	USBD_ERR_EP_INVALID_TYPE	Invalid endpoint type.
404	USBD_ERR_EP_NONE_AVAIL	Physical endpoint NOT available.
405	USBD_ERR_EP_ABORT	Device driver abort transfer for an endpoint failed.
406	USBD_ERR_EP_STALL	Device driver stall endpoint failed.
407	USBD_ERR_EP_IO_PENDING	I/O operation pending on endpoint.

H-6 OS LAYER ERROR CODES

500	USBD_ERR_OS_INIT_FAIL	OS layer initialization failed.
501	USBD_ERR_OS_SIGNAL_CREATE	OS signal NOT successfully created.
502	USBD_ERR_OS_FAIL	OS object Pend/Post failed.
503	USBD_ERR_OS_TIMEOUT	OS object timeout.
504	USBD_ERR_OS_ABORT	OS object abort.
505	USBD_ERR_OS_DEL	OS object delete.

H-7 URB ERROR CODES

| 600 | USBD_ERR_URB_ALLOC | USB request block allocation failed. |

H-8 DEVICE CONTROLLER DRIVER ERROR CODES

| 700 | USBD_ERR_DRV_EP_BUSY | USB request block queuing in the driver failed. |

H-9 MSC ERROR CODES

1000	USBD_ERR_MSC_INVALID_CBW	Invalid Command Block Wrapper.
1001	USBD_ERR_MSC_INVALID_DIR	Mismatch between direction indicated by CBW and SCSI command.
1002	USBD_ERR_MSC_MAX_LUN_EXCEED	Maximum number of logical units reached.
1003	USBD_ERR_SCSI_UNSUPPORTED_CMD	SCSI command not supported.
1004	USBD_ERR_SCSI_MORE_DATA	Read or write requires more data to be read or written.
1005	USBD_ERR_SCSI_LU_NOTRDY	Logical unit not ready to perform any operations.
1006	USBD_ERR_SCSI_LU_NOTSUPPORTED	Logical unit number not supported.
1007	USBD_ERR_SCSI_LU_BUSY	Logical unit number is busy with other operations,
1008	USBD_ERR_SCSI_LOG_BLOCK_ADDR	Logical block address out of range.
1009	USBD_ERR_SCSI_MEDIUM_NOTPRESENT	Medium not present.
1010	USBD_ERR_SCSI_MEDIUM_NOT_RDY_TO_RDY	Medium transitions from not ready to ready state.
1011	USBD_ERR_SCSI_MEDIUM_RDY_TO_NOT_RDY	Medium transitions from ready to not ready state.
1012	USBD_ERR_SCSI_LOCK	Medium lock failed.
1013	USBD_ERR_SCSI_LOCK_TIMEOUT	Medium lock timed out.
1014	USBD_ERR_SCSI_UNLOCK	Medium successfully unlocked.

I

Memory Footprint

μC/USB-Device's memory footprint can be scaled to contain only the features required for your specific application. Refer to Chapter 5, "Configuration" on page 109 to better understand how to configure the stack and your application. This appendix will provide a reference to μC/USB-Device's memory footprint for each associated device class offered by Micrium. Each class presents a table of device configuration values that represents the configuration used for the footprint calculation. All footprint values calculated in this appendix has been obtained with the environment configuration shown in Table I-1 and μC/USB-Device general configuration shown in Table I-2.

Note that any Device Controller Driver offered by the μC/USB-Device stack can allocate internal data structures from the heap. You can use memory functions from μC/LIB, common standard library functions, macros and constants developed by Micrium, to determine the amount of heap that has been allocated for the Device Controller Driver. Refer to μC/LIB documentation for more information.

Specification	Configuration
Architecture	generic 32-bit CPU
Toolchain	IAR
Compiler Optimization	High for Size and Speed
OS	μC/OS-III

Table I-1 **Memory Footprint Environment Configuration**

Device Configuration	Value
USBD_CFG_OPTIMIZE_SPD	DEF_DISABLED
USBD_CFG_MAX_NBR_DEV	1
USBD_CFG_MAX_NBR_CFG	1

Table I-2 **Memory Footprint µC/USB Device Configuration**

I-1 COMMUNICATIONS DEVICE CLASS

The Communication Device Class (CDC) configuration is presented in Table I-3 and its associated memory footprint table is shown in Table I-4.

Configuration	Value
USBD_CFG_MAX_NBR_IF	2
USBD_CFG_MAX_NBR_IF_ALT	2
USBD_CFG_MAX_NBR_IF_GRP	1
USBD_CFG_MAX_NBR_EP_DESC	3
USBD_CFG_MAX_NBR_EP_OPEN	5
USBD_CDC_CFG_MAX_NBR_DEV	1
USBD_CDC_CFG_MAX_NBR_CFG	2
USBD_CDC_CFG_MAX_NBR_DATA_IF	1
USBD_ACM_SERIAL_CFG_MAX_NBR_DEV	1

Table I-3 **CDC Configuration for Memory Footprint**

Module	Code (kB)	Constant (kB)	Data (kB)
Device Core	20.62	-	0.47
Device RTOS Port	0.76	-	1.39
Device Controller Driver	6.74	0.21	Data allocated from heap.
CDC	2.55	-	0.07
ACM Subclass	2.20	-	0.04
Total:	32.87	0.21	1.97

Table I-4 **CDC Memory Footprint**

I-2 HUMAN INTERFACE DEVICE CLASS

The Human Interface Device (HID) Class configuration is presented in Table I-5 and its associated memory footprint table is shown in Table I-6. Note that there is an optional Interrupt OUT endpoint that you may add during HID initialization that has been omitted in the configuration below. Also note that the Data size shown for HID class does not take into account memory allocated for input report buffer(s), output report and feature report buffers from the heap. You can use memory functions from µC/LIB to determine the amount of heap that has been allocated for these HID reports. Refer to µC/LIB documentation for more information.

Configuration	Value
USBD_CFG_MAX_NBR_IF	1
USBD_CFG_MAX_NBR_IF_ALT	1
USBD_CFG_MAX_NBR_IF_GRP	0
USBD_CFG_MAX_NBR_EP_DESC	1
USBD_CFG_MAX_NBR_EP_OPEN	3
USBD_HID_CFG_MAX_NBR_DEV	1
USBD_HID_CFG_MAX_NBR_CFG	2
USBD_HID_CFG_MAX_NBR_REPORT_ID	16
USBD_HID_CFG_MAX_NBR_REPORT_PUSHPOP	0

Table I-5 **HID Configuration for Memory Footprint**

Module	Code (kB)	Constant (kB)	Data (kB)
Device Core	19.17	-	0.78
Device RTOS Port	0.76	-	1.31
Device Controller Driver	6.74	0.21	*Data allocated from heap.
HID	6.29	-	0.52 *Input, Output and/or Feature Report buffers allocated from heap. Refer to section I-2 "Human Interface Device Class" on page 611 for details.
HID RTOS Port	1.05	-	1.39
Total:	34.01	0.21	4.00

Table I-6 **HID Memory Footprint**

I-3 MASS STORAGE CLASS

The Mass Storage Class (MSC) configuration is presented in Table I-7 and its associated memory footprint table is shown in Table I-8.

Configuration	Value
USBD_CFG_MAX_NBR_IF	1
USBD_CFG_MAX_NBR_IF_ALT	1
USBD_CFG_MAX_NBR_IF_GRP	0
USBD_CFG_MAX_NBR_EP_DESC	2
USBD_CFG_MAX_NBR_EP_OPEN	4
USBD_MSC_CFG_MAX_NBR_DEV	1
USBD_MSC_CFG_MAX_NBR_CFG	2
USBD_MSC_CFG_MAX_LUN	1
USBD_MSC_CFG_DATA_LEN	2048

Table I-7 **MSC Configuration for Memory Footprint**

Module	Code (kB)	Constant (kB)	Data (kB)
Device Core	19.13	-	0.85
Device RTOS Port	0.76	-	1.35
Device Controller Driver	6.74	0.21	*Data allocated from heap.
MSC	7.57	0.03	2.55
MSC RTOS Port	0.68	-	1.27
RAMDisk Storage	0.36	-	*RAMDisk Storage layer allocates data sections to simulate a memory area from a media storage. This memory area size is configured in app_cfg.h.
Total:	35.24	0.24	6.02

Table I-8 **MSC Memory Footprint**

I-4 PERSONAL HEALTHCARE DEVICE CLASS

The Personal Healthcare Device Class (PHDC) configuration is presented in Table I-9 and its associated memory footprint table is shown in Table I-10. Note that there is an optional Interrupt IN endpoint that you may add during PHDC initialization that has been omitted in the configuration below. Also note that the memory footprint is taken for both QOS Based Scheduler enabled and disabled configurations. The memory footprint for the PHDC RTOS layer therefore reflects the differences when it is one configuration or the other.

Configuration	Value
USBD_CFG_OPTIMIZE_SPD	DEF_DISABLED
USBD_CFG_MAX_NBR_DEV	1
USBD_CFG_MAX_NBR_CFG	1
USBD_CFG_MAX_NBR_IF	1
USBD_CFG_MAX_NBR_IF_ALT	1
USBD_CFG_MAX_NBR_IF_GRP	0
USBD_CFG_MAX_NBR_EP_DESC	2
USBD_CFG_MAX_NBR_EP_OPEN	4
USBD_PHDC_CFG_MAX_NBR_DEV	1
USBD_PHDC_CFG_MAX_NBR_CFG	2
USBD_PHDC_CFG_DATA_OPAQUE_MAX_LEN	43
USBD_PHDC_OS_CFG_SCHED_EN	DEF_ENABLED/DEF_DISABLED

Table I-9 **PHDC Configuration for Memory Footprint**

Module	Code (kB)	Constant (kB)	Data (kB)
Device Core	19.82	-	0.85
Device RTOS Port	0.76	-	1.35
Device Controller Driver	6.74	0.21	Data allocated from heap.
PHDC	4.70	-	0.21
PHDC RTOS Port (QOS Based Scheduler Enabled)	1.56	-	1.62
PHDC RTOS Port (QOS Based Scheduler Disabled)	0.66	-	0.11
Total (QOS Based Scheduler Enabled/ Disabled):	33.58 / 32.68	0.21	4.03 / 2.52

Table I-10 **PHDC Memory Footprint**

I-5 VENDOR CLASS

The Vendor Class configuration is presented in Table I-11 and its associated memory footprint table is shown in Table I-12. Note that there is a pair of Interrupt IN/OUT endpoints that you may add during Vendor Class initialization that has been omitted in the configuration below.

Configuration	Value
USBD_CFG_MAX_NBR_IF	1
USBD_CFG_MAX_NBR_IF_ALT	1
USBD_CFG_MAX_NBR_IF_GRP	0
USBD_CFG_MAX_NBR_EP_DESC	2
USBD_CFG_MAX_NBR_EP_OPEN	4
USBD_VENDOR_CFG_MAX_NBR_DEV	1
USBD_VENDOR_CFG_MAX_NBR_CFG	2

Table I-11 **Vendor Class Configuration for Memory Footprint**

Module	Code (kB)	Constant (kB)	Data (kB)
Device Core	18.18	-	0.85
Device RTOS Port	0.76	-	1.35
Device Controller Driver	6.74	0.21	Data allocated from heap.
Vendor	1.05	-	0.09
Total:	26.73	0.21	2.29

Table I-12 **Vendor Class Memory Footprint**

μC/USB Device™

Universal Serial Bus Device Stack

and the
Renesas RX63N

The Micrium USB Team

Micrium
Press

Weston, FL 33326

Micriµm Press
1290 Weston Road, Suite 306
Weston, FL 33326
USA
www.micrium.com

For bulk orders, please contact Micriµm Press at: +1 954 217 2036

ISBN: 978-1-935772-01-9
100-uC-USB-Device-Renesas-RX63N-001

Micriµm
Press

Foreword

The application of USB is increasingly expanding in various fields, from personal computers and digital appliances to audio/video equipment, embedded devices and personal healthcare. Currently, nearly 100% of all personal computers are equipped with USB which has become the standard for computers and peripheral devices.

As a member of the USB Implementers Forum (USB-IF) Board of Directors, Renesas Electronics has been actively involved in the development and support of specifications and technologies surrounding the USB protocol. Over the years, Renesas Electronics has established solid credibility in the field, for example, by releasing the world's first USB 2.0 host controller with Large Scale Integration (LSI) technology "µPD720100" in April 2000, by steadily expanding its lineup with hub controller LSI and other products, and by proactively acquiring USB certification for all its commercial LSI.

By the end of 2008, Renesas Electronics has shipped over 160 million USB-related products in its Application Specific Standard Products (ASSP) business alone.

Through the development of USB 2.0 LSI, Renesas Electronics established core USB 2.0 technologies such as software drivers and various IPs. And through extensive partnerships, Renesas Electronics has also worked to streamline the provision of complete USB solutions, from connectors to testing environment and certification. By enhancing the partnerships, and by fully utilizing our rich USB 2.0 technology asset, we strive to become the global leader in the development of complete solutions.

This time we have partnered with Micriµm and TotalPhase to bring you a complete USB device solution based on the Renesas RX63N MCU.

The solution is delivered in the form of a book that teaches you not only the essentials of USB 2.0, but also brings you the theory accompanied of ready-to-run applications, an evaluation board and word-class USB and embedded development tools.

Starting out new with USB can be quite daunting. With the USB 2.0 specification at 650 pages one could easily be put off just by the sheer size of the standard. This is only the beginning of a long list of associated standards for USB. With this book, we reduce the important areas that you need to consider when designing a product with USB connectivity.

The book starts by teaching the theory behind USB 2.0, the µC/USB-Device stack and the most important USB classes such as the Mass Storage Class used in USB removable storage devices, the PHDC class which is becoming the standard for new medical devices, or the Human Interface Device Class which is the one used for computer peripherals such as keyboards and mice.

The second part of the book proceeds to applying that theory to real world USB devices that you can run immediately and use as a reference to create your own USB devices.

We are convinced that this package, loaded with proven hardware and software will streamline your USB application development process and help you get to market faster.

Peter Carbone
VP Marketing
Renesas Electronics America

1

Introduction

USB has probably been the most successful communication interface in the history of computer systems and has become the de-facto standard for connecting computer peripherals. Part II of this book demonstrates how the Renesas YRDKRX63N Demonstration Kit and Micriµm's µC/USB-Device stack can be used as the cornerstone to build a USB device that relies on a combination of proven hardware and software platforms. Micriµm's µC/USB-Device is a USB device stack designed for embedded systems. It was built from the ground up with Micriµm's quality, scalability and reliability and has gone through a very rigorous validation process to comply with the USB 2.0 specification. Renesas' ultra-low-power RX63N MCU is at the core of the YRDKRX63N board that incorporates communication functions suitable for networking equipment such as Ethernet controller, USB 2.0 full-speed (host or device), and CAN. In addition, with a RTC (Real-Time Clock) that can operate on a dedicated power supply as a low power feature, standby power consumption can be reduced by approximately 90% compared to existing products.

The examples in this part of the book include USB devices with the most basic functionality that will allow you to understand the USB concepts covered in the first part of this book and at the same time, they provide a framework to quickly build devices such as:

- USB-to-serial adapter (Communications Device Class)

- Mouse or keyboard (Human Interface Device Class)

- Removable storage device (Mass Storage Class)

- USB medical device (Personal Healthcare Device Class)

- Custom device (Vendor Class)

All the five examples are based on the key elements illustrated in Figure 1-1:

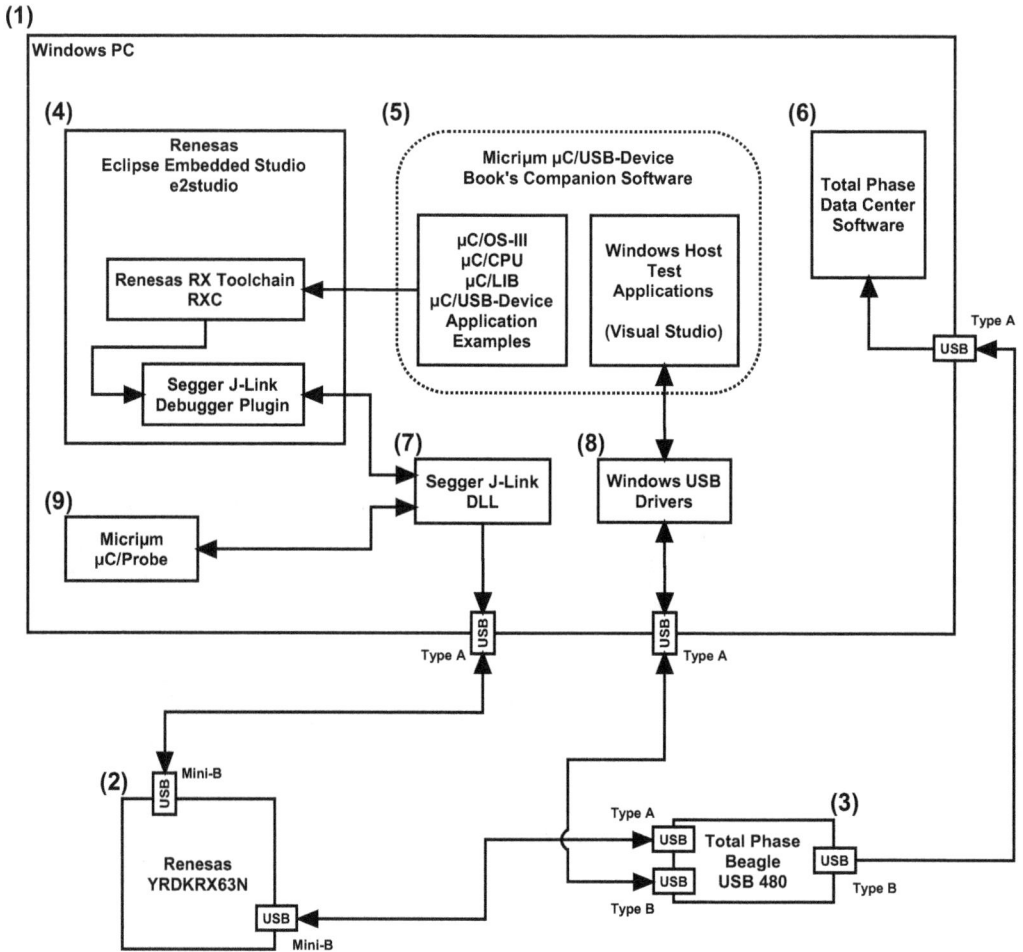

Figure 1-1 **USB Device Application Examples Overview**

F1-1(1)   In order to run the USB device application examples included with the book, you need a PC running Windows XP or Windows 7 with at least three USB Type-A receptacles. One of the receptacles will be used to download and debug the code and the other two will be used to connect to the USB device and capture the USB traffic for protocol analysis purposes.

F1-1(2)   The Renesas Demonstration Kit YRDKRX63N is available from Renesas. The board includes two USB Mini-B ports. One of them is tied to the J-Link in-circuit debugger while the other is tied to the RX63N USB controller. For more information on how to setup the board, see section 2-2-1 "Renesas Demonstration Kit YRDKRX63N" on page 635.

F1-1(3)   The Beagle™ USB 480 protocol analyzer from Total Phase is a low cost, non-intrusive high-speed USB 2.0 bus monitor that includes real-time USB class-level decoding. This piece of hardware is not required to run the examples but it is highly recommended in order to understand the protocol and in case you are building a USB device, it is definitely a must have. For more information on how to connect the protocol analyzer see section 2-2-2 "USB Protocol Analyzer BeagleTM USB 480" on page 638.

F1-1(4)   In order to build and debug the example code, you must download the Renesas e2studio from the Renesas website. You also need to download the RXC toolchain from the Renesas website and integrate it into e2studio. For more information on installing the e2studio IDE and the RXC toolchain see section 2-1-2 "Renesas Eclipse Embedded Studio e2studio" on page 629 and section 2-1-3 "Renesas RXC Toolchain" on page 630 respectively.

F1-1(5)   The book's companion software is available for download from the Micriµm website. The software includes not only the application examples, but also the µC/OS-III source code and µC/USB-Device in precompiled linkable object form among other Micriµm modules. Moreover, some examples will require custom Windows applications that are distributed as part of the book's companion software package in the form of Visual Studio source code. For more information on installing the required software from Micriµm see section 2-1-5 "µC/USB-Device Book's Companion Software" on page 630.

F1-1(6)   The Data Center Software from Total Phase is a free protocol analysis software that is included with the Beagle™ USB 480 Protocol Analyzer. For more information on installing the Data Center Software see section 2-1-4 "Total Phase Data Center Software" on page 630.

F1-1(7)   The YRDKRX63N board includes a J-Link in-circuit debugger from Segger. When you install e2studio, it also installs the appropriate Windows J-Link drivers for the RX600 series of microcontrollers.

F1-1(8)   In order to run the examples, the Windows PC needs to have some drivers installed. Some examples such as the ones implementing the HID and MSC classes make use of Windows native drivers. Other examples implementing classes such as CDC, PHDC and Vendor specific, require Windows drivers that come as part of the book's companion software package.

F1-1(9)   You can download a trial version of µC/Probe from the Micriµm website in order to not only monitor the application variables at run time but also the µC/USB Device stack and µC/OS-III internal variables. For more information on installing µC/Probe see section 2-1-6 "µC/Probe" on page 633.

This book and the Renesas YRDKRX63N make an excellent platform for engineers interested in creating their own USB devices.

The application examples in this book are provided solely as a reference to help engineers use Micriµm and Renesas products.

There are no express or implied copyright licenses granted hereunder to design or fabricate any USB devices based on the information in this book.

Micriµm and Renesas make no warranty, representation or guarantee regarding the suitability of these examples for any particular purpose, nor does Micriµm and Renesas assume any liability arising out of the application or use of any example design, and specifically disclaims any and all liability, including without limitation consequential or incidental damages.

1-1 PART II CHAPTER CONTENTS

Figure 1-2 shows the layout and flow of Part II of the book. This diagram should be useful in understanding the relationship between chapters and appendices.

The first column on the left indicates chapters that should be read in order to understand µC/USB-Device's structure as well as the examples. The columns to the right hand side consist of miscellaneous appendices that further expand on the information presented in the first columns on the left.

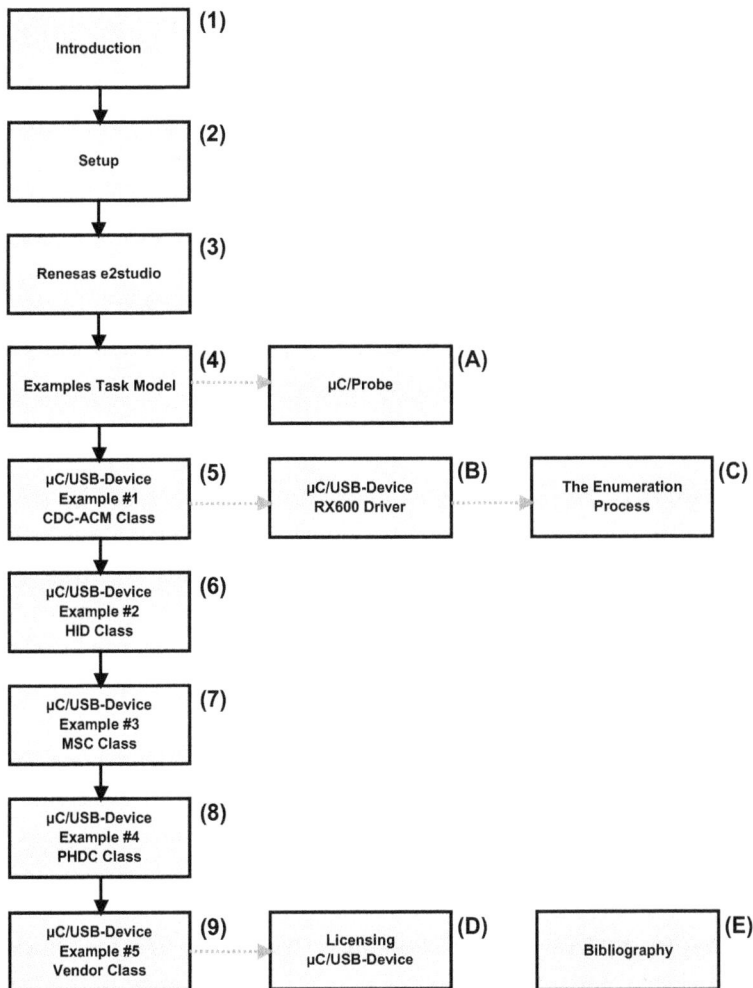

Figure 1-2 **Part II Chapter Layout**

F1-2(1)   **Chapter 1, Introduction.** This chapter.

F1-2(2)   **Chapter 2, Setup.** This chapter explains how to set up the environment to run the μC/USB-Device examples. It describes where to download and how to install the required software and, where to buy and how to connect the required hardware.

F1-2(3)   **Chapter 3, Renesas Eclipse Embedded Studio e2studio** This chapter provides a brief description of e2studio and how to compile and debug embedded applications.

F1-2(4)   **Chapter 4, Examples Task Model.** This chapter describes the task model supported by μC/OS-III for all the examples featured in this book. Each example will run at least 10 different tasks and most of them are common to all the examples. This chapter aims at describing each task.

F1-2(5)   **Chapter 5, Example #1: Communications Device Class.** This chapter explains how to get the μC/USB-Device stack up and running. It shows you how to send and receive serial data from a USB device through a virtual COM port using the CDC class and ACM subclass. It also introduces the USB Protocol Analyzer from Total Phase as an indispensable tool for the development of USB applications.

F1-2(6)   **Chapter 6, Example #2: Human Interface Device.** The project features a simulated mouse that exercises input reports sent to the host computer. It basically makes the mouse pointer in Windows move back and forth. The theory described in the first part of the book keeps getting complemented by describing some of the most important USB protocol bus traffic transactions captured with the Beagle USB 480 Protocol Analyzer.

F1-2(7)   **Chapter 7, Example #3: Mass Storage Class.** This chapter shows you how to create a solid state USB drive using the μC/USB-Device stack and the MSC class. It shows you how to run the example and then it explains how it works by describing code listings and USB traffic captures.

F1-2(8)   **Chapter 8, Example #4: Personal Healthcare Device Class.** This chapter provides a demonstration of Micriμm's implementation of the PHDC class. You can use the demo as the cornerstone to build not only any type of medical device with USB connectivity, but also its corresponding Windows host application; as the example is accompanied by a Visual Studio project that interfaces with PHDC devices that you can use as a reference.

F1-2(9)   **Chapter 9, Example #5: Vendor Specific Class.** In case your next USB application does not conform with any of the aforementioned USB classes you can define your own with the Vendor Specific Class. This chapter provides an example of defining your own USB vendor specific class.

F1-2(J)   **Appendix A, Introduction to µC/Probe.** This appendix provides a brief description of Micriµm's µC/Probe, which easily allows users to display and change target variables at run time.

F1-2(11)   **Appendix B, RX600 µC/USB-Device Driver.** This appendix provides a brief description of the RX600 USB controller driver for µC/USB-Device.

F1-2(12)   **Appendix C, The Enumeration Process.** This appendix provides a brief description of the enumeration process in terms of USB traffic captures.

F1-2(M)   **Appendix D, Licensing µC/OS-III and µC/USB-Device.**

F1-2(N)   **Appendix E, Bibliography.**

1-2 ACKNOWLEDGEMENTS

Micriµm Press would like to thank Rob Dautel and Todd DeBoer, from Renesas, who helped see the project through to completion. They made this possible by fostering collaborative relationships between Renesas and Micriµm.

Thanks to the rest of the fine team at Renesas for their support, for designing the YRDKRX63N board and for providing access to the Eclipse Embedded Studio e2studio and RXC tools. e2studio is a great IDE and we are sure readers of this book will appreciate the ability to try out µC/USB-Device on the YRDKRX63N board.

We would also like to thank Total Phase for providing samples of the Beagle USB 480 Protocol Analyzer. This protocol analyzer and their Data Center software are a great tool that we consider indispensable in the development of any USB based application.

Finally, thanks to the Micriµm USB Team for providing not only a world-class USB Device Stack but also all the material in this book:

Christian Légaré *is Micriµm's CTO. He has a Master's degree in Electrical Engineering from the University of Sherbrooke, Québec, Canada. Before joining Micriµm, Christian spent 22 years in the telecom industry as an executive in such large-scale organizations as Teleglobe Canada and other engineering and R&D startups. He is a regular speaker at the Embedded Systems conferences in Boston and Silicon Valley and has published several articles on embedded systems including the book µC/TCP-IP The Embedded Protocol Stack.*

Cédric Migliorini *is an Embedded Software Engineer and leader of the USB team at Micriµm. He graduated from École Polytechnique de Montréal with a Master's degree in Computer Engineering in 2008. During his time at Micriµm, he has improved and maintained the USB device and host stacks. While completing his master's degree, Cédric worked in a codesign laboratory where he explored on-chip bus communication by using an Electronic System Level method.*

Jean-François Deschênes *is an Embedded Software Engineer at Micriµm in Montréal, Canada. He received his B.S. degree in Electrical Engineering from the École de Technologie Supérieure in Canada. He joined Micriµm as part of the USB Team in 2011 where he leads the work on the µC/USB-Host product. While completing his B.S. degree, he worked on the embedded software of a nanosatellite and on the development of an extra planetary autonomous rover project at the Canadian Space Agency.*

Juan P. Benavides *is an Applications Engineer at Micriµm in Weston, Florida. He received his B.S. degree in Electrical Engineering from the University of the Andes, Bogotá, Colombia in 1999. Since then, he has held positions in the industry designing and developing multiple embedded systems using a wide variety of hardware and software architectures in different industries such as medical, power generation, marine and industrial control and instrumentation. Prior to joining Micriµm he was the Lead Software Developer at Swantech, a division of the Curtiss-Wright Corporation.*

2

Setup

In this chapter you will learn how to setup an environment to run the μC/USB-Device application projects included with the book. In the following sections we will consider the Software and Hardware that need to be setup. Please follow the instructions below in the exact order.

2-1 SOFTWARE

2-1-1 WINDOWS PC SYSTEM REQUIREMENTS

All the required software is officially supported on Windows XP (SP2 or later, 32-bit and 64-bit), and Windows 7 (32-bit and 64-bit).

It requires a computer with an Intel or AMD processor running at a minimum speed of 2.0 GHz, 1GB of physical RAM, at least one high-speed USB port and two full-speed USB ports (or faster).

2-1-2 RENESAS ECLIPSE EMBEDDED STUDIO e2studio

The examples provided with this book were tested using the Renesas Eclipse Embedded Studio e2studio version 1.0.1.14. You can download the complete e2studio IDE installation including debug and build phase support from the Renesas website at:

```
http://www.renesas.com/products/tools/ide/
ide_e2studio/downloads.jsp
```

The toolchain (compiler, assembler, linker, etc.) is not included with the download.

We recommend to execute the installer with administrative privileges and into an installation directory outside of the typical *Program Files*.

2-1-3 RENESAS RXC TOOLCHAIN

The examples were built using the Renesas RXC Toolchain. You can download a free trial version from the Renesas website. Look for *C/C++ Compiler Package for the RX Family*.

    http://www.renesas.com/products/tools/coding_tools/
    c_compilers_assemblers/rx_compiler/downloads.jsp

Make sure that e2studio is not running while you install the toolchain. Once the installation completes you can open e2studio and the IDE will detect the new toolchain and ask you if you want to integrate it.

2-1-4 TOTAL PHASE DATA CENTER SOFTWARE

The Data Center^{TM} Software from Total Phase is a free bus monitoring software that captures and displays USB, I2C, SPI and CAN bus data in real time through the Beagle^{TM} line of hardware protocol analyzers.

The Data Center^{TM} Software can be downloaded from the following link:

    http://www.totalphase.com/products/data_center/

Download the appropriate zip file for your version of Windows and extract to a folder in your computer. Create a shortcut on your desktop to the application file **Data Center.exe** as the download does not include an installer.

2-1-5 μC/USB-DEVICE BOOK'S COMPANION SOFTWARE

The book's companion software includes:

■ μC/OS-III for the RX63N (source code)

■ μC/CPU for the RX63N (source code)

■ μC/LIB (source code)

■ μC/USB-Device for the RX63N (precompiled linkable object)

▦ Application Examples (source code)

You can download all the software you need from the following link:

    http://micrium.com/page/downloads/uc-usb-device_files

Once the zip file is downloaded, you can extract the files to any location in your computer and the directory structure should look like the one illustrated in Figure 2-1:

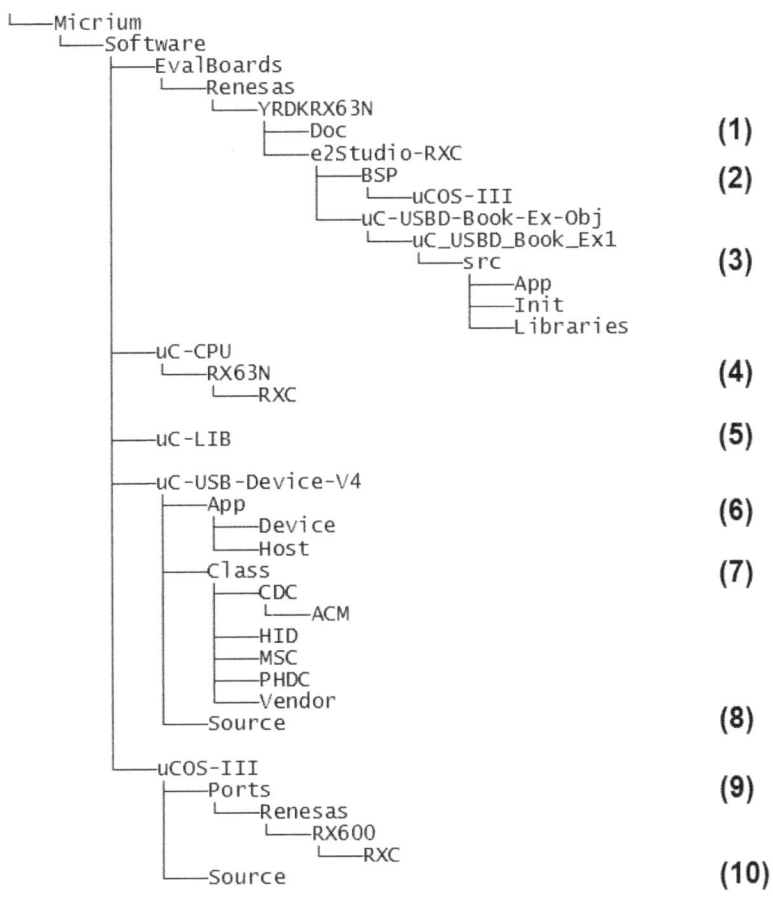

```
└──Micrium
    └──Software
        ├──EvalBoards
        │   └──Renesas
        │       └──YRDKRX63N
        │           ├──Doc                              (1)
        │           └──e2Studio-RXC
        │               ├──BSP                          (2)
        │               │   └──uCOS-III
        │               └──uC-USBD-Book-Ex-Obj
        │                   └──uC_USBD_Book_Ex1
        │                       └──src                  (3)
        │                           ├──App
        │                           ├──Init
        │                           └──Libraries
        ├──uC-CPU
        │   └──RX63N                                    (4)
        │       └──RXC
        ├──uC-LIB                                       (5)
        ├──uC-USB-Device-V4
        │   ├──App                                      (6)
        │   │   ├──Device
        │   │   └──Host
        │   ├──Class                                    (7)
        │   │   ├──CDC
        │   │   │   └──ACM
        │   │   ├──HID
        │   │   ├──MSC
        │   │   ├──PHDC
        │   │   └──Vendor
        │   └──Source                                   (8)
        └──uCOS-III
            ├──Ports                                    (9)
            │   └──Renesas
            │       └──RX600
            │           └──RXC
            └──Source                                   (10)
```

Figure 2-1 µC/USB-Device Book's Companion Software

F2-1(1)   The documentation for the YRDKRX63N, including the hardware manual and schematics is in this folder.

F2-1(2)   The **BSP** folder for the YRDKRX63N not only includes functions to initialize the peripherals on the board such as the LCD, LEDs, push buttons and the microphone, but also other μC/OS-III related functions.

F2-1(3)   The **src** folder contains some of the source code, including the application level code and hardware initialization. There is also a folder named **Libraries** that contains the precompiled library object for the μC/USB-Device stack.

F2-1(4)   The μC/CPU module defines portable data-types and critical section macros for specific processor architectures and compilers such as the RX63N and the RXC compiler. The μC/USB-Device examples make reference to the portable data types defined by this μC/CPU module.

F2-1(5)   The μC/LIB module replaces some of the C standard library functions in order to simplify third-party certification. The μC/USB-Device examples make reference to the functions and macros defined by this μC/LIB module.

F2-1(6)   The μC/USB-Device stack's application level code is in this folder.

    ■ Device: includes the application examples that run on the device.

    ■ Host: includes the windows applications and INF files for the host.

F2-1(7)   The μC/USB-Device classes code is in this folder for all μC/USB-Device licensees. See Appendix D, "μC/OS-III and μC/USB-Device Licensing Policy" on page 819 for more details on how to purchase a license for a μC/USB-Device class.

F2-1(8)   The μC/USB-Device stack core source code is in this folder for all μC/USB-Device licensees. See Appendix D, "μC/OS-III and μC/USB-Device Licensing Policy" on page 819 for more details.

F2-1(9)   The μC/OS-III port for the RX63N is in this folder. It includes the functions for context switching and system ticker among others.

F2-1(10)   The μC/OS-III source code is available for free short-term evaluation, see Appendix D, "μC/OS-III and μC/USB-Device Licensing Policy" on page 819 for more details.

2-1-6 µC/PROBE

µC/Probe is a Windows application that allows users to display or change the value (at run-time) of virtually any variable or memory location on a connected embedded target. See Appendix A, "Introduction to µC/Probe" on page 789 for a brief introduction.

µC/Probe is used in the examples described in Chapter 1, "Introduction" on page 621 to gain run-time visibility. There are two versions of µC/Probe:

- The Full Version allows users to display or change an unlimited number of variables.

- The Trial Version is not time limited, but only allows users to display or change up to five application variables. However, the trial version also allows users to monitor any µC/OS-III variables because µC/Probe is µC/OS-III aware.

Both versions are available from Micriµm's website. Simply point your browser to:

    http://www.micrium.com/probe

CONFIGURING µC/PROBE TO WORK WITH J-LINK FOR THE RX600

The YRDKRX63N board comes with a J-Link in-circuit debugger from Segger.

The J-Link debugger not only allows you to download and debug the code but also to communicate with µC/Probe. The best thing of all is that you can run the e2studio debugger and µC/Probe at the same time as illustrated in Figure 2-2:

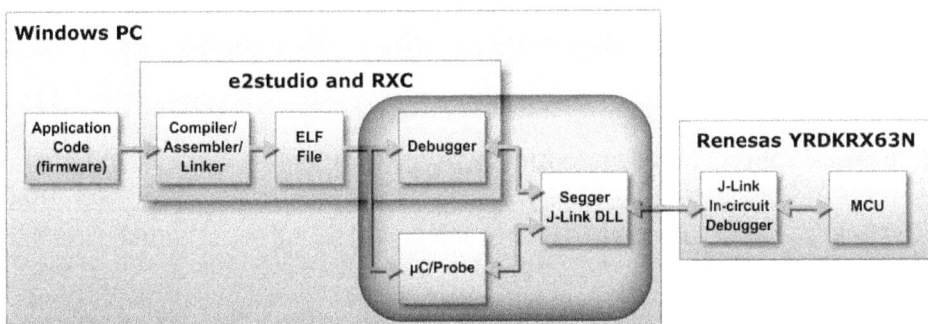

Figure 2-2 **µC/Probe and e2studio via J-Link**

If you followed the installation instructions for e2studio, then the J-Link drivers for the RX600 family of microcontrollers are already installed in your computer. It is necessary to configure µC/Probe with the path in your file system to the J-Link driver.

Open µC/Probe and click the *Settings* button on the top toolbar and the application will open the configuration screen shown in Figure 2-3:

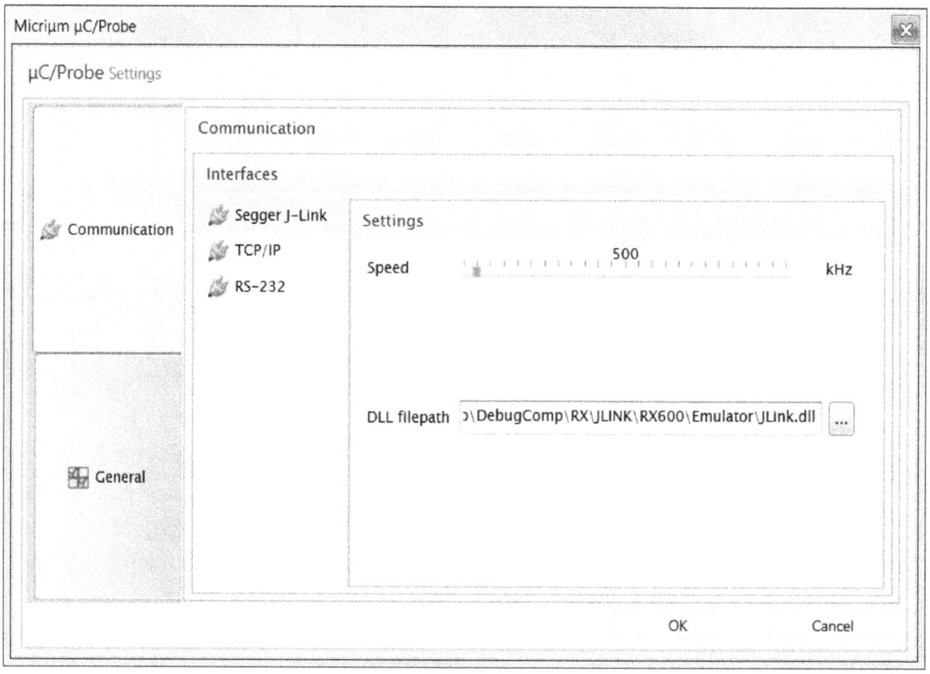

Figure 2-3 **µC/Probe Configuration Screen**

Configure the J-Link driver's DLL path by browsing to the following folder in your file system:

```
$\Renesas\e2studio\DebugComp\RX\JLINK\RX600\Emulator\JLink.dll
```

Click *OK* and the J-Link driver will be used the next time you want to interface with the YRDKRX63N board.

This configuration screen also allows you to specify the speed which can be increased for better performance.

2-2 HARDWARE

Before connecting the hardware, make sure that all the required software has been installed as described in section 2-1 "Software" on page 629.

2-2-1 RENESAS DEMONSTRATION KIT YRDKRX63N

The YRDKRX63N board shown in Figure 2-4 is available for purchase through any of the Renesas Electronics sales channels. Go online to the Renesas website and find a distributor or sales representative in your area:

http://www.renesas.com/yrdkrx63n.

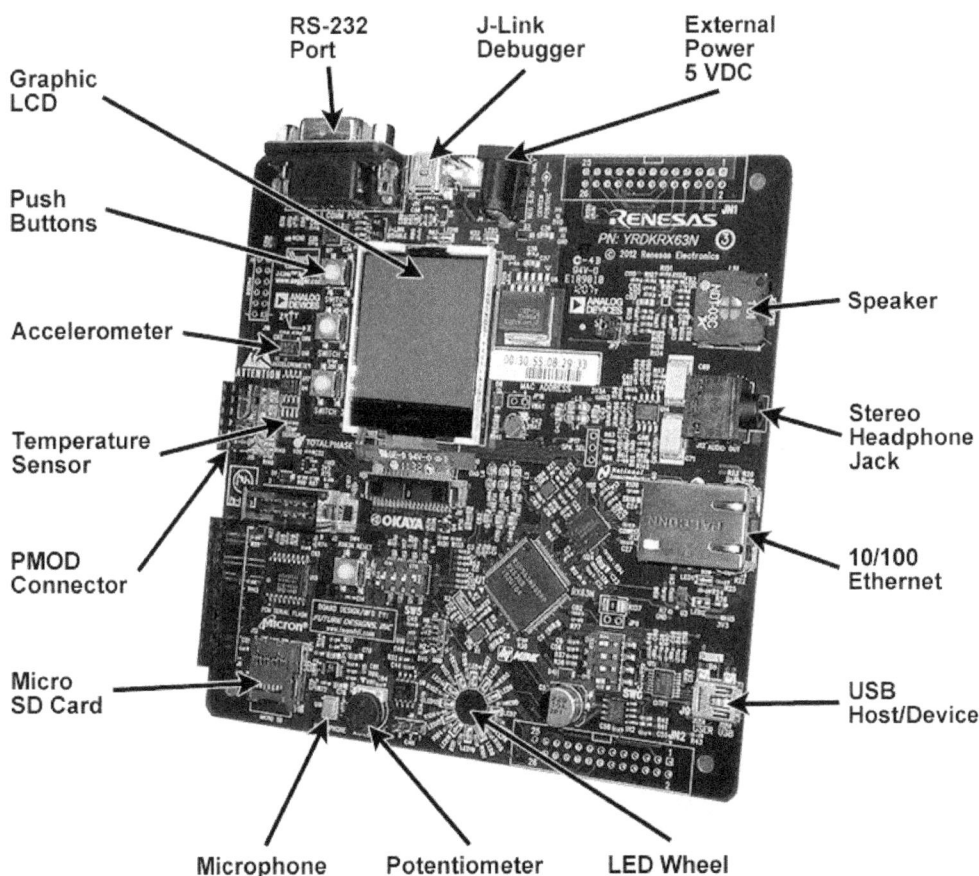

Figure 2-4 **Renesas Demonstration Kit YRDKRX63N**

The following figures illustrate the most important things to configure before running the µC/USB-Device examples.

Connect a USB cable to the USB Mini-B port on J14 of the YRDKRX63N board and into a USB Type A port in the PC. This cable is used to download and debug the code through the in-circuit J-Link debugger.

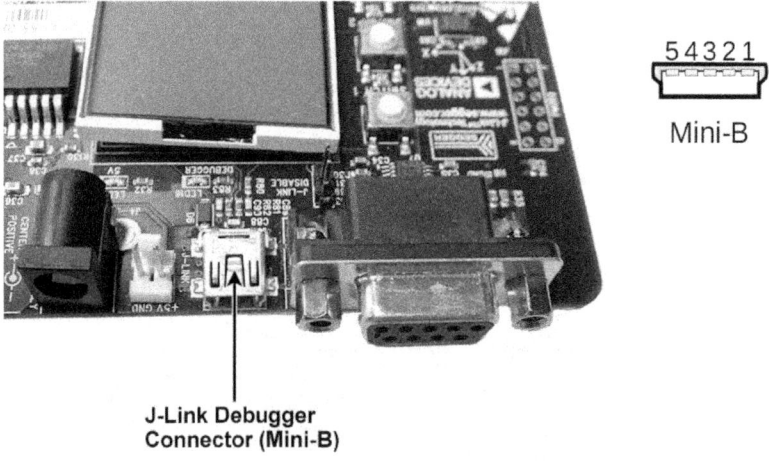

Figure 2-5 **J-Link In-Circuit Debugger on J14**

Make sure that J-Link is enabled by leaving the jumper on JP13 out:

Figure 2-6 **J-Link Disable Jumper on JP13**

Set the DIP switch on SW5 into *Debug mode* by setting the positions to OFF-OFF-OFF-ON:

MCU Mode
DIP Switch

Figure 2-7 **MCU Mode DIP Switch on SW5**

Configure the on-chip USB controller to operate as a USB-Device by setting the DIP switch on SW6 to lever positions ON-OFF-OFF-ON as shown in Figure 2-8:

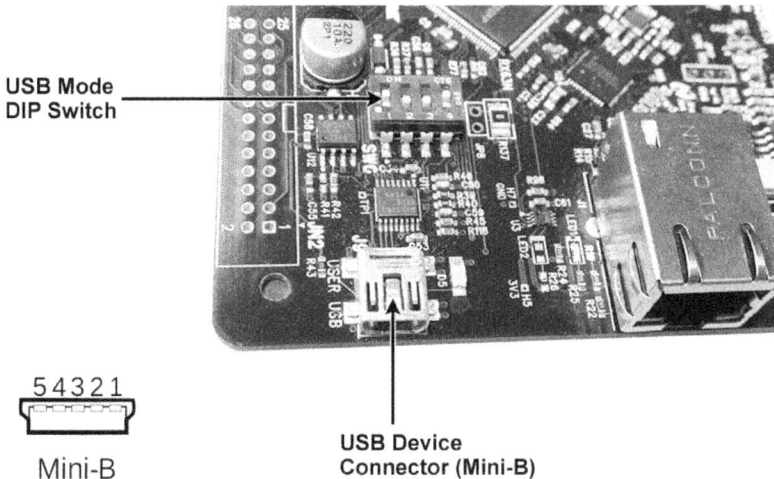

USB Mode
DIP Switch

5 4 3 2 1

Mini-B

USB Device
Connector (Mini-B)

Figure 2-8 **USB Mode DIP Switch on SW6**

The USB Mini-B connector on J9 needs to be left disconnected for the moment and will only be attached to the host computer while one of the examples is actually running.

For more information on the YRDKRX63N, please refer to the Renesas documentation.

2-2-2 USB PROTOCOL ANALYZER BEAGLE^{TM} USB 480

The Beagle^{TM} USB 480 Protocol Analyzer from Total Phase is a non-intrusive bus monitor which allows you to see and analyze serial bus data in real time as it appears on the bus.

For pricing and ordering information go online to:

    http://www.totalphase.com/products/beagle_usb480/

On one side of the Beagle USB 480 monitor is a single USB Type-B receptacle. This is the *Analysis side* as shown in Figure 2-9. This port connects to the analysis computer that is running the Beagle Data Center software. This side must be connected at all times to ensure that all connections are properly powered.

Figure 2-9 **Beagle USB 480 Protocol Analyzer: Analysis Side**

The opposite side is the *Capture side* and as shown in Figure 2-10, it contains a USB Type-A and USB Type-B receptacles. These are used to connect the target host computer to the target device (YRDKRX63N). The target host computer can be the same computer as the analysis computer, although it may not be optimal under certain conditions.

The Capture side acts as a USB pass-through. In order to remain within the USB 2.0 specification, no more than 16 feet of USB cable should be used in total between the target host computer and the target device.

Figure 2-10 **Beagle USB 480 Protocol Analyzer: Capture Side**

The top of the Beagle USB 480 Protocol Analyzer has three LED indicators as shown in Figure 2-11. The green LED serves as an Analysis Port connection indicator. The green LED will be illuminated when the Beagle analyzer has been correctly connected to the analysis computer and is receiving power from USB. The amber LED serves as a Target Host connection indicator. The amber LED will be illuminated when the target host computer is connected to the analyzer. Finally, the red LED is an activity LED. Its blink rate is proportional to the amount of data being sent across the monitored bus. If no data is seen on the bus, but the capture is active, the activity LED will simply remain on.

Figure 2-11 **Beagle USB 480 Protocol Analyzer: LED Indicators**

In order to monitor the USB bus on the YRDKRX63N, connect the Windows PC (target host) to the USB Type-B receptacle on the Capture side of the Beagle USB analyzer, and connect the YRDKRX63N (target device) to the USB Type-A receptacle on the Capture side of the Beagle USB analyzer by using the setup illustrated in Figure 2-12:

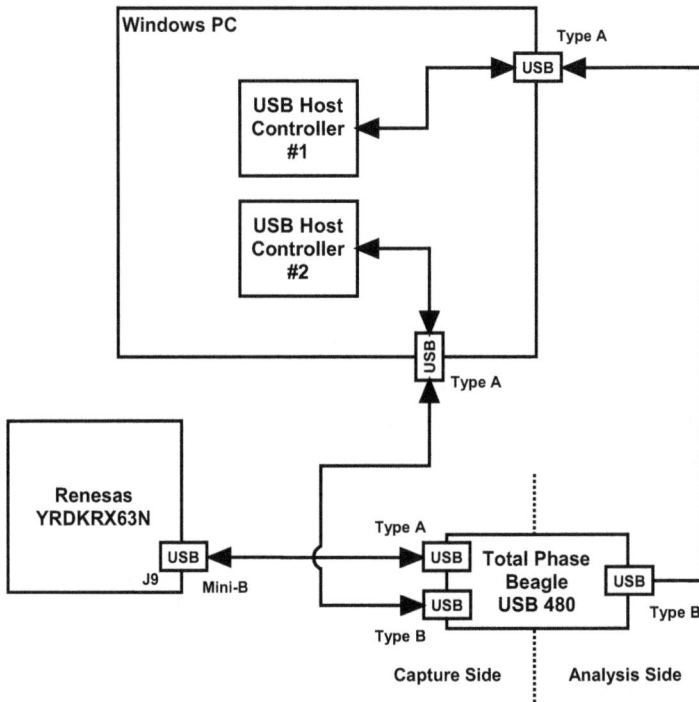

Figure 2-12 **Beagle USB 480 Protocol Analyzer: Connections**

Desktop and laptop computers usually have more than one USB host controller. It is highly recommended to keep the Analysis and Capture sides separated by connecting them to different USB host controllers. This is to avoid that the Beagle analyzer ends up capturing some of its own traffic. Typically, the USB receptacles in the back of a desktop computer are connected to one host controller while the ones in the front are connected to a different host controller. Similarly, in laptop computers, receptacles on the left and right sides of the laptop are tied to different host controllers respectively. In case your computer does not have multiple host controllers you can use a separate computer to run the Data Center Software and connect to the analysis side of the Beagle USB 480.

For more information on the Beagle USB 480 consult the user's guide on their website.

3

Renesas Eclipse Embedded Studio e2studio

Renesas Eclipse Embedded Studio, also known as e2studio, is a complete development and debug environment based on the popular Eclipse platform (v3.6 – Helios) and the associated C/C++ Development Tooling (CDT) project. The e2studio IDE covers build support (editor, compiler, and linker control), as well as debug support based on an extended GNU debugger interface (GDB).

This chapter provides general information on e2studio as well as a quick start guide that describes how to compile and debug with e2studio. Unless you are already familiar with Eclipse-based IDEs you must read this chapter before running the book examples.

3-1 e2studio GENERAL INFORMATION

3-1-1 TARGET DEVICES

e2studio has been developed to support the RX600 series among other families of Renesas microcontrollers and as new devices are released from Renesas, e2studio can easily be updated from within the IDE to add the necessary support files and debugger extensions without having to re-install the entire application. Some of the current target devices are:

- RL78

- RX (RX600, RX200)

- V850

- SH-2/SH-2A

3-1-2 BUILD PLUG-INS

e2studio allows a range of compilers to be integrated in order to provide a flexible build environment for a variety of development projects. The examples featured in this book make use of the Renesas RX toolchain which when combined with the extremely powerful editor functionality and project management tools automatically built into Eclipse CDT, offers a state-of-the-art coding environment for Renesas embedded controllers.

Other build plug-ins include:

- Renesas RX toolchain

- KPIT GNU toolchains

- IAR toolchains (via build plug-ins)

3-1-3 TARGET DEBUGGERS AND EMULATORS

To complete the development cycle, Renesas has developed a range of GDB debuggers to interface between the coding environment and a range of on-chip debuggers and in-circuit emulators. The Renesas E1, E20, and IECUBE, as well as the Segger J-Link, are supported by e2studio. The YRDKRX63N board comes with a J-Link in-circuit debugger which is the debugger chosen for the examples featured in this book.

Other third-party debuggers are supported via plug-ins from those vendors.

3-1-4 DEBUG PLUG-INS AND FEATURES

The standard GDB debugger supplied as part of the Eclipse CDT includes support for common debug functionality such as CPU registers display, memory manipulation, simple breakpoints and run control. In addition, Renesas has developed a number of extensions to enable access to advanced debug functionality available on the target devices. Extended debugger plug-ins are supplied in e2studio to support advanced debugging features like trace, real-time memory view, peripheral registers display, complex hardware event breakpoints, and more. The exact debug feature support depends on the device family and debug hardware used.

The examples featured in this book offer the following debugging features:

- Basic debugging features

  - Connect / Disconnect

  - Run / Stop (Resume / Suspend)

  - Software breakpoints

  - Source step / disassembly step

  - Variable and Expression views

  - Register view

  - Basic Memory view

  - Endian selection

- Advanced debugging features

  - Renesas Debug view with Call Stack

  - I/O Registers view

  - Trace view

  - Event points view

  - Real-time Expression view

  - Real-time Memory view

  - Real-time Chart view (data visualization)

3-1-5 PROJECT GENERATORS

Although the examples featured in this book are ready to build and run, e2studio includes project generators to speed up the initial project setup. The software engineer is offered a selection of device, initial compiler options, and debuggers. e2studio will then prepare a preconfigured, ready to build and debug project with all the necessary support files such as the device-specific header file.

3-1-6 PRICING AND AVAILABILITY

The e2studio IDE, as well as the KPIT GNU compilers, are available free of charge.

The Renesas RX compiler, as well as the IAR compiler, require the purchase of a commercial license.

The examples featured in this book make use of the Renesas RX toolchain. The evaluation version of this toolchain is provided with the same functionality as the commercial version except that link size will be restricted to 128 Kbytes on and after the 61st day from when you begin using the compiler.

3-1-7 SUPPORTED OS PLATFORMS

■ Windows XP (32-bit)

■ Windows 7 (32-bit)

■ Windows 7 (64-bit)

3-2 e2studio QUICK START GUIDE

3-2-1 LOADING A WORKSPACE IN e2studio

Open e2studio by clicking the shortcut on your desktop:

Figure 3-1 **e2studio Shortcut**

When e2studio is launched, the first thing you see is a dialog box that allows you to select where the workspace should be located. The workspace is the directory where your work will be stored. Feel free to select a path that it is easy to remember as your workspace, as long as e2studio has writing privileges. We recommend creating a new empty folder and then browse to it as shown in Figure 3-2:

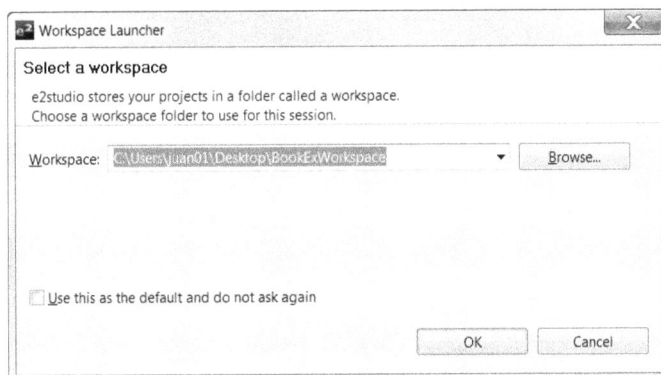

Figure 3-2 **Workspace Launcher**

3-2-2 IMPORTING A PROJECT IN e2studio

The C project included in your book's companion software package needs to be imported into your new workspace before building and running the examples for the first time.

In order to import a project into your new workspace select *File -> Import...* as shown in Figure 3-3:

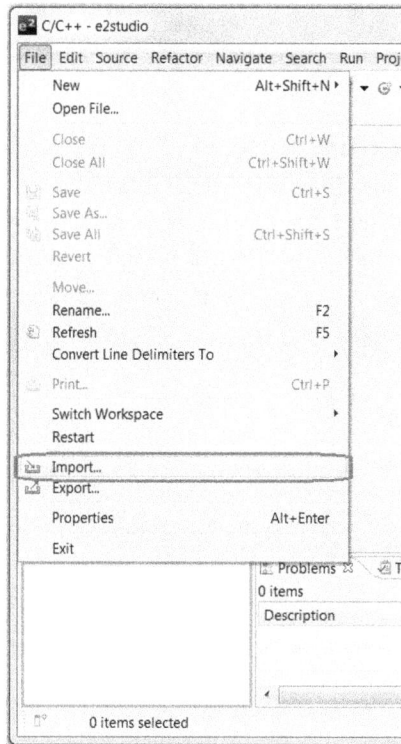

Figure 3-3 **Importing a Project in e2studio: Step 1**

A couple of dialog windows will guide you through the importing process.

Select *General -> Existing Projects into Workspace* and click *Next* to continue.

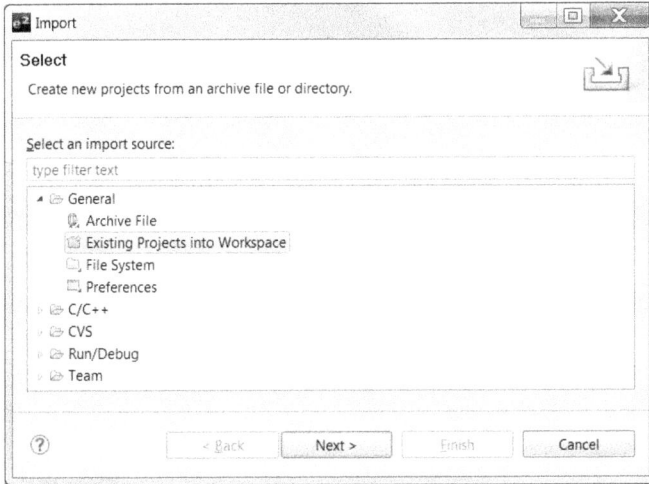

Figure 3-4 **Importing a Project in e2studio: Step 2**

The last step in the importing process is to provide e2studio with the path to the project.

The screen shown in Figure 3-5 allows you to do so. Click *Browse* and select the folder where you extracted the book's companion software:

```
$\Micrium\Software\EvalBoards\Renesas\YRDKRX63N\
    e2studio-RXC\uC-USBD-Book-Ex-Obj
```

Verify that your dialog screen looks similar to the one shown in Figure 3-5 and click *Finish* to import the project.

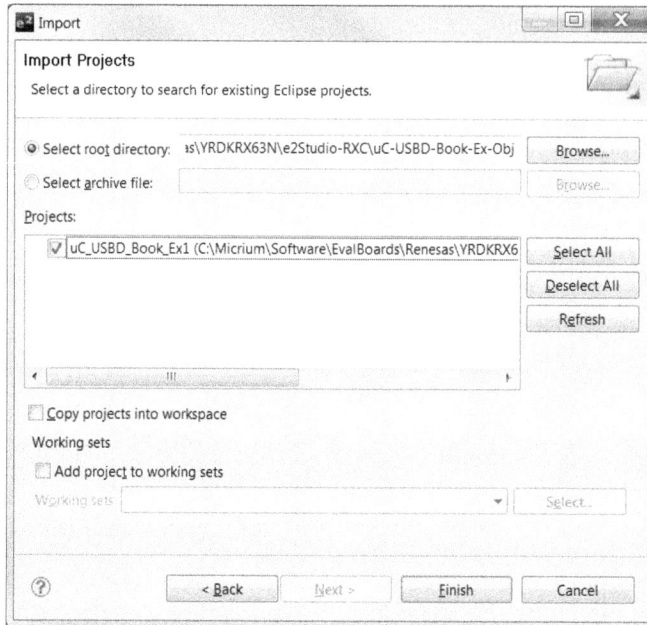

Figure 3-5 **Importing a Project in e2studio: Step 3**

Keep in mind that importing the C project into your workspace is something you only need to do once for all the examples.

3-2-3 BUILDING A PROJECT IN e2studio

In order to compile a project in e2studio, first make sure to select the correct build configuration active. In the *Project Explorer* view, select your project by making right-click over the project name and activate the build configuration labeled as *HardwareDebug (Debug on Hardware)* as shown in Figure 3-6:

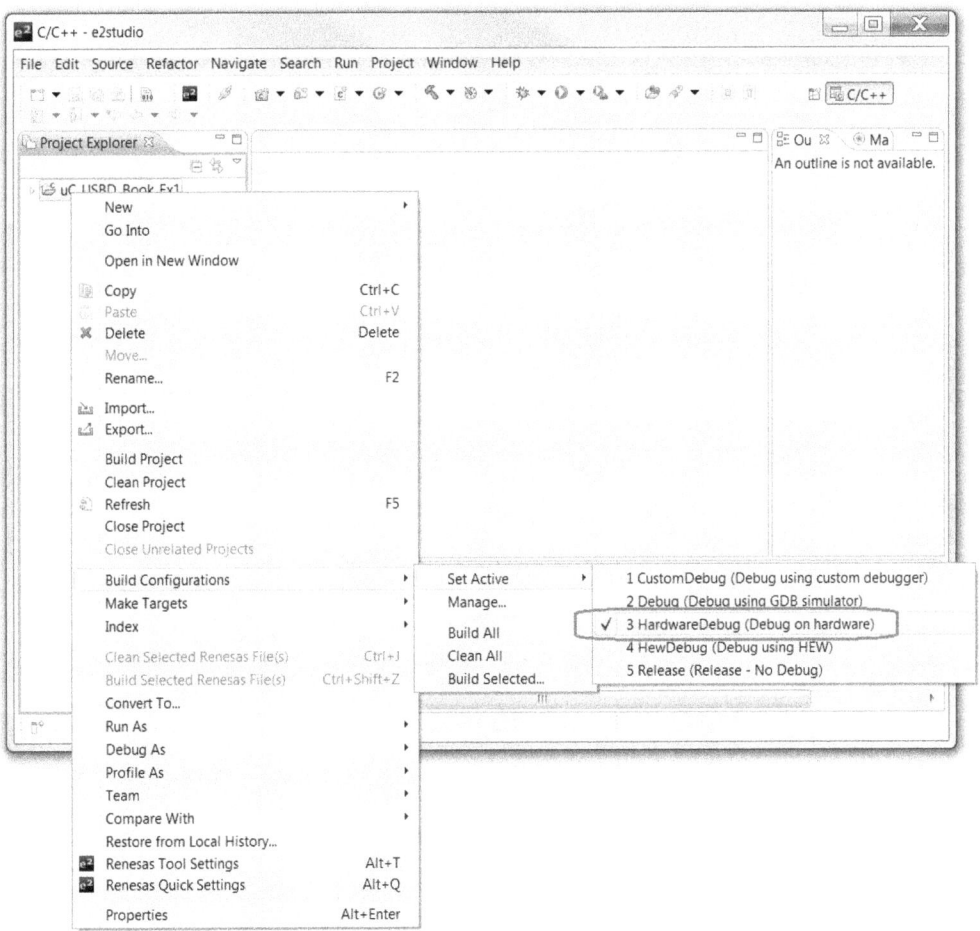

Figure 3-6 **Selecting the Correct Build Configuration**

Next, in the *Project Explorer* view, select your project and press **Ctrl+B** or right-click over the project name and select *Build Project* as shown in Figure 3-7:

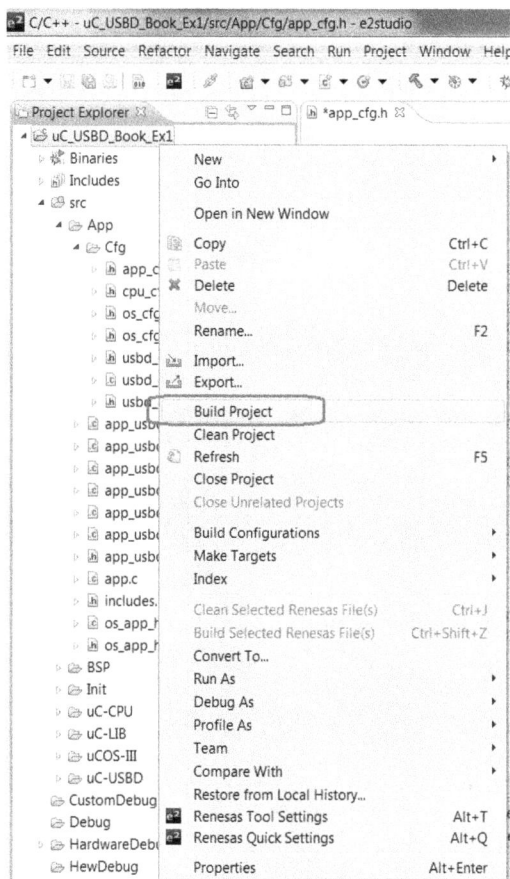

Figure 3-7 **Building a Project**

A progress bar similar to the one shown in Figure 3-8 indicates the progress of all the different building stages:

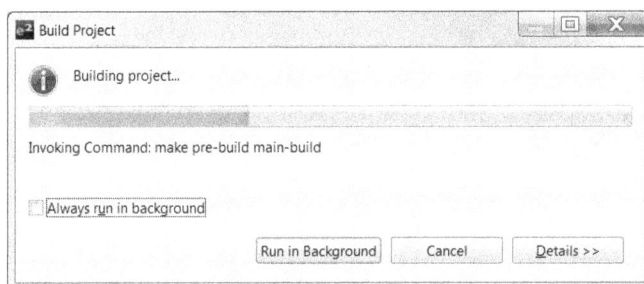

You can also see the output and results of the build command in the *Console* view at the bottom of e2studio. Click on its tab to bring the view forward if it is not currently visible. If for some reason it is not present, you can open it by selecting *Window -> Show View -> Console*. If the building process finishes without any errors, it will create what is called the *Executable and Linkable Format* file (ELF). Figure 3-9 shows the console view and the final success message you should receive:

Figure 3-9 **Building a Project: Console**

3-2-4 CREATING A DEBUG SESSION IN e2studio

A new debug session needs to be created in your new workspace before building and running the examples for the first time.

In order to create a new debug session in e2studio, you need to build the ELF file as described in the previous section. Once you get a success message in the console window, you will notice that the new ELF file is under the new folder *Binaries* in the project explorer. Select the ELF file **uC_USBD_Book_Ex1.x**, right-click over the name and select *Debug As -> Debug Configurations...* as shown in Figure 3-10:

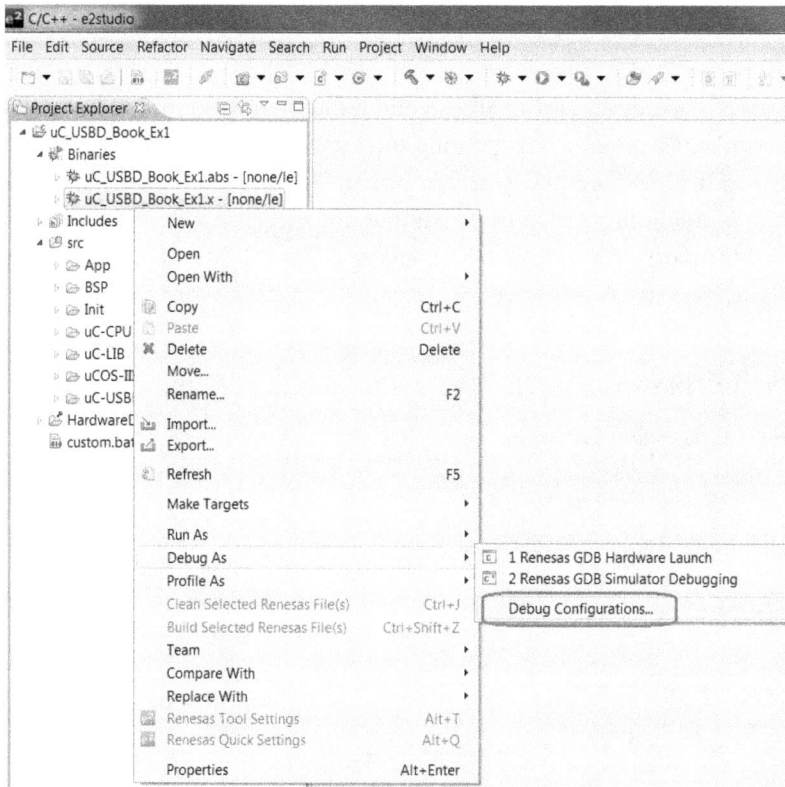

Figure 3-10 **Creating a Debug Session: Step 1**

A series of dialog windows will guide you through the process of creating a new debug session in your workspace.

Select the debugging type *Renesas GDB Hardware Debugging* and press the *New* button as indicated in Figure 3-11:

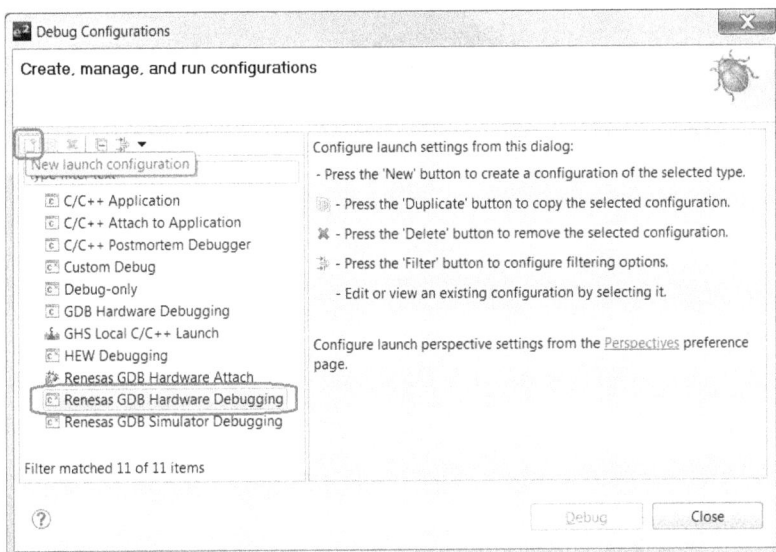

Figure 3-11 **Creating a Debug Session: Step 2**

The new debug session will be created with default settings that you need to change to match those from the YRDKRX63N board.

Make sure the settings in the *Main* tab look exactly like the ones shown in Figure 3-12:

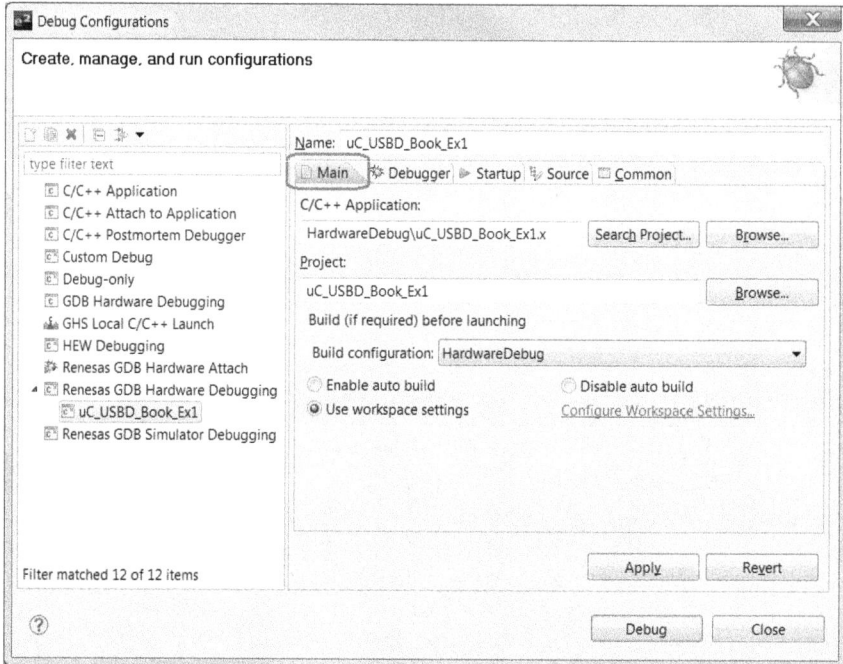

Figure 3-12 **Creating a Debug Session: Step 3**

Finally, make sure that the debugging hardware in the *Debugger* tab, is configured to *Segger JLink* and press the *Close* button as indicated in Figure 3-13:

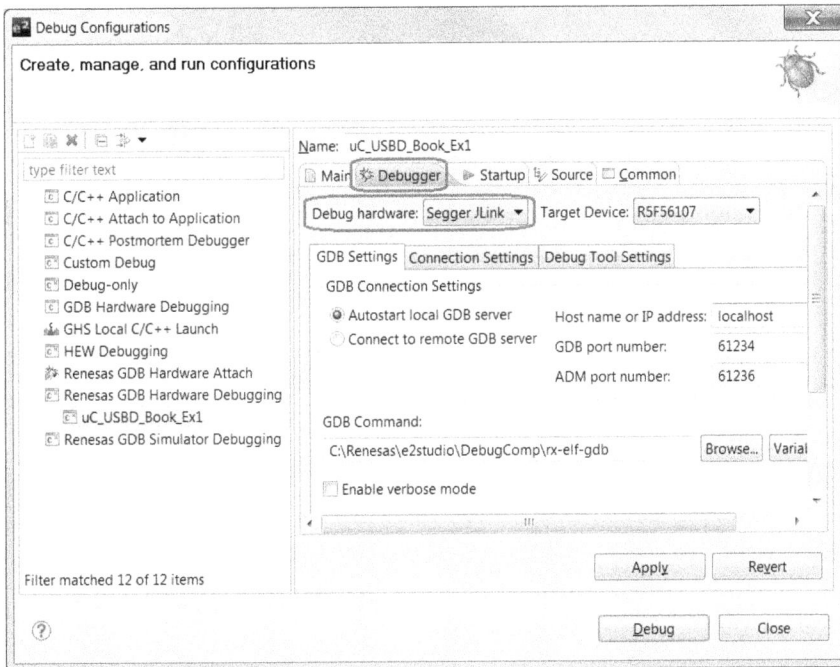

Figure 3-13 **Creating a Debug Session: Step 4**

3-2-5 LAUNCHING A DEBUG SESSION IN e2studio

In order to launch a debug session, you need to build the ELF file as described in section 3-2-3 on page 648. Once you get a success message in the console window, you will notice that the new ELF file is under the new folder *Binaries* in the project explorer. Select the ELF file uC_USBD_Book_Ex1.x, click on the debug button (the one with the bug icon) and select the debugging session named *uC_USBD_Book_Ex1* as shown in Figure 3-14:

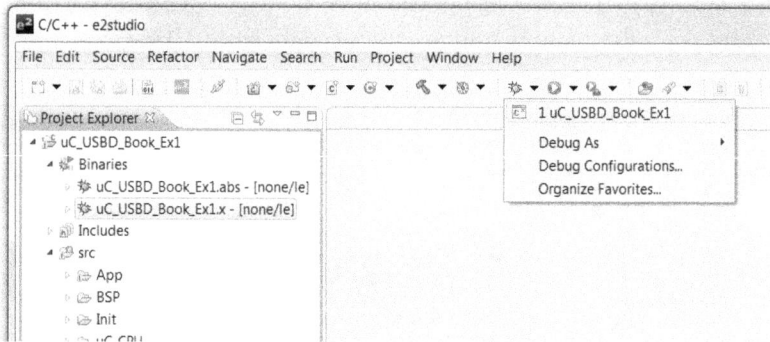

Figure 3-14 **Launching the Debugging Session**

e2studio will prompt you if you prefer to change the appearance of your IDE (perspective) to one more suitable for debugging:

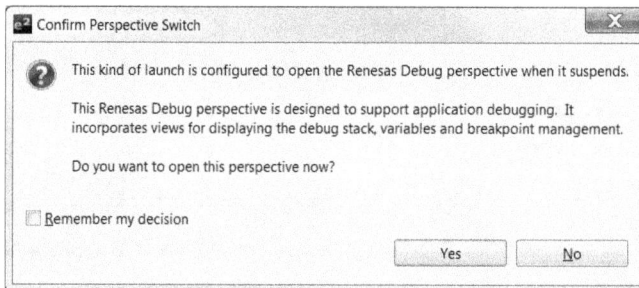

Figure 3-15 **IDE Perspectives**

Select *Yes* and your IDE will switch to the debugging perspective shown in Figure 3-16:

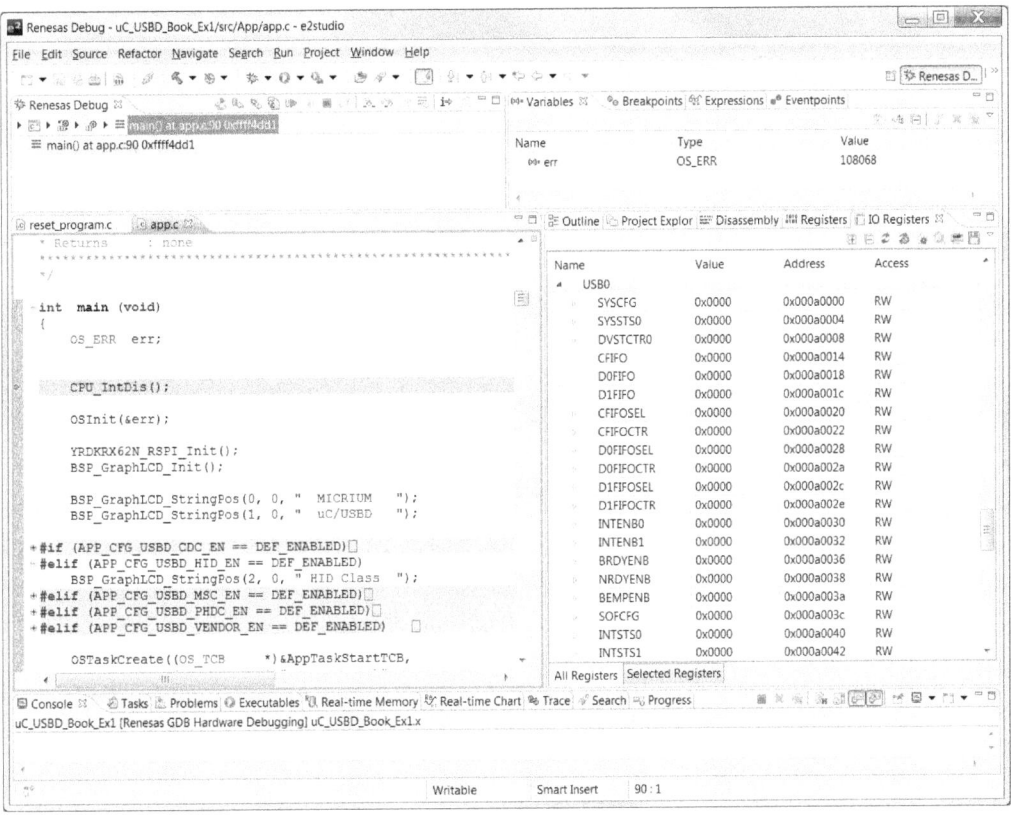

Figure 3-16 **Debugging Perspective**

At this point you can use any of the typical debugging tools such as Variable Watch and I/O Register Windows and, you can step through the source code as shown in Figure 3-17:

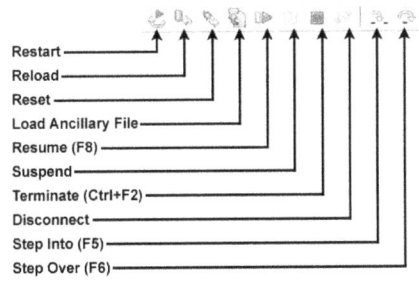

Restart
Reload
Reset
Load Ancillary File
Resume (F8)
Suspend
Terminate (Ctrl+F2)
Disconnect
Step Into (F5)
Step Over (F6)

Figure 3-17 **Debugging Toolbar**

Chapter 3

Examples: Task Model

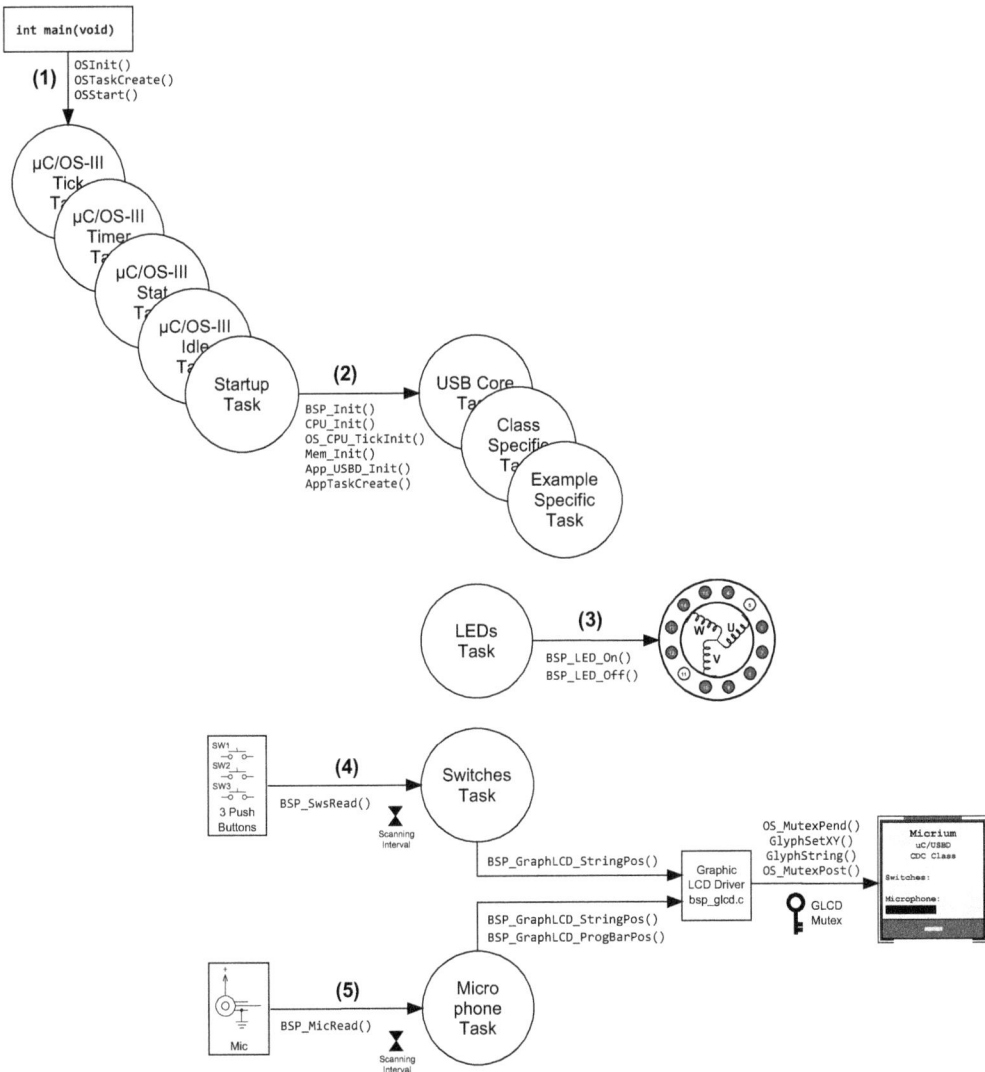

Figure 4-1 **Examples Task Model**

All the examples featured in this book are not only in the same e2studio workspace and project, but also share the same base application. You get to enable one class and example by configuring a series of preprocessor macros.

The base application features a task model supported by µC/OS-III that includes the tasks illustrated in Figure 4-1.

F4-1(1)   The main entry point is declared in **app.c**. The **main()** starts by initializing µC/OS-III through a call to **OSInit()** which in turn creates the following internal tasks:

■ *Tick Task*: **OS_TickTask()** is used by µC/OS-III to keep track of tasks waiting for time to expire or, for tasks that are pending on kernel objects with a timeout. **OS_TickTask()** is a periodic task that waits for signals from the tick ISR.

■ *Timer Task*: **OS_TimerTask()** is used by µC/OS-III to provide countdown timer services that perform an action when the counter reaches zero.

■ *Statistics Task*: **OS_StatTask()** is used by µC/OS-III to calculate run-time statistics such as CPU usage.

■ *Idle Task*: **OS_IdleTask()** is used by µC/OS-III to run whenever there are no other tasks that are ready to run.

The **main()** continues by creating the *Startup Task* and starting the multi-tasking process by calling **OSStart()**.

F4-1(2)   The *Startup Task* is implemented by **AppTaskStart()** in **app.c** and it is used to initialize various hardware and software modules including the µC/USB-Device stack and class example. They are initialized by calling **App_USBD_Init()** which in turn creates the following tasks:

■ *USB Core Task*: **USBD_OS_CoreTask()** is used by the µC/USB-Device stack to process all the stack's core events and operations as described in section 4-2 "Task Model" on page 102 of the first part of the book.

- *Class-specific Task*: Depending on the class you enable, you may have one or two tasks that are specific to the USB class under test. Refer to the class specific chapter in the first part of the book to learn more about a class task model.

- *Example-specific Task*: Depending on the example you enable, you may have one or two tasks that are specific to the example under test.

The *Startup Task* finishes the startup process by creating the rest of application tasks, described in the next figure annotations.

F4-1(3)   The *LEDs Task* is implemented by `AppTaskLEDs()` in `app.c` and it is used by the application to toggle the LEDs in four different sequences.

F4-1(4)   The *Switches Task* is implemented by `AppTaskSws()` in `app.c` and it is used by the application to read the state of the push buttons. Any button press is indicated on the LCD display. Three global variables of boolean data type store the status of each push button: `AppSwitch1, AppSwitch2` and `AppSwitch3`.

F4-1(5)   The *Microphone Task* is implemented by `AppMicTask()` in `app.c` and it is used by the application to read the output from the microphone. The noise level is displayed in the form of a bar graph on the LCD display. Three global variables store the readings:

- `AppSoundLevel`: instantaneous sound level in 12-bit ADC raw counts.

- `AppSoundWave[1000]`: non-sliding 1000-samples array (burst mode).

- `AppSoundPct`: instantaneous sound level percentage.

F4-1(6)   The Graphic LCD onboard the YRDKRX63N is accessed via an SPI interface. As multiple tasks intend to gain access to the SPI bus, we need to protect the shared resource with a mutual exclusion semaphore. The *mutex* is called `GLCD_Mutex` and it is declared in the BSP's OS layer for µC/OS-III, in file `bsp_os.c`.

4-1 THE TASK MODEL AS SEEN FROM µC/PROBE

µC/Probe is µC/OS-III-aware and Figure 4-2 shows the Kernel Awareness screen for the PHDC example:

CPU Usage	7.80 %														

	Task(s)							Performance				Task Stack			
Item	Name	Priority	State	Pending On Object	Pending On	Ticks Remaining	CPU Usage	CtxSwCtr	Interrupt Disable Time (Max)	Scheduler Lock Time (Max)	#Used	#Free	Size	Stack Usage	
0	Switches Task	4	Delayed			17	7.54 %	6,040	0.0	0.0	90	166	256	35.16 %	
1	Microphone Task	3	Delayed			0	6.05 %	60,813	0.0	0.0	110	146	256	42.97 %	
2	LEDs Task	5	Delayed			170	0.00 %	646	0.0	0.0	51	205	256	19.92 %	
3	USB Device PHDC tx comm	15	Delayed			100	0.01 %	597	0.0	0.0	52	204	256	20.31 %	
4	USB Device PHDC rx comm	16	Delayed			100	0.01 %	598	0.0	0.0	72	184	256	28.13 %	
5	USB PHDC Scheduler	8	Pending	Multiple Objects		0	0.00 %	0	0.0	0.0	47	209	256	18.36 %	
6	USB Core Task	6	Pending	Task Message Queue	Task Q	0	0.00 %	0	0.0	0.0	56	456	512	10.94 %	
7	Startup Task	2	Delayed			51	0.01 %	648	0.0	0.0	86	170	256	33.59 %	
8	uC/OS-III Timer Task	6	Pending	Task Semaphore	Task Sem	0	0.42 %	15,438	8.0	8.0	49	463	512	9.57 %	
9	uC/OS-III Stat Task	14	Delayed			100	0.62 %	1,182	0.0	0.0	73	439	512	14.26 %	
10	uC/OS-III Tick Task	1	Pending	Task Semaphore	Task Sem	0	1.61 %	65,078	0.0	0.0	20	364	384	5.21 %	
11	uC/OS-III Idle Task	63	Ready			0	84.93 %	59,726	0.0	0.0	53	459	512	10.35 %	

Figure 4-2 µC/Probe Kernel Awareness Screen

As you keep adding more features to any of the following examples you are going to find µC/Probe very useful for tuning and debugging purposes. For more information, see Appendix A, "Introduction to µC/Probe" on page 789 and section "Configuring µC/Probe to work with J-Link for the RX600" on page 633.

Example CDC ACM: USB-to-Serial Converter

The CDC class along with its ACM (Abstract Control Model) subclass were presented in the first part of the book on section "Communications Device Class" on page 163. The chapter finished presenting a demonstration application. This chapter describes how to run the CDC ACM class demonstration example on the YRDKRX63N using e2studio and the Beagle USB 480 protocol analyzer.

The USB CDC Class and its ACM subclass allow a USB device to be accessible by a host computer for data transfer purposes. The USB device appears to the host computer as a serial device (virtual COM port), thus enabling the transfer of data via read and write functions.

The example featured in this book implements a USB-to-serial converter which can be used in applications such as the ones illustrated in Figure 5-1:

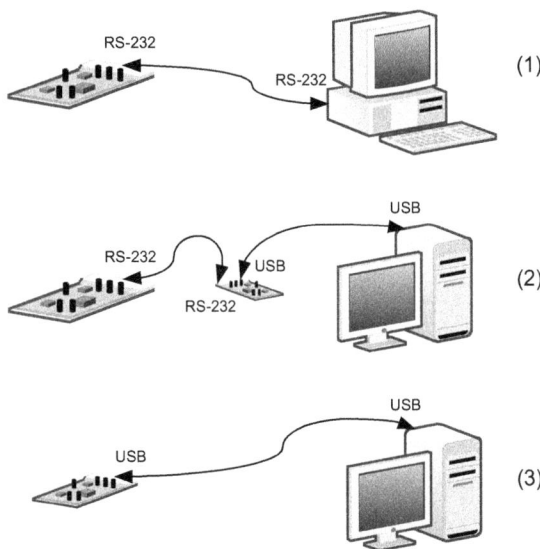

Figure 5-1 **Serial Application Examples**

F5-1(1)   As odd as it may sound the majority of embedded systems and equipment used in industrial applications are designed for serial communication. Some examples include PLCs, RTUs, sensors, meters and control panels.

F5-1(2)   CDC ACM allows you to create a USB-to-serial converter to place in the middle of an old serial device and newer host computer that does not have any serial ports. Both, the serial device and the host software can remain unchanged, as the converter emulates the USB as serial port (virtual COM port).

F5-1(3)   CDC ACM allows you to upgrade an old serial device design into a new USB based device. At the same time you can replace the host computer with a new one without having to change the old host software.

The example featured in this chapter implements a USB-to-serial converter. You will be able to open a serial terminal program and exercise the µC/USB-Device stack and its CDC and ACM subclass by echoing characters as shown in Figure 5-2:

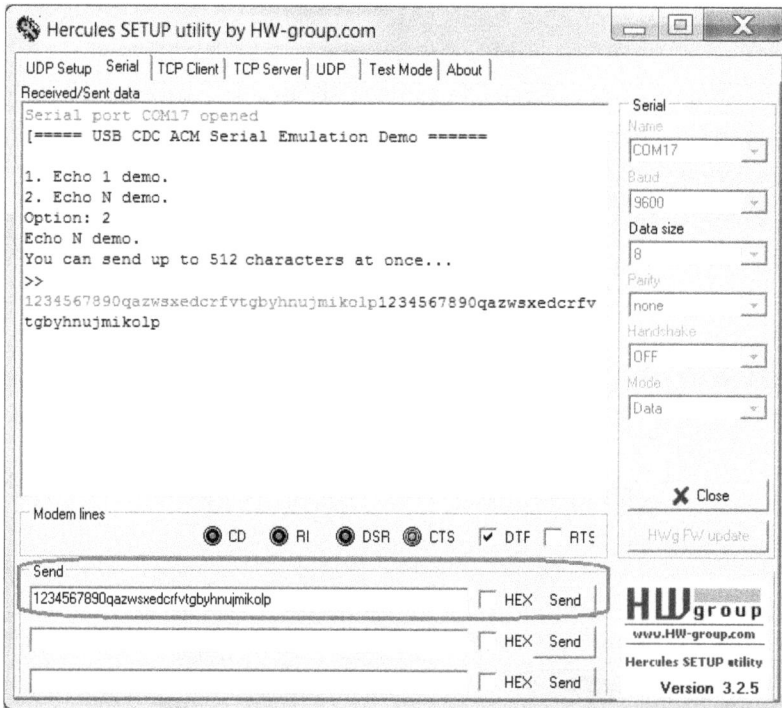

Figure 5-2 **USB-to-Serial Converter Example**

5-1 LOADING THE PROJECT IN e2studio

In order to load this project you first need to import the C project included in the book's companion software package. You only need to do this once for all the examples and the procedure is described in sections 3-2-1 and 3-2-2 on page 645.

If you already went through that procedure, all you need to do is start e2studio and launch the workspace you created in the path of your choice.

5-2 CONFIGURING THE USB-TO-SERIAL CONVERTER EXAMPLE

Open the header file **app_cfg.h** from the *Project Explorer* view as shown in Figure 5-3:

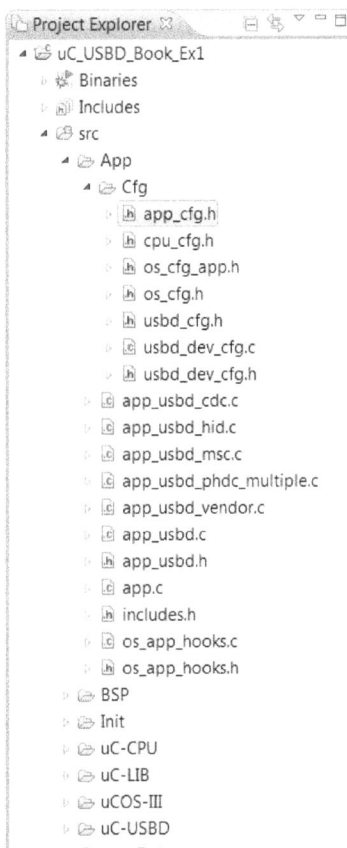

Figure 5-3 **Project Explorer: Configuration File**

5-2-1 ENABLING AND DISABLING CLASSES

All the examples featured in this book are not only in the same workspace but also in the same project and Code Listing 5-1 shows the lines of code in **app_cfg.h** that need to be edited in order to enable the CDC ACM class and the USB-to-serial converter example:

```
/*
*****************************************************************************
*                        uC/USB-DEVICE DEMO CONFIGURATION
*****************************************************************************
*/

#define  APP_CFG_USBD_VENDOR_EN              DEF_DISABLED          (1)
#define  APP_CFG_USBD_CDC_EN                 DEF_ENABLED           (2)
#define  APP_CFG_USBD_HID_EN                 DEF_DISABLED          (3)
#define  APP_CFG_USBD_MSC_EN                 DEF_DISABLED          (4)
#define  APP_CFG_USBD_PHDC_EN                DEF_DISABLED          (5)


#define  APP_CFG_USBD_CDC_SERIAL_TEST_EN     DEF_ENABLED           (6)
.
.
.
```

Listing 5-1 **Configuring the USB-to-Serial Converter Example: app_cfg.h**

L5-1(1)   In order to run the USB-to-Serial converter example, make sure the Vendor class is disabled by setting **APP_CFG_USBD_VENDOR_EN** to **DEF_DISABLED.**

L5-1(2)   Make sure the CDC class is enabled by setting **APP_CFG_USBD_CDC_EN** to **DEF_ENABLED.**

L5-1(3)   Make sure the HID class is disabled by setting **APP_CFG_USBD_HID_EN** to **DEF_DISABLED.**

L5-1(4)   Make sure the MSC class is disabled by setting **APP_CFG_USBD_MSC_EN** to **DEF_DISABLED.**

L5-1(5)   Make sure the PHDC class is disabled by setting **APP_CFG_USBD_PHDC_EN** to **DEF_DISABLED.**

L5-1(6)   Finally, make sure the actual USB-to-serial converter example is enabled by setting **APP_CFG_USBD_CDC_SERIAL_TEST_EN** to **DEF_ENABLED.**

5-3 BUILDING THE USB-TO-SERIAL CONVERTER EXAMPLE PROJECT

In order to build the project press *Ctrl+B* as described in section 3-2-3 "Building a Project in e2studio" on page 648.

5-4 RUNNING THE USB-TO-SERIAL CONVERTER EXAMPLE PROJECT

In order to run the example project, you need to follow the next steps including the preparation of an INF file which Windows will use to load one of its own native drivers.

5-4-1 CONNECTING THE BOARD

Connect the board as illustrated in Table 2-12, "Beagle USB 480 Protocol Analyzer: Connections," on page 640 and make sure that the USB cable on J9 of the YRDKRX63N board *is not* connected yet.

5-4-2 LAUNCHING THE DEBUGGING SESSION

Launch a debugging session as described in section 3-2-5 "Launching a Debug Session in e2studio" on page 655 and press *F8* to let the program run freely.

5-4-3 VERIFYING THE APPLICATION

In order to make sure that you are actually running the CDC class example, take a look at the LCD screen on the YRDKRX63N as it should look like the one illustrated in Figure 5-4:

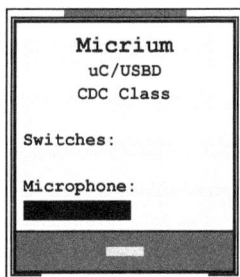

Figure 5-4 **CDC Class Example Screen**

The LCD screen also helps you verify that the application is running correctly as it indicates if any of the 3 push buttons on the YRDKRX63N has been pressed. At the same time, the horizontal bar graph shows the current noise level as detected by the microphone on U16. These two features are implemented in the form of two μC/OS-III tasks. So, if you see anything changing on the LCD screen as you make any noise or press the buttons, it means that μC/OS-III is multi-tasking. Besides that, the LEDs wheel should also be blinking as it is also driven by another μC/OS-III task.

5-4-4 INSTALLING THE CDC DEVICE

At this time, the μC/USB-Device stack should be running and waiting for any USB events, such as connecting the USB device. Go ahead and connect the USB cable from J9 of the YRDKRX63N board and into the Capture Side of the Beagle USB 480 as illustrated in Table 2-12, "Beagle USB 480 Protocol Analyzer: Connections," on page 640. In case you do not have a USB protocol analyzer, you can still connect the other end of the cable directly into any available USB receptacle on your host computer.

The first time you run the example, the host computer will install the YRDKRX63N as a *virtual COM port*. You will be notified that the device is installing by the typical Windows messages shown in the notification area on the bottom right corner of your desktop as shown in Figure 5-5:

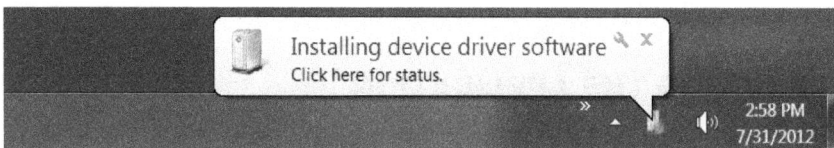

Figure 5-5 **Windows Installing the CDC Device**

If it is the first time you install the device, Windows will fail to do so, because this particular example, even though it uses one of the Windows native drivers, it requires an INF file to load the driver.

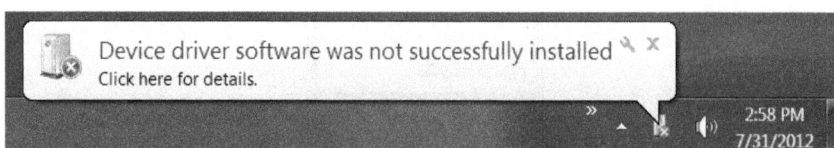

Figure 5-6 **Windows Notifying Failure Installing the Device**

The subject of INF files was briefly described in section 3-1-1 "About INF Files" on page 90. The book companion's software that you installed in section 2-1-5 "µC/USB-Device Book's Companion Software" on page 630 includes the required INF file for this example. You only need to make sure that both the INF file and your CDC Device's hardware IDs match. In order to do so, open the following INF file in a text editor such as *Notepad*:

`$\Micrium\Software\uC-USB-Device-V4\App\Host\OS\Windows\CDC\INF\usbser.inf`

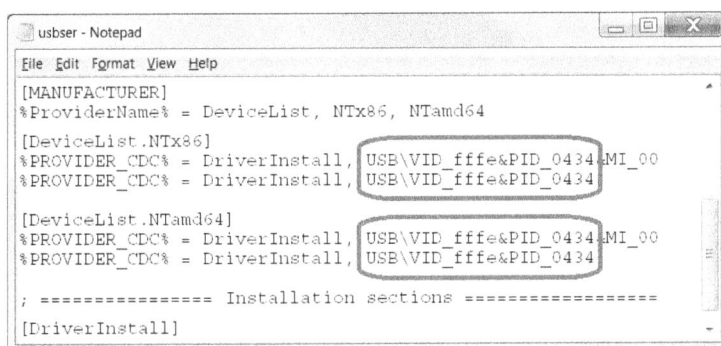

Figure 5-7 **Updating the INF File**

Locate the lines that specify the *Vendor ID* = **FFFEh** and *Product ID* = **0434h** as indicated in Figure 5-7 and make sure that they match with the hardware IDs configured in **usbd_dev_cfg.c** as shown in Code Listing 5-2:

```
/*
********************************************************************************
*                          USB DEVICE CONFIGURATION
********************************************************************************
*/

USBD_DEV_CFG  USBD_DevCfg_RX63N = {
    0xFFFE,                            /* Vendor   ID.                       */
    0x0434,                            /* Product ID (CDC).                  */
    0x0100,                            /* Device release number.             */
    "OEM MANUFACTURER",                /* Manufacturer  string.              */
    "OEM PRODUCT",                     /* Product       string.              */
    "1234567890ABCDEF",                /* Serial number string.              */
    USBD_LANG_ID_ENGLISH_US            /* String language ID.                */
};
```

Listing 5-2 **USB CDC Device Configuration**

If you open Windows Device Manager, you are going to find a new entry for the CDC device that failed to install. Windows lists this device under the group *Other Devices* as shown in Figure 5-8:

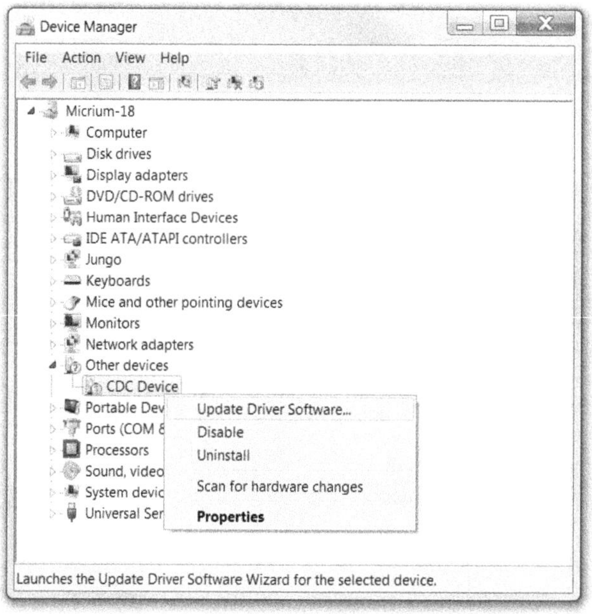

Figure 5-8 **Windows Device Manager**

In order to install the device with the appropriate driver, you need to provide Windows with the newly updated INF file. In order to do so, right-click over the device's name on the Device Manager list and select *Update Driver Software* as shown in Figure 5-8.

Windows will launch a series of dialogs to specify the driver's options. Select the option to *Browse my computer for driver software* as shown in Figure 5-9:

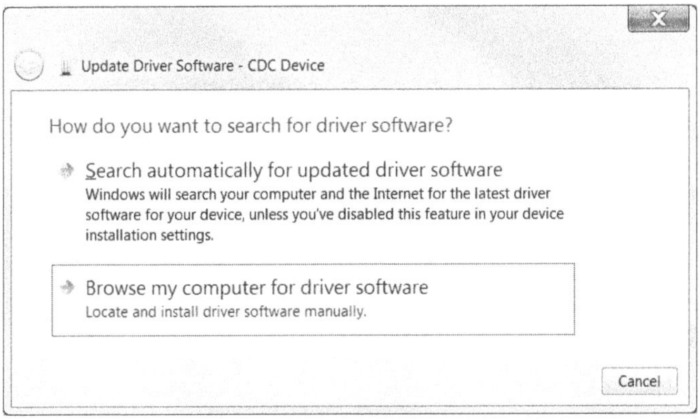

Figure 5-9 **Update Driver Software: Browse**

Browse to the path where you saved the newly updated INF file **usbser.inf** as shown in Figure 5-10:

Figure 5-10 **Update Driver Software: INF File Path**

Windows will probably give you a warning message because the driver has not been digitally signed. It is safe to ignore the warning and select *Install this driver software anyway* as shown in Figure 5-11:

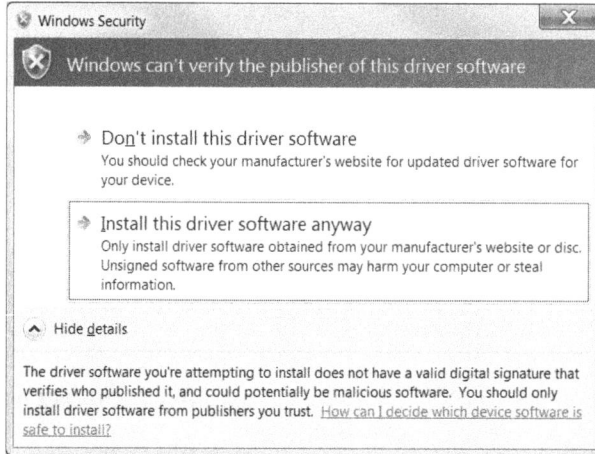

Figure 5-11 **Update Driver Software: Warning Message**

Windows will take a few seconds while it installs the new CDC ACM device and makes a copy of the INF file into the directory $\Windows\inf.

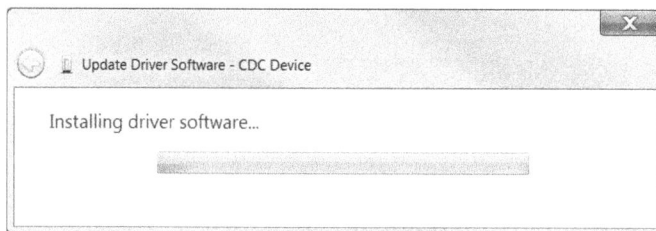

Figure 5-12 **Update Driver Software: Installing**

Windows will finish the installation by displaying the message box shown in Figure 5-13:

Figure 5-13 **Update Driver Software: Finish**

You should see now a new entry in your Device Manager under the group *Ports (COM &* *LPT)* similar to the one shown in Figure 5-14. Make a note of the serial COM port number:

Figure 5-14 **Device Manager Showing the Newly Installed Device**

5-4-5 TESTING THE NEW VIRTUAL SERIAL PORT

Now that the CDC ACM device has been installed successfully as a virtual COM port, you can exercise the µC/USB-Device stack and its CDC ACM class by opening a serial console and echoing some characters.

We recommend a serial terminal program capable of controlling the signal *Data Terminal Ready (DTR)* such as *Hercules Setup* from HW group s.r.o. The Hercules Setup utility is a very useful serial port terminal (RS-485 or RS-232 terminal), UDP/IP terminal and TCP/IP Client Server terminal. It was created for HW group internal use only, but today it has been released as freeware, and has become very popular. Hercules Setup can be downloaded from: `http://www.hw-group.com/products/hercules/index_en.html`.

In case you prefer to use other serial terminal, Table 8-10 in the first part of the book Table 8-10, "Serial Terminals and CDC Serial Demo," on page 183 provides a list of other serial terminals you can use.

Launch *Hercules Setup* and open a serial connection to the virtual COM port as shown in Figure 5-15:

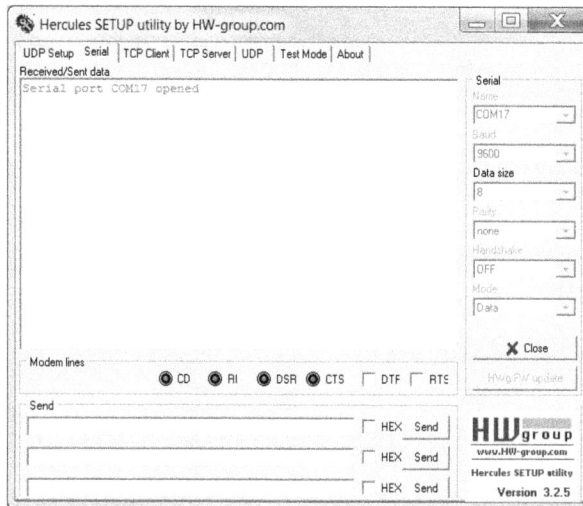

Figure 5-15 **Hercules Setup: Open Connection**

The example application running on the YRDKRX63N should print an options menu that will allow you to select one of two tests:

- Echo 1 demo: echo one single character.

- Echo N demo: echo up to 512 characters.

The CDC device will not display the options menu until the host computer sends a DTR (Data Terminal Ready) signal. In order to send such signal, select the checkbox *DTR* as shown in Figure 5-16:

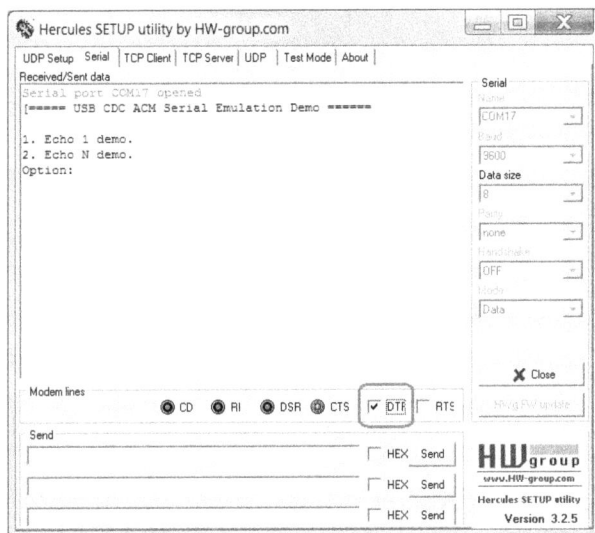

Figure 5-16 **Hercules Setup: Sending a DTR Signal**

In order to execute the echo test, select the option number 2 by typing in *2 <enter>*.

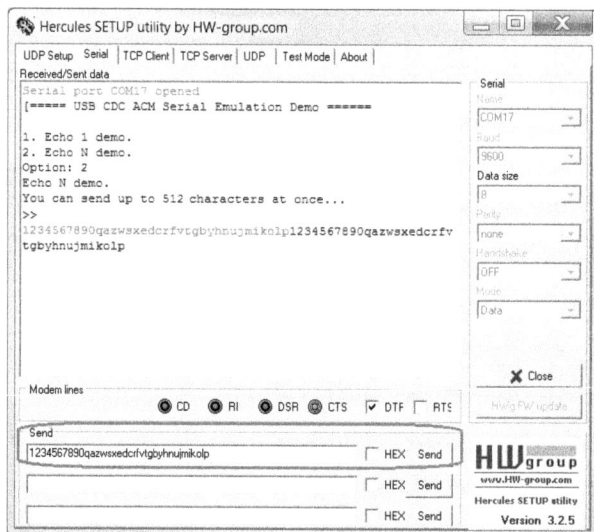

Figure 5-17 **Hercules Setup: Echo N test**

In this test, you can send up to 512 characters at once as indicated by the terminal in Figure 5-17. Enter the characters to send in one of the three output buffers (text boxes) in the terminal and press the respective *Send* button to send the characters. The terminal should show you the echoed characters back as shown in Figure 5-17.

In order to go back to the main menu to select a different test, you can send the ASCII code for **Ctrl+C** which is *03h*. You can type in 03 in one of the three output buffers (text boxes), select the hexadecimal format checkbox and press the respective *Send* button to send **Ctrl+C** as shown in Figure 5-18:

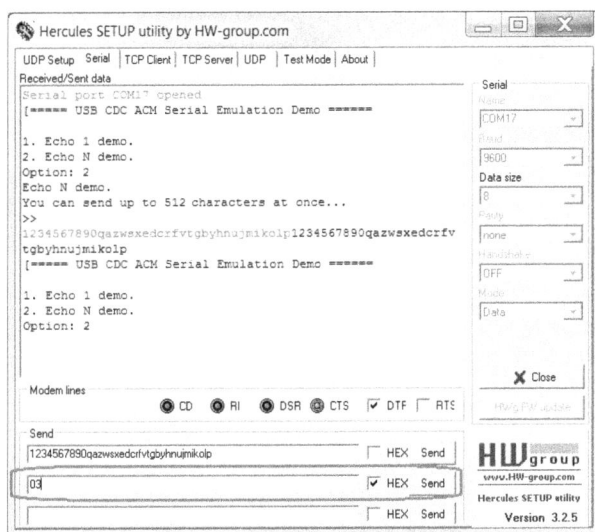

Figure 5-18 **Hercules Setup: Going Back to the Main Menu**

5-5 HOW THE CODE WORKS

5-5-1 INITIALIZATION

The function to initialize the CDC class, ACM subclass and USB-to-serial example is declared at the application level in file **app_usbd_cdc.c.** The following code listings describe the initialization process:

```
CPU_BOOLEAN  App_USBD_CDC_Init (CPU_INT08U  dev_nbr,
                                CPU_INT08U  cfg_hs,
                                CPU_INT08U  cfg_fs)
{
    USBD_ERR    err;
    USBD_ERR    err_fs;
    CPU_INT08U  subclass_nbr;
#if (APP_CFG_USBD_CDC_SERIAL_TEST_EN == DEF_ENABLED)
    OS_ERR      os_err;
#endif

    APP_TRACE_DBG(("Initializing CDC class ... \r\n"));

    USBD_CDC_Init(&err);                                                        (1)
    if (err != USBD_ERR_NONE) {
        APP_TRACE_DBG(("... could not initialize CDC class w/err = %d\r\n\r\n", err));
        return (DEF_FAIL);
    }

    APP_TRACE_DBG(("Initializing ACM serial subclass ... \r\n"));

    USBD_ACM_SerialInit(&err);                                                  (2)
    if (err != USBD_ERR_NONE) {
        APP_TRACE_DBG(("... could not initialize ACM serial subclass w/err = %d\r\n\r\n", err));
        return (DEF_FAIL);
    }
    .
    .
    .
```

Listing 5-3 **Initializing the USB-to-Serial Example**

L5-3(1)   The **USBD_CDC_Init()** function is declared in **usbd_cdc.c** and it is used to initialize all internal structures and variables that the class needs. For more information on this function, see "USBD_CDC_Init()" on page 422.

L5-3(2)   The **USBD_ACM_SerialInit( )** function is declared in **usbd_acm_serial.c**. The function is responsible for initializing the ACM serial emulation subclass by allocating memory for the buffers and initializing other internal structures and variables. This function and all functions prefixed by **USBD_ACM_** are well documented in Appendix C, "CDC ACM Subclass Functions" on page 437.

The next step in the initialization process is to add the new instance of the ACM subclass and register the serial line coding and control line callback functions as shown in code Listing 5-4:

```
        subclass_nbr = USBD_ACM_SerialAdd(100u, &err);                        (1)
        if (err != USBD_ERR_NONE) {
            APP_TRACE_DBG(("... could not create ACM serial subclass instance
                            w/err = %d\r\n\r\n", err));
            return (DEF_FAIL);
        }

                                /* Register line coding and ctrl line change callbacks. */
        USBD_ACM_SerialLineCodingReg(       subclass_nbr,
                                            App_USBD_CDC_SerialLineCoding,
                                    (void *)0,
                                            &err);                            (2)

        USBD_ACM_SerialLineCtrlReg(         subclass_nbr,
                                            App_USBD_CDC_SerialLineCtrl,
                                    (void *)0,
                                            &err);                            (3)
```

*Listing 5-4 **Instantiating the ACM Subclass***

L5-4(1)   The function **USBD_ACM_SerialAdd( )** is also part of usbd_acm_serial.c. The function is responsible for adding a new instance of the ACM subclass for serial emulation purposes. The first argument in this function is the polling interval in frames or microframes for line state notification. The next section will show you some of the records captured by the Beagle USB 480 that represent these notifications.

L5-4(2)   The function **USBD_ACM_SerialLineCodingReg()** is used to register a callback function in response to a notification for a change in the serial line coding (i.e. 9600-8-N-1).

L5-4(3)   The function **USBD_ACM_SerialLineCtrlReg()** is also used to register a callback function, although in this case, in response to a notification for a change in the serial control line state (i.e. DTR and RTS signals).

Both callback functions are declared at the application level in **app_usbd_cdc.c**.

The next step in the initialization process is common for all USB classes; Adding the previously created instances to the full-speed device configuration as shown in Listing 5-5:

```
    •
    •
    •
                                    /* Add ACM subclass to FS dflt cfg.        */    (1)
    USBD_ACM_SerialCfgAdd(subclass_nbr, dev_nbr, cfg_fs, &err_fs);
    if (err_fs != USBD_ERR_NONE) {
        APP_TRACE_DBG(("... could not add ACM subclass instance #%d to FS configuration
                      w/err = %d\r\n\r\n", subclass_nbr, err_fs));
    }
    •
    •
    •
```

Listing 5-5 Adding the ACM Subclass Instance to the Full-Speed Configuration

L5-5(1)   Proceed to add the new ACM instance to this full-speed configuration. The **USBD_ACM_SerialCfgAdd()** function returns **DEF_YES** if the ACM subclass instance can be added into the USB device configuration without any problems such as memory allocation, invalid arguments, etc.

For more information on this function parameters and return error codes, see section C-2-3 "USBD_ACM_SerialCfgAdd()" on page 439.

The last thing to do for the **App_USBD_CDC_Init()** function is to create the μC/OS-III task that implements the echo terminal. If you are familiar with μC/OS-III you already know that the function **OSTaskCreate()** is used to have μC/OS-III manage the execution of a task. Notice how the ACM subclass number is passed as the fourth argument. The fourth argument of **OSTaskCreate()** is a pointer to an optional data area which can be used to pass parameters to the task when the task first executes. In the next section 5-5-2, you will learn that the function that implements this task requires the variable **subclass_nbr** to make reference to this particular instance of the ACM subclass:

```
    .
    .
    .
    OSTaskCreate(          &App_USBD_CDC_SerialTaskTCB,
                           "USB Device CDC ACM Test",
                           App_USBD_CDC_SerialTask,
                 (void *)subclass_nbr,
                           APP_CFG_USBD_CDC_SERIAL_TASK_PRIO,
                           &App_USBD_CDC_SerialTaskStk[0],
                           APP_CFG_USBD_CDC_SERIAL_TASK_STK_SIZE / 10u,
                           APP_CFG_USBD_CDC_SERIAL_TASK_STK_SIZE,
                           0u,
                           0u,
                 (void *)0,
                           OS_OPT_TASK_STK_CHK | OS_OPT_TASK_STK_CLR,
                           &os_err);
    if (os_err != OS_ERR_NONE) {
        APP_TRACE_DBG(("... could not add CDC ACM serial test task
                        w/err = %d\r\n\r\n", os_err));
        return (DEF_FAIL);
    }
```

Listing 5-6 **Creating the μC/OS-III Task that Implements the Echo Terminal**

5-5-2 THE SERIAL TASK

The serial task is declared in **app_usbd_cdc.c** as an infinite loop in function **App_USBD_CDC_SerialTask( )**. The task implements the echo terminal in the form of a 3-state machine as illustrated in Figure 5-19:

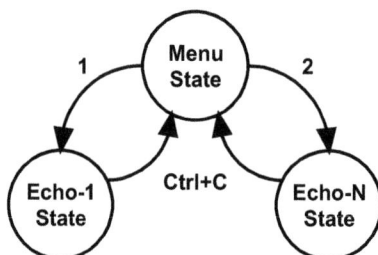

Figure 5-19 **Serial Task State Machine**

THE MENU STATE

During the menu state identified as **APP_USBD_CDC_STATE_MENU**, the task displays an options menu by sending characters with the function **USBD_ACM_SerialTx( )** as shown in Listing 5-7:

```
(void)USBD_ACM_SerialTx( subclass_nbr,
                         "===== USB CDC ACM Serial Emulation Demo ======"
                         "\r\n"
                         "\r\n"
                         "1. Echo 1 demo.\r\n"
                         "2. Echo N demo.\r\n"
                         "Option: ",
                          92u,
                          APP_USBD_CDC_TX_TIMEOUT_mS,
                         &err);
```

Listing 5-7 **Printing the Options Menu**

The functions to send and receive characters along with any other functions prefixed with **USBD_ACM_Serial** are part of the ACM subclass for serial emulation whose API is referenced in Appendix C, "CDC ACM Subclass Functions" on page 437.

Right after printing the menu, the task will not transition to any other state until the user sends the character that represents the type of demo he wants to execute. The function `USBD_ACM_SerialRx()` is used to read characters. You can specify a timeout or you can make it a blocking function by passing a timeout of 0 as shown in Listing 5-8:

```
                                      /* Wait for character.              */
        (void)USBD_ACM_SerialRx( subclass_nbr,
                         &ch,
                         1u,
                         APP_USBD_CDC_RX_TIMEOUT_mS,
                         &err);
```

Listing 5-8 Waiting for a Menu Choice

The variable `ch` contains the choice made by the user and the state machine will transition to either the Echo-1 State or Echo-N state.

THE ECHO-1 STATE

During the Echo-1 State identified as `APP_USBD_CDC_STATE_ECHO_1` the task will wait for the user to send one single character. This is accomplished by calling the `USBD_ACM_SerialRx()` function with a buffer for one single character and a timeout of 0 which was similar to what the menu state did in Listing 5-8.

The only difference in this state is that if the received character is different than `Ctrl+C` (03h in ASCII), then the single character is echoed back by calling the function `USBD_ACM_SerialTx()`. Otherwise, the state machine will transition back to the menu state.

THE ECHO-N STATE

During the Echo-N State identified as `APP_USBD_CDC_STATE_ECHO_N` the task will wait for the user to send any number of characters (maximum of 512 characters). This is accomplished by calling the `USBD_ACM_SerialRx()` function with a buffer for 512 characters and a timeout of 0.

Similar to the Echo-1 State, if the received character is different than `Ctrl+C` (03h in ASCII), then the series characters are echoed back by calling the function `USBD_ACM_SerialTx()`. Otherwise, the state machine will transition back to the menu state.

5-6 ANALYZING THE USB TRAFFIC

In order to capture USB traffic, you need to connect the Beagle USB 480 as illustrated in the Setup section Figure 2-12 "Beagle USB 480 Protocol Analyzer: Connections" on page 640.

When monitoring USB traffic, it is best to attach the Beagle USB 480's analysis side and start the capture *before* attaching the YRDKRX63N. That means that before starting a capture, make sure the USB cable on J9 of the YRDKRX63N is disconnected from the Beagle USB 480 capture side. This allows the Beagle USB 480 to capture the descriptor information that is communicated during the enumeration phase.

Start the Total Phase Data Center software by using the shortcut created during Setup section 2-1-4 "Total Phase Data Center Software" on page 630 or, go to the folder where the software package was extracted and run *Data Center.exe*.

Figure 5-20 **Data Center Software Icon**

Once the application starts it will detect the Beagle and will connect it automatically.

You can tell the Beagle USB 480 is properly connected by looking at the LEDs on the top which should have the Red and Green LEDs lit up.

Press *Ctrl+R* or click the *Run Capture* button in the toolbar to start the capture.

You should see a couple of new rows in the grid that read something like *Capture Started*.

At this point, you can attach the CDC device by connecting the USB cable on J9 of the YRDKRX63N.

Complete the installation of the CDC device by following the steps described in the previous section section 5-4-4 "Installing the CDC Device" on page 668 and then proceed to send a couple of characters by following the instructions in section 5-4-5 "Testing the New Virtual Serial Port" on page 674.

As traffic is seen on the bus, it will be displayed in real-time in the *transactions grid*. You should start to see not only some of the typical records captured during enumeration such as *Get Device Descriptor, Set Address, Get Configuration Descriptor, Get String Descriptor* and *Set Configuration* described in Appendix C, "The Enumeration Process" on page 811, but also a new series of rows in the transactions grid including the transactions for *Serial Line Coding* and *Control Line State* as shown in Figure 5-21:

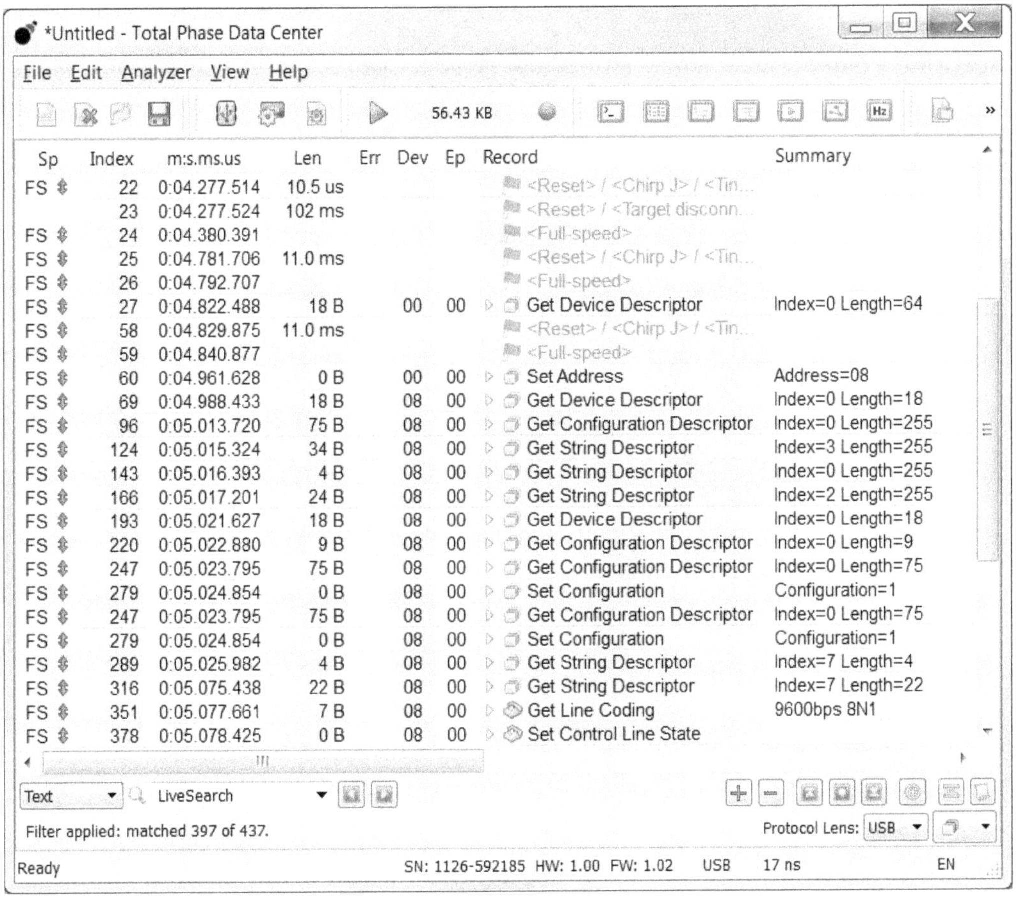

Figure 5-21 **Capturing USB Traffic**

In order to avoid filling up the transactions grid with more records than you really need to analyze, you can stop the capture by pressing **Ctrl+R** or the *Stop* button.

5-6-1 GET CONFIGURATION DESCRIPTOR

General — Radix: auto
Timestamp	0:03.126.455.550
Duration	468.166 us
Length	75 Bytes

Configuration Descriptor — Radix: auto
bLength	9
bDescriptorType	CONFIGURATION (0x02)
wTotalLength	75
bNumInterfaces	2
bConfigurationValue	1
iConfiguration	Not Requested (4)
bmAttributes.Reserved	0
bmAttributes.RemoteWakeup	RemoteWakeup Not Supported (0b0)
bmAttributes.SelfPowered	Self Powered (0b1)
bMaxPower	100mA (0x32)

Interface Association Descriptor — Radix: auto
bLength	8
bDescriptorType	INTERFACE_ASSOCIATION (0x0b)
bFirstInterface	0
bInterfaceCount	2
bFunctionClass	Communications and CDC Control (0x02)
bFunctionSubClass	Abstract Control Model (0x02)
bFunctionProtocol	AT Commands: V.250 etc (0x01)
iFunction	CDC Device (7)

Interface Descriptor — Radix: auto
bLength	9
bDescriptorType	INTERFACE (0x04)
bInterfaceNumber	0
bAlternateSetting	0
bNumEndpoints	1
bInterfaceClass	Communications and CDC Control (0x02)
bInterfaceSubClass	Abstract Control Model (0x02)
bInterfaceProtocol	AT Commands: V.250 etc (0x01)
iInterface	None (0)

Interface Descriptor — Radix: auto
bLength	9
bDescriptorType	INTERFACE (0x04)
bInterfaceNumber	1
bAlternateSetting	0
bNumEndpoints	2
bInterfaceClass	CDC Data (0x0a)
bInterfaceSubClass	Unknown (0x00)
bInterfaceProtocol	No class specific protocol required (0x00)
iInterface	None (0)

Class-Specific Descriptor Header Format — Radix: auto
bFunctionLength	5
bDescriptorType	CS_INTERFACE (0x24)
bDescriptorSubtype	Header Functional Descriptor (0x00)
bcdCDC	1.20 (0x0120)

Endpoint Descriptor — Radix: auto
bLength	7
bDescriptorType	ENDPOINT (0x05)
bEndpointAddress	1 IN (0b10000001)
bmAttributes.TransferType	Bulk (0b10)
wMaxPacketSize.PacketSize	64
bInterval	0

Union Interface Functional Descriptor — Radix: auto
bFunctionLength	5
bDescriptorType	CS_INTERFACE (0x24)
bDescriptorSubtype	Union Functional Descriptor (0x06)
bControlInterface	0
bSubordinateInterface0	1

Endpoint Descriptor — Radix: auto
bLength	7
bDescriptorType	ENDPOINT (0x05)
bEndpointAddress	2 OUT (0b00000010)
bmAttributes.TransferType	Bulk (0b10)
wMaxPacketSize.PacketSize	64
bInterval	0

Abstract Control Management Functional Descriptor — Radix: auto
bFunctionLength	4
bDescriptorType	CS_INTERFACE (0x24)
bDescriptorSubtype	Abstract Control Management (0x02)
bmCapabilities.CommFeature	Supported (0b1)
bmCapabilities.LineStateCoding	Supported (0b1)
bmCapabilities.SendBreak	Supported (0b1)
bmCapabilities.NetworkConnection	Unsupported (0b0)

Call Management Functional Descriptor — Radix: auto
bFunctionLength	5
bDescriptorType	CS_INTERFACE (0x24)
bDescriptorSubtype	Call Management Functional Descriptor (0x01)
bmCapabilities.CallManagement	Handles call management (0b1)
bmCapabilities.DataClass	Call Management over Comm Class interface (0b0)
bDataInterface	0

Endpoint Descriptor — Radix: auto
bLength	7
bDescriptorType	ENDPOINT (0x05)
bEndpointAddress	6 IN (0b10000110)
bmAttributes.TransferType	Interrupt (0b11)
wMaxPacketSize.PacketSize	64
wMaxPacketSize.Transactions	One transaction per microframe if HS (0b00)
bInterval	100

Figure 5-22 **Get Configuration Descriptor Capture**

The example in this chapter as specified by the *Get Configuration Descriptor* capture shown in the previous page, Figure 5-22, features a CDC ACM device with 2 interfaces:

- Interface 0: Communications Class Interface (CCI)

  - Endpoint 6: Interrupt IN

- Interface 1: Data Class Interface (DCI)

  - Endpoint 1: Bulk IN

  - Endpoint 2: Bulk OUT

These two interfaces were described in the CDC Overview in section 8-1 on page 164. If you open the *Navigator* window in the *Data Center Software* you will find a summary of the device configuration, including the 2 interfaces and their respective endpoints as shown in Figure 5-23:

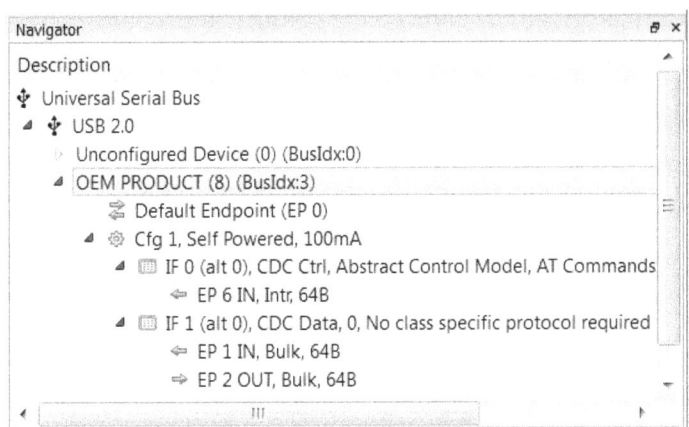

Figure 5-23 **CDC Device Interfaces and Endpoints**

Any transactions through Endpoint 6 (Interrupt IN) are meant for device management and optionally call management. The device management includes not only device configuration and control, but also event notifications such as serial line state. Whereas the call management includes transactions to enable the establishment and termination of calls.

If you want to focus on the transactions through one particular endpoint, you can do so by using the Data Center software filter mechanism.

The following sections describe some of the most important transactions during the capture of USB traffic for this particular CDC ACM device.

5-6-2 GET AND SET LINE CODING

If you scroll around the transactions grid, you will find a series of records titled *GetLineCoding* and *SetLineCoding* similar to the ones shown in Figure 5-24 and Figure 5-25. These pair of transactions are piped through the default control endpoint 0 and represent the moment when the host computer opens up a serial connection to the CDC device via the virtual COM port.

GET LINE CODING

During the *GetLineCoding* request shown in Figure 5-24, the host computer sends this request to get the current ACM settings (baud rate, stop bits, parity, data bits). For a serial emulation such as this example, serial terminals send this request automatically during virtual COM port opening.

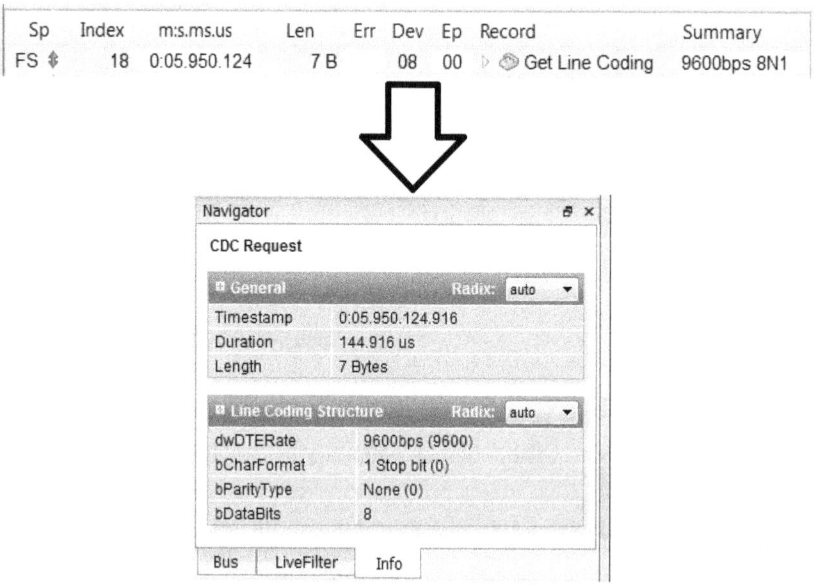

Figure 5-24 **GetLineCoding Request**

SET LINE CODING

During the *SetLineCoding* request shown in Figure 5-25, the host computer sends this request to configure the ACM device settings such as baud rate, number of stop bits, parity type and number of data bits. For a serial emulation, this request is sent automatically by a serial terminal each time you configure the serial settings for an open virtual COM port.

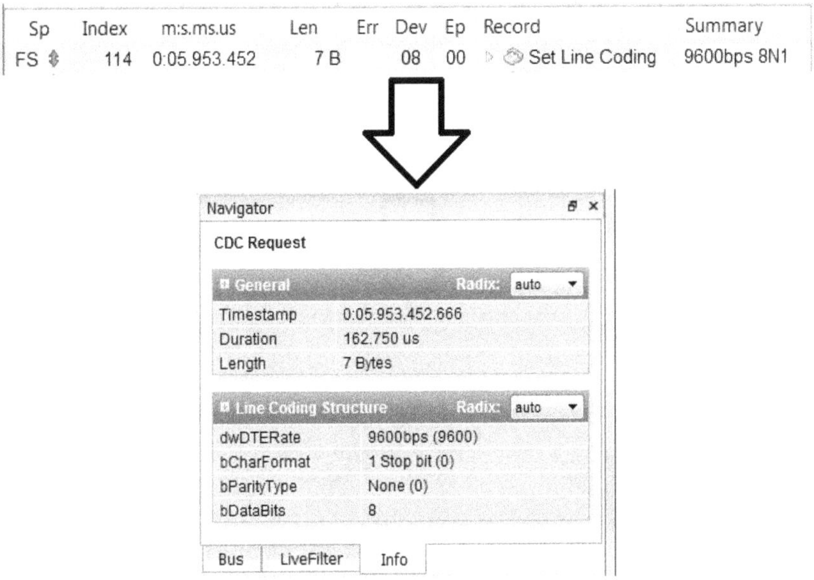

Figure 5-25 **SetLineCoding Request**

5-6-3 SET CONTROL LINE STATE

Locate a transaction titled *SetControlLineState*, similar to the one shown in Figure 5-26. The host computer sends this ACM request to control the carrier for half duplex modems and indicate that *Data Terminal Equipment (DTE)* is ready or not.

In this particular example of serial emulation, the DTE is the *Hercules Setup* serial terminal and the request gets sent when you click on the DTR checkbox as described in section Figure 5-16 "Hercules Setup: Sending a DTR Signal" on page 675.

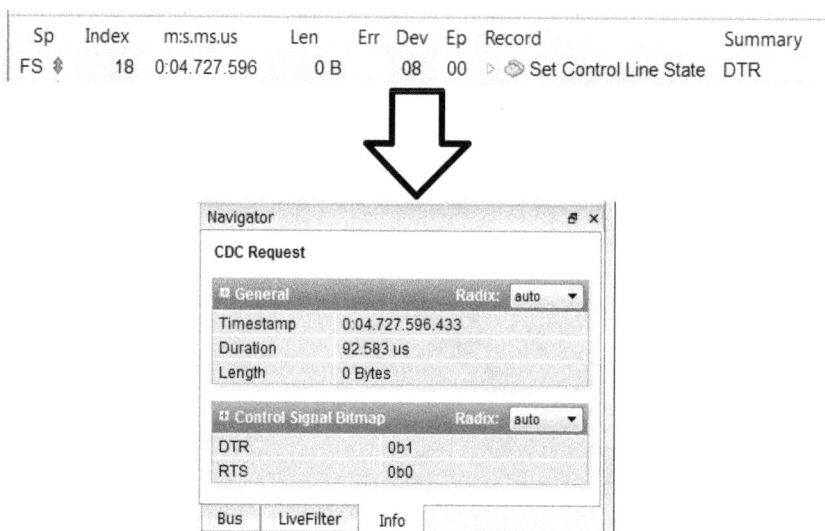

Figure 5-26 **SetControlLineState Request**

5-6-4 CDC IN/OUT DATA

If you exercised the µC/USB-Device stack and its CDC ACM class by echoing a couple of characters, you should have captured a series of records titled CDC OUT Data and CDC IN Data similar the ones shown in Figure 5-27:

Total Phase Data Center capture showing CDC IN/OUT transactions:

Sp	Index	m:s.ms.us	Len	Err	Dev	Ep	Record	Summary	ASCII
FS	18	0:04.304.037	1 B		08	02	◢ CDC OUT Data	78	x
FS	19	0:04.304.037	1 B		08	02	◢ OUT txn	78	x
FS	20	0:04.304.037	3 B		08	02	○ OUT packet	E1 08 49	..I
FS	21	0:04.304.040	4 B		08	02	DATA1 packet	4B 78 40 9D	Kx@.
FS	22	0:04.304.044	1 B		08	02	✓ ACK packet	D2	.
FS	23	0:04.000.018	1 B		08	01	◢ CDC IN Data	78	x
FS	24	0:04.000.018	1 B		08	01	◢ IN txn [20014 POLL]	78	x
FS	25	0:04.000.018	304 ms		08	01	[20014 IN-NAK]		
FS	26	0:04.304.100	3 B		08	01	○ IN packet	69 88 D0	i..
FS	27	0:04.304.104	4 B		08	01	DATA0 packet	C3 78 40 9D	.x@.
FS	28	0:04.304.107	1 B		08	01	✓ ACK packet	D2	.

Text ▾ LiveSearch ▾

Filter applied: matched 24 of 41.

Protocol Lens: USB ▾

Ready   SN: 1126-592185 HW: 1.00 FW: 1.02   USB   17 ns   EN

Figure 5-27 **CDC IN/OUT Data Transaction**

As you can see, these transactions are piped through the Data Class Interface (DCI) endpoints 1 and 2 (Bulk IN and Bulk OUT respectively) as described in the first part of the book section Table 8-1 "CDC Endpoint Usage" on page 166.

The transactions shown in Figure 5-27 represent the moment when a user sends an 'x' character from the host computer (*CDC OUT Data*) and the subsequent echo (*CDC IN Data*) replied by the `SerialTask` running on the YRDKRX63N as described in this chapter section section 5-5-2 "The Serial Task" on page 682.

5-7 SUMMARY

The example featured in this chapter is a great reference for creating your own CDC ACM device or to upgrade an existing RS-232/485-based embedded system design without creating host software incompatibilities.

The chapter showed you how to run the example and then went into explaining how the code works by describing code listings and USB traffic captures. It kept on showing you more of the features of the Total Phase Data Center Software by describing the most important USB traffic captures found in CDC devices.

Analyzing the USB traffic captures is a great hands-on exercise that maximizes learning by complementing the topics described in the first part of the book.

6

Example HID: Mouse

The HID class enables USB connectivity of computer peripherals such as mice, keyboards and game controllers among others. It was presented in the first part of the book on Chapter 9, "Human Interface Device Class" on page 185. The chapter finished presenting a couple of demonstration applications. This chapter describes how to run the HID class demonstration example on the YRDKRX63N using e2studio and the Beagle USB 480 protocol analyzer.

A computer mouse is a relative pointing device. In other words, the coordinates returned by the mouse are the amount of movement since it last reported.

When it comes time for the host computer to update the screen, the computer sums the total reported mouse movement in the x-axis and the y-axis and moves the pointer that much relative to its current position.

This example simulates the movement of a mouse by sending in an infinite loop a report data that contains the values 50 for the x-axis and 50 for the y-axis. The task delays for 100 milliseconds and then it sends another report data that contains the values -50 for the x-axis and -50 for the y-axis. The result is that the mouse pointer in the host computer will move back and forth on the screen as illustrated in Figure 6-1:

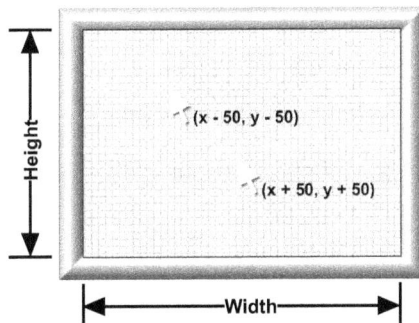

Figure 6-1 **Mouse Example**

6-1 LOADING THE PROJECT IN e2studio

In order to load this project you first need to import the C project included in the book's companion software package. You only need to do this once for all the examples and the procedure is described in sections 3-2-1 and 3-2-2 on page 645.

If you already went through that procedure, all you need to do is start e2studio and launch the workspace you created in the path of your choice.

6-2 CONFIGURING THE MOUSE EXAMPLE

Open the header file **app_cfg.h** from the *Project Explorer* as shown in Figure 6-2:

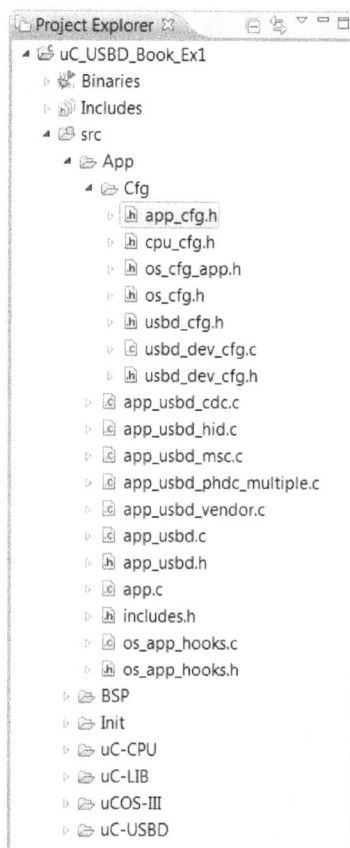

Figure 6-2 **Project Explorer: Configuration File**

All the examples featured in this book are not only in the same workspace but also in the same project and Code Listing 6-1 shows the lines of code in **app_cfg.h** that need to be edited in order to enable the HID class and the Mouse example:

```
/*
*******************************************************************************
*                       uC/USB-DEVICE DEMO CONFIGURATION
*******************************************************************************
*/

#define  APP_CFG_USBD_VENDOR_EN               DEF_DISABLED          (1)
#define  APP_CFG_USBD_CDC_EN                  DEF_DISABLED          (2)
#define  APP_CFG_USBD_HID_EN                  DEF_ENABLED           (3)
#define  APP_CFG_USBD_MSC_EN                  DEF_DISABLED          (4)
#define  APP_CFG_USBD_PHDC_EN                 DEF_DISABLED          (5)


#define  APP_CFG_USBD_HID_TEST_MOUSE_EN       DEF_ENABLED           (6)
.
.
.
```

Listing 6-1 **Configuring the Mouse Example: app_cfg.h**

L6-1(1)   In order to run the Mouse example, make sure the Vendor class is disabled by setting **APP_CFG_USBD_VENDOR_EN** to **DEF_DISABLED**.

L6-1(2)   Make sure the CDC class is disabled by setting **APP_CFG_USBD_CDC_EN** to **DEF_DISABLED**.

L6-1(3)   Make sure the HID class is enabled by setting **APP_CFG_USBD_HID_EN** to **DEF_ENABLED**.

L6-1(4)   Make sure the MSC class is disabled by setting **APP_CFG_USBD_MSC_EN** to **DEF_DISABLED**.

L6-1(5)   Make sure the PHDC class is disabled by setting **APP_CFG_USBD_PHDC_EN** to **DEF_DISABLED**.

L6-1(6)   Finally, make sure the actual Mouse example is enabled by setting **APP_CFG_USBD_HID_TEST_MOUSE_EN** to **DEF_ENABLED**.

6-3 BUILDING THE MOUSE EXAMPLE PROJECT

In order to build the project press *Ctrl+B* as described in section 3-2-3 "Building a Project in e2studio" on page 648.

6-4 RUNNING THE MOUSE EXAMPLE PROJECT

In order to run the example project, you do not need to install any drivers on the host computer as the example implements a standard USB mouse that Windows installs with its native drivers.

6-4-1 CONNECTING THE BOARD

Connect the board as illustrated in Table 2-12, "Beagle USB 480 Protocol Analyzer: Connections," on page 640 and make sure that the USB cable on J9 of the YRDKRX63N board *is not* connected yet.

6-4-2 LAUNCHING THE DEBUGGING SESSION

Launch a debugging session as described in section 3-2-5 "Launching a Debug Session in e2studio" on page 655. Press *F8* to let the program run freely.

6-4-3 VERIFYING THE APPLICATION

In order to make sure that you are actually running the HID class example, take a look at the LCD screen on the YRDKRX63N as it should look as the one illustrated in Figure 6-3:

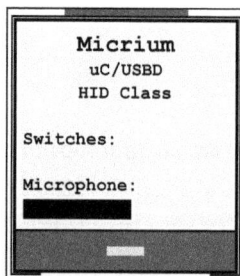

```
      Micrium
       uC/USBD
      HID Class

Switches:

Microphone:
```

Figure 6-3 **HID Class Example Screen**

The LCD screen also helps you verify that the application is running correctly as it indicates if any of the 3 push buttons on the YRDKRX63N has been pressed. At the same time, the horizontal bar graph shows the current noise level as detected by the microphone on U16. These two features are implemented in the form of two µC/OS-III tasks. So, if you see anything changing on the LCD screen as you make any noise or press the buttons, it means that µC/OS-III is multi-tasking. Besides that, the LEDs wheel should also be blinking as it is also driven by another µC/OS-III task.

6-4-4 INSTALLING THE HID DEVICE

At this time, the µC/USB-Device stack should be running and waiting for any USB events, such as connecting the USB device. Go ahead and connect the USB cable from J9 of the YRDKRX63N board, to the Capture Side of the Beagle USB 480 as illustrated in Table 2-12, "Beagle USB 480 Protocol Analyzer: Connections," on page 640. In case you do not have a USB protocol analyzer, you can still connect the other end of the cable directly into any available USB receptacle of the host computer.

The first time you run the example, the host computer will install the YRDKRX63N as a mouse. You will be notified that the device is installing by the Windows messages shown in the notification area on the bottom right corner of your desktop as shown in Figure 6-4:

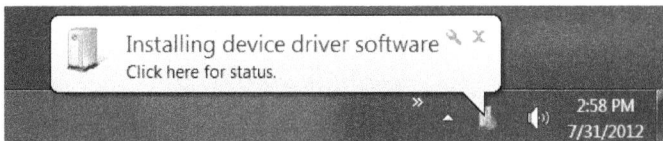

Figure 6-4 **Windows Installing the HID Device**

If you click on the bubble message shown in Figure 6-4, a more detailed message box will pop up describing the installation process. If Windows is able to install the device properly, you will be notified with a message similar to the one shown in Figure 6-5:

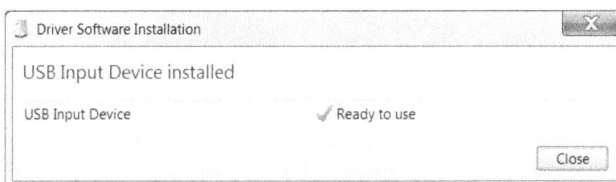

Figure 6-5 **Windows Notifying that the HID Device is Ready to Use**

At this point you should see the mouse pointer moving back and forth on your screen.

Since your mouse becomes pretty much unusable you can disconnect the USB cable on J9 of the YRDKRX63N to stop the mouse pointer.

You can try opening your Windows Device Manager from the Control Panel and reconnect the USB cable again to see how the newly installed HID device gets included in the list of devices as shown in Figure 6-6:

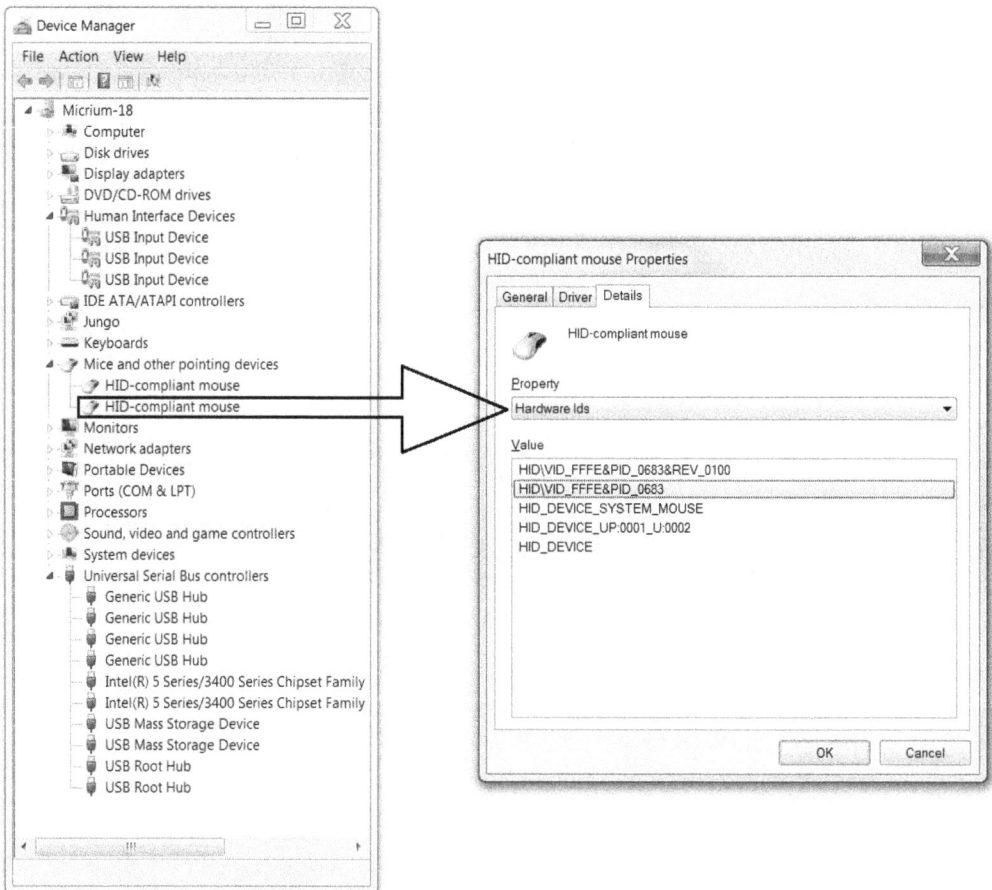

Figure 6-6 **Device Manager Showing the Newly Installed Device**

You can stop program execution by pressing `Ctrl+F2` or by clicking on the *Stop* button on the debugging toolbox as shown in section Figure 3-17 "Debugging Toolbar" on page 657.

6-5 HOW THE CODE WORKS

The function to initialize the HID class and mouse example is listed below:

```
CPU_BOOLEAN  App_USBD_HID_Init (CPU_INT08U  dev_nbr,
                                CPU_INT08U  cfg_hs,
                                CPU_INT08U  cfg_fs)
{
    USBD_ERR    err;
    USBD_ERR    err_fs;
    CPU_INT08U  class_nbr;
    OS_ERR      os_err;


    err_hs = USBD_ERR_NONE;
    err_fs = USBD_ERR_NONE;

    App_USBD_HID_X = 101;
    App_USBD_HID_Y = 101;

    APP_TRACE_DBG(("Initializing the HID class ... \r\n"));

    USBD_HID_Init(&err);                    /* Init HID class.              */   (1)
    if (err != USBD_ERR_NONE) {
        APP_TRACE_DBG(("... could not initialize HID class
                        w/err = %d\r\n\r\n", err));
        return (DEF_FAIL);
    }
                                            /* Create a HID class instance. */   (2)
    class_nbr = USBD_HID_Add(               USBD_HID_SUBCLASS_BOOT,
                                            USBD_HID_PROTOCOL_MOUSE,
                                            USBD_HID_COUNTRY_CODE_NOT_SUPPORTED,
                                            &App_USBD_HID_ReportDesc[0],
                                            sizeof(App_USBD_HID_ReportDesc),
                             (CPU_INT08U *)0,
                                            0u,
                                            2u,
                                            2u,
                                            DEF_YES,
                                            &App_USBD_HID_Callback,
                                            &err);
    if (err != USBD_ERR_NONE) {
        APP_TRACE_DBG(("... could not instantiate a HID class
                        w/err = %d\r\n\r\n", err));
        return (DEF_FAIL);
    }
```

Listing 6-2 **Initializing the Mouse Example**

L6-2(1)   The **USBD_HID_Init()** function is declared in **usbd_hid.c** and it is used to initialize all internal structures and variables that the class needs including the HID OS layer and HID report module. For more on this function, consult the HID API reference on section D-1-1 "USBD_HID_Init()" on page 456.

L6-2(2)   The **USBD_HID_Add()** function is also declared in **usbd_hid.c**. The function is responsible for creating a new HID class instance. Here is where you specify which protocol from the HID class to use. In this example we will use the *Mouse protocol* as defined in the USB HID specification. This function also sets the *Mouse Report descriptor* as described in section Figure 9-1 "Report Descriptor Content from a Host HID Parser View" on page 190 and section Listing 9-2 "Mouse Report Descriptor Example" on page 198.

The same **App_USBD_HID_Init()** function continues the initialization process by adding the new instance of the HID class into the USB full-speed device configuration as shown in code Listing 6-3:

```
    .
    .
    .
                                /* Add HID class to FS dflt cfg.              */   (1)
    USBD_HID_CfgAdd(class_nbr, dev_nbr, cfg_fs, &err_fs);
    if (err_fs != USBD_ERR_NONE) {
        APP_TRACE_DBG(("... could not add HID class instance #%d to FS configuration
                      w/err = %d\r\n\r\n", class_nbr, err_fs));
    }


    if (err_fs != USBD_ERR_NONE) {     /* If FS cfg fails, stop class init.     */   (2)
        return (DEF_FAIL);
    }
    .
    .
    .
```

Listing 6-3 **Adding the HID Class Instance to the Full-Speed Configuration**

L6-3(1)   Proceed to add the new HID instance to this full-speed configuration.

L6-3(2)   The **USBD_HID_CfgAdd()** function returns error code **USBD_ERR_NONE** if the HID class instance can be added into the USB device configuration without any problems such as memory allocation, invalid arguments, etc.

For more information on this function parameters and return error codes, see the HID API Reference section D-1-3 "USBD_HID_CfgAdd()" on page 459.

The last thing to do for the **App_USBD_HID_Init()** function is to create a µC/OS-III task that will simulate the mouse. Code Listing 6-4 shows how to create the task. If you are not familiar with µC/OS-III, we recommend downloading the PDF version of the book *µC/OS-III The Real-Time Kernel for the Renesas RX62N* from the Micriµm website.

```
        .
        .
        .
    OSTaskCreate(      &App_USBD_HID_MouseTaskTCB,
                       "USB Device HID Mouse",
                       App_USBD_HID_MouseTask,
                (void *)class_nbr,
                       APP_CFG_USBD_HID_MOUSE_TASK_PRIO,
                       &App_USBD_HID_MouseTaskStk[0],
                       APP_CFG_USBD_HID_TASK_STK_SIZE / 10u,
                       APP_CFG_USBD_HID_TASK_STK_SIZE,
                       0u,
                       0u,
                (void *)0,
                       OS_OPT_TASK_STK_CHK | OS_OPT_TASK_STK_CLR,
                       &os_err);
    if (os_err != OS_ERR_NONE) {
        APP_TRACE_DBG(("... could not add HID mouse task w/err = %d\r\n\r\n", os_err));
        return (DEF_FAIL);
    }
```

Listing 6-4 **Creating the Mouse Task**

The first part of the book on section 9-1-1 "Report" on page 186 described that the reports are the data structures used by the USB host and a HID device to exchange data. In this example the report is well-defined by Microsoft and the structure is declared in **app_usbd_hid.c** as **App_USBD_HID_ReportDesc[]**. An example of this descriptor is shown in Table 9-2, "Mouse Report Descriptor Example," on page 198.

The host computer will poll periodically the YRDKRX63N through an Interrupt IN endpoint which according to the RX63N hardware manual can be one of the endpoints in the range from 6 to 9. The report data which has a length of 4-bytes, is sent back to the host in response to the poll token. The 4-bytes of data contain the values for each x-axis and y-axis displacements.

Code Listing 6-5 shows the function that updates the data report with the displacements. Since the purpose of the example is to move the mouse pointer back and forth, the displacements are set to 50 and the global boolean variables **App_USBD_HID_X** and **App_USBD_HID_Y** serve as state flags to switch the movement back and forth:

```
static void  App_USBD_HID_MouseSetReport (CPU_INT08U  *p_buf)
{
    CPU_SR_ALLOC();


    p_buf[0] = 0;
    p_buf[1] = 0;

    CPU_CRITICAL_ENTER();
    p_buf[2] = (App_USBD_HID_X > 0) ? 50 : -50;
    p_buf[3] = (App_USBD_HID_Y > 0) ? 50 : -50;

    App_USBD_HID_X = !App_USBD_HID_X;
    App_USBD_HID_Y = !App_USBD_HID_Y;
    CPU_CRITICAL_EXIT();

}
```

Listing 6-5 **Preparing the Report Data**

This function **App_USBD_HID_MouseSetReport()** is called by the Mouse Task every 100 milliseconds as shown in Listing 6-6:

```
static void App_USBD_HID_MouseTask (void *p_arg)
{
    CPU_INT08U   class_nbr;
    CPU_BOOLEAN  conn;
    USBD_ERR     err;
    OS_ERR       os_err;


    class_nbr = (CPU_INT08U)(CPU_ADDR)p_arg;

    while (DEF_TRUE) {                                               (1)
        conn = USBD_HID_IsConn(class_nbr);                          (2)
        while (conn != DEF_YES) {                                   (3)
            OSTimeDlyHMSM(0, 0, 0, 250, OS_OPT_TIME_HMSM_STRICT, &os_err);

            conn = USBD_HID_IsConn(class_nbr);
        }

        App_USBD_HID_MouseSetReport(&App_USBD_HID_ReportBuf[0]);    (4)

        (void)USBD_HID_Wr( class_nbr,
                          &App_USBD_HID_ReportBuf[0],
                           APP_USBD_HID_REPORT_LEN,
                           0u,
                          &err);                                    (5)

        OSTimeDlyHMSM(0, 0, 0, 100, OS_OPT_TIME_HMSM_STRICT, &os_err);
    }
}
```

Listing 6-6 **Mouse Task**

L6-6(1)   If you are familiar with µC/OS-III, you already know that a typical µC/OS-III task is implemented as an infinite loop.

L6-6(2)   The **USBD_HID_IsConn()** function is declared in **usbd_hid.c** and it returns **DEF_TRUE** if both, the USB device and the instance of the HID class are in the *configured state*.

L6-6(3)   In case the **USB_HID_IsConn()** function returns with **DEF_FALSE**, the while loop keeps checking the status of the Device and the instance of the HID class until they transition into the configured state.

L6-6(4)   The function **App_USBD_HID_MouseSetReport()** was described in Code Listing 6-5, it basically updates the report data with the x-axis and y-axis displacements.

L6-6(5)   The **USBD_HID_Wr()** function is declared in **usbd_hid.c** and it is called to send data to the host computer through an Interrupt IN endpoint, which in the case of the RX63N it is endpoint 6 or EP6. Since the fourth argument of this function (timeout) is zero, the function call blocks until the data is sent. It will keep doing this every 100 milliseconds which means the mouse pointer on your host computer will move back and forth every 100 milliseconds.

6-6 ANALYZING THE USB TRAFFIC

In order to capture USB traffic, you need to connect the Beagle USB 480 as illustrated in Table 2-12, "Beagle USB 480 Protocol Analyzer: Connections," on page 640.

When monitoring USB traffic, it is best to attach the Beagle USB 480's analysis side and start the capture *before* attaching the YRDKRX63N. That means that before starting a capture, make sure the USB cable on J9 of the YRDKRX63N is disconnected from the Beagle USB 480 capture side. This allows the Beagle USB 480 to capture the descriptor information that is communicated during the enumeration phase.

Start the Total Phase Data Center software by using the shortcut created during Setup section 2-1-4 "Total Phase Data Center Software" on page 630 or, go to the folder where the software package was extracted and run *Data Center.exe*.

Figure 6-7 **Data Center Software Icon**

Once the application starts it will detect the Beagle and will connect it automatically.

You can tell the Beagle USB 480 is properly connected by looking at the LEDs on the top which should have the Red and Green LEDs lit up.

Press *Ctrl+R* or click the *Run Capture* button in the toolbar to start the capture.

You should see a couple of new rows in the grid that read something like *Capture Started*.

At this point, you can attach the HID device by connecting the USB cable on J9 of the YRDKRX63N. As traffic is seen on the bus, it will be displayed in real-time in the *transactions grid*. The first transactions you should see are those common to all USB classes during the process of enumeration, which is described in Appendix C, "The Enumeration Process" on page 811. Once the device is enumerated successfully by the host, you should start to see not only the mouse pointer moving back and forth on your screen but also a whole bunch of new rows in the grid that indicate that a mouse report is being sent to the host as shown in Figure 6-8:

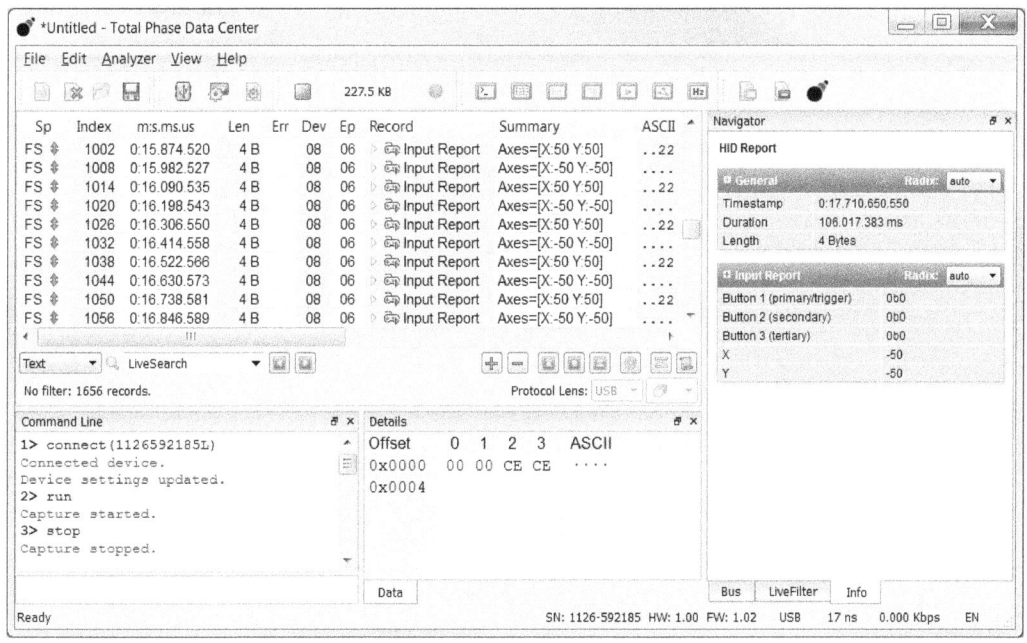

Figure 6-8 **Capturing USB Traffic**

Since you cannot use the mouse to stop the capture, you can either press *Ctrl+R* again to stop the capture or you can detach the HID device by disconnecting the USB cable from J9 on the YRDKRX63N and proceed to analyze the USB capture.

6-6-1 GET CONFIGURATION DESCRIPTOR

The *Get Configuration Descriptor* shown below in Figure 6-9, specifies the configuration(s) available. The Get Configuration Descriptor includes interface descriptors and endpoint descriptors that further describe the available interfaces and endpoints respectively. In this example there is only one configuration with a single interface and a single endpoint.

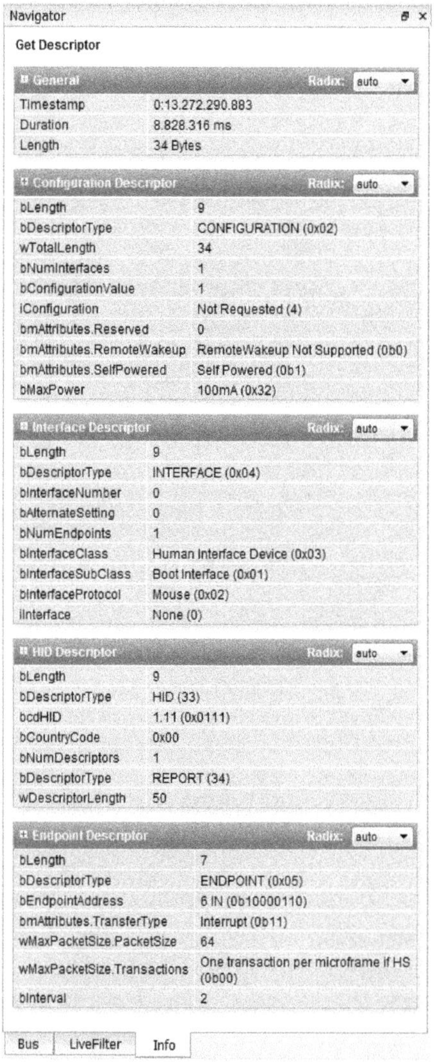

Figure 6-9 **Get Configuration Descriptor**

6-6-2 GET REPORT DESCRIPTOR

One of the *Get Descriptor* requests specific to the HID class is the one in the transactions grid titled *Get Report Descriptor* shown in Figure 6-10. This row represents the moment when the YRDKRX63N describes to the host computer the report's data format by sending the report descriptor listed in Table 9-2, "Mouse Report Descriptor Example," on page 198.

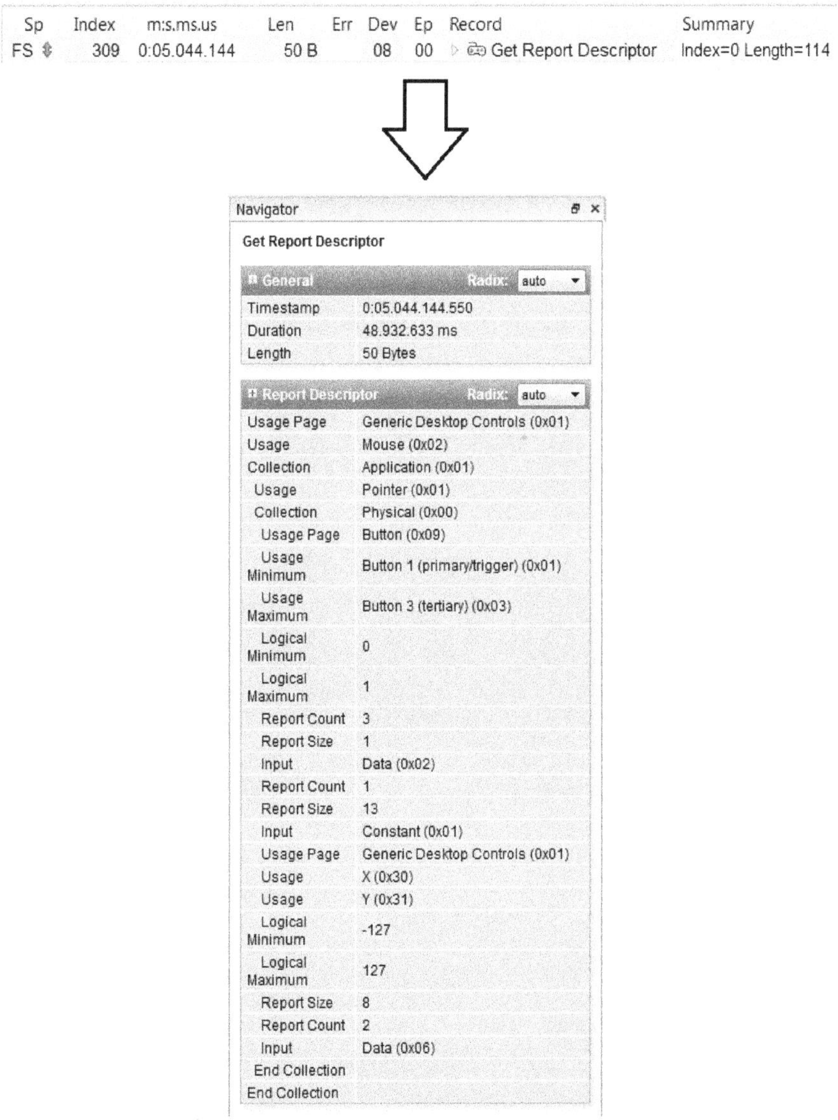

Figure 6-10 **Get Report Descriptor Capture**

6-6-3 THE MOUSE INPUT REPORT

Once the device has moved from the *addressed* state to the *configured* state as described in section 1-4 "Bus States" on page 31, the device is ready to use. You will find a series of *Input Report* records similar to the one shown in Figure 6-11. You can easily find the record in the transactions grid because that is the one that gets captured the most as the data report is sent at an interval of 100 milliseconds according to the mouse task shown in Code Listing 6-6.

Locate the *Input Report* record in the transactions grid and notice how the Info Pane in the Navigator window reports the x-axis and y-axis displacements of 50 as set by the function `App_USBD_HID_MouseSetReport()` declared in `app_usbd_hid.c`.

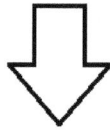

Figure 6-11 **Input Report Capture**

Also notice in Figure 6-11 how the *Ep* column shows the Endpoint number 6 which is the Interrupt IN endpoint that is meant to be used in HID class applications for data communication as described in Chapter 9, "Human Interface Device Class" on page 185.

The Block View shown in Figure 6-12 provides an alternate representation of the selected record that combines the hierarchical layout of the transaction grid with the detailed information found in the Info Pane.

The record tree that the selected record belongs to is displayed in the Block View, with the selected record highlighted in blue. Rows that have an arrow next to the first block can be expanded to reveal hidden fields.

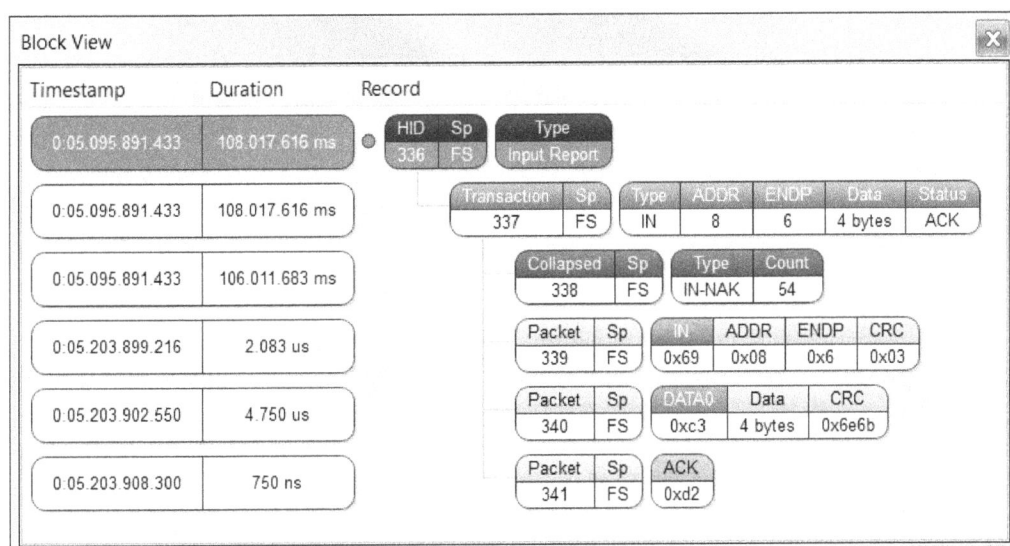

Figure 6-12 **Input Report as seen from the Block View**

6-7 SUMMARY

The example featured in this chapter is a great reference for creating your own HID device. It demonstrated the importance of having a USB protocol analyzer for debugging purposes and introduced you to the µC/USB-Device stack and the HID class. The chapter showed you how to run the example and then went into explaining how the code works by describing code listings and USB traffic captures.

The Renesas YRDKRX63N board is a great platform and if you want to take this example one step further, you can do so easily by using the push buttons and the accelerometer to create your own tilt mouse for game controlling purposes.

Example MSC: Removable Storage

The MSC class was presented in the first part of the book on Chapter 10, "Mass Storage Class" on page 215. The chapter finished presenting a demonstration application. This chapter describes how to run the MSC class demonstration example on the YRDKRX63N using e2studio and the Beagle USB 480 protocol analyzer.

The USB Mass Storage Class defines a protocol that allows a USB device to be accessible by a host computer for file transfer purposes. The USB device appears to the host computer as a removable storage device, thus enabling the transfer of files via drag-and-drop.

The example featured in this chapter implements a USB removable storage device with a capacity of 32 kilobytes. You will be able to create a small text file to test the µC/USB-Device stack and its MSC class as shown in Figure 7-1:

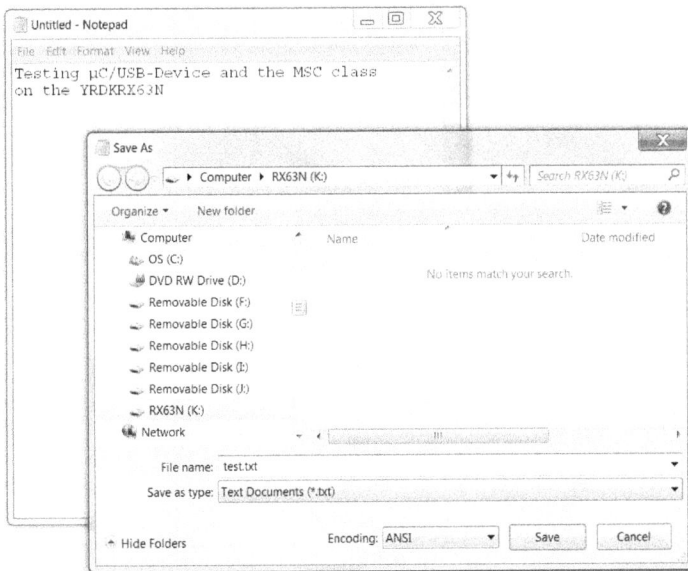

Figure 7-1 **Removable Storage Example**

7-1 LOADING THE PROJECT IN e2studio

In order to load this project you first need to import the C project included in the book's companion software package. You only need to do this once for all the examples and the procedure is described in sections 3-2-1 and 3-2-2 on page 645.

If you already went through that procedure, all you need to do is start e2studio and launch the workspace you created in the path of your choice.

7-2 CONFIGURING THE REMOVABLE STORAGE EXAMPLE

Open the header file **app_cfg.h** from the *Project Explorer* as shown in Figure 7-2:

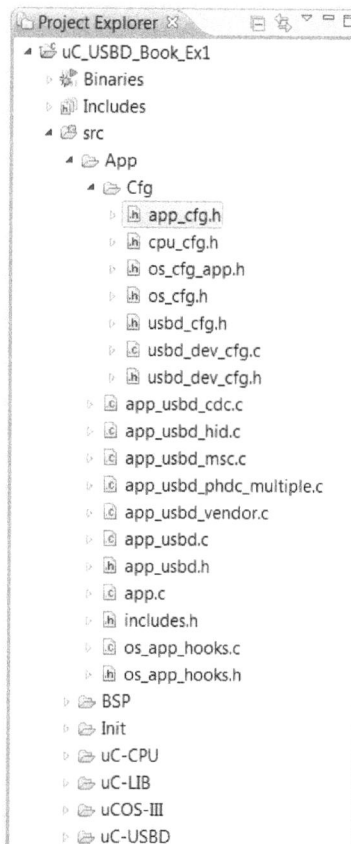

Figure 7-2 **Project Explorer: Configuration File**

7-2-1 ENABLING AND DISABLING CLASSES

All the examples featured in this book are not only in the same workspace but also in the same project and Code Listing 7-1 shows the lines of code in **app_cfg.h** that need to be edited in order to enable the MSC class and the Removable Storage example:

```
/*
*****************************************************************************
*                        uC/USB-DEVICE DEMO CONFIGURATION
*****************************************************************************
*/

#define  APP_CFG_USBD_VENDOR_EN                 DEF_DISABLED              (1)
#define  APP_CFG_USBD_CDC_EN                    DEF_DISABLED              (2)
#define  APP_CFG_USBD_HID_EN                    DEF_DISABLED              (3)
#define  APP_CFG_USBD_MSC_EN                    DEF_ENABLED               (4)
#define  APP_CFG_USBD_PHDC_EN                   DEF_DISABLED              (5)
  .
  .
  .
```

Listing 7-1 **Configuring the Removable Storage Example: app_cfg.h**

L7-1(1)   In order to run the removable storage example, make sure the Vendor class is disabled by setting **APP_CFG_USBD_VENDOR_EN** to **DEF_DISABLED.**

L7-1(2)   Make sure the CDC class is disabled by setting **APP_CFG_USBD_CDC_EN** to **DEF_DISABLED.**

L7-1(3)   Make sure the HID class is disabled by setting **APP_CFG_USBD_HID_EN** to **DEF_DISABLED.**

L7-1(4)   Make sure the MSC class is enabled by setting **APP_CFG_USBD_MSC_EN** to **DEF_ENABLED.**

L7-1(5)   Make sure the PHDC class is disabled by setting **APP_CFG_USBD_PHDC_EN** to **DEF_DISABLED.**

7-2-2 CONFIGURING THE STORAGE CAPACITY

The example featured in this chapter will use some blocks of RAM from the RX63N. Such blocks of memory will be treated as if the memory were non-volatile memory. This is known as *RAMDisk* and even though the data stored in this type of media will be lost whenever you switch off the board, it will be enough to demonstrate the MSC class. Of course, you always have the option to use a file system stack such as Micriµm's µC/FS or even utilize a file system storage medium of your own. In the event you use a file system storage medium of your own, you will need to create a storage layer port to communicate your storage medium to the µC/USB MSC Device. Please refer to section 10-6 "Porting MSC to a Storage Layer" on page 236 to learn how to implement this storage layer.

In order to configure the RAMDisk in `app_cfg.h`, you must specify the location in RAM where to allocate the blocks, the number of blocks and the block size.

You do not need to change any of these settings for this example, but Code Listing 7-2 shows you the set of preprocessor directives for your own reference:

```
#define   USBD_RAMDISK_CFG_BASE_ADDR         0u              (1)
#define   USBD_RAMDISK_CFG_NBR_UNITS         1u              (2)
#define   USBD_RAMDISK_CFG_BLK_SIZE        512u              (3)
#define   USBD_RAMDISK_CFG_NBR_BLKS         64u              (4)
```

Listing 7-2 **RAMDisk Configuration**

L7-2(1)   RAMDisk base address in memory. This constant is used to define the data area of the RAMDisk. If set to 0, the RAMDisk's data area will be represented as a table from the program's data area.

L7-2(2)   Number of logical units within the RAMDisk area.

L7-2(3)   RAMDisk block size in bytes.

L7-2(4)   RAMDisk logical unit's number of blocks. In this example, 64 times 512 amounts to a total capacity of 32768 bytes. Keep in mind that part of that capacity will be reserved for the file system of your choice.

7-3 BUILDING THE REMOVABLE STORAGE EXAMPLE PROJECT

In order to build the project press *Ctrl+B* as described in section 3-2-3 "Building a Project in e2studio" on page 648.

7-4 RUNNING THE REMOVABLE STORAGE EXAMPLE PROJECT

In order to run the example project, you do not need to install any drivers on the host computer as the example implements a standard removable storage device that Windows installs with its native drivers.

7-4-1 CONNECTING THE BOARD

Connect the board as illustrated in Table 2-12, "Beagle USB 480 Protocol Analyzer: Connections," on page 640 and make sure that the USB cable on J9 of the YRDKRX63N board *is not* connected yet.

7-4-2 LAUNCHING THE DEBUGGING SESSION

Launch a debugging session as described in section 3-2-5 "Launching a Debug Session in e2studio" on page 655.

Press *F8* to let the program run freely.

7-4-3 VERIFYING THE APPLICATION

In order to make sure that you are actually running the MSC class example, take a look at the LCD screen on the YRDKRX63N as it should look like the one illustrated in Figure 7-3:

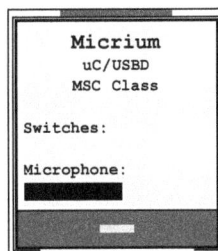

Figure 7-3 **MSC Class Example Screen**

The LCD screen also helps you verify that the application is running correctly as it indicates if any of the 3 push buttons on the YRDKRX63N has been pressed. At the same time, the horizontal bar graph shows the current noise level as detected by the microphone on U16. These two features are implemented in the form of two µC/OS-III tasks. So, if you see anything changing on the LCD screen as you make any noise or press the buttons, it means that µC/OS-III is multi-tasking. Besides that, the LEDs wheel should also be blinking as it is also driven by another µC/OS-III task.

7-4-4 INSTALLING THE MSC DEVICE

At this time, the µC/USB-Device stack should be running and waiting for any USB events, such as connecting the USB device. Go ahead and connect the USB cable from J9 of the YRDKRX63N board and into the Capture Side of the Beagle USB 480 as illustrated in Table 2-12, "Beagle USB 480 Protocol Analyzer: Connections," on page 640. In case you do not have a USB protocol analyzer, you can still connect the other end of the cable directly into any available USB receptacle on your host computer.

The first time you run the example, the host computer will install the YRDKRX63N as a removable storage device. You will be notified that the device is installing by the typical Windows messages shown in the notification area on the bottom right corner of your desktop as shown in Figure 7-4:

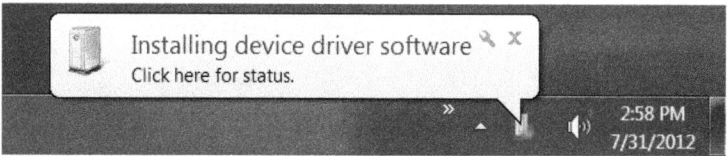

Figure 7-4 **Windows Installing the MSC Device**

7-4-5 FORMATTING THE NEW REMOVABLE STORAGE DEVICE

If it is the first time you install the device, Windows will ask you to format the disk drive with a prompt window similar to the one shown in Figure 7-5:

Figure 7-5 **Windows Formatting the New Removable Storage Device**

It is safe to format the device as it will only affect those blocks of RAM configured in `app_cfg.h`.

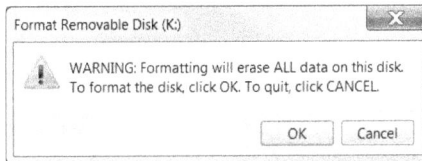

Figure 7-6 **Windows Format Warning**

Configure the volume label with a name you can easily recognize in the future such as *RX63N*. You can select whatever file system you want, this example was tested with the FAT file system as shown in Figure 7-7:

Figure 7-7 **Windows Format Configuration**

Once the format is complete, Windows will notify you with a message box similar to the one shown in Figure 7-8:

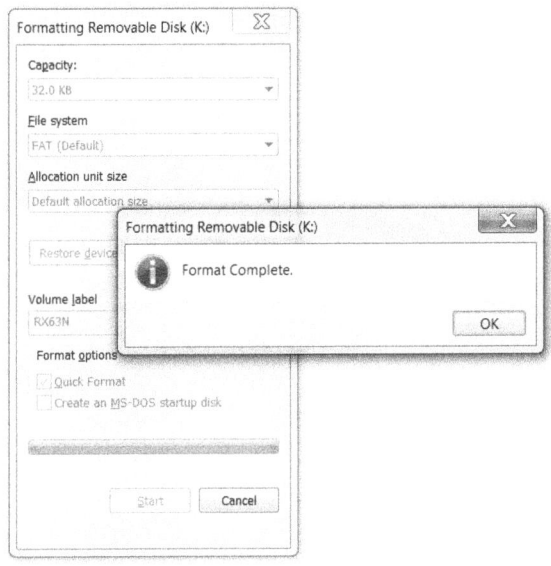

Figure 7-8 **Windows Format Complete**

7-4-6 EXPLORING THE NEW REMOVABLE STORAGE

Some versions of Windows will open Windows Explorer automatically to your new Removable Storage Device path, otherwise open Windows Explorer and locate your new MSC device:

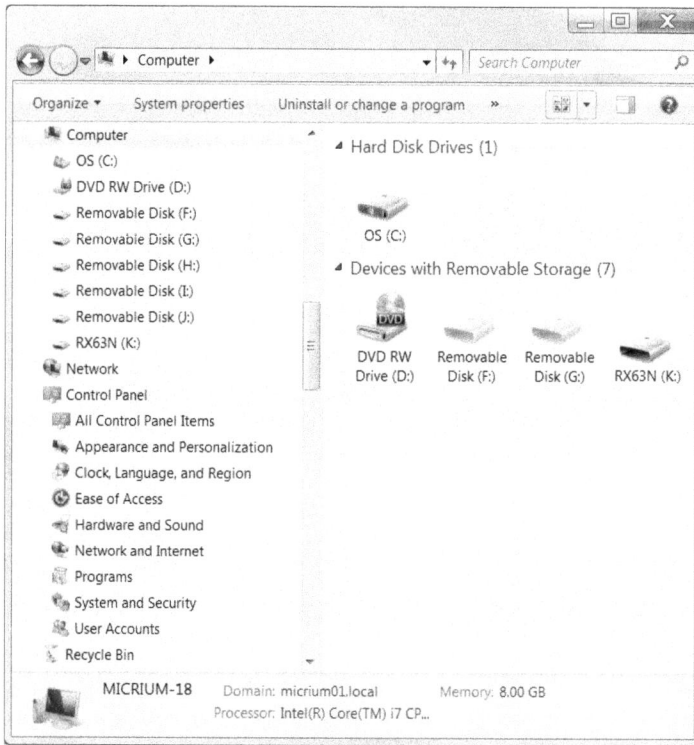

Figure 7-9 **Windows Explorer Showing the New Removable Storage Device**

Right-click over the icon that represents your new removable storage device and select *Properties* to look at the capacity as shown in Figure 7-10:

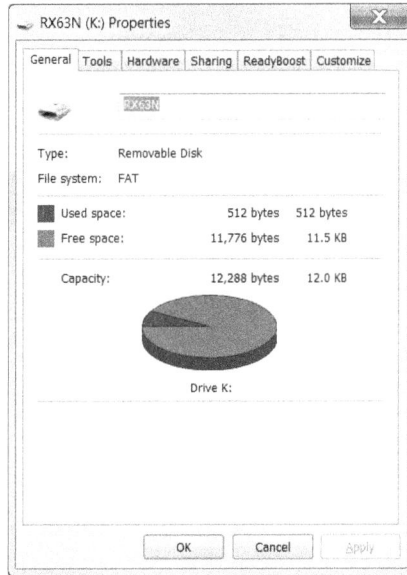

Figure 7-10 **Windows Displaying the New Removable Storage Capacity**

Notice how Windows reports a capacity of 12,288 bytes, whereas the capacity that you configured the RAMDisk in **app_cfg.h** was 32 KB. That is because part of the RAMDisk is reserved for special sectors needed by the FAT file system.

You can also try opening your Windows Device Manager from the Control Panel to see how the newly installed MSC device gets included in the list of devices as shown in Figure 7-11:

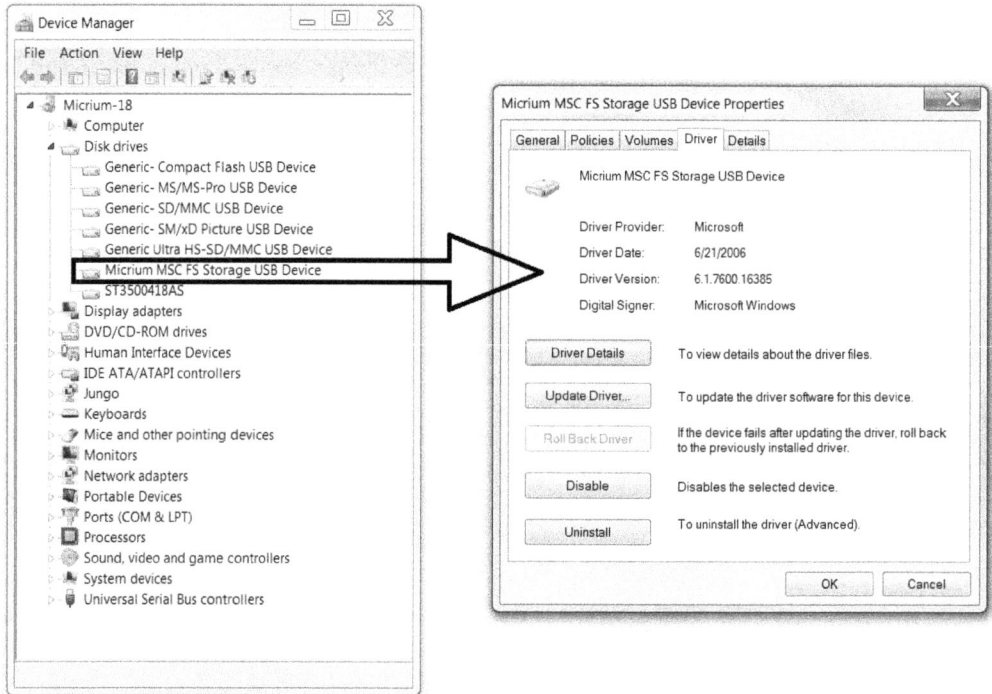

Figure 7-11 **Device Manager Showing the Newly Installed Device**

7-4-7 TESTING THE NEW REMOVABLE STORAGE DEVICE

At this point you can exercise the µC/USB-Device stack and its MSC class by writing some data to the new device.

Open *Notepad*, write some text for test and save it into your new device as shown in Figure 7-12:

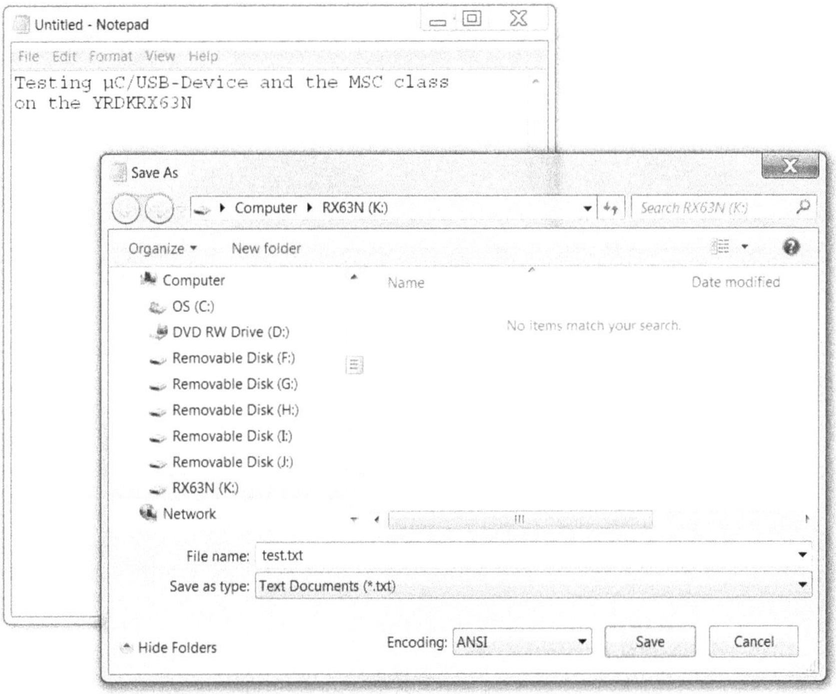

Figure 7-12 **Notepad Test**

The file will remain in memory as long as the YRDKRX63N is powered on, which means that if you keep supplying power by the USB cable attached to the J-Link port in J14 of the YRDKRX63N, you can disconnect the other USB cable on J9, reconnect it again and see how Windows opens up your removable storage with your test file in it.

You can stop program execution by pressing **Ctrl+F2** or by clicking on the *Stop* button on the debugging toolbox as shown in section Figure 3-17 "Debugging Toolbar" on page 657.

7-5 HOW THE CODE WORKS

The function to initialize the MSC class and removable storage example is declared at the application level in file **app_usbd_msc.c.** The following code listings describe the initialization process:

```
CPU_BOOLEAN  App_USBD_MSC_Init (CPU_INT08U  dev_nbr,
                                CPU_INT08U  cfg_hs,
                                CPU_INT08U  cfg_fs)
{
    USBD_ERR     err;
    CPU_INT08U   msc_nbr;
    CPU_BOOLEAN  valid;

    APP_TRACE_DBG(("Initializing MSC class ... \r\n"));

    USBD_MSC_Init(&err);                                                    (1)
    if (err != USBD_ERR_NONE) {
        APP_TRACE_DBG(("... could not initialize MSC class w/err = %d\r\n\r\n", err));
        return (DEF_FAIL);
    }

    msc_nbr = USBD_MSC_Add(&err);                                          (2)
    .
    .
    .
```

Listing 7-3 **Initializing the Removable Storage Example**

L7-3(1)   The **USBD_MSC_Init()** function is declared in **usbd_msc.c** and it is used to initialize all internal structures and variables that the class needs including the initialization of the MSC task handler. The MSC task handler is responsible for implementing the MSC protocol by allowing the communication between the device and the host. For more information on this function, consult the MSC API reference on section E-1-1 "USBD_MSC_Init()" on page 488.

L7-3(2)   The **USBD_MSC_Add()** function is also declared in **usbd_msc.c**. The function is responsible for creating a new instance of the MSC class. The function returns the class number after successfully allocating the new class. This class number identifies the instance and is used as an input argument for all MSC API functions.

The next step in the initialization process is to add the new instance of the MSC class into the USB full-speed device configuration as shown in code Listing 7-4:

```
    .
    .
    .
                                /* Add MSC class to FS dflt cfg.            */    (1)
    valid = USBD_MSC_CfgAdd(msc_nbr, dev_nbr, cfg_fs, &err);
    if (valid != DEF_YES) {
        APP_TRACE_DBG(("... could not add MSC class instance #%d to FS configuration
                        w/err = %d\r\n\r\n", msc_nbr, err));
        return (DEF_FAIL);
    }
    .
    .
    .
```

Listing 7-4 Adding the MSC Class Instance to the Full-Speed Configuration

L7-4(1)   Proceed to add the new MSC instance to this full-speed configuration. The **USBD_MSC_CfgAdd()** function returns **DEF_YES** if the MSC class instance can be added into the USB device configuration without any problems such as memory allocation, invalid arguments, etc.

For more information on this function parameters and return error codes, see the MSC API Reference section E-1-3 "USBD_MSC_CfgAdd()" on page 490.

The last thing to do for the **App_USBD_MSC_Init()** function is to add a logical unit number to the MSC interface, by calling **USBD_MSC_LunAdd()** as shown in Listing 7-5. Here is where you get to specify the logical unit's type and volume among other device details such as vendor ID and product ID. Logical units are added by a device driver string name composed of the storage device driver name (i.e. RAMDisk) and the logical unit number starting from 0. In this example the pointer to the logical unit driver is called *ram:0*.

```
     .
     .
     .
     USBD_MSC_LunAdd((void *)"ram:0:",         /* Pointer to logical unit driver         */
                        msc_nbr,               /* Add Logical Unit to MSC interface #    */
                 (void *)"Micrium",            /* Vendor  ID                             */
                 (void *)"MSC FS Storage",     /* Product ID                             */
                        0x00,                  /* Product revision level                 */
                        DEF_FALSE,             /* Read-only?                             */
                        &err);
     if (err != USBD_ERR_NONE) {
        return (DEF_FAIL);
     }


     return (DEF_OK);
}
```

Listing 7-5 **Adding the Logical Unit to the MSC Class Instance**

7-6 ANALYZING THE USB TRAFFIC

In order to capture USB traffic, you need to connect the Beagle USB 480 as illustrated in Figure 2-12, "Beagle USB 480 Protocol Analyzer: Connections," on page 640.

When monitoring USB traffic, it is best to attach the Beagle USB 480's analysis side and start the capture *before* attaching the YRDKRX63N. That means that before starting a capture, make sure the USB cable on J9 of the YRDKRX63N is disconnected from the Beagle USB 480 capture side. This allows the Beagle USB 480 to capture the descriptor information that is communicated during the enumeration phase.

Start the Total Phase Data Center software by using the shortcut created during Setup section 2-1-4 "Total Phase Data Center Software" on page 630 or, go to the folder where the software package was extracted and run *Data Center.exe.*

Figure 7-13 **Data Center Software Icon**

Once the application starts it will detect the Beagle and will connect it automatically.

You can tell the Beagle USB 480 is properly connected by looking at the LEDs on the top which should have the Red and Green LEDs lit up.

Press *Ctrl+R* or click the *Run Capture* button in the toolbar to start the capture.

You should see a couple of new rows in the grid that read something like *Capture Started*.

At this point, you can attach the MSC device by connecting the USB cable on J9 of the YRDKRX63N.

Complete the steps to format the new removable storage device and create a test file by following the steps described in the section 7-4 "Running the Removable Storage Example Project" on page 715.

As traffic is seen on the bus, it will be displayed in real-time in the *transactions grid*. The first transactions you should see are those common to all USB classes during the process of enumeration, which is described in Appendix C, "The Enumeration Process" on page 811.

Once the device is enumerated successfully by the host, you should start to see not only the Windows dialogs to format the new removable storage device but also a whole bunch of new rows in the transactions grid including the rows that represent the SCSI commands described in section Table 10-3 "SCSI Commands" on page 221.

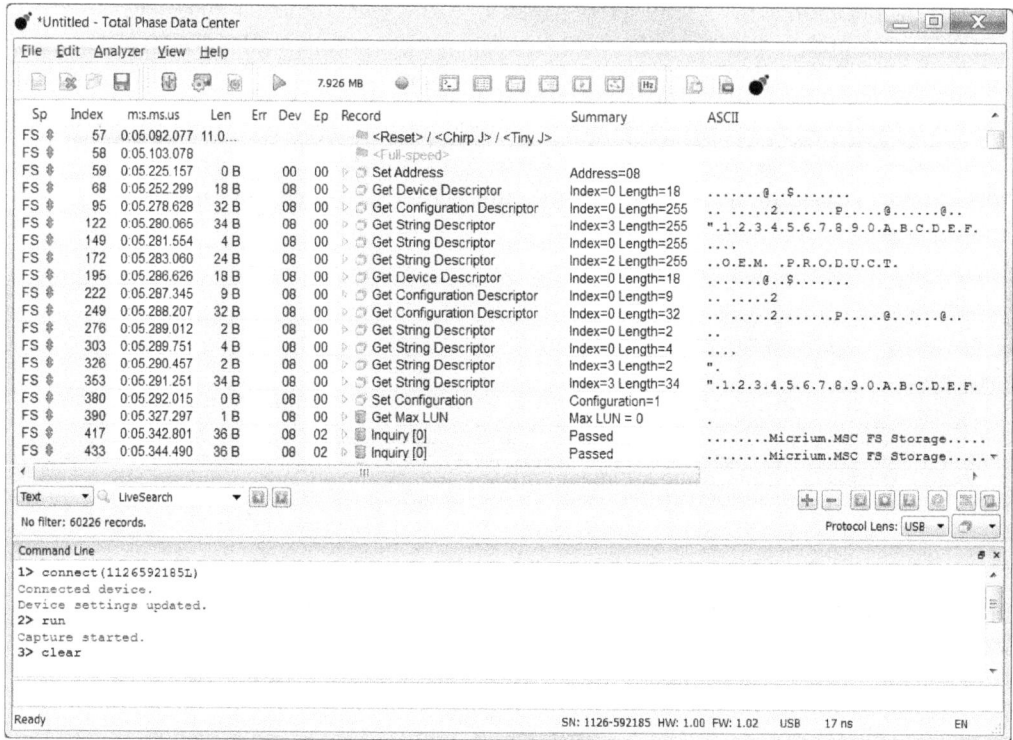

Figure 7-14 **Capturing USB Traffic**

You can press *Ctrl+R* again to stop the capture and proceed to analyze the USB capture.

7-6-1 GET CONFIGURATION DESCRIPTOR

The host computer gets the capabilities of the device by a series of get descriptor requests such as the record in the transactions grid titled *Get Configuration Descriptor* shown in Figure 7-15. This row represents the moment when the YRDKRX63N describes to the host computer the possible device configuration by describing the available endpoints for MSC.

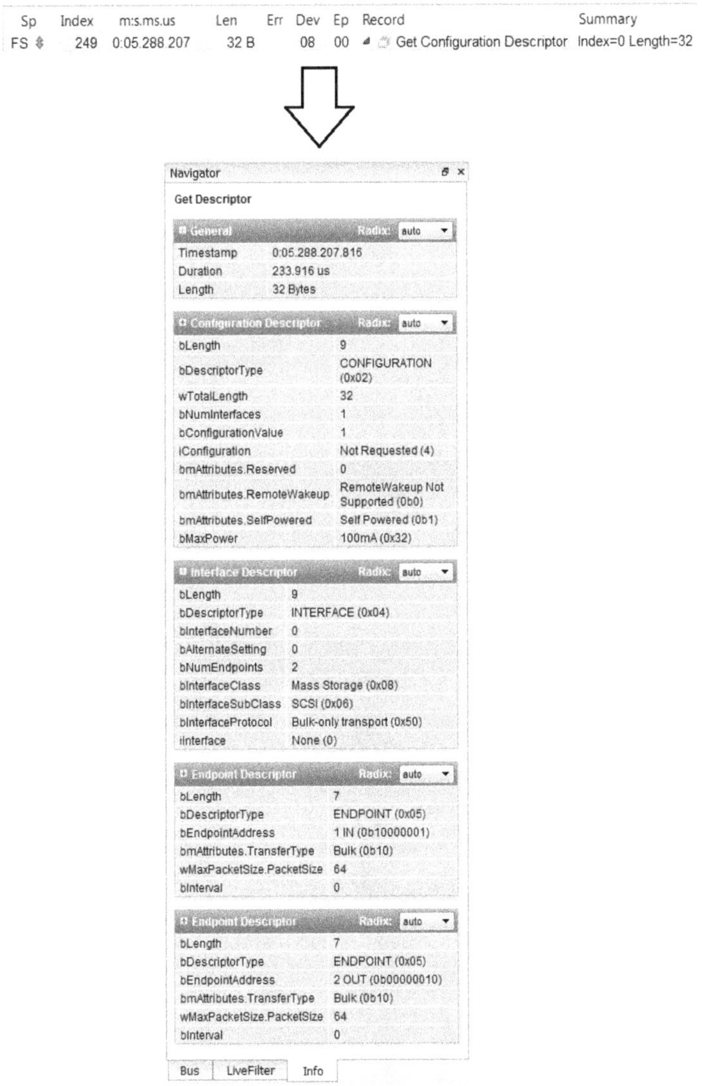

Sp	Index	m:s.ms.us	Len	Err	Dev	Ep	Record	Summary
FS	249	0:05.288.207	32 B		08	00	Get Configuration Descriptor	Index=0 Length=32

Navigator

Get Descriptor

General — Radix: auto

Timestamp	0:05.288.207.816
Duration	233.916 us
Length	32 Bytes

Configuration Descriptor — Radix: auto

bLength	9
bDescriptorType	CONFIGURATION (0x02)
wTotalLength	32
bNumInterfaces	1
bConfigurationValue	1
iConfiguration	Not Requested (4)
bmAttributes.Reserved	0
bmAttributes.RemoteWakeup	RemoteWakeup Not Supported (0b0)
bmAttributes.SelfPowered	Self Powered (0b1)
bMaxPower	100mA (0x32)

Interface Descriptor — Radix: auto

bLength	9
bDescriptorType	INTERFACE (0x04)
bInterfaceNumber	0
bAlternateSetting	0
bNumEndpoints	2
bInterfaceClass	Mass Storage (0x08)
bInterfaceSubClass	SCSI (0x06)
bInterfaceProtocol	Bulk-only transport (0x50)
iInterface	None (0)

Endpoint Descriptor — Radix: auto

bLength	7
bDescriptorType	ENDPOINT (0x05)
bEndpointAddress	1 IN (0b10000001)
bmAttributes.TransferType	Bulk (0b10)
wMaxPacketSize.PacketSize	64
bInterval	0

Endpoint Descriptor — Radix: auto

bLength	7
bDescriptorType	ENDPOINT (0x05)
bEndpointAddress	2 OUT (0b00000010)
bmAttributes.TransferType	Bulk (0b10)
wMaxPacketSize.PacketSize	64
bInterval	0

Bus | LiveFilter | Info

Figure 7-15 **Get Configuration Descriptor Capture**

7-6-2 THE MSC PROTOCOL

The MSC protocol was introduced in section 10-1-1 "Mass Storage Class Protocol" on page 216, where we described that each command in MSC is exchanged between the host and device through a three phase mechanism. Figure 7-16 illustrates the three phases during a command to read the capacity of the device:

Sp	Index	m:s.ms.us	Len	Dev	Ep	Record	Summary
FS	811	0:03.460.565	8 B	08	02	◢ 🖥 Read Capacity [0]	Passed
FS	812	0:03.460.565	31 B	08	02	▷ 🖥 Command Transport	
FS	817	0:03.461.109	8 B	08	01	▷ 🖥 Data Transport	00 00 00 3F 00 00 02 00
FS	823	0:03.468.625	13 B	08	01	▷ 🖥 Status Transport	Passed

Navigator   🗗 ✕

Mass Storage Transfer

⊟ General   Radix: auto ▾

Timestamp	0:03.460.565.650
Duration	8.075.983 ms
Length	8 Bytes

⊟ Command Block Wrapper   Radix: auto ▾

dCBWSignature	Correct (0x43425355)
dCBWTag	0xc7a18c0
dCBWDataTransferLength	8
bmCBWFlags.Direction	Data-In (0b1)
bCBWLUN	0
bCBWCBLength	10

⊟ SCSI Command   Radix: auto ▾

Opcode	Read Capacity (10) (0x25)
Logical Block Address	0
Partial Medium Indicator	0b0
Control	0b0

⊟ Read Capacity (10) Data   Radix: auto ▾

Returned Logical Block Address	63
Logical Block Length (Bytes)	512
Total capacity	31.512 kB

⊟ Command Status Wrapper   Radix: auto ▾

dCSWSignature	Correct (0x53425355)
dCSWTag	0xc7a18c0
dCSWDataResidue	0
bCSWStatus	Passed (0x0)

Bus   LiveFilter   Info

Figure 7-16 **MSC Protocol's Three Phases**

7-6-3 THE SCSI COMMANDS

Once the device has moved from the *addressed state* to the *configured state* as described in section 1-4 "Bus States" on page 31, the device is ready to use. You will find a series of records similar to the ones shown in Figure 7-17. Those records represent the Small Computer System Interface (SCSI) commands sent by the host computer. These commands set specific requests for transfer of blocks of data and status, and control information such as a device's capacity and readiness to exchange data. These particular SCSI commands shown in Figure 7-17 represent the moment when Windows formatted the new removable storage device:

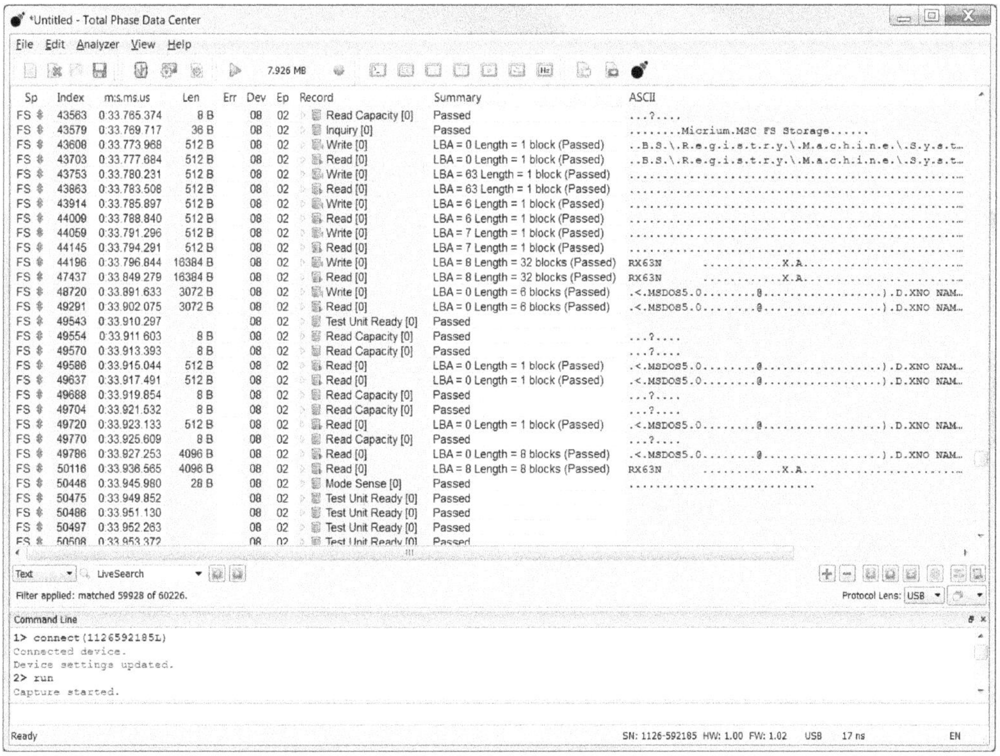

Figure 7-17 **SCSI Commands During Formatting**

The SCSI interface for the µC/USB-Device stack is implemented in file **usbd_scsi.c** and includes the SCSI commands listed in Table 10-3, "SCSI Commands," on page 221.

Also notice in Figure 7-17 how the *Ep* column shows the Endpoint number 2 which is the Bulk OUT endpoint that is meant to be used in MSC class applications for data communication as described in Chapter 10, "Mass Storage Class" on page 215.

The Endpoint Table for the YRDKRX63N is declared as part of the µC/USB-Device driver's board support package in file **usbd_bsp_yrdkrx63n.c** (See Appendix B, "Endpoint Information Table for the RX63N" on page 798).

WRITE COMMAND

Now focus your attention to one of the SCSI commands. The *Write* command shown in Figure 7-18 was captured during the part when you save the test file with *Notepad*:

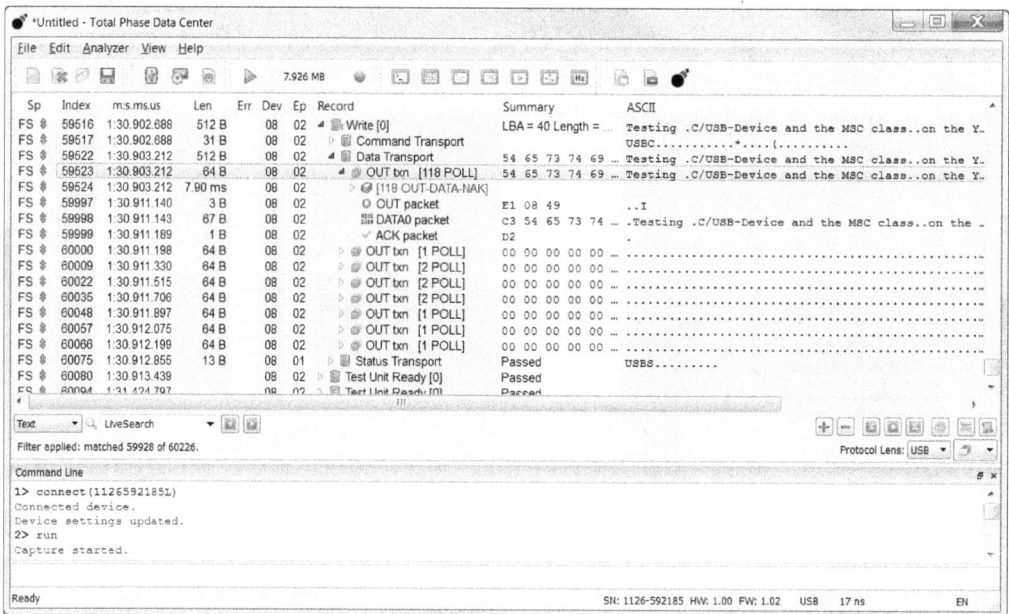

Figure 7-18 **The Write Command**

Notice how the *Write* command includes the MSC protocol's 3 phases described in section section 7-6-2 "The MSC Protocol" on page 730.

Also notice the amount of NAK records; 180 NAK records for a total of 7.90 milliseconds. This is completely normal, the NAK handshake packet is generally used for flow control to indicate that a USB device is temporarily unable to transmit or receive data.

7-7 SUMMARY

The example featured in this chapter is a great reference for creating your own MSC device. It introduced you to the µC/USB-Device stack and the MSC class. The chapter showed you how to run the example and then went into explaining how the code works by describing code listings and USB traffic captures.

The Renesas YRDKRX63N board is a great platform and if you want to take this example further, you can do so easily by adding a File System stack such as µC/USB-FS and using the Micro SD card on J13 of the YRDKRX63N, to create a non-volatile removable storage device.

Chapter 7

Example PHDC: Communication Monitor

The μC/USB-Device stack and its PHDC class enable USB connectivity among medical devices by complying with medical industry standards. The PHDC class was presented in Chapter 11, "Personal Healthcare Device Class" on page 239. The chapter finished presenting a demonstration application. This chapter describes how to run the PHDC class demonstration example on the YRDKRX63N using e2studio and the Beagle USB 480 protocol analyzer.

The example featured in this book includes not only source code for the embedded application running on the YRDKRX63N, but also a Visual Studio project for the software on the Windows PC as illustrated in Figure 8-1:

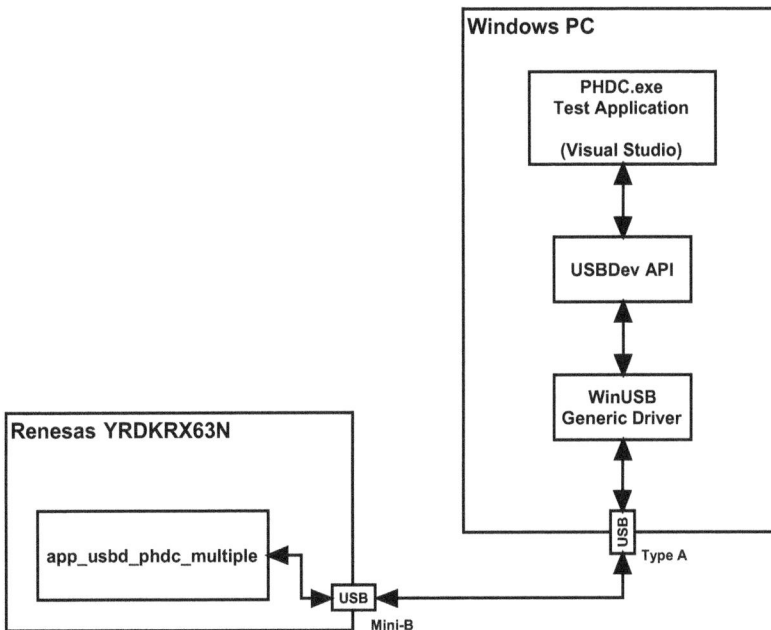

Figure 8-1 **PHDC Example**

The example application demonstrates how to transfer data items back and forth between the YRDKRX63N and the host computer by using different combinations of latency/reliability (Quality of Service) as shown in Table 8-1:

Quality of Service (QoS) (Latency / Reliability)	Latency	Raw info rate	Transfer direction	Typical use
Low / good	< 20ms	50 bits/sec to 1.2M bits/sec	IN	Real-time monitoring, with fast analog sampling rate.
Medium / good	< 200ms	50 bits/sec to 1.2M bits/s	IN	
Medium / better	< 200ms	10s of byte range	IN	Data from measured parameter collected off-line and replayed or sent real-time.
Medium / best	< 200ms	10s of byte range	IN, OUT	Events, notifications, request, control and status of physiological and equipment functionality.
High / best	< 2s	10s of byte range	IN, OUT	Physiological and equipment alarms.
Very high / best	< 20s	10s of byte range to gigabytes of data	IN, OUT	Transfer reports, histories or off-line collection of data.

Table 8-1 **QoS Levels**

8-1 LOADING THE PROJECT IN e2studio

In order to load this project you first need to import the C project included in the book's companion software package. You only need to do this once for all the examples and the procedure is described in sections 3-2-1 and 3-2-2 on page 645.

If you already went through that procedure, all you need to do is start e2studio and launch the workspace you created in the path of your choice.

8-2 CONFIGURING THE PHDC EXAMPLE

Open the header file **app_cfg.h** from the *Project Explorer* as shown in Figure 8-2:

Figure 8-2 **Project Explorer: Configuration File**

8-2-1 ENABLING AND DISABLING CLASSES

All the examples featured in this book are not only in the same workspace but also in the same project and Code Listing 8-1 shows the lines of code in **app_cfg.h** that need to be edited in order to enable the PHDC class and example:

```
/*
*********************************************************************************
*                       uC/USB-DEVICE DEMO CONFIGURATION
*********************************************************************************
*/
#define  APP_CFG_USBD_VENDOR_EN                  DEF_DISABLED          (1)
#define  APP_CFG_USBD_CDC_EN                     DEF_DISABLED          (2)
#define  APP_CFG_USBD_HID_EN                     DEF_DISABLED          (3)
#define  APP_CFG_USBD_MSC_EN                     DEF_DISABLED          (4)
#define  APP_CFG_USBD_PHDC_EN                    DEF_ENABLED           (5)

#define  APP_CFG_USBD_PHDC_ITEM_DATA_LEN_MAX     255u                  (6)
#define  APP_CFG_USBD_PHDC_ITEM_NBR_MAX          10u                   (7)
```

Listing 8-1 **Configuring the PHDC Example: app_cfg.h**

L8-1(1)   In order to run the PHDC example, make sure the Vendor class is disabled by setting **APP_CFG_USBD_VENDOR_EN** to **DEF_DISABLED**.

L8-1(2)   Make sure the CDC class is disabled by setting **APP_CFG_USBD_CDC_EN** to **DEF_DISABLED**.

L8-1(3)   Make sure the HID class is disabled by setting **APP_CFG_USBD_HID_EN** to **DEF_DISABLED**.

L8-1(4)   Make sure the MSC class is disabled by setting **APP_CFG_USBD_MSC_EN** to **DEF_DISABLED**.

L8-1(5)   Make sure the PHDC class is enabled by setting **APP_CFG_USBD_PHDC_EN** to **DEF_ENABLED**.

L8-1(6)   The maximum number of bytes that can be transferred as data must be >= 5.

L8-1(7)   The maximum number of items that the application supports must be at least 1.

8-3 BUILDING THE PHDC EXAMPLE PROJECT

In order to build the project press *Ctrl+B* as described in section 3-2-3 "Building a Project in e2studio" on page 648.

8-4 RUNNING THE PHDC EXAMPLE PROJECT

In order to run the example project, you need to follow the next steps including the preparation of an INF file which Windows will use to load one of its own native drivers.

8-4-1 CONNECTING THE BOARD

Connect the board as illustrated in section Figure 2-12 "Beagle USB 480 Protocol Analyzer: Connections" on page 640 and make sure that the USB cable on J9 of the YRDKRX63N board *is not* connected yet.

8-4-2 LAUNCHING THE DEBUGGING SESSION

Launch a debugging session as described in section 3-2-5 "Launching a Debug Session in e2studio" on page 655 and press *F8* to let the program run freely.

8-4-3 VERIFYING THE APPLICATION

In order to make sure that you are actually running the PHDC class example, take a look at the LCD screen on the YRDKRX63N as it should look like the one illustrated in Figure 8-3:

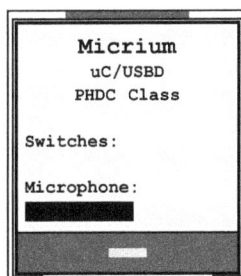

```
         Micrium
          uC/USBD
         PHDC Class

    Switches:

    Microphone:
```

Figure 8-3 **PHDC Class Example Screen**

The LCD screen also helps you verify that the application is running correctly as it indicates if any of the 3 push buttons on the YRDKRX63N has been pressed. At the same time, the horizontal bar graph shows the current noise level as detected by the microphone on U16. These two features are implemented in the form of two µC/OS-III tasks. So, if you see anything changing on the LCD screen as you make any noise or press the buttons, it means that µC/OS-III is multi-tasking. Besides that, the LEDs wheel should also be blinking as it is also driven by another µC/OS-III task.

8-4-4 INSTALLING THE PHDC DEVICE

At this time, the µC/USB-Device stack should be running and waiting for any USB events, such as connecting the USB device. Go ahead and connect the USB cable from J9 of the YRDKRX63N board and into the Capture Side of the Beagle USB 480 as illustrated in Figure 2-12, "Beagle USB 480 Protocol Analyzer: Connections," on page 640. In case you do not have a USB protocol analyzer, you can still connect the other end of the cable directly into any available USB receptacle on your host computer.

The first time you run the example, the host computer will install the YRDKRX63N as a *PHDC Device*. You will be notified that the device is installing by the typical Windows messages shown in the notification area on the bottom right corner of your desktop as shown in Figure 8-4:

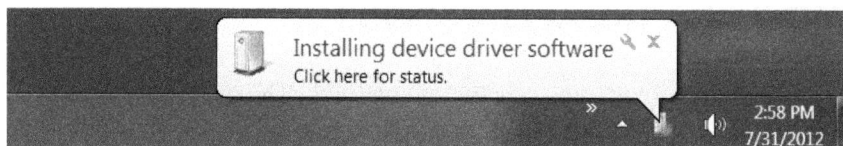

Figure 8-4 **Windows Installing the PHDC Device**

If it is the first time you install the device, Windows will fail to do so, because this particular example, even though it uses one of the Windows native drivers, it requires an INF file to load the driver.

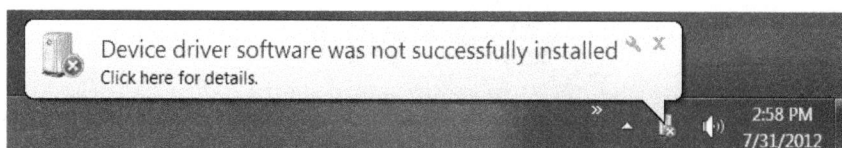

Figure 8-5 **Windows Notifying Failure Installing the Device**

The subject of INF files was briefly described in section 3-1-1 "About INF Files" on page 90. The book companion's software that you installed in section 2-1-5 "µC/USB-Device Book's Companion Software" on page 630 includes the required INF file for this example. You only need to make sure that both the INF file and your PHDC Device's hardware IDs match. In order to do so, open the following INF file in a text editor such as *Notepad*:

`$\Micrium\Software\uC-USB-Device-V4\App\Host\OS\Windows\PHDC\INF\WinUSB_single.inf`

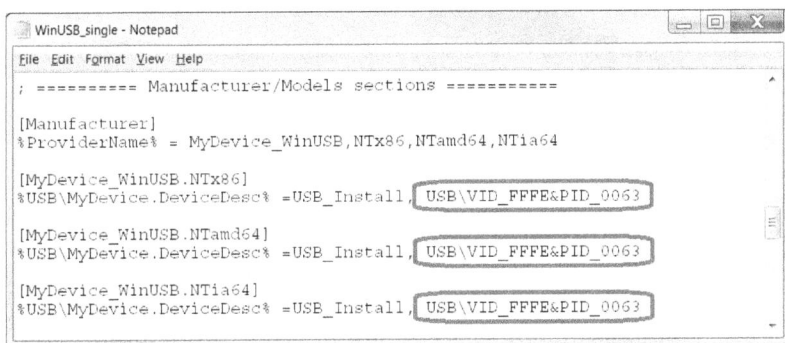

Figure 8-6 **Updating the INF File**

Locate the lines that specify the *Vendor ID* = **FFFEh** and *Product ID* = **0063h** as indicated in Figure 8-6 and make sure that they match with the hardware IDs configured in `usbd_dev_cfg.c` as shown in Code Listing 8-2:

```
/*
*************************************************************************************
*                             USB DEVICE CONFIGURATION
*************************************************************************************
*/

USBD_DEV_CFG   USBD_DevCfg_RX63N = {
    0xFFFE,                              /* Vendor   ID.                  */
    0x0063,                              /* Product ID (PHDC).            */
    0x0100,                              /* Device release number.        */
    "OEM MANUFACTURER",                  /* Manufacturer  string.         */
    "OEM PRODUCT",                       /* Product      string.          */
    "1234567890ABCDEF",                  /* Serial number string.         */
    USBD_LANG_ID_ENGLISH_US              /* String language ID.           */
};
```

Listing 8-2 **USB PHDC Device Configuration**

If you open Windows Device Manager, you are going to find a new entry for the PHDC device that failed to install. Windows lists this device under the group *Other Devices* as shown in Figure 8-7:

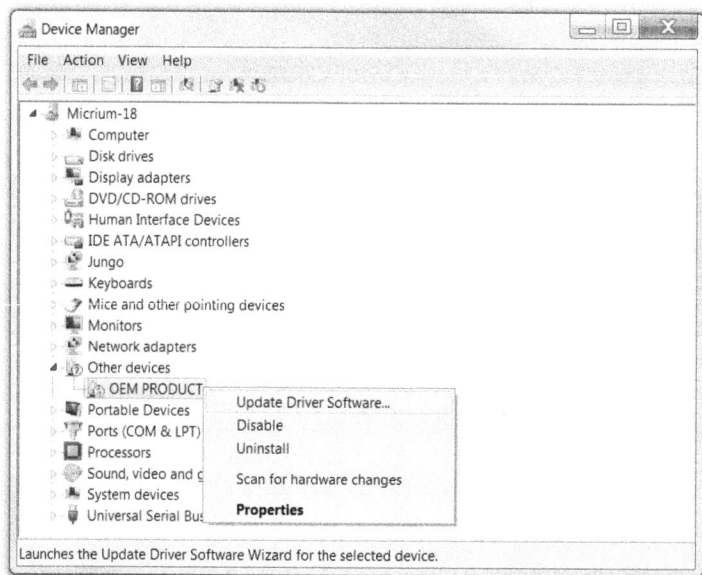

Launches the Update Driver Software Wizard for the selected device.

Figure 8-7 **Windows Device Manager**

In order to install the device with the appropriate driver, you need to provide Windows with the newly updated INF file. In order to do so, right-click over the device's name on the Device Manager list and select *Update Driver Software* as shown in Figure 8-7.

Windows will launch a series of dialogs to specify the driver's options. Select the option to *Browse my computer for driver software* as shown in Figure 8-8:

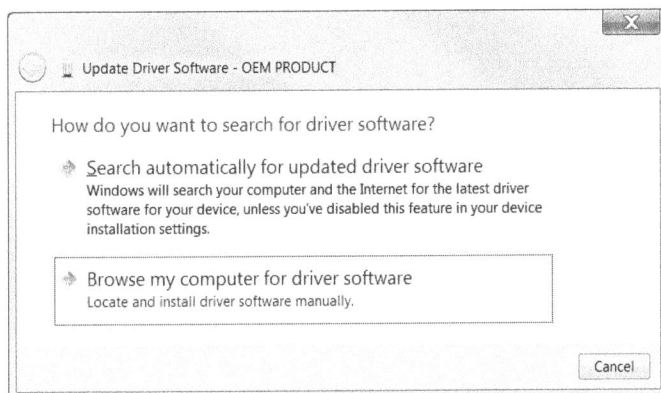

Figure 8-8 **Update Driver Software: Browse**

Browse to the path where you saved the newly updated INF file WinUSB_single.inf as shown in Figure 8-9:

Figure 8-9 **Update Driver Software: INF File Path**

Windows will probably give you a warning message because the driver has not been digitally signed. It is safe to ignore the warning and select *Install this driver software anyway* as shown in Figure 8-10:

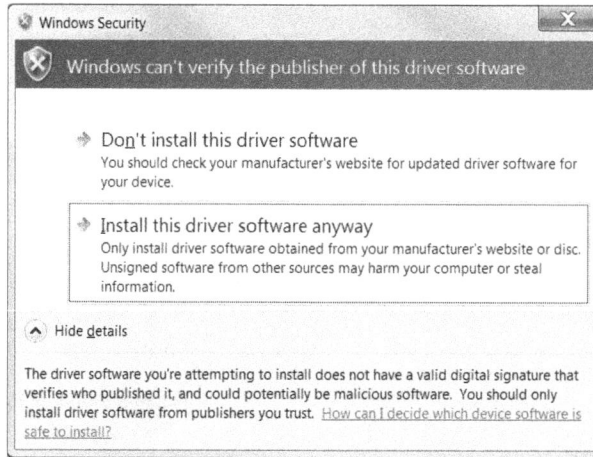

Figure 8-10 **Update Driver Software: Warning Message**

Windows will take a few seconds while it installs the new PHDC device and makes a copy of the INF file into the directory `$\Windows\inf`.

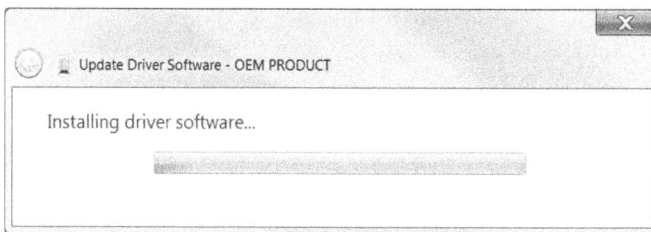

Figure 8-11 **Update Driver Software: Installing**

Windows will finish the installation by displaying the message box shown in Figure 8-12:

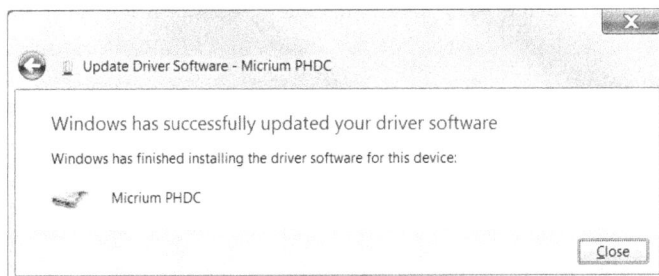

Figure 8-12 **Update Driver Software: Finish**

You should see now a new entry in your Device Manager under the group *USB Sample Class* similar to the one shown in Figure 8-13:

Figure 8-13 **Device Manager Showing the Newly Installed Device**

745

8-4-5 TESTING THE NEW PHDC DEVICE

Now that the PHDC device has been installed successfully, you can exercise the µC/USB-Device stack and its PHDC class by using the *PHDC Monitor* included with the Book's companion software.

The PHDC Monitor is a Windows application distributed in the form of a Visual Studio project. You can either try executing the file located at:

$\Micrium\Software\uC-USB-Device-V4\App\Host\OS\Windows\PHDC\Visual Studio 2010\exe\PHDC.exe

Or, you can rebuild the executable by opening the Visual Studio solution file located at:

$\Micrium\Software\uC-USB-Device-V4\App\Host\OS\Windows\PHDC\Visual Studio 2010\PHDC.sln

The PHDC Monitor shown in Figure 8-14 is a console application that allows you to exercise the µC/USB-Device and PHDC class running on the YRDKRX63N by:

- Sending commands to the YRDKRX63N to continuously send data of different QoS level and using a given periodicity.

- Compute and display traffic statistics such as Mean and Standard Deviation for each of the data transfers.

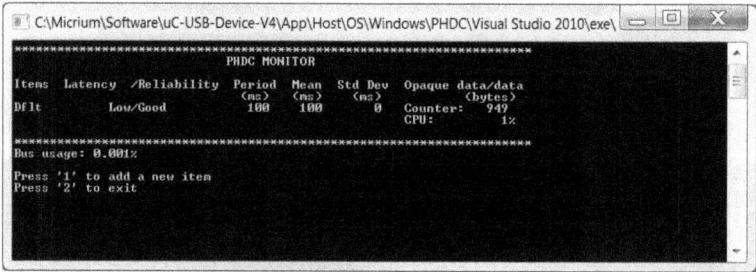

Figure 8-14 **PHDC Monitor Console Application**

Each request to send data at a certain QoS and periodicity is called a *Data Item*. Table 8-2 shows the properties of each *Data Item*:

Property Name	Description	Example
Periodicity	Periodicity of the transfer	100 ms
QoS	Quality of Service (Latency/Reliability of the transfer)	Low/Good
Opaque Data	Application data that is not visible to the PHDC class.	"Opaque Data"
Data	Data that is visible to the PHDC class.	"Data"

Table 8-2 **Data Item Properties**

When you first execute the PHDC monitor, the application sends a command to the YRDKRX63N to create a default item at a QoS level of *Low/Good* and a periodicity of *100 ms*. You can create more items to evaluate different QoS levels by pressing '1' at the console.

The console application will prompt you for the properties of the item as shown in Figure 8-15

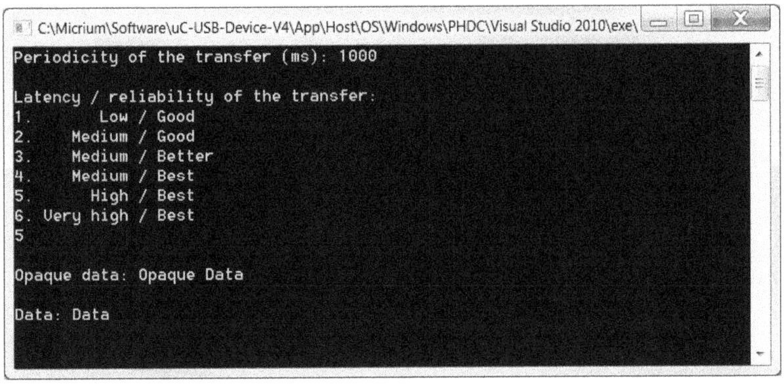

```
C:\Micrium\Software\uC-USB-Device-V4\App\Host\OS\Windows\PHDC\Visual Studio 2010\exe\
Periodicity of the transfer (ms): 1000

Latency / reliability of the transfer:
1.       Low / Good
2.    Medium / Good
3.    Medium / Better
4.    Medium / Best
5.      High / Best
6. Very high / Best
5

Opaque data: Opaque Data

Data: Data
```

Figure 8-15 **PHDC Monitor Adding an Item**

Try adding more items to evaluate different QoS and periodicities, you can end up with a console application similar to the one shown in Figure 8-16:

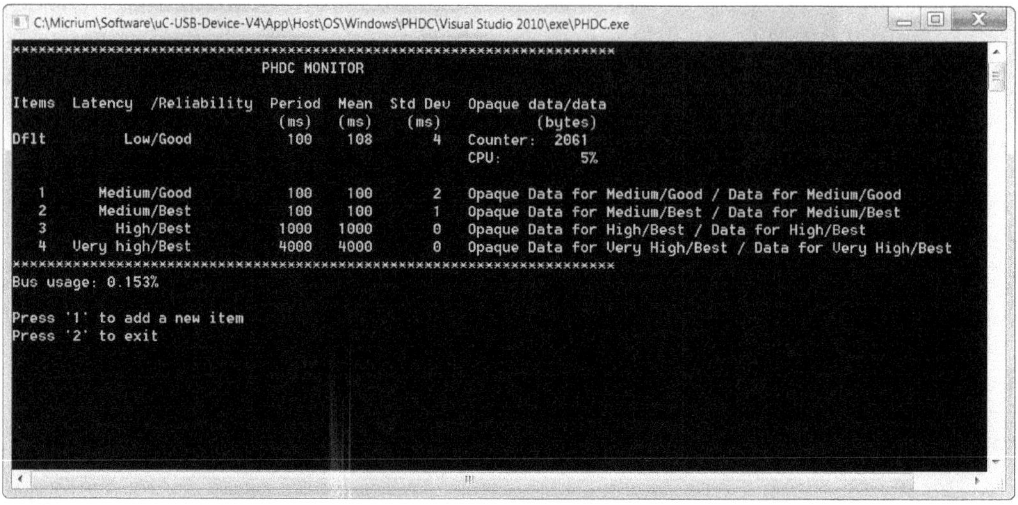

Figure 8-16 **PHDC Monitor Multiple Items**

8-5 HOW THE CODE WORKS

The PHDC class example is implemented in **app_usbd_phdc_multiple.c** in the form of a Reception Task named **App_USBD_PHDC_RxCommTask()** and one or more Transmission Task(s) named **App_USBD_PHDC_TxCommTask()** as illustrated in Figure 8-17:

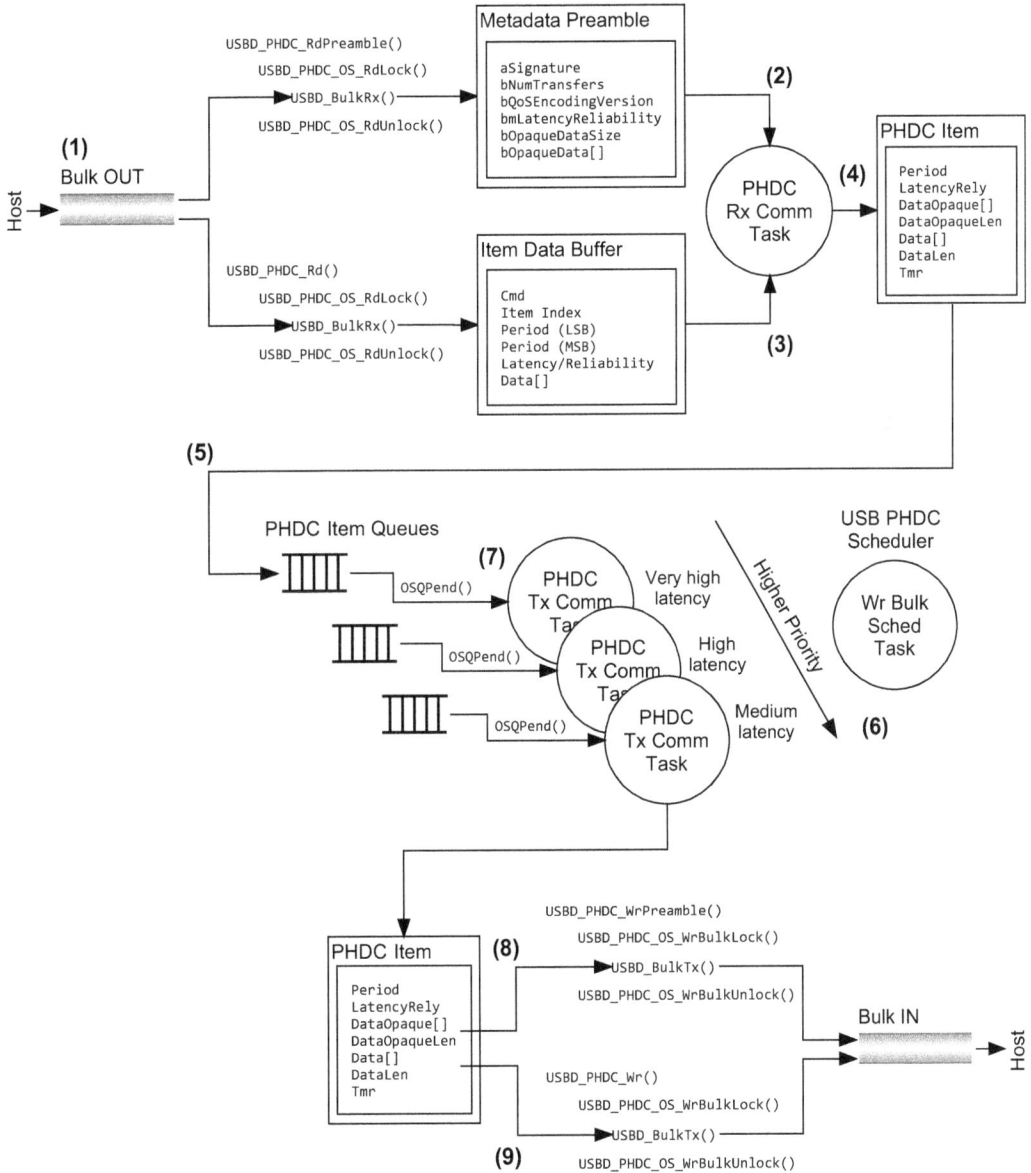

Figure 8-17 **PHDC Class Example**

F8-17(1)   This example features PHDC transfers with a QoS of very high, high and medium latency. Therefore, the operational model requires from the RX63N a Bulk OUT endpoint and a Bulk IN endpoint as described in the PHDC section 11-1-2 "Operational Model" on page 242.

F8-17(2)   The μC/OS-III task responsible for all QoS data receptions is implemented by the function `App_USBD_PHDC_RxCommTask()` in `app_usbd_phdc_multiple.c`.

The metadata message preamble is disabled by default, and only the host can enable or disable it. If enabled, the `RxCommTask` will read the preamble by calling the function `USBD_PHDC_RdPreamble()` in order to learn not only the QoS of the next transfer, but also the number of transfers to which this QoS applies, among other settings. For more information on the metadata message preamble see Table 11-3, "Metadata Preamble," on page 243.

F8-17(3)   The next transfer by the host is the actual data which contains not only the command to add a new item to the test, but also the new item's properties such as QoS and periodicity. The `RxCommTask` calls the function `USBD_PHDC_Rd()` to read this data. For more information on this function see the PHDC API reference in section F-1-9 "USBD_PHDC_Rd()" on page 531.

F8-17(4)   The `RxCommTask` creates a new PHDC item with the information from the last received message's preamble and data.

F8-17(5)   The PHDC item gets inserted into a queue. Part of the PHDC item includes a one-shot timer responsible for posting a signal at timeout according to the item's periodicity.

F8-17(6)   One of the nicest features of Micrium's implementation of the PHDC class is the ability to have one transmission task in charge of only transfers of certain QoS level. Therefore, in this example you can have as many `TxCommTasks` as QoS levels. The PHDC class includes an internal task that is responsible for scheduling the use of the bulk IN endpoint for data transfers to the host. The PHDC scheduler will give more priority to those transfers that require a lower latency. The PHDC scheduler is OS-dependent and it is implemented at the OS layer in the function `USBD_PHDC_OS_WrBulkSchedTask()` in `usbd_phdc_os.c`.

F8-17(7)   The `TxCommTask` waits for a signal to de-queue the next item to transmit. The periodicity of items transmission is defined by the PHDC item's timer and the task is allowed to use the bulk IN endpoint by the PHDC scheduler according to its QoS.

F8-17(8) In similar fashion to the receptions task, the **TxCommTask** transmits a metadata message preamble if enabled by the host. The preamble contains the item's opaque data and it is transmitted by calling the function **USBD_PHDC_WrPreamble()**.

F8-17(9) The **TxCommTask** prepares the data to transmit by incrementing a counter and reading the current CPU usage. These two readings are part of the message data and get transmitted by calling the function **USBD_PHDC_Wr()**.

8-5-1 INITIALIZATION

The function to initialize the PHDC class and example is declared at the application level in the file **app_usbd_phdc_multiple.c.** The following code listings describe the initialization process:

```
CPU_BOOLEAN  App_USBD_PHDC_Init (CPU_INT08U  dev_nbr,
                                 CPU_INT08U  cfg_hs,
                                 CPU_INT08U  cfg_fs)

{
    CPU_BOOLEAN         valid_cfg_fs;
    CPU_INT08U          cnt;
    USBD_ERR            err;
    OS_ERR              os_err;
    OS_TICK             tmr_period;
    LATENCY_RELY_FLAGS  latency_rely_flags;
    APP_USBD_PHDC_ITEM  *p_dflt_item;

    USBD_PHDC_Init(&err);                    /*------------- INIT PHDC --------------- */  (1)
    if (err != USBD_ERR_NONE) {
        return (DEF_FAIL);
    }
                                             /* Add PHDC instance.                 */  (2)
    App_USBD_PHDC_ClassNbr = USBD_PHDC_Add(DEF_NO,
                                           DEF_YES,
                                           App_USBD_PHDC_SetPreambleEn,
                                           10,
                                           &err);

    if (err != USBD_ERR_NONE) {
        return (DEF_FAIL);
    }
    .
    .
    .
```

Listing 8-3 **Initializing the PHDC Example**

L8-3(1)   The **USBD_PHDC_Init()** function is declared in **usbd_phdc.c** and it is used to initialize all internal structures and variables that the class needs. For more information on this function, consult the PHDC API reference on section F-1-1 "USBD_PHDC_Init()" on page 516.

L8-3(2)   The **USBD_PHDC_Add()** function is also declared in **usbd_phdc.c** and it is responsible for creating a new PHDC class instance. If there is not any errors during the allocation, the function returns a number that is assigned to a global variable **App_USBD_PHDC_ClassNbr** for identification purposes.

The next step in the initialization process is to configure the read and write pipes with the correct QoS and opaque data as shown in code Listing 8-4:

```
    .
    .
    .
    latency_rely_flags = USBD_PHDC_LATENCY_VERYHIGH_RELY_BEST  |
                         USBD_PHDC_LATENCY_HIGH_RELY_BEST      |
                         USBD_PHDC_LATENCY_MEDIUM_RELY_BEST;
                                 /* Cfg rd xfers with all possible latency/rely flags.  */
    USBD_PHDC_RdCfg(App_USBD_PHDC_ClassNbr,
                    latency_rely_flags,
                    App_USBD_PHDC_OpaqueDataRx,
                    sizeof(App_USBD_PHDC_OpaqueDataRx),
                    &err);                                                             (1)

    if (err != USBD_ERR_NONE) {
        return (DEF_FAIL);
    }

    latency_rely_flags = USBD_PHDC_LATENCY_VERYHIGH_RELY_BEST  |
                         USBD_PHDC_LATENCY_HIGH_RELY_BEST      |
                         USBD_PHDC_LATENCY_MEDIUM_RELY_BEST    |
                         USBD_PHDC_LATENCY_MEDIUM_RELY_BETTER  |
                         USBD_PHDC_LATENCY_MEDIUM_RELY_GOOD;
                                 /* Cfg very high, high and medium xfers with metadata. */
    USBD_PHDC_WrCfg(App_USBD_PHDC_ClassNbr,
                    latency_rely_flags,
                    App_USBD_PHDC_OpaqueDataTx,
                    sizeof(App_USBD_PHDC_OpaqueDataTx),
                    &err);                                                             (2)
```

```
    if (err != USBD_ERR_NONE) {
        return (DEF_FAIL);
    }
                                    /* Cfg low latency xfers with specific metadadata.    */
    USBD_PHDC_WrCfg(App_USBD_PHDC_ClassNbr,
                    USBD_PHDC_LATENCY_LOW_RELY_GOOD,
                    App_USBD_PHDC_OpaqueDataTxLowLatency,
                    sizeof(App_USBD_PHDC_OpaqueDataTxLowLatency),
                    &err);                                                         (3)


    if (err != USBD_ERR_NONE) {
        return (DEF_FAIL);
    }
    .
    .
    .
```

Listing 8-4 **Configuring the QoS**

L8-4(1)   The function **USBD_PHDC_RdCfg( )** is also part of **usbd_phdc.c.** The function is responsible for configuring the communication pipe that will carry the data from the host to the device. The function takes arguments such as the QoS and a pointer to the opaque data buffer among others. The latencies configured in this step (very high, high and medium) require a Bulk OUT pipe from the RX63N.

L8-4(2)   The function **USBD_PHDC_WrCfg( )** is very similar to the previous one, except that it configures the pipe that carries data from the device to the host. The types of latencies configured in this step (very high, high and medium) require a Bulk IN pipe from the RX63N.

L8-4(3)   Low latency data transfers from the device to the host such as those for real-time monitoring and/or high sampling rate are accomplished by using an Interrupt IN pipe. In this step the function **USBD_PHDC_WrCfg( )** is called to configure such pipe.

The next step in the initialization process is adding the new PHDC instance to the full-speed device configuration as shown in Listing 8-5:

```
     .
     .
     .
   valid_cfg_fs = USBD_PHDC_CfgAdd(App_USBD_PHDC_ClassNbr,
                              dev_nbr,
                              cfg_fs,
                              &err);          /* Add PHDC class to FS dflt cfg.      */

   if (valid_cfg_fs == DEF_NO) {
       return (DEF_FAIL);
   }
     .
     .
     .
```

Listing 8-5 Adding the PHDC Class Instance to the Full-Speed Configuration

The last series of steps in the initialization process is the actual application initialization. The first thing to do is to create the *default item*. If you recall from section section 8-4-5 "Testing the New PHDC Device" on page 746, when you first start the console application, it already has a default item configured at a periodicity of 100-ms and a QoS level of low latency / good reliability. Code   shows the part where the function **App_USBD_PHDC_Init()** creates the default item:

```
     .
     .
     .
                                    /* --------------- INIT APP ----------------- */
                                    /* Init dflt item.                            */
   p_dflt_item                  = &App_USBD_PHDC_Items[0];
   p_dflt_item->Period          = APP_USBD_PHDC_ITEM_DFLT_PERIOD;
   p_dflt_item->LatencyRely     = USBD_PHDC_LATENCY_LOW_RELY_GOOD;
   p_dflt_item->DataLen         = APP_USBD_PHDC_ITEM_DATA_LEN_MIN + 3;
   p_dflt_item->DataOpaqueLen   = 0;
   p_dflt_item->Data[1]         = 0;          /* See Note 1 of APPLICATION ITEM section.   */
   p_dflt_item->Data[2]         = (CPU_INT08U)APP_USBD_PHDC_ITEM_DFLT_PERIOD;
   p_dflt_item->Data[3]         = (CPU_INT08U)(APP_USBD_PHDC_ITEM_DFLT_PERIOD >> 8);
   p_dflt_item->Data[5]         = 0;          /* Ctr value, 0 by dflt.           */
   p_dflt_item->Data[6]         = 0;
   p_dflt_item->Data[7]         = OSStatTaskCPUUsage;
```

```
tmr_period = ((((OS_TICK)APP_USBD_PHDC_ITEM_DFLT_PERIOD *
                     OSCfg_TmrTaskRate_Hz)  + 1000u - 1u) / 1000u);

                                    /* Create tmr for dflt item.              */
OSTmrCreate(             &p_dflt_item->Tmr,
            (CPU_CHAR *)0,
                         tmr_period,
            (OS_TICK  )0,
                         OS_OPT_TMR_ONE_SHOT,
                         App_USBD_PHDC_TmrCallback,
            (void     *)p_dflt_item,
                         &os_err);

if (os_err != OS_ERR_NONE) {
    APP_TRACE_DBG(("Could not add default item timer w/err = %d\r\n", os_err));
    return (DEF_FAIL);
}
.
.
.
```

Listing 8-6 **Creating the Default Item**

Depending on the maximum number of PHDC priorities, the initialization function creates a µC/OS-III-based message queue that will hold the next item to transmit. The µC/OS-III function **OSQCreate( )** is used to allocate the new message queues as shown in Listing 8-7:

```
                                    /* Create one Q per xfer priority.        */
for (cnt = 0; cnt < APP_USBD_PHDC_MAX_NBR_PRIO; cnt++) {
    OSQCreate(&App_USBD_PHDC_ItemQ[cnt],
              "PHDC application item Q",
               APP_USBD_PHDC_ITEM_Q_NBR_MAX,
              &os_err);
    if (os_err != OS_ERR_NONE) {
        APP_TRACE_DBG(("Could not create item Q w/err = %d\r\n", os_err));
        return (DEF_FAIL);
    }
}
```

Listing 8-7 **Creating the Message Queues**

If you recall from the annotation on figure F8-17(2) on page 750, the **RxCommTask** is responsible for all data reception transfers and this part of the code creates this task:

```
                                    /* Create task that will handle rd procedures. */
        OSTaskCreate(       &App_USBD_PHDC_RxCommTaskTCB,
                            "USB Device PHDC rx comm",
                            App_USBD_PHDC_RxCommTask,
                   (void *)App_USBD_PHDC_ClassNbr,
                            APP_CFG_USBD_PHDC_RX_COMM_TASK_PRIO,
                            &App_USBD_PHDC_RxCommTaskStk[0],
                            APP_CFG_USBD_PHDC_TASK_STK_SIZE / 10u,
                            APP_CFG_USBD_PHDC_TASK_STK_SIZE,
                            0u,
                            0u,
                   (void *)0,
                            OS_OPT_TASK_STK_CHK | OS_OPT_TASK_STK_CLR,
                            &os_err);

    if (os_err != OS_ERR_NONE) {
        APP_TRACE_DBG(("Could not add PHDC rx comm task w/err = %d\r\n", os_err));
        return (DEF_FAIL);
    }
```

Listing 8-8 Creating the RxCommTask

Finally, in similar fashion to the creation of the message queues, the initialization process finishes by creating one **TxCommTask** per PHDC priority as shown in Code Listing 8-9:

```
                                       /* Create one tx task per prio (QoS).        */
    for (cnt = 0; cnt < APP_USBD_PHDC_MAX_NBR_PRIO; cnt++) {
        OSTaskCreate(       &App_USBD_PHDC_TxCommTaskTCB[cnt],
                            "USB Device PHDC tx comm",
                            App_USBD_PHDC_TxCommTask,
                   (void *)cnt,
                            APP_CFG_USBD_PHDC_TX_COMM_TASK_PRIO,
                            &App_USBD_PHDC_TxCommTaskStk[cnt][0],
                            APP_CFG_USBD_PHDC_TASK_STK_SIZE / 10u,
                            APP_CFG_USBD_PHDC_TASK_STK_SIZE,
                            0u,
                            0u,
                   (void *)0,
                            OS_OPT_TASK_STK_CHK | OS_OPT_TASK_STK_CLR,
                            &os_err);

        if (os_err != OS_ERR_NONE) {
            APP_TRACE_DBG(("Could not add PHDC tx comm task w/err = %d\r\n", os_err));
            return (DEF_FAIL);
        }
    }

    return (DEF_OK);
}
```

Listing 8-9 **Creating the TxCommTask(s)**

8-6 ANALYZING THE USB TRAFFIC

In order to capture USB traffic, you need to connect the Beagle USB 480 as illustrated in Figure 2-12, "Beagle USB 480 Protocol Analyzer: Connections," on page 640.

When monitoring USB traffic, it is best to attach the Beagle USB 480's analysis side and start the capture *before* attaching the YRDKRX63N. That means that before starting a capture, make sure the USB cable on J9 of the YRDKRX63N is disconnected from the Beagle USB 480 capture side. This allows the Beagle USB 480 to capture the descriptor information that is communicated during the enumeration phase.

Start the Total Phase Data Center software by using the shortcut created during Setup section 2-1-4 "Total Phase Data Center Software" on page 630 or, go to the folder where the software package was extracted and run *Data Center.exe*.

Figure 8-18 **Data Center Software Icon**

Once the application starts it will detect the Beagle and will connect it automatically.

You can tell the Beagle USB 480 is properly connected by looking at the LEDs on the top which should have the Red and Green LEDs lit up.

Press *Ctrl+R* or click the *Run Capture* button in the toolbar to start the capture.

You should see a couple of new rows in the grid that read something like *Capture Started*.

At this point, you can attach the PHDC device by connecting the USB cable on J9 of the YRDKRX63N.

Complete the installation of the PHDC device by following the steps described in the previous section section 8-4-4 "Installing the PHDC Device" on page 740 and then proceed to send the default item by following the instructions in section 8-4-5 "Testing the New PHDC Device" on page 746.

As traffic is seen on the bus, it will be displayed in real-time in the *transactions grid*. The first transactions you should see are those common to all USB classes during the process of enumeration, which is described in Appendix C, "The Enumeration Process" on page 811.

8-6-1 GET CONFIGURATION DESCRIPTOR

The *Get Configuration Descriptor* shown below in Figure 8-19, specifies one of the configurations available, which for the majority of devices is usually no more than one. The *Get Configuration Descriptor* includes interface descriptors and endpoint descriptors that further describe the available interfaces and endpoints respectively. In this example there is only one configuration that includes one interface and three endpoints.

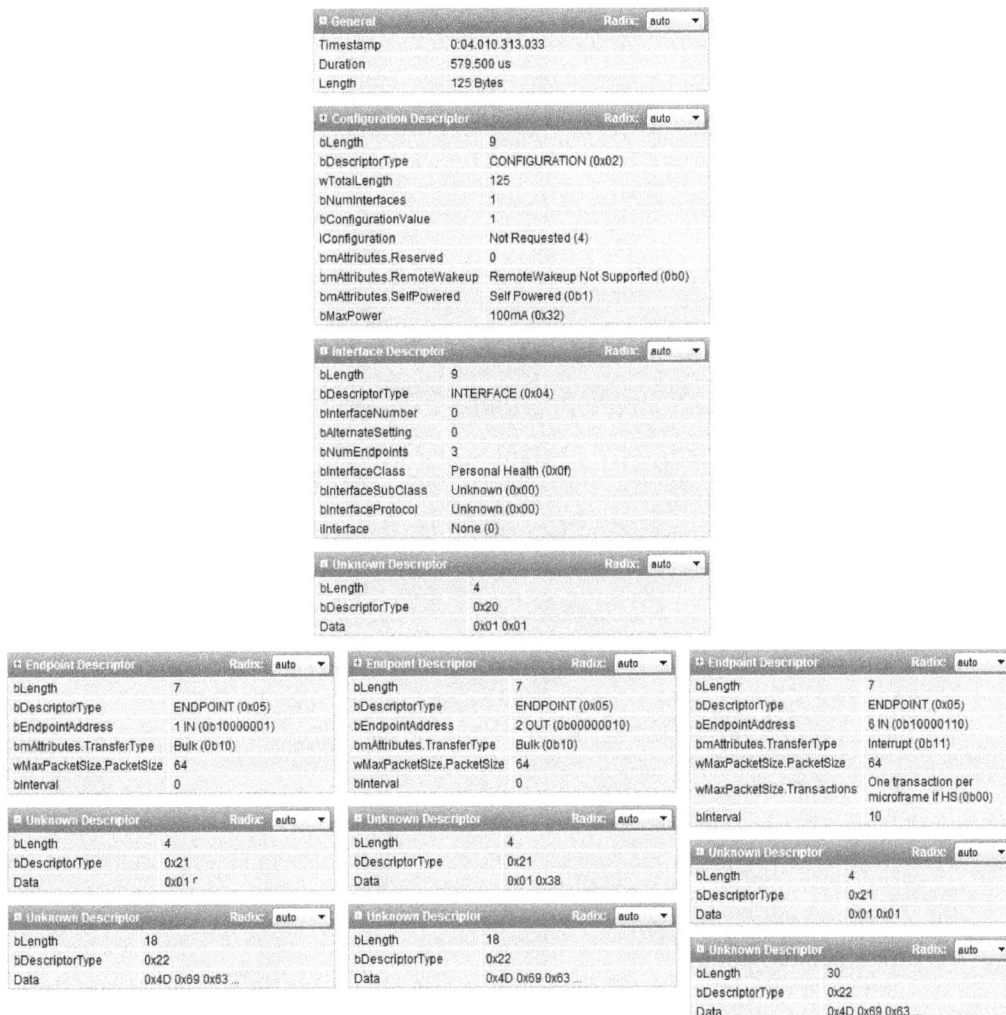

Figure 8-19 **Get Configuration Descriptor Capture**

Notice that some of the descriptors are not decoded correctly by the software due to its current limited support of the PHDC class.

They are the PHDC QoS and meta-data descriptors titled as *unknown descriptor.*

Once the host issues a *Set Configuration* request as described in Appendix C, "Set Configuration" on page 818, the enumeration process is finished and a summary of the enumeration is provided by the Data Center software. Open the enumeration summary by opening the *Navigator* window and selecting the *Bus* tab and the *Enumeration* tab as shown in Figure 8-20:

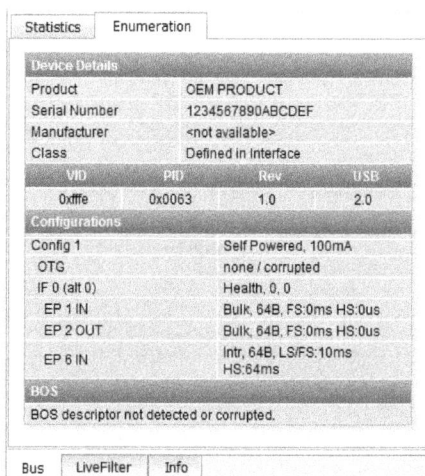

Statistics	Enumeration		
Device Details			
Product	OEM PRODUCT		
Serial Number	1234567890ABCDEF		
Manufacturer	<not available>		
Class	Defined in Interface		
VID	**PID**	**Rev**	**USB**
0xfffe	0x0063	1.0	2.0
Configurations			
Config 1	Self Powered, 100mA		
OTG	none / corrupted		
IF 0 (alt 0)	Health, 0, 0		
EP 1 IN	Bulk, 64B, FS:0ms HS:0us		
EP 2 OUT	Bulk, 64B, FS:0ms HS:0us		
EP 6 IN	Intr, 64B, LS/FS:10ms HS:64ms		
BOS			
BOS descriptor not detected or corrupted.			

Bus	LiveFilter	Info

Figure 8-20 **PHDC Enumeration Summary**

Notice how the configuration includes the three endpoints configured by the part of `App_USBD_PHDC_Init()` shown in Code section Listing 8-4 "Configuring the QoS" on page 753.

If the enumeration process is successful and you scroll down the transactions grid you will find a record named *Control Transfer* which is described in the first part of the book in the section "Control Transfers" on page 49, and it is shown in Figure 8-21:

Sp	Index	m:s.ms.us	Len	Err	Dev	Ep	Record
FS ✦	440	0:45.298.406	0 B		08	00	◢ ⎙ Control Transfer
FS ✦	441	0:45.298.406	8 B		08	00	◢ ⎙ SETUP txn
FS ✦	442	0:45.298.406	3 B		08	00	O SETUP packet
FS ✦	443	0:45.298.409	11 B		08	00	▦ DATA0 packet
FS ✦	444	0:45.298.418	1 B		08	00	✓ ACK packet
FS ✦	445	0:45.298.427	0 B		08	00	◢ ⎙ IN txn [1 POLL]
FS ✦	446	0:45.298.427	4.00 us		08	00	⊟ [1 IN-NAK]
FS ✦	447	0:45.298.510	3 B		08	00	O IN packet
FS ✦	448	0:45.298.513	3 B		08	00	▦ DATA1 packet
FS ✦	449	0:45.298.516	1 B		08	00	✓ ACK packet

Figure 8-21 **PHDC Control Transfer**

The capture of this control transfer represents the moment when the PHDC monitor console application running on the host computer, opens a pipe.

In this case, the pipe opened by the host is the one that leads to endpoint 6, which according to the RX63N hardware manual corresponds to an Interrupt IN endpoint.

If you recall from the PHDC section 11-1-2 "Operational Model" on page 242 and section 1-8-3 "Transfers" on page 49, any PHDC data that requires a latency below 100 ms, requires an Interrupt endpoint.

The reason why the host is requesting to open this endpoint is because the only item in the test is the *default item*, which if you recall from the initialization of the application, it was configured at a QoS of low latency / good reliability (see section Listing 8-4 "Configuring the QoS" on page 753).

Right after the control transfer request you should see the Interrupt IN transactions sent every 100 milliseconds through endpoint 6 by the default item as shown in Figure 8-22:.

Sp	Index	m:s.ms.us	Len	Err	Dev	Ep	Record
FS ⬍	450	0:45.403.517	8 B		08	06	▷ 🖥 IN txn
FS ⬍	457	0:45.411.518	8 B		08	06	▷ 🖥 IN txn [12 POLL]
FS ⬍	464	0:45.515.525	8 B		08	06	▷ 🖥 IN txn [12 POLL]
FS ⬍	469	0:45.619.533	8 B		08	06	▷ 🖥 IN txn [12 POLL]
FS ⬍	474	0:45.723.540	8 B		08	06	▷ 🖥 IN txn [12 POLL]
FS ⬍	479	0:45.827.548	8 B		08	06	▷ 🖥 IN txn [12 POLL]
FS ⬍	484	0:45.931.555	8 B		08	06	▷ 🖥 IN txn [12 POLL]
FS ⬍	489	0:46.035.563	8 B		08	06	▷ 🖥 IN txn [12 POLL]
FS ⬍	494	0:46.139.570	8 B		08	06	▷ 🖥 IN txn [12 POLL]
FS ⬍	499	0:46.243.578	8 B		08	06	▷ 🖥 IN txn [12 POLL]
FS ⬍	504	0:46.347.585	8 B		08	06	▷ 🖥 IN txn [12 POLL]
FS ⬍	509	0:46.451.592	8 B		08	06	▷ 🖥 IN txn [12 POLL]
FS ⬍	514	0:46.555.600	8 B		08	06	▷ 🖥 IN txn [12 POLL]
FS ⬍	519	0:46.659.608	8 B		08	06	▷ 🖥 IN txn [12 POLL]
FS ⬍	524	0:46.763.615	8 B		08	06	▷ 🖥 IN txn [12 POLL]
FS ⬍	529	0:46.867.622	8 B		08	06	▷ 🖥 IN txn [12 POLL]
FS ⬍	534	0:46.971.630	8 B		08	06	▷ 🖥 IN txn [12 POLL]
FS ⬍	539	0:47.075.637	8 B		08	06	▷ 🖥 IN txn [12 POLL]
FS ⬍	544	0:47.179.645	8 B		08	06	▷ 🖥 IN txn [12 POLL]
FS ⬍	549	0:47.283.652	8 B		08	06	▷ 🖥 IN txn [12 POLL]

Figure 8-22 **Default Item Transactions**

At this point go ahead and add new items from the PHDC monitor console application for the QoS level you need to evaluate, and notice that if the latency is configured to very high, high and medium, as opposed to the default item's low latency, then the transactions will be carried over the bulk endpoint instead of the interrupt endpoint.

Figure 8-23 shows the transactions over the bulk endpoints typically used for items with a QoS above low latencies. The capture was taken after adding a new item with a periodicity of 1000 ms and a QoS of High / Best (Latency / Reliability). Since you have more than one QoS running at the same time, you can use the Data Center Software's filter mechanisms to show only those transactions over the bulk endpoints 1 and 2. Or, you can also apply a filter to exclude any transactions over the interrupt endpoint 6.

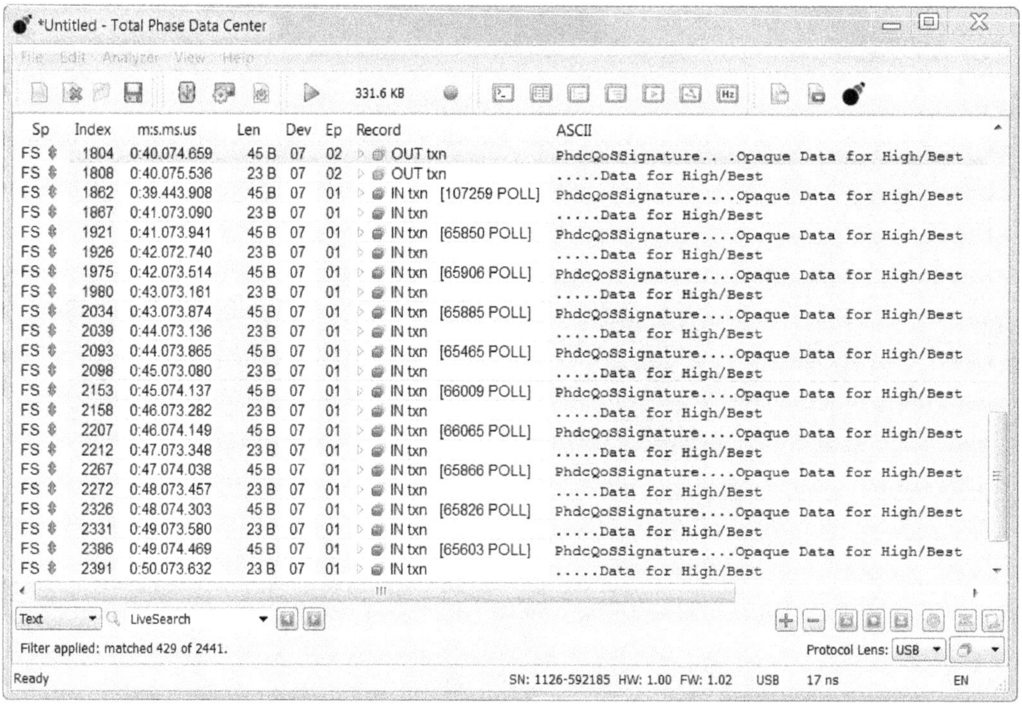

Figure 8-23 **Bulk Transactions**

8-7 SUMMARY

The example featured in this chapter is a great reference for adding USB connectivity to your medical device. It allows you to evaluate the performance of the μC/USB-Device stack and its PHDC class by letting you test the transfer of data at the QoS you expect your biomedical signal to be transferred from the PHDC device.

The chapter showed you how to run the example and then went into explaining how the code works by describing a flow diagram, code listings and USB traffic captures.

9

Example Vendor: Bulk Sync/Async Communications

The μC/USB-Device stack and its Vendor specific class enable USB connectivity among devices that do not necessarily comply with any of the other USB classes described in the previous chapters. The vendor class allows you to specify your own proprietary protocol while maintaining your device under a USB class that is certifiable by the USB implementers forum. The vendor class was presented in Chapter 12, "Vendor Class" on page 263. The chapter finished presenting a demonstration application. This chapter describes how to run the vendor class demonstration example on the YRDKRX63N using e2studio and the Beagle USB 480 protocol analyzer.

The example featured in this book includes not only source code for the embedded application running on the YRDKRX63N, but also a Visual Studio project for the software on the Windows PC as illustrated in Figure 9-1:

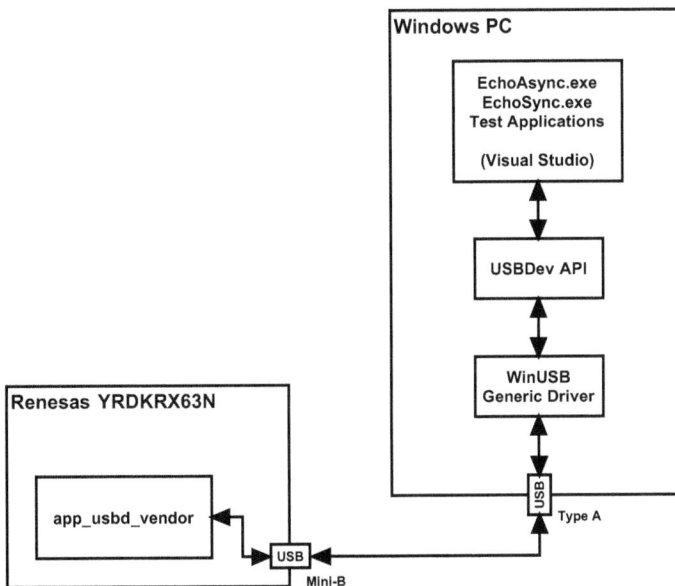

Figure 9-1 **Vendor Class Example**

The example application demonstrates how to transfer data back and forth between the YRDKRX63N and the host using two types of communication:

- Synchronous communication: the transfer blocks the application.

- Asynchronous communication: the transfer does not block the application.

For the sake of brevity, the following sections will describe the example running on asynchronous communication only. However, you can try the same example using a synchronous communication or even both at the same time, by enabling and/or disabling the corresponding configuration macros (section 9-2-1 on page 768). In case you enable both interfaces, you would be creating a composite device.

9-1 LOADING THE PROJECT IN e2studio

In order to load this project you first need to import the C project included in the book's companion software package. You only need to do this once for all the examples and the procedure is described in sections 3-2-1 and 3-2-2 on page 645.

If you already went through that procedure, all you need to do is start e2studio and launch the workspace you created in the path of your choice.

9-2 CONFIGURING THE VENDOR CLASS EXAMPLE

Open the header file **app_cfg.h** from the *Project Explorer* as shown in Figure 9-2:

Figure 9-2 **Project Explorer: Configuration File**

9-2-1 ENABLING AND DISABLING CLASSES

All the examples featured in this book are not only in the same workspace but also in the same project and Code Listing 9-1 shows the lines of code in `app_cfg.h` that need to be edited in order to enable the Vendor class and the example:

```
/*
*********************************************************************************
*                        uC/USB-DEVICE DEMO CONFIGURATION
*********************************************************************************
*/

#define  APP_CFG_USBD_VENDOR_EN                    DEF_ENABLED               (1)
#define  APP_CFG_USBD_CDC_EN                       DEF_DISABLED              (2)
#define  APP_CFG_USBD_HID_EN                       DEF_DISABLED              (3)
#define  APP_CFG_USBD_MSC_EN                       DEF_DISABLED              (4)
#define  APP_CFG_USBD_PHDC_EN                      DEF_DISABLED              (5)

#define  APP_CFG_USBD_VENDOR_ECHO_SYNC_EN          DEF_DISABLED              (6)
#define  APP_CFG_USBD_VENDOR_ECHO_ASYNC_EN         DEF_ENABLED
     .
     .
     .
```

Listing 9-1 **Configuring the Vendor Class Example: app_cfg.h**

L9-1(1)   In order to run the Vendor class example, make sure the Vendor class is enabled by setting **APP_CFG_USBD_VENDOR_EN** to **DEF_ENABLED**.

L9-1(2)   Make sure the CDC class is disabled by setting **APP_CFG_USBD_CDC_EN** to **DEF_DISABLED**.

L9-1(3)   Make sure the HID class is disabled by setting **APP_CFG_USBD_HID_EN** to **DEF_DISABLED**.

L9-1(4)   Make sure the MSC class is disabled by setting **APP_CFG_USBD_MSC_EN** to **DEF_DISABLED**.

L9-1(5)   Make sure the PHDC class is disabled by setting **APP_CFG_USBD_PHDC_EN** to **DEF_DISABLED**.

L9-1(6)   Select the communication type: synchronous and/or asynchronous.

9-3 BUILDING THE VENDOR CLASS EXAMPLE PROJECT

In order to build the project press *Ctrl+B* as described in section 3-2-3 "Building a Project in e2studio" on page 648.

9-4 RUNNING THE VENDOR CLASS EXAMPLE PROJECT

In order to run the example project, you need to follow the next steps including the preparation of an INF file which Windows will use to load one of its own native drivers.

9-4-1 CONNECTING THE BOARD

Connect the board as illustrated in Figure 2-12, "Beagle USB 480 Protocol Analyzer: Connections," on page 640 and make sure that the USB cable on J9 of the YRDKRX63N board *is not* connected yet.

9-4-2 LAUNCHING THE DEBUGGING SESSION

Launch a debugging session as described in section 3-2-5 "Launching a Debug Session in e2studio" on page 655 and press *F8* to let the program run freely.

9-4-3 VERIFYING THE APPLICATION

In order to make sure that you are actually running the Vendor class example, take a look at the LCD screen on the YRDKRX63N as it should look like the one illustrated in Figure 9-3:

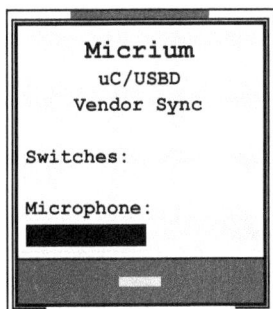

```
APP_CFG_USBD_VENDOR_ECHO_SYNC_EN    DEF_ENABLED
APP_CFG_USBD_VENDOR_ECHO_ASYNC_EN   DEF_DISABLED
```

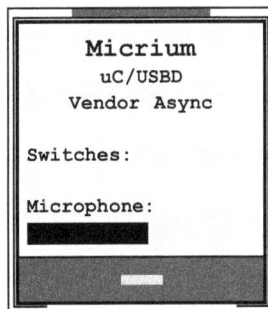

```
APP_CFG_USBD_VENDOR_ECHO_SYNC_EN    DEF_DISABLED
APP_CFG_USBD_VENDOR_ECHO_ASYNC_EN   DEF_ENABLED
```

Figure 9-3 **Vendor Class Example Screen**

The LCD screen also helps you verify that the application is running correctly as it indicates if any of the 3 push buttons on the YRDKRX63N has been pressed. At the same time, the horizontal bar graph shows the current noise level as detected by the microphone on U16. These two features are implemented in the form of two µC/OS-III tasks. So, if you see anything changing on the LCD screen as you make any noise or press the buttons, it means that µC/OS-III is multi-tasking. Besides that, the LEDs wheel should also be blinking as it is also driven by another µC/OS-III task.

9-4-4 INSTALLING THE VENDOR SPECIFIC DEVICE

At this time, the µC/USB-Device stack should be running and waiting for any USB events, such as connecting the USB device. Go ahead and connect the USB cable from J9 of the YRDKRX63N board and into the Capture Side of the Beagle USB 480 as illustrated in Figure 2-12, "Beagle USB 480 Protocol Analyzer: Connections," on page 640. In case you do not have a USB protocol analyzer, you can still connect the other end of the cable directly into any available USB receptacle on your host computer.

The first time you run the example, the host computer will install the YRDKRX63N as a *Vendor Device.* You will be notified that the device is installing by the typical Windows messages shown in the notification area on the bottom right corner of your desktop as shown in Figure 9-4:

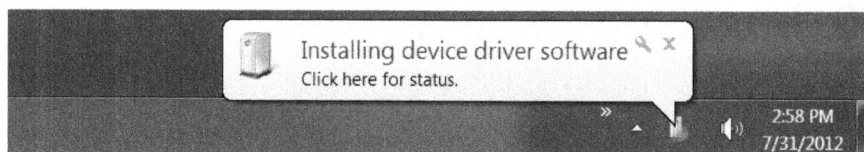

Figure 9-4 **Windows Installing the Vendor Specific Device**

If it is the first time you install the device, Windows will fail to do so, because this particular example, even though it uses one of the Windows native drivers, it requires an INF file to load the driver.

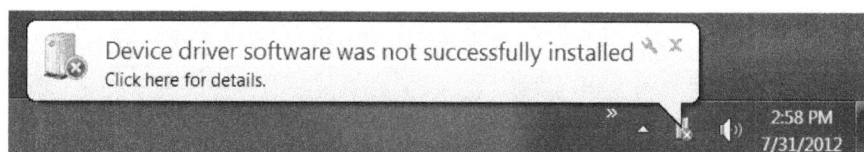

Figure 9-5 **Windows Notifying Failure Installing the Device**

The subject of INF files was briefly described in section 3-1-1 "About INF Files" on page 90. The book companion's software that you installed in section 2-1-5 "µC/USB-Device Book's Companion Software" on page 630 includes the required INF file for this example. You only need to make sure that both the INF file and your Vendor specific device's hardware IDs match. In order to do so, open the following INF file in a text editor such as *Notepad*:

```
$\Micrium\Software\uC-USB-Device-V4\
    App\Host\OS\Windows\Vendor\INF\WinUSB_single.inf
```

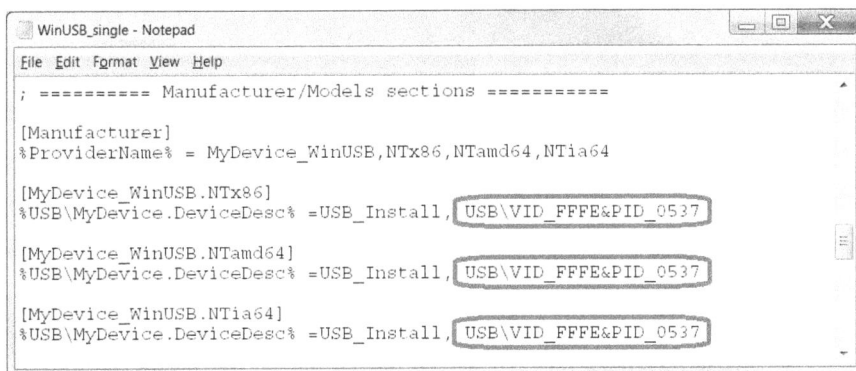

Figure 9-6 **Updating the INF File**

Locate the lines that specify the *Vendor ID* = **FFFEh** and *Product ID* = **0537h** as indicated in Figure 9-6 and make sure that they match with the hardware IDs configured in **usbd_dev_cfg.c** as shown in Code Listing 9-2:

```
/*
******************************************************************************
*                          USB DEVICE CONFIGURATION
******************************************************************************
*/

USBD_DEV_CFG  USBD_DevCfg_RX63N = {
    0xFFFE,                              /* Vendor  ID.                    */
    0x0537,                              /* Product ID (Vendor).           */
    0x0100,                              /* Device release number.         */
    "OEM MANUFACTURER",                  /* Manufacturer  string.          */
    "OEM PRODUCT",                       /* Product       string.          */
    "1234567890ABCDEF",                  /* Serial number string.          */
    USBD_LANG_ID_ENGLISH_US              /* String language ID.            */
};
```

Listing 9-2 **USB Vendor Specific Device Configuration**

If you open Windows Device Manager, you are going to find a new entry for the Vendor specific device that failed to install. Windows lists this device under the group *Other Devices* as shown in Figure 9-7:

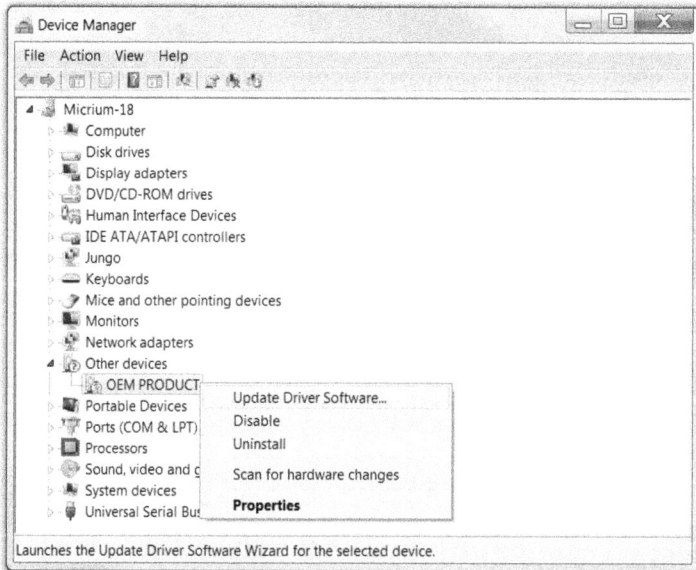

Figure 9-7 **Windows Device Manager**

In order to install the device with the appropriate driver, you need to provide Windows with the newly updated INF file. In order to do so, right-click over the device's name on the Device Manager list and select *Update Driver Software* as shown in Figure 9-7.

Windows will launch a series of dialogs to specify the driver's options. Select the option to *Browse my computer for driver software* as shown in Figure 9-8:

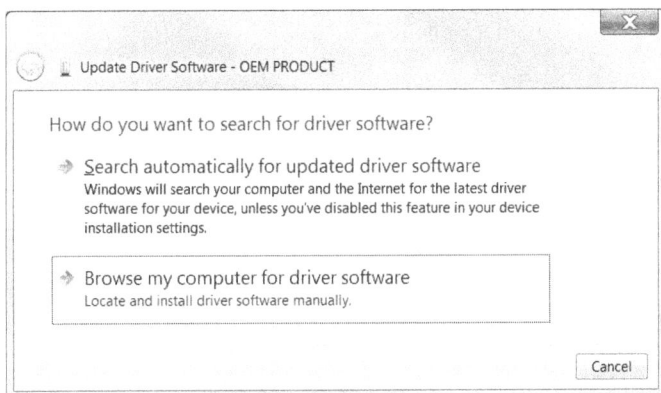

Figure 9-8 **Update Driver Software: Browse**

Browse to the path where you saved the newly updated INF file `WinUSB_single.inf` as shown in Figure 9-9:

Figure 9-9 **Update Driver Software: INF File Path**

Windows will probably give you a warning message because the driver has not been digitally signed. It is safe to ignore the warning and select *Install this driver software anyway* as shown in Figure 9-10:

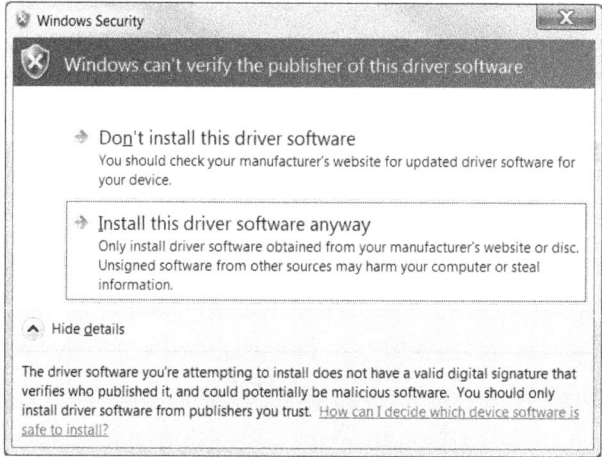

Figure 9-10 **Update Driver Software: Warning Message**

Windows will take a few seconds while it installs the new vendor specific device and makes a copy of the INF file into the directory `$\Windows\inf`.

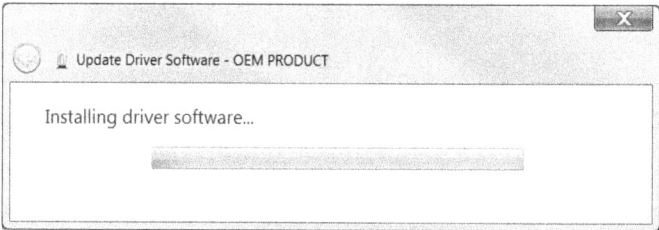

Figure 9-11 **Update Driver Software: Installing**

Windows will finish the installation by displaying the message box shown in Figure 9-12:

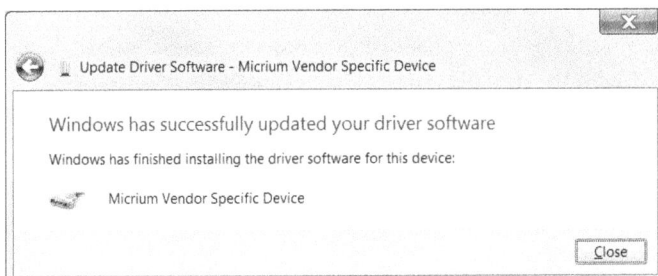

Figure 9-12 **Update Driver Software: Finish**

You should see now a new entry in your Device Manager under the group *USB Sample Class* similar to the one shown in Figure 9-13:

Figure 9-13 **Device Manager Showing the Newly Installed Device**

9-4-5 TESTING THE NEW VENDOR SPECIFIC DEVICE

Now that the Vendor specific device has been installed successfully, you can exercise the µC/USB-Device stack and its vendor class by using the *Echo Sync* or *Echo Async* Console application included with the Book's companion software.

In order to run one or the other you need to execute the appropriate Windows application:

- **EchoSync.exe**: The *Echo Sync* example exercises, by using the synchronous mode of WinUSB, the device's synchronous and/or the asynchronous communication API described in sections section 12-2-4 "Synchronous Communication" on page 269 and section 12-2-5 "Asynchronous Communication" on page 270.

- **EchoAsync.exe**: The *Echo Async* example exercises, by using the asynchronous mode of WinUSB, the device's synchronous and/or the asynchronous communication API described in sections section 12-2-4 "Synchronous Communication" on page 269 and section 12-2-5 "Asynchronous Communication" on page 270.

These Windows applications are distributed in the form of a Visual Studio project. You can either try executing the files located at:

- Windows 64-bit:

  `$\Micrium\Software\uC-USB-Device-V4\App\Host\OS\Windows\Vendor\Visual Studio 2010\exe\x64\`

- Windows 32-bit:

  `$\Micrium\Software\uC-USB-Device-V4\App\Host\OS\Windows\Vendor\Visual Studio 2010\exe\x86\`

Or, you can rebuild the executable with a certain configuration (see Table 12-7, "Windows Application Constants Configuration," on page 281) by opening the Visual Studio solution file located at:

`$\Micrium\Software\uC-USB-Device-V4\App\Host\OS\Windows\Vendor\Visual Studio 2010\Vendor.sln`

The Echo Sync or Echo Async shown in Figure 9-14 is a console application that allows you to exercise the µC/USB-Device and Vendor class running on the YRDKRX63N by sending a data packet and waiting for the echo back in response, similar to network utilities such as *ping*.

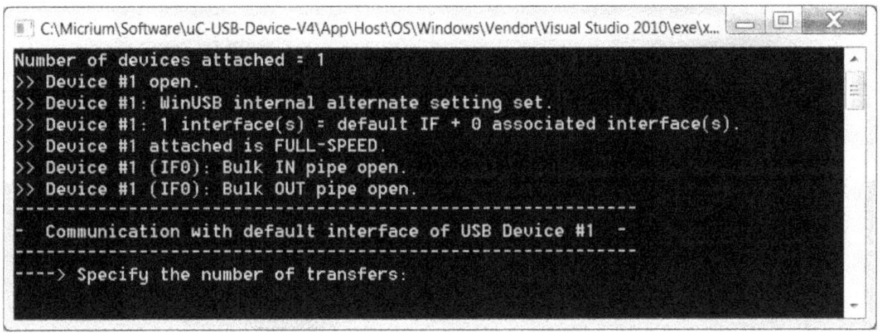

```
■  C:\Micrium\Software\uC-USB-Device-V4\App\Host\OS\Windows\Vendor\Visual Studio 2010\exe\x...
Number of devices attached = 1
>> Device #1 open.
>> Device #1: WinUSB internal alternate setting set.
>> Device #1: 1 interface(s) = default IF + 0 associated interface(s).
>> Device #1 attached is FULL-SPEED.
>> Device #1 (IF0): Bulk IN pipe open.
>> Device #1 (IF0): Bulk OUT pipe open.
-------------------------------------------------------------
- Communication with default interface of USB Device #1  -
-------------------------------------------------------------
---> Specify the number of transfers:
```

Figure 9-14 **Vendor Class Console Application**

When you first execute the Echo Sync or Async console, the application prompts for the number of transfers to test. The image below shows the results of testing 10 transfers:

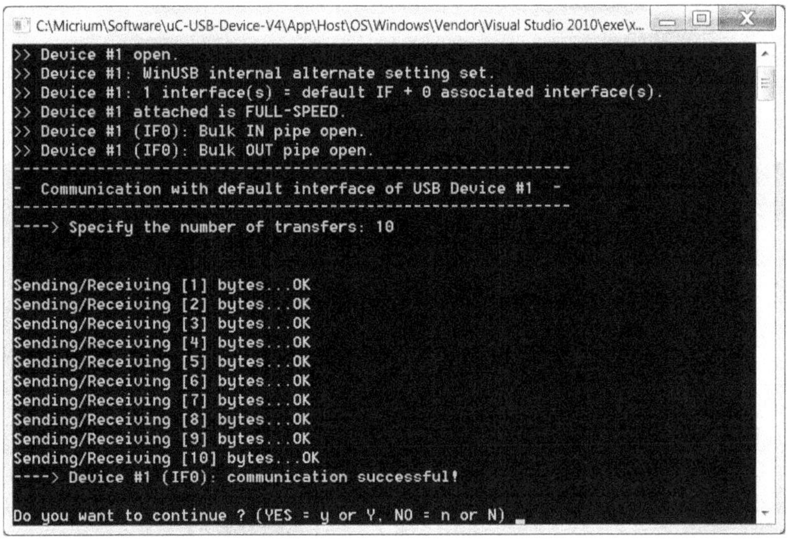

```
■  C:\Micrium\Software\uC-USB-Device-V4\App\Host\OS\Windows\Vendor\Visual Studio 2010\exe\x...
>> Device #1 open.
>> Device #1: WinUSB internal alternate setting set.
>> Device #1: 1 interface(s) = default IF + 0 associated interface(s).
>> Device #1 attached is FULL-SPEED.
>> Device #1 (IF0): Bulk IN pipe open.
>> Device #1 (IF0): Bulk OUT pipe open.
-------------------------------------------------------------
- Communication with default interface of USB Device #1  -
-------------------------------------------------------------
---> Specify the number of transfers: 10

Sending/Receiving [1] bytes...OK
Sending/Receiving [2] bytes...OK
Sending/Receiving [3] bytes...OK
Sending/Receiving [4] bytes...OK
Sending/Receiving [5] bytes...OK
Sending/Receiving [6] bytes...OK
Sending/Receiving [7] bytes...OK
Sending/Receiving [8] bytes...OK
Sending/Receiving [9] bytes...OK
Sending/Receiving [10] bytes...OK
---> Device #1 (IF0): communication successful!

Do you want to continue ? (YES = y or Y, NO = n or N) _
```

Figure 9-15 **Vendor Class Console Application Results**

The image below illustrates the third set of transactions in the test represented on the console by the label *"Sending/Receiving [3] bytes...OK"*:

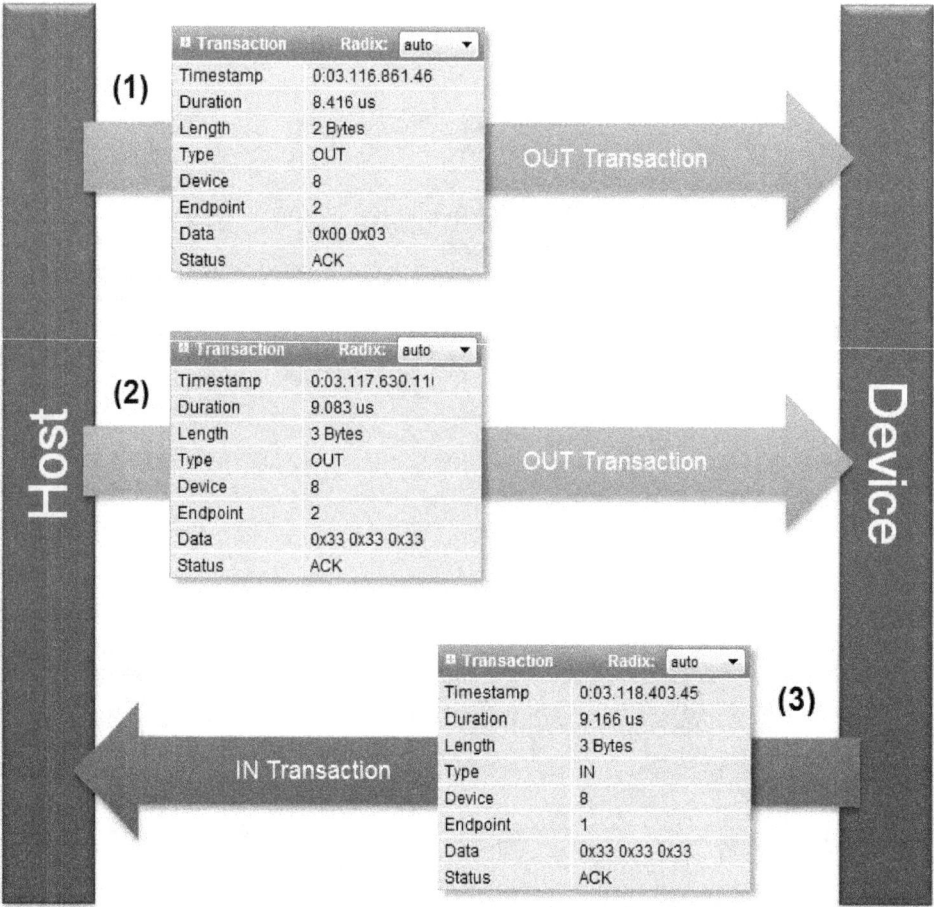

Figure 9-16 **Vendor Class Example**

F9-16(1)   The host initiates the third test by sending a 2-byte message header that contains the number of bytes the payload to follow will have (in this case, since it is the third set in the test, the length of the payload will be 3-bytes).

F9-16(2)   Then, the host sends the actual payload (in this case the ASCII code for the number "3", three times: 0x33 0x33 and 0x33).

F9-16(3)   The device receives the payload and echoes back the same payload.

9-5 HOW THE CODE WORKS

9-5-1 SYNCHRONOUS COMMUNICATION

The Vendor specific class synchronous communication example is implemented in **app_usbd_vendor.c** in the form of a task named *EchoSyncTask* as illustrated below in Figure 9-17:

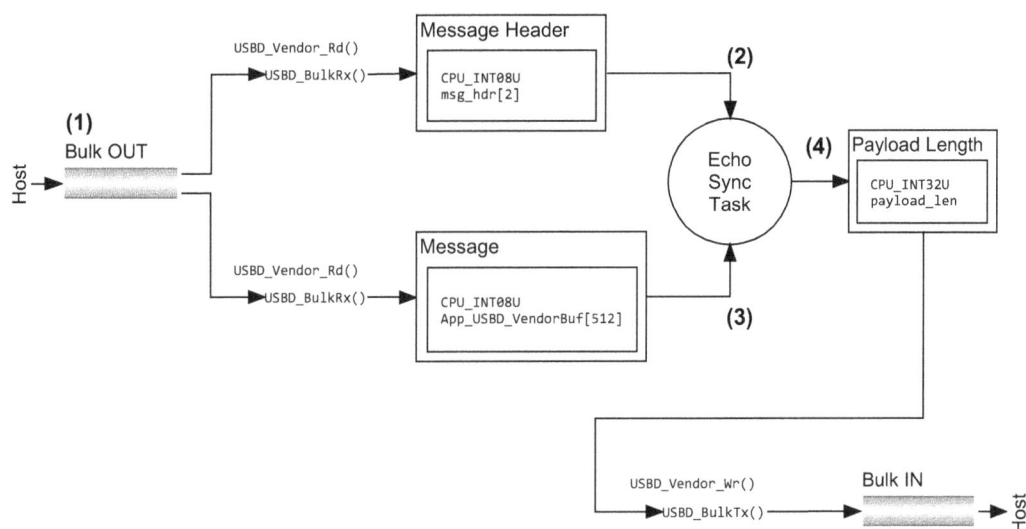

Figure 9-17 **Vendor Class Echo Sync**

F9-17(1)   The operational model for this example requires from the RX63N a Bulk OUT endpoint and a Bulk IN endpoint as described in the Vendor Class section 12-1 "Overview" on page 264.

The host starts by sending a *Message Header* through a bulk OUT pipe.

F9-17(2)   The µC/OS-III task responsible for all the synchronous reception and transmission transactions is implemented in **app_usbd_vendor.c** by the function **App_USBD_Vendor_EchoSyncTask( )**.

The **EchoSyncTask** will read the 2-byte message header by calling the function **USBD_Vendor_Rd( )** in order to learn how many bytes the following payload will have.

F9-17(3)   The next transfer by the host is the actual data payload. The host sends the data in chunks of up to 512-bytes. For each chunk of data, the host waits for a response back with the same chunk of data.

Meanwhile, the device reads the chunk of data by calling the blocking function `App_USBD_Vendor_Rd( )`.

F9-17(4)   The `EchoSyncTask` sends back the same payload by calling the function `App_USBD_Vendor_Wr( )` and it goes back to F9-17(3) to send the next chunk of data until all the payload gets sent.

9-5-2 ASYNCHRONOUS COMMUNICATION

The Vendor specific class asynchronous communication example is also implemented in **app_usbd_vendor.c** in the form of a task named *EchoAsyncTask* and other kernel objects such as the semaphore *EchoAsyncSem* as illustrated in Figure 9-18:

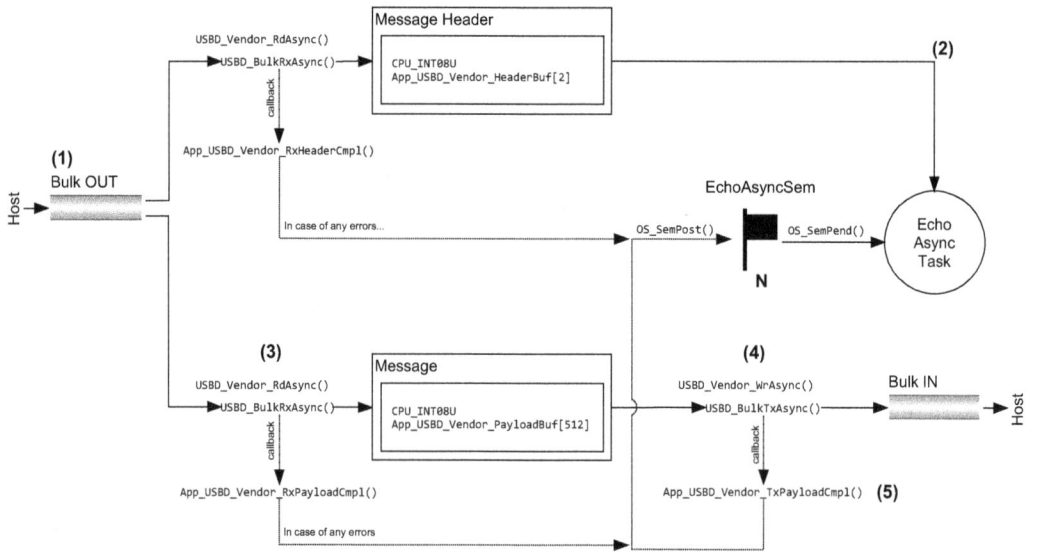

Figure 9-18 **Vendor Class Echo Async**

F9-18(1)   The operational model for this example requires a Bulk OUT endpoint and a Bulk IN endpoint from the RX63N as described in the Vendor Class Chapter 12, "Overview" on page 206. The host starts by sending a Message Header through a bulk OUT pipe.

F9-18(2)   The **EchoAsyncTask** prepares the reception of the message header by calling the non-blocking function **USBD_Vendor_RdAsync()** with a pointer to the header's buffer **App_USBD_Vendor_HeaderBuf[2]** and the name of the callback function **App_USBD_Vendor_RxHeaderCmpl()** which will be called by the device stack on completion.

F9-18(3)   Once the transfer of the message header has completed, the callback function **App_USBD_Vendor_RxHeaderCmpl()** is called by the device stack which in turn, not only parses the message header to calculate the total length of the payload, but also prepares the reception of the payload by calling the non-blocking function **USBD_Vendor_RdAsync()** with a pointer to the payload's buffer **App_USBD_Vendor_PayloadBuf[512]** and the name of the callback function **App_USBD_Vendor_RxPayloadCmpl()**.

F9-18(4)   Once the transfer of the payload, or at least the chunk of data has completed, the callback function **App_USBD_Vendor_RxPayloadCmpl()** is called by the device stack which prepares the transmission of the payload (echo) by calling the non-blocking function **USBD_Vendor_WrAsync()** with a pointer to the chunk of data's buffer **p_buf** and the name of the callback function **App_USBD_Vendor_TxPayloadCmpl()**.

F9-18(5)   Once the transfer of the payload or a chunk of it has completed, the callback function **App_USBD_Vendor_TxPayloadCmpl()** is called by the device stack which in turn, either prepares the reception of the next chunk of data or a new message header.

At the end of each callback function the results of the transactions are evaluated. In case of any errors a signal is posted to the semaphore **App_USBD_Vendor_EchoAsyncSem** which will trigger the task **EchoAsyncTask** to restart the sequence by preparing the reception of the message header over again.

9-5-3 INITIALIZATION

The function to initialize the Vendor specific class and the Echo Sync and Async example is declared at the application level in the file **app_usbd_vendor.c.** The following code listings describe the initialization process:

```
CPU_BOOLEAN  App_USBD_Vendor_Init (CPU_INT08U  dev_nbr,
                                   CPU_INT08U  cfg_hs,
                                   CPU_INT08U  cfg_fs)
{
    USBD_ERR    err;
    USBD_ERR    err_fs;
    CPU_INT08U  class_nbr_0;
#if ((APP_CFG_USBD_VENDOR_ECHO_SYNC_EN  == DEF_ENABLED) || \
     (APP_CFG_USBD_VENDOR_ECHO_ASYNC_EN == DEF_ENABLED))
    OS_ERR      os_err;
#endif
#if ((APP_CFG_USBD_VENDOR_ECHO_SYNC_EN  == DEF_ENABLED) && \
     (APP_CFG_USBD_VENDOR_ECHO_ASYNC_EN == DEF_ENABLED))
    CPU_INT08U  class_nbr_1;
#endif


    err_fs = USBD_ERR_NONE;

    APP_TRACE_DBG(("Initializing Vendor class ... \r\n"));

    USBD_Vendor_Init(&err);                 /* Init Vendor class.         */   (1)
    if (err != USBD_ERR_NONE) {
        APP_TRACE_DBG(("      ... could not initialize Vendor class w/err = %d\r\n\r\n", err));
        return (DEF_FAIL);
    }
                                            /* Create a Vendor class instance.    */   (2)
    class_nbr_0 = USBD_Vendor_Add(DEF_FALSE, 0u, App_USBD_Vendor_VendorReq, &err);
    if (err != USBD_ERR_NONE) {
        APP_TRACE_DBG(("... could not instantiate a Vendor class w/err = %d\r\n\r\n", err));
        return (DEF_FAIL);
    }
    .
    .
    .
```

Listing 9-3 **Initializing the Vendor Specific Example**

L9-3(1)   The **USBD_Vendor_Init()** function is declared in **usbd_vendor.c** and it is used to initialize all internal structures and variables that the class needs. For more information on this function, consult the Vendor Class API reference in section G-1-1 "USBD_Vendor_Init()" on page 548.

L9-3(2)   The **USBD_Vendor_Add( )** function is also declared in **usbd_vendor.c** and it is responsible for creating a new Vendor class instance. If there is not any errors during the allocation, the function returns the class number for identification purposes. Here is also the opportunity to register a callback function where you can implement any vendor-specific processing such as decoding of any proprietary requests.

The next step in the initialization process is adding the new Vendor class instance to the full-speed device configuration as shown in Listing 9-4:

```
                                    /* Add vendor class to FS dflt cfg.      */
    USBD_Vendor_CfgAdd(class_nbr_0, dev_nbr, cfg_fs, &err_fs);
    if (err_fs != USBD_ERR_NONE) {
        APP_TRACE_DBG(("... could not add Vendor class instance #%d to FS
                        configuration w/err = %d\r\n\r\n", class_nbr_0, err_fs));
    }

    if (err_fs != USBD_ERR_NONE) {      /* If FS cfg fails, stop class init.     */
        return (DEF_FAIL);
    }
```

Listing 9-4 **Adding the Vendor Class Instance to the Full-Speed Configuration**

The last series of steps in the initialization process is the actual application initialization. This includes the creation of all the necessary kernel objects such as the tasks and semaphore described in the previous section section 9-5-1 "Synchronous Communication" on page 779 and section section 9-5-2 "Asynchronous Communication" on page 780.

9-6 ANALYZING THE USB TRAFFIC

In order to capture USB traffic, you need to connect the Beagle USB 480 as illustrated in Figure 2-12, "Beagle USB 480 Protocol Analyzer: Connections," on page 640.

When monitoring USB traffic, it is best to attach the Beagle USB 480's analysis side and start the capture *before* attaching the YRDKRX63N. That means that before starting a capture, make sure the USB cable on J9 of the YRDKRX63N is disconnected from the Beagle USB 480 capture side. This allows the Beagle USB 480 to capture the descriptor information that is communicated during the enumeration phase.

Start the Total Phase Data Center software by using the shortcut created during Setup section 2-1-4 "Total Phase Data Center Software" on page 630 or, go to the folder where the software package was extracted and run *Data Center.exe*.

Figure 9-19 **Data Center Software Icon**

Once the application starts it will detect the Beagle and will connect it automatically.

You can tell the Beagle USB 480 is properly connected by looking at the LEDs on the top which should have the Red and Green LEDs lit up.

Press *Ctrl+R* or click the *Run Capture* button in the toolbar to start the capture.

You should see a couple of new rows in the grid that read something like *Capture Started*.

At this point, you can attach the Vendor specific device by connecting the USB cable on J9 of the YRDKRX63N.

Complete the installation of the Vendor specific device by following the steps described in the previous section on section 9-4-4 "Installing the Vendor Specific Device" on page 770.

As traffic is seen on the bus, it will be displayed in real-time in the *transactions grid*. The first transactions you should see are those common to all USB classes during the process of enumeration, which is described in Appendix C, "The Enumeration Process" on page 811.

9-6-1 GET CONFIGURATION DESCRIPTOR

The *Get Configuration Descriptor* shown below in Figure 9-20, specifies one of the configurations available, which for the majority of devices is usually no more than one. The *Get Configuration Descriptor* includes interface descriptors and endpoint descriptors that further describe the available interfaces and endpoints respectively. In this example there is only one configuration with a single interface and two endpoints.

Navigator   ₽ ✕

Get Descriptor

General   Radix: auto ▾

Timestamp	0:05.375.050.050
Duration	239.500 us
Length	32 Bytes

Configuration Descriptor   Radix: auto ▾

bLength	9
bDescriptorType	CONFIGURATION (0x02)
wTotalLength	32
bNumInterfaces	1
bConfigurationValue	1
iConfiguration	Not Requested (4)
bmAttributes.Reserved	0
bmAttributes.RemoteWakeup	RemoteWakeup Not Supported (0b0)
bmAttributes.SelfPowered	Self Powered (0b1)
bMaxPower	100mA (0x32)

Interface Descriptor   Radix: auto ▾

bLength	9
bDescriptorType	INTERFACE (0x04)
bInterfaceNumber	0
bAlternateSetting	0
bNumEndpoints	2
bInterfaceClass	Vendor Specific (0xff)
bInterfaceSubClass	Unknown (0xff)
bInterfaceProtocol	Unknown (0xff)
iInterface	None (0)

Endpoint Descriptor   Radix: auto ▾

bLength	7
bDescriptorType	ENDPOINT (0x05)
bEndpointAddress	1 IN (0b10000001)
bmAttributes.TransferType	Bulk (0b10)
wMaxPacketSize.PacketSize	64
bInterval	0

Endpoint Descriptor   Radix: auto ▾

bLength	7
bDescriptorType	ENDPOINT (0x05)
bEndpointAddress	2 OUT (0b00000010)
bmAttributes.TransferType	Bulk (0b10)
wMaxPacketSize.PacketSize	64
bInterval	0

Figure 9-20 **Get Configuration Descriptor**

A summary of the enumeration process is provided by the Data Center software.

See the enumeration summary by opening the *Navigator* window and selecting the *Bus* tab and the *Enumeration* tab as shown in Figure 9-21:

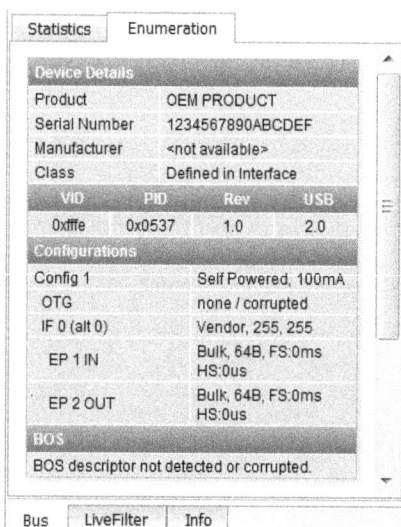

Figure 9-21 **Vendor Class Enumeration Summary**

Notice how the configuration includes two Bulk IN and OUT endpoints, which is the operational model required by the two setups described in section Figure 9-17 "Vendor Class Echo Sync" on page 779 and section Figure 9-18 "Vendor Class Echo Async" on page 780.

Proceed to send some echo requests with one of the console applications as described in a previous section section 9-4-5 "Testing the New Vendor Specific Device" on page 776.

If you configure the console application to send 10 echo requests, you should be able to capture 10 sets of transactions. Each set contains the message header and payload transactions from the host and then the payload transaction from the device as shown in Figure 9-22.

Sp	Index	m:s.ms.us	Len	Err	Dev	Ep	Record	Summary	ASCII
FS ⬍	8	0:03.111.475	2 B		08	02	▷ 🖮 OUT txn	00 01	. .
FS ⬍	12	0:03.112.579	1 B		08	02	▷ 🖮 OUT txn	31	1
FS ⬍	16	0:03.113.429	1 B		08	01	▷ 🖮 IN txn	31	1
FS ⬍	20	0:03.114.379	2 B		08	02	▷ 🖮 OUT txn	00 02	. .
FS ⬍	24	0:03.115.223	2 B		08	02	▷ 🖮 OUT txn	32 32	22
FS ⬍	28	0:03.115.983	2 B		08	01	▷ 🖮 IN txn	32 32	22
FS ⬍	32	0:03.116.861	2 B		08	02	▷ 🖮 OUT txn	00 03	. .
FS ⬍	36	0:03.117.630	3 B		08	02	▷ 🖮 OUT txn	33 33 33	333
FS ⬍	40	0:03.118.403	3 B		08	01	▷ 🖮 IN txn	33 33 33	333
FS ⬍	44	0:03.119.255	2 B		08	02	▷ 🖮 OUT txn	00 04	. .
FS ⬍	48	0:03.120.021	4 B		08	02	▷ 🖮 OUT txn	34 34 34 34	4444
FS ⬍	52	0:03.120.605	4 B		08	01	▷ 🖮 IN txn	34 34 34 34	4444
FS ⬍	56	0:03.121.388	2 B		08	02	▷ 🖮 OUT txn	00 05	. .
FS ⬍	60	0:03.122.223	5 B		08	02	▷ 🖮 OUT txn	35 35 35 35 35	55555
FS ⬍	64	0:03.122.943	5 B		08	01	▷ 🖮 IN txn	35 35 35 35 35	55555
FS ⬍	68	0:03.123.742	2 B		08	02	▷ 🖮 OUT txn	00 06	. .
FS ⬍	72	0:03.124.351	6 B		08	02	▷ 🖮 OUT txn	36 36 36 36 36 36	666666
FS ⬍	76	0:03.125.034	6 B		08	01	▷ 🖮 IN txn	36 36 36 36 36 36	666666
FS ⬍	80	0:03.125.856	2 B		08	02	▷ 🖮 OUT txn	00 07	. .
FS ⬍	84	0:03.126.566	7 B		08	02	▷ 🖮 OUT txn	37 37 37 37 37 37 37	7777777
FS ⬍	88	0:03.127.225	7 B		08	01	▷ 🖮 IN txn	37 37 37 37 37 37 37	7777777
FS ⬍	92	0:03.127.976	2 B		08	02	▷ 🖮 OUT txn	00 08	. .
FS ⬍	96	0:03.128.745	8 B		08	02	▷ 🖮 OUT txn	38 38 38 38 38 38 38 38	88888888
FS ⬍	100	0:03.129.353	8 B		08	01	▷ 🖮 IN txn	38 38 38 38 38 38 38 38	88888888
FS ⬍	104	0:03.130.224	2 B		08	02	▷ 🖮 OUT txn	00 09	. .
FS ⬍	108	0:03.131.046	9 B		08	02	▷ 🖮 OUT txn	39 39 39 39 39 39 39 39 39	999999999
FS ⬍	112	0:03.131.609	9 B		08	01	▷ 🖮 IN txn	39 39 39 39 39 39 39 39 39	999999999
FS ⬍	116	0:03.132.354	2 B		08	02	▷ 🖮 OUT txn	00 0A	. .
FS ⬍	120	0:03.133.035	10 B		08	02	▷ 🖮 OUT txn	3A 3A 3A 3A 3A 3A 3A 3A 3A 3A	::::::::::
FS ⬍	124	0:03.133.612	10 B		08	01	▷ 🖮 IN txn	3A 3A 3A 3A 3A 3A 3A 3A 3A 3A	::::::::::

Figure 9-22 **Echo Transactions**

9-7 SUMMARY

The example featured in this chapter is a great reference for adding USB connectivity to any vendor specific device. It allows you to evaluate the performance of the µC/USB-Device stack and its Vendor class by letting you test the transfer of data IN and OUT of bulk endpoints.

The chapter showed you how to run the example and then went into explaining how the code works by describing a couple of flow diagrams, code listings and USB traffic captures. It kept on showing you more of the features of the Total Phase Data Center Software by describing the most important USB traffic captures found in vendor specific devices.

Chapter 9

Introduction to μC/Probe

This appendix aims at briefly introducing μC/Probe. μC/Probe is a Windows application designed to read and write the memory of any embedded target processor during run-time. Memory locations are mapped to a set of virtual controls and indicators placed on a dashboard. Figure A-1 shows an overview of the system and data flow.

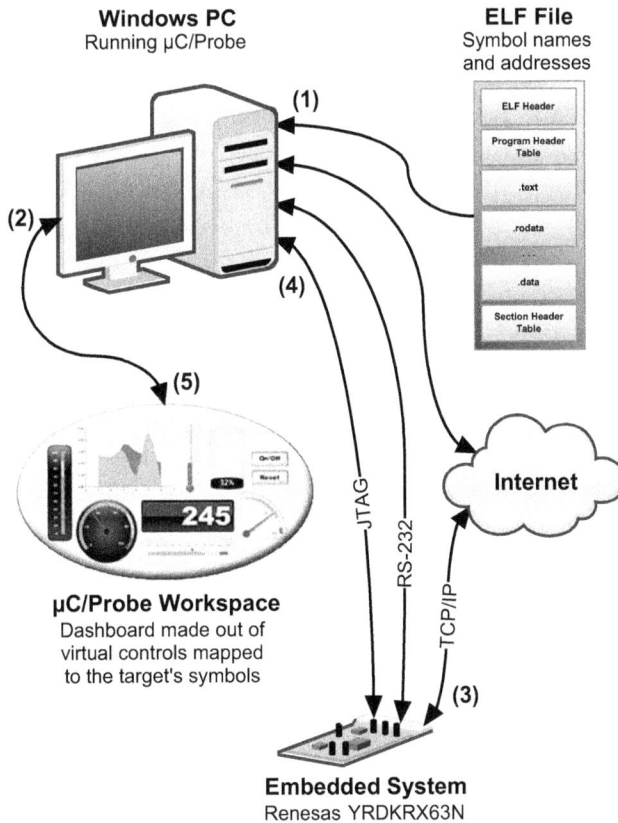

Figure A-1 **μC/Probe Data Flow Diagram**

FA-1(1)   You have to provide μC/Probe with an ELF file with DWARF-2 debugging information. The ELF file is generated by Renesas RXC toolchain's linker. μC/Probe parses the ELF file and reads the addresses of each of the embedded target's symbols (i.e. global variables) and creates a catalog known as *symbol browser*, which will be used by you during design-time to select the symbols you want to display on your dashboard. For more information on building ELF files with e2studio, see section 3-2-3 "Building a Project in e2studio" on page 648.

FA-1(2)   During design-time, you create a workspace using a Windows PC and μC/Probe. You design your own dashboard by dragging and dropping virtual controls and indicators onto a *data screen*. Each virtual control and indicator needs to be mapped to an embedded target's symbol by selecting it from the symbol browser.

FA-1(3)   Before proceeding to the run-time stage, μC/Probe needs to be configured to use one of the three communication interfaces: JTAG, RS232 or TCP/IP. The examples featured in the book use the J-Link interface, see section "Configuring μC/Probe to work with J-Link for the RX600" on page 633 for more details. In order to start the run-time stage, you click the *Play* button and μC/Probe starts making requests to read the value of all the memory locations associated with each virtual control and indicator (i.e. buttons and gauges respectively). At the same time, μC/Probe sends commands to write the memory locations associated with each virtual control (i.e. buttons on a click event).

FA-1(4)   In the case of a reading request, the embedded target responds with the latest value. In the case of a write command, the embedded target responds with an acknowledgement. Because the examples in this book use the J-Link interface, no resident firmware is necessary on the YRDKRX63N board. Any other type of interface such as RS-232 or TCP/IP requires target code available from Micriμm.

FA-1(5)   μC/Probe parses the responses from the embedded target and updates the virtual controls and indicators.

Figure A-2 provides an example of a Data Screen using bitmap animations to display the status of the push buttons on the YRDKRX63N and a numeric indicator and graph to display the noise level captured by the microphone as described in section Figure 4-1 "Examples Task Model" on page 659.

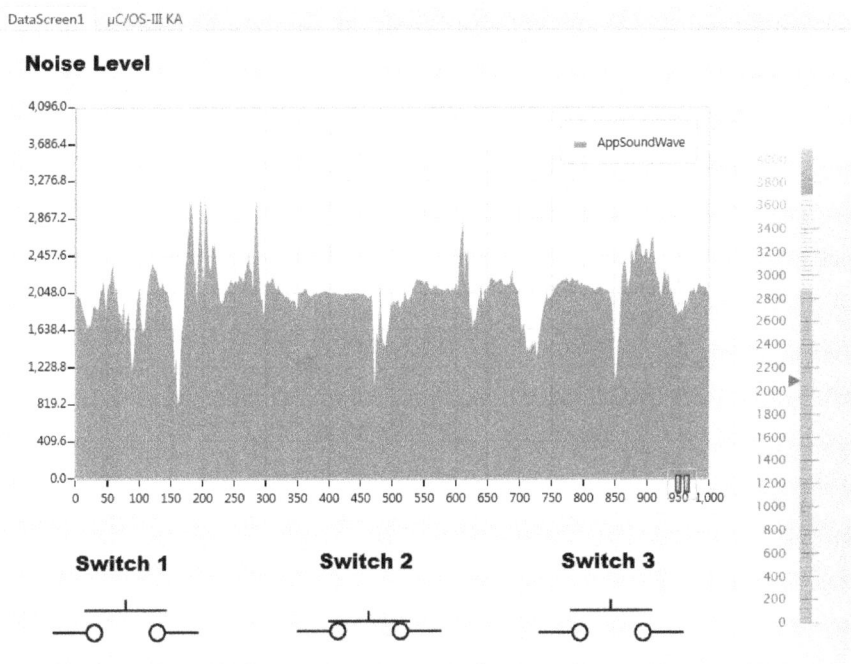

Figure A-2 **µC/Probe Example of a Data Screen**

A-1 FURTHER READING

The µC/Probe page on the Micriµm website is filled with instructional videos and the official documentation. Go online to:

    http://www.micrium.com/probe

- Download the document *µC/Probe Target Manual* for more information about the firmware that resides on the Embedded System.

- Download the document *µC/Probe User's Manual* for more information about the Windows PC side of the system.

B

The RX600 USB Device Driver

The μC/USB-Device stack is designed to operate with a wide variety of USB device controllers as it features a hardware abstraction layer that allows porting the stack to any new USB device controllers. There are many USB device controllers available on the market and each requires a driver to work with μC/USB-Device. Micriμm offers many USB device controller drivers and additional drivers are added on a regular basis.

This chapter describes the μC/USB-Device driver for the RX600 series of MCUs which is included precompiled in linkable object form with this book's companion software. To access source code, a license must be obtained from Micriμm (see Appendix D, "μC/OS-III and μC/USB-Device Licensing Policy" on page 819).

The chapter starts by describing some of the main features of the RX63N USB device controller. The chapter proceeds at explaining a few details about the YRDKRX63N before describing the driver code.

Micriμm provides a USB Device Driver API and data type naming conventions. By following these naming conventions, as well as standard Micriμm conventions and software development patterns, the process of device driver debugging and testing is simplified, allowing developers to become familiar with device drivers authored by others.

It is important to develop a driver to be re-entrant, as μC/USB-Device supports multiple interfaces of the same type. By avoiding global macros and variables (e.g., using the device data area, and defining macros within the driver's **.c** file), driver developers ensure that projects containing multiple device driver files are able to compile.

Chapter 6, "Device Driver Guide" on page 125 provides the guidelines for the architecture of a USB Device Controller Driver. Micriμm also provides a μC/USB-Device driver template that is located in the following directory:

```
$\Micrium\Software\uC-USB-Device-V4\Drivers\Template
```

The μC/USB-Device driver for the RX63N has been validated for compliance with the USB 2.0 specification. The USB Implementers Forum (USB-IF) at www.usb.org offers a software tool called USB Command Verifier to evaluate USB devices for conformance to the USB Device Framework (Chapter 9), HID class, MSC class and PHDC class among others.

B-1 RX63N ON-CHIP USB 2.0 HOST/DEVICE CONTROLLER

The Renesas RX63N on-chip USB controller operates as a full-speed host or device controller. The module has an internal USB transceiver and supports all of the transfer types described in section 1-8-3 "Transfers" on page 49.

Some of the most important features of the module operating as a USB Device controller are:

▦   Complies with USB-IF certification standards

▦   USB 2.0 full-speed transfers (12 Mbps)

▦   Integrated USB 2.0 transceiver (PHY)

▦   Four transfer types: Control, Bulk, Interrupt and Isochronous

▦   Ten endpoints

   ▦   One dedicated control IN endpoint and one dedicated control OUT endpoint

   ▦   Eight configurable IN or OUT endpoints

▦   Auto-response function for *SET_ADDRESS* request

▦   Buffer memory for USB communications

B-2 RENESAS DEMONSTRATION KIT YRDKRX63N

Products of the RX63N incorporate a USB 2.0 full-speed host/device module (USB0) and a USB 2.0 device-only module (USB1), for two USB ports.

On board the YRDKRX63N demonstration kit, the RX63N on-chip USB controller is configured to operate as Host, Device, or OTG using the USB0 module.

In order to configure the YRDKRX63N board to operate as a USB device, simply put the SW6 DIP switches 1 and 4 on the ON position and switches 2 and 3 on the OFF position as shown in Figure 2-8 on Chapter 2, "Setup" on page 629.

This device mode does not take any external power circuitry to implement and the USB circuitry is tied to the Mini-B connector on J9 of the YRDKRX63N board.

The following sections provide the implementation of a driver for the RX63N integrated USB device controller based on the driver template in:

    $\Micrium\Software\uC-USB-Device-V4\Drivers\Template

B-3 DEVICE DRIVER CONVENTIONS

All USB device drivers are named **usbd_drv_<controller>.c** and **.h**, where **<controller>** represents the name of the USB device controller. The names for the purposes of this book are **usbd_drv_rx600.c** and **usbd_drv_rx600.h** and are located in the directory shown in Figure B-1:

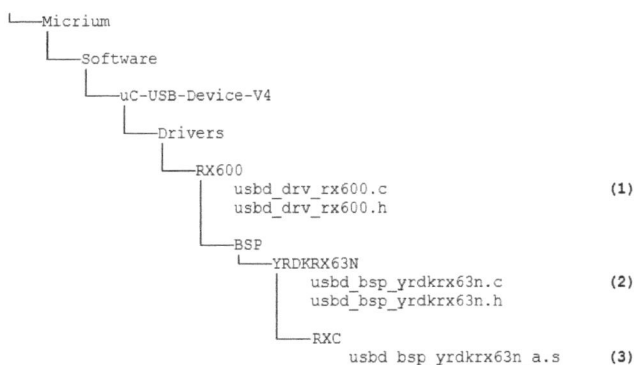

```
 └──Micrium
     └──Software
         └──uC-USB-Device-V4
             └──Drivers
                 └──RX600
                         usbd_drv_rx600.c              (1)
                         usbd_drv_rx600.h
                     └──BSP
                         └──YRDKRX63N
                                 usbd_bsp_yrdkrx63n.c      (2)
                                 usbd_bsp_yrdkrx63n.h
                             └──RXC
                                     usbd_bsp_yrdkrx63n_a.s    (3)
```

Figure B-1 µC/USB-Device Driver Source Code for the Renesas RX63N

The USB controller in the Renesas RX600 series of microcontrollers is the same and that is why the µC/USB-Device driver for the RX63N was designed as a generic RX600 series driver with a BSP abstraction layer as illustrated in Figure B-1 to take into account some differences among boards.

FB-1(1)   The files **usbd_drv_rx600.c** and **usbd_drv_rx600.h** implement the driver API and it will be described in great detail in section B-4 "Device Driver API" on page 798.

FB-1(2)   The files **usbd_bsp_yrdkrx63n.c** and **usbd_bsp_yrdkrx63n.h** are meant to be the layer of code that abstracts details such as clocks, interrupt controllers and GPIO pins among others. In the case of the RX63N driver, these files not only define the hardware register addresses for the interrupt controller as implemented in the YRDKRX63N board but also implement the functions to initialize, connect and disconnect the USB device controller. It also defines the endpoint information table.

FB-1(3)   The file **usbd_bsp_yrdkrx63n_a.s** abstracts any assembly code specific to a compiler and CPU architecture. In the case of this driver, it implements the USB controller interrupt service routines.

B-3-1 ENDPOINT VARIABLE NAMES

Endpoints are the fundamental unit of communication in USB. They were described in section 1-8-1 "Endpoint" on page 48 and through the source code, they are identified by the following numbers:

- Endpoint Address: **ep_addr**

- Endpoint Physical Number: **ep_phy_nbr**

- Endpoint Logical Number: **ep_log_nbr**

These variables are widely used in the source code of the µC/USB-Device stack and the driver for the RX600 series keeps the same naming conventions.

Figure B-2 illustrates the meaning of each of the endpoint variables names.

Endpoint Address (ep_addr)

b15	b14	b13	b12	b11	b10	b9	b8	b7	b6	b5	b4	b3	b2	b1	b0
-	-	-	-	-	-	-	-	0/1	-	-	-	0/1	0/1	0/1	0/1

Endpoint Direction:
0: OUT (host-to-dev)
1: IN   (dev-to-host)

Endpoint Number
(ep_log_nbr):
From 0 to 15

Physical Endpoint Number (ep_phy_nbr)

Endpoint Direction:
0: OUT (host-to-dev)
1: IN   (dev-to-host)

$+$

$\left(\begin{array}{c} \text{Endpoint Number} \\ \text{(ep\_log\_nbr):} \\ \text{From 0 to 15} \end{array} \times 2 \right)$

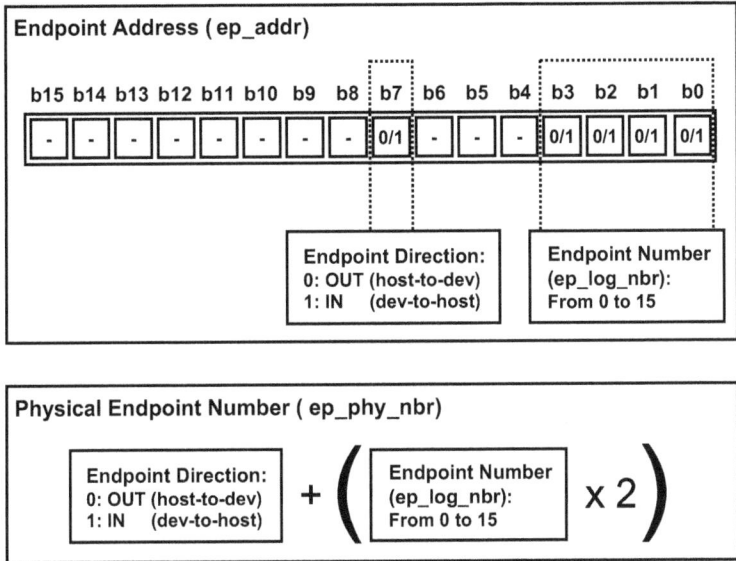

Figure B-2 **Endpoint Variable Names**

B-3-2 ENDPOINT INFORMATION TABLE

As described in section 1-8-1 "Endpoint" on page 48, each USB device controller is designed with a set of endpoints which are the point of origin or the point of destination for data. The RX600 USB-Device controller has 10 endpoints including the default endpoint zero EP0. The capabilities of these endpoints are defined in the endpoint information table as described in section 6-5-1 "Endpoint Information Table" on page 135 and for the RX600 driver it is declared in **usbd_bsp_yrdkrx63n.c** as shown in Listing B-1:

```
USBD_DRV_EP_INFO  USBD_DrvEP_InfoTbl_RX63N[] = {
    {USBD_EP_INFO_TYPE_CTRL | USBD_EP_INFO_DIR_OUT,      0u,  64u},
    {USBD_EP_INFO_TYPE_CTRL | USBD_EP_INFO_DIR_IN,       0u,  64u},
    {USBD_EP_INFO_TYPE_BULK | USBD_EP_INFO_TYPE_ISOC |
     USBD_EP_INFO_DIR_OUT   | USBD_EP_INFO_DIR_IN,       1u, 256u},
    {USBD_EP_INFO_TYPE_BULK | USBD_EP_INFO_TYPE_ISOC |
     USBD_EP_INFO_DIR_OUT   | USBD_EP_INFO_DIR_IN,       2u, 256u},
    {USBD_EP_INFO_TYPE_BULK | USBD_EP_INFO_DIR_OUT   |
     USBD_EP_INFO_DIR_IN,                                3u,  64u},
    {USBD_EP_INFO_TYPE_BULK | USBD_EP_INFO_DIR_OUT   |
     USBD_EP_INFO_DIR_IN,                                4u,  64u},
    {USBD_EP_INFO_TYPE_BULK | USBD_EP_INFO_DIR_OUT   |
     USBD_EP_INFO_DIR_IN,                                5u,  64u},
    {USBD_EP_INFO_TYPE_INTR | USBD_EP_INFO_DIR_OUT   |
     USBD_EP_INFO_DIR_IN,                                6u,  64u},
    {USBD_EP_INFO_TYPE_INTR | USBD_EP_INFO_DIR_OUT   |
     USBD_EP_INFO_DIR_IN,                                7u,  64u},
    {USBD_EP_INFO_TYPE_INTR | USBD_EP_INFO_DIR_OUT   |
     USBD_EP_INFO_DIR_IN,                                8u,  64u},
    {USBD_EP_INFO_TYPE_INTR | USBD_EP_INFO_DIR_OUT   |
     USBD_EP_INFO_DIR_IN,                                9u,  64u},
    {DEF_BIT_NONE,                                       0u,   0u}
};
```

Listing B-1 **Endpoint Information Table for the RX63N**

B-4 DEVICE DRIVER API

As described in the first part of the book in Chapter 6, "Device Driver Guide" on page 125, all device drivers must declare an instance of the appropriate device driver API structure as a global variable within the source code. The API structure is an ordered list of function pointers utilized by the µC/USB-Device stack when device hardware services are required. Such API structure is declared in **usbd_drv_rx600.c** as shown in code Listing B-2:

```
/*
*********************************************************************************
*                       USB DEVICE CONTROLLER DRIVER API
*********************************************************************************
*/

USBD_DRV_API  USBD_DrvAPI_RX600 = { USBD_DrvInit,
                                    USBD_DrvStart,
                                    USBD_DrvStop,
                                    USBD_DrvAddrSet,
                                    USBD_DrvAddrEn,
                                    USBD_DrvCfgSet,
                                    USBD_DrvCfgClr,
                                    USBD_DrvGetFrameNbr,
                                    USBD_DrvEP_Open,
                                    USBD_DrvEP_Close,
                                    USBD_DrvEP_RxStart,
                                    USBD_DrvEP_Rx,
                                    USBD_DrvEP_RxZLP,
                                    USBD_DrvEP_Tx,
                                    USBD_DrvEP_TxStart,
                                    USBD_DrvEP_TxZLP,
                                    USBD_DrvEP_Abort,
                                    USBD_DrvEP_Stall,
                                    USBD_DrvISR_Handler,
};
```

Listing B-2 **µC/USB-Device Driver API for the RX600 Series**

Each driver API function accepts a pointer to a structure of the type **USBD_DRV** as one of its parameters. Through this structure, you are able to access the following fields:

```
typedef  const  struct  usbd_drv_cfg {
    CPU_ADDR          BaseAddr;    /* Base address of device controller hardware regs. */  (1)
    CPU_ADDR          MemAddr;     /* Base address of device controller dedicated mem. */  (2)
    CPU_ADDR          MemSize;     /* Size        of device controller dedicated mem. */  (3)
    USBD_DEV_SPD      Spd;         /* Speed       of device controller.               */
    USBD_DRV_EP_INFO *EP_InfoTbl;  /* Device controller EP information table.         */  (4)
} USBD_DRV_CFG;


typedef usb_drv {
    CPU_INT08U        DevNbr;                                                                (5)
    USBD_DRV_API      *API_Ptr;    /* Device controller API.                          */  (6)
    USBD_DRV_CFG      *CfgPtr;     /* Device controller configuration.                */  (7)
    void              *DataPtr;    /* Device controller local data.                   */  (8)
    USBD_DRV_BSP_API *BSP_API_Ptr; /* Device controller board specific API.           */  (9)
} USBD_DRV;
```

Listing B-3 **USB Device Driver Data Type**

LB-3(1)   Base address of the RX63N USB device hardware registers.

LB-3(2)   This setting is not used as the RX63N USB controller does not have a dedicated memory available.

LB-3(3)   This setting is not used as the RX63N USB controller does not have a dedicated memory available.

LB-3(4)   RX63N endpoint information table.

LB-3(5)   Unique index to identify device.

LB-3(6)   Pointer to USB device controller driver API.

LB-3(7)   Pointer to USB device controller driver configuration.

LB-3(8)   Pointer to USB device controller driver specific data.

LB-3(9)   Pointer to USB device controller BSP for the YRDKRX63N.

You will notice that almost every driver API function will first get a reference through this structure's pointer to the RX63N hardware registers and also to the BSP API, before doing anything else.

A general description of each device driver API function is provided in Appendix B, "Device Controller Driver API Reference" on page 391.

If you have purchased a license for the µC/USB-Device stack, then you have full access to the driver's source code. Otherwise, the following sections provide the details specific to the RX600 series of USB controllers in the form of a C-comments outline.

B-4-1 USBD_DrvInit()

```
static  void  USBD_DrvInit (USBD_DRV  *p_drv,
                            USBD_ERR  *p_err)
{
                        /* Allocate driver's internal data.                 */
                        /* Store drv internal data ptr.                     */
                        /* Get a reference to the USB hardware registers.   */
                        /* Get driver BSP API reference.                    */
                        /* Call board/chip specific device controller ...   */
                        /* ... initialization function.                     */
                        /* Transition the USB0 module from the stop state.  */
                        /* Disable USB module.                              */
                        /* Supply 48-Mhz clock signal to the USB module.    */
                        /* Enable USB module.                               */
                        /* Enable the default interrupt registers.          */
                        /* Enable VBUS interrupt.                           */
                        /* Enable Resume interrupt.                         */
                        /* Enable Device State Transition interrupt.        */
                        /* Enable Control Transfer Stage Transition interrupt. */
                        /* Enable Buffer Empty interrupt.                   */
                        /* Enable Buffer Ready interrupt.                   */
                        /* Enable Buffer Ready interrupt for the control pipe. */
                        /* Buffer Not Ready interrupt are not used.         */
                        /* Enable Buffer Empty interrupt for the control pipe. */
}
```

Listing B-4 **USBD_DrvInit() for the RX600 USB Device Driver**

B-4-2 USBD_DrvStart()

```
static  void  USBD_DrvStart (USBD_DRV   *p_drv,
                             USBD_ERR   *p_err)
{
                    /* Get a reference to the USB hardware registers.     */
                    /* Get a reference to the driver's BSP API.           */
                    /* Call board/chip specific connect function.         */
                    /* Connect to host by activating the pull-up on D+ pin. */
                    /* If D+ pin is enabled, disable D+ pin.              */
                    /* Enable pulling up of the D+ line.                  */
}
```

Listing B-5 **USBD_DrvStart() for the RX600 USB Device Driver**

B-4-3 USBD_DrvStop()

```
static  void  USBD_DrvStop (USBD_DRV  *p_drv)
{
                    /* Get a reference to the USB hardware registers.     */
                    /* Get a reference to the driver's BSP API.           */
                    /* Disable pulling up of the D+ line.                 */
}
```

Listing B-6 **USBD_DrvStop() for the RX600 USB Device Driver**

B-4-4 USBD_DrvAddrSet()

```
static  void  USBD_DrvAddrSet (USBD_DRV    *p_drv,
                               CPU_INT08U  dev_addr)
{
                    /* Allocate driver's internal data.                  */
                    /* Get a reference to the driver's internal data.    */
                    /* There is no need to send a ZLP as the USB ...     */
                    /* ... controller responds automatically to SET_ADDRESS.*/
}
```

Listing B-7 **USBD_DrvAddrSet() for the RX600 USB Device Driver**

B-4-5 USBD_DrvAddrEn()

```
static  void  USBD_DrvAddrEn (USBD_DRV   *p_drv,
                              CPU_INT08U  dev_addr)
{
                      /* No need to do anything as the controller handles ... */
                      /* ... the SET_ADDRESS request automatically.           */
}
```

Listing B-8 **USBD_DrvAddrEn() for the RX600 USB Device Driver**

B-4-6 USBD_DrvCfgSet()

```
static  CPU_BOOLEAN  USBD_DrvCfgSet (USBD_DRV   *p_drv,
                                     CPU_INT08U  cfg_val)
{
                      /* No need to do anything.                              */
}
```

Listing B-9 **USBD_DrvCfgSet() for the RX600 USB Device Driver**

B-4-7 USBD_DrvCfgClr()

```
static  void  USBD_DrvCfgClr (USBD_DRV   *p_drv,
                              CPU_INT08U  cfg_val)
{
                      /* No need to do anything.                              */
}
```

Listing B-10 **USBD_DrvCfgClr() for the RX600 USB Device Driver**

B-4-8 USBD_DrvGetFrameNbr()

```
static  CPU_INT16U  USBD_DrvGetFrameNbr (USBD_DRV  *p_drv)
{
                        /* Get a reference to the USB hardware registers.    */
                        /* Frame Number Register (FRMNUM).                   */
}
```

Listing B-11 **USBD_DrvGetFrameNbr() for the RX600 USB Device Driver**

B-4-9 USBD_DrvEP_Open()

```
static  void  USBD_DrvEP_Open (USBD_DRV     *p_drv,
                              CPU_INT08U   ep_addr,
                              CPU_INT08U   ep_type,
                              CPU_INT16U   max_pkt_size,
                              CPU_INT08U   transaction_frame,
                              USBD_ERR     *p_err)
{
                        /* Get the physical endpoint number.                 */
                        /* Configure the endpoint.                           */
                        /* Get a reference to the driver's internal data.    */
                        /* Attempt to get a pipe of the specified type.      */
                        /* Check to see if pipe is valid.                    */
                        /* Set the associated pipe in the endpoint table.    */
                        /* Set the associated endpoint in the pipe table.    */
                        /* Remove pipe on error.                             */
}
```

Listing B-12 **USBD_DrvEP_Open() for the RX600 USB Device Driver**

B-4-10 USBD_DrvEP_Close()

```
static  void  USBD_DrvEP_Close (USBD_DRV    *p_drv,
                                CPU_INT08U   ep_addr)
{
                         /* Get a reference to the driver's internal data.       */
                         /* Reset selected pipe and remove from internal bitmaps. */
                         /* Remove pipe references from internal data structures. */
}
```

Listing B-13 **USBD_DrvEP_Close() for the RX600 USB Device Driver**

B-4-11 USBD_DrvEP_RxStart()

```
static  void  USBD_DrvEP_RxStart (USBD_DRV    *p_drv,
                                  CPU_INT08U   ep_addr,
                                  CPU_INT08U  *p_buf,
                                  CPU_INT32U   buf_len,
                                  USBD_ERR    *p_err)
{
                         /* Use current pipe for USB transfer.                    */
}
```

Listing B-14 **USBD_DrvEP_RxStart() for the RX600 USB Device Driver**

B-4-12 USBD_DrvEP_Rx()

```
static  CPU_INT32U  USBD_DrvEP_Rx (USBD_DRV    *p_drv,
                                   CPU_INT08U   ep_addr,
                                   CPU_INT08U  *p_buf,
                                   CPU_INT32U   buf_len,
                                   USBD_ERR    *p_err)
{
                    /* Get a reference to the USB hardware registers.    */
                    /* Get a reference to the driver's internal data.    */
                    /* Use current pipe for USB transfer.                */
                    /* Decrement data length on read.                    */
                    /* Port access 16-bit width.                         */
                    /* Select the pipe to be read from.                  */
                    /* Clear the FIFO for zero packet read.              */
                    /* Check that FIFO is ready to be read.              */
                    /* Get packet length.                                */
                    /* Clear the FIFO for zero packet read.              */
                    /* If packet length is not a multiple of a word length. */
                    /* Indicate that an extra packet is to be read.      */
                    /* Read data from the FIFO one word at a time.       */
                    /* If an extra byte is to be read.                   */
                    /* Read one byte of data from the FIFO.              */
}
```

Listing B-15 **USBD_DrvEP_Rx() for the RX600 USB Device Driver**

B-4-13 USBD_DrvEP_RxZLP()

```
static  void  USBD_DrvEP_RxZLP (USBD_DRV    *p_drv,
                                CPU_INT08U   ep_addr,
                                USBD_ERR    *p_err)
{
                    /* Get a reference to the USB hardware registers.      */
                    /* Read zero length packet.                            */
                    /* Use current pipe for USB transfer.                  */
                    /* Enable the status stage of the control transfer...  */
                    /* ... to be completed.                                */
}
```

Listing B-16 **USBD_DrvEP_RxZLP() for the RX600 USB Device Driver**

B-4-14 USBD_DrvEP_Tx()

```
static  CPU_INT32U  USBD_DrvEP_Tx (USBD_DRV    *p_drv,
                                   CPU_INT08U   ep_addr,
                                   CPU_INT08U  *p_buf,
                                   CPU_INT32U   buf_len,
                                   USBD_ERR    *p_err)
{
                    /* Get a reference to the USB hardware registers.     */
                    /* Get a reference to the driver's internal data.     */
                    /* Use current pipe for USB transfer.                 */
                    /* Port access 16-bit width.                          */
                    /* Pipe selected in write mode.                       */
                    /* Select the pipe to be read from.                   */
                    /* If a zero packet is to be sent (see Note #1).      */
                    /* If packet length is not a multiple of a word length. */
                    /* Indicate that an extra packet is to be written.    */
                    /* Write data into the FIFO one word at a time.       */
                    /* If an extra byte is to be written.                 */
                    /* Port access 8-bit width.                           */
                    /* Write one byte of data to the FIFO.                */
    return (bytes_txd);
}
```

Listing B-17 **USBD_DrvEP_Tx() for the RX600 USB Device Driver**

B-4-15 USBD_DrvEP_TxStart()

```
static  void  USBD_DrvEP_TxStart (USBD_DRV    *p_drv,
                                  CPU_INT08U   ep_addr,
                                  CPU_INT08U  *p_buf,
                                  CPU_INT32U   buf_len,
                                  USBD_ERR    *p_err)
{
                    /* Get a reference to the USB hardware registers.     */
                    /* Data has been completely written to the FIFO buffer. */
                    /* Use current pipe for USB transfer.                 */
}
```

Listing B-18 **USBD_DrvEP_TxStart() for the RX600 USB Device Driver**

B-4-16 USBD_DrvEP_TxZLP()

```
static  void  USBD_DrvEP_TxZLP (USBD_DRV      *p_drv,
                                CPU_INT08U    ep_addr,
                                USBD_ERR      *p_err)
{
                    /* Get a reference to the driver's internal data.     */
                    /* Do not send a zero length packet if the flag is set. */
}
```

Listing B-19 **USBD_DrvEP_TxZLP() for the RX600 USB Device Driver**

B-4-17 USBD_DrvEP_Abort()

```
static  CPU_BOOLEAN  USBD_DrvEP_Abort (USBD_DRV      *p_drv,
                                       CPU_INT08U    ep_addr)
{
                    /* Get a reference to the USB hardware registers.     */
                    /* Get a reference to the driver's internal data.     */
                    /* Use current pipe for USB transfer.                 */
                    /* Clear the pipe's FIFO.                             */
}
```

Listing B-20 **USBD_DrvEP_Abort() for the RX600 USB Device Driver**

B-4-18 USBD_DrvEP_Stall()

```
static  CPU_BOOLEAN  USBD_DrvEP_Stall (USBD_DRV      *p_drv,
                                       CPU_INT08U    ep_addr,
                                       CPU_BOOLEAN   state)
{
                    /* Get a reference to the driver's internal data.     */
                    /* Make a transition to STALL state.                  */
}
```

Listing B-21 **USBD_DrvEP_Stall() for the RX600 USB Device Driver**

B-4-19 USBD_DrvISR_Handler()

The first part of the ISR consists of reading the RX63N interrupts status registers and masking any interrupts that are not enabled as outlined in Listing B-22:

```
void  USBD_DrvISR_Handler (USBD_DRV  *p_drv)
{
                        /* Get a reference to the USB hardware registers.    */
                        /* Get a reference to the driver's internal data.    */

                        /* Read all the Interrupt Status Registers:          */

                        /* Interrupt Status Register 0 (INTSTS0).            */
                        /* Interrupt Status Register 1 (INTSTS1).            */
                        /* BRDY Interrupt Status Register (BRDYSTS).         */
                        /* BEMP Interrupt Status Register (BEMPSTS).         */
                        /* NRDY Interrupt Status Register (NRDYSTS).         */

                        /* Mask all non-enabled interrupts:                  */
                        /* BRDY Interrupt Enable Register (BRDYENB).         */
                        /* BEMP Interrupt Enable Register (BEMPENB).         */
                        /* NRDY Interrupt Enable Register (NRDYENB).         */
        .
        .
        .
```

Listing B-22 **USBD_DrvISR_Handler() for the RX600 USB Device Driver**

The second part of the ISR consists of processing each interrupt. Some of them just require clearing the flag, while others require to not only clearing the flag but also posting the event to the µC/USB-Device stack by calling one of the functions described in Table 6-1, "Status Notification API," on page 132.

```
                    /* Process each of the interrupt flags:              */

                    /* VBUS Interrupt Status.                            */
                    /* Resume event detected.                            */
                    /* Post resume event to the USBD stack.              */
                    /* Device state change detected.                     */
                    /* Mask all non relevant bits.                       */
                    /* Device has entered the powered state.             */
                    /* Device has entered the default state.             */
                    /* Post the bus reset event to the USBD stack.       */
                    /* Device has entered the addressed state.           */
                    /* Device has entered the configured state.          */
                    /* Device has entered the suspended state.           */
                    /* Post the bus suspend event to the USBD stack.     */
                    /* Setup packet has been received.                   */
                    /* Handle the setup packet.                          */
                    /* Post the setup packet to the USBD stack.          */
                    /* Start of frame interrupt.                         */
                    /* Control transfer status change detected.          */
                    /* Mask all non relevant bits.                       */
                    /* Control read status stage.                        */
                    /* Control write (no data) status stage.             */
                    /* Idle or setup stage.                              */
                    /* Control read data stage.                          */
                    /* Control write data stage.                         */
                    /* Control write status stage.                       */
                    /* Control transfer sequence error.                  */
                    /* Overcurrent interrupt.                            */
                    /* Bus change interrupt.                             */
                    /* Attach interrupt.                                 */
                    /* Detach interrupt.                                 */
                    /* EOF error interrupt.                              */
                    /* Setup packet error interrupt.                     */
                    /* Setup packet transfer complete interrupt.         */
                    /* Buffer Ready Interrupt Status.                    */
                    /* Post the successful completion to the USBD stack. */
                    /* Buffer Empty Interrupt Status.                    */
                    /* Post the successful completion to the USBD stack. */

}
```

Listing B-23 **USBD_DrvISR_Handler() for the RX600 USB Device Driver**

C

The Enumeration Process

The process of enumeration is used by the host to learn about the device's capabilities and set the device's configuration as described in the first part of the book in section 1-12 "Enumeration" on page 58.

This appendix describes the enumeration process in terms of USB captures using the Beagle USB 480.

C-1 CAPTURING USB TRAFFIC

In order to capture USB traffic, you need to connect the Beagle USB 480 as illustrated in Figure 2-12, "Beagle USB 480 Protocol Analyzer: Connections," on page 640.

When monitoring USB traffic, it is best to attach the Beagle USB 480's analysis side and start the capture *before* attaching the YRDKRX63N. That means that before starting a capture, make sure the USB cable on J9 of the YRDKRX63N is disconnected from the Beagle USB 480 capture side. This allows the Beagle USB 480 to capture the descriptor information that is communicated during the enumeration phase.

Start the Total Phase Data Center software by using the shortcut created during Setup in section 2-1-4 "Total Phase Data Center Software" on page 630 or, go to the folder where the software package was extracted and run *Data Center.exe*.

Figure C-1 **Data Center Software Icon**

Once the application starts it will detect the Beagle USB 480 and will connect it automatically.

You can tell the Beagle USB 480 is properly connected by looking at the LEDs on the top which should have the Red and Green LEDs lit up.

Press *Ctrl+R* or click the *Run Capture* button in the toolbar to start the capture.

You should see a couple of new rows in the grid that read something like *Capture Started*.

At this point, you can attach the device by connecting the USB cable on J9 of the YRDKRX63N.

Complete the installation of the USB device by following the steps described in the corresponding example chapter, as referenced in Table C-1:

USB Class	Example	Chapter and Page Number
CDC ACM	USB-to-Serial Converter	section 5-4-4 "Installing the CDC Device" on page 668
HID	Mouse	section 6-4-4 "Installing the HID Device" on page 697
MSC	Removable Storage	section 7-4-4 "Installing the MSC Device" on page 716
PHDC	Communication Monitor	section 8-4-4 "Installing the PHDC Device" on page 740
Vendor	Bulk Sync/Async Communication	section 9-4-4 "Installing the Vendor Specific Device" on page 770

Table C-1 **Device Installation References**

As traffic is seen on the bus, it will be displayed in real-time in the *transactions grid*. You should start to see a group of standard requests that look the same for all USB classes and another group that even though is similar among different USB classes, it varies in number, size and content depending on the USB class being enumerated. These groups of requests are illustrated in Figure C-2.

Sp	Index	m:s.ms.us	Len	Dev	Ep	Record	Summary
	0	0:00.000.000				Capture started (Aggregate)	[09/06/12 11:42:00]
	1	0:00.000.000				\<Host connected>	
	6	0:01.856.094				\<Host disconnected>	
	7	0:01.856.297				\<Host connected>	
	8	0:01.869.088	733 ns			\<Reset> / \<Chirp K> / \<Tiny K>	
	9	0:01.869.089	302 us			\<Reset> / \<Target disconnected>	
	10	0:01.869.392	4.13 us			\<Reset> / \<Chirp J> / \<Tiny J>	
FS	11	0:01.869.396				\<Full-speed>	
FS	12	0:01.984.326	11.0 ms			\<Reset> / \<Target disconnected>	
FS	13	0:01.995.327	5.20 us			\<Reset> / \<Chirp J> / \<Tiny J>	
FS	29	0:02.247.039				\<Full-speed>	
FS	30	0:02.560.246	11.0 ms			\<Reset> / \<Chirp J> / \<Tiny J>	
FS	31	0:02.571.247				\<Full-speed>	
FS	32	0:02.601.242	18 B	00	00	Get Device Descriptor	Index=0 Length=64
FS	63	0:02.602.116	11.0 ms			\<Reset> / \<Chirp J> / \<Tiny J>	
FS	64	0:02.613.118				\<Full-speed>	
FS	65	0:02.735.409	0 B	00	00	Set Address	Address=08
FS	74	0:02.762.142	18 B	08	00	Get Device Descriptor	Index=0 Length=18
FS	101	0:02.786.403	125 B	08	00	Get Configuration Descriptor	Index=0 Length=255
FS	133	0:02.787.737	34 B	08	00	Get String Descriptor	Index=3 Length=255
FS	160	0:02.789.131	4 B	08	00	Get String Descriptor	Index=0 Length=255
FS	187	0:02.790.147	24 B	08	00	Get String Descriptor	Index=2 Length=255
FS	214	0:02.792.676	18 B	08	00	Get Device Descriptor	Index=0 Length=18
FS	241	0:02.793.653	9 B	08	00	Get Configuration Descriptor	Index=0 Length=9
FS	268	0:02.794.629	125 B	08	00	Get Configuration Descriptor	Index=0 Length=125
FS	300	0:02.805.085	2 B	08	00	Get Device Status	
FS	327	0:02.805.776	0 B	08	00	Set Configuration	Configuration=1

Figure C-2 **Enumeration Process**

The first port reset operations identified by the *\<Reset>* tag, are attempts to get the USB device into a *Port Enabled and Connected* state where the USB device will be able to respond to any requests addressed to the default device address 0. The next sections will describe the subsequent requests.

C-1-1 GET DEVICE DESCRIPTOR

The first request by the host is one represented by a record titled *Get Device Descriptor* similar to the one shown in Figure C-3.

The request is addressed to device 0 and the row represents the moment when the YRDKRX63N describes to the host computer information about the entire USB device such as the supported USB version, control endpoint's maximum packet size, vendor ID, product ID and the number of possible configurations the device can have (most of this information is declared in **usbd_dev_cfg.c**). This is the first step of the enumeration process:

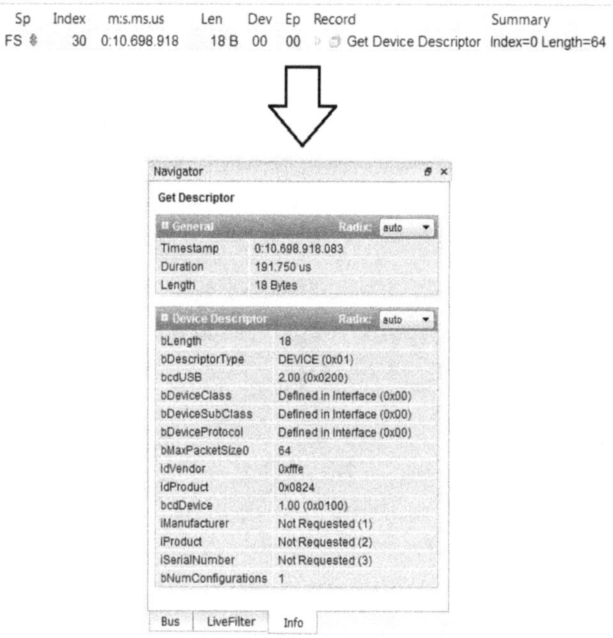

Figure C-3 **Get Device Descriptor Capture**

If the request for the device descriptor succeeds, all subsequent control transactions will use the maximum packet size of 64 bytes as specified by the Device Descriptor shown above in Figure C-3.

A second port reset is performed in preparation for the next enumeration state.

C-1-2 SET ADDRESS

The next step in the enumeration process is for the host controller to assign a unique address to the device. Right after *Get Device Descriptor* record and the second port reset, you will find a *Set Address* record similar to the one shown in Figure C-4 that represents the moment when the host computer assigns a unique address of 8 to the USB device.

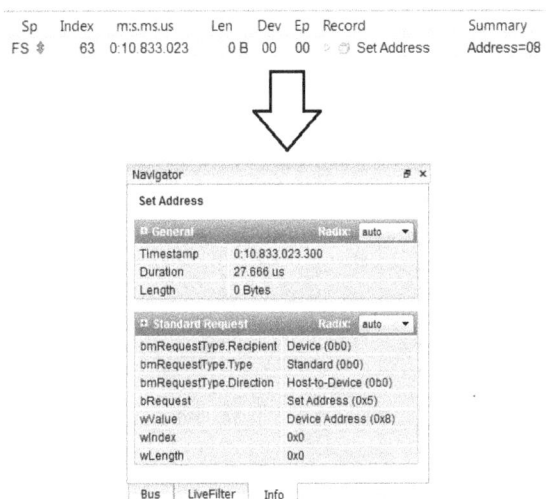

Figure C-4 **Set Address Capture**

Notice how up until this record all the previous transactions have been broadcasted to the default device address 0 (column header *Dev*). From now on, any future transactions will be addressed to device address 8.

The *Info Pane* in the *Navigator* window shown at the bottom of Figure C-4 provides a parsed view of the package for your convenience.

If the device is assigned an address successfully, a second device descriptor request is issued to the new device address before issuing a series of *Get Configuration Descriptor* and *Get String Descriptor* requests to learn about the capabilities of the device.

C-1-3 GET STRING DESCRIPTOR

The records titled *Get String Descriptor* represent the moment when the device provides optional human readable information such as the product's name, manufacturer and serial number which are part of the device's configuration set in **usbd_dev_cfg.c**.

The *Get String Descriptors* shown in Figure C-5 also include a language ID to allow the support of multiple languages:

Sp	Index	m:s.ms.us	Len	Dev	Ep	Record	Summary	ASCII
FS ⊕	133	0:02.787.737	34 B	08	00	▷ ⊘ Get String Descriptor	Index=3 Length=255	".1.2.3.4.5.6.7.8.9.0.A.B.C.D.E.F.
FS ⊕	160	0:02.789.131	4 B	08	00	▷ ⊘ Get String Descriptor	Index=0 Length=255	....
FS ⊕	187	0:02.790.147	24 B	08	00	▷ ⊘ Get String Descriptor	Index=2 Length=255	..O.E.M. .P.R.O.D.U.C.T.

Get Descriptor

General	Radix: auto ▼
Timestamp	0:02.787.737.983
Duration	627.083 us
Length	34 Bytes

String Descriptor	Radix: auto ▼
bLength	34
bDescriptorType	STRING (0x03)
bString	1234567890ABCDEF

Get Descriptor

General	Radix: auto ▼
Timestamp	0:02.789.131.416
Duration	149.750 us
Length	4 Bytes

String Descriptor	Radix: auto ▼
bLength	4
bDescriptorType	STRING (0x03)
wLANGID[0]	English (United States) (0x0409)

Get Descriptor

General	Radix: auto ▼
Timestamp	0:02.790.147.416
Duration	208.500 us
Length	24 Bytes

String Descriptor	Radix: auto ▼
bLength	24
bDescriptorType	STRING (0x03)
bString	OEM PRODUCT

Figure C-5 **Get String Descriptors**

C-1-4 GET CONFIGURATION DESCRIPTOR

A USB device can implement many different configurations. The configuration descriptor is just a header for the interface descriptors. Therefore, the capture of the *Get Configuration Descriptor* looks different depending on the USB class or application configuration. See the different *Get Configuration Descriptors* in the corresponding example's chapter as referenced in Table C-2:

USB Class	Example	Chapter and Page Number
CDC ACM	USB-to-Serial Converter	section 5-6-1 "Get Configuration Descriptor" on page 686
HID	Mouse	section 6-6-1 "Get Configuration Descriptor" on page 706
MSC	Removable Storage	section 7-6-1 "Get Configuration Descriptor" on page 729
PHDC	Communication Monitor	section 8-6-1 "Get Configuration Descriptor" on page 758
Vendor	Bulk Sync/Async Communications	section 9-6-1 "Get Configuration Descriptor" on page 785

Table C-2 **Get Configuration Descriptors by USB Class**

Be aware that for the USB traffic, the Data Center Software is able to decode some standard USB classes such as HID, CDC ACM and MSC so that the transactions can be displayed in a convenient way. Unfortunately, the support of classes such as PHDC and Vendor is limited, and only raw data related to the USB protocol will be decoded.

C-1-5 SET CONFIGURATION

The enumeration process finishes with the host selecting one of the active configurations. The record titled *Set Configuration* represents this moment and it should look similar to the one in Figure C-6:

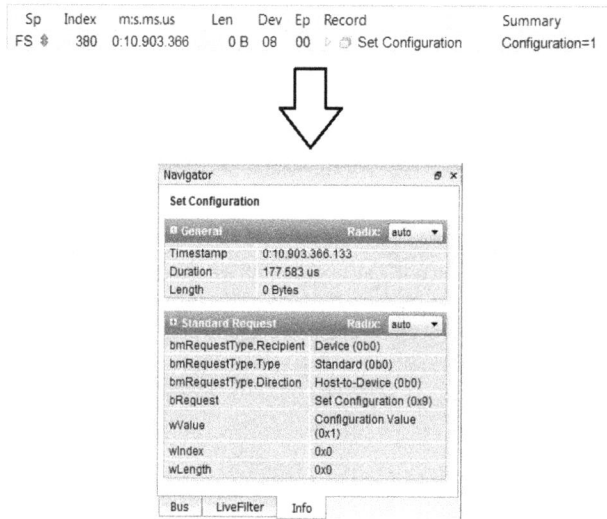

Sp	Index	m:s.ms.us	Len	Dev	Ep	Record	Summary
FS	380	0:10.903.366	0 B	08	00	Set Configuration	Configuration=1

Navigator

Set Configuration

General — Radix: auto

Timestamp	0:10.903.366.133
Duration	177.583 us
Length	0 Bytes

Standard Request — Radix: auto

bmRequestType.Recipient	Device (0b0)
bmRequestType.Type	Standard (0b0)
bmRequestType.Direction	Host-to-Device (0b0)
bRequest	Set Configuration (0x9)
wValue	Configuration Value (0x1)
wIndex	0x0
wLength	0x0

Bus | LiveFilter | Info

Figure C-6 **Set Configuration Capture**

The *Set Configuration* request enables the USB device to start communication through the endpoints specified in the desired configuration.

µC/OS-III and µC/USB-Device Licensing Policy

This book includes µC/OS-III in source form for free short-term evaluation, for educational use or for peaceful research. We provide ALL the source code for your convenience and to help you experience µC/OS-III. The fact that the source is provided does NOT mean that you can use it commercially without paying a licensing fee. Knowledge of the source code may NOT be used to develop a similar product either. The book also includes µC/USB-Device precompiled in linkable object form.

The reader can purchase the Renesas Demonstration Kit YRDKRX63N separately from Renesas and may use µC/OS-III and µC/USB-Device with the YRDKRX63N. It is not necessary to purchase anything else, as long as the initial purchase is used for educational purposes. Once the code is used to create a commercial project/product for profit, however, it is necessary to purchase a license.

It is necessary to purchase this license when the decision to use µC/OS-III and/or µC/USB-Device in a design is made, not when the design is ready to go to production.

If you are unsure about whether you need to obtain a license for your application, please contact Micrium and discuss the intended use with a sales representative.

D-1 µC/USB-DEVICE MAINTENANCE RENEWAL

Licensing µC/USB-Device provides one year of technical support, maintenance and source code updates. Renew the maintenance agreement for continued support and source code updates. Contact sales@Micrium.com for additional information.

D-2 µC/USB-DEVICE SOURCE CODE UPDATES

If you are under maintenance, you will be automatically emailed when source code updates become available. You can then download your available updates from Micrium's customer portal. If you are no longer under maintenance, or forget your Micrium username or password, please contact sales@Micrium.com.

D-3 µC/USB-DEVICE SUPPORT

Support is available for licensed customers. Please visit the customer support section in www.Micrium.com. If you are not a current user, please register to create your account. A web form will be offered to you to submit your support question.

Licensed customers can also use the following contact:

CONTACT MICRIUM

Micriµm
1290 Weston Road, Suite 306
Weston, FL 33326

+1 954 217 2036
+1 954 217 2037 (FAX)

E-Mail: sales@Micrium.com
Website: www.Micrium.com

Appendix

E

Bibliography

▦ Labrosse Jean J. *μC/OS-III, The Real-Time Kernel for the Renesas RX62N*. Micriμm Press, 2010, ISBN 978-0-9823375-7-8.

▦ Renesas Electronics. *RX63N Group User's Manual: Hardware*. Rev. 0.9. December 1, 2011. Available at: www.renesas.com/products/mpumcu/rx/rx600/Documentation.jsp.

▦ Total Phase, Inc. *Beagle Protocol Analyzers Data Sheet v4.20*. January 31, 2012. Available at: www.totalphase.com.

▦ Total Phase, Inc. *Data Center Software Manual v6.20*. July 12, 2012. Available at: www.totalphase.com.

▦ Compaq, Hewlett-Packard, Intel, Lucent, Microsoft, NEC, Philips. *Universal Serial Bus Specification Revision 2.0*. April 27, 2000. Available at: www.usb.org/developers/docs.

▦ USB Implementers Forum, Inc. *Universal Serial Bus, Class Definitions for Communications Devices, Revision 1.2*. November 3, 2010. Available at: www.usb.org/developers/devclass_docs.

▦ USB Implementers Forum, Inc. *Universal Serial Bus, Communications, Subclass for PSTN Devices, Revision 1.2*. February 9, 2007. Available at: www.usb.org/developers/devclass_docs.

▦ USB Implementers Forum, Inc. *Device Class Definition for Human Interface Devices (HID), Version 1.11*. June 27, 2001. Available at: www.usb.org/developers/devclass_docs.

▦ USB Implementers Forum, Inc. *Universal Serial Bus HID Usage Tables, Version 1.12*. October 28, 2004. Available at: www.usb.org/developers/ devclass_docs.

E

▨ USB Implementers Forum, Inc. *Universal Serial Bus Mass Storage Class Specification Overview, Revision 1.3.* September 5, 2008. Available at: www.usb.org/developers/devclass_docs.

▨ USB Implementers Forum, Inc. *Universal Serial Bus Mass Storage Class Bulk-Only Transport, Revision 1.0.* September 31, 1999. Available at: www.usb.org/developers/devclass_docs.

▨ USB Implementers Forum, Inc. *USB Device Class Definition for Personal Healthcare Devices, Release 1.0,* November 8, 2007. Available at: www.usb.org/developers/devclass_docs.

Analog Devices Products Featured in the Renesas Demonstration Kit

ADXL345 Low Power, 3-Axis Digital *i*MEMS Accelerometer
- ±2 g, ±4 g, ±8 g, and ±16 g ranges
- Ultralow power
  - From 30 µA to 140 µA in full measurement mode
  - 0.1 µA in standby mode at VS = 2.5 V (typ)
- Supply Voltage: 2.0 V to 3.6 V
- 10-bit to 13-bit / 4mg resolution
- SPI and I²C digital interfaces
- Temp range: −40°C to +85°C
- 3 mm × 5 mm × 1 mm LGA package

ADMP401 Analog Output, Omni-Directional *i*MEMS Microphone
- SNR: 62 dBA
- Flat Frequency Response: 100 Hz to 15 kHz
- PSRR: 70 dBV
- Sensitivity: -42 dBV
- Current Consumption: < 250 µA
- 4.72 mm × 3.76 mm × 1.00 mm SMT package

SSM2167 Low Power Microphone Preamp
- Low shutdown current < 2 µA
- Adjustable compression ratio and noise gate threshold
- Low noise and distortion: 0.2% THD + N
- 20 kHz bandwidth
- Single 3 V operation

ADT7420 High Accuracy, 16-Bit Digital Temp Sensor
- ±0.25°C temp accuracy from −20°C to +105°C
- I²C-compatible interface
- Supply voltages: 2.7 V to 5.5 V
- Operating temperature: −40°C to +150°C
- LFCSP package

ADM3101 ±15 kV ESD Protected, Single-Channel RS-232 Line Driver/Receiver
- Conforms to EIA/TIA-232E and CCITT V.28 Specifications
- Data Rate: 460 kbps
- 0.1 µF charge pump capacitors
- Contact discharge: ±8 kV ap discharge: ±15 kV

www.analog.com

ANALOG DEVICES

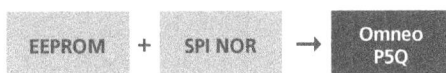

National Semiconductor
10/100 PHYTER®

DP83640

The IEEE 1588 Precision Time Protocol (PTP) is an important improvement to Ethernet systems that provides precise time synchronization for applications such as test and measurement, factory automation, and telecommunications. National Semiconductor's DP83640 Precision PHYTER transceiver is the industry's first to add the IEEE 1588 PTP functionality to a fully-featured, 10/100 Mbps Ethernet PHY.

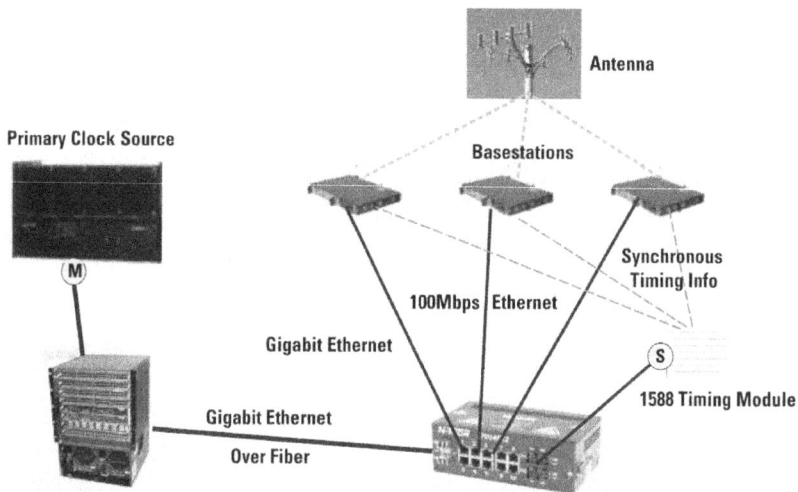

Wireless BTS Timing Sync Using IEEE 1588

High-Speed Industrial Ethernet

Product ID	Temp Range (°C)	Number of Ports	Interface	Typ Power (mW)	Package
DP83640*	-40 to 85	10/100 Single	MII/RMII	280	LQFP-48
DP83848I	-40 to 85	10/100 Single	MII/RMII/SNI	265	LQFP-48
DP83848VYB	-40 to 105	10/100 Single	MII/RMII/SNI	265	LQFP-48
DP83848J	-40 to 85	10/100 Single	MII/RMII	265	LLP-40
DP83849I	-40 to 85	10/100 Dual	MII/RMII	300/Port	TQFP-80

*IEEE 1588

national.com/ethernet

National Semiconductor

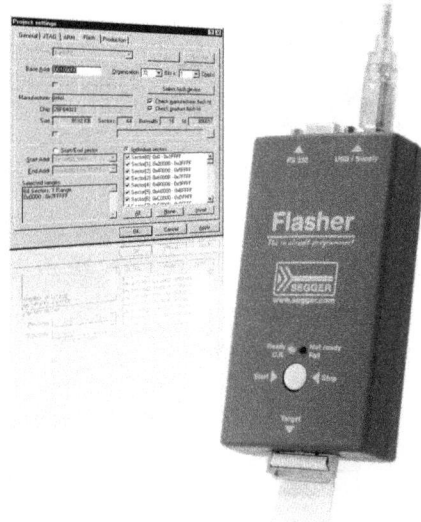

NDT-03C: Small Surface Mount Speaker Solution

The NDT-03C dynamic speaker from Star Micronics is the ideal small surface mount solution for automotive telematics, handheld devices, medical, and many other applications.

With its unique design, high SPL rating, and flat frequency response, the NDT-03C delivers clear sound in a variety of tones. The NDT-03C is perfect for applications with audio outputs including polyphonic tones, voice and music. The NDT-03C features a top sound port and is reflowable. With availability in tape and reel packaging, NDT-03C speaker is ideal for automatic mounting in high volume applications.

NDT-03C Features include:

- *Top Sound Port*
- *Reflowable (Conforms to EIAJ ED-4702)*
- *Flat Frequency response with a high sound level*
- *Excellent Durability in Severe Environments*
- *Compact 15 x 15 x 4 mm size*

Always Leading - Always Innovating

Star Micronics America, Inc.
1150 King Georges Post Rd.
Edison, NJ 08837
800-782-7636 ext. 986
www.starmicronics.com/NDT-03C

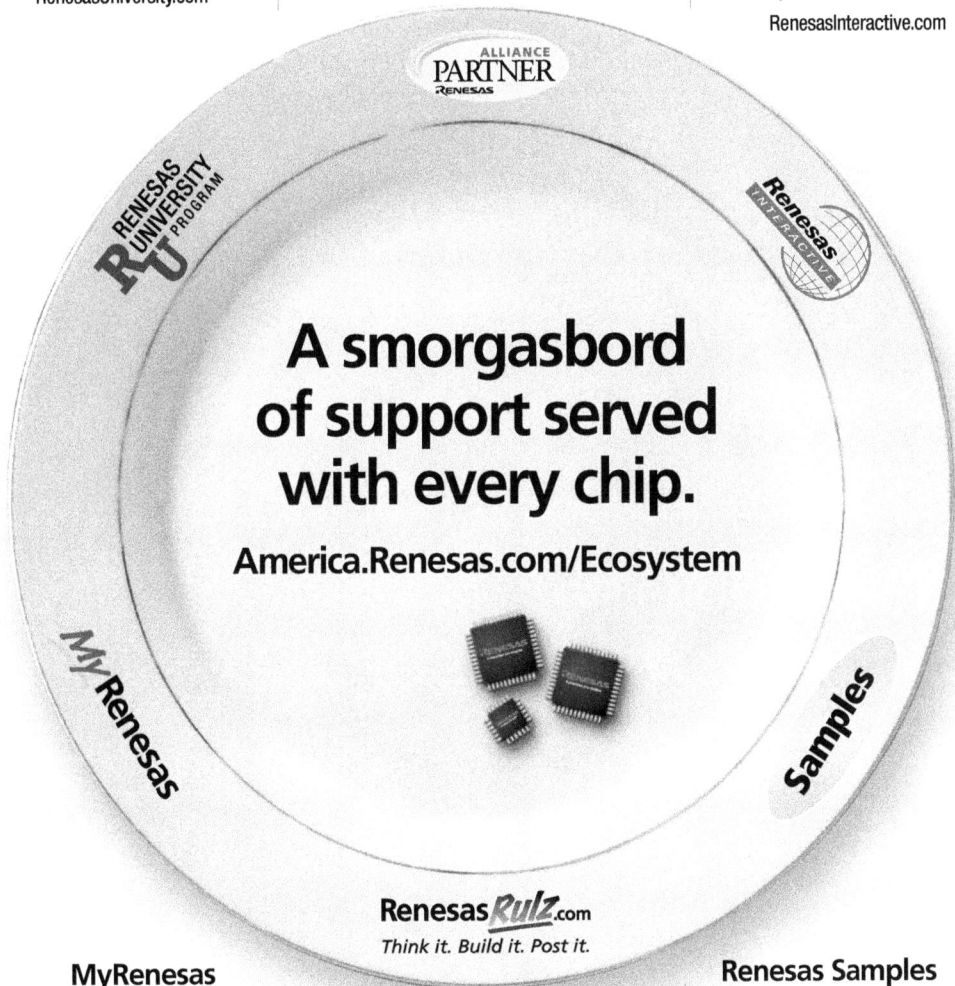

Index

D

E

F

www.ingramcontent.com/pod-product-compliance
Lightning Source LLC
Chambersburg PA
CBHW062009190326
41458CB00009B/3022